9/10

PRAIRIES AND PLAINS

The Reference Literature

of a Region

PRAIRIES AND PLAINS

The Reference Literature

of a Region

ROBERT BALAY
General Editor

Contributors

Mel Bohn   Jean Piper Burton   Jeanetta Drueke

Gayla Koerting   Larry McDonald   Lisa Mitten   Marcella Stark

Under Sponsorship of
Mountain Plains Library Association
and
Center for Great Plains Studies, University of Nebraska-Lincoln

KWS
PUBLISHERS
Chicago ❖ London

Published in 2009 by
KWS Publishers

1516 North State Parkway
Chicago 60610

81 Oxford Street
London W1D 2EU

Cataloging-in-Publication Data is available from the Library of Congress and the British Museum.

First published in the United States and United Kingdom in 2009

Typeset by Chicago Advertising and Design
Printed by Edwards Brothers
Cover design by Peter Aristedes, Chicago Advertising and Design

Cover photo: *Cottonwood, Colorado High Plains*, reproduced with the permission of Richard Balay

107.50

For

SELECTION OFFICERS

*Who take care that the titles students and scholars will need are
on hand in libraries*

INTERLIBRARY LOAN STAFF

Who locate sources local libraries lack

THE MOUNTAIN PLAINS LIBRARY ASSOCIATION

and

THE CENTER FOR GREAT PLAINS STUDIES, UNIVERSITY OF NEBRASKA-LINCOLN

Sympathetic and uncomplaining sponsors

Table of Contents

Foreword

Anyone who grew up on the Great Plains or has spent much time there will be familiar with the complaint that the Plains are featureless, barren, boring, and, heaven knows, flat. The cry often comes from travelers from the East who dread the drive across from Kansas City or Omaha or Fargo or Winnipeg on their way to the mountains or the Coast. Natives come to resent the chorus of censure, especially when voiced by people who live in places like New Jersey, Chicago, the sweaty Gulf Coast, or Los Angeles, and who are consequently ill-placed to cast stones at other regions. Plains people sometimes long to find a way to correct the scorn directed at the place where they live. Their region has endured slurs for two centuries, from Edwin James's "Great American Desert" through "the billiard table of the gods" (William Least Heat-Moon's phrase, himself a chronicler and admirer of the Plains).

Some years ago, reading Stephen Ambrose's *Undaunted Courage*, an account of the Lewis and Clark Expedition (1803-1806), I was struck by the reaction of the leaders of the Corps of Discovery to their first exposure to the Plains environment. "This immence river [the Missouri]…" Lewis wrote to his mother in 1804, "waters one of the fairest portions of the globe, nor do I believe that there is in the universe a similar extent of country, equally fertile, well watered, and intersected by such a number of navigable streams…. I had been led to believe that the open prarie country was barren, steril and sandy; but on the contrary I found it fertile in the extreme, the soil being from one to 20 feet in debth, consisting of a fine black loam [with] luxuriant growth of grass and other vegetables." In 1805, heading west from Fort Mandan, Lewis recorded in his journal, "The country is as yesterday beatifull in the extreme," and "The country on both sides of the missouri from the tops of the river hills, is one continued level fertile plain as far as the eye can reach, in which there is not even a solitary tree or shrub to be seen." Best of all, the country teemed with game that provided food for the Expedition members all the way to the mountains. I recalled that Indian peoples who inhabited the Plains traveled up and down the expanse of the region where they lived following the migrations of game (chiefly bison), and that there is no recorded instance that they wearied of the Plains' supposed sterility; indeed, they objected strenuously to its being invaded by whites and fought to keep it.

I felt called upon to see what I might do that would in some way help overcome the image the Prairies-Plains region had acquired. I remembered the region with affection; I grew up in the urban Plains in Wichita, and images of that place acquired during childhood and youth crowd my imagination to this day. I began to cast about for some way to pay homage to that memory and help draw Prairies-Plains to the attention of readers, especially those who scoffed at it. I was advised by a friend at a publishing house not to compile a bibliography, since in the Internet age nobody buys bibliographies, but instead to prepare an encyclopedia. I had just begun to think seriously about how to go about putting such a thing together when I had the luck to stumble across on the Internet site of the Center for Great Plains Studies in Lincoln an announcement that the Center had just such a work in development, with publication expected in about a year. That encyclopedia is listed in this guide, record number **AA4**.

I returned to the idea of a bibliography, and interested my son Christopher in creating a database program where records could be entered. I had the unfocused notion that the database could be used as the basis for an Internet site that would help students and scholars and would assist libraries in building collections. I began loading records, identifying candidates for entry by searching bibliographies in encyclopedias and monographs that were concerned in whole or part with the Prairies-Plains region. I realized after loading a few hundred records that a generous share of them were the bibliographies, encyclopedias, dictionaries, collective biographies, directories, and the like that librarians identify as reference works. A good first use for the database, it seemed, would be to assemble a guide to Prairies-Plains reference titles that would provide full bibliographic descriptions and annotations, using as a model the American Library Association publication, *Guide to Reference Books*.[1]

At early stages, I was able to interest as sponsor the Mountain Plains Library Association. MPLA has been a source of support and encouragement during preparation of this Guide, even when it seemed it might never see the light of day. I was joined by seven collaborators, all librarians, four of them affiliated with *Choice* magazine as reviewers (Mel Bohn, Jean Burton, Jeanetta Drueke, and Marcella Stark), one a Choice editor (Lisa Mitten), and two volunteers (Gayla Koerting and Larry McDonald). All except Lisa have connections with the Prairies-Plains region, now or in the past, and four are presently associated with libraries at Plains institutions; Lisa, the exception, has wide knowledge of Indian culture and history, an important consideration in a literature so heavily weighted toward Indian studies. Working together, we have assembled the guide we present here in about three years, dating from a planning conference at the ACRL Conference in Minneapolis in April, 2005. At a later stage, the Center for Great Plains Studies at the University of Nebraska at Lincoln also agreed to stand as sponsor.

We hope that the Guide will assist students beginning study of the Prairies-Plains region, those who are looking for sources for more advanced study, scholars seeking sources to support research projects, reader service librarians helping library users searching for specific information or source materials, and collection development librarians building library collections. We recognize that the *Guide* is a first step toward a more complete description of the resources that will support study of the region, and that some portions of the *Guide* are more satisfactorily complete than others. Specialists in the areas we cover will doubtless know the literature of their subjects thoroughly, and will be able to point out omissions. We invite comments and suggestions by readers, addressed to the General Editor at Prairies and Plains, 97 Livingston Street, New Haven, CT 06511, or arebee@prairiesandplains.com. — *RB*

*   *   *   *   *

No project of this size can come into being without help from many people who offer advice, encouragement, and assistance. We extend our heartfelt thanks to the following libraries and individuals who gave help and counsel during compilation.

-- At West Chester University of Pennsylvania: K im Klaus, Carol Gerhart, and Neal Kenney of the Interlibrary Loan office and Tracie Meloy and Dana McDonnell of the Circulation Department.
-- At the Burton family collection: Gerry Burton, J.C. Burton, Bryan Burton.
-- At the University of Nebraska-Lincoln: Beth McNeil, Richard Voeltz (Biology and Chemistry Librarian); the staff of the Interlibrary Loan Office.
-- At the Great Plains Art Museum, Lincoln, NE: Reese Summers.
-- At the Nebraska State Historical Library: Cindy Drake and other staff.
-- At the Nebraska Library Commission: Beth Goble and other staff.
-- At the I.D. Weeks Library, University of South Dakota: Muriel Schamber and Joan Olson of the Interlibrary Loan office, and Joe Edelen, Executive Secretary of the Mountain Plains Library Association.
-- At Yale University: The entire Research Services and Collections staff (Alan Solomon, Head), Privileges Office (Sue Crockford-Peters, Head), Music Library, and Map Collection (especially Margit Kaye), all at Sterling Memorial Library; the Government Publications unit at the Mudd Library (especially Debbie Falvey); the Beinecke Rare Book and Manuscript Library (especially George Miles, Curator of the Western Americana Collection and a fruitful source of early advice); the Divinity Library (especially Susanne Estelle Holmer and the Librarian, Paul Stuehrenberg); the Film Study Center; the Forestry and Environmental Studies Library (especially its Librarian, Carla Heister); the Geology Library (especially John Morgan); the Kline Science Library (especially Lori Bronars); the Law Library; and the Ornithology Library.
-- At Trinity College, Hartford, CT: Peter Knapp and Jeff Kaimowitz of the Watkinson Library.
-- At the Newberry Library, Chicago, IL: Brian Hosmer.

*   *   *   *   *

[1] This work has a new title, *Guide to Reference*, and has been released in a 12th edition under the editorship of Robert Kieft, recently Librarian at Haverford College, now Librarian at Occidental College (see http://www.guidetoreference.org/HomePage.aspx).

Introduction

In this *Guide*, we have tried to identify as many titles of reference value as we could that relate in whole or part to the region of the United States and Canada we are calling Prairies and Plains. The titles we list vary widely in content and comprehensiveness, and represent those we selected that we were able to examine at the shelf or over the Internet. The annotations that accompany entries attempt to describe the works in such a way that seasoned reference librarians will be able to visualize the sources and use them readily. Some annotations make recommendations concerning a source's usefulness, usually positive, but evaluative comments are by no means lacking; indeed, contributors have not been laid under obligation to suppress personal opinion in writing about any source, since the judgments of working reference librarians are among the most reliable appraisals reference titles are likely to receive.

The Region.

The Prairies-Plains region is that part of the United States called by Edwin James (chronicler of Stephen Long's expedition that explored overland the country west of St. Louis as far as the Rocky Mountains) the "Great American Desert." Its geophysical characteristics were specified by Walter Prescott Webb in *The Great Plains* (1931) as treeless, flat, and semiarid. Webb noted the change that occurred in the region's geophysical nature somewhere around the 100th meridian: east of that indefinite boundary, rainfall was more dependable and vegetation relatively luxuriant—it is the tallgrass Prairie. West of the 100th meridian, rainfall drops below 20 inches per year and often becomes undependable; in good years, enough rain falls to support conventional agriculture, but cycles of drought often render the land fit at best for grazing. It is the shortgrass Prairie, often called the Great Plains or High Plains.

We define the Prairies-Plains as the region west of the Missouri River to the Rocky Mountains, stretching from the Rio Grande River at the border with Mexico to the Parkland Belt in the Prairie provinces of western Canada. It includes the states of Kansas, Nebraska, and North and South Dakota in their entirety; western portions of Oklahoma and Texas; eastern portions of New Mexico, Colorado, Wyoming, and Montana; southern portions of Manitoba, Saskatchewan, and Alberta; and, recognizing its importance in the history and development of the region, the Missouri River watershed from source to mouth. Except for the latter, the region in which we are interested does not differ in any important respect from the Great Plains described with such care by David Wishart in *Encyclopedia of the Great Plains*, p. xiii-xviii.

But no region is adequately described by simply specifying its boundaries or describing its rainfall or physiography. The heart of a region lies in the interaction between its physical surroundings and the people who live there. When a storm blows up in harvest season on the Plains of North Dakota, everyone stops to see whether the clouds may bring hail, which could lay the wheat to the ground and cause grave economic hardship not just for farmers but for everyone nearby, nearly all of whom depend on agriculture for their livelihood. Throughout the Prairies-Plains, travelers and residents cannot escape a sense of space and distance. On a brilliant summer day on the High Plains, the land runs without hindrance to the horizon, the blue sky arching to meet it, an immense prospect in which people often feel insignificant. Many find the experience intimidating. Prairies-Plains was one of the last regions of the continental United States and Canada to be settled, is still sparsely populated, and is predominantly rural. Cities are confined primarily to the region's perimeter (Denver, Cheyenne, Edmonton, Winnipeg, Fargo, Omaha, Kansas City, Tulsa, Dallas); cities sitting unprotected on the Plains are rare (Saskatoon, Lincoln, Wichita, Amarillo). Residents who live on farms contend with loneliness as a constant fact of life, and look forward to church services, quilting bees, rodeos, trips into town, and in an earlier age, trapper rendezvous, as

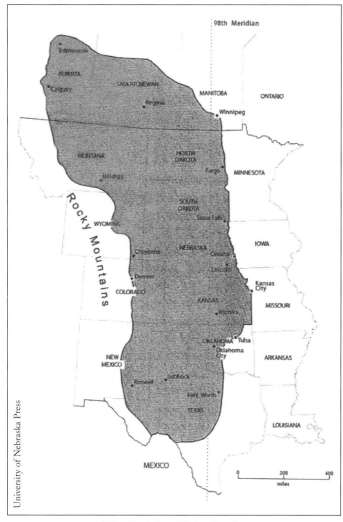

The Prairies-Plains Region

social opportunities. It is not a country for the faint of heart.

In compiling this *Guide*, we have been anxious to encourage a view that regards Prairies-Plains as a region remarkable in its diversity but whose people share both common experiences and reactions to the Plains environment they inhabit. We have learned to our disappointment that the overwhelming share of reference sources are concerned with individual states. Bibliographies, histories, field guides, and encyclopedias tend to be concerned only with, say, Nebraska or North Dakota, making the unvoiced assumptions that birds do not cross state boundaries or that citizens of North Dakota are uninfluenced by what happens in Saskatchewan or Montana or South Dakota. That mindset may well be dictated by the funding of research projects—money nearly always comes from a state, whose officials, in the Plains as elsewhere, have little interest in research that concerns itself with other states. The surveyors' lines that established state boundaries have set barriers that draw strict political lines. Even works that take a regional approach, however helpful they may be for research about the region, often define the Plains as a specific group of states, pushing some parts of Prairies-Plains into other regions (e.g., **AA3**, **AA6**, **AA10**). *Encyclopedia of the Great Plains* (**AA4**) and *A Great Plains Reader* (**AA5**), by contrast, both take a regional approach that is one of the greatest contributions these titles make to raising the view of researchers interested in Prairies-Plains topics. Both give voice to a regional consciousness that is, we hope, gaining strength around the region at research institutes like the Center for Great Plains Studies in Lincoln, the Center for Western Studies at Augustana College in Sioux Falls, and the Canadian Plains Research Center in Regina (see Site List 1, p. 2). Prairies-Plains is a region that crosses state, provincial, and international boundaries.

Audience.

We intend the *Guide* primarily for scholars and students interested in studying the Prairies-Plains region. We include some sources that will help younger readers, but primarily aim for an audience of educated adults. Like other guides, this one also hopes to be helpful to reference staff looking for sources that will help readers or refresh the memories of reference librarians concerning titles they use infrequently, and to collection staff seeking to build collections.

Since the chosen audience will be familiar with bibliographic entry format, entries in the *Guide* follow a version of the format specified by the International Standard Bibliographic Description, except that titles appear in boldface rather than italic. We find boldface easier to read than italic, and it provides some visual relief on the printed page.

We are not happy with the format we use for Internet sites, although entries for these sites are drawn from descriptions we found for the most part in standard catalogs, principally those available online from the Library of Congress and the Online Catalog Library Center. In its brief life, the Internet and its associated communications standard, Hypertext Transfer Protocol, have ridden off in so many directions libraries have been unable to keep up. It would be helpful to readers if providers included with each site the official site name, the producer, the size of the file, the date the site first became available, and the date of last revision. Some national organizations such as the Modern Language Association supply satisfactory specifications for citing individual articles or locations drawn from Internet sites, but a national or international standard for describing the sites themselves has not appeared. The MARC format, developed for books, is not very satisfactory for Internet sites.

Scope.

We restrict the kinds of sources we list to published books, periodical sets, and Internet sites. Some in all three categories are government publications, and a handful are academic theses. We exclude periodical articles but include lists of periodicals and periodical indexes, and also exclude newspaper articles, but cite lists of newspapers.

There is no restriction as to language, although apart from English, we list chiefly dictionaries in Spanish and French, together with dictionaries of Indian languages. We also held the *Guide* open to all subjects, but found that resources in greatest number treat history, biology, and Indians. We assumed that we would find few sources in the natural sciences, since mathematics, physics, and chemistry are not often regionally oriented, but that there would be lively interest in the natural resources of the Prairies-Plains region, in its flora and fauna, and in the region's climate and underlying geology. The resources we found bore out both assumptions. We also thought we would find ample sources that would support research in the social sciences, but, except for history, found that not to be the case. In all the social sciences except for history, reference sources were thin and frequently devoted to narrow subtopics. In a number of subjects that have a rich American national literature--music, theater, literature, medicine, education--the Plains sources are simply anemic in both numbers and coverage. We suspect that reasons for this lie in the relatively recent settlement of the Prairies-Plains region, its sparse population, and the existence there of relatively few of the institutions that have interest in producing scholarly reference titles—publishers, learned societies, and front-rank universities.

The positive aspect to this is that the field lies open to institutions and researchers who have interest in the region. We can envision a range of titles that would enrich the Prairies-Plains reference literature: films of the Plains, a survey of Plains rivers and drainage basins, a first-rate encyclopedia of Plains literature, another of Plains music, an index to Plains-related periodicals, a directory of Plains institutions that hold primary materials of interest to historians and other researchers. Although histories exist for most of the region's states and provinces, we have found no general history of the region.

We also made no restriction as to dates of either publication or coverage, but recognized that little publication, especially of reference sources, could be expected before the 20th century. We include imprint lists that go back to the earliest years of white settlement in the Plains, and also include bibliographies and other works that cover the earliest non-Indian exploration of the Prairies-Plains, dating from Coronado's expedition in 1540-1541 through the late 19th century, featuring American explorations beginning with Lewis and Clark's expedition to the Pacific, 1803-1806.

We have tried to compensate for the paucity of sources restricted to Prairies-Plains by citing more general sources that cover the North American continent, the United States, Canada, or the trans-Mississippi West. All provide some form of coverage of the Prairies-Plains region, which as the largest plains region in the Western Hemisphere, can scarcely be ignored. Annotations for these sources describe the degree of Prairies-Plains coverage and often cite where in each source Plains material may be found.

Arrangement.

Entries in the text are arranged by 29 sections, AA, "The Prairies-Plains Region," through H, "Military Science; War." The sections present an arrangement by subject of the titles we cite in the book, and while this may fall short of the desirable characteristics found in a full-fledged classification, which would proceed from the general to the specific and collocate like entries, they group related fields in sections of general works, history, humanities, social sciences, sciences, agriculture, and military science.

Besides the formal entries (there are about 1,270 records), the *Guide* offers 18 Site Lists that group sources which share an emphasis (e.g., WPA guides to the states, Historical Records Surveys, Agricultural Statistics Services), but which are better presented together than scattered through the book or through a section. They serve to supplement entries in the main list. Some are simply institutional sites, but we think it may prove helpful to call their existence to the attention of readers, and hope that grouping them may add weight to the reference utility of the *Guide*. Jeanetta Drueke had the idea for the Site Lists, and prepared them all.

A few words concerning terminology. We use "Blacks" in preference to "African Americans" in recognition that not all African Americans are black, and "Latinos" as a general term for emigrants from Mexico, Central America, South America, the Spanish-speaking Caribbean, and the Iberian peninsula. We use "Indians" rather than "Native Americans" as a compromise term that will include native peoples from the entire international region and will be readily recognized. This usage does nothing to resolve contentions among Indians themselves in both the United States and Canada concerning appropriate labels; "Indians" is simply a term of convenience.

Record structure.

For books, records have a common structure, consisting of three parts: Bibliographic entry, Notes, and Annotation. Entries are based on International Standard Bibliographic Description, arranged in the following pattern:

Author [if any]. – **Title : Subtitle** / Statement of Responsibility. – Edition. – Place: Publisher, Date, Pagination – (Series [if any]).

The Notes section supplements the entry with items that will assist collection officers in deciding whether to purchase a title (Library of Congress Control Number, International Standard Book and Serial Numbers, OCLC numbers). Notes also provide items that give publication history (earlier editions, cessations, or resumptions), occasionally list a volume's contents when that may help readers decide whether the title may help them, or any other information that may shed light on the publication's origin.

The annotation section describes the book, attempts to give some notion of its arrangement, assesses its usefulness to Prairies-Plains researchers, and often appraises the title's stature in its field and its value to students and scholars. Annotations, signed with the initials of the contributors, are preceded by a symbol •.

For Internet sites, record structure differs. All Internet sites have title entry, indicate whether the site charges for access or is available free, and because sites change frequently, indicate the date (month and year) when the contributor viewed the site.

The pattern:

Title : Subtitle / Statement of Responsibility (personal or institutional, if available). – Place : Producer, Date (if available). – URL.

Readers familiar with searching the Internet will know that sites arise and disappear with rapidity but without notice, and that the network is in a state of continual flux and development. It is attended by a cavalier disregard for standards, the needs of users, and the requirements of bibliographic description: the people responsible for a site are seldom named, the title may be given in several versions at the site or may be identical with the issuing agency, the date of first issue is not to be discovered, any indication of a site's scope or size is lacking, or the URL may change, as may the issuing agency (particularly if the chief administrator or the political party in control has changed). Readers are advised, instead of relying on URLs, to search for specific sites by using an Internet search engine.

Indexes.

Indexes of names, titles, and subjects follow the main list of entries. In the Names index, all authors, editors, or compilers from the entry are listed (but not illustrators, series editors, photographers, cartographers, or other ancillary contributors), as well as authors cited in annotations. The Titles index lists titles occurring in the entry, notes, or annotations, but omits titles of chapters or papers listed in Contents notes.

*   *   *   *   *

We cannot pretend that the *Guide* is comprehensive. We identified a fairly large number of titles we hoped to include that we had to drop because we could not examine them. Copies were not available in libraries to which we had access, and we were unable to persuade libraries that owned copies to release them through interlibrary loan, although many libraries were exceedingly generous in lending reference titles.

We are also uneasy that titles we might have included have simply eluded our efforts to locate all the reference titles that might be pertinent to Prairies-Plains studies. We encourage librarians and scholars to notify us of titles we have omitted, at Prairies and Plains, 97 Livingston Street, New Haven, CT 06511, or to the General Editor at our editorial e-mail, arebee@prairiesandplains.com.

Abbreviations

bk.	book
ca.	circa (about)
cm.	centimeters
Co.	Company
col.	colored, in color
comp., comps.	compiler, compilers
Dept.	Department
distr.	distributed
Div.	Division
ed., eds.	editor(s), edition(s)
enl.	enlarged
facsim.; facsims.	facsimile; facsimiles
front.	frontispiece
Govt. Print. Off.	Government Printing Office [U.S.]
html, HTML	Hypertext Markup Language
http	Hypertext Transfer Protocol
ill.	illustration, illustrations
introd.	introduction
ISBN	International Standard Book Number
ISSN	International Standard Serial Number
JPEG	Joint Photographic Experts Group
LCCN	Library of Congress Control Number
no., nos.	number, numbers
OCLC	Online Catalog Library Center
p.	page, pages
pbk.	paperback
pdf	Portable Document Format
PhD	Doctor of Philosophy
port., ports.	portrait, portraits
Pr.	Press
pt., pts.	part, parts
publ.	published, publisher, publication
Publ.	Publishing, Publisher (in names of publishers)
rev.	revised
rtf	rich text format
s.l.	sine loco (place unknown)
s.n.	sine nomine (name unknown)
Supt. of Docs.	Superintendent of Documents [U.S.]
U.S.	United States
Univ.	University
URL	Uniform Resource Locator
v.	volume, volumes

In bibliographic entries, states of the United States and provinces of Canada are indicated by two-letter postal abbreviations (e.g., KS for Kansas, SK for Saskatchewan)

A   General Works

AA : THE PRAIRIES–PLAINS REGION

Scope   This section lists works that take as their subject all aspects of the entire Prairies-Plains region. Works larger in scope (the North American continent, Canada, the United States, the trans-Mississippi West) will be found under D, History, as will works concerned with portions of the region – its states, provinces, or territories, or its counties, cities, and towns. Works taking up individual topics (e.g., birds of the Great Plains) will be found with their subject.

AA1   Adelman, Charlotte, 1937?-   . - **Prairie Directory of North America : The United States and Canada** / by Charlotte Adelman & Bernard L. Schwartz. - Wilmette, IL : Lawndale Enterprises Book, 2001. - 354 p. ; ill., maps.

> Class Numbers:
>   Library of Congress QH104
> ISBN 0971509603
> LCCN 2001-98353
> Notes:
>   Includes bibliographical references (p. 345-348)

• A directory describing the locations of prairie remnants located in North America that covers all the Prairies-Plains states and the Prairie provinces of Canada. Arranged alphabetically by state, then county; Canadian provinces are sub-arranged by prairie name. Includes both shortgrass and long grass prairies. Entries give prairie name, area, type of wildlife and vegetation, description (occasionally running as long as a page), direction and distance to nearest town, contact address and telephone. Glossary, four-page bibliography arranged by title, index of subjects but none of prairie names, occasional illustrations, two outline maps of the central U.S. and Canadian Prairie provinces. — *RB*

AA2   The **American Midwest : An Interpretive Encyclopedia** / general eds., Richard Sisson, Christian Zacher, and Andrew Cayton. - Bloomington, IN : Indiana Univ. Pr., 2006. - 1916 p. ; ill.

> Class Numbers:
>   Library of Congress F351
> ISBN 0253348862 9780253348869
> OCLC 70676538
> LCCN 2006-23198
> Notes:
>   Includes bibliographical references; index

Table of contents: http://www.loc.gov/catdir/toc/ecip0617/2006023198.html

• Like other recent compilations, *American Midwest* signals a renewal of regional consciousness. It celebrates a region that stretches from the eastern border of Ohio to the western border of the Plains states of Kansas, Nebraska, and the Dakotas, and from the Ohio River and the southern borders of Kansas and Missouri to the Canadian border and the Great Lakes. In nearly 2,000 pages, its editors, advisors, and contributors (who are named with the articles they wrote but for whom there is no roster) treat many aspects of the region they acknowledge to be "flyover country." Articles are arranged under five broad headings: "Landscapes and People," "Society and Culture," "Community and Social Life," "Economy and Technology," and "Public Life," subdivided into 22 headings more modest in scope ("Images of the Midwest," "Literature," "Religion," "Small-Town Life," "Labor Movements and Working-Class Culture"). In the initial subsection, "Portraits of the Twelve States," contributors are given license to write personal essays, which some of them use to write of their feelings about the region and their growing-up process there. Many individual essays are biographical sketches of Midwesterners (politicians, poets, sports and entertainment figures), and most essays are followed by brief bibliographies. Each subsection begins with a table of contents for the section that lists all the section's articles; that and the index (which the editors advise is the best way to locate specific topics), allow readers to find their way into this immense work. Some oddities deserve mention: there is no word about Wounded Knee, Indians are mentioned primarily as 18th-century residents of the region (although there is a long list of the region's other peoples), and of institutions of higher education, only the University of Chicago deserves a separate entry; there is neither general bibliography nor chronology. Nevertheless, a splendid achievement that covers a significant portion of the Prairies-Plains region and fulfills admirably the promise of its subtitle. — *RB*

AA3   Brodie, Carolyn S., ed. - **Exploring the Plains States Through Literature**. - Phoenix, AZ : Oryx Pr., 1994. - 124 p. - (Exploring the United States through Literature Series).

> Class Numbers:
>   Library of Congress F591 ; Z1251.G85
> ISBN 0897747623
> OCLC 29389126
> LCCN 93-42065
> Notes:
>   Includes bibliographical references; index

• Covers the states of Iowa, Kansas, Missouri, Nebraska, North Dakota, and South Dakota in chapters contributed by different persons. Supplies for each state a bibliography of sources. Nonfiction sources are arranged by Dewey Decimal Classification number. Other sections are biography, fiction, and periodicals.

Site List 1

Plains Research Centers

Research institutes devoted to study of the Prairies-Plains region and its residents' concerns may be found throughout the region, some sponsored by state governments, some by universities, some private.

General

Canadian Plains Research Center [Regina, SK]
> http://www.cprc.ca
> To "improve understanding and appreciation of the Canadian Plains region, its people, and its resources." Affiliated with the University of Regina.

Center for Great Plains Studies [Lincoln, NE]
> http://www.unl.edu/plains
> "To promote a greater understanding of the people, cul ture, history, and environment of the Great Plains through a variety of research, teaching, [publishing] and outreach programs." Affiliated with University of Nebraska-Lincoln.

Center for Great Plains Studies [Emporia, KS]
> http://www.emporia.edu/cgps/
> "Emphasizes the study of the grasslands as one of its pri mary responsibilities to Kansas and the region." Affiliated with Emporia State University.

Center for Western Studies [Sioux Falls, SD]
> http://www.sdhistory.org/soc/Hist_Orgs/
> CWS.htm
> "Collecting, preserving and interpreting prehistoric, his toric and contemporary materials that document native and immigrant cultures of the northern prairie/plains." Affiliated with Augustana College.

Institute for Regional Studies and University Archives [Fargo, ND]
> http://www.lib.ndsu.nodak.edu/ndirs/
> "To foster understanding of regional life through research … teaching … and service to … the Red River Valley, the state of North Dakota, the plains of North America … and comparable regions." Affiliated with North Dakota State University.

Humanities

Plains Humanities Alliance (Lincoln, NE]
> http://www.unl.edu/rcplains/index.html
> "Preserving and promoting the cultural heritage of the Great Plains region." The Alliance defines the Plains as Kansas, Nebraska, Oklahoma, and the Dakotas. The site offers a calendar of events, a list of 500 "Great Books of the Great Plains," and is planning a Plains Gateway project, an online directory of Plains cultural resources. Affiliated with the University of Nebraska-Lincoln and the National Endowment for the Humanities.

Agriculture

Agricultural Research Service, U.S. Department of Agriculture
> http://www.ars.usda.gov
> "Finding solutions to agricultural problems that affect Americans every day, from field to table." A "People and Places" section links to regional headquarters, research centers, human nutrition centers, research locations, and worksites.

Archaeology

Midwest Archeological Center, National Park Service
> http://www.cr.nps.gov/mwac
> "Study, interpretation and preservation of archaeological resources" in the Great Plains and beyond. Maintains the Archeological Sites Management Information System, which inventories, documents, and evaluates sites.

Environment

Center for Grassland Studies [Lincoln, NE]
> http://www.grassland.unl.edu/index.htm
> To "implement focused, interdisciplinary research, edu cational and service programs and activities that emphasize the role of grasslands as a natural resource and conservation measure and that enhance the effi ciency, profitability, sustainability, and aesthetic value of grasslands, wetlands, and turfs."

Land Institute [Salina, KS]   H
> http://www.landinstitute.org
> "To develop an agricultural system with the ecological stability of the prairie and a grain yield comparable to that from annual crops." See also G4.

Northern Prairie Wildlife Research Center
> http://www.npwrc.usgs.gov
> To "provide the scientific information needed to conserve and manage the Nation's biological resources, with an emphasis on the species and ecosystems of the nation's interest."

Prairies Forever
> http://www.prairies.org
> "Dedicated to promoting the ecological and cultural sig nificance of the American prairie through education, outreach, and public engagement."

Each entry contains bibliographic data, interest level, Sears subject headings, an annotation, and suggested student projects. — *MB*

AA4   **Encyclopedia of the Great Plains** / David J. Wishart, ed. - Lincoln, NE : Univ. of Nebraska Pr., 2004. - 919 p. ; ill., maps.

> Class Numbers:
> Library of Congress F591
> ISBN 0803247877
> LCCN 2003-21037
> Notes:
> Includes bibliographical references; index
> Overview [Appreciations] by William Ferris, Linda M. Hasselstrom, Andrew C. Isenberg: *Great Plains Quarterly* 26.2 (spring 2006): 117-127
> Table of contents: http://www.loc.gov/catdir/toc/ ecip049/2003021037.html
> See also *Encyclopedia of the Great Plains Indians* (**CD23**).

• Requiring more than ten years in planning and production, EGP was compiled principally at the Center for Great Plains Studies at the University of Nebraska-Lincoln, where its editor teaches in the Department of Geography. It displays the hallmarks of reference titles that librarians rely on in day-to-day reference work: its range and limits are carefully defined; it exerts organization over its materials; it is firmly based on scholarly research and enrolled practicing scholars (nearly 1,000 of them) as contributors; it supplies scholarly aids (bibliographies with most entries, cross-references, a thorough index); its illustrations are relevant to the text, carefully captioned, and located near the text they illustrate; it provides context not only in the text itself but in the 27 categories under which articles appear and the introductions that open each section; and it promises to become the seed-ground that will generate fresh scholarship in years to come. EGP's 1,300 articles include many persons and places that are known nationally or internationally (Eisenhower, Sitting Bull, Gwendolyn Brooks; Denver, Wounded Knee) but also those known primarily in the Plains region (Kate O'Hare, Gabrielle Roy, Charles Siringo; Nicodemus, KS, Sandhills, NE). The 27 sections cover topics everyone will expect (art, literature, politics and government), but others are important chiefly to the Plains (water) or their presence in a work about the Plains may surprise outsiders ("Images and Icons," "Protest and Dissent"). EGP's (and its editor's) devotion to geography are revealed in articles that show a deep, abiding interest in the Plains environment ("Tornadoes," "Shelterbelts," "Victorian Women Travelers"). Diverse ethnic groups living on the Plains may be found in sections on African, Asian, European, Hispanic, and of course, Native Americans, the region's most intensively studied population. Although the articles are written by specialists who have the range of Plains scholarship at their call, the style is intended for educated adults and can be understood by a wide range of readers. Readers may quarrel with EGP's choice of topics, but the breadth and balance of its coverage and special love for the Plains region are not to be doubted. EGP lacks a classified arrangement; the 27 categories are simply arranged alphabetically, which makes difficult the collocation of like subjects and the progression from general to specific that characterize a classification. EGP, for example, separates the five sections on ethnic groups. The contributors are simply listed by name in an index that points to page numbers for their articles; only there is their affiliation given. The index is thorough, but some entries ("Canada," "Literature") are heavily posted and difficult to read. A chronology and a general bibliography that collected the sources cited in the articles would have made the book more useful (if larger). EGP is likely to be the centerpiece of reference collections about the Prairies-Plains region for a long time. — *MB, RB*

AA5   **A Great Plains Reader** / ed. by Diane D. Quantic and P. Jane Hafen. - Lincoln, NE ; London : Univ. of Nebraska Pr., 2003. - xxii, 730 p.

> Class Numbers:
> Library of Congress F591
> ISBN 0803238029 0803288530 (pbk.)
> LCCN 2002031968
> Notes:
> Includes bibliographical references; index
> Review by Philip R. Coleman-Hull: *Great Plains Quarterly* 24.3 (summer 2004): 210-211

• Anthologies are seldom included in bibliographies of reference works, but this one deserves mention here both because the reference literature that treats the entire Prairies-Plains is so thin and because Quantic and Hafen have so carefully selected key texts, written such knowledgeable supporting materials, and provide so good a bibliography of sources and reading lists for every writer, all of it supplying a highly useful introduction to Plains literature. Not just literature, either: the editors include writing about Plains natural history, travelers' and newcomers' accounts, settlers' stories, facing up to the weather, and building communities. The stories, poems, and excerpts are arranged in five sections ("The Lay of the Land," "Natives and Newcomers," "Arriving and Settling In," "Adapting to a New Country," "The Great Plains Community") and an epilogue. The 70-odd writers include some early luminaries (Twain, Cooper, Parkman, Irving), the famous Plains voices (Stafford, Butala, Frazier, Erdrich, Cather, Morris, Sandoz), Indians (Zitkala-Sa, Neihardt, Ella Deloria), and naturalists (Johnsgard, Madson, Cutler). The selections themselves and the readings to which they point constitute an education in the Plains surroundings and the mindset of Plains people. Beginning students of the Plains could do worse than to read straight through as a way of gaining familiarity with the region and those who love it (or sometimes hate it). — *RB*

AA6   The Greenwood Encyclopedia of American Regional Cultures / William Ferris, consulting ed. - Westport, CT : Greenwood, 2004. - 8 v. (3200 p.) ; ill., maps.

> Class Numbers:
> Library of Congress F351
> ISBN 0313332665 (set)   0313327335 (v. 1)
> 031332817X (v. 6) 0313328056 (v. 8)
> LCCN   2004-56060
> Notes:
> Includes bibliographical references; index

• Although volume I is called "The Great Plains Region," three of the eight volumes cover states of the Prairies-Plains region: v. 1 covers North Dakota, South Dakota, Nebraska, Kansas, and Oklahoma, v. 6, Montana, Wyoming, and Colorado, and v. 8, New Mexico and Texas. Focusing on the diverse histories and cultures of each region, each volume has chapters on architecture, art, ecology and environment, ethnicity, fashion, film and theater, folklore, food, language, literature, music, religion, and sports and recreation. Numerous sidebars on Plains topics include excerpts from memoirs, profiles, and recipes, as well as Indian language families, six-man football, gourd dancing in powwows, buffalo soldiers, women's clubs, and fine art. Resource guides at the end of each chapter include print titles, Internet sites, films, recordings, events, organizations, and manuscript collections. Each volume has an introduction to the region, maps, a timeline of major events, footnotes, a bibliography of general sources, and an index. For the editor, regions are coterminous with a set of states: the Plains are seen to cease at the western borders of five states rather than being determined by topography, climate, vegetation, or animal life. For students and scholars. — *JD*

AA7   Jones, Stephen R., 1947– . - A Field Guide to the North American Prairie / [by] Stephen R. Jones and Ruth Carol Cushman. - Boston, MA : Houghton Mifflin, 2004. - 510 p. ; col. ill., col. maps. - (The Peterson field guide series).

> Class Numbers:
> Library of Congress QH102
> ISBN 0618179291 0618179305 (pbk.)
> LCCN 2002-191338 2003-66253
> Notes:
> Includes bibliographical references (p. 488-496)

• Using the familiar and readable Peterson format, this field guide covers the ten states and three Canadian provinces of the Prairies-Plains, as well as Illinois, Iowa, Minnesota, and Wisconsin. Following an introduction to the ecology of prairie plants, wildlife and humans, a state-by-state viewing guide describes grasslands, preserves, refuges, parks, recreation areas, and other sites. Entries, illustrated by numerous color photographs, highlight two to three plant or animal species; hiking, boating, rockhounding, and camping facilities; best times to visit; information numbers; and how to get there. Mean temperatures and precipitation and selected wildlife of special interest are included. Appendixes list prairie preserves in other states and common and scientific plant names. References and index by species common name, location, geological features and Indian peoples. — *JD*

AA8   Stubbendieck, James L. - An Identification of Prairie in National Park Units in the Great Plains / by James Stubbendieck and Gary Wilson. - [Atlanta, GA] : U.S. Dept. of the Interior, National Park Service, 1986. - 307 p. ; maps. - (National Park Service occasional paper, 7).

> Class Numbers:
> Library of Congress QK135
> OCLC 14966489
> LCCN 86-607903
> Notes:
> Includes bibliographies

• The authors account for sections of prairie that are found within the boundaries of 32 National Park Service units located in the Great Plains. Their interest is not recreational but botanical. They carefully specify the kinds of vegetation that grow in sections of prairie, using vegetation types described by A.W. Kuchler ("Potential Natural Vegetation of the Conterminous United States," *American Geographical Society Special Publication 36* [1964]). The region covered stretches from Indiana Dunes (IN) on the southeastern shore of Lake Michigan to Bighorn Canyon (MT), and from Fort Union Trading Post (MT-ND) to Lyndon B. Johnson National Historical Park (TX). For each unit they identify, the authors supply a description of the National Park unit, a map of it showing the prairie portion, specification of Kuchler vegetation type(s), present vegetation type and prairie management history, land use and vegetation within one mile of the Park boundary, and "Prairie Research"–that is, research conducted in the Park unit. A long classed bibliography (p. 227-307) collects all the entries from the "Prairie Research" sections. There is no index, but apart from the bibliography, none is needed; there, one would allow entries to be located without sifting its 80 pages. — *RB*

AA9   U.S. National Archives and Records Administration : Central Plains Region [Internet Site]. - [Washington, DC] : U.S. National Archives and Records Administration, 2000s- . - http://www. archives.gov/central-plains/

> Access Date: June 2006
> Fees: None

• NARA maintains regional centers where citizens and others may consult archival materials of regional interest. The regional center for Prairies-Plains is the Central Plains Region in Kansas City, MO; other regional centers relevant to Plains study are the Rocky Mountain region in Denver, CO and the Southwest region in Austin, TX. The Central Plains facility provides copies of the most heavily used records held at the central NARA facility in Washington, DC, and makes some attempt to provide holdings tailored to the region. Among subjects of local interest are: frontier and territorial history, American Indians native to the Northern Great Plains, the development of natural resources, and certain court cases. Records for nearly 100 federal agencies in Kansas, Nebraska, North Dakota, and South Dakota are also archived. Finding aids are not available online though request forms for court case transcripts are. A subject index for the NARA Internet site links to other agencies and collections of interest. Prairies-Plains researchers will find it best to consult the Internet site's information for the public and contact the facility before making a visit. A pdf file, "General Information Leaflet" for genealogical and historical researchers, outlines procedures and lists the available NARA record groups. Two presidential libraries, that for Eisenhower in Abilene, KS and for Truman in Independence, MO, are within easy reach; NARA has jurisdiction over all presidential libraries. — *JD*

AA10   Winckler, Suzanne, 1946–   . - **The Plains States** / text by Suzanne Winckler ; special photography by Jonathan Wallen, Tim Thompson ; editorial director, Roger G. Kennedy. – Rev. ed. - New York : Stewart, Tabori & Chang, 1998. - 461 p. ; ill (some col.), col. maps. - (The Smithsonian Guides to Historic America).

    Class Numbers:
        Library of Congress F595.3
    ISBN 1556701233 155670125X (pbk.)
    OCLC 19670134
    LCCN 89-4624
    Notes:
        Index

• Winckler's lavishly illustrated guidebook features historic sites in what the Smithsonian considers the states of the Plains–Missouri, Kansas, Nebraska, Iowa, and the Dakotas. Other Plains states are in three other Smithsonian regions. Double-spread outline maps for each state show roads, rivers, forts, missions, parks, and historic sites, all described in varying detail in the text, where sites of historic interest are shown in boldface. Index of persons and places. Useful as a guide to historic sites, and notable primarily for its illustrations, some historic, others present-day photographs. — *RB*

AA11   Winckler, Suzanne, 1946-   . - **Prairie : A North American Guide.** - Iowa City, IA : Univ. of Iowa Pr., 2004. - 132 p. ; maps. - (A Bur Oak guide).

    Class Numbers:
        Library of Congress GB571
    ISBN 0877458839 (pbk.)
    Notes:
        Includes bibliographical references; index

• Winckler provides a guidebook to the remaining patches of the tallgrass and shortgrass prairies that once covered the central U.S. and the Prairie provinces of Canada. Sections in her book are arranged north to south, Canada to Texas, providing brief descriptions of preserves and parks where the prairie environment may still be seen, some public, some in private hands. Each chapter begins with an outline map that shows major roads and locations of prairie sections, marked with icons that indicate size in acres. Winckler supplies driving directions for each location. A bibliography divided into a general section and one for each state includes Internet sites and is followed by two indexes, one alphabetical by place, the other arranged by state, then alphabetical by place. A single section covers the Canadian Prairie provinces, another both Dakotas; Iowa, Illinois, Minnesota, and Missouri are included, but not Montana, Wyoming, Colorado, or New Mexico. — *RB*

AB : Periodicals

Scope Includes directories and lists of periodicals, periodical indexes, and lists and indexes of newspapers.

General Works

AB1   Gale Directory of Publications and Broadcast Media. -122nd ed. (1990)–   . Detroit, MI : Gale Research, 1990–   . Annual.

> Ed. 140 publ. Aug. 2005
> Former titles: Ayer *Directory of Publications* (v. 1 [1880]-v. 114 [1982]. Philadelphia, PA : Ayer). Annual. (Title varies: *N.W. Ayer and Son's Directory of Newspapers and Periodicals*; 1970-71; 1960-1969, *Ayer Directory: Newspapers, Magazines ...*); The IMS ... Ayer *Directory of Publications* (Ed. 115 [1983]-ed. 117 [1985]. Fort Washington, PA: IMS Pr.) Annual.; *IMS Directory of Publications* (Ed. 118 [1986]); *Gale Directory of Publications* (Ed. 119 [1987]-ed. 121 [1989]. Detroit, MI: Gale Research).
> OCLC 39072647
> Notes:
>> Available as part of Gale's *Ready Reference Shelf* at subscribing libraries:
>> http://galenet.gale.com/m/mcp/db/grr/

• The five volumes of *Gale Directory* cover printed newspapers, magazines, journals, and other periodicals, but exclude newsletters and directories. Media entries list radio and television stations and cable television systems. Volumes 1-2 arrange entries alphabetically by state for the U.S. and by province for Canada. Each entry distinguishes between print and media, gives a general description and location, advertising rates, and lists contact personnel (giving their Internet and e-mail addresses where known). Volume 3 has subject indexes and a master index for all entries; volume 4 provides a regional marketing index; and volume 5 lists international publications and broadcast media. *Gale Directory* covers all media, including those in rural areas; for example, South Dakota entries include small-town newspapers. —*JB*

AB2   Kanellos, Nicólas. - Hispanic Periodicals in the United States, Origins to 1960 : A Brief History and Comprehensive Bibliography / by Nicólas Kanellos and Helvetia Martell. - Houston, TX : Arte Publico Pr., 2000. - 359 p.
> Class Numbers:
>> Library of Congress PN4885.S75 Z6853.5.S66

ISBN 1558852530
LCCN 98-28341
Notes:
> Indexes

• The introductory history notes that the first printing press, news sheets, periodicals, and newspapers in the Americas appeared in the Spanish Empire in 1533, 1541, 1693 and 1722, respectively. Today, an extensive Hispanic press performs cultural and information functions for audiences on both sides of the border. The not-so-brief, well-documented history describes the development and spread of the Hispanic press. The bibliography of 1,700 periodicals includes no less than 900 with no known extant issues. While places of publication are located throughout the U.S., the majority are in New Mexico and Texas. Entries include titles, places, publishers, dates, frequencies, brief print histories, languages, and sources of documentation. Holdings are not noted but many titles are documented in OCLC. Geographical index by state and city; chronological index by date of first issue; and subject index with names, titles, and topics. —*JD*

AB3   The Literary Magazine and Press Directory / [sponsored by] Council of Literary Magazines and Presses. - 2005-2006 ed. (2005)-   . - Brooklyn, NY : Soft Skull Pr., 2005–   . Annual.

> Class Numbers:
>> Library of Congress PN2; Z6513
> Notes:
>> Preceding titles: *The Directory of Literary Magazines and Presses* (20th ed., 2002 – 21st ed., 2003); *Directory of Literary Magazines* (New York: Coordinating Council of Literary Magazines, 1984-2001; ISSN 0884-6006)
>> Publisher varies: 20th ed. publ. by: San Francisco [CA]: Manic D Pr.

• Typically, annual editions of this useful directory include alphabetic lists of literary magazines, literary presses, literary magazine/presses, and online publishers. Each entry includes some of a long list of possible information items (addresses, subject matter, recent authors, reading period, payment, staff size, and the like). Indexes are alphabetical (all the magazines, presses, and online publishers interfiled), by editorial focus, by state, nonprofit literary publishers, and distributors. An introduction offers well-considered and blessedly brief advice to aspiring writers on getting published and on negotiating with editors. The index by state makes identifying titles published in Prairies-Plains states a cinch, but not foolproof: *Minnesota Review* is edited in Columbia, MO. — *RB*

AB4   Wynar, Lubomyr Roman, 1932-   . - Encyclopedic Directory of Ethnic Newspapers and Periodicals in the United States / [by] Lubomyr R. Wynar and Anna T.

Wynar. – 2nd ed. - Littleton, CO : Libraries Unlimited, 1976. – 248 p.

Class Numbers:
    Library of Congress Z6953.5.a1
ISBN 0872871541
LCCN 76-23317
Notes:
    1st ed., 1972

• Based on surveys of ethnic presses and organizations, the Wynars' directory is a guide to primary and secondary sources on the historical and sociological study of ethnic groups. Though in need of both an update and a geographical index, it is useful in reference or collection development for identifying ethnic presses either located in the Prairies-Plains region or significant to the Plains. The many titles that began in the 19th century are important sources on early migration and immigrant cultures. The work does not include the numerous ceased titles, non-English trade and professional publications titles, or American Indian and black presses, which are covered in other sources (*A Register and History of Negro Newspapers in the United States, 1827-1950*, **AB16**; *American Indian and Alaska Native Newspapers and Periodicals* **CD121**; or *Negro Newspapers on Microfilm*, **AB15**). Organized by ethnic group, entries total 977 titles from 63 ethnic groups and include a translation for non-English titles, year of origin, directory information, language, sponsor, circulation, frequency, subscription rate, and annotation. Statistical analyses are included in the introduction and appendix. A quick browse shows Swedish presses in Colorado; Spanish in New Mexico and Texas; and Jewish in Colorado, Oklahoma, and Nebraska. Most titles will be available through *United States Newspaper Program* (**AB14**). Indexed by title. — *JD*

Indexes

AB5   **19th Century Masterfile [Internet Site]**. - Sterling, VA : Paratext, 1990s–   . - http://www.paratext.com/

Class Numbers:
    Library of Congress AI3
OCLC 51647919
Access Date : Mar. 2006
Notes:
    Contents: 1. – Poole's and other multititle periodical indexes: *Poole's Index to Periodical Literature* (1802-1906); *Stead's Index to Periodicals* (1890-1906); Jones & Chipman's *Index to Legal Periodical Literature* (1786-1922); Richardson's *Index to Periodical Articles in Religion* (1890-1899); 2. – 19th century book and periodical bibliographic records; 3. – *New York Times* and other newspaper indexes: *New York Times Index* (1863-1905); *New York Daily Tribune Index* (1875-

1906); Palmer's *Index to The Times* (London) (1880-1890); Index to the *Oregon Spectator* (1846-1854); 4. – Individual title indexes with full text links: *Harpers Magazine Index* (1850-1892); *Atlantic Monthly Index* (1857-1901); *North American Review* (1815-1877); *Library Journal Index* (1876-1897); 5. – Patent and government publication indexes: *Subject Matter Index of Patents Issued by the U.S.* (1790-1873); *Descriptive Catalog of the Gov. Pubns. of the U.S.* (1774-1881); *Compilation of the Messages and Papers of the Presidents* (1789-1897); *Hansard's Index to Debates*, House of Commons only (1803-1830); *Hansard's Index to Debates*, House of Lords only (1803-1830); Cobbett's *Parliamentary History of England* (1066-1803).
    Originally released as: *Poole'sPlus*
    Fees: Subscription

• The producers combine several printed indexes to provide citations to 8,000 popular and scholarly periodicals plus books, government publications, and patents. Though the site focuses on the 19th century, some late 18th- and early 20th-century works are included. *Masterfile* has five series, which are available separately. Indexes of particular interest for Plains research are *Poole's* 1802-1906, Richardson's *Index to Periodical Articles in Religion* 1890-1899, and *Index to Legal Periodical Literature* 1786-1922, all in Series I. The index is not ideal for either identifying or accessing works. The search engine is basic, with results organized by index and ranked by relevancy. Entries consist of citations that unhappily have not been enhanced from the original printed indexes, so they lack abstracts and offer few indexing terms. The search "Great American Desert," for example, retrieved only nine results while the same search retrieved 771 records in ProQuest's *American Periodicals Series Online* (**AB6**). Though *American Periodicals Series* has full text, better functionality, a more powerful search engine, and special features, *19th Century Masterfile* has wider coverage of 19th-century works. The index is open-URL compliant, allowing easy linkage to other full-text collections, but many of *Masterfile's* sources have not been digitized and may be difficult to find. — *JD*

AB6   **American Periodicals Series Online, 1740-1900 [Internet Site]**. - [Ann Arbor, MI] : ProQuest Information and Learning Co., 2000–   . - http://www.proquest.com/

OCLC 48159241
LCCN 2004-354457
Access Date : Mar. 2006
Notes:
    Alternate title: *APS Online*
    Fees: Subscription

• Derived from the APS Series I, II, and III on microfilm, the online version indexes all elements in all pages of more than 1,100 periodicals that began publishing between 1740 and 1900, with coverage for some extending into the 20th century. It contains digitized images of the documents as well as images of the full pages showing layout, typography and accompanying material. Searches can be limited by type of publication (including magazines, newspapers, trade publications, scholarly journals, and reports) or by type of document (advertisements, cartoons, letters, obituaries, photographs, poems, recipes, reviews, statistics, comics, and illustrations). The index reveals numerous documents written about the Plains or read by Plains people. The site provides a quick way to find a Great Northern Railway advertisement for "low rates west"; an illustration of the Dodge City "Peace Commission"; an exposé on the travails of the Ponca in Indian Territory; or a news article on the 1860 famine in Kansas. APS uses an early and broad definition of newspaper, which can lead to some confusion for researchers seeking specific types of publications. — *JD*

AB7   Bibliography of Old West Characters from Selected Western Periodical Literature, 1953-2003 [CD-ROM] / by Larry J. Walker. - [La Pine, OR : Magazine House], 2004.

> OCLC 79401360
> Access Date : May 2008
> Notes:
>   1 CD-ROM, 4-3/4 in.
>   Based on James A. Browning, *The Western Reader's Guide*
> Fees: None

• Consists of about 650 pages of citations arranged alphabetically by author. References to materials published 1991-1996 were derived from the files of James A. Browning, compiler of *The Western Reader's Guide;* the remainder were compiled by the author using magazines with titles such as *Old West, True West, Frontier West,* and *The West.* The bibliography is available as both pdf and rtf files. There is no index so searchers must use the "Find" command to locate materials, which, since most searchers will be looking for proper names, will retrieve relevant sources. Individuals known both by a given name and another designation (e.g., Emily Morgan, the "Yellow Rose of Texas") will need to be searched using both names. — *MS*

AB8   Index to Texas Magazines and Documents. - [v. 1], (1986)- . Victoria, TX : Victoria College/Univ. of Houston-Victoria Library, 1988- . Quarterly.

> Notes:
>   Annual, 1986-1987
>   Quarterly with annual cumulation

• "A non commercial venture" (Introd.). Indexes approximately 40 periodicals consisting of general interest maga-

zines, regional historical journals, trade, professional, and government magazines. Journals covered include *Journal of Big Bend Studies, Panhandle-Plains Historical Journal, West Texas Historical Association Yearbook, Texas Highways,* and *Texas Heritage.* Materials are indexed using *Library of Congress Subject Headings* as subject authority. Some entries include annotations. Book and movie reviews are presented separately in two indexes, both separate from the main index. — *MS*

AB9   Oklahoma Periodicals Index : An Index to Four Key Oklahoma Periodicals [Internet Site] / Oklahoma State Univ. Library. - Stillwater, OK : Oklahoma State Univ. Library, 2000-   . - http://www.library.okstate.edu/database/perindex.htm

> Access Date: July 2005
> Fees: None

• A topical index to the most recent five years of four periodicals relating to Oklahoma, with some coverage outside the state. The periodical titles, all currently published, are those published in Oklahoma that are held by the largest number of Oklahoma libraries: *Chronicles of Oklahoma, Oklahoma Today, Outdoor Oklahoma,* and *Persimmon Hill.* The index covers 2000 to the present; articles in issues for 1999 and earlier years are being added. The site gives no information about the total number of entries. The search engine, Reference Web Poster, supports as many as eight search terms, will search five individual fields (author, title, keyword, etc.), all indexed fields, or all unindexed fields, and allows Boolean operators. Displays (not in standard MLA format) give full citations that supply inclusive pagination, but provide neither abstracts nor full text. Records may be printed (if instructions for printing records under "Search Tips" are followed carefully) or saved to disk, but may not be e-mailed. The site will be useful to readers exploring Oklahoma topics, but including additional titles and pushing indexing back to the beginning of publication for each title will increase its usefulness. — *RB*

AB10   Periodicals Index Online : [PIO] [Internet Site]. - [Cambridge, UK] : Chadwyck-Healey, 1996-   . - http://pio.chadwyck.com/

> Access Date : May 2006
> Notes:
>   Preceding title: *Periodicals Contents Index*
>   Updated weekly
> Fees: Subscription

• One of the largest indexing efforts ever attempted, PIO presently holds some 15 million records of articles from journals drawn from more than 4,800 journal titles in 40 languages. For every title, the intention is to index the entire run back to its initial issue, with a goal of more than 5,000 titles and more than 20 million records. The publishers claim to add one million records per year. PIO restricts subject matter to humanities and social sciences (including history), both scholarly titles and popular titles that provide research materials of interest to scholars. The index includes monographs in series, but excludes newspapers, publications that are mainly pictorial, and journals that are themselves indexes. Users may access entries for individual journal titles, see which issues have been indexed, and view the tables of contents of individual issues. The tables of contents form the basis for the index itself; the actual articles are not seen by indexing staff. PIO links to a full-text source, *Periodicals Archive Online*, which offers full text for 400 journal titles (though the publishers do not reveal whether the full run is available in full text) and provides links to JSTOR and Project MUSE. The journals indexed are also arranged by 37 subject categories, the only arrangement by subject the site provides. The search engine allows searching the entire file by keyword, but since this commonly produces fewer responses than the more detailed searching in "Article Search," it should be avoided. In "Article Search," users may search by keyword(s), article title keyword(s), author, journal title, language, journal subject (i.e., the 37 categories), year of publication, and ISSN, or by any combination of fields. Many of the journals PIO indexes are indexed elsewhere, but only PIO indexes back to the first issue, and this access over the entire run of any journal constitutes PIO's great advantage. Some sample searches: "Great Plains," 901 articles, the earliest 1858 (simple keyword search produced only 609); "Great American Desert," 53, earliest 1888; "Lewis and Clark," 537, earliest 1807; "Sandhills," 76 (but many not relevant; "Sandhills Nebraska"produced five); "Moose Jaw," 17, earliest 1913; "Coronado," 277, earliest 1864 (many not relevant). Responses do not highlight the search statement, so longer records require careful scanning. PIO's long temporal coverage promises to support Prairies-Plains research, producing citations otherwise not findable, but in such an immense file, users will do well to refine search strategy before submitting any query in order to avoid responses that are off target. PIO will be useful in Plains studies because of its large base of journals and its unrivalled coverage into the 19th (and in some cases, the 18th) century. — *RB*

AB11 **South Dakota Periodicals Index** / Clark N. Hallman, project director. - [1st] (1982-1986)- . - Brookings, SD : Reference Dept., Hilton M. Briggs Library, South Dakota State Univ., 1987- . - Irregular.

Class Numbers:

Library of Congress Z1283
OCLC 16515930
Notes:
Funded in part by a grant from the South Dakota Committee on the Humanities

• A subject and author index to articles contained in 26 South Dakota periodicals published 1987-1991 intended for a general audience and concentrating on state events, people, and locations. The subject section, arranged alphabetically by subject heading, lists articles, citing author, title, periodical, volume and issue number, inclusive pages, and date; an author index follows. — *GK*

AB12 Winther, Oscar Osburn, 1903-1970. - A **Classified Bibliography of the Periodical Literature of the Trans-Mississippi West (1811-1967)** / [by] Oscar Osburn Winther [and] Richard A. Van Orman. - Westport, CT : Greenwood Pr., 1972, 1961. - xxvi, 626, xxv, 340 p. - (Indiana University publications. Social science series, 19, 26).

Class Numbers:
Library of Congress Z1251.W5
ISBN 0837164753
OCLC 929094
LCCN 72-6218
Notes:
Reprint. Originally publ.: Bloomington, IN: Indiana Univ. Pr., 1961, covering 1811-1957 (ISBN 0253384265; LCCN 61-63869); Supplement, 1970, covering 1957-1967 (ISBN 023384265)

• This reprint binds together the 1961 edition and the 1970 supplement without attempting to merge the two titles or renumber the entries, the page numbers, or the indexes. The first part cites 9,244 articles, the second 4,559. The structure of the two parts is highly similar: both arrange entries under categories that are usually broad, and interfile geographical and topical headings alphabetically ("Kansas" is followed by "Lewis and Clark Expedition"). Topical changes are summarized in the preface to the Supplement (p. v-vi). The entire trans-Mississippi West is covered, including Alaska but not Hawaii. Sections pertinent to Plains study include, e.g., "Great Plains" (two pages), "Indian Territory," "Kansas" (as well as other Plains states), "Range and Cattle," "Immigrant Groups." Most categories are subdivided by topic, and entries are subarranged alphabetically under topic. Detailed author indexes follow both the basic list and the Supplement. Cross-references appear at the head of each category. Although the basic index and the Supplement each index fewer than 100 periodical titles, this is an important index to the periodical literature of the West and will be essential to students of either the West or the Plains. — *MB*

NEWSPAPERS

United States

AB13 Riley, Sam G. - **Biographical Dictionary of American Newspaper Columnists**. - Westport, CT : Greenwood Pr., 1995. - 411 p.

    Class Numbers:
        Library of Congress PN4871
        ISBN 0313291926 031033298X (electronic bk.)
        LCCN 95-7185
    Notes:
        Electronic book:
            http://www.ebooks.greenwood.com/reader.jsp?x=
            0313291926&p=cover
        Includes bibliographical references (p. [367]-374); index

• Brief sketches of approximately 600 columnists who wrote in areas such as politics, humor, and all-purpose lifestyle; columnists in more specialized areas such as finance, health, and various hobbies are excluded. Entries include a short biography, summary of career, information about the column, books written, and reference sources. In addition to national figures with roots in the Great Plains such as Eric Sevareid (North Dakota), Damon Runyon (Kansas), and Jeanne Kirkpatrick (Oklahoma), a large number of local columnists are included. The index contains the titles of newspapers such as *Wichita Eagle-Beacon*, *Tulsa Tribune*, and *Omaha World Herald*; a careful reading yields papers such as *The Forum* (Fargo, ND). Provides a means to identify columnists associated with the Plains region and lesser-known columnists not in the various volumes of *American Newspaper Journalists* ("Dictionary of Literary Biography," volumes 23, 25, 29, and 43). — *JD*

AB14 **United States Newspaper Program [Internet Site]** / National Endowment for the Humanities. - [Washington, DC] : National Endowment for the Humanities, 2000s-   . - http://www.neh.gov/projects/esnp.html#ENR

    Access Date : June 2006
    Fees: None

• Printed newspaper finding aids have generally been made obsolete by *U.S. Newspaper Program*, which worked with partners in all 50 states and eight national repositories to inventory, catalog, and microfilm all extant newspapers; to house the microfilm in state repositories; and to make the microfilm reels available through Interlibrary Loan. The NEH Internet site gives directory information and links to the repository in each state. Some links go directly to a newspaper holdings list or search page; others require some negotiation of the institution's Internet site. A few state repositories, including the Colorado Historical Society, do not yet list the holdings on their sites. Cataloging for all titles may be found in OCLC. Provision of full-text access and indexing are not part of the program. Invaluable for identifying and acquiring Great Plains newspapers. — *JD*

Black Newspapers

AB15 Library of Congress. Photoduplication Service. - **Negro Newspapers on Microfilm : A Selected List**. - Washington, DC : Library of Congress. Photoduplication Service, 1953. - 8 p.

    Class Numbers:
        Library of Congress Z6944.N39
        LCCN 53-60015

• A brief list of titles and holdings of microfilmed black newspapers held at the Library of Congress. Support for filming was awarded by the Committee on Negro Studies of the American Council of Learned Societies. Positive copies may be purchased from LC's Photoduplication Service. Newspaper titles are listed alphabetically by state; entries give dates, missing issues, and number of reels. The largest number of titles from Plains states are from Kansas and Nebraska, but there are also titles for Oklahoma, Texas, and Colorado. — *JB*

AB16 Pride, Armistead Scott. - **A Register and History of Negro Newspapers in the United States, 1827-1950**. - Evanston, IL : Pride, 1973. - 426 leaves.

    Class Numbers:
        Library of Congress Z6944.N39
    Notes:
        Dissertation [PhD?]: Northwestern Univ., 1973.
        Includes bibliographical references (leaves 423-426)
        Photocopy of typescript. Ann Arbor, MI: Univ.
            Microfilms, 1975

• A photocopy of a dissertation that derived from a project initiated by the Committee on Negro Studies of the American Council of Learned Societies (1946). A lengthy introduction explains the process and significance of the research. An initial section discusses black newspapers by state, giving background, publishing history, and their place in the U.S. social framework. The register proper follows, listing all known newspapers by state, library locations, and indicating for which titles no known copies have been found. States of interest to Prairies-Plains researchers will be Kansas, Nebraska, and Texas, with the richest archives in Kansas. — *JB*

Colorado

AB17 Oehlerts, Donald E. - **Guide to Colorado Newspapers, 1859-1984.** - Greeley, CO : Univ. of Northern Colorado, James A. Michener Library, 1984. - 183 p.

> Class Numbers:
> Library of Congress Z6952.C7
> OCLC 10807054

• Oehlerts lists 2,844 titles of newspapers published in Colorado, 1859-1984; of these, complete files could be located for 320 titles (11 percent), but for 1,959 (70 percent) no file at all could be found. The earliest titles, both published in Denver, began in 1859–*Cherry Creek Pioneer* and *Rocky Mountain News*; the *Pioneer* did not last out the year, but the *News* ran until 1925, competing with a rival paper by the same name, still published (and sometimes referred to locally as "Rocky Mountain Spotted News"). Entries are arranged alphabetically by county, then by town; titles for each town are arranged chronologically by beginning date. Holdings (where any exist) follow the entry, with libraries identified with NUC symbols (most are in Colorado, supplemented by holdings in 19 libraries outside the state). Entries give title, frequency, publishing dates, and holdings. A map of Colorado shows counties and numbered place-names. Index of town names and newspaper titles. — *RB*

Kansas

AB18 Anderson, Aileen, comp. - **Kansas Newspapers : A Directory of Newspaper Holdings in Kansas** / produced by the Kansas Library Network Board. - Topeka, KS : Kansas Library Network Board, 1984. - 268 p.

> Class Numbers:
> Library of Congress PN4897.K3 Z6952.K2
> OCLC 12557851
> LCCN 85-620570
> Notes:
> Indexes

• "Only in Kansas," writes State Archivist Eugene Decker in the preface, "could a newspaper be published before there was news to print." This union list of newspaper holdings is incomplete, since at publication time the holdings of the largest collection in the state, at the Kansas State Historical Society in Topeka, were still being inventoried; their holdings can be found at the Society's Internet site (**AB19**) or at the site of the *United States Newspaper Program* (**AB14**). This union list is arranged by county, then town, then alphabetically by title. Notes link each title to earlier or later versions, and holdings notations cite holding institution (chiefly libraries), dates of holdings, and format (paper or film). Indexes of towns and cities (which refer to county names), and of newspaper titles. A supplementary list gives addresses of holding institutions. Useful because it gives holdings of many smaller institutions. — *RB*

AB19 **Newspapers in Kansas [Internet Site]** / Kansas State Historical Society. - Topeka, KS : Kansas State Historical Society, 2000s- . - http://www.kshs.org/library/news.htm

> Access Date : May 2007
> Notes:
> Part of the Kansas State Historical Society Internet site, http://www.kshs.org/
> Fees: None

• The KSHS Internet site includes this site, intended to provide access to newspapers, principally those published in Kansas, but adding titles from other locations as well. Several subsidiary files list specialized newspapers: black newspapers, Kansas Civilian Conservation Corps, labor, Populist, Socialist, and papers of the territorial period. Clicking on any of the subsidiary files displays titles, publication dates, publisher, and holdings. The site is intended only to indicate holdings of newspapers, either on paper or microfilm. A typical search ("Wichita *Eagle*" for 1929-1930) produces a month-by-month list of microfilm reels for that period, 40 in all. The home page claims that KSHS owns a "virtually complete collection of all Kansas newspapers published from 1875 to the present." Readers should not expect any information concerning the history of any title (except in the subsidiary files); the site is a finding list, and other information about any title–publisher, dates, early or famous editors, political stance (if known)–must be sought elsewhere. — *RB*

New Mexico

AB20 Grove, Pearce S., 1930- , ed. - **New Mexico Newspapers : A Comprehensive Guide to Bibliographical Entries and Locations** / Pearce S. Grove, Becky J. Barnett, Sandra J. Hansen, eds. ; with the research assistance of Edward A. Richter and Bill D. Sheridan ; cartography by William J. Mettenet. - Albuquerque, NM : Univ. of New Mexico Pr., 1975. – xxxvi, 641 p. ; maps.

> Class Numbers:
> Library of Congress Z952.N55
> ISBN 0826303366
> OCLC 1531635
> LCCN 74-84232

• Confining themselves to the present boundaries of the state, the editors arrange the index by counties. For each county they provide an outline map that shows towns and cities with published newspapers. Entries by town cite past and current titles of newspapers, years of publication, location of copies, volumes and issues held, and format. Entries include notes about special issues and preceding and succeeding titles. Ten plates depict newspaper offices and editors from various parts of the state. The editors claim accuracy to date of publication of this list. Useful in identifying New Mexico newspaper titles. — *JB*

North Dakota

AB21   State Historical Society of North Dakota. - **The North Dakota Newspaper Inventory**. - Bismarck, ND : State Historical Society of North Dakota, 1992. - 295 p.

Class Numbers:
    Library of Congress Z6945
    OCLC 28498841
    LCCN 93-120554

• A catalog of newspapers held by the State Historical Society of North Dakota; it forms part of the North Dakota Newspaper Project completed in 1991. Entries provide information on original newsprint copies, microfilm holdings, and master microfilm holdings. Entries are arranged by state or province, then by city or town. Under towns, entries are listed alphabetically by title. Title merges are indicated. At the front are lists of non-English-language and combined language newspapers published in North Dakota. — *JB*

South Dakota

AB22   **South Dakota State Newspapers [Internet Site]**. – Pierre, SD : South Dakota State Historical Society, 2000s. - http://www.sdhistory.org/arc/newspaper/default. asp

Access Date : Mar. 2005
Fees: None
Notes:
    Also publ. in print: *South Dakota Newspapers on Microfilm, 1859-2001*, ed. by LaVera Rose. Pierre, SD: South Dakota State Archives, 2002. 112 p.

• LaVera Rose (Project Director, South Dakota Newspaper Project) has compiled a comprehensive list of South Dakota newspapers available on microfilm from the State Archives in Pierre. The Archives house over 14,000 reels of newspapers on microfilm as part of NEH's *United States Newspaper Program* (**AB14**). The work is organized in two parts: newspapers listed by city and newspapers listed by title. For general readers, an Access database was mounted in 2002. Individuals can also search the South Dakota Library

Network's online catalog for information regarding state newspapers. — *GK*

Texas

AB23   Historical Records Survey (TX). - **Texas Newspapers, 1813-1939 : A Union List of Newspaper Files Available in Offices of Publishers, Libraries, and a Number of Private Collections** / prepared by Historical Records Survey Program, Div. of Professional and Service Projects, Work Projects Administration of Texas. - Houston, TX : San Jacinto Museum of History Association, 1941. - 293 p. - (San Jacinto Museum of History Association. [Publications, v. 1]).

Class Numbers:
    Library of Congress Z6952.T5
    OCLC 1535636
    LCCN 41-27316
Notes:
    Reproduced from typescript

• A union list of Texas newspapers held by libraries and other institutions across the U.S., the largest number of depositories being in Texas. The list is arranged by town, Abernathy to Yorktown, giving for each town the titles of newspapers published there during the specified period, and supplying dates of publication and in many cases issue-specific holdings. Since many titles were selected from *Union List of Newspapers* (1937), holdings from that list are indicated by an asterisk preceding the holding institution. The union list is followed by a chronological list of titles published prior to 1877, and an index of titles (all the papers called *Lone Star*, for example). A list of libraries with their symbols precedes the union list. To be used with caution, since in a list more than 60 years old, some titles will have disintegrated, been replaced by microfilm or online files, been discarded, or in some cases the depositories themselves may no longer exist. — *RB*

CANADA

AB24   **Canadian Newsstand Prairies [Internet Site]**. - [Ann Arbor, MI] : ProQuest Information and Learning Co., 1999. - http://www.il.proquest.com/products_pq/descriptions/canadian_newsstand.shtml

Access Date : Jan. 2006
Fees: Subscription

• This regional subset of *Canadian Newsstand* contains the full text of the *Calgary Herald, Edmonton Journal, Leader-Post* (Regina), *Moose Jaw Times Herald, Prince Albert Daily Herald, Regina Sun, Saskatoon Sun,* and *Star-Phoenix*

(Saskatoon). It oddly also includes the *Whitehorse Star* (Yukon Territory), but no newspapers from Manitoba, an omission the vendor eventually plans to remedy. Classifieds, death notices, and illustrations are among the few elements omitted. Coverage varies, with some papers going back to the late 1980s; the site is updated daily, with a two-day delay. Basic and advanced search modes use the standard ProQuest interface. A welcome alternative to the tedium of using microfilm. — *LMcD*

Alberta

AB25 Strathern, Gloria M. - **Alberta Newspapers, 1880-1982 : An Historical Directory**. - Edmonton, AB : Univ. of Alberta Pr., 1988. - 568 p. ; ill.

> Class Numbers:
> Library of Congress PN4919.A45 Z6954.C2
> ISBN 0888641370 0888641389 (pbk.)
> 1417592923 (electronic bk.)
> OCLC 20630820
> LCCN 89-134955
> Notes:
> Electronic book: http://www.ourfutureourpast.ca/
> loc_hist/toc.aspx?id=1108
> Includes index and bibliographical references (p. 545-568)

• A comprehensive guide to 1,090 newspapers, with an additional 23 titles that may never have existed noted for good measure. The arrangement is by place of publication, with titles listed in chronological order. Dates of publication, frequency, special interest or ethnic affiliation, and language are indicated. Notes untangle complicated title relationships, provide brief chronologies and histories, indicate special features and supplements, and summarize the editors and publishers of each paper. Two hundred pages of biographical sketches. Chronological, ethnic, subject and title indexes provide multiple approaches to Alberta newspaper history. — *LMcD*

Manitoba

AB26 Loveridge, D. M. - **A Historical Directory of Manitoba Newspapers, 1859-1978**. – Winnipeg, MB : Univ. of Manitoba Pr., 1981. - 233 p.

> Class Numbers:
> Library of Congress PN4917.M32 ; Z6954.C2
> OCLC 7592746
> LCCN 81-179578
> Notes:
> Bibliography: p. 180-186
> Includes indexes

• Loveridge begins with an extended essay tracing the evolution of newspapers within the social and historical context of Manitoba. The directory proper consists of three sections listing English and French papers of rural Manitoba, English and French papers of the Winnipeg area, and ethnic newspapers. Within each section, entries are arranged by the geographic or ethnic community which they addressed, subarranged in order of first publication. Entries indicate frequency, dates of publication, notes on title changes and mergers, and library holdings. The subject index lists agricultural, commercial, fraternal, labor, religious, and alternative papers. The somewhat cryptic symbols and abbreviations used throughout require frequent referral to the key on p. 32-34. — *LMcD*

AB27 Manitoba Library Association. - **Manitoba Newspaper Checklist with Library Holdings, 1859-1986** / Manitoba Library Association with the assistance of Legislative Library of Manitoba, National Library of Canada, Manitoba Heritage Federation. - [Winnipeg, MB] : Manitoba Library Association, 1986. - 106 p.

> Class Numbers:
> Library of Congress Z6954.C2
> ISBN 0969281404
> OCLC 16180550

• A brief but comprehensive listing. Arrangement is by place with newspapers published outside Winnipeg listed first, followed by Winnipeg papers. Publication dates, history including title changes, and holdings are noted. Indexes by title, decade, language and subject. Extends the coverage of *A Historical Directory of Manitoba Newspapers, 1859-1978* (**AB26**). — *LMcD*

Saskatchewan

AB28 MacDonald, Christine. - *Historical Directory of Saskatchewan Newspapers, 1878-1983*. - Regina, SK : Saskatchewan Archives Board, 1984. - 87 p. : ill. - (Saskatchewan Archives reference series, 4).

> Class Numbers:
> Library of Congress PN4917.S3   Z6954.C2
> ISBN 0969144539
> OCLC 12265644
> LCCN 86-121600
> Notes:
> Revised ed. of: *Historical Directory of Saskatchewan*
> *Newspapers, 1878-1950* (1951)

• Arranged by place of publication rather than the more customary place of coverage, requiring frequent use of cross-references. Beginning date, frequency, chronological listing of owners, editors and publishers, variant titles, mergers, and splits are traced in painstaking detail. Holdings of the Saskatchewan Archives Board are indicated. Although lacking some of the useful features of provincial counterparts such as *Alberta Newspapers, 1880–1982* (**AB25**), the work simplifies the complex histories of many newspapers in an easy-to-use fashion. — *LMcD*

AB29 Saskatchewan News Index [Internet Site]. - Saskatoon, SK : Univ. of Saskatchewan Libraries, 2000s - . - http://library.usask.ca/sni/

   OCLC 45363118
   Access Date : Apr. 2006
   Fees: None

• Indexes four daily newspapers (*Leader-Post* [Regina], *Moose Jaw Times Herald*, *Prince Albert Daily Herald*, *Star-Phoenix* [Saskatoon] and their antecedents); the weekly *Western Producer*; and several community papers. Dates of coverage differ. Generally indexes only articles originating in the province; birth/wedding/funeral announcements, editorials, and most sports stories are excluded. Searching is by title, subject, and keyword; "Browse" offers ten searchable fields, with "Subject (Exact)" giving the most systematic results. "Advanced" provides Boolean searching, limits by year and newspaper (including, unaccountably, three from Winnipeg), and sorting. "Search History" permits combining of sets; results can be e-mailed. The only full text is in a "Top News Stories" feature that contains a selection of representative articles under 11 broad categories such as agriculture, arts, and politics. SNI is useful for researching more than a century of history and development. *Canadian Newsstand Prairies* (**AB24**) contains the full text of six Saskatchewan newspapers. — *LMcD*

AC : Collective Biographies

Scope Lists collective biographies with an international or national base, and those that are general whose base is a state or province. Collective biographies that feature persons active in a profession (e.g., geologists), that concentrate on a topic (e.g., art), or that are concerned with an ethnic group (e.g., Mexican Americans) will be found with that topic.

General Works

AC1 Biography Resource Center [Internet Site]. - Farmington Hills, MI : Gale Group, c2002– . - http://infotrac.galegroup.com/

> LCCN 2002-556415
> Access Date: Feb. 2006
> Fees: Subscription

• This general resource is so vast it permits numerous entries to be found concerning both contemporary and historical figures important to Prairies-Plains study. Its interface allows users to locate easily materials in four categories of sources: narrative biographies, thumbnail biographies, magazine articles, and Internet sites. It combines more than 422,000 biographies from 135 Gale Group sources with over half a million full-text articles from 300 magazines. Simple searches can begin with a name fragment or "name contains" (e.g., first name). It is possible to search by groups (rock bands, sports teams); search results yield information about both the group and its members. Advanced search permits searching by full text, keyword, or source document and combining these using Boolean operators. "Biographical Facts Search" allows searching by occupation or nationality (from controlled lists), gender, birth and death year, and location. Keyword searches can be used to identify entries containing place-names, but with less satisfying results. Online help supplies search tips, including truncation, operators, and date range searches. A helpful "Research Guide" assists in developing search strategy, while a more extensive help screen gives advice about advanced search techniques and navigating results. Recent search histories are saved and can be re-used. Displays resemble the printed source publications, and sometimes contain a small black-and-white portrait. — *MB*

AC2 In the First Person : An Index to Letters, Diaries, Oral Histories and Personal Narratives [Internet Site]. - Alexandria, VA : Alexander Street Pr., 2006 – . - http://www.inthefirstperson.com/firp/index.aspx

> Access Date: Feb. 2006
> Fees: None

• An index to personal names appearing in letters, diaries, personal narratives, and oral histories, published and unpublished, that are to be found in Internet collections available from Alexander Street Press. The collections so far covered are *North American Women's Letters and Diaries* (**CH1**); *The American Civil War: Letters and Diaries*; and *British and Irish Women's Letters and Diaries.* Coverage of persons of interest to Prairies-Plains students and scholars is therefore spotty (nearly 100 mentions of Willa Cather but none of Mari Sandoz), but Alexander Street promises that *North American Indian Biographical Database* (**CD46**) will be searchable soon, which will greatly increase the site's usefulness for Plains studies. The index allows searching personal names in any of the sources covered by the site, showing the names in a brief contextual setting and providing access to full text of the original. A good source for locating personal writing by a wide range of individuals. Unlike other Alexander Street sites, this one is free. — *RB*

United States

General Works

AC3 American National Biography / general eds., John A. Garraty, Mark C. Carnes. - New York : Oxford Univ. Pr., 1999. - 24 v.

> Class Numbers:
> Library of Congress CT213
> ISBN 0195206355 (set)
> LCCN 98-20826
> Notes:
> "Conceived as the successor to *Dictionary of American Biography*, first publ. between 1926 and 1937." — v. 1, p. xvii
> Contents: v. 1-24, A-Z
> Includes bibliographical references ; index
> Kept up to date by supplements
> Publ. under auspices of the American Council of Learned Societies
> Available as fee-based Internet site: http://www.anb.org/

• The replacement for *Dictionary of American Biography* (AC4) and, like it, published under the auspices of the American Council of Learned Societies, ANB is the record of accomplishment of notable Americans, "loosely defined as [those] whose significant actions occurred during his or her residence within what is now the United States or whose life and career directly influenced the course of American history" (Preface, v. 1, p. xvii). The subjects all died before 1996, and the editors (Garraty, history, Columbia Univ., and Carnes, history, Barnard College) used utility as their primary criterion for admission: "Would researchers want to know something about a particular figure?" (Preface, v. 1, p. xvii-xviii). They also attempted to emphasize the experience and contribution of ordinary citizens, often women or members of ethnic groups or racial minorities that earlier compilations ignored, and to pay careful attention to recent scholarship and to emergence of new fields of study. Candidates for inclusion are grouped by categories that are chiefly occupational (politics, performing arts, medicine, religion), but American Indians are put together in a single category. Like any large compilation concerned with the entire U.S., ANB will include subjects associated with the Prairies-Plains region, and indexes in the final volume offer some assistance in identifying them: all the persons who have separate entries are listed alphabetically; a roster of contributors lists the articles each wrote; subjects are listed by place of birth inside and outside the U.S. (less helpful than it might seem); and an index by occupations and "Realms of Renown" that lists subjects by their field of specialization. The latter has entries for, e.g., explorers, ethnologists, dramatists, cowboys, murder victims, and Indian cultural intermediaries, all categories that include Prairies-Plains figures, but even here they must be extracted from their fellows. The scholars who write the essays were chosen with care and intelligence (David Wishart on Pierre Chouteau Jr., James Woodress on Cather, Vernon Maddux on Jesse Chisholm), and all the entries end with bibliographies that attempt to point readers to sources where they may begin to seek additional information. Highly useful, and now the standard collective biography for noted Americans, ANB will provide background reading for Prairies-Plains figures, once readers have found them in the set. — *RB*

AC4   Dictionary of American Biography / [publ.] under the auspices of the American Council of Learned Societies. - New York : Scribner, 1928-1936. - 20 v. ; index ; supplements.

    Class Numbers:
        Library of Congress E176
        OCLC 167545
        LCCN 28-28500
        Notes:
            Comprehensive Index. New York: Scribner, 1990. 1001 p.
            Supplements 1-8. New York: Scribner, 1944-1988. 8 v. —

Contents: Suppl. 1, to Dec. 31, 1935, ed. by Harris E. Starr; Suppl. 2, 1936-1940, ed. by Robert L. Schuyler and Edward T. James; Suppl. 3, 1941-1945, ed. by Edward T. James; Suppl. 4, 1946-1950, ed. by John A. Garraty and Edward T. James; Suppl. 5, 1951-1955, ed. by John A. Garraty; Suppl. 6, 1956-1960, ed. by John A. Garraty; Suppl. 7, 1961-1965, ed. by John A. Garraty; Suppl. 8, 1966-1970, ed. by John A. Garraty and Mark C. Carnes
        Contents: v. 1-20, A-Z
        Editors; v. 1-3, Allen Johnson; v. 4-7, Allen Johnson and Dumas Malone; v. 8-20, Dumas Malone

• For decades, DAB stood as the standard collective biography about persons of the first importance in the American colonies and, after independence, in the United States. Now great in years, it is primarily suited to acquiring a picture of prominent American citizens as viewed by scholars of an earlier age. It includes only persons who have died, persons born outside the U.S. who "identified with the country and contributed notably to its history" (Introd., v. 1, p. vii), but no persons who never lived in the territory occupied by the United States, nor British officers who served in America after independence. The biographical sketches were written by specialists, who are listed with their entries (but with no affiliations) in the Index volume. The largest number of subjects are from the Eastern seaboard, and people of interest to Prairies-Plains study seem to be admitted only when their importance is so marked it cannot be ignored: Lewis and Clark, Pike, William Jennings Bryan, Sacajawea. Since living persons are excluded, supplemental volumes must be searched for the period of a person's death to find whether they have been admitted; Cather is in Supplement 4, 1946-1950. Although the Index volume lists in its "Occupations" section such professions as oarsman, cantor, and cabalist alongside expected professions in politics, literature, finance, the clergy, etc., and both "Indian Chief" and "Indian Leader," it lists for "Negro Leader" only four names and has no entry at all for women. (Feminists who wish to retain their composure should not read the v. 1 introduction.) The bibliographies, especially in the basic set, are too old to be of much use. Nevertheless, DAB is a work of great learning, written by scholars thoroughly familiar with their subjects, hence is well worth reading for its view of persons important to the founding and development of the United States. — *RB*

AC5   Kaplan, Louis, 1909-   . - A Bibliography of American Autobiographies / comp. by Louis Kaplan in association with James Tyler Cook, Clinton E. Colby Jr. [and] Daniel C. Haskell. - Madison, WI : Univ. of Wisconsin Pr., 1961. - 372 p.

    Class Numbers:
        Library of Congress Z1224

OCLC 552856
LCCN 61-5499

• Now more than half a century old, Kaplan's book needs revision, but can still be useful in locating autobiographies (that most self-serving genre) of Americans. Kaplan excludes several categories of publication: episodic accounts (e.g., Indian captivities), works in which the autobiographical element is insignificant (e.g., travel, exploration), autobiographies appearing in works of genealogy or collective biographies, manuscript autobiographies, spurious works, works known to be fictional, and works published after 1945. Entries, arranged alphabetically, include author (with date of birth), title, edition, publisher, date of publication, pagination, library holding the copy examined, and annotation (commonly very brief). Entries are numbered serially. The index, which refers to the serial numbers, lists subjects (principally occupations), where the biographees lived, and important historical events. For Prairies-Plains study, two geographic categories hold promise, "West North Central States" and "West South Central States" but several "occupational" categories also will have interest: cowboys, explorers, farmers and farm life, governors, immigrants (by country of origin), Indian agents, Indian fighters, Indians, missionaries, pioneers, railroad workers, ranchers and ranch life. Many index entries are heavily posted, so patience will be required. For its period of coverage, a useful work. — *RB*

AC6   The National Cyclopaedia of American Biography. - New York : J.T. White, 1892-1984. - 63 v. ; ill.

Class Numbers:
  Library of Congress E176
OCLC 1759175
LCCN 21-21756
Notes:
  Index. Clifton, NJ: J.T. White, 1984. 576 p.
  Published: Clifton, NJ, 1973-1984
  Supplement: New York: J.T. White, 1930-1978.
    Vol. A-M
  Vols. 53 through N-63 have title *National Cyclopedia of American Biography*

• Long standing as the Other Collective Biography of Americans (providing more entries than *Dictionary of American Biography* [AC4] but lacking the scholarly background its contributors could claim), *Cyclopaedia* endured for 80 years. Its first volume began bravely with a long biography of Washington, adding sketches of his cabinet, but eventually became principally a source for figures of business and industry. Many sketches include engraved portraits, for which the publisher required payment, but the suspicion that paying for a picture was the price of admission to the *Cyclopaedia*'s pages was denied by the publisher. It includes far more biographees than DAB, and is useful as a source of information about lesser-known Americans. For

Plains students, the Index volume will be essential, since it will help identify Plains figures by name (Bryan, Meriwether Lewis, Pike, Frémont, Cabeza de Vaca) and by topic (all Prairies-Plains states including their governors, agriculture, woman leaders [who are listed not alphabetically but in order of their occurrence in the set], farm management ["Farmer" appears only as a name], cattle, petroleum subdivided geographically). Useful principally for the more obscure people it includes. — *RB*

Current

AC7   Who's Who in the Midwest. - [1st ed.] -   . Chicago, IL : A.N. Marquis, 1949–   . Biennial.

Class Numbers:
  Library of Congress E176
Notes:
  Later volumes publ.: New Providence, NJ: Marquis Who's Who
  Preceding title: *Who's Who in the Central States*
  Volumes for 1965-66– include men and women of Canada, Manitoba, and western Ontario
  Prairies-Plains states and provinces covered: Kansas, Nebraska, North and South Dakota, Manitoba

AC7a   Who's Who in the South and Southwest. - 33rd ed. - New Providence, NJ: Marquis Who's Who Inc., 2006. - 750 p.

Class Numbers:
  Library of Congress E176
Notes:
  Prairies-Plains states covered: Oklahoma, Texas

AC7b   Who's Who in the West. - 12th ed. (1970/1971) –   . Chicago, IL: Marquis Who's Who Inc., 1971 –   . Biennial.

Class Numbers:
  Library of Congress E176
OCLC 5282690
LCCN 87-647966 sc 80-466   cn 88-39013
Notes:
  Prairies-Plains states and provinces covered: Colorado, New Mexico, Wyoming, Alberta, Saskatchewan
  Later volumes publ.: New Providence, NJ: Marquis Who's Who

• Alphabetical lists of persons who in the Marquis editors' judgment demonstrate "distinction" (a term nowhere defined), and whose entries display the highly structured Marquis format that identifies the subject's field, gives birth date (only living persons are included), education, marriage, children, positions held, memberships, publications, honors, address. Since the information is provided by the subject, length of entries varies considerably; readers should be aware that information the subject wishes to conceal will not appear. The entry for financier Warren Buffett, for example, is astonishingly brief. From the 12th through the 31st editions, the number of subjects has been held at about 15,000. A "Professional Index" is arranged by profession with subsections for states and provinces, then cities and towns, an arrangement sometimes helpful in locating Prairies-Plains personalities. An Internet version, *Marquis Who's Who on the Web*, http://www.marquiswhoswho.com/, combines entries for some 30 Marquis biographical publications. For quick facts about persons encountered in other sources. — *RB, MB*

Colorado

AC8   Monett, John H. - *Colorado Profiles : Men and Women Who Shaped the Centennial State* / [by] John H. Monett and Michael McCarthy. - Niwot, CO : Univ. Pr. of Colorado, 1996. - 329 p. ; ill.

    Class Numbers:
       Library of Congress F776
    ISBN 0870814397 0585022240 (electronic bk.)
    LCCN 96-31144
    Notes:
       Electronic book: http://www.netLibrary.com/urlapi.asp?
          action=summary&v=1&bookid=195
       Includes bibliographical references (p. [311]-321) ; index

• In their introduction, the authors profess to provide only a sampling of people who helped settle Colorado--known, unknown, stalwart, and notorious. Each biographical sketch considers its subject's life and contribution to Colorado history in informative but entertaining style. Some sketches are accompanied by portraits. Bibliographic notes are collected at the end. Some personalities of interest: Black Kettle, Tom Horn, Ann Bassett, Casimiro Barela, Jack Stillwell. — *JB*

Kansas

AC9   **Kansas Biographical Name Index [Internet Site].** - Topeka, KS : Kansas State Historical Society, 2007-   . - http://www.kshs.org/

    Access Date: May 2007
    Fees: None

• Name index only for a small number of state histories and biographical works dealing with Kansas; entries give citation information, not content. Similar in intent, if not scale,

to *North Dakota Biography Index* (**DB59**). Apparently a project in progress, its value for genealogical and historical purposes will increase as it expands to include additional material. —*LMcD*

Nebraska

AC10   700 Famous Nebraskans : Nationally Distinguished Nebraskans : A Brief Biobibliography of 700 Individuals [Internet Site] / by E. A. Kral. - Lincoln, NE : Nebraska State Education Association, 2004. - http://www.nsea.org/

    Access Date: Feb. 2005
    Fees: None

• Kral, a 30-year veteran of public school teaching in Livingston, CA, and Lincoln and Grand Island, NE, is preparing a collective biography (with bibliographies) of more than 700 distinguished Nebraska citizens. He makes this preliminary version available at the NSEA Internet site as a courtesy. To be included, candidates had to meet most or all of a list of criteria that include being a pioneer in a field, founder, inventor, developer, creator, opinion maker, leader, record holder, performer, or philanthropist; being listed in reputable national compilations; having longevity and magnitude of accomplishment; being recognized by peers; and receiving major national awards, honors, or recognition. Subjects consist of "any nationally distinguished person . . . born in Nebraska or who resided in the state for any length of time after 1854 [year of passage of the Kansas-Nebraska Act]" (Introd.) Entries treat both contemporary and historical figures and are arranged alphabetically in 22 general areas of accomplishment (e.g., business, literature, medicine, sports). Entries are brief, ranging from a sentence to approximately 200 words. Each entry cites one or more additional biographical sources, and there is an alphabetical index of all entrants. A pdf file at this page can be printed to create a printed form of the Internet version. — *MB*

AC11   Johnson, John Reuben, 1897-   . - **Representative Nebraskans** / ill. by Clarence E. Struble. - Lincoln, NE : Johnsen Publ. Co., 1954. - 198 p. ; ill.

    Class Numbers:
       Library of Congress F665
    LCCN 54-3445
    Notes:
       Includes bibliographical references

• Thirty-five notable Nebraskans (as of 1954), including the likes of Willa Cather, William Jennings Bryan, Father Flanagan, and J. Sterling Morton. Entries are arranged alphabetically with brief bibliographical notes; each entry has a line drawing of the subject, birth and death dates, and a substantial essay. — *MB*

New Mexico

AC12   New Mexican Lives : Profiles and Historical Stories / ed. by Richard W. Etulain. - Albuquerque, NM : Univ. of New Mexico Pr ; publ. in cooperation with the UNM Center for the American West, 2002. - 334 p. ; ill., maps.

Class Numbers:
Library of Congress F796.5
ISBN 0826324339 (pbk.) 08263244320 9780826324320
OCLC 48265524
LCCN 2001-6432
Notes:
Includes bibliographical references; index

• Although the contributors to this work (chiefly from universities in Arizona and New Mexico) consider only about 15 figures who had importance in New Mexico history, Popé and Juan de Oñate through Tony Hillerman, their book deserves inclusion on the strength of its bibliographic essay on New Mexico history (p. 310-322). Written by Richard Etulain, the dean of his subject, it takes a gratefully brief glance at the reference titles and basic histories students will need to know. — *RB*

North Dakota

See also **North Dakota Biography Index [Internet Site], DB59**

AC13   Rolfsrud, Erling Nicolai, 1912- . - Extraordinary North Dakotans. - Alexandria, MN : Lantern Books, 1954. - 228 p. ; ill.

Class Numbers:
Library of Congress F635
LCCN 54-44007

AC13a   Rolfsrud, Erling Nicolai, 1912- . - Notable North Dakotans. - Farwell, MN : Lantern Books, 1987. - 110 p. ; ill.

Class Numbers:
Library of Congress CT253
ISBN 0914689118 (pbk.)
LCCN 88-134658

Notes:
Bibliography: p. [113]

• These two volumes compile vignettes about white North Dakota residents, some famous, others lesser-known, from Territorial times to the early 1980s. The subjects influenced those around them or became successful in the face of adversity. Among them: Missouri River boat captain Grant March; Helen Carlson, educator and superintendent of the Anne Carlson School for children with disabilities; John Christiansen, German immigrant who followed Lakota advice that plowing the prairie was "wrong side up," becoming one of the state's first dairy farmers; Ida Parker Lee, an artist who used natural resources for her pictures and sculptures; Governor John Burke, who brought reform to the state and its political parties; and Laura Taylor Hughes, who created Rosemead pottery. Photographs of subjects are scattered throughout both titles. *Notable North Dakotans* supplies additional entries and updates many that first appeared in *Extraordinary North Dakotans*. Rolfsrud presents the sketches with style and humor. — *JB*

CANADA

General Works

AC14   Dictionary of Canadian Biography. - Toronto, ON : Univ. of Toronto Pr., 1966– (In progress). - 15 v.

Class Numbers:
Library of Congress F1005
National Library of Canada FC25
ISBN 0802034128 (set)
OCLC 1566617
LCCN 66-31909
Notes:
Contents: v. 1, 1000-1700 ; v. 2, 1701-1740 ; v. 3, 1741-1770 ; v. 4, 1771-1800 ; v. 5, 1801-1820 ; v. 6, 1821-1835; v. 7, 1836-1850 ; v. 8, 1851-1860 ; v. 9, 1861-1870; v. 10, 1871-1880 ; v. 11, 1881-1890 ; v. 12, 1891-1900 ; v. 13, 1901-1910 ; v. 14, 1911-1920 ; v. 15, 1921-1930
Includes bibliographical references

• Scholarly accounts of significant figures in the history of Canada; the approximately 8,400 individuals presented in the 15 volumes published to date represent every aspect of Canadian life. Each volume in the chronologically ordered set contains from 500 to 700 biographies, arranged alphabetically, varying in length from 500 to 15,000 words. Death dates generally determine which volume a subject is located in. Entries are signed and contain extensive bibliographies. Volumes conclude with a general bibliography of archival and manuscript collections, newspapers, published sources and theses; contributors; index of identifications (primarily professions); geographical index, listing biographees under birthplace and location of career; and index of names mentioned in the particular volume. A printed index to volumes 1-12 was published in 1991; a CD-ROM covering volumes 1-14 appeared in 2000. — *LMcD*

AC14a   Dictionary of Canadian Biography Online=Dictionnaire biographique du Canada en ligne [Internet Site] / Ramsay Cook, general ed. ; Réal Bélanger, directeur général adjoint . - [Montréal, QC] : Université Laval, 2003– . http://www.biographi.ca/EN/index.html (English version) ; http://www.biographi.ca/FR/index.html (French version)

> Class Numbers:
> Library of Congress F1005
> Access Date: Jan. 2005
> Notes:
> "... provides access to the 14 volumes already in print. ..."
> Available in print and CD-ROM versions
> Fees: None

• The Internet site makes freely available volumes 1-14 and a selection of biographies from volumes not yet published. "Quick Biography Search" provides searching by keyword and browsing by surname. "Advanced Search," available in Flash and HTML versions, has date range of death, geography, gender, and identification (generally occupations) options. Combinations such as biographies of noteworthy Blackfoot Indians in Alberta or male lawyers who practiced in Manitoba and died in the 1890s are easily constructed. The Internet version makes an important source of Prairie biography even more indispensable. — *LMcD*

AC15   Who's Who in Western Canada : A Biographical Dictionary of Notable Living Men and Women of Western Canada. - [1st] (1911)-92nd (2001). Vancouver, BC ; Portland, OR [etc.] : Canadian Press Association, Ltd., 1911-2001. Irregular.

> Class Numbers:
> Library of Congress F1005
> National Library of Canada FC25
> LCCN 21-17520

• Provided 3,000 biographical entries for individuals of varying degrees of prominence, with 88 pages of portraits, in its first edition. Contact information, educational background, and a brief statement of career experience and highlights constituted most accounts. After its initial appearance, the directory moved beyond its regional outlook and changed title to *Who's Who and Why* in 1912 and eventually to *Who's Who in Canada* in 1922 before ceasing publication in 2001. In later years entries became more extensive and increasingly bilingual and added elements such as corporate, professional and industry indexes, but

geographical indexes are wanting, making it difficult to identify persons associated with particular provinces. *Canadian Who's Who*, a competing directory from the Univ. of Toronto Pr., continues to be published. — *LMcD*

Alberta

AC16   Who's Who in Southern Alberta. - 1988/1989 (1988) – . Lethbridge, AB : Historical Research Centre, [1988] – . Biennial.

> Class Numbers:
> Library of Congress F1075.8
> National Library of Canada FC3655
> OCLC 19898665
> LCCN cn 89-32073

• Almost 6,000 very brief entries, largely based on information supplied by the individuals themselves, giving details such as occupation, education, family, and address. — *LMcD*

Manitoba

See also **Harvey, Pioneers of Manitoba, DB147**
Manitoba Library Association. **Pioneers and Early Citizens of Manitoba, DB148**
Dorge, **Introduction à l'étude des Franco-Manitobains, CC32**

AC17   Bumsted, J. M. - Dictionary of Manitoba Biography. - Winnipeg, MB : Univ. of Manitoba Pr., 1999. - 273 p. ; map.

> Class Numbers:
> Library of Congress F1061.8
> National Library of Canada FC3355
> ISBN 0887551696 0887556620 (pbk.)
> OCLC 43278672
> Notes:
> Includes bibliographical references: p. x
> Electronic book: http://www.mhs.mb.ca/docs/people/index.shtml

• Bumsted (history, Univ. of Manitoba) provides brief sketches of more than 1,600 deceased individuals who resided in Manitoba at some point and either had an impact on the province or were influenced by it. Both the well-known (novelist Margaret Laurence, prime minister Arthur Meighen, explorer La Vérendrye) and the more obscure are included, representing all aspects of Manitoba life. Surprises abound: for example, Lila Wallace, cofounder of

Reader's Digest, was born in Virden. Biographies range from a short paragraph to 550 words for the longest entries; they tend to assemble the essential facts without adornment or interpretation. Many entries have a cross-reference to more complete accounts in the *Dictionary of Canadian Biography* (**AC14, AC14a**). The work would have benefited from indexes for names, places, professions, religions, etc. A useful source of information on noteworthy Manitobans, supplemented as necessary by DCB. — *LMcD*

AC18 **Representative Men of Manitoba, History in Portraiture : a Gallery of Men whose Energy, Ability, Enterprise and Public Spirit have Produced the Marvellous Record of the Prairie Province**. - Winnipeg, MB : Tribune Pub. Co., 1902. - xxxi p., 151 p. of ports.

> Class Numbers:
>   Library of Congress F1061.8
>   National Library of Canada FC 3355
> OCLC 28238040
> Notes:
>   Electronic book: http://peel.library.ualberta.ca/cocoon/peel/2653.html

• A brief history of the province (p.[v]-xxviii) is followed by portraits of approximately 280 individuals considered important at the turn of the previous century. Occupation, employer, and location are the sole identifying elements included with each photograph. Not arranged in surname order; index of names. About the work, the introduction offers the view "...that in years to come it will possess historical worth beyond computation..." (p. iv); perhaps. — *LMcD*

Saskatchewan

AC19 Clemence, Verne, 1937-   . - **Saskatchewan's Own : People Who Made a Difference**. - Calgary, AB ; Allston, MA : Fifth House, 2004. - 234 p. ; ports.

> Class Numbers:
>   Library of Congress CT297
>   National Library of Canada FC3505
> ISBN 1894004906
> OCLC 53847322
> LCCN 2004-396983
> Notes:
>   Includes bibliographical references (p. 230-231); index

• The 44 individuals profiled are a varied lot, stretching from a socialist premier (Tommy Douglas) to a Conservative prime minister (John Diefenbaker), novelists such as

W.O. Mitchell (**BC74** and **BC75**) and Sinclair Ross (**BC76**), Grey Owl (apparently a native conservationist but in fact a transplanted Englishman named Archie Belaney), and a Finnish immigrant obsessed with building an ocean-going ship on his prairie farm. An interesting mix of well-known and less-celebrated people chronicling the history of the province. — *LMcD*

AC20 Lapointe, Richard. - **100 noms : petit dictionnaire biographique des Franco-Canadiens de la Saskatchewan**. - Régina, SK : Société historique de la Saskatchewan, 1988. - 434 p. : ill., ports.

> Class Numbers:
>   National Library of Canada FC3550 .5
> ISBN 0920895026
> OCLC 17233854
> Notes:
>   Includes bibliographical references ; index

• Biographical sketches, typically three or four pages in length, of deceased French Saskatchewanians. Those included represent the range of the provincial francophone community, religious and lay, well-known and obscure, from a variety of occupations and accomplishments. Also available, with additional material, in *Musée Virtuel Francophone de la Saskatchewan* (http://www.societehisto.com/Musee/) on the Internet site of the Société historique de la Saskatchewan. — *LMcD*

AC21 **The Saskatchewanians**. - [Regina, SK] : Saskatchewan Diamond Jubilee and Canada Centennial Corporation, 1967. - 100 p. ; ports.

> Class Numbers:
>   Library of Congress F1070.8
>   National Library of Canada COP.SA.2709
> OCLC 133095
> LCCN 73-491505

• Brief biographical accounts, originating as a newspaper series in 1965-67, celebrating the achievements of 100 individuals of significance to the province. Those profiled range from the explorer Henry Kelsey, who traveled the prairies in 1690-1692, to politicians, clergy, artists and other prominent figures. Not arranged alphabetically. — *LMcD*

AD : GENEALOGY

Scope   Lists works, especially bibliographies, directories, and guides intended to help readers interested in establishing descent from a group of ancestors or in hanging leaves on their family trees. Highly selective, since genealogists are tireless researchers and prolific publishers.

UNITED STATES

Kansas

AD1   Kansas Pioneers. - Topeka, KS : Topeka Genealogical Society, 1976-   . - 1 v. ; ill.

> Class Numbers:
> Library of Congress F680
> OCLC 2985105
> LCCN 76-52757
> Notes:
> Indexes

• Primarily of genealogical interest, this volume contains 356 brief numbered articles. It began with the intention of covering only Shawnee County (of which Topeka is the seat) but later expanded to include 82 of the 105 counties in Kansas. There is no perceptible order to the entries, which lead off with "Wilson Beauty Shop," followed immediately by "David Bonecutter" and "Charles A. Wells." Entries are signed and some are illustrated with old photos. Most of the articles are concerned with individuals or families, but some have wider interest (e.g., "An Early Country Store," "Shoe Factory in Topeka"). The entries were printed as submitted, without checking for accuracy or authenticity. At the end are a needless numerical index to the entries and a comprehensive name index. — *MB*

Nebraska

AD2   Nimmo, Sylvia. - Nebraska Local History and Genealogy Reference Guide : A Bibliography of County Research Materials in Selected Repositories ... / [by] Sylvia Nimmo, Mary Cutler. - Papillion, NE : S. Nimmo, 1987. - 242 p. ; [3]p. of plates, maps.

> Class Numbers:
> Library of Congress F665; Z1307
> OCLC 17546523
> LCCN 87-129281

• While dated, this county-by-county guide to local archival records is a significant resource for genealogists and histo-

rians. Thirty-one outline maps of Nebraska counties and unorganized territory, 1854-1925, can help researchers determine where records might exist and their dates of coverage. For each county, the compilers list libraries, local historical societies, and genealogical societies, followed by relevant holdings in six national and state repositories (Library of Congress, National DAR Library, Omaha Public Library, University of Nebraska Libraries, Nebraska State Historical Society, and the Family History Library of the Church of Jesus Christ of Latter-Day Saints). Sources cited include published maps, directories, articles, and local histories; unpublished church, birth, death records (including cemetery); marriage, military, land, court, tax, naturalization, and school records; and newspaper indexes and censuses. At a time when access to genealogical information is amply available online, many sources in this bibliography are not listed elsewhere and have not been digitized. — *JD*

New Mexico

AD3   Daniel, Karen Stein. - Genealogical Resources in New Mexico. - Albuquerque, NM : New Mexico Genealogical Society, 2002. - 100 p.

> Class Numbers:
> Library of Congress F795
> OCLC 49510044
> LCCN 2002-449211
> Notes:
> Rev. ed. of: Robert Esterly, *Genealogical Resources in New Mexico* (1997)

• Daniel (New Mexico Genealogical Society) cites resources of interest for researchers and the repository locations for these materials or collections. The work has three parts: repositories (churches, counties, mortuaries, libraries, archives, and museum records); record groups and collections (manuscripts, census, land, online, maps, atlas, military, Native American, newspapers, adoption, school, and vital records); and societies (contact information for genealogical, historical, lineage, and fraternal/ethnic organizations). Includes important dates in New Mexico history, a timeline, and a selected annotated bibliography. — *GK*

Oklahoma

AD4   Follett, Paul, 1958-   . - Printed Sources for Oklahoma Research. - [Wyandotte, OK : Gregath Publ. Co.] ; Lawton, OK : Southwest Oklahoma Genealogical Society, 2004. - 670 p. ; maps.

> Class Numbers:
> Library of Congress F693
> Notes:
> Indexes

• The book's three sections each provide contact information for records repositories, libraries, and citations to historical materials. Citations refer to newspapers, newsletters, church and county histories, and journals published by county and state historical societies. "Indian Sources" covers all Native peoples in Oklahoma, but limits information about the Five Civilized Tribes to their Oklahoma experience. The largest section (486 p.) covers counties. The appendix provides bibliographic information for all journals and newsletters cited. Two indexes: a list of towns noting their county location, and subjects. Two maps: Indian Territory 1866-1889 and Oklahoma counties. — *MS*

AD5 Follett, Paul, 1958- . - **Printed Sources for Oklahoma Genealogical and Historical Research**. - [Wyandotte, OK : Gregath Publ. Co.] ; Lawton, OK : Southwest Oklahoma Genealogical Society, 2003. - 670 p. ; maps.

Class Numbers:
Library of Congress F693
OCLC 57618167
Notes:
Indexes

• Follett provides ample information for genealogists in three parts: "Oklahoma Sources," "Indian Sources," and "County Sources." Among subtopics for Oklahoma are archives, atlases, churches, court records, directories, land records, and migration; for Indian sources, arrangement is alphabetical by tribal names, giving the tribal office address and telephone and listing printed sources alphabetically by title; and county sources, arranged alphabetically by county, supplying address and telephone for the courthouse, libraries, and societies, and listing townships and the date the county was established. Topical divisions for printed sources vary from county to county, but most include atlases, business and industry, cemeteries, churches, court records, schools, vital records, and town histories. Appendixes list periodicals cited, and towns and communities showing location in their counties. Indexes of museums, libraries, and societies, and a general subject index. — *JB*

AD6 Huffman, Mary, comp. - **Family Histories : A Bibliography of the Collections in the Oklahoma Historical Society** / with the assistance of Nancy Laub. - Oklahoma City, OK : Library Resources Div., Oklahoma Historical Society, 1992. - 403 p.

Class Numbers:
Library of Congress F694
ISBN 0941498662
OCLC 28952203

• Huffman compiles a bibliographic guide for 2,000 family histories housed at the Oklahoma Historical Society's

Library Resources Division as an aid to genealogical research. Arranged alphabetically by surname (includes variant spellings), entries include title of book, publication date, and call number of book, microfilm, or microcard. Author-title index; newsletter and journals section. — *GK*

AD7 Koplowitz, Bradford S. - **Guide to the Historical Records of Oklahoma**. - Rev. ed. - Bowie, MD : Heritage Books, 1997. - 219 p. ; map.

Class Numbers:
Library of Congress F693   Z1325
ISBN 0788407309
OCLC 38519243

• The greater part of this bibliography lists resource materials found in public offices in Oklahoma's 77 counties and about 100 of its cities. For each county or city, items are arranged by the office that maintains the records (e.g., for Adair County, the County Clerk maintains deed record books and the Court Clerk maintains divorce records). The bibliography also notes when agencies do not maintain public records (e.g., in Hughes County neither the sheriff nor assessor keeps records that may be examined by the public). Records at historical societies and the Univ. of Oklahoma are also cited. — *MB*

Texas

AD8 Kennedy, Imogene Kinard. - **Genealogical Records in Texas** / by Imogene Kinard Kennedy & J. Leon Kennedy. - Baltimore, MD : Genealogical Publ. Co., 1987. - 248 p. ; ill.

Class Numbers:
Library of Congress F386
ISBN 0806311851
OCLC 15791165
LCCN 86-83384
Notes:
Bibliography: p. 240-248

• Six concise chapters cover early governmental organization, list early municipalities, colonies and land districts, cover Mexican laws concerning colonization, and provide and translate the Spanish terms used in land grants. Chapter 7, the longest (126 pages), describes the formation and organization of counties. Entries for each county consist of a brief history, note repositories of county records, and are accompanied by a map. There is a list of counties whose records have been destroyed. Record repositories at the state level, and libraries that specialize in genealogy, are covered in the remaining chapters. A bibliography provides full records for sources cited in the individual chapters. — *MS*

CANADA

Prairie Provinces

AD9   Census of the Northwest Provinces, 1906 [Internet Site]. - [Ottawa, ON] : Library and Archives Canada, 2003. - http://www.collectionscanada.ca/genealogy/index-e.html

> Access Date : Apr. 2006
> Fees: None

• Records of a special Census that documents major political and demographic changes in the Prairies: Alberta and Saskatchewan became provinces in 1905 when a large influx of settlers and immigrants was under way. Records provide "tombstone" information: name, address, age, sex, marital status, and country of origin. Images scanned from microfilm are searchable by province, census district name and number, and subdistrict number; a list of census districts and maps identifies areas. Provides detailed help searching and interpreting results, but names are not searchable on the site. The *Alberta Family Histories Society* (http://www.afhs.ab.ca) and *Automated Genealogy* (http://automatedgenealogy.com) Internet sites provide free searching by name. A valuable source for genealogists, historians, and demographers interested in prairie settlement. — *LMcD*

AD10   Index to the Census of Canada 1891 / Eileen P. Condon, ed. - Regina, SK : Regina Branch, Saskatchewan Genealogical Society, 1988-   . - v. ; maps.

> Class Numbers:
>   Library of Congress CS88.S39
> ISBN 0969333803 ([v.1])   0969333846 ([v.2])
>   1895859085 ([v.3])   1895859026 ([v.4])
> OCLC 18644035
> LCCN 89-196643
> Notes:
>   Contents: [v. 1] Assiniboia West; [v. 2] Assiniboia
>   East; [v. 3] District of Alberta; [v. 4] District of
>   Saskatchewan
>   Cover title: *Index to the 1891 Census*

• Each volume covers one of the territorial districts that existed before Alberta and Saskatchewan became provinces in 1905. District and provincial boundaries differ, requiring use of the maps. Entries list surname, given names, sex, age, birthplace, subdivision, and page number on microfilm reels; the microfilm provides additional information such as religion, occupation, and birthplace of parents. Useful for genealogical research. — *LMcD*

AD11   Obee, Dave, 1953-   . - Back to the Land : A Genealogical Guide to Finding Farms on the Canadian Prairies. - Victoria, BC : D. Obee, 2003. - 61 p. ; maps.

> Class Numbers:
>   Library of Congress CS88.P69
> ISBN 0968502695
> LCCN 2004-396072
> Notes:
>   Includes bibliographical references (p. 61)

• A handbook to the somewhat cryptic elements of legal land description, as used in homestead records and early census returns. A glossary of surveying terms follows a description of the Dominion Land Survey, the agency that mapped the prairies prior to large-scale settlement. Most of the book is an index to land descriptions in the 1901 Census; township/range/meridian numbers are given their subdistrict and district names as well as microfilm numbers (Library and Archives Canada, in Ottawa; Family History Library, in Salt Lake City). The guide demystifies the numbering scheme used in official land documents, early directories, and some local histories. — *LMcD*

AD12   Obee, Dave, 1953-   . - Western Canadian Directories on Microfiche and Microfilm. - Victoria, B.C. : D. Obee, 2003. - 74 p. ; ill.

> Class Numbers:
>   Library of Congress Z5771.4.C2
> ISBN 0968502660
> Notes:
>   First ed. pub. in 1999

• From their first appearance in Winnipeg in 1871 to their discontinuance in Canada in 2000 because of federal privacy laws, city directories recorded the evolution of Prairie communities. Arranged by surname, they typically indicated occupation, employer, spouse, address, and phone number; the reverse directory section listed people by address. They often also included a classified business directory and ads that provide a feel for the commercial life of an area. The guide is organized by province, with regional directories followed by individual cities. Each year indicates microform record number and number of microforms. The *Peel Bibliography on Microfiche* (**DA78**) includes directories for several cities: Calgary, Edmonton, Lethbridge, and Medicine Hat (AB); Moose Jaw, Prince Albert, North Battleford, Regina, Saskatoon, Swift Current, and Yorkton (SK); Brandon and Winnipeg (MB). Coverage in Peel ends with 1953 but the finding aid indicates other microform collections. A useful guide for genealogists wishing to obtain information not yet available in unreleased census records. — *LMcD*

AD13   Our Roots : Canada's Local Histories Online = Nos racines : les histoires locales du Canada en ligne [Internet Site]. – Calgary, AB : Univ. of Calgary ; Sainte-Foy, QC : Université Laval, 2002–   . - http://www.ouroots.ca/

OCLC 51840239

Access Date: Apr. 2005

Notes:

In English and French versions

Fees: None

• *Our Roots* makes available digitized versions of published local histories that focus on some aspect of Canadian culture, history, environment, or biography. The home page and introductory matter concentrate on classroom use of local history and explain in detail some recent projects for which the site was used as a resource. The heart of the site, however, is its collection of local history resources, digitized in full text, and searchable by author, title, subject, or keyword. Although the total number of resources is not revealed, and new titles are continuously added, for the Prairie provinces there are about 250 titles for Alberta, 160 for Manitoba, and 150 for Saskatchewan. The file may also be browsed alphabetically by author, title, or NLC subject, and individual sources examined page by page. Beyond its classroom emphasis, the site will be useful to genealogists, community historians, and general readers or scholars interested in Canadian history. — *LMcD*

AD14 The Western Canadians, 1600-1900 : An Alphabetized Directory of the People, Places and Vital Dates / ed. by Noel Montgomery Elliot. - Toronto, ON : Genealogical Research Library, 1994. - 3 v.

Class Numbers:

Library of Congress CS88.C265

National Library of Canada CS88

ISBN 0919941311 (set)

OCLC 31684873

LCCN 94-203625

Notes:

Contents: v. 1-3, A-Z

Includes bibliographical references and indexes

• An alphabetical index of approximately 300,000 names, an indeterminate number of which are from Alberta and Saskatchewan. (Manitoba is included in the companion set *The Central Canadians, 1600-1900*, also published by Genealogical Research Library in 1994 in 3 v.) Entries are sketchy, consisting of little more than a single line giving name, occupation or some identifying term, where and when the person lived, and a code for the source of information. Names are drawn from a disparate collection of local histories, federal census microfilms, and city directories ca. 1910-1915. Each volume has a place-name index situating communities by township or district. — *LMcD*

AD15 Western Land Grants (1870-1930) [Internet Site]. - [Ottawa, ON] : Library and Archives Canada, 2003. - http://www.collectionscanada.ca/genealogy/index-e.html

Access Date: Apr. 2006

Fees: None

• Land grants in the prairies and a narrow slice of British Columbia issued by the Lands Patent Branch of the Canadian Department of the Interior. Records contain only the name of the grantee, land description, and date granted. Searchable by name, section, township, range, and meridian. — *LMcD*

Alberta

AD16 Alberta Genealogical Society. Edmonton Branch. - Alberta, Formerly a Part of the North-West Territories : Index to Birth, Marriage and Death Registrations. - Edmonton, AB : Alberta Genealogical Society, 1995- . -

Class Numbers:

Library of Congress CS88.A46

ISBN 09214749629 (v.1)

OCLC 35933366

• An index to registration documents located at the Provincial Archives of Alberta, arranged by surname in a single sequence. Entries include names, parents or spouse, sex, event (birth/marriage/death), age, place, and archival number. The original documents often include additional information such as occupation, maternal maiden name, birthplace, marriage witnesses, religion, cause of death, and district of registration. Of interest to those searching for elusive elements of family history. — *LMcD*

AD17 Alberta, Formerly a Part of the North-West Territories : Index to Birth, Marriage and Death Registrations. - Edmonton, AB : Alberta Genealogical Society, Edmonton Branch, 1999-2004. - 5 v. ; maps.

Class Numbers:

Library of Congress CS88.A46

National Library of Canada FC3217.1

ISBN 1551940604 ([v.1])   1551940647 ([v.2])

1551940620 ([v.3])   1551940639 ([v.4])

1551940612 ([v.5])

OCLC 44651030

• Index for the region that became the provinces of Alberta and Saskatchewan. Surnames are followed by given names, relationship to head of household, place and year of birth, census subdistrict, and page numbers on microfilm reels; the microfilm contains additional information such as nationality, origin, and year of naturalization. Searching by name and birthplace, with optional limits by birth year, age, district, and subdistrict is available on the Internet site of the *Alberta Genealogical Society, Edmonton Branch* (http://www.agsedm.edmonton.ab.ca/). Useful for genea-logical research. — *LMcD*

AD18   Proof-of-Age Documents in Alberta : A Surname Index 1863-1969. – Edmonton, AB : Documentary Heritage Society of Alberta, 1998. - 208 p.

Class Numbers:
National Library of Canada CD3645 A3
ISBN 0968325505
OCLC 38753593
Notes:
Published in cooperation with the Provincial Archives of Alberta

• An index to original documents (birth certificates, naturalization papers, passports, and the like), many in languages other than English, submitted to prove age eligibility for seniors' and disability pensions. Arranged by name of applicant. Entries include type of document, year of "event" (birth, marriage, citizenship), year certificate prepared, and file information for the originals at the Provincial Archives. Useful source for genealogists and demographers. — *LMcD*

Manitoba

AD19   An Index of Marriage and Death Notices from Manitoba Newspapers / Kathleen Rooke Stokes [et al.]. - [Winnipeg, MB] : Manitoba Genealogical Society, 1986- . – 5 v.

Class Numbers:
National Library of Canada CS88 M34
ISBN 096922110X (v.1)   0921622171 (v. 2)
092162221X (v. 3)   0921622295 (v. 4)
0921622406 (v. 5)
OCLC 17875281
Notes:
"Manitoba Genealogical Society Inc. special projects publication"–Cover
Contents: v. 1. 1859-1881; v. 2. 1882-1884; v. 3. 1885; v. 4 1886; v. 5 1887
Vols. 2-3 have title: *An Index of Birth, Marriage and Death Notices from Manitoba Newspapers*

• Covers 27 English and French newspapers. Marriages, deaths, and births are in separate sequences, with marriages indexed by both bride and groom. Entries give basic facts only, with references to name and date of newspaper for complete notices. Useful for 19th-century genealogy. — *LMcD*

AD20   Jonasson, Eric. - Surname Index to the 1870 Census of Manitoba and Red River. – Winnipeg, MB : Wheatfield Pr., 1981. - 27 p. ; ill.

Class Numbers:
Library of Congress CS88.M27
ISBN 0920374042
OCLC 8363926
LCCN 83-129254
Notes:
"Surname index compiled from Public Archives of Canada microfilm C-2170" (Title page verso)

• A nominal index facilitating genealogical exploration of a significant document of Manitoba history. — *LMcD*

AD21   Lareau, Paul J., comp. - Manitoba Marriages = Mariages du Manitoba / comp. and ed. by Paul J. Lareau and Julien Hamelin. - Ottawa, ON : Centre de généalogie, 1984. - 3 v. (1557 p.); ill. - (Publication généalogique, 45).

Class Numbers:
Library of Congress CS88.M27
OCLC 11290846
LCCN 84-174213
Notes:
Contents: v. 1. A-G; v. 2. H-R; v. 3. S-Z

• An index to records from 23 parishes, mostly French, in the region of St. Boniface. Brides and grooms are listed in one sequence; date and place of ceremony follow the parents' names. An unusual feature is the "Index of Mothers" (p. 1319-1957) by maiden name, identifying matrilineal descent. — *LMcD*

AD22   Main, Lorne W. - Index to 1881 Canadian Census of Manitoba with Extensions & East Rupert's Land. - [Vancouver, BC : L.W. Main], 1984. - 238 p. ; maps.

Class Numbers:
Library of Congress F1062
National Library of Canada HA741.5 1881
ISBN 0969109326
OCLC 18234331

• Arranged by enumeration area, then by surname. The lack of a name index complicates efficient use of the work. — *LMcD*

Saskatchewan

AD23   Saskatchewan Homestead Index [Internet Site]. - [Regina, SK] : Saskatchewan Genealogical Society, [2005]. - http://www.saskhomesteads.com/

Access Date: Apr. 2006
Notes:
A project of the Saskatchewan Genealogical Society

and the Saskatchewan Archives Board
Fees: None

• Database of 360,000 settlers who homesteaded 1872-1930, searchable by name, legal land description (section, township, range, median), and remarks. Homestead records may indicate nationality and place of origin, and contain naturalization papers, letters, and other documents. Files will eventually be digitized; in the meantime, they can be ordered from the Saskatchewan Archives Board. The site is a boon for genealogists, historians, and researchers studying Prairie land settlement. — *LMcD*

AD24   Tracing Your Saskatchewan Ancestors : A Guide to the Records and How to Use Them / ed. by Laura M. Hanowski. - 3rd ed. - Regina, SK : Saskatchewan Genealogical Society, 2006. - 160 p. : ill., maps.

Class Numbers:
    Library of Congress CS88.S39
ISBN 1895859077 9781895859072
OCLC 74554795
Notes:
    Includes bibliographical references and index

• Handbook of genealogical resources related to Saskatchewan. The first chapter, appropriately, concerns the process of tracking aboriginal forebears. Lists of archives, libraries, and museums follow. Arrangement is by type of record, with chapters or sections treating records from cemeteries, censuses, churches, courts, educational institutions, ethnic colonies, immigration agencies, land titles, military organizations, municipalities, newspapers, and vital records. The origin, function, location, and use of each type are clearly spelled out; hints and cautionary notes are interspersed throughout. Although directed to genealogists, the guide should also prove useful for those seeking primary sources in Saskatchewan history, demography, and settlement patterns. — *LMcD*

Cemeteries

AD25   Carved in Stone : Manitoba Cemeteries and Burial Sites / ed. by Kathleen Rooke Stokes. - Rev. ed., 2nd ed. - Winnipeg, MB : Manitoba Genealogical Society, 1997. - 106 p. ; ill., maps.

Class Numbers:
    National Library of Canada CS88
ISBN 0921622236
OCLC 37489844

• Arranged by rural municipality or local government district, lists cemeteries by name and location (section, township, and range). Also lists cemeteries on native reservations and named graveyards elsewhere in the province. — *LMcD*

AD26   Pierce, Barbara, comp. - **Oklahoma Cemeteries : A Bibliography of the Collections in the Oklahoma Historical Society** / comp. by Barbara Pierce and Brian Basore. - Oklahoma City, OK : Oklahoma Historical Society. Library Resources Div., 1993. - 236 p.

Class Numbers:
    Library of Congress F695
ISBN 0941498670
OCLC 28957586
Notes:
    Index

• One of a series of bibliographies produced by the Historical Society that deal with single aspects of Oklahoma history. Entries are arranged by county, then alphabetically by cemetery. A user's guide explains how to read entries and lists abbreviations used in the book. The bibliography was created from index files held by the Society's library. The cutoff date is March 1, 1993. Useful in historical and genealogical research. — *JB*

AE : Directories

Scope   Directories that are general in nature, or that include organizations of a single type (e.g., museums).

AE1   Associations Canada : The Directory of Associations in Canada = Le répertoire des associations du Canada. – [1st] (1991) - . - Toronto, ON : Canadian Almanac & Directory Pub. Co. 1991- . – Annual.

Class Numbers:
National Library of Canada HS17
OCLC 25066491
LCCN 92-641105; ce 92-30119
Notes:
Preceding title: *Directory of Associations in Canada*
Some vols. have subtitle: *An Encyclopedic Directory = Un*

répertoire encyclopédique
Vols. for 1998/99- publ.: Toronto: IHS/Micromedia

• Among the almost 20,000 Canadian and related international organizations in this annual directory are approximately 3,700 located in the Prairie provinces. Ranging from mainstream to decidedly arcane, their interests lie in areas such as education, arts, business, health, and many others. Profiles typically contain contact information, scope, membership, publications, and activities. Subject, geographical, acronym, executive, charitable status, budget, conference, and mailing list indexes. The online version, produced by Micromedia ProQuest (http://www.micromedia.ca/ Directories/Associations.htm), is updated monthly. It permits greater precision with customized searching of 26 aspects of associations and provides features such as lateral searching, hotlinks, and exporting to spreadsheets. — *LMcD*

AE2   Encyclopedia of Associations : Regional, State, and Local Organizations. - 1st ed. (1988-89)- . Detroit,

---

Site List 2
State and Province Museum Directories

AAM Internet site (American Association of Museums)
http://www.aam-us.org
The AAM site offers two directories with both overlapping and different entries, "Museum Directory" of 3000 AAM members and "List of Accredited Museums" covering about 800 museums accredited by the AAM. The Directory, found under "About/Find a Museum," can be browsed or searched by name, location, or type. Entries have basic directory information and links to Internet sites. Links to regional, state, local, and other organizations, which often offer their own online directories, are in the FAQ section.

MuseumsUSA
http://www. museumsusa.org
Well-established and growing, this commercial site provides over 15,000 entries that offer minimal directory information but links to museum Internet sites. Its higher number of entries include smaller museums that may not be affiliated with the AAM or do not themselves have Internet sites. Museums can be browsed by name, state, and type. The site also includes links to regional, state, local, and other associations such as the American Association of State and Local History, which in turn offer online directories.

Official Museum Directory (**AE3**)
National Register Publishing
An annual printed source. Supplements directory information with lengthy entries on attendance, facilities, personnel, hours, fees, collections, and governing authority. Volume 2 is an index by type.

International Council of Museums
http://www.icom.museum
The ICOM "Resources" section provides information on print museum directories and links to online directories worldwide.

Mountain Plains Museum Association
http://www.mpma.net

The MPMA Internet site links to state and other organizations with online directories in all ten of the Plains states.

State and provincial museum associations with online directories

Colorado-Wyoming Association of Museums
http://www.mpma.net

Kansas Museums Association
http://www.ksmuseums.org

Museums Association of Montana
http://www.montanamuseums.org

Nebraska Museums Association
http://www.nebraskamuseums.org

New Mexico Association of Museums
http://www.nmmuseums.org

Museums in North Dakota
http://www.nd.gov/hist/mind.htm

Oklahoma Museums Association
http://www.okmuseums.org

Association of South Dakota Museums
http://www.sdmuseums.org

Texas Association of Museums
http://www.io.com/~tam

Museums Alberta
http://www.albertaheritage.net/museums

Association of Manitoba Museums
http://www.museumsmanitoba.com/

Museums Association of Saskatchewan
http://www.saskmuseums.org/

MI : Gale Research Co., 1989– . Annual.

Class Numbers:
   Library of Congress AS22
LCCN 87-640488 ; sn 87-2813
Notes:
   16th ed., 2006
   Also available as part of CD-ROM: *Encyclopedia of*
      Associations on CD-ROM
   Contents: v. 1, Great Lakes States; v. 2, Northeastern
      States; v. 3, Southern and Middle Atlantic States; v. 4,
      South Central and Great Plains States; v. 5, Western
      States
   Frequency varies: Biennial, 1988/1989-1994/1995

• A standard directory of nonprofit membership organizations in the U.S. that are "organized and function at the regional (both interstate and intrastate), state, county, city, neighborhood, and local levels" (v.1, p. vii). For Prairies-Plains purposes, the two relevant volumes are v. 4, which covers Kansas, Nebraska, Oklahoma, Texas, and the Dakotas, and v. 5, which covers Montana, Wyoming, Colorado, and New Mexico. Entries are arranged by state, then alphabetically by community, and provide name of organization, address, phone, e-mail, URL, contact, level of organization (local, state, etc.), brief description, and institutional affiliations. The editors disclaim completeness, since organizations are born, die, fade, and grow unpredictably, and entries are generated from information supplied by the organizations themselves. Useful in finding names of local organizations. — *RB*

Museums

AE3   **The Official Museum Directory**. 36th ed. (1999)- . New Providence, NJ : National Register Publ., 1999- . Biennial.

Class Numbers:
   Library of Congress AM10.A2
OCLC 1264511
LCCN 79-144808
Notes:
   Companion publ.: *The Official Museum Products and*
      Services Directory, 1981-1992; absorbed that
      publication, 1993
   Publ. 1971-1998: Washington, DC: American
      Association of Museums

• A very full and thorough directory of museums of all types in U.S. states and territories. It lists 6,000-7,000 museums, arranging them by state, then city or town, providing for each its congressional district (reflecting the importance of federal funding), personnel, governing authority, type of museum, collections, research fields, facilities, activities, publications, hours and admission fees, and membership fees. All the Prairies-Plains states are included. No online equivalent is yet available. — *RB*

B   Humanities

BA : Religion

Scope   Includes all forms of religious conviction as practiced in the United States or Canada, especially in the Prairies-Plains region. Includes both religious belief and practice brought from Europe and religion as practiced by Natives before white arrival and afterward.

General Works

Bibliographies

BA1   Etulain, Richard W., comp. - **Religion in the Twentieth-Century American West : A Bibliography**. - Albuquerque, NM : Center for the American West, Dept. of History, Univ. of New Mexico, 1991. - 69 leaves. - (University of New Mexico. Center for the American West. Occasional papers, 4).

> Class Numbers:
>   Library of Congress Z7757.U5
> LCCN 93-620163

• Like Etulain's other compilations, this one (intended to be a brief descriptive list covering 1970-1990) begins with a list of pertinent reference sources and another of general works, followed in this instance by sections for individual persuasions (Roman Catholics, Mormons) or groups (mainline Protestants, evangelicals/fundamentalists). Separate sections cover "Women's Roles," "Ethnicity and Religion" (Native American, Hispanics, and other), and "Communities and Cults." Except for the general works section, articles and books are listed together alphabetically by author, but most government publications, popular press items, master's theses, and personal memoirs are omitted. Although a fair number of entries have to do with religion in the Prairies-Plains region, the absence of an index makes them a trial to find. Reproduced from typescript. — *RB*

BA2   Turner, Harold W. - **Bibliography of New Religious Movements in Primal Societies**. - Boston, MA : G.K. Hall, 1977-1992. - 6 v. - (v. 1, Bibliographies and guides in African studies).

> Class Numbers:
>   Library of Congress BP603   Z7835.C86
> ISBN 0816179271
> LCCN 77-4732
> Notes:

Contents: v. 1, Black Africa; v. 2, North America; v. 3, Oceania; v. 4, Europe and Asia; v. 5, Latin America; v. 6, The Caribbean
Indexes

• Turner's very full bibliography covers movements in all parts of the world "which arise in the interaction of a primal society with another society where there is a great disparity of power or sophistication" (v. 2, p. vii). Volume 2 has greatest interest for Prairies-Plains study, dealing with the U.S., Canada, and northern Mexico. Among the movements in the U.S. section are ghost dances, Kennekuk, Midéwiwin and drum religion, sun dance, Yuwipi, and at greatest length, three sections on peyote. Volume 2 offers more than 1,600 entries, all annotated, arranged in sections Classed "Theory," "General," then U.S.; Canada, Alaska, and Greenland; and northern Mexico. In each section, entries are alphabetical by author. The section for Canada omits metis and is much briefer than the U.S. section. Entries are carefully thorough. Indexes: authors and sources; films, records, and tapes; main movements and Indian individuals. Fearsomely complete, although dates of coverage vary by volume (volume 2 was published 1978). — *RB*

Encyclopedias

BA3   Laderman, Gary, ed. - **Religion and American Culture : An Encyclopedia of Traditions, Diversity, and Popular Expressions** / Gary Laderman and Luis León, eds. ; foreword by Amanda Porterfield. - Santa Barbara, CA : ABC-CLIO, 2003. - 3 v. (1046 p.) ; ill.

> Class Numbers:
>   Library of Congress BL2525
> ISBN 157607238X
> OCLC 52109129
> LCCN 2003-8644
> Includes bibliographical references (p. 969-1001); index

• Laderman (Emory Univ.) and León (Univ. of California-Berkeley) attempt to present the varied religious expressions encountered in American culture, using as their starting point Clifford Geertz's definition of religion, "a system of symbols which acts to establish powerful, pervasive, and long-lasting moods and motivations" (*Religion as a Cultural System*, 1973). The first volume covers religions practiced by various groups in America (hence they provide a section, "Native American Religions and Politics"), traditional religions (e.g., Buddhism, Catholicism, Islam) as they have been affected by the American context, and new religions, including New Age. The second volume takes up cultural topics ("idioms"), demonstrating their spiritual content and genesis (mourning, advertising, lynching, abortion, Las Vegas). The third volume reproduces documents that bear on the religious experience of Americans. The contributors consciously depart from American exceptionalism,

Christian agendas, and Protestant church history in a set that celebrates diversity and shows American society permeated by religious belief. All volumes have a table of contents for the set, and v. 3 has a long bibliography, roster of contributors, and index. The set touches on Plains concerns at a number of points, but will be primarily useful to Plains students for its summary of Native religions. — *RB*

Almanacs ; Yearbooks

BA4 Yearbook of American and Canadian Churches. - 41st (1973)- . Nashville, TN : Abingdon Pr., 1973- . Annual.

> Class Numbers:
> Library of Congress BR513
> OCLC 1798538
> LCCN 75-640866
> Notes:
> Preceding title: *Yearbook of American Churches*.
> ISSN 0084-3644
> Vols. for 1973– prepared in the Office of Research, Evaluation and Planning of the National Council of Churches of Christ in the U.S.A.

• A directory section lists cooperative organizations; religious bodies, arranged alphabetically and by family, with descriptions; organizational sources of religion-related research; regional and local ecumenical bodies by state and province, with a subject index of their programs; theological seminaries and Bible colleges; religious periodicals; and church archives and historical records collections. A statistical section has membership statistics, selected church finance statistics, and trends in seminary enrollment. A three-year church calendar and indexes by organizations and individuals are included. Though only ecumenical bodies are listed by state or province and there is no geographical index, the directory is a unique compilation and an excellent way to begin research on contemporary churches in the Prairies-Plains. A serial number inside the back cover of each printed volume allows access to an electronic version, but that requires opening a charge account with the publisher or using a bankcard. The one-account-per-book limit will be problematic for libraries. The Internet site is updated biennially but appears to have no value-added search features. — *JD*

Atlases

BA5 New Historical Atlas of Religion in America / [by] Edwin Scott Gaustad and Philip L. Barlow ; with the special assistance of Richard W. Dishno. - New York : Oxford Univ. Pr., 2001. - 1 atlas (xxiii, 435 p.) ; col. maps ; 34 cm.

> Class Numbers:
> Library of Congress G1201.E4
> ISBN 019509168X
> OCLC 46660732
> LCCN 00-300001
> Notes:
> "Denominational Predominance: 1990" (col. map foldout in pocket)
> Includes bibliographical references; index
> Rev. ed. of: Edwin Scott Gaustad, *Historical Atlas of Religion in America* (1976)
> Scales vary

• Environment, this classic work suggests, influences the nature and progress of religion across the U.S. The atlas attempts to represent that position statistically with text, maps, and charts. Because it presents detailed information by state and county over a long period of time, it is an excellent source on the status of religion in the Great Plains and how historical and geographical influences have shaped it. Primary features include maps that show the strength of each denomination and excellent histories of each religious group. This welcome revision reorganizes and expands information about ethnic groups and non-Christian religious groups. Part 1 covers institutional and ethnic religion before 1800 and the establishment of colonial patterns in the eastern U.S. Part 2 covers 1800-1990, a period of expansion and diversity. Maps show county by county the distribution of churches of each denomination in 1890 and 1990. Religious practices of Native Americans and other ethnic groups are covered. Part 3 examines the distribution and growth of Lutherans, Roman Catholics, and Mormons in greater detail. Part 4 moves beyond denominations, examining such topics as camp meetings and the geography of faith and unbelief. Pie charts for each state show the proportionate strength of denominations in 1890 and 1990; the 1890 charts include Indian Territory. Data are drawn from reports of denominations and from the U.S. Census, which gathered information on churches from 1850 to 1936. Charts and maps also illustrate mergers in religious groups, demographics, locations of missions and Mormon settlements, overall growth of denominations, and other factors influencing religion. Appendixes note sources and provide tables of the mapped data, maps of counties, and an index by subject to text and illustrations. Illustrations are clear and attractive. —*JD*

BA6 Newman, William M. - **Atlas of American Religion : The Denominational Era, 1776-1990** / [by] William M. Newman, Peter L. Halvorson. - Walnut Creek, CA : AltaMira Pr., 2000. - 176 p. ; maps 30 cm.

> Class Numbers:
> Library of Congress BR515
> LCCN 99-6320

• The authors (both University of Connecticut) rely on numerous early compilations of religious data, much of it collected in the 18th and 19th centuries, to compile a picture of the spread of various shades of religious belief across the United States at four key periods: 1850, 1890, 1952, and 1990. They confine their data to Christian denominations and Jews, and show the weight of denominational belief on maps of the continental U.S., two for each denomination, that use color to present total adherents by county in 1990, and geographic change by county for as many of the key periods as the data reported. They also classify denominations into four categories: national denominations (Catholics, Methodists, Presbyterians), multiregional denominations (Lutherans, United Churches of Christ), classic sects (Mennonites, Moravians), multiregional sects (Brethren, Friends), and national sects (Nazarenes, Mormons, Seventh-Day Adventists). The Plains were late in accepting certain Eastern seaboard denominations, partly by reason of late settlement, partly because the frontier proved hostile to them. It is fascinating to see the spread of denominations and sects across the country, and to see which have had success in the Prairies-Plains region. The introductory matter of this fascinating compilation requires close reading. The bibliography cites sources used in compilation. — *RB*

Statistical Compendiums

BA7   Religious Congregations & Membership in the United States : An Enumeration by Region, State and County Based on Data Reported for 149 Religious Bodies / [ed. by] Dale E. Jones [et al.]. - Nashville, TN : Glenmary Research Center, 2002– . Semimonthly.

Class Numbers:
Library of Congress BL2525
LCCN 2002-111833
Notes:
Accompanied by a CD-ROM that contains the printed data. 1 computer optical disc
Earlier eds. publ. under title: *Churches & Church Membership in the United States*
The Association of Statisticians of American Religious Bodies (ASARB) sponsored the study on which this report is based

• A statistical survey of the affiliation American residents maintain with 149 religious bodies or congregations. The principal part of the report is a survey by state, then county, of the numbers of churches, synagogues, mosques, or temples; the numbers of communicant, confirmed, or full members; number of attendees; number of adherents (members and others who attend); and for adherents, percentages of the total population and of total adherents for the unit surveyed (county, state, etc.). That survey is preced-

ed by summary surveys by United States, by region (Prairies-Plains states fall into three regions), and by state. A set of 24 outline maps of the U.S. in color show percentages of various religious bodies by county. Appendixes define various religious groups and summarize data-gathering procedures. All Prairies-Plains states are represented. — *RB*

Women

BA8   Tucker, Cynthia Grant. - **Prophetic Sisterhood : Liberal Women Ministers of the Frontier, 1880-1930**. - Bloomington, IN : Indiana Univ. Pr., 1994, 1990. - 298 p. ; ill.

Class Numbers:
Library of Congress BX9867
ISBN 025321822X
LCCN 93-22699
Notes:
Includes bibliographical references (p. 271-284); index
Originally publ.: Boston, MA: Beacon Pr., c1990

• Tucker (English, Memphis State Univ.) documents the lives of nine Unitarian/Universalist female ministers in the late 19th century (Florence Buck, Caroline Bartlett Crane, Eleanor Gordon, Marie Jenney Howe, Ida Hultin, Marion Murdock, Mary Stafford, Eliza Wilkes, and Celia Parker Wooley). Part 1 focuses on the economic, political, and legal reasons these women moved to Iowa and the surrounding Great Plains states; Part 2 examines their pastoring methods; Part 3 looks at their grass-roots success; and Part 4 focuses on their efforts to spread the word of God outside the pulpit. Eight illustrations. — *GK*

Anabaptists

See also **Hutterian-English Dictionary, BB8**

BA9   Anderson, Alan B., 1939-. - **German, Mennonite and Hutterite Communities in Saskatchewan : An Inventory of Sources**. – Saskatoon, SK : Saskatchewan German Council, 1988. - [42] p.

Class Numbers:
Library of Congress F1074.7.G37
National Library of Canada Z1392 S27
OCLC 22483265

• An initial historical overview, both religious and geographical, of Saskatchewan's large German population is followed by detailed notes on sources. Separate sections cover the three groups; arrangement is by very specific form of publication. Approximately 500 citations, although some are listed in more than one section. Extends the coverage, backward and forward, of V. Wiebe's *Alberta Saskatchewan Mennonite and Hutterite Bibliography 1962-1981* (**BA13**). — *LMcD*

BA10   Kraybill, Donald B. - **Anabaptist World USA /** [by] Donald B. Kraybill, C. Nelson Hostetter. - Scottdale, PA : Herald Pr., 2001. - 296 p. ; ill.

> Class Numbers:
> Library of Congress BX4933.U6
> ISBN 0836191633
> LCCN 2001-24423
> Notes:
> Includes bibliographical references (p. 222-230); indexes

• Although strongest in Pennsylvania and Ohio, Anabaptist "tribes" (as this work calls its various sects, with shadings of belief and practice among Amish, Brethren, Mennonites, and Hutterites) may be found in greater or lesser strength in all the Prairies-Plains states, and in the Canadian Prairie provinces. The authors begin with interpretive essays about history and belief, and discuss the tribes and their penetration into U.S. and Canadian society. Section 2, "Resources," provides statistics by state of congregations and their membership and ends with a nine-page bibliography. Part 3 is a directory of congregations by state. There is no index. — *RB*

BA11   Riley, Marvin P. - **The Hutterite Brethren : An Annotated Bibliography with Special Reference to South Dakota Hutterite Colonies**. - Brookings, SD : Sociology Dept., Agricultural Experiment Station, South Dakota State Univ., 1965. - 188 p. ; map. - (South Dakota Agricultural Experiment Station. Bulletin, 529).

> Class Numbers:
> Library of Congress Z7845.H86
> OCLC 2510153
> LCCN 66-64560

• Riley (rural sociology, South Dakota State Univ.) prefaces this work with a general history of the Hutterites, 1528-1964. Topical categories for the 332 entries include general information, history, religious beliefs, music, family, conscientious objection, statistical information, agricultural methods, crafts, psychological aspects, intergroup relations, legal issues, social change, affiliated colonies, and funeral/burial rites. Author index; one map (location of South Dakota Hutterite colonies). — *GK*

BA12   Smucker, Donovan Ebersole, 1915-   . - **The Sociology of Canadian Mennonites, Hutterites, and Amish : A Bibliography with Annotations**. - Waterloo, ON : Wilfrid Laurier Univ. Pr., 1977-1990. - 2 v.

> Class Numbers:
> Library of Congress BX8111 Z7845.M4
> ISBN 0889200521 (v. 1)   0889200513 (v. 1 : pbk.)
>   0889509995 (v. 2)
> OCLC 3695499
> LCCN 78-317456
> Notes:
> Indexes
> Vol. 2 has title: *The Sociology of Mennonites, Hutterites, and Amish* and special title: 1977-1990

• The estimated 1,400 items listed by Smucker examine elements of the social and cultural life of three religious groups descended from the Anabaptist Reformation of the 16th century. An introductory essay establishes the context of their origin and provides an overview of methodological trends in the studies. The first chapter covers reference works and social theory, followed by chapters devoted to each group separately. Each is arranged by type of publication: books and pamphlets, theses, articles, and unpublished sources. Acculturation, education, immigration, farming, and socialization are among the recurring areas of examination. The second volume extends the range of the bibliography to include the United States. Name and subject indexes, although the subject portion is not consistently reliable in identifying studies of specific communities, either in the plains or elsewhere. Appendixes in v. 2 include a church member profile, sectarian research libraries and bookstores, and special collections of Amish material. Most items in the bibliography are in English, with a few in German. — *LMcD*

BA13   Wiebe, Victor G. - **Alberta Saskatchewan Mennonite and Hutterite Bibliography 1962-1981**. - Saskatoon, SK : Mennonite Historical Society of Alberta and Saskatchewan, 1981. - 10 p.

> Class Numbers:
> Library of Congress Z7845.M4
> National Library of Canada Z7845
> OCLC 8822531

• A list of 122 works dealing with two distinctive religious denominations in the 16th-century Anabaptist tradition. Books, pamphlets, and theses are included; articles and non-Mennonite works by Mennonite authors are excluded. Although not annotated, some entries have very brief explanatory notes. The period before 1962 is covered by *Mennonite Bibliography, 1631-1961* (Scottsdale, AZ: Herald Pr., 1977; 2 v.), compiled by N.P. Springer and A.J. Klassen. — *LMcD*

BA14   Wiebe, Victor G. - **Saskatchewan Mennonite Bibliography, 1962-1995**. - Saskatoon, SK : Mennonite Historical Society of Saskatchewan, 1995. - 48 p.

Class Numbers:

    Library of Congress Z7845.M4

    OCLC 35368971

• Wiebe's bibliography emphasizes studies of the Mennonite presence in the province but includes some material on the Hutterian Brethren as well. Creative writings (poetry, drama, novels) by Mennonites are included, but most works on non-Mennonite subjects are not. The 365 items are organized into sections on general works, genealogy, and local history; some entries are briefly annotated. Title index. Although narrower in geographical scope than the author's earlier work (**BA13**), it extends the chronological coverage. — *LMcD*

Anglicans

BA15   MacDonald, Wilma, 1939-   . - **Guide to the Holdings of the Archives of the Ecclesiastical Province and Dioceses of Rupert's Land**. - Winnipeg, MB : St. John's College Pr., 1986. - 208 p. - (Records of the Anglican Church of Canada, 1).

Class Numbers:

    Library of Congress CD3649.W563

    National Library of Canada CD3649 R96

    ISBN 0920291015

    OCLC 18053219

    LCCN 87-167075

    Notes:

        Includes bibliographical references and indexes

• A guide to collections in the archives of ten western dioceses of the Anglican Church, half of which are Prairie-based. Under each diocese, parish records arranged by place follow administrative records. Entries briefly describe the contents, inclusive dates, and size of each collection, identifying primary sources for Prairie church history and Anglican missionary, educational, and social endeavors. Short biographies and separate indexes for names and places complete the volume. For Calgary in particular, see *A Guide to the Records of the Anglican Diocese of Calgary* (**BA16**). — *LMcD*

BA16   Kynaston, Donna, 1957-   . - **A Guide to the Records of the Anglican Diocese of Calgary**. - Calgary, AB : Anglican Diocese of Calgary, 1992. - 188 p. : ill., ports.

Class Numbers:

    National Library of Canada BX5617 C34

    ISBN 0969634404

    OCLC 31777604

• Records date from 1881 to 1990, with most located in

Special Collections at the Univ. of Calgary. Parish records are arranged by place and parish. Entries begin with a short history, followed by registers of baptisms, confirmations, marriages and burials, and minutes and papers of parish organizations. Synod records consist of parish files (chiefly correspondence, with parishes listed by place), clergy files, and various institutional series. The final sections describe records of women's auxiliaries and special formats such as maps and photographs. The guide identifies primary sources for the social and religious history of southern Alberta. — *LMcD*

Baptists

BA17   Early, Joseph Everett, 1970-   . - **A Handbook of Texas Baptist Biography**. - Bloomington, IN : AuthorHouse, 2004. - 238 p.

Class Numbers:

    Library of Congress BX6248.T4

    ISBN 1418446963 (pbk.)   1418456748 (e-book)

    OCLC 57028889

    LCCN 2005-298525

    Notes:

        Includes bibliographical references

• Consists of 300 entries organized alphabetically. Those profiled had to have made a significant contribution to church growth, evangelism, missions, or philanthropy. All are deceased, and a great majority were not native Texans. The entries, 50-700 words in length, emphasize church work, and provide minimal personal information. Although the compiler notes information was derived from church and seminary archives, interviews, and genealogies, only references to published sources accompany the entries. No index. — *MS*

Church of Jesus Christ of Latter-Day Saints

BA18   **Encyclopedia of Mormonism** / ed. by Daniel H. Ludlow. - New York : Macmillan, 1992. - 5 v. ; ill.

Class Numbers:

    Library of Congress BX8605.5

    ISBN 0028796004 (v. 1) 0028796012 (v. 2)

      0028796020 (v. 3)   0028796039 (v. 4)

      0028796047 (v. 5) 002904040X (set)

    OCLC 24502140

    LCCN 91-34255

    Notes:

        Includes bibliographical references; index

• The Mormon presence in the Prairies-Plains region is not

large, although settlements have been founded by adherents of the Church (whose official name is Church of Jesus Christ of Latter-Day Saints) in Alberta, Wyoming, and New Mexico. Mormons have been the targets of lawsuits and persecution virtually since the church's founding in the 1830s. This encyclopedia, sanctioned by the Church leadership, covers all aspects of Church belief and history, and touches on aspects of Mormon migration, starting from settlements in Nauvoo, IL, Council Bluffs, IA, and Winter Quarters in Nebraska, across Nebraska and Wyoming to Utah in 1847, and the migration of the handcart companies in the mid-1850s. Volume 4 includes an index, biographies of Church officers, excerpts from Joseph Smith's translation of the Bible, and, leaving no stone unturned, a selection of hymns with music. Volume 1 lists all the articles and has a roster of contributors, and volume 5 reprints *The Book of Mormon*, *The Doctrine and Covenants*, and *The Pearl of Great Price*. Important for study of the Church, or for accounts of the Mormons' passages across the Plains. — *RB*

BA19   Flake, Chad J., ed. - **A Mormon Bibliography, 1830-1930 : Books, Pamphlets, Periodicals, and Broadsides Relating to the First Century of Mormonism** / ed. by Chad J. Flake and Larry W. Draper ; introd. by Dale L. Morgan. - Provo, UT : Brigham Young Univ., 2004. - 2 v.

Class Numbers:
    Library of Congress BX8638
ISBN 084252570X
Notes:
    Includes bibliographical references; index

• Flake's bibliography is arranged alphabetically by main entry in the first volume (1978). Entries are brief, but each lists libraries that hold the item. The 10,145 items in the parent volume are numbered consecutively. An index to item numbers by year (starting in 1811) allows publications to be tracked chronologically. A smaller ten-year supplement (1989), is likewise alphabetical, but its entries are numbered to fit them into place with entries in the parent volume; 2542a and 2542b belong alphabetically between 2542 and 2543 in the parent volume. The supplement contains a title index to its own entries but not to the parent volume, and a chronological index. — *MB*

Protestants

BA20   Lindquist, Emory Kempton, 1908-   . - **The Protestant Church in Kansas : An Annotated Bibliography**. - Wichita, KS : Univ. of Wichita, 1956. - 28 p. - (Wichita State University. University studies. Bulletin, 35 ; University of Wichita bulletin, v. 31 no. 4).

Class Numbers:
    Library of Congress AS36

OCLC 2546485
LCCN 57-717

• This pamphlet cites 152 books and journal articles, arranged alphabetically by author, relating to the origin and growth of the Protestant church in Kansas. The compiler made no attempt to include congregational histories or official printed records of various denominations. Most items cited were published in the first half of the 20th century. — *MB*

Roman Catholics

BA21   **Catholic Archives of Texas [Internet Site]**. - Austin, TX : Catholic Archives of Texas, 2000?-   . - http://www.onr.com/user/cat/

Access Date: May 2008
Fees: None

• The Archives house a rare book, map, and archives collection that includes an extensive collection of Spanish and Mexican manuscripts. A 2,000-volume Kasner Reference Library focuses on Catholics and Texas history and culture. The Archives site offers finding guides to its extensive collections of personal, corporate, manuscript, and sacramental records as well as information on hours, staff, contacts, and use policies. It also links to *National Union Catalog of Manuscript Collections* (NUCMC), *Texas Catholic Historical Society*, and *Catholic Southwest: A Journal of History and Culture*. The Archive is intended for serious church or Texas historians. A detailed guide to Spanish and Mexican manuscripts is available in print only: *Guide to the Spanish and Mexican Manuscript Collection at the Catholic Archives of Texas*, comp. by Dedra S. McDonald, ed. by Kinga Perzynska (Austin, TX : Catholic Archives of Texas, 1994; 147 p.). — *JD*

BA22   Owens, Brian M. - **A Guide to the Archives of the Oblates of Mary Immaculate, Province of Alberta-Saskatchewan** / [by] Brian M. Owens and Claude M. Roberto. - Edmonton, AB : Missionary Oblates, Grandin Province, 1989. - 138, 143 p. ; + 17 microfiches (negative).

Class Numbers:
    Library of Congress CD3649.E36
ISBN 0969384408
OCLC 28291741
LCCN 89-217615
Notes:
    Records are housed at Provincial Archives of Alberta
    Text in English and French; microfiches in French only
    Title on added t.p. inverted: *Guide pour les Archives des Oblats de Marie Immaculée, Province d'Alberta-Saskatchewan*

• Guide to records documenting the extensive missionary and educational activities of the Oblates, the most influential Catholic religious order in western Canada. The written material spans 1842 to 1984 and is mainly in French. Much of the material is administrative in nature (correspondence, minutes) but there are also 30,000 photographs and hundreds of recordings in various native languages. Detailed lists of personal papers of individual Oblates and institutional records of more than a hundred parishes and missions. Inventory file listings appear on the microfiche. Useful guide to primary sources on early religious efforts, Indian residential schools, and native languages. — *LMcD*

United Church of Canada

BA23   Mychajlunow, Lorraine. - **A Guide to the Archives of the United Church of Canada, Alberta and Northwest Conference** / Lorraine Mychajlunow and Keith Stotyn. - Edmonton, AB : United Church of Canada, Alberta and Northwest Conference, 1991. - 167 p.

Class Numbers:
    National Library of Canada CD3649 A45
    ISBN 0886223024
    OCLC 23838360
    Notes:
        11 microfiches in back pocket

• The records of the Church and its constituent predecessor denominations (Presbyterian Church in Canada, Methodist Church, and Congregational Union of Canada) are housed at the Provincial Archives of Alberta. The material is mostly written but also includes photos, maps and plans; it ranges from 1831 to 1990. The guide outlines documents related to administrative and home mission activities at the General Council, Alberta Conference, and presbytery levels. It also lists records of approximately 650 parishes and pastoral charges. Personal papers of individual ministers are noted. A detailed inventory file on microfiche is included. A useful guide to primary sources on the Protestant religious and social history of Alberta. — *LMcD*

Indians

BA24   Crawford, Suzanne J. - **American Indian Religious Traditions : An Encyclopedia** / [by] Suzanne J. Crawford and Dennis F. Kelley. - Santa Barbara, CA : ABC-CLIO, 2005. - 3 v. (ccvii, 1269 p.) ; ill., maps.

Class Numbers:
    Library of Congress E98.R3
    National Library of Canada E98
    ISBN 1576075206 (electronic bk.)
    OCLC 57143246

LCCN 2004-28169
Notes:
    Contents: v. 1-3, A-Z
    Electronic book: http://www.ebooks.abc-clio.com
    Includes bibliographical references; index
    Table of contents: http://www.loc.gov/catdir/toc/
        ecip054/2004028169.html

• An abundance of Native contributors enhance these lengthy, scholarly alphabetical encyclopedia entries. It covers the entire U.S. (Canada, Mexico, and Hawai'i were deliberately, if regrettably, omitted). Editors Crawford and Kelley took pains to be sensitive to and respectful of Native feelings about sharing religious traditions, and many subjects were, as they say, "intentionally left out" in deference to those concerns. This is not political correctness run amok, but simple respect. Entries range across the usual topics, but some subjects are addressed in separate entries by region, culture area, or tribe. Consequently, there are entries for "Art (Traditional and Contemporary), Plains," "Ceremony and Ritual, Lakota," "Missionization, Northern Plains," "Oral Traditions, Western Plains," and "Religious Leaders, Plains," as well as more specific regional entries (e.g., "Kiowa Indian Hymns," "Ella Deloria," "Sun Dance, Crow," and "Buffalo/Bison Restoration Project"). A detailed, 80-page index refers to terms throughout the articles, such as "Owls—in Dakota traditions," and includes words in Native languages, referring to their appearance in encyclopedia entries. An excellent work with much of relevance to the region. — *LM*

BA25   Hirschfelder, Arlene B. - **Encyclopedia of Native American Religions : An Introduction** / [by] Arlene Hirschfelder [and] Paulette Molin ; foreword by Walter L. Echo-Hawk. - Updated ed. - New York : Facts on File, 2001. - 390 p. ; ill., map, ports. - (Facts on File library of American history).

Class Numbers:
    Library of Congress E98.R3
    ISBN 0816039496
    LCCN 99-21586
    Notes:
        Includes bibliographical references (p. 349-363); indexes
        Previous ed.: New York: Facts on File, 1992

• Entries arranged alphabetically briefly describe spiritual beliefs and practices of Native American and First Nations people before and after Western contact. To avoid compromising sacred and private traditions, information is based on published works. Entries include biographies of Native religious practitioners and Catholic and Protestant missionaries. Native medicine, legislation, court cases, sacred sites and structures, ceremonial races, games, and clowns are covered, but detailed interpretations of cosmologies, stories, songs, prayers, and poetry are not. Although individual tribes do not have entries, a classified list of subjects names specific ceremonies, leaders, and themes associated with each tribe. The authors supply introductions to topics that are complex and difficult to research, but also provide an excellent bibliography for further reading. Subject index. — *JD*

BA26   Lyon, William S. - **Encyclopedia of Native American Shamanism : Sacred Ceremonies of North America**. - Santa Barbara, CA : ABC-CLIO, 1998. - xxxvii, 468 p. ; ill., maps.

> Class Numbers:
> Library of Congress E98.M4
> ISBN 0874369339
> LCCN 98-34582
> Notes:
> Includes bibliographical references (p. 411-437); index

• Religious studies professor Lyon takes that discipline's approach to this continuation of his earlier work, *Encyclopedia of Native American Healing* (**CD100**). His new work provides information on all the ways that "shamans" (a term used throughout by Lyon and other scholars but shunned by Native peoples), or medicine people, manifest their powers beyond healing, although some additional materials on healing are included as well. Lyon intends both works to be used together, tying references in *Shamanism* to entries in the earlier work; but the two encyclopedias may be used separately. Excluded from both works is plant usage and herbalism, but *Shamanism* includes a bibliography on ethnobotany in addition to a 20-page list of references. Fifteen culture area maps list tribes within each culture, and the maps for Plains, Midwest, and Plateau, and the Canadian Eastern Woodlands and Mackenzie-Yukon enable users to identify tribes in these regions. Encyclopedia entries list tribe and culture area immediately after the entry title. Entries often contain lengthy quotations from source materials, fully cited. Unhappily, the only way to search for regional entries is by tribe in the detailed index, but one must know the various names by which a people are known, since the index has no cross-references. For example, there is no entry for "Sioux," but "Santee" and "Teton" both have entries, and there are entries in plenty under "Lakota" and "Dakota," with no way to tie these entries for the same people together. A scholarly work that requires some previous knowledge and provides information not found in the usual general works. — *LM*

BA27   White, Phillip M., comp. - **The Native American Sun Dance Religion and Ceremony : An Annotated Bibliography**. - Westport, CT : Greenwood Pr., 1998. - xxiv, 115 p. - (Bibliographies and indexes in American history).

> Class Numbers:
> Library of Congress Z1209.83.
> ISBN 03131306281
> LCCN 98-15332

• White's extensively annotated bibliography of 335 titles is preceded by an introduction and a "core collection" list of 14 titles. The bibliography itself is arranged alphabetically by 19 tribes, Arapaho to Ute. All published materials are included; excluded are unpublished manuscripts, diaries, letters, personal papers, musical recordings, and fiction. Most entries in the index refer to individuals. An essential title. — *LM*

BB : LANGUAGES ; LINGUISTICS

Scope   Lists works concerned with linguistics, with individual languages (especially glossaries and dictionaries) spoken in the Prairies-Plains region, and with Indian languages.

LINGUISTICS

BB1   Allen, Harold Byron, 1902–   . - **The Linguistic Atlas of the Upper Midwest**. - [Minneapolis, MN] : Univ. of Minnesota Pr., 1973-1976. - 3 v. ; ill.

> Class Numbers:
> Library of Congress PE2912
> ISBN 0816606862 (v. 1)
> LCCN 72-96716
> Notes:
> Bibliography: v. 1, p. 141-144 ; v. 2, p. 5

• Allen's comprehensive study, sponsored by the Univ. of Minnesota where he was a specialist in linguistic geography, analyzes dialectal variants drawn from 208 interviews collected 1949-62. The set, part dictionary, part atlas, illustrates speech patterns used by informants in Upper Midwest states (Minnesota, Iowa, Nebraska, North Dakota, and South Dakota). Chapters discuss the history of the project, states covered by the study, survey methodology (selection of communities, informants, and preparation of fieldworkers). Each volume contains detailed statistical data and maps showing distribution of variants and phonetic anomalies. Regional coordinators (some of whom provided financial assistance) were Albert H. Marckwardt and Hans Kurath (Univ. of Michigan), Rachael Kirkpatrick (Univ. of Iowa), G.E. Giescke (North Dakota State Univ.), and Joseph Giddings (South Dakota State Univ.). — *GK*

BB2   **International Encyclopedia of Linguistics** / William Bright, ed.-in-chief. - New York : Oxford Univ. Pr., 1992. - 4 v. ; ill., maps.

> Class Numbers:
> Library of Congress P29.I58 1991
> ISBN 0195051963 (set)
> LCCN 91-7349
> Notes:
> Includes bibliographical references; index

• Bright provides a comprehensive source on all branches of linguistics (descriptive, historical, comparative, typological,

functionalist, and formalist) aimed at scholars and students. The relationship of linguistics to other disciplines receives extensive coverage–e.g., ethnolinguistics, sociolinguistics, and psycholinguistics. The work is arranged alphabetically; longer essays run 5,000 words. Advisors and topic editors consist of 37 scholars and the work contains a synoptic outline of contents that includes topic areas, languages of the world, language families, and areas. Sections addressing the languages of indigenous or ethnic Great Plains groups include Czech, Slovak, German, Polish, Scandinavian, Indo-European, Siouan, and Spanish. Cross-references, abbreviations, symbols, glossary, maps, illustrations, tables, directory of contributors. — *GK*

BB3   Teschner, Richard V., ed. - **Spanish and English of United States Hispanos : A Critical, Annotated, Linguistic Bibliography** / Garland D. Bills and Jerry R. Craddock, associate eds. - Arlington, VA : Center for Applied Linguistics, 1975. - xxii, 352 p.

> Class Numbers:
> Library of Congress PC4826 Z2695.D5
> ISBN 0872810429
> OCLC 1923912
> LCCN 75-21564
> Notes:
> Index

• Intended as a comprehensive bibliography of books, articles, and theses that relate, in whole or part, to the English, Spanish, or bilingual speech and language behavior of U.S. residents of Hispanic background, Teschner et al.'s book is primarily about Mexican Americans but also covers the influences of Spanish and English upon one another. Most of the 675 items are linguistic but others stem from disciplines ranging from folklore to speech pathology. Only language education of Mexican Americans is excluded. The citations are arranged by culture and subcategorized by location. Two sections are devoted to Mexican Americans in New Mexico and south-central Colorado, and in Texas. Other Plains states are included in the subcategory for Mexican Americans "elsewhere." Entries include extensive annotations, references to previous bibliographies and reviews, and cross-references to related items in other sections. Author index. A substantial scholarly work marred only by the extensive use of abbreviations in the citations and cross-references. — *JD*

ENGLISH

Dictionaries

BB4   Blevins, Winfred. - **Dictionary of the American West : Over 5,000 Terms and Expressions from Aarigaa! to**

Zopilote. - Seattle, WA : Sasquatch Books, c2001. - 429 p. ; ill., maps.

Class Numbers:
  Library of Congress PE2970.W4 B5 2001
  ISBN 1570613044
  LCCN 2001-40063
  Notes:
    Includes bibliographical references (p. 427-429)
    Previous ed.: New York: Facts on File, 1993

• Blevins, a Western novelist and writer, supplies a glossary for 5,000 terms or expressions used by residents of the American West (defined as the Rocky Mountains, the Southwest, the Great Basin, and the Great Plains) in their work and everyday life during the 19th century. He does not attempt to present or supplant the technical vocabulary used in logging, mining, firefighting, or stock raising, but the word stock encountered in casual conversation in the street or the workplace. He draws words and phrases from French, Spanish, and Indian languages, and carefully includes terms that are inclusive of gender, race, and ethnic groups, and terms used by missionaries, immigrants, Mormons, and French Canadians. He does not pretend to be a professional lexicographer, so ignores etymology (although he accounts for the sources of some words), parts of speech, and in most cases pronunciation, concentrating instead on lexical meaning and usage and on the special meanings words acquired in the West. Illustrations are used effectively (not to be missed is the buffalo hide yard, p. 48). Section of further readings. Highly useful in Plains studies and in reading early accounts of the West. — *GK, RB*

Dictionaries, Regional

BB5   Adams, Ramon Frederick, 1889-1976. - **Western Words : A Dictionary of the American West**. - New edition, rev. and enl. - Norman, OK : Univ. of Oklahoma Pr., 1968. - 355 p.

Class Numbers:
  Library of Congress PE2970.W4
  LCCN 68-31369
  Notes:
    First edition published as *Western Words: A Dictionary of the Range, Cow Camp and Trail* (1944)

• Often metaphorical or highly specialized, the vocabulary used on cattle ranches can be difficult to interpret. Entries in Adams's dictionary include clear definitions, anecdotes, origins, and notes about regional variations. The second edition adds terms used by western sheepherders, trappers, freighters and packers, buffalo hunters, boatmen, loggers, sawmill workers, miners, and gamblers. Cross-references from common terms are both plentiful and necessary. The

entry "horse" refers readers to over 150 terms including "parada," "peg pony," and "pie biter." Sources are cited for some definitions but most are based on observation and interviews. — *JD*

BB5a   Adams, Ramon Frederick, 1889-1976. – **The Cowboy Dictionary : The Chin Jaw Words and Whing-Ding Ways of the American West**. – New York : Perigee Books, 1993. – 355 p.

Class Numbers:
  Library of Congress PE3727.C6
  ISBN 0399518665
  OCLC 28676763
  LCCN 93-30210

• To this reprint of the first edition, which defined common and obscure terms associated with the West and the cattle industry, Adams adds a discussion of how cowhand language evolved from the informant's sketchy education and borrowed from Spanish horsemen, Indians, French trappers, riverboat gamblers, and outlaws, among others. Entries have value for the information they give beyond lexical meaning; for example, the entry for "dally" includes information on the word's derivation and the changes it endured. — *JB*

BB6   Cassidy, Frederick Gomes, 1907–2000, ed. - **Dictionary of American Regional English**. - Cambridge, MA : Belknap Pr. of Harvard Univ. Pr., 1985–   . - 4 v. ; ill., maps. (In progress).

Class Numbers:
  Library of Congress PE2843
  ISBN 0674205111 (v. 1)067420512X (v. 2)
    0674205197 (v. 3)   0674000847 (v. 4)
  LCCN 84-29025
  Notes:
    An online version, http://polyglot.lss.wisc.edu/dare/dare. html, describes the set, provides a sample of about 100 entries, and lists editors and advisors ("Board of Visitors")
    Contents: v. 1-4, A-Sk. A 5th volume will complete the alphabet and a 6th contain bibliography, maps, responses to questionnaires, etc.
    Vol. 2-4: Joan Houston Hall, associate ed.

• Cassidy's innovative dictionary illustrates language usage for specific words and phrases and includes specialized maps that display variations such as the frequency and distribution of "cougar" versus "mountain lion" in the Plains and the Spanish influence on the pronunciation of "coyote" in New Mexico. In a map of the U.S., state shapes are distorted to display population density rather than boundaries; Wyoming is a tiny rectangle and Texas is a largish area shaped somewhat like Illinois. The map is filled with dots representing 1,002 communities distributed throughout the states according to population density; Wyoming has three dots and Texas 46. One questionnaire with 1,847 questions in 41 categories was completed in each community, often using more than one informant. Entries give parts of speech, pronunciation, variant spellings, etymology, geographical labels, usage, quotations, cross-references, and definitions. Entries with distinct regional variations include maps that plot the communities in which informants used the word or expression in the same context as the definition. A detailed methodology, list of informants, text of the questionnaire, analyses of regional variations, and a pronunciation guide are included in the introduction. No geographical index. — *JD*

BB7   Chariton, Wallace O. - **This Dog'll Hunt** / introd. by Ann Richards ; ill. by Wayde Gardner. - Plano, TX : Wordware Publ., 1989. - 277 p. ; ill.

> Class Numbers:
> Library of Congress PE3101.T4
> ISBN 1556221266
> OCLC 18908554
> LCCN 88-33865
> Notes:
> > Index
> > Continued by Chariton's *This Dog'll Really Hunt: An Informative and Entertaining Texas Dictionary*. Plano, TX: Republic of Texas Pr., 1999. 307 p.

• Chariton's English-to-Texan dictionary groups the commonest regional colloquial terms under the corresponding standard English term of the same meaning. Many are familiar but others have a flavor more local; e.g., the Texan term corresponding to "frugal" would be "chews close and spits tight." The appeal of Chariton's volume is that it lists entries under standard English rather than the colloquial word or phrase. — *JB*

BB8   Hoover, Walter B. - **Hutterian-English Dictionary : Compendium of the Common Vocabulary of the Hutterian Prairie People at Langham, Saskatchewan (1901-2001)**. - Centennial ed. - Saskatoon, SK : W.B. Hoover, 2001. - 164 p.

> Class Numbers:
> National Library of Canada PF5625
> OCLC 47948065
> Notes:
> > First published (1997) covering 1905-1997

• Approximately 3,800 terms in "hutrish," the German dialect brought to Saskatchewan by 19th-century Hutterite pioneers from Russia. Multiple English equivalents and examples of usage. The dictionary provides proof of linguistic tenacity on the prairies. — LMcD

BB9   Sandilands, John. - **Western Canadian Dictionary and Phrase Book**. – Edmonton, AB : Univ. of Alberta Pr., 1977 [1997]. - 51 p.

> Class Numbers:
> Library of Congress PE3237
> ISBN 0888640218
> OCLC 4569467
> LCCN 78-325287
> Notes:
> > Facsim. of the 1913 ed. published by Telegram Job Printers, Winnipeg, with a new introd. by John Orrell
> > Cover has sub-title: *Picturesque Language of the Cowboy and Bronco-Buster*

• Reprint of a guide to colloquialisms and distinctive words used by western Canadians, originally intended for new arrivals to the Prairies. Fascinating as a reflection of regional life, customs, and attitudes of almost a century ago. *Cold as a Bay Street Banker's Heart* (**BB10**) is somewhat a contemporary equivalent in recording unusual features of Prairie vocabulary. — *LMcD*

BB10   Thain, Chris, 1937-   . - **Cold as a Bay Street Banker's Heart**. - Calgary, AB : Fifth House, 2003, 1987. - 196 p. ; ill.

> Class Numbers:
> Library of Congress PE3245.P73
> ISBN 189485621X
> OCLC 51086289
> LCCN 2004-444427
> Notes:
> > Originally published: Saskatoon, SK.: Western Producer Prairie Books, 1987

• A dictionary of colorful terms and phrases (e.g., "klootch," "buffalo chips," "nanny whamming") used by Prairie residents. Captures words that reflect shared experience and elements of the social history of the region. Not a scholarly work (Thain solicited suggested terms from newspaper readers in western Canada) but a rarity among reference books: both informative and entertaining. — *LMcD*

BB11   Watts, Peter Christopher. - **A Dictionary of the Old West, 1850-1900**. - New York : Wings Books ; distr. Avenel, NJ : Random House Value Publ., 1994, 1977. - 399 p. ; ill., map.

> Class Numbers:
> Library of Congress PE2970 .W4
> ISBN 0517119137
> OCLC 30545024
> LCCN 94-18340
> Notes:
> > Includes bibliographical references (p. [379]-399)
> > Originally publ.: New York: Knopf, 1977

• Primarily designed to help readers understand some of the distinctive words and phrases of the Old West, as an aid to understanding its literature. Headwords are arranged alphabetically; the dictionary section ends with a short list of works cited and consulted. Definitions include, as appropriate, cross-references, variants, and word origin (e.g., Spanish, French). Works cited for the definition are included in most cases but not all. Entries range from a few words to entire pages. Numerous line drawings throughout. The author, a Briton living in London, is himself an author of Western novels and short stories. — *MB*

Cowhand Language

See also **Adams, Western Words (BB5) and The Cowboy Dictionary (BB5a)**.

BB12   Adams, Ramon Frederick, 1889-1976. - **Cowboy Lingo** / ill. by Nick Eggenhofer ; foreword by Elmer Kelton. - Boston, MA : Houghton Mifflin, 2000, 1936. - 253 p. ; ill.

  Class Numbers:
    Library of Congress PE3727.C6
  ISBN 0518083499 (pbk.)
  OCLC 44727734
  LCCN 00-61321
  Notes:
    Index

• Adams provides descriptive essays on commonly used cowboy jargon, expressions, and terms. Chapter topics include the ranch, duties, costume, riding and riding equipment, roping, cattle, horses, roundups, brands, trails, commissary, outlaws, guns, nicknames, dances, and figures of speech. Adams recognizes that the vocabulary he includes is not comprehensive and that jargon will change over time. Illustrations and examples of brands. — *GK*

BB13   Smead, Robert Norman, 1954–   . - **Vocabulario Vaquero/Cowboy Talk : A Dictionary of Spanish Terms from the American West** / ill. by Ronald Kil ; foreword by Richard W. Slatta. - Norman, OK : Univ. of Oklahoma Pr., 2004. - xxxiii, 197 p. ; ill.

  Class Numbers:
    Library of Congress PE3727.C6 S64 2004
   ISBN 0806135948
   LCCN 2003061298
  Notes:
    Bibliography: p. 195-197

• The language of Western cattle culture contains many words of Spanish origin. One of several recent efforts to affirm the diversity of ethnic influences in the West,

Smead's dictionary is a scholarly record of this lexical borrowing. The foreword is a history of borrowed ranching and cowboying terms and a review of the literature. An introductory essay explains the lexical borrowing process and the methodology used to determine derivations. The dictionary lists as English headwords 416 phrases borrowed from Spanish, along with 347 related terms. Entries give the Spanish model, etymology, English and Spanish dictionaries citing the term, the date of first appearance in print in English, and a definition. A few entries, mostly for cowboy gear, are illustrated with drawings. — *JD*

French

BB14   Gaborieau, Antoine. - **À l'écoute des Franco-Manitobains**. - Saint-Boniface, MB : Éditions des Plaines, 1985. - 146 p.

  Class Numbers:
    Library of Congress PC3645.M35
  ISBN 0920944523
  OCLC 21678652
  LCCN 86-181920
  Notes:
    Includes bibliographical references (p. 146)

• Dictionary of distinctive elements in the vocabulary of French as spoken in Manitoba. For each of the approximately 950 words or phrases, identified through fieldwork interviews, the part of speech and gender are indicated as well as derivation (Old French, dialect, Anglicism). A sentence illustrates usage in the Manitoba context; the final element of each entry is a definition or equivalent word in standard French. Gaborieau's *La langue de chez nous* (Éditions des Plaines, 1999; 286 p.) considerably expands the number of words treated. A spirited defense of the legitimacy of French linguistic variation in Manitoba. — *LMcD*

BB15   Rodriguez, Liliane, 1949-   . - **Mots d'hier, mots d'aujourd'hui**. - Saint-Boniface, MB : Éditions des Plaines, 1984. - 95 p.

  Class Numbers:
    Library of Congress PC3645.M35
  ISBN 0920944442
  OCLC 13240923
  LCCN 85-148076
  Notes:
    Includes bibliographical references (p. 91-94)

• A study of archaic elements (phonetic, lexical, morphological, and syntactical) in the French language as used in Manitoba. More scholarly but less widely useful than *À l'écoute des Franco-Manitobains* (**BB14**). — *LMcD*

Spanish

BB16 Cobos, Rubén. - **A Dictionary of New Mexico and Southern Colorado Spanish**. - Santa Fe, NM : Museum of New Mexico Pr., 1983. - 189 p. ; ill.

Class Numbers:
Library of Congress PC4829.N4
ISBN 0890131414   0890131422 (pbk.)
OCLC 9082915
LCCN 82-22528
Notes:
Includes bibliographical references (p. 181-189)

• Cobos supplies a vocabulary of about 7,200 words in a dialect of Spanish spoken in a region of the Plains and mountains in southern Colorado and northern New Mexico bounded roughly by Durango and Walsenburg, CO and Santa Fe, Raton, and Tierra Amarillo, NM; a map on the page facing the title shows the region. The dictionary is arranged by headwords in Spanish and provides part of speech, rudimentary derivation, lexical meaning, and, often, discussion of circumstances in which words are used and of their cultural background. Most headwords are derived from Spanish, but some are borrowings or derivations from English or Náhuatl, some from older Mexican or Rio Grande dialects. A bibliography cites sources. There is no English-Spanish vocabulary. Carefully prepared, notable for its background notes. — *RB*

BB17 Galván, Roberto A., comp. - **El diccionario del español chicano = The Dictionary of Chicano Spanish** / comp. by Roberto A. Galván, Richard V. Teschner. - Silver Spring, MD : Institute of Modern Languages, 1977. - 144 p.

Class Numbers:
Library of Congress PC4829.T4
ISBN 0884991466
OCLC 3511829
LCCN 77-155911
Notes:
First ed. publ. under title: *El diccionario del español de Tejas* (c1975)
Includes bibliographical references (p. 142-144)

• Has a vocabulary of about 9,000 words in Chicano dialects of Spanish, spoken and written. All headwords are Spanish; there is no equivalent section for English-Spanish. Entries sometimes offer usage labels ("slang," "vulg."), but greatest attention is given to lexical meaning. — *RB*

INDIAN LANGUAGES

BB18 Campbell, Lyle. - **American Indian Languages : The Historical Linguistics of Native America**. - New York

: Oxford Univ. Pr., 1997. - 512 p. ; maps. - (Oxford studies in anthropological linguistics, 4).

Class Numbers:
Library of Congress PM108 .C36 1997
National Library of Canada PM108
ISBN 0195094271   058537161X (electronic bk.)
LCCN 95031905
Notes:
Electronic book: http://www.netLibrary.com/urlapi.asp?
action=summary&v=1&bookid=53410
Includes bibliographical references (p. 429-482); indexes

• Campbell's survey of the history of Native American languages includes North, Central, and South American languages, hence only a small part will relate to Plains study. Plains language families include Algonquian, Siouan, Muskogean, Caddoan, and Kiowa. Besides describing language families and the nations associated with each, the book presents a linguistic tree of groups within each family. Twenty-seven maps help identify the geographic distribution of languages, one of which is a map of the Plains linguistic area. Notes appear just before the lengthy bibliography. The index of language families is detailed and includes many cross-references and see references. Author-subject index. — *MB*

BB19 Evans, G. Edward, 1937-   . - **Bibliography of Language Arts Materials for Native North Americans : Bilingual, English as a Second Language, and Native Language Materials, 1965-1974** / G. Edward Evans, principal investigator ; Karin Abbey, research director ; Dennis Reed, research assistant. - Los Angeles, CA : Univ. of California, American Indian Studies Center, 1977. - 283 p.

Class Numbers:
Library of Congress PM206 ; Z7118
OCLC 4693710
LCCN 92-217165
Notes:
Index

• Produced by the American Indian Studies Center at UCLA and largely based on their library holdings, this directory and bibliography of sources for English as Second Language teaching materials is intended for speakers of American Indian languages. Its more than 800 titles are grouped by Native language; that arrangement is the only way to identify materials relevant for Plains and Prairies studies. Language distribution is very uneven, based as much as anything on individual tribes' success in grant writing. Tribes with large numbers of native language speakers are not necessarily well-represented; only ten titles are cited for the Sioux (all three dialects), eight for the Ojibwa, and 16 for the Cree (a group, ironically, that is publishing an abundance of high-quality language materials). Though useful as a historical record of materials produced during the late 1960s through early 1970s, the heyday of federal funding for bilingual education programs for American Indians, most of these locally-produced works are no longer available, and since few libraries will have acquired these titles at the time of their publication, the usefulness of this bibliography is limited. — *LM*

BB20   The Languages of Native America : Historical and Comparative Assessment / ed. by Lyle Campbell and Marianne Mithun. - Austin, TX : Univ. of Texas Pr., c1979. - 1034 p. ; map.

> Class Numbers:
> Library of Congress PM108 .L35
> ISBN 0292746245
> LCCN 79-65784
> Notes:
> Includes bibliographies ; index

• Campbell and Mithun appraise studies of North American Indian languages, offering comparative and historical descriptions of language families including the Siouan, Caddoan and others spoken by Plains tribes and tribes removed to Indian Territory. Entries introduce each family's range, development, subgroups, and morphological patterns and survey the historical linguistic studies of major researchers. The introductions are accessible to students and general readers while the surveys are intended for experts. Each entry includes a bibliography of the works cited. The final chapter reviews linguistic lacunae and research trends. Indexed by subgroup. — *JD*

BB21   Mithun, Marianne. - The Languages of Native North America. - Cambridge, UK ; New York : Cambridge Univ. Pr., 1999. - xxi, 773 p. ; maps. - (Cambridge language surveys).

> Class Numbers:
> Library of Congress PM108.L35 1999
> ISBN 0521232287
> LCCN 98053576
> Notes:
> Table of contents: http://www.loc.gov/catdir/toc/
> cam024/98053576.html
> Includes bibliographical references (p. 617-750); index

• Linguistics professor Mithun, an authority on Native American languages, presents a thorough scholarly overview of the histories and language structures of North American language families. Attempts to understand and categorize the nearly 300 different languages spoken north of the Rio Grande began with the first Europeans, and the schemes and classifications have been in a state of flux ever since. Although European languages are classified in three families, Native American languages have over 50. Mithun tries to make sense of this in her fine survey. Languages spoken in the Plains and Prairies, fortunately, fall into only a few of these diverse families. Hence, discussions of these language groups–chiefly Algonquian, Siouan, Uto-Aztecan, Caddoan, Kiowa-Tanoan, and Athabaskan–form the relevant sections of this work. An essential resource. — *LM*

BB22   Singerman, Robert. - Indigenous Languages of the Americas : A Bibliography of Dissertations and Theses. - Lanham, MD : Scarecrow Pr., 1996. - xxix, 311 p. - (Native American Bibliographical Series, 19).

> Class Numbers:
> Library of Congress PM108
> ISBN 0810830329
> OCLC 32893105
> LCCN 95-35046
> Notes:
> Includes bibliographical references; indexes

• Much of the current work on Native American languages is published in master's theses and doctoral dissertations. Singerman has done the linguistic and Native communities a service with this bibliography of 1,679 titles accepted, 1892-1992. He took special care to locate the very elusive master's theses from colleges and universities in the U.S., Canada, and the U.K. A preface by Mary Kay Ritchie gives a history of academic research on Native languages over the century covered. Singerman's introduction sets out his arrangement, methodology, and scope. He covers the entire Western Hemisphere, and includes anthropological linguistics as well as pure linguistics. The theses and dissertations are arranged alphabetically by language within language families, then by author. Many titles have brief one- or two-sentence annotations. Relevance for Plains studies requires that users know the language families represented by Plains and Prairies tribes (predominantly Algonquian, Siouan, and Kiowa-Tanoan). Indexes of authors and of languages, dialects, and tribes, the latter enabling users to pinpoint specific languages and peoples. Recommended. — *LM*

Blackfoot

BB23   Frantz, Donald. - Blackfoot Dictionary of Stems, Roots, and Affixes / Donald Frantz and Norma Jean Russell. - 2nd ed. – Toronto, ON : Univ. of Toronto Pr., 1995. - xxiv, 442 p.

> Class Numbers:
> Library of Congress PM2343
> ISBN 0802007678 0802071368 (pbk.)
> OCLC 33839769
> LCCN 95-236599
> Notes:

First ed. published in 1989

Includes bibliographical references (p. xviii-xix)

• Blackfoot is spoken by the Siksika, Blood, and Peigan First Nations of southern Alberta and the Blackfoot of northwestern Montana. The dictionary lists approximately 4,000 "words" (the stems, roots, and affixes of the title) assembled from interviews with native speakers. Entries indicate morphological categories, variants, and related terms; sample English sentences follow. The English-Blackfoot section contains 5,000 words and is an index to the Blackfoot entries. An appendix describes the alphabet and spelling conventions used. Updates *An English-Blackfoot Vocabulary* and *A Blackfoot-English Vocabulary*, both based on material from the southern Peigans, by C.C. Uhlenbeck and R.H. van Gulik (New York: AMS Pr., 1979-1984, which reprinted the 1930-1934 ed. published in Amsterdam by Noord-Hollandsche uitgevers-maatschappij). Useful for linguists as well as fluent speakers. — *LMcD*

Cheyenne

BB24   Petter, Rodolphe Charles, 1865-1947. - **English-Cheyenne Dictionary**. - Kettle Falls, WA : Valdo Petter, 1915. - 1126 p.

> Class Numbers:
> Library of Congress PM795.Z5
> OCLC 15011622
> Notes:
> Printed in the interest of the Mennonite Mission among the Cheyenne Indians of Oklahoma and Montana

• This massive self-published work was printed in only 100 copies. Petter, a Mennonite missionary to the Cheyenne in Oklahoma, found that if he were to succeed as a missionary, he would need to speak Cheyenne. His original intent was to provide "anthropologic data as well as special details in fauna and flora" (p.iv). Since scientific institutions and libraries showed little interest, Petter published the linguistic material of greatest use to his missionary work. He states that a Cheyenne-English dictionary, a Cheyenne grammar, and Cheyenne tales "exist in manuscript form." The English entries contain very thorough Cheyenne equivalents, as well as extensive historical and ethnographic background when available. Petter often refers to other works to support his material, but there is no source bibliography. Of great use for those libraries fortunate to own a copy of this work, since the Cheyenne are historically one of the more prominent Plains peoples. — *LM*

Choctaw

BB25   Byington, Cyrus, 1793-1868. - **A Dictionary of the Choctaw Language** / ed. by John R. Swanton and

Henry S. Halbert. - Idabel, OK : LEA, 1985, 1915. - 611 p. ; front. (port.). - (Smithsonian Institution. Bureau of American Ethnology. Bulletin, 46).

> OCLC 30321962
> Notes:
> Reproduction of 1915 ed.
> With portrait and biographical sketch of the author

• The first written record of the Choctaw language, Byington's dictionary is one of the most significant of the many linguistic works by missionaries ministering to Native Americans in the 19th century. The author spent much of his 50 years with the Choctaw nation, one of the "Five Civilized Tribes" removed to Indian Territory in southeastern Oklahoma, compiling the dictionary for use in translating Bible passages, hymns, and tracts. It has two parts, Choctaw to English and English to Choctaw; though some style and content may be dated, it remains the only complete lexicon of the nuanced language. The terms and definitions also reveal some of the culture of the tribe. — *JD*

Comanche

BB26   Rejón, Manuel Garcia, comp. - **Comanche Vocabulary** / tr. and ed. by Daniel T. Gelo. - Austin, TX : Univ. of Texas Pr., 1995. - xxvii, 76 p. ; ill. - (Texas archaeology and ethnohistory series).

> Class Numbers:
> Library of Congress PM921.Z5
> ISBN 0292727828   0292727836 (pbk.) 0292727844
> OCLC 32130496
> LCCN 95-7813
> Notes:
> Includes bibliographical references (p. [69]-76)
> Text in English, tr. from Spanish; vocabulary lists in English, Comanche, and Spanish

• A new translation of a work originally published in Spanish in Mexico (1865). Like many early works on Native American languages, the original publication has been difficult to find and was archaic in terminology. Anthropologist Gelo has translated the work into English, making this a trilingual word list, and provides an introduction that places the work in historical context. Early vocabularies and word lists like this are invaluable as Native peoples seek to revitalize their languages, many of which are on the verge of extinction. Gelo updates the Spanish colloquialisms and spellings, and appends a Comanche-English vocabulary, as well as a bibliography. A useful title on an important Plains language. — *LM*

BB27   Robinson, Lila Wistrand, 1931- . - **Comanche Dictionary and Grammar** / Lila Wistrand Robinson and James Armagost. - Dallas, TX : Summer Institute of

Linguistics ; [Arlington, TX] : University of Texas at Arlington, 1990. - 338 p. ; ill. - (Summer Institute of Linguistics and the University of Texas at Arlington publications in linguistics, publication 92).

Class Numbers:
Library of Congress PM921.Z5
ISBN 0883127156
OCLC 22722333
LCCN 89-63029

• Covers an Indian language of western Oklahoma. The Comanche-English portion indicates regional variations, grammatical categories, basic etymology, and representative sentences. Appendixes list fauna, flora, body parts, months, and personal names. The English-Comanche section is followed by a grammar explaining the syntax and morphology of the language. Partly based on fieldwork done by Elliott Canonge between 1945 and 1963. — *LMcD*

Cree

BB28   Online Cree Dictionary = Nehiyaw Masinahikan [Internet Site]. - [Hobbema, AB] : Miyo Wahkohtowin Community Education Authority, 2007-   . - http://www.creedictionary.com/

Access Date : May 2007
Fees: None

• This multimedia dictionary provides 36,000 words in Plains Cree (Maskwacis Plains and Saskatchewan Plains) and Woods Cree. "Basic Search" includes Roman orthography, Cree syllabics, English, definition, and keyword options. "Advanced" offers searching by dialect, usage category (current, old, ritual), meaning category (family, animals, plants, etc.), source, geographic region, and resource type (sound, video). The site includes a version for children, syllabics tables, converter, and links to related resources; additional curriculum material is to be developed. A work in progress, it initially consists of Arok Wolvengrey's *Cree: Words* (**BB30**) and *Alberta Elders' Cree Dictionary*, by Nancy LeClaire and George Cardinal, edited by Earle H. Waugh (Edmonton, AB: Univ. of Alberta Pr., 1998). The flexibility and search capabilities make this a welcome addition to the increasing number of Cree dictionaries. — *LMcD*

BB29   Wolfart, H. Christoph. - The Student's Dictionary of Literary Plains Cree : Based on Contemporary Texts / [by] H.C. Wolfart & Freda Ahenakew. - Winnipeg, Man. : Algonquian and Iroquoian Linguistics, 1998. - 425 p. - (Memoir [Algonquian and Iroquoian Linguistics], 15).

Class Numbers:
Library of Congress PM988

ISBN 0921064152
OCLC 40538984
LCCN 00-364083

• A dictionary of the Cree language as used in the central prairies of Saskatchewan and Alberta, intended as a reference work for serious students rather than an introductory lexicon. Compiled by Plains Cree linguist Ahenakew and linguistics professor Wolfart, this dictionary sets down the vocabulary used by older speakers of Plains Cree in relating oral literary works of traditional narrative, mythological texts, and pedagogical and religious discourses (p.vi). The work reflects contemporary formal usage, and offers no comparisons with other dialects of Cree. For scholars of Cree. — *LM*

BB30   Wolvengrey, Arok, 1965-   . - Nehiawewin : itwewina = Cree : Words / comp. by Arok Wolvengrey ; ed. by members of the Cree Editing Council, Freda Ahenakew [et al.] ; with Mary Bighead [et al.]. - Regina, SK : Canadian Plains Research Center, Univ. of Regina, 2001. - 2 v. (lxxxxiv, 622 p.). - (Canadian plains reference works, 3).

Class Numbers:
Library of Congress PM988
ISBN 0889771278
OCLC 47691175
LCCN 2004-444574
Notes:
Contents: v. 1 Cree-English; v. 2. English-Cree

• One of several works on Native and indigenous languages to appear in recent years that result from intensive collaboration between Native speakers and linguists and non-Native linguistics scholars. This set (Cree-English and English-Cree) features work with the Cree Language Retention Committee's Cree Editing Council, a group of "Cree Elders and professionals in the field of education" (p.ix) that includes the respected Freda Ahenakew. The Cree-English volume features a thorough, accessible, scholarly, but nontechnical 52-page introduction to the Cree language, "Cree: Pronunciation and Orthography" that considers at length dialects, writing systems, parts of speech, and word formation. This volume has a vocabulary of over 15,000 Cree and over 35,000 English entries, as a single Cree word may appear under several different English entries. Some Woods Cree and western Swampy Cree variations are indicated. Cree entries are arranged according to Roman orthography with accompanying Cree syllabic symbols. Clean, attractive format; should be a required resource in the wide geographical areas where Cree is spoken–primarily Manitoba, Saskatchewan, Alberta, and Rocky Boy, Montana. — *LM, LMcD*

Creek

BB31   Martin, Jack B., 1961-   . - A Dictionary of Creek/Muskogee : With Notes on the Florida and

Oklahoma Seminole Dialects of Creek / [by] Jack B. Martin, Margaret McKane Mauldin. - Lincoln, NE : Univ. of Nebraska Pr. in cooperation with the American Indian Studies Research Institute, Indiana Univ., Bloomington, 2000. - xxxviii, 353 p. ; [4] p. of plates, ill., map. - (Studies in the anthropology of North American Indians).

Class Numbers:
Library of Congress PM991.Z5
ISBN 0803232071 0803283024 (pbk.)
9780803283022 (pbk.) 9780803232075
OCLC 43561668
LCCN 00-27202
Notes:
Includes bibliographical references

• The Creek people of the southeast U.S., following the Red Stick War in the early 1800s, split into the Creek (Muskogee) and Seminole groups. Most Creeks and many Seminole were forcibly moved to Oklahoma under the Indian Removal Act of 1830, while most Seminoles remained in Florida. This migration has resulted today in three Creek dialects: in Oklahoma, Muskogee and Oklahoma Seminole; in Florida, Seminole Creek. As the subtitle indicates, this comprehensive, highly useable dictionary and overview focuses on the Oklahoma Creek language, so is an excellent resource for Plains collections. After Cherokee, Oklahoma Creek has more speakers than any other Native language in the state. The extensive introduction explains the historical interactions between white settlers and Creeks and the movement of the people from the southeast to Oklahoma, and provides an overview of the language and its three dialects, with a pronunciation guide and an excellent discussion of Creek spelling conventions. The bulk of the work is divided into a 7,000-word Creek-English and a 4,000-word English-Creek dictionary. The Creek-English section also has word lists of topical information such as months and days, common expressions, numbers, and clans and dances, and a chronology of both Creek and Oklahoma Seminole chiefs. A 16-page, 400-item section of Creek language place-names in Oklahoma, Alabama, Georgia, and Florida round out this key resource of an important language. — *LM*

Hidatsa

BB32 Matthews, Washington, 1843-1905. - **Grammar and Dictionary of the Language of the Hidatsa.** - New York : AMS Pr., 1983. - 168 p.

Class Numbers:
Library of Congress PM1331
ISBN 0404157874
OCLC 10022069
LCCN 76-44080
Notes:
Originally published: New York: Cramoisy Pr., 1873-1874. (Shea's American linguistics. Series II , no. 1-2)

• Compiled by an army surgeon and anthropologist stationed in North Dakota in the 1860s and 1870s, this dictionary is the earliest published work on Hidatsa, used on the Fort Berthold Reservation. A brief description of Hidatsa-Mandan culture precedes a section on grammar. Has sections both for Hidatsa-English and English-Hidatsa. Although dated linguistically, it retains value as a historical record of a language in decline. — *LMcD*

Lakota/Dakota

BB33 Boas, Franz. - **Dakota Grammar** / by Franz Boas and Ella Deloria. - New York : AMS Pr., 1976, 1941. - 183 p. 29 cm. - (National Academy of Sciences [U.S.]. Memoirs, v. 23, 2nd memoir).

Class Numbers:
Library of Congress PM1022 .B6 1976
ISBN 0404118291
OCLC 1973768
LCCN 74-7942
Notes:
"Presented to the Academy at the annual meeting, 1939."
Reprint. Originally publ.: Washington, DC: U.S. Govt. Print. Off., 1941 as 2nd memoir, v. 23 in *Memoirs of the National Academy of Sciences*

• Contains 171 numbered sections that discuss points of grammar of the Dakota language under the broad headings of phonetics (items 2-23) and morphology and syntax (items 24-171). In the first category, sections are divided into vowels, consonants, and consonant clusters. The larger second section is divided into parts of speech and word structures such as compounding, verb endings, and suffixes. Sample Teton, Santee, and Assiniboine texts are included for illustrative purposes. There is no index, but the table of contents is extremely detailed. Boas is an authority on Native American languages. A seminal resource. — *MB*

BB34 Buechel, Eugene. - **Lakota Dictionary : Lakota-English/English-Lakota** / comp. and ed. by Eugene Buechel and Paul Manhart. - Lincoln, NE : Univ. of Nebraska Pr., c2002. - xxi, [22], 530 p.

Class Numbers:
Library of Congress PM1024.Z9 L333
ISBN 0803213050
LCCN 2002-18109
Notes:
Includes bibliographical references (p. [529]-530); index
Rev. ed. of: *A Dictionary of the Teton Dakota Sioux Language* (1970)

• Serves primarily as a Lakota-English dictionary; the section for English to Lakota is much briefer. The introduction includes a guide to pronunciation, an explanation of how to use the dictionary, and a brief guide to Lakota grammar with examples of how sentences are structured. Charts explain such linguistic concerns as verb classes, common prepositions, and word origins. Lakota entries, arranged alphabetically by romanized spelling, include pronunciation, part of speech, and definition. — *MB*

BB35   Durand, Paul C. - **Where the Waters Gather and the Rivers Meet : (Ó-ki-zu wa-kpá) (To Meet, To Unite) : An Atlas of the Eastern Sioux** / ed. by Robin Siev Durand ; Valerie Maisonneuve, programmes culturels ; ill. by Rene E. Durand . - [Prior Lake, MN : P.C. Durand, 1994]. - 138 p. ; ill. 24 cm.

> Class Numbers:
>   Library of Congress E99.D1
>   ISBN 0964146908   9780964146907
>   OCLC 32050105
>   LCCN 94-71463
>   Notes:
>   Index

• Durand's "atlas" is in fact a dictionary of place-names in Dakota and Ojibwa. It is arranged in three sections: an introduction with a pronunciation guide; Dakota and Ojibwa (Chippewa) place-names, alphabetically arranged; and two cross-indexes for Dakota and Ojibwa place-names by subject (beliefs/traditions, camp sites/villages, effigies, lakes, islands, rapids/waterfalls, rivers/creeks, topography, trails). The work includes 12 illustrations and one folded map. — *GK*

BB36   Karol, Joseph S., ed. - **Everyday Lakota : An English-Sioux Dictionary for Beginners** / assistant ed., Stephen L. Rozman. - Lincoln, NE : Univ. of Nebraska, Nebraska Curriculum Development Center, 1971. - 121 p.

> Class Numbers:
>   Library of Congress PM1023
>   OCLC 1935170

• "This little book ..." Karol explains, "is intended to enable speakers of English to begin to learn Lakota..." (p. vi). Shortly after it was published, it began appearing in craft supplies catalogs around Indian Country, and has proved useful for its intended purpose. Containing only about 3,800 words and some 300 phrases, this practical booklet is an introduction to more extensive study of this still widely-spoken and important Plains language. The word list is alphabetically arranged by English equivalent; one can look up "white man," for example, and easily locate the familiar *wasicun*, with diacritics to indicate accurate pronunciation. A smattering of common phrases (in no discernible order) concludes the word list, followed by about a dozen brief examples of idiomatic conversation and handy lists of times of the day, days of the week, months of the year, cardinal

numbers, lists of native birds and animals, etc. Brief, simple rules of syntax and pronunciation conclude this handy reference. There is no Lakota-English section. — *LM*

BB37   Riggs, Stephen Return, 1812-1883. - **Dakota Grammar, Texts, and Ethnography** / ed. by James Owen Dorsey. - New York : AMS Pr., 1976, 1893. - xxxii, 239 p. - (Contributions to North American ethnology, v. 9).

> Class Numbers:
>   Library of Congress PM1021
>   ISBN 0404118917
>   LCCN 74-7998
>   Notes:
>   At head of title: Department of the Interior, U.S.
>   Geographical and Geological Survey of the Rocky
>   Mountain Region
>   Includes bibliographical references; index
>   Originally publ. as v. 9 of *Contributions to North American
>   Ethnology* (1893)

• Riggs's introduction to Dakota has three sections. The first treats grammar and is divided into subsections on phonology, morphology, and syntax. The latter two are further divided into parts of speech for detailed analysis. The second section consists of 11 selected texts with commentary and translations into English. The third section, "Ethnography," has seven chapters that address such topics as Dakota law, dance, religion, and migration. A brief subject index ends the volume. Serves as an introduction to the Dakota language, compiled with the great advantage of direct contact with native speakers, but is now more than a century old. — *MB*

BB38   Riggs, Stephen Return, 1812-1883. - **A Dakota-English Dictionary** / ed. by James Owen Dorsey ; with a new foreword by Carolynn I. Schommer. - St. Paul, MN : Minnesota Historical Society Pr., 1992, 1890. - 665 p. - (Borealis books).

> Class Numbers:
>   Library of Congress PM1023
>   ISBN 0873512820   9780873512824
>   OCLC 26397344
>   LCCN 92-28736
>   Notes:
>   Reprint. Originally publ.: Washington, DC: U.S. Govt.
>   Print. Off., 1890

• Dictionary of an estimated 20,000 words of the Dakota language, today used principally in a number of dialects in Minnesota and South Dakota. Compiled through 19th-century missionary efforts and unrevised apart from the introduction by an Upper Sioux scholar. Of approximately the same vintage as Williamson's *An English-Dakota Dictionary* (**BB40**). —*LMcD*

BB39   Riggs, Stephen Return, 1812-1883, ed. - **Grammar and Dictionary of the Dakota Language** / collected by members of the Dakota Mission ; ed. by Rev. S.R. Riggs ... under the patronage of the Historical Society of Minnesota. - [Washington, D.C.] : Smithsonian Institution, 1852. - 64, 338 p. - (Smithsonian contributions to knowledge, v. 4).

> Class Numbers:
> Library of Congress Q11
> LCCN s 13-20
> Notes:
> "Dakota bibliography": verso of p. xix

• Using an alphabet developed by missionaries, this Dakota dictionary was compiled by missionaries and Indian informants in order to "preach the Gospel to the Dakotas in their own language." The first such dictionary, it established the written form of the Dakota language, so closely related to Lakota that they are now generally considered dialects of the same language. Following an introduction to Dakota history and language and a grammar, Dakota-English and English-Dakota sections show parts of speech, pronunciation, variant forms, and lexical meanings. Includes a Dakota bibliography of children's books, religious tracts, hymns, catechisms, and parts of the Bible. Though prepared for practical use by missionaries, an important scholarly work. — *JD*

BB40   Williamson, John P. - **An English-Dakota Dictionary = Wasícun k.a Dakota Ieska Wowapi**. - Minneapolis, MN : Ross & Haines, Inc., c1902, 1970. - xviii, 264 p.

> OCLC 36937167
> Notes:
> Reprint of 1902 ed.

• Originally compiled by Presbyterian missionary Williamson, this English-Dakota dictionary is arranged alphabetically by English words (there is no Dakota-English section). A 13-page introduction contains "The Dakota Alphabet" and an overview of parts of speech. Entries often contain Lakota and Nakota variants. Useful, especially when paired with Lakota/Dakota-English dictionaries such as Buechel (**BB34**). — *LM*

Omaha

BB41   Stabler, Elizabeth, 1905-1985. - **Umonhon iye of Elizabeth Stabler : A Vocabulary of the Omaha Language** / comp. by Mark J. Swetland. - Winnebago, NE : Nebraska Indian Pr., 1977. - 203 p. ; ill., ports.

> Class Numbers:
> Library of Congress PM2071.Z5
> OCLC 5362534

• Published in an edition of 488 copies, the prefatory material in this work provides terms associated with good and bad traits, translated from Omaha to English. Following that, a pronunciation guide offers comment about specific consonant and vowel sounds. The dictionary itself is arranged alphabetically in columns, the English word on the left and Omaha equivalents on the right. Parts of speech are shown in parentheses. Omaha terms are sometimes explained–e.g., railroad is literally "self runner" and March is "little frog moon." There are no Omaha-English entries. Illustrated with a number of sketches and black-and-white photos. Finally, a supplementary section explains "terms of relationships," e.g., nephew, younger sister. — *MB*

Osage

BB42   La Flesche, Francis, d. 1932. - **A Dictionary of the Osage Language**. - Phoenix, AZ : Indian Tribal Series, 1975, 1932. - 406 p. - (Smithsonian Institution. Bureau of American Ethnology. Bulletin, 109).

> Class Numbers:
> Library of Congress PM2081.Z5
> OCLC 2679034
> Notes:
> Electronic book: http://gallica.bnf.fr/ark:/12148/
> bpt6k27551b
> Reprint. Originally publ.: Washington, DC: Smithsonian Institution, Bureau of American Ethnology. Bulletin 109 (1932)

• Osage-English and English-Osage dictionary for an almost extinct Siouan language of north central Oklahoma. Phonetic key for the orthography, influenced by Omaha-Ponca. The appendix gives days and months, descriptions of rituals known as *wi-gi-es*, translations of legends, paraphrases of rituals, sayings and expressions, and a few Osage stories in English. — *LMcD*

Saulteaux

BB43   **The Saulteaux Language Dictionary** / [comp. by Mary Ellen Scott et al.]. - [Edmonton, AB] : Duval House Pub. ; [Saskatchewan] : Kinistin First Nation, 1995. – 118 p.

> Class Numbers:
> Library of Congress PM853
> ISBN 1895850517
> OCLC 35574474
> LCCN 95-230561

• A dictionary of approximately 1,500 words of Saulteaux, also known as Plains Ojibwa, prepared for the Kinistin First Nation of Saskatchewan. Arranged by themes such as colors, food, kinship, and occupations, rather than direct alphabetical order. Includes English-Saulteaux section. — *LMcD*

Place-Names

BB44   Bright, William. - **Native American Placenames of the United States**. - Norman, OK : Univ. of Oklahoma Pr., 2004. - 600 p.

> Class Numbers:
> Library of Congress E98.N2
> ISBN 080613576X   0806135980 (pbk.)
> LCCN 2003-61395
> Notes:
> Includes bibliographical references (p. 587-600)
> Review by A.L. Posas: *Choice* 42.8 (Apr. 2005): review
> 42-4385

• Attempting to account for place-names in the U.S. that can be traced to Indian origins or associations, Bright worked from the Geographical Names Information System maintained by the U.S. Board on Geographic Names, extracting from it all names that could be identified as having an Indian association. His introduction accounts for the various sources of place-names and the etymological uncertainties that surround them. Entries, in alphabetical order, consist of a headword (in boldface), its locations, pronunciation, and as much etymology as can be reliably determined. Includes numerous Prairies-Plains places (Cahola, Monango, Nepesta, Potawatomi), but, alas, there is no index of states to identify them, so Bright's book is useful principally to identify individual names. Bibliography of sources. — *RB*

BC : Literature

Scope. Lists general literary titles all or portions of which bear on the Prairies and Plains region, a few works pertaining to all or part of the region or concerned with individual genres, and works about individual writers. Includes some materials about writers who were born and grew up in the Prairies-Plains region but made their reputations elsewhere.

UNITED STATES
Guides

BC1 Bryer, Jackson R., ed. - **Sixteen Modern American Authors: A Survey of Research and Criticism**. - Durham, NC: Duke Univ. Pr., 1969. - 673 p.

> Class Numbers:
> Library of Congress PS221
> LCCN 72-97454

• Of the writers surveyed in this volume, only Cather is closely associated with Prairies-Plains, but the essay about her, written by Bernice Slote, one of the foremost Cather authorities, by itself makes the book worthwhile for Prairies-Plains researchers. The format is narrative, beginning with a bibliographic essay; then come commentary on editions of Cather's books, information on manuscripts and letters, biography, and criticism (both general and specific). This edition includes a supplementary section that adds new information in the same categories. The index is exhaustive. — *MB*

BC2 Nemanic, Gerald, ed. - **A Bibliographical Guide to Midwestern Literature**. - Iowa City, IA: Univ. of Iowa Pr., c1981. - xxiv, 380 p.

> Class Numbers:
> Library of Congress Z1251.W5 PS273
> ISBN 087745079X
> LCCN 81-4087

• The bibliographies are arranged in two broad sections, by subject and author. Subject bibliographies are subdivided by literature and language, history and society, folklore, personal narratives, architecture and graphics, Chicago, black literature, Indians, and literary periodicals, each subdivided as appropriate. The literature, history, and folklore sections are arranged by state, but some of the states the volume covers (e.g., Indiana) are off the Prairies-Plains map. The subject bibliographies are chiefly book-length publications.

The author section, which is longer, compiled by specialists, and arranged alphabetically, covers 120 Midwestern authors. Each entry includes a brief essay about the writer, a list of major works, and a checklist of secondary sources. Lesser-known writers are accorded nearly as much attention as major writers. Appendix A lists 101 additional writers and appendix B, 101 additional Midwestern narratives. Mari Sandoz and Toni Morrison are listed only in Appendix A, whereas many writers less often read are in the author bibliography section, perhaps reflecting the critical perspective at the time of publication. — *MB*

Bibliographies

BC3 Etulain, Richard W., ed. - **A Bibliographical Guide to the Study of Western American Literature** / ed. by Richard W. Etulain and N. Jill Howard. - Albuquerque, NM: Univ. of New Mexico Pr. in cooperation with the Univ. of New Mexico, Center for the American West, 1995. - 471 p.

> Class Numbers:
> Library of Congress PS271Z1251.W5
> ISBN 0826316441
> LCCN 95-4418
> Notes:
> 1st ed.: 1982
> Index

• Etulain and Howard arrange nearly 6,500 entries in sections for bibliographies and reference sources, anthologies, general works, and special topics (local color and regionalism, popular fiction including dime novels, film, Indian literature, Mexican American literature, the environment and Western literature, women and families, the Beats, and Canadian Western literature). The largest section lists studies of more than 300 writers associated with the West, chiefly the montane West and the Pacific Coast. Among Plains writers covered are Guthrie, Momaday, Morris, Sandoz, Steinbeck, Kuzma, Wilder, Woiwode, and, of course, Cather. Most of the items listed in the first edition (1982) are repeated; new entries cover the period 1981-1994. Bibliographic descriptions are carefully complete. Index of names. Despite its geographic emphasis, broad enough in scope to be useful for students of the Plains. — *MB*

BC4 Etulain, Richard W. - **Western American Literature: A Bibliography of Interpretive Books and Articles**. - Vermillion, SD: Dakota Pr., 1972. - 137 p.

> Class Numbers:
> Library of Congress Z1225
> ISBN 0882490109
> OCLC 369990
> LCCN 72-78188

• Etulain (then at Idaho State Univ.) presents a checklist later expanded into his and Jill Howard's *A Bibliographical Guide to the Study of Western American Literature* (1995; BC3). It cites about 2,500 secondary studies with no annotations, in sections for bibliographies, anthologies, general works, three topics ("The Beats," "Local Color and Regionalism," and "The Western"), and 100 pages on individual writers. The section on regionalism has a smattering of studies on Plains literature; among the authors are Aldrich, Dobie, Zane Grey, McMurtry, Parkman, Rhodes, Rølvaag, William Stafford, and Cather. No index, a handicap in locating topical material. — *RB*

BC5   Fifty Western Writers: A Bio-Bibliographical Sourcebook / ed. by Fred Erisman and Richard W. Etulain. - Westport, CT: Greenwood Pr., 1982. - 562 p.

Class Numbers:
    Library of Congress PS271
    ISBN 0313221677
    LCCN 81-13462
Notes:
    Index

• The editors' West consists of the continental stretch between the Mississippi River and the Pacific Ocean. Since this reach includes the Prairies-Plains region, some of the 50 writers are Plains authors (e.g., Andy Adams, Capps, Cather, DeVoto, Manfred, Momaday, Wright Morris, Neihardt, Rølvaag, Sandoz, Stafford, Stegner). The biographical entries are written by specialists (e.g., the entry for Mari Sandoz is written by her principal biographer, Helen Stauffer). Some writers (Owen Wister) are identified with the mountain West. Both 19th- and 20th-century authors are included, ranging from Bret Harte (born 1836) to Larry McMurtry (born 1936), but writers from the Canadian West are excluded. Entries follow a standard format: biography, major themes, survey of criticism, and bibliography (works by and works about). The volume concludes with a general index of names, titles, and topics in which "Great Plains" has only two references, and with a roster of contributors. — *MB*

BC6   Modern Language Association International Bibliography [Internet Site] / Modern Language Association. - New York: Modern Language Association, 1963– . - http://www.proquest.com/

Access Date: Mar. 2006
Fees: Subscription

• With its printed predecessors, MLA constitutes the premier source for tracking world publications in language and literature. There is little need to rehearse the characteristics of a source so well-known other than to say it covers literature, folklore, language and linguistics, literary theory, dra-matic arts, printing and publishing, and teaching; that it covers monographs and collections, 4,400 journals, reference works, working and conference papers, and dissertations listed in *Dissertation Abstracts International*; that it makes available about 1.8 million records, adding 60,000 per year in monthly updates; that it incorporates a thesaurus used in preparing the index; and that it is available both by direct subscription and through Chadwyck-Healey's *Literature Online* where it is cross-searchable with *ABELL*. Period of coverage is made needlessly cloudy in the introductory matter, but seems to be 1963 to the present. "Standard Search" allows searching in nine fields and limiting by form of publication; "Advanced Search" will search 13 fields, adds a greatly expanded subject search capability, and adds peer-reviewed journals to publication limits. Topics of interest to Plains studies are liberally represented: Ted Kooser by 14 records, William Inge 59, Plains 912, Dodge City 3, Sandoz 62, Butala 13, Red Cloud 12, *One of Ours* 38. Essential for language and literature study; important for Plains students. — *RB*

BC7   Nilon, Charles H. - Bibliography of Bibliographies in American Literature. - New York: R.R. Bowker Co., 1970. - 483 p.

Class Numbers:
    Library of Congress Z1225
    ISBN 0835202593
    OCLC 127604
    LCCN 73-103542

• Nilon arranges his work in four sections: general and basic items; specific authors, by century; genre; and category. The latter is the section helpful for Plains studies, where relevant sections include "Folklore and Myth," "Indian Language and Literature," "Regions and Regionalism," "States," and "Travel." For example, "States," under North Dakota, lists two bibliographies about North Dakota writers which were published in periodicals. The authors section provides citations to a number with Plains connections, including Willa Cather and William Inge. Entries are unannotated. Detailed index. — *MB*

BC8   Twentieth Century Western Writers / ed., Geoffrey Sadler; preface, Christine Bold. – 2nd ed. - Chicago, IL: St. James Pr., 1991. - xxv, 848 p. - (Twentieth Century Writers Series).

Class Numbers:
    Library of Congress PS271
    ISBN 0912289988 978091289984
    OCLC 27430045
    LCCN 91-61741
Notes:
    Includes bibliographical references (p. xxi-xxiv)

• This edition lists about 550 writers who had some association with the West. For each writer (they are alphabetically arranged), the editor supplies the basic facts of the writer's life in a who's-who paragraph. In most cases a bibliography of publications and sometimes a list of critical writings are supplied, occasionally the writer gives a comment about his or her approach to writing, and a contributor provides a sometimes lengthy critical assessment. An index supplies titles of novels and story collections, and the book closes with a roster of contributors. Not a few of the writers covered have a Plains association (Manfred, Rølvaag, Sandoz), and the scholar writing the critical assessment is often intelligently chosen (Susan Rosowski on Cather), but Plains writers must be identified elsewhere; nothing in this compilation will allow them to be isolated. — *RB*

BC9   VanDerhoof, Jack Warner, 1921–   . - **A Bibliography of Novels Related to American Frontier and Colonial History**. - Troy, NY: Whitston Publ. Co., 1971. - 501 p.

> Class Numbers:
> Library of Congress Z1231.F4
> ISBN 087875007X
> OCLC 141962
> LCCN 70-150333

• A typescript publication, suggesting lack of editorial review. The 6,439 numbered entries are arranged alphabetically by author or by title if the author cannot be identified. The book's lack of index or subject access limits its usefulness, but most entries include a few words to describe content–e.g., "Dakota homesteading," "Kansas–1850s,"

"Western–Romance." See also *Encyclopedia of Frontier Literature* (**BC12**). — *MB*

Encyclopedias

BC10   Dictionary of Literary Biography. - Detroit, MI: Gale, 1978–   . - 322 v. [In progress].

• A large ongoing project that intends to cover literary figures in many countries and regions, paying closest attention to writers of the United States, Canada, and Western Europe writing in English. Writers of particular interest to students of the Prairies and Plains are scattered through a number of volumes (listed below), but no volume in the series is devoted to Prairies-Plains writers. No end is in sight for the series, which now occupies more than 300 volumes. — *RB*

BC10a   American Novelists, 1910-1945 / ed. by James J. Martine; foreword by Orville Prescott. - 1981 - 3 v.; ill. - (*Dictionary of literary biography*, v. 9).

> Class Numbers:
> Library of Congress PS129
> ISBN 08810309318
> OCLC 7735451
> LCCN 81-6834
> Notes:
> Includes bibliographical references (v. 3, p. 317-326); index

• Martine includes a few Plains writers in this three-volume set–e.g., Cather, Walter Van Tilburg Clark, Neihardt,

---

Site List 3
Humanities Councils

Internet sites for humanities councils offer calendars of events, speaker directories, research links, and links to local organizations related to history, literature, language, philosophy, law, archaeology, religion, ethics, art history and theory, and social sciences. The National Endowment for the Humanities Internet site (http://www.neh.gov) has links and directory information for all affiliates.

Colorado Endowment for the Humanities
    http://www.ceh.org

Kansas Humanities Council
    http://www.kansashumanities.org

Montana Committee for the Humanities
    http://www2.umt.edu/lastbest

Nebraska Humanities Council
    http://www.nebraskahumanities.org

New Mexico Humanities Council
    http://www.nmeh.org

North Dakota Humanities Council
    http://www.nd-humanities.org

Oklahoma Humanities Council
    http://www.okhumanitiescouncil.org

South Dakota Humanities Council
    http://sdhc.sdstate.org

Texas Council for the Humanities
    http://www.humanitiestexas.org

Wyoming Humanities Council
    http://uwadmnweb.uwyo.edu/HUMANITIES

Sandoz, Rølvaag, William Allen White–and includes some others who can claim only one Plains-related title–e.g., Wister, Conrad Richter, Emerson Hough, Howard Fast. Like many another catalog of Western writers, this one requires that the reader have specific writers in mind before visiting it. — *RB*

BC10b   American Novelists Since World War II: Sixth Series / ed. by James R. Giles and Wanda H. Giles. - 2000 - xxi, 431 p.; ill. - (Dictionary of literary biography, v. 227).

> Class Numbers:
>   Library of Congress PS379
>   ISBN 0787631361
>   LCCN 00-34139
>   Notes:
>   Includes bibliographical references (p. 353-361); index

• Entries for a few writers associated with the Prairies-Plains region. Southerner Truman Capote's *In Cold Blood* forever ties him to Kansas, North Dakotan William H. Gass is known for his contributions to postmodern literature, and Jane Smiley's novels portray farm and university life in the Midwest. — *MB*

BC10c   American Poets, 1880-1945: Third Series / ed. by Peter Quartermain. - 1987 - 2 v.; ports. - (Dictionary of literary biography, v. 54, pts. 1-2).

> Class Numbers:
>   Library of Congress PS324
>   ISBN 081031732X
>   LCCN 86-19562
>   Notes:
>   Includes bibliographical references (v. 2, p. 677-688);
>   index

• Poets of interest to Prairies-Plains studies include Willa Cather, better known for her novels, whose book of poetry, *April Twilights*, was published in 1903, ten years before *O Pioneers!* Another Nebraskan, John G. Neihardt, wrote poetry somewhat tortuous to read. Each entry contains a selective bibliography, photos, and references for further reading. — *MB*

BC10d   American Poets Since World War II: Second Series / ed. by R.S. Gwynn. - 1991 - 403 p.; ill. - (Dictionary of literary biography, v. 105).

> Class Numbers:
>   Library of Congress PS323.5
>   ISBN 0810345854
>   LCCN 91-10848
>   Notes:
>   Includes bibliographical references (p. 323-331); index

• Contains entries for a number of authors associated with the Prairies-Plains region. At the region's edge are Amy Clampitt (born in Iowa) and Philip Dacey (Missouri). Dave Etter's works are associated with various locations in the region (*Cornfields* and *Riding the Rock Island through Kansas*). The poetry of Ted Kooser (Poet Laureate of the United States for 2004-05) has always been closely identified with his native Nebraska. Walter McDonald, a Texas poet, has also written novels. — *MB*

BC10e   American Travel Writers, 1776-1864 / ed. by James Schramer and Donald Ross. - 1997 - xxvi, 418 p.; ill., ports. - (Dictionary of literary biography, v. 189).

> Class Numbers:
>   Library of Congress PS366.T73
>   ISBN 0787610720 0787610739
>   LCCN 97-26928
>   Notes:
>   Includes bibliographical references (p. 342-351); index

• Contains entries for a number of authors associated with the Prairies-Plains region. A few writers of this period wrote about travels in the region, then being explored and settled by Europeans. Perhaps deservedly best known is George Catlin, who described the terrain and the natives in both words and sketches. Horace Greeley ("Go west, young man ...") described travel across the plains in *An Overland Journey*. — *MB*

BC10f   Canadian Writers, 1890-1920 / ed. by William H. New. - 1990 - 472 p.; ill. - (Dictionary of literary biography, v. 92).

> Class Numbers:
>   Library of Congress PR9180.2
>   National Library of Canada PS8081
>   ISBN 0810345722
>   LCCN 89-48355
>   Notes:
>   Includes bibliographical references; index

• Entries for a number of authors associated with the Prairies-Plains region. Ralph Connor, born in Ontario, traveled widely in the Canadian West and the Prairie provinces, writing about them in such books as *The Foreigner: A Tale of Saskatchewan*. Grey Owl, a pseudonym for A. S. Belaney, was born in England but wrote several books about Canada's heartland. Frederick Philip Grove, one of the first to write about the Canadian prairies, wrote, e.g., *Over Prairie Trails* and *Settlers of the Marsh*. Nellie McClung, best known for her contributions to women's suffrage, lived in Manitoba and Alberta. Martha Ostenso's best known work, *Wild Geese*, tells of her years in Manitoba. Manitoba was also the setting for much of Ernest Thompson Seton's work; he wrote extensively about both Indians and wild animals of the region (buffalo, bear, and fox). Although he lived in Ontario, Arthur Stringer is best known for his trilogy of prairie novels, including *The Prairie Wife*. — *MB*

BC10g   Canadian Writers Since 1960: First Series / ed. by William H. New. - 1986 - 445 p.; ill. - (Dictionary of literary biography, v. 53).

> Class Numbers:

Library of Congress PR9186.2
ISBN 0810317311
LCCN 86-14892
Notes:
    Bibliography: p. 383-389; index

• Covers only a few authors associated with the Canadian prairies, but two are major figures in Canadian literature. Robert Kroetsch, a renowned novelist, poet, essayist, and literary critic, was born in Alberta but spent most of his life in Manitoba. His subject matter includes all Western Canada, Manitoba to the Yukon. Margaret Laurence's novels and stories focus almost exclusively on growing up in Manitoba. Saskatchewan author Eli Mandel is perhaps less well-known. Each entry contains a selective bibliography, photos, and references for further reading. — *MB*

BC10h   Nineteenth-Century American Western Writers / ed. by Robert L. Gale. - 1997 - 469 p.; ill. - (Dictionary of literary biography, v. 186).

    Class Numbers:
        Library of Congress PS271
    ISBN 0787616826
    LCCN 97-40333
    Notes:
        Includes bibliographical references; index

• A number of these Western writers are associated with the Prairies-Plains region. Ned Buntline and George Catlin have close association with the Plains region, while the lesser-known Thomas J. Dimmesdale is tied specifically to Montana history. Explorer John Charles Frémont traveled widely throughout the region and recorded his impressions in a number of books. Hamlin Garland wrote about the region in books like *Prairie Songs and Prairie Folks*. Josiah Gregg published *Commerce of the Prairies* in 1844. Lieutenant Charles King wrote about campaigns with General George Crook through Sioux territory and battles that ensued. Meriwether Lewis and William Clark, who require no introduction, are covered in a single entry. Francis Parkman (*The Oregon Trail*) and John Wesley Powell (*Report on the Lands of the Arid Region of the United States*) touched on the Plains region, as did Frederic Remington, best known as a painter of Western scenes. Owen Wister deserves inclusion for his novel *The Virginian* and historian Frederick Jackson Turner for his seminal theory on the significance of the frontier in American history (1893). — *MB*

BC10i   Twentieth-Century American Western Writers: First Series / ed. by Richard H. Cracroft. - 1999 - 379 p.; ill. - (Dictionary of literary biography, v. 206).

    Class Numbers:
        Library of Congress PS271
    ISBN 0787631000
    LCCN 99-13127
    Notes:
        Includes bibliographical references (p. 311-313); index

• Among authors associated with the Prairies-Plains region are Ivan Doig (Montana) and Native American Louise Erdrich (North Dakota). Ernest Haycox wrote pulp fiction about cowboys and gunfights. Both poet Richard Hugo and novelist Dorothy M. Johnson, like Doig, are known for their Montana connections, as is Norman Maclean (*A River Runs Through It*). Best-selling author Barbara Kingsolver used the Plains as setting for some of her novels (*Pigs in Heaven*). Louis L'Amour, prolific writer of Westerns, was born in North Dakota but also lived in Oklahoma. Wright Morris (Nebraska) has a reputation both as a photographer of the Plains and as a writer (*Plains Song*). Rounding out the book are Kansas-born poet William Stafford and the legendary Wallace Stegner, who grew up in Montana, North Dakota, and, especially, Saskatchewan (*Wolf Willow*). — *MB*

BC10j   Twentieth-Century American Western Writers: Second Series / ed. by Richard H. Cracroft. - 1999 - 374 p.; ill. - (Dictionary of literary biography, v. 212).

    Class Numbers:
        Library of Congress PS271
    ISBN 078763106X
    LCCN 99-35556
    Notes:
        Includes bibliographical references (p. 305-307); index

• Authors of interest to Prairies-Plains studies include Rick Bass, who grew up in Texas but also writes about Montana, and Oklahoman Matt Braun, who writes about the Old West, and has produced a book on how to write Westerns. J. Frank Dobie makes Texas and its folk life the subject of most of his work. Gerda Ehrlich has been dubbed "Walt Whitman of Wyoming." Montana author A.B. Guthrie's best-known work is *The Big Sky*, and William Kittredge writes extensively about Montana. Scandinavian-born O.E. Rølvaag described pioneer life in South Dakota. Nebraskan Mari Sandoz, best known for *Old Jules*, published many works about Native Americans and pioneers on the Plains. Entries contain a selective bibliography, photos, and lists of further readings. — *MB*

BC10k   Twentieth-Century American Western Writers: Third Series / ed. by Richard H. Cracroft. - 2002 - xxi, 418 p.; ill. - (Dictionary of literary biography, v. 256).

    Class Numbers:
        Library of Congress PS271
    ISBN 0787652504
    LCCN 2002-20018
    Notes:
        Includes bibliographical references (p. 341-343); index

• Prairies-Plains writers include Mary Clearman Blew (Montana), who writes short stories and essays, and Benjamin Capps (Texas), who focuses on the Old West, emphasizing Native Americans. Willa Cather, Nebraska's premier author, is known primarily for her novels of pioneer life, and the prolific Max Brand tells tales of the Old West, as does Luke Short. Linda M. Hasselstrom writes of ranch life in South Dakota, and Elmer Kelton's subject is Texas cowboys. Larry McMurtry, whose Plains novels have been made into movies or television series, is most closely associated with North Texas. Among writers identified with Indian themes are N. Scott Momaday (Oklahoma), John G. Neihardt, author of *Black Elk Speaks* (Nebraska), and James Welch, who writes about the Indian Wars. Laura Ingalls Wilder's "Little House" series rounds out the book. Each entry contains a selective bibliography, photos, and references for further reading. — *MB*

BC11   Dictionary of Midwestern Literature / Philip A. Greasley, general ed. - Bloomington, IN: Indiana Univ. Pr., c2001- (In progress). - v. 1.

> Class Numbers:
> > Library of Congress PS273 D53
> Notes:
> > Contents: v. 1: The authors
> > Entries created by the members of the Society for the Study of Midwestern Literature
> > Includes bibliographical references and index

• Briefly covers the lives and writings of about 400 significant Midwestern authors, past and present, and criticism of their work. The region defined as the Midwest includes seven states of the Upper Midwest and the Prairies-Plains states of Kansas, Nebraska, Missouri, and the Dakotas. Introductory material includes an introduction describing Midwestern literature and an essay on its origins. Entries include author's name, dates, any pseudonyms, biographical information, selected works, and a short list of suggested readings. Entries are signed, and a few have photos of the author. The best-known Plains writers are included–Wright Morris, William Inge, Mari Sandoz, Bess Streeter Aldrich, Willa Cather, Larry Woiwode, Laura Ingalls Wilder, Zitkala-Sa. Although coverage is for the most part excellent, especially when compared to many rival publications, there are notable absences—Canadian Robert Kroetsch, novelist Larry McMurtry, and Poet Laureate Ted Kooser. Canadian authors are largely ignored. Supplementary material identifies contributors by institutional affiliation and academic accomplishments. The subject index is extensive and easily accessible. A second volume that is to contain topical entries is in preparation. — *MB*

BC12   Snodgrass, Mary Ellen. - Encyclopedia of Frontier Literature. - New York: Oxford Univ. Pr., 1997. - 540 p.

> Class Numbers:
> > Library of Congress PS169.F7
> ISBN 0195133188 (pbk.)
> LCCN 99-11766
> Notes:

Reprint; originally publ. Santa Barbara, CA: ABC-CLIO, 1997

• Covering the settlement of the North American continent by Europeans from the earliest incursions through the confinement of Plains Indians to reservations in the 1890s, Snodgrass's encyclopedia concentrates on literature but unavoidably bridges into other concerns. Entries, some several pages long, treat such matters as Indians, European writers, motifs (captivity, cowboys, law and order), ethnic groups, women, and the usual suspects among American writers (Dee Brown, Cather, Irving, Richter, Sandoz, Wilder). Some writers that hold great interest for Plains studies (Wright Morris) are omitted, presumably because they do not write about the frontier. Several appendixes have special interest: timelines of frontier literature (1532-1996) and of films based on literature, lists of major works, major authors, and primary sources (books, audiocassettes, videos, CD-ROMs, Web sites). There is a general bibliography. An index covers names, titles, and topics. The compiler, an independent scholar who specializes in reference book compilation, wrote all the entries, most of which are clear and avoid overstatement. She seems at ease with the concept of the frontier, whose validity is under suspicion, especially by the New West historians. A useful place to begin research on literature of the frontier, and for Plains studies to the extent it covers people and topics related to the region. — *RB*

BC13   Tuska, Jon. - Encyclopedia of Frontier and Western Fiction / Jon Tuska and Vicki Piekarski, eds.-in-chief. - New York: McGraw-Hill, 1983. - 365 p.; ports.

> Class Numbers:
> > Library of Congress PS374.W4
> ISBN 0070655871
> LCCN 82-14831
> Notes:
> > Includes bibliography

• A work perhaps better titled "Encyclopedia of Frontier and Western Fiction Writers," since all but five of its entries are about writers, not topics. Tuska, a prolific author of books on Western literature and film, has made better contributions to the field. His subject is "cowboy and pioneer" fiction, so his book includes writers of the mountain West as well as the Great Plains. Some entries (not many) have photos of the authors, usually poor in quality. Each entry discusses the author's work in general terms, but fights shy of literary criticism, presenting only a general summation of the author's place in Western fiction. No index. — *MB*

BC14   Western Literature Association (U.S.). - A Literary History of the American West / sponsored by the Western Literature Association. - Fort Worth, TX: Texas Christian Univ. Pr., 1987. - xliii, 1353 p.; ill.

> Class Numbers:

Library of Congress PS271
ISBN 087565021X
LCCN 85-50538
Notes:
Bibliography: p. 1317-1323; index
Hypertext and pdf version: http://www.tcu.edu/depts/prs/
amwest/

• A literary history whose individual sections are written by
more than 70 scholars, most associated with the Western
Literature Association. Topics of interest to Prairies and
Plains students and scholars are buried in articles and in
sections whose principal concern is the trans-Mississippi
West, but sections are clearly identified (e.g., Far West,
Southwest, Midwest). The volume has three major divi-
sions, each with subsections: "Encountering the West,"
"Settled In: Many Wests," and "Rediscovering the West."
Part 1 deals with exploration, including oral tradition, trav-
el narratives, and other precursors. Part 2 is subdivided geo-
graphically, the Midwest being the section most important
for Plains studies (with articles about Cather, Rølvaag,
Krause, Neihardt, Sandoz, Wright Morris), but other sections include the likes of Stafford, Dobie, McMurtry,
DeVoto, and Stegner. Part 3 addresses the contributions of
Native Americans, Mexican Americans, Asian Americans,
and black Americans and describes present trends in
Western poetry, fiction, drama, and nonprint media.
Articles are signed and end with bibliographies. Especially
useful in establishing context for the study of Western lit-
erature, since it begins with both historical and literary
chronologies, establishes a classification of sorts for
Western literature, and near the end offers a seven-page

"Major Reference Sources on the West." — MB, RB

GENRES

Autobiographies

See Kaplan, **A Bibliography of American Autobiographies,
AC5**

Fiction

BC15   Coan, Otis Welton. - **America in Fiction: An
Annotated List of Novels that Interpret Aspects of Life in
the United States, Canada, and Mexico** / [by] Otis Welton
Coan [and] Richard Gordon Lillard. - 5th ed. - Palo Alto,
CA: Pacific Books, 1967. - 232 p.

Class Numbers:
Library of Congress Z1361.C6
LCCN 66-28118

• The editors, whose affiliations are not revealed, list fictional treatments of various aspects of American life that
are suitable for educated adults, undergraduates, and upper-
division secondary students. Entries have brief annotations,
but citations are abbreviated (short title, publisher, date).
Arranged by rough classification. Titles relating to Prairies
and Plains occur principally in the section "Grass: The
Plains Country" under "Pioneering" and in "The
Southwest" under "Farm and Village Life." Titles in other

sections occasionally treat Plains subjects, but they must be found by scanning, since the index lists only authors. Now seriously out of date. — *RB*

BC16   Critical Survey of Long Fiction / ed. by Frank N. Magill; academic director, Walton Beacham. - Englewood Cliffs, NJ: Salem Pr., 1983. - 8 v. (3352, xlviii p.).

> Class Numbers:
> Library of Congress PR821
> ISBN 0893563595
> LCCN 83-61341
> Notes:
> Contents: v. 1-7, Authors, A-Z; v. 8, Essays; Index
> Includes bibliographies; index

• Since this set covers long fiction in English, it includes American, British, and Canadian authors. Some are of interest to Plains studies, including Willa Cather, Margaret Laurence, Larry McMurtry, Wright Morris, and Sinclair Ross. Of particular interest is the essay, "The Western Novel," in volume 8. The supplemental volume includes North Dakota authors William H. Gass and Larry Woiwode. Entries for each writer are substantial; they include birth and death dates (where applicable), principal long fiction, achievements, biography, analysis, and a short bibliography of works about the author. The analysis section usually runs several pages. — *MB*

BC17 Johannsen, Albert, 1871-1962. - **The House of Beadle and Adams and Its Dime and Nickel Novels: The Story of a Vanished Literature** / with a foreword by John T. McIntyre. - Norman, OK: Univ. of Oklahoma Pr., 1950-1962. - 3 v.; ill., ports., facsims.

> Class Numbers:
> Library of Congress Z1231.F4
> LCCN 50-8158
> Notes:
> E-book: http://www.netLibrary.com/urlapi.asp?action-
>   summary&v=1&bookid=15666
> Bibliography: v. 2, p. 328-338
> Contents: v. 1, A history of the firm. Numerical lists of the
>   various series of Beadle novels; v. 2, The authors and
>   their novels. Appendix; v. 3, Supplement, addenda, cor
>   rigenda, etc.

• The dedication of this remarkable work reads: "Written for Collectors of Americana, Librarians, and Booksellers and for those who are nostalgic for Books of their Youth." In 1860 Beadle inaugurated its tremendously successful dime novel series, many of them set in the Plains; the series shaped many peoples' view of the region. The bibliographic information, collected from extant titles, advertisements, and research on Beadle authors, required special treatment.

The novels were reprinted and condensed many times; books were given new titles or titles and subtitles were reversed; names of authors were changed; dates of publication were often lacking; none of the firm's records remained; and its staff and authors were long dead. Part 1 has a history of dime novels and an essay on authors, artists, and readers, part 2 is a history of the firm, and part 3 offers numerical lists of the many series (e.g., "Beadle's Half-Dime Novelettes" and "New Dime Novels") and lists the novels in each series. Synopses are included to help distinguish among titles. Part 4 has biographical sketches of the usually obscure authors with portraits, references, and publication lists. Part 5, appendixes, presents a chronology of principle Beadle series; the firm's changes in name and address by date; the number of reprints in each series; reprints in the "Deadwood Dick" and "Frontier Libraries" series; an author pseudonyms list; an essay on condition and value; an essay on pre-Beadle novels; a bibliography of newspaper and magazine articles by date; an index of titles and subtitles; and a general index. An index of principal story localities—states, towns, tribes, and settings—is particularly useful. Northern Illinois University Libraries is digitizing the bibliography and the novels for *Beadle and Adams Dime Novel Digitization Project* at http://www.niulib.niu.edu/badndp/. — *JD*

BC18   Mort, John, 1947-   . - **Read the High Country: Guide to Western Books and Films.** - Westport, CT: Libraries Unlimited, 2006. - 488 p. - (Genreflecting Advisory Series).

> Class Numbers:
> Library of Congress PS374.W4 Z1231.W58
> ISBN 1591581346 97871591581345
> OCLC 70830926
> LCCN 2006-23647
> Notes:
> Filmography: p. 343-414
> Includes bibliographical references (p. 427-431); indexes

• Mort's survey of Western fiction and film provides a fair if opinionated overview of the genre (the "Genreflecting" series is intended for readers' advisory services in public libraries). He provides a brief history of the genre, followed by "Six Great Western Writers" (Grey, Brand, Haycox, L'Amour, Kelton, and McMurtry), and sections on traditional Westerns, nontraditional Westerns, and films. He confines comment about Cather to a dismissive paragraph and a swift review of *Death Comes for the Archbishop*, and believes Cormac McCarthy's early work before *All the Pretty Horses* "occupies the literary high ground." A decent beginning, but no serious student, even of Western fiction and movies, will be content with Mort's selection or critical stance. At the end are a list of Western writing awards, a bibliography, a time line, an author/title/subject index, and a film index. — RB

POETRY

BC19 Sanders, Mark, 1955-. - **A Bibliographic Introduction to Poetry in Nebraska**. - Ord, NE: Sandhills Pr., 1992. - 20 p. - (Sandhills Press MonoGraph, 1).

Class Numbers:
   Library of Congress PS3569.A5128
   OCLC 43051731
   Notes:
      "Presented at the 1989 meeting of the Nebraska Writers' Guild; an earlier draft ... was distributed during poetry readings at the University of Nebraska-Kearney and University of Nebraska-Lincoln in 1991."

• Sanders (Nebraska poet and small press publisher) provides four useful lists. The first, a selected list of books by 41 Nebraska poets, includes some who are well known (Weldon Kees, Ted Kooser) and others lesser known. A list of related readings includes books and articles covering Nebraska and Plains poetry. Lists of defunct and active presses and journals complete the work. While slim, the bibliography adds to the scant published information on the hearty community of Nebraska poets and other writers. An update would be welcome. — *JD*

REGIONAL LITERATURE: UNITED STATES

BC20 **A Companion to the Regional Literatures of America** / ed. by Charles L. Crow. - Malden, MA: Blackwell Publ., 2003. - 606 p.; ill., maps. - (Blackwell companions to literature and culture, 21).

Class Numbers:
   Library of Congress PS169.R45
   ISBN 0631226311
   LCCN 2002-38288
   Notes:
      Electronic book: http://www.netLibrary.com/urlapi.asp?action=summary&v=1&bookid=108712
      Includes bibliographical references; index
      Review by Kathleen A. Boardman: *Great Plains Quarterly* 24.4 (fall 2004): 298-299

• A collection of essays, all but two original, having to do with regional literatures of the U.S. Students of Prairies-Plains will be interested in the essays on frontier literature, the Great Plains, humor and grotesque in the Southwest, Montana, Texas and the Southwest, Cather, and Stegner. The contributors are intelligently chosen–e.g., Diane Quantic (Wichita State Univ.) on her specialty, Plains literature, and Robert Thacker (St. Lawrence Univ.) on Cather. Bibliographies, sometimes of novels and other genres by the writers discussed, more often of general scholar-

ly sources. The index of names and topics has no geographic approach. — *RB*

Iowa

BC21 Paluka, Frank. - **Iowa Authors: A Bio-Bibliography of Sixty Native Writers**. - Iowa City, IA: Friends of the Univ. of Iowa Libraries, 1967. - 243 p.

Class Numbers:
   Library of Congress PS283.I8
   LCCN 67-31800

• A bibliography of 60 Iowa authors, each of whom published at least five titles. Some are little known, others are household names. Of special interest to Prairies-Plains are Bess Streeter Aldrich, William F. Cody, Herbert Hoover, Meridel Lesueur, Wallage Stegner, and Carl Van Vechten. The 60 entries, arranged chronologically by the author's date of birth, each contain a short biobibliographical essay, and a chronological listing of the author's books. Translations and later editions are listed for each work. Articles in periodicals are mentioned only in passing. There is no table of contents, but an author index at the back lists the writers alphabetically. — *MB*

Kansas

BC22 Fox, Maynard. - **Book-Length Fiction by Kansas Writers, 1915-1938**. - Topeka, KS: Kansas State Printing Plant, 1944. - 44 p. - ([Kansas. Fort Hays State College, Hays] Fort Hays Kansas State College studies. Language and literature series, 2).

Class Numbers:
   Library of Congress AS36.K3 no. 2
   LCCN 44-42189
   Notes:
      Bibliography: p. 42-44

• An appraisal of fiction by Kansas writers during the period between the beginning of World War I and the cusp of World War II. The record is assuredly thin; the only writers likely to be still recognized are Dorothy Canfield and Edgar Howe. The author does not identify himself. For students of Kansas literature, primarily in identifying authors and titles. — *RB*

Nebraska

BC23 Cox, Gerry, 1930- . - **Guide to Nebraska Authors** / [by] Gerry Cox, Carol MacDaniels. - Lincoln, NE: Dageforde Publ., 1998. - 271 p.

Class Numbers:
   Library of Congress PS283.N2

ISBN 1886225354 (pbk.)
OCLC 39695817
LCCN 98-36889
Notes:
    Indexes

• The compilers present brief biographical information about some 700 Nebraska authors, established (Willa Cather, Mari Sandoz) and aspiring. They include writers of fiction and nonfiction books, screenplays, poetry, essays, and short stories, and both historical and contemporary figures (welfare activists Edith and Grace Abbott, Poet Laureate Ted Kooser, author and illustrator of children's books about Native Americans Paul Goble, clinical psychologist Mary Pipher, mystery writer Mignon Eberhart, anthropologist Loren Eiseley, humorist Roger Welsch). Many writers have only local reputation and interest. Entries, arranged alphabetically, range from a sentence to two pages, and cite sources; many were supplied by the writers themselves or by the Heritage Room of Nebraska Authors at the Lincoln City Library. The compilers include a list of wildflower photos and indexes of Nebraska cities and towns, names cited by authors, and authors appearing on the "Nebraska Literary Map with Native Wildflowers." The wildflower list and index of cities and towns are only marginally useful; lists of published works are incomplete. — *MB, JD*

BC24   Harvey, Alice G. - **Nebraska Writers**. - Rev. ed. - [Omaha, NE: Citizen Printing Co.], 1964. - 183 p.
    Class Numbers:
        Library of Congress PS283.N2
    Notes:
        Originally publ.: [Omaha, NE: Citizen Printing Co.], 1934. LCCN 34-25546 (pbk.)

• Produced by a local writer who was a supporter of other writers, this enthusiastic collective biography includes writers born and reared in Nebraska who are "thoroughly imbued with [its] history, environment, and spirit" and residents who "have caught the vision and inspiration which helped them portray life a little clearer." (Pref.) Part 1 is arranged by categories for "Early Writers," "Nebraska Poets," "Our Fiction Writers," "Writers of Drama," "Miscellaneous Writers," "Historical Writers," "Newspaper Writers and Columnists," "Literary Organizations," "Nebraska Literary Publications." Biographical sketches (half a page to two pages) cover significant authors (e.g., 22 authors of fiction) and appear to be based on personal acquaintance and interviews. Sketches cover writing habits, character, health, hobbies, opinions, childhood dreams. Part 2 is an index of authors associated with Nebraska, supplying sketchy bibliographical entries for

each, arranged chronologically. Some writers listed in the index do not appear in Part 1. — *MB, JD*

BC25   Hawkins, Lynn. - **Alive and Writing in Nebraska** / [by] Lynn Hawkins and Muffy Fisher-Vrana; [cover design by Marie Christian]. - Lincoln, NE: Media Production and Marketing, 1986. - 120 p.; ill., ports.
    Class Numbers:
        Library of Congress PS283.N2
    ISBN 0939644223 (pbk.)
    Notes:
        "Funding . . . provided . . . by a grant from the Nebraska Committee for the Humanities . . . to the Nebraska Writers Guild."
    Directory: p. 109-118
    Index

• An index of 37 selected authors arranged by category: "Poets," "Literary, Social, and Natural History," "Folklore, Storytellers, Humorists," "Novelists," "Children and Young Adult," "Motivation and Inspiration." Each entry includes a photo, biographical information, and samples of the writer's work. — *MB*

BC26   Kauffman, Bernice, comp. - **Nebraska Centennial Literary Map and Guide to Nebraska Authors** / map by Jack Brodie. - [Lincoln, NE?]: Nebraska Centennial Commission in cooperation with the Nebraska Arts Council, [1967]. - 62 p.; folded map (in pocket).
    Class Numbers:
        Library of Congress PS28.N2 K3
    OCLC 1129327
    LCCN 67-5855
    Notes:
        Bibliography: p. 59-62

• Covers writers born in Nebraska or resident there for a significant period. It focuses on belles lettres, general culture, and Nebraska, excluding scholarly or technical works but does not pretend to be a comprehensive list of either authors or titles. Entries for authors, a paragraph long, supply brief biographical sketches and citations to important works. Ends with a list of works consulted. The literary map, which locates the areas where 70 major writers lived, is a bonus. Kauffman, a longtime reference librarian at Lincoln City Libraries, cites their Nebraska Author Information File as a primary source. That file has become the online *Nebraska Author Information Link* (NAIL), which has entries for 3,400 Nebraska writers. NAIL, together with extensive vertical file and book collections, forms the research component of the Library's Heritage Room of Nebraska Authors. The NAIL database includes biographical and bibliographical information, and Heritage Room maintains vertical files (2,000 items) and 11,000 volumes about Nebraska authors. While a public Internet site is planned, queries may be submitted to Heritage Room staff (136 South14th, Lincoln, NE 68508-1899, 402-441-8516, or at the "Ask a Librarian" service at the Library's Internet site, http://www.lcl.lib.ne.us). — *JD*

BC27 McCleery, David. - **Resource Guide to Six Nebraska Authors** / ed. by David McCleery & Kira Gale. - Lincoln, NE: Slow Tempo Pr., 1991. - 93 p.; ill.

> Class Numbers:
> Library of Congress PS283.N2
> OCLC 25402622
> Notes:
> Includes bibliographical references
> Major funding provided by the Nebraska Humanities Council, a state program of the National Endowment for the Humanities
> Produced in cooperation with Nebraska Center for the Book and Friends of Nebraska Literature

• Selected for their potential value for teachers, all six authors (Bess Streeter Aldrich, Willa Cather, Loren Eiseley, Wright Morris, John G. Neihardt, and Mari Sandoz) have national reputations, speak to timeless issues, and are tied to the Nebraska landscape. The biographies include personal and professional histories; annotated bibliographies of major works arranged by type; works adapted to other media; recommended readings; research archives; audiovisual materials and other programs; places to visit such as homes, museums, book settings, and cemeteries; tours; annual events such as festivals, dinners and scholarships; seminars and workshops; and organizations such as foundations and literary societies. Excerpts from writings and photographs of the authors are included with each entry. Enhancements: a map shows the Nebraska settings of the authors' works; photographs of busts of the authors in the rotunda of the State Capitol Building; and videos, speakers, and collections offered by local organizations. — *JD*

BC27a McCleery, David. - **Resource Guide to Six Nebraska Authors: Volume 2**. - Lincoln, NE: Slow Tempo Pr., 1992. - 57 p.

> Class Numbers:
> Library of Congress PS283 N2
> OCLC 27731746
> Notes:
> Produced by the Nebraska Center for the Book. Major funding provided by the Nebraska Humanities Council, a state program of the National Endowment for the Humanities.

• Biographies of Dorothy Canfield Fisher, Weldon Kees, Malcolm X, Tillie Olsen, Louis Pound, and Sophus Keith

Winther follow the format of those in v. 1, but limit elements to single portraits, biographies, annotated bibliographies of works by and about the authors, and research archives. — *JD*

BC28 **Nebraska Center for Writers** [Internet Site]. - [Omaha, NE]: Nebraska Center for Writers, 1995–   . - http://mockingbird.creighton.edu/NCW/

> Access Date: May 2005
> Fees: None

• An Internet page intended for writers that will also be useful to readers and researchers. "The Life" supplies directories and links to Nebraska literary organizations, places, workshops, conferences, public readings, and academic programs. A directory of published writers with Nebraska connections offers biographies, bibliographies, critiques and commentaries, and excerpts. "The Lit" is a directory of literary magazines, book publishers, and booksellers in Nebraska. "Saddle Up for a Literary Tour of Nebraska" is not a tour (the galloping horse icon notwithstanding) but a tidy summary of Nebraska literature with links to additional information. The site also includes reference sources, writing software, literary agents, jobs for writers, writers' colonies, and national organizations. — *JD*

BC29 Uzendoski, Emily Jane. - **A Handlist of Nebraska Authors**. - Lincoln, NE: Nebraska Dept. of Education, 1977. - 275 leaves.

> Class Numbers:
> Library of Congress PS28.N2; Z1307.U9
> Notes:
> Originally publ. as author's dissertation, Univ. of Nebraska–Lincoln, 1976

• Lists 3,444 titles by 1,139 authors, including writers born or resident in Nebraska, or those a significant part of whose published output has Nebraska or the Great Plains as setting. Uzendoski cites only separately published books or parts of books of 64 pages or more, and books of poetry of any length. The compiler intends to "incorporate and extend previous bibliographical catalogs" of Nebraska writers, hence includes names from Harvey (**BC24**) and Kauffman (**BC26**). Excluded are commercial, religious, promotional, highly specialized or technical publications, and works intended for a limited audience. The largest category of works is community histories and personal recollections (journals, diaries, memoirs, oral histories, travel, and biographies and autobiographies) written before 1910, followed by fiction. The volume is arranged alphabetically by author, but lacks table of contents and index. Citations include book titles with single-word descriptions (drama, novel, memoir), but do not enumerate edition variants.

Particularly useful in identifying personal accounts of pioneer life. — *MB, JD*

New Mexico

BC30 Lewis, Tom, 1932- . - **Storied New Mexico: An Annotated Bibliography of Novels with New Mexico Settings**. - Albuquerque, NM: Univ. of New Mexico Pr., 1991. - 224 p.

Class Numbers:
Library of Congress PS283.N6 Z1315
ISBN 0826312233 9780826312235
OCLC 22957075
LCCN 90-26834
Notes:
Indexes

• Lewis cites and briefly annotates some 1,200 novels set (however tangentially) in New Mexico. The basic list is arranged by author, listed by pseudonym when one was used on the title page (e.g., Tom Cutter), and gives full publishing information. The annotations note, for example, that four pages of *Lonesome Dove* take place in New Mexico, and that *Death Comes for the Archbishop* is "the pre-eminent New Mexico novel." Indexes by title, theme (i.e., subject) and genre, place-names, regions, and time periods. A brief list cites novels that were excluded because their New Mexico content was too slight. Useful; but Cormac McCarthy is omitted, though most of his work postdated 1991. — *RB*

North Dakota

BC31 Torgerson, Lowell E. - **Bibliography of North Dakota Authors & Poets**. - Minot, ND: Torgerson, 1982. - 109 leaves.

Class Numbers:
Library of Congress PS571.N9
OCLC 9047532
Notes:
Reproduced from typescript

• An annotated bibliography of poets, authors, and books. The preface, dated 1982, as is the imprint, makes it likely that few publications are later than 1980. The bibliography is divided into poetry and books, with titles in each section arranged alphabetically by author. There are topical listings for Norwegian American Studies, George Armstrong Custer, and Theodore Roosevelt. Unfortunately, there has been no supplement. — *JB*

Oklahoma

BC32 Marable, Mary Hays. - **A Handbook of Oklahoma Writers** / by Mary Hays Marable and Elaine Boylan. - Norman, OK: Univ. of Oklahoma Pr., 1939. - 308 p.

Class Numbers:
LIbrary of Congress PS283.O5
OCLC 1454916
LCCN 39-27387
Notes:
"Bibliography of Oklahoma Writers": p. 226-304

• Attempts to take stock of Oklahoma writers of all stripes who had emerged by 1939. First come biographical sketches of writers of fiction, poets, dramatists, historians, and writers of nonfiction, then a list of literary honors and awards won by Oklahoma writers, a list of writers arranged by town, a bibliography arranged by author, and an index of names. A wide net is cast, catching such writers as Hubert Collins, who wrote manuals about steam engines and their ancillary systems, but also mentioning Angie Debo before she wrote the works of history in which her reputation rests, Lynn Riggs before his play *Green Grow the Lilacs* had been reworked into *Oklahoma!*, Andy Adams, Stanley Vestal, Vernon Parrington, and George Milburn. A fascinating glimpse of writers in a developing state (in both senses of the term). — *RB*

Texas

BC33 **Texas Women Writers: A Tradition of Their Own** / ed. by Sylvia Ann Grider & Lou Halsell Rodenberger. - College Station, TX: Texas A&M Univ. Pr., 1997. - 461 p. - (Tarleton State University southwestern studies in the humanities, 8).

Class Numbers:
Library of Congress PS266.T4
ISBN 0890967520 0890967652 (pbk.)
LCCN 97-7048
Notes:
Includes bibliographical references (p. [359]-432); index

• A collection of essays, chiefly by women academics, about women writers associated with Texas by birth, residence (permanent or temporary), or treatment of Texas subjects in their writing. Some nonfiction writers are treated, but the emphasis rests on writers of literature. Sections cover prose writers 1830-1995, Tejana and black American writers, poets, and dramatists. The most useful section is a selected (but very full) bibliography (73 p.) that lists general studies followed by sections for individual writers (including some not covered by the text), citing primary and secondary sources. — *RB*

ETHNIC LITERATURE

See also Inglehart, **Image of Pluralism in American Literature, CC5**

Latino

BC34   **Latino Literature: Poetry, Drama, and Fiction [Internet Site]**. - Alexandria, VA: Alexander Street Pr., 2004- . - http://alexanderstreet.com/products/lali.htm

> Access Date: Dec. 2005
> Notes:
>> Available through outright purchase or subscription

• This full-text database contains a wealth of work, largely post-1965, by Latino writers in the U.S. Currently about 80 percent complete, it will ultimately contain 100,000 pages of poetry and fiction and 450 plays. Most of the works are presented in English but some in Spanish; almost 30 percent are unpublished or considered rare. The "Geographical Locations" section of the subject index identifies Plains content at the level of region (Great Plains States), state (Kansas) and city (Tulsa). Individual theaters and theatrical companies such as the Omaha Magic Theater are indicated. Alexander Street products are noted for the depth and quality of their indexing and the database can be browsed or searched from a wide variety of perspectives. The search engine is described at **CD46**. The site assembles a large number of texts representing the diversity of Latino literature, both as imaginative creation and as a reflection of the Latino experience in the U.S. — *LMcD*

BC35   Martínez, Julio A., ed. - **Chicano Literature: A Reference Guide** / ed. by Julio A. Martínez and Francisco A. Lomelí. - Westport, CT: Greenwood Pr., 1985.

> Class Numbers:
>> Library of Congress PS153 .M4
>> ISBN 0313236917
>> LCCN 83-22583
> Notes:
>> Includes bibliographical references (p. [469]-480); index

• The editors identify Chicano literature as writings by Mexican Americans from 1848 (the year in which Anglo culture began to dominate in the Southwest) to the present. Entries are arranged alphabetically by topic, both subjects (e.g., theater) and persons interfiled. Essays are signed. Since the guide is concerned exclusively with Chicanos and their literature, some of the headings ("Chicano Literary Criticism," "Chicano Poetry") might have omitted "Chicano." Appendixes include a chronology, glossary, and general bibliography. A modest index and information about contributors complete the volume. — MB

INDIVIDUAL WRITERS

Cather

BC36   Arnold, Marilyn, 1935- . - **Willa Cather: A**

Reference Guide. - Boston, MA: G.K. Hall, 1986. - xxii, 415 p. - (A reference guide to literature).

> Class Numbers:
>> Library of Congress PS3505.A87 Z8155.65
>> ISBN 0816186545
>> LCCN 86-14277
> Notes:
>> Indexes
>> Supplemented by: Marilyn Arnold. *Willa Cather: A Reference Guide, Update 1984-1992: Annotated Bibliography*. [Red Cloud, NE?]: Willa Cather Pioneer Memorial and Educational Foundation, 1999. 1 v.

• Arnold's annotated bibliography of writings about Willa Cather, 1895-1984, is arranged chronologically by year then alphabetically by main entry. It includes all items Arnold could locate about Cather, both scholarly and informal. Many early entries are from local newspapers and book review sources. Included also are book chapters, dissertations, and some non-English-language items. Good author and subject indexes refer to year and item (e.g., 1955.13). — *MB*

BC37   Crane, Joan St. C. - **Willa Cather: A Bibliography** / foreword by Frederick B. Adams. - Lincoln, NE: Univ. of Nebraska Pr., 1982. - xxviii, 412 p.

> Class Numbers:
>> Library of Congress PS3505.A87 Z8155.65
>> ISBN 0803214154
>> LCCN 81-23134
> Notes:
>> Index

• A comprehensive descriptive bibliography of works by Cather, not a listing of critical writings about her work. The separate publications are arranged chronologically with a formal title page transcription, collation, notes on physical features (illustrations, paper, typefaces, binding, dust jackets), printing history, and editions. Major textual changes are noted. Anthologies and edited works have the same structure. Separate sections treat Cather's poetry, short fiction, articles, and essays, also chronologically but in less detail. Translations, pirated editions, Braille and recorded books, and adaptations are itemized. Largely replaces JoAnna Lathrop's *Willa Cather: A Checklist of her Published Writing* (Lincoln, NE: Univ. of Nebraska Pr., 1975; 118 p.). The definitive work on one of the most important figures in the literature of the Great Plains. — *LMcD*

BC38   March, John, 1905?-ca. 1990. - **A Reader's Companion to the Fiction of Willa Cather** / [by] John March; ed. by Marilyn Arnold, with Debra Lynn Thornton. - Westport, CT: Greenwood Pr., 1993. - xxix, 846 p.

Class Numbers:

Library of Congress PS3505.A87

ISBN 0313287678

LCCN 92-42434

Notes:

Includes bibliographical references

• The late March and his editors attempt to give background information about all persons and objects mentioned in Cather's fiction. The editors exclude entries for Cather's poetry and essays, although March had included them in the original manuscript. Entries, alphabetically arranged, are coded to identify genre, title, book or chapter, and section; a key to symbols used in coding precedes the entries. Some entries are quite long, others are simply cross-references. — *MB*

BC39 Stout, Janis P., ed. - **A Calendar of the Letters of Willa Cather**. - Lincoln, NE: Univ. of Nebraska Pr., 2002. - 334 p.

Class Numbers:

Library of Congress PS3505.A87

ISBN 080324293X

LCCN 2001-34723

Notes:

Indexes

• As the title indicates, the 1,817 entries are arranged chronologically. Entries supply name of recipient, date, place, description, and the collection where the item can be found. The content of each letter or postcard is summarized in 20 to 200 words as appropriate; most summaries run about 100 words. A biographical directory briefly identifies addressees or persons mentioned in the letters. The chronological arrangement makes necessary indexes of addressees, names and Cather titles mentioned, and a less useful index to the 64 repositories holding her correspondence; all indexes refer to item numbers. A very useful addition to Cather scholarship, since her will and subsequent legal decisions regarding copyright prohibit the text of her letters being published until 2017. — *MB*

Erdrich

BC40 Beidler, Peter G. - **A Reader's Guide to the Novels of Louise Erdrich** / [by] Peter G. Beidler and Gay Barton. - Rev. and expanded ed. - Columbia, MO: Univ. of Missouri Pr., 2006. - 435 p.; ill.

Class Numbers:

Library of Congress PS3555.R42

ISBN 0826216706   0826216714 (pbk.)

9780826216700   9780826216717

OCLC 65400532

LCCN 2006-10717

Notes:

1st ed., 1999

Includes bibliographical references (p. 399-422); index

Table of contents: http://www.loc.gov/catdir/toc/ ecip0611/2006010717.html

• The authors are concerned with the related novels *Love Medicine*, *Beet Queen*, *Tracks*, *Bingo Place*, *Tales of Burning Love*, and *The Antelope Wife*, which revolve around a fictitious Indian reservation in eastern North Dakota. The guide begins by describing the geography, genealogy, and chronology of the novels' location and characters. A second section presents detailed entries for major characters, followed by a briefer section for minor characters. Lengthy bibliography; detailed index. — *JB*

BC41 Stookey, Lorena Laura. - **Louise Erdrich: A Critical Companion**. - Westport, CT: Greenwood Pr., 1999. - 168 p. - (Critical companions to popular contemporary writers).

Class Numbers:

Library of Congress PS3555.R42

ISBN 0313306125

LCCN 99-21709

Notes:

Electronic access: http://site.ebrary.com/lib/niagara/ Doc?id=5005097

Includes bibliographical references (p. [143]-162); index

• Stookey discusses the fiction of Erdrich, Indian writer and North Dakota resident. Chapter 1 provides a brief biography, chapter 2 an overview of her fiction. Erdrich's six books are each treated in a separate chapter, divided into discussion of plot, characters, and themes. Brief notes end each chapter. Preceding the index, an extensive bibliography of primary and secondary works has sections on criticism of individual works. — *MB*

Grey

BC42 Scott, Kenneth William, 1923-   . - **Zane Grey, Born to the West: A Reference Guide**. - Boston, MA: G.K. Hall, 1979. - 179 p. - (Reference publication in literature).

Class Numbers:

Library of Congress PS3513.R6545   Z869.2633

ISBN 0816178755

LCCN 79-715

Notes:

Index

• Following the narrative introduction is a list of the adult fiction by Zane Grey, some 65 books published 1903-1977. Of these, about two dozen published after his death are of questionable authorship. "Zane Grey on Film" lists chronologically the more than 100 movies based on his novels and short stories, giving studio, date, director, and cast. The greater part of Scott's guide is an annotated list of works about Grey, arranged chronologically, 1904-1977. The combined index, too brief to be very useful, lists hardly any subjects. The text is reproduced from typescript, suggesting the publisher had no role in editing copy. — *MB*

Hughes

BC43   Dickinson, Donald C. - **A Bio-Bibliography of Langston Hughes, 1902-1967** / with a preface by Arna Bontemps. - 2nd, revised ed. - [Hamden, CT]: Archon Books, 1967. - 273 p.; port.

> Class Numbers:
> Library of Congress PS3515.U274
> ISBN 0208012699
> LCCN 70-181877
> Notes:
> An expansion of the author's dissertation, Univ. of
> Michigan
> Bibliography: p. 257-262

• Just under half this volume consists of a narrative biography of Hughes that includes a chronology, a discussion of significant eras in his life, and an appendix regarding his foreign reception. The bibliography section includes books by Hughes, books he edited and translated, and works by him published in languages other than English for which there is no English edition. Other sections list his contributions to collections, and the publications where his prose, drama, and poetry have appeared. The book ends with a bibliography of works about Hughes and general references. The subject index is too short to be useful. — *MB*

Inge

BC44   McClure, Arthur F., ed. - **A Bibliographical Guide to the Works of William Inge** (1913-1973) / ed. by Arthur F. McClure, C. David Rice. - Lewiston, NY: E. Mellen Pr., 1991. - 166 p. - (Studies in American literature, v. 14).

> Class Numbers:
> Library of Congress PS3517.N265   Z8437.5
> ISBN 0773496882 088946166X (series)
> OCLC 24319191
> LCCN 91-30669
> Notes:
> Index

• Inge, an important dramatist of the mid-20th century, was born in Kansas and set plays such as *Picnic* and *Bus Stop* there. A chronology of Inge precedes a list of his published work, arranged by genre; it includes reviews written for the St. Louis *Star-Times*, 1943-1946. A chapter on biographical sources is followed by one covering critical articles and reviews. General studies are followed by reviews of plays, arranged by date of first production. Chapters on film and television adaptations are organized by date of release. The book concludes with a description of the Inge Collection at Independence Community College Library and the annual Inge Festival, both in Independence, KS.

§   Richard Leeson's *William Inge: A Research and Production Sourcebook* (Westport, CT: Greenwood Pr., 1994; Modern Dramatists Research and Production Sourcebook, 5) covers much the same territory but with a slightly different emphasis. Entries for the plays, arranged alphabetically, supply lists of characters, extended plot summary, productions and credits, reviews, and a critical overview. Separate sections list Inge's writings (arranged by form), reviews, and books and articles, organized chronologically and annotated. Both books are useful, Leeson's somewhat more so, given its annotations and additional features. — *LMcD*

Manfred

BC45   Mulder, Rodney J. - **Frederick Manfred: A Bibliography and Publishing History** / [by] Rodney J. Mulder, John H. Timmerman. - Sioux Falls, SD: Center for Western Studies, Augustana College, 1981. - 139 p.

> Class Numbers:
> Library of Congress PS3525.A52233
> ISBN 093117015X
> OCLC 8218340
> LCCN 81-67077

• A description of Manfred's body of work, this bibliography is intended for collectors and researchers. Manfred's 25 Western novels were widely read and admired from his first novel in 1944 to his last in 1980, especially in the Minnesota-South Dakota-Nebraska-Iowa region he called Siouxland. Chapters cover Manfred's original books and other writings, along with critical studies and book reviews. The entries for original works, which have a confusing format, include bibliographical information; contents notes; edition; lengthy descriptions of cover and dust jacket; place of composition; publication date; press run; price; and notes on composition, publishing history, and reception. The chapter on other works by Manfred includes student writings, short stories, poems, articles, published letters, book reviews, and interviews. The critical studies, which include books, articles, dissertations and theses, are annotated; the book reviews are not. A narrative interview with Manfred in the closing chapter provides additional background.— *JD*

Porter

BC46   Kiernan, Robert F. - **Katherine Anne Porter and Carson McCullers: A Reference Guide**. - Boston, MA: G.K.

Hall, 1976. - 194 p. - (Reference guides in literature, 9).

Class Numbers:
    Library of Congress PS3531.O752
    LCCN 76-2357

• Born and schooled in Texas, Katherine Anne Porter drew instant acclaim on publication of her first book of stories, *Flowering Judas* (1930). Although critics hedged their praise when she published later collections, short novels (*Old Mortality* [1937], *Noon Wine* [1937], and *Pale Horse, Pale Rider* [1939]), and a single novel, *Ship of Fools* (1962), she enjoys a high reputation as a stylist and practitioner of the short story. Kiernan's book reviews the critical writings about her, arranged chronologically, 1924-1974, an exercise that reveals perhaps less about Porter herself than about her critics. The other half of the book, about Carson McCullers, falls outside the Prairies-Plains interest. — *RB*

Rhodes

BC47   Hutchinson, William Henry, 1910-1990. - **A Bar Cross Liar: Bibliography of Eugene Manlove Rhodes Who Loved the West-That-Was When He Was Young**. - Stillwater, OK: Redlands Pr., 1959. - 94 p.

Class Numbers:
    Library of Congress Z8741
    LCCN 60-17854

• The author of popular magazine short stories and novels, Rhodes was known for combining realistic depictions of ranch life with admirable cowhand characters. Most of his works were set in New Mexico, which was also the home of the Bar Cross ranch, Rhodes's favorite and most frequent employer. The bibliography begins with annotated citations, along with original payments, for his magazine pieces, many of which were serialized. The book list includes original prices, printing and publishing histories, annotations, and excerpts from reviews. A list of five motion pictures includes review excerpts. Two sections entitled "Association Items" and "In the Dust of the Drag" cite works about Rhodes and mentions of Rhodes in published letters, bibliographies, dedications, conference papers, newspapers, and other sources. Lists of characters, their real-life counterparts, and real and fictional communities and cowboy outfits confirm that Rhodes's work was grounded in real life in the West. The uncritically admiring compiler concludes with a selection of his favorite lines, among them: "She was wild and sweet and witty. Let's not say dull things about her" and "He had a wholesome sense of humor that went far to soften and ameliorate his many virtues." —*JD*

Sandoz

BC48   Greenwell, Scott L. - **Descriptive Guide to the Mari Sandoz Collection**. - Lincoln, NE: Univ. of Nebraska, 1980. - 109 p. - (University of Nebraska studies, n.s., 63; ISSN 0077-6386).

Class Numbers:
    Library of Congress E175.5.S24   Z6616.S163 G74
    OCLC 7143400

• Inventories the Mari Sandoz Collection at the University of Nebraska-Lincoln. The guide is organized in broad sections: Sandoz's personal library, her research files, manuscripts and publications, personal materials, and miscellaneous items (e.g., awards, paintings, maps). Personal library items often contain Sandoz's marginal notes, making them valuable for research. The research files include 68 boxes of materials, which are briefly described, and 45,000 3x5 index cards, organized into 11 categories. The publications section lists all editions of her works, including non-English-language editions, as well as articles and manuscripts. — *MB*

Stegner

BC49   Colberg, Nancy. - **Wallace Stegner: A Descriptive Bibliography** / introd. by James R. Hepworth. - Lewiston, ID: Confluence Pr., 1990. - xxxvi, 280 p.; ill. - (Confluence American authors series, 3).

Class Numbers:
    Library of Congress Z8838.3
    ISBN 0917652800
    LCCN 89-82163
    Notes:
        Index

• Although frequently labeled a Western writer, Stegner has a strong claim to Plains identity through life experience (early years in North Dakota and Montana, among other places), novels such as *On a Darkling Plain*, and *Wolf Willow*, in part a memoir of his family's pioneering years in the Cypress Hills region of Saskatchewan. The bibliography describes Stegner's voluminous production to 1988 as physical objects, transcribing title pages and recording details such as binding colors, dust jackets, publication history, and printing variants. Works are arranged chronologically within formats: books, chapters, articles, short stories, and miscellaneous items; translations are organized by language and manuscripts are listed by repository. A brief section lists secondary material about Stegner and his work. Valuable for scholars, less directly so for students. In 2001 Colberg transferred her personal collection to Montana State University as the Wallace Stegner Research Collection, 1942-1996; a detailed finding aid is located at http://www.lib.montana.edu/collect/spcoll/findaid/2443.html. — *LMcD*

Wilder

BC50   Mooney-Getoff, Mary J. - **Laura Ingalls Wilder, a Bibliography: Writings by and about Laura Ingalls Wilder, Audio Visual Resources: for Researchers, Writers, Teachers, Students, and Those Who Enjoy Reading about Laura**. - Southold, NY: Wise Owl Pr., 1980. - 40 p.

Class Numbers:
   Library of Congress Z8975.6
OCLC 7614822
LCCN 81-119775

• Mooney-Getoff's annotated bibliography intends to assist researchers and librarians in locating literary criticism about Wilder. It includes books, journals, audiovisual materials, articles, and dissertations about the author and her family. Newspaper articles are limited to entries for the *New York Times* and the *Times Literary Supplement*. Three appendixes record information received late; other indexes consulted to prepare the work; and addresses of publishers, library associations, and historical societies that have more information about Wilder. — *GK*

BC51 Subramanian, Jane M., 1950- . - **Laura Ingalls Wilder: An Annotated Bibliography of Critical, Biographical, and Teaching Studies**. - Westport, CT: Greenwood Pr., 1997. - 115 p. - (Bibliographies and Indexes in American Literature, 24).

Class Numbers:
   Library of Congress PS35345.I342   Z8975.6
ISBN 0313299994 9780313299995
OCLC 35110369
LCCN 96-33047
Notes:
   Indexes

• Subramanian (librarian, SUNY College-Potsdam) lists only secondary works in sections of criticism, biographical works, teaching aids, teaching kits, serials, and book reviews. As one hopes in a source prepared by a librarian, entries are carefully complete, and annotations describe content and critical stance. Indexes of sources (i.e., titles), younger readers (titles appropriate for that age group), authors, and subjects refer to numbered entries. A good place to locate studies of this author, who is admired by teachers and children, and respected by social historians. — *RB*

REGIONAL LITERATURE: CANADA

General Works

BC52 **Auteurs francophones des Prairies**. - Saint-Boniface, MB: Centre de ressources éducatives françaises du Manitoba, 1981. - 47 p.; ports.

Class Numbers:
   National Library of Canada PS8081
OCLC 19846891

• Short biobibliographies of Prairie authors, most from Manitoba, writing in French. Among the 25 profiled, Gabrielle Roy is the most prominent. — *LMcD*

BC53 **Canadian Writers and Their Works: Fiction Series** / ed. by Robert Lecker, Jack David, Ellen Quigley; introd. by George Woodcock. - Downsview, ON: ECW Pr., 1983- . - v. 1- (In progress).

Class Numbers:
   Library of Congress PR9192.2
ISBN 0920802435   0920802451 (v. 1)
LCCN 84-115108
Notes:
   Includes bibliographies; indexes

• Volume 1 covers writers of the 18th and 19th centuries, including Catharine Parr Traill and Susanna Moodie; volume 4 Martha Ostenso, Frederick Philip Grove, W.O. Mitchell, and Sinclair Ross; volume 9 Rudy Wiebe, Marian Engel, and Margaret Laurence; volume 10 Manitoba writer Robert Kroetsch among others; and volume 12 Manitoba's Sandra Birdsell and Alberta (and Iowa's) W.P. Kinsella. Each volume includes only four or five writers, providing detailed information about each. Entries, written by specialists, provide a biography of the writer, a critical overview, discussions of specific works, and bibliographies, primary and secondary. Each volume is separately indexed. — *MB*

BC54 Dagg, Anne Innis. - **The Feminine Gaze: A Canadian Compendium of Non-Fiction Women Authors and Their Books, 1836-1945**. - Waterloo, ON: Wilfrid Laurier Univ. Pr., 2001. - 346 p.

Class Numbers:
   Library of Congress PR9188
   National Library of Canada Z1376 W65
ISBN 0889203555
OCLC 46769681
Notes:
   Includes bibliographical references (p. 333-335); index

• Surveys the writings of 476 women, mostly Canadian, who wrote nonfiction in Canada's early years. Writers of fiction are included if they also produced nonfiction, and non-Canadians (e.g., Isabella Lucy Bird) are listed for their works about Canadian topics. Only women writing in English are included. After an informative introduction, entries follow, arranged alphabetically, each containing a brief bibliography of works by and about the writer. Three appendixes, a general bibliography, and index. Includes writers from the Prairie provinces. — *MB*

BC55 **ECW's Biographical Guide to Canadian Novelists**. - Don Mills, ON: ECW Pr., 1993. - 252 p.; ill.

Class Numbers:
    Library of Congress PR9192.2
    ISBN 1550221515
    LCCN 93-227237
    Notes:
        Includes bibliographical references

• The publishers claim that all major Canadian authors are included, but French Canadian writers are not. Even among English Canadians, many popular authors are absent (L.M. Montgomery, W.P. Kinsella, W.D. Valgardson, several others). Aboriginal Canadians are not well represented, and women are underrepresented relative to their contributions to Canadian literature. None of the writers included was born within the past 60 years. The book has neither preface nor introduction, and entries are listed chronologically by writers' birthdates. Since there is no alphabetical index, it is tedious to determine whether a given author is included. Selection criteria are not explained, nor are the credentials of contributors given. Entries vary substantially in length, and there is no standard format. Not recommended. — *MB*

BC56   Jones, Joseph, 1947- . - **Reference Sources for Canadian Literary Studies**. - Toronto, ON: Univ. of Toronto Pr., 2005. - 464 p.

Class Numbers:
    Library of Congress Z1375
    National Library of Canada Z1375
    ISBN 080208740X
    Notes:
        Includes bibliographical references; indexes
        Review by M.S. Brown-Sica: *Choice* 43.1 (Sep. 2005):
           review 43-0021

• Annotated bibliography arranged by type of reference work and literary genre. The Prairies section (p. 434-436) of the regional subject index identifies works devoted to the area as well as the individual provinces. — *LMcD*

BC57   McLeod, Gordon Duncan. - **A Descriptive Bibliography of the Canadian Prairie Novel, 1871-1970**. - Ottawa, ON: National Library of Canada, 1974. - 253 leaves. - (Canadian theses on microfiche; no. 20399).

Class Numbers:
    Library of Congress Z1377.F4
    OCLC 5751210
    Notes:
        Includes bibliographical references: leaves 227-245
        Reproduction: microfiche of typescript (Ottawa: National
           Library of Canada, 1975); 3 sheets, 10.5 x 15 cm.
        Thesis (PhD) — Univ. of Manitoba, 1974

• McLeod defines the Prairie novel as written either by Prairie residents, regardless of subject, or by former resi-

dents on a Prairie theme; 88 novelists are examined. A biographical sketch justifying the writer's inclusion is followed by a chronological list of novels. Each title has at least one subject heading and a brief summary of plot and setting. Other features include lists of novels by publication date, category or genre (pioneer, depression, historical, etc.), and title. Useful for identifying some obscure authors and for the novel synopses. — *LMcD*

BC58   Morcos, Gamila. - **Dictionnaire des artistes et des auteurs francophones de l'Ouest canadien** / Gamila Morcos; établi avec la collaboration de Gilles Cadrin, Paul Dubé, Laurent Godbout. - [Sainte-Foy, QC]: Presses de l'Université Laval, 1998. - lxiii, 366 p.; col. ill., col. maps.

Class Numbers:
    Library of Congress NX513.A1
    National Library of Canada FC3208
    ISBN 2763775667
    OCLC 38748236
    LCCN 98-165119
    Notes:
        Published in collaboration with the Faculté Saint-Jean

• A collective biography of more than 400 French Canadian artists and writers who have lived in the West (the Prairies, British Columbia, or the Territories), and who produced original work or contributed to strengthening the French presence. Besides literary authors and artists of all types, it includes musicians, journalists, professors, architects, and a small number of scientists. The introduction presents a historical overview of the French population in the region as a whole as well as in individual jurisdictions, tables and graphs of assimilation rates, and statistics on official linguistic minorities by province; it concludes with a thematic bibliography (p. lix-lxiii). Entries are arranged alphabetically and indicate province or territory of association, profession, biographical sketch, separate lists of works and articles, a quotation characterizing the subject, list of criticism, and references to the works in the table of abbreviations (p. xv-xxxiii). Index of names on a grid indicating area of specialty; index of names by province or territory. Useful reference work on an aspect of the prairies that is sometimes overlooked. — *LMcD*

BC59   Stouck, David, 1940– . - **Major Canadian Authors: A Critical Introduction**. - 2nd ed., 1988 - Lincoln, NE: Univ. of Nebraska Pr., 1988. - 330 p.; ill.

Class Numbers:
    Library of Congress PR9184.3
    ISBN 080324195X 0803291384 (pbk.)
    LCCN 87-38089
    Notes:
        1st ed.: Lincoln, NE: Univ. of Nebraska Pr., 1984
        Bibliography: p. [323]-324; index

• Stouck covers 18 of the most famous Canadian authors who write in English, only a few of whom are closely associated with the Prairie provinces. Entries are arranged chronologically by date of birth, beginning with Thomas Haliburton (b. 1796), continuing through Margaret Atwood (b. 1939). Of the 18, Sinclair Ross and Margaret Laurence are associated with the Plains of Saskatchewan and Manitoba, respectively, but many others have ties to Ontario, which verges on the plains. Absent are other notable writers of the Prairie provinces—e.g., Robert Kroetsch. Each entry contains a critical essay, a full-page photo of the author, and a short selective list of writings. — *MB*

BC60   Weiss, Allan Barry, comp. - **A Comprehensive Bibliography of English-Canadian Short Stories, 1950-1983.** - Toronto, ON: ECW Pr., 1989 (c1988). - 973 p.

Class Numbers:
    Library of Congress PR9192.52 Z1375
    ISBN 0920763677
    LCCN 89-157854
    Notes:
        Includes bibliographical references

• The compiler attempts to cite every appearance of every short story published by a Canadian during the 33-year period. The result is a substantial volume, which includes nearly 20,000 appearances of 14,314 short stories by just under 5,000 authors. Following a brief introduction wherein the compiler presents his methodology, there is a listing of the periodicals and collections cited. Most of the volume consists of citations to the stories, arranged alphabetically by author. The remainder of the volume is an alphabetical index of titles. Since references to the works of better-known authors are available elsewhere, the usefulness of this book is to provide access to lesser-known writers. Writers from the Prairie provinces are represented in direct correspondence to their productivity. — *MB*

Alberta

BC61   **Alberta Novelists.** - [Edmonton, AB]: Alberta Culture, Library Services, 1979. - 16 p.

Class Numbers:
    Library of Congress Z1392.A4
    OCLC 9280412
    LCCN 82-205312

• A brief inventory of 54 writers either residents of Alberta or with a substantial influence on the province. Familiar names include Robert Kroetsch, Nellie McClung, Edward McCourt, and George Ryga, as well as lesser-known novelists. Author arrangement followed by a list of novels. — *LMcD*

BC62   Reineberg Holt, Faye, ed. - **Alberta Plays and**

Playwrights: Alberta Playwrights' Network Catalogue. - Edmonton, AB: Jasper Printing Group, 1992. - 80 p.

Class Numbers:
    Library of Congress PR9198.2.A4
    National Library of Canada Z1377 D7
    ISBN 0969545908
    OCLC 35227142

• A guide to the Alberta theater scene. Arranged by playwright with brief biography, contact information, and list of plays. Each play has a plot summary and an indication of genre, audience, length, sets, and number of male and female characters. Production history includes theater, director, date, run, and awards. Title and genre indexes. Useful source for regional dramatic activity. — *LMcD*

Manitoba

BC63   **Books by Manitoba Authors: A Bibliography** / Manitoba Writers' Guild. - Winnipeg, MB: Manitoba Writers' Guild, 1986. - 88 p.

Class Numbers:
    Library of Congress Z1392
    National Library of Canada Z1392 M35
    ISBN 0969252501
    OCLC 17826805

• An annotated list of 148 books, works of the imagination as well as nonfiction, published 1972-1986. Title index uses a grid designating genre, locale, and level. None of the writers is included in *Manitoba Authors* (**BC64**). — *LMcD*

BC64   **Manitoba Authors = Écrivains du Manitoba.** - Ottawa, ON: National Library of Canada, 1970. - [122] p.; ill., ports.

Class Numbers:
    Library of Congress Z1392.M35
    OCLC 204707
    LCCN 70-855054

• The introduction to this catalog of an exhibition for the province's centennial gives an overview of the development of a distinctive body of Manitoba writing. Sections consist of significant examples of early printing, travel accounts, pioneer reminiscences, historical works, poetry, and prose. Annotations in English and French. — *LMcD*

Saskatchewan

BC65   Marchildon, Michel. - **Les publications littéraires francophones de la Saskatchewan.** - Régina, SK:

Commission culturelle fransaskoise, 1989. - 63 p.

Class Numbers:
    National Library of Canada PS9255.S3

• A preliminary effort to document the literary production of Francophone writers of Saskatchewan. Although the majority of the estimated 350 works included fall into expected genres such as novels, plays, and poetry, a substantial number are nonfiction and cover history, politics, religion, and other subjects. The final section lists translations and English works by francophones. Some entries have very brief annotations and author notes. The categories used to organize the bibliography are not particularly helpful, given the lack of a subject index. Some of the writers included appear to have a tenuous connection with Saskatchewan: Gabrielle Roy and Maurice Constantin-Weyer, for example, are more likely to be claimed by Manitoba. Caveats aside, the bibliography does serve a purpose in bringing together material that otherwise might be overlooked. — *LMcD*

BC66   Hodgson, Heather, ed. - **Saskatchewan Writers: Lives Past and Present**. - Regina, SK: Univ. of Regina, Canadian Plains Research Center, 2004. - 247 p.; ports. - (The Saskatchewan lives past and present series).

Class Numbers:
    Library of Congress PR9198.2.S2
    National Library of Canada PS8081.1
    ISBN 0889771634
    OCLC 56490524
    LCCN 2004-484828

• Biographical accounts of approximately 175 creative writers, residing in Saskatchewan or having a significant connection to the province, and with at least one book to their credit. Many of the sketches were written by the authors themselves, adding a welcome personal element and stylistic variation not always found in reference works. Instead of a formal bibliography of each author, the titles of major works are interwoven with the narrative. Most entries conclude with a statement on the art of writing as viewed by the individual author. A very useful source for Saskatchewan literature that would have been more useful if it had an index. — *LMcD*

BC67   Jain, Sushil Kumar. - **Saskatchewan in Fiction: A Bibliography of Works of Fiction about Saskatchewan & Fiction Written by Saskatchewanians**. - Regina, SK: Regina Campus Library, Univ. of Saskatchewan, 1966. - 20 leaves.

Class Numbers:
    Library of Congress Z1392.S2

OCLC 33256
LCCN 78-5954

• Brief unannotated bibliography; leaves 14-20 list Saskatchewan autobiographies. Dated but serviceable. — *LMcD*

BC68   Regina Book Festival Committee. - **Forty Saskatchewan Poets**. - Regina, SK: Regina Book Festival Committee, 1980. - 48 p.

Class Numbers:
    National Library of Canada PS8081
    OCLC 25442794

• Biographical sketches with bibliographies; useful for identifying some lesser-known regional writers. — *LMcD*

BC69   Saskatchewan Books!: A Selected Annotated Bibliography of Saskatchewan Literature. - Regina, SK: Saskatchewan Writers Guild, 1990. - 65 p.

Class Numbers:
    National Library of Canada Z1392 S27
    ISBN 0969038771
    OCLC 23652004
Notes:
    Cover title: *SWG presents Saskatchewan books!*

• Briefly lists both fiction and nonfiction. Arranged alphabetically with publication information, category (e.g., children's folklore) and audience level. Genre index. — *LMcD*

BC70   **Saskatchewan Literary Arts Handbook** / 4th ed. rev. and updated by Heather Wood. - Regina, SK: Saskatchewan Writers Guild, 1994. - 150 p.

Class Numbers:
    Library of Congress PN147
    ISBN 096903878X

• Aimed at writers both novice and experienced, the guide provides practical advice in areas such as manuscript submission, copyright, and marketing; educational opportunities (colleges, writers' colonies); financial assistance; and competitions. Includes lists of Saskatchewan and selected Canadian periodicals, publishers, media outlets, bookstores, and libraries. Much of the directory information is out of date and should be supplemented by later sources such as *Canadian Writer's Market* (Toronto: McClelland & Stewart, 2004; 16th ed.) — *LMcD*

BC71   Saskatchewan Writes!: A Learning Resource Guide about Saskatchewan Writers and their Works. -

Regina, SK: Saskatchewan Writers Guild, 1994. - 186 p.; ports.

Class Numbers:
   National Library of Canada PS8131.S2
   OCLC 56238746
Notes:
   Electronic book: http://www.skwriter.com/

• Directory of approximately 140 contemporary writers; indicates contact information, genres, publications, awards, and author availability. An index grid connects authors and genre, availability, and grade level. Intended for schools. The version on the Saskatchewan Writers Guild Internet site updates profiles and provides searching by location, type of writing, and willingness to participate in curricula, readings, panels, etc. — *LMcD*

INDIVIDUAL WRITERS

Kroetsch

BC72 University of Calgary. Libraries. Special Collections Division. - **The Robert Kroetsch Papers, First Accession: An Inventory of the Archive at the University of Calgary Libraries** / comp., Jean F. Tener, Sandra Mortensen, Marlys Chevrefils; eds., Jean F. Tener, Apollonia Steele; biocritical essay, Aritha van Herk. - Calgary, AB: Univ. of Calgary Pr., 1986. - xlvii, 371 p. - (Canadian archival inventory series; Literary papers, 3).

Class Numbers:
   Library of Congress PR9199.3.K7 Z6616.K712
   ISBN 0919813453 0585113777 (electronic bk.)
   OCLC 44958686
   LCCN 87-142964
Notes:
   Bibliography: p. xxxix; indexes
   Electronic book: http://www.netLibrary.com/urlapi.
      asp?action=summary&v=1&bookid=17539

• A detailed guide to the archives of the postmodern writer perhaps best known for works such as *The Studhorse Man* and *Gone Indian*. The collection encompasses Kroetsch's literary endeavors, 1945-1976, and consists of 1,873 items including correspondence, drafts, galleys, and reviews. Correspondence is arranged, for the most part, by the title of the work discussed, then by date; a summary accompanies each of the almost 1,000 letters. Manuscripts of fiction are arranged by form (anthologies, novels, poetry, etc.) and date; nonfiction manuscripts (speeches, essays, reviews) are listed by title. The final sections describe published works, miscellaneous items, interviews, and material by other writers. Title and name indexes; letters are indexed by both

recipient and date. An additional volume, implied by the title of the guide, has not yet appeared. — *LMcD*

Livesay

BC73 University of Manitoba Libraries. Dept. of Archives and Special Collections. - **The Papers of Dorothy Livesay: A Research Tool** / comp. by the staff of Dept. of Archives and Special Collections, Univ. of Manitoba Libraries. - [Winnipeg, MB]: Univ. of Manitoba, 1986. - xxviii, 419 p.; ill.

Class Numbers:
   Library of Congress PR9199.3.L56
   National Library of Canada PS8523
   ISBN 0919932231
   OCLC 17305492
Notes:
   Includes bibliographical references; index

• A detailed guide to the archives of the Canadian author and social activist. Descriptive essays helpfully introduce each section: personal papers, correspondence, and individual literary genres (poems, short stories, essays, etc.). Separate sections itemize photos, tapes, and the writer's own library. Appendixes describe Livesay holdings in other repositories, later additions to the collection not included in the main sequence, and other Prairie authors whose papers are also at the Univ. of Manitoba. Extensive index (p. 347-419). — *LMcD*

Mitchell

BC74 Latham, Sheila. - **W.O. Mitchell: An Annotated Bibliography**. - Downsview, ON: ECW Press, 1981. - p. 323-364.

Class Numbers:
   Library of Congress Z1392.M35
   National Library of Canada Z8581.53
   OCLC 15915439
Notes:
   Includes index
   Offprint from *Annotated Bibliography of Canada's Major
      Authors*, v. 3

• Latham lists, by genre, almost 270 works of the prolific Saskatchewan writer; despite extensive effort, the radio plays section is incomplete. (This area was later covered by T.J. Zeman's *An Annotated Bibliography of the Radio Drama of W.O. Mitchell in the Special Collections of the University of Calgary Libraries*, a 1993 master's thesis for the Univ. of Alberta.) Critical works, including theatrical reviews, are arranged by format. The bibliography is useful when supplemented by literary databases such as MLA. — *LMcD*

BC75   University of Calgary. Libraries. - **The W.O. Mitchell Papers: An Inventory of the Archive at the University of Calgary Libraries** / comp., Marlys Chevrefils ... [et al.]; ed., Jean F. Tener, Apollonia Steele; biocritical essay, Catherine McLay. - Calgary, AB: Univ. of Calgary Pr., 1986. - xxxix, 218 p.; ill. - (Canadian archival inventory series. Literary papers, 2).

Class Numbers:
    Library of Congress PR9199.3.M54Z6616.M643
    National Library of Canada PS8526 I9765
  ISBN 0919813488
  OCLC 19129211
  LCCN 87-208707

• Archival inventory for the author of the classic Saskatchewan novel *Who Has Seen the Wind* and numerous other works. An opening essay traces the centrality of the prairies throughout Mitchell's work. The guide organizes the 4,026 items in series: family papers, 1888-1977; scrapbooks, 1940-49; photographs, 1934-76; personal and business correspondence, 1942-77; manuscripts, 1942-77; published works, 1933-76; audiovisuals, 1953-74; works by other writers, 1945-77; and miscellaneous material, 1910-54. Indexes of Mitchell's works by title and genre; alphabetical and chronological lists of letters. General index. — *LMcD*

Ross

BC76   Latham, David. - **Sinclair Ross: An Annotated Bibliography**. - Downsview, ON: [ECW Press], 1981. - p. 365-395.

Class Numbers:
    Library of Congress Z8757.9
  OCLC 15941966
  Notes:
    Offprint from *Annotated Bibliography of Canada's Major Authors*, no. 3

• Latham's bibliography covers works by and about Ross, best-known for his prairie novels, including *As for Me and My House*. Criticism is arranged by form (books, articles, theses, interviews, book reviews) and date. The approximately 120 works provide a useful starting point, supplemented by databases such as MLA for later commentary. — *LMcD*

Ryga

BC77   University of Calgary. Libraries. Special Collections Division. - **The George Ryga Papers: George Ryga Fonds, Renée L. Paris Fonds, George Ryga & Associates Fonds: an**

Inventory of the Archive at the University of Calgary Library / comp., Juanita Walton and Sandra Mortensen; ed., Marlys Chevrefils and Apollonia Steele; biocritical essay, James Hoffman. - Calgary, AB: Univ. of Calgary Pr., 1995. - xl, 463 p.; facsims. - (Canadian archival inventory series, 13).

Class Numbers:
    Library of Congress PR9199.3.R9
    National Library of Canada PS8585
  ISBN 1895176662
  OCLC 33864115
  Notes:
    Electronic book: http://www.netLibrary.com/urlapi.asp?
      action=summary&v=1&bookid=17613

• The guide documents the career of Alberta-born Ryga, author of plays such as *The Ecstasy of Rita Joe* and works collected as *The Prairie Novels* (Vancouver, B.C.: Talonbooks, 2004). Organized by archival series: personal correspondence, 1944-87 and business correspondence, 1958-88; manuscripts, 1957-87; published works, 1958-87; audiovisuals, 1964-77; scrapbooks, 1961-69; works by other authors, 1966-88; and miscellaneous items. The guide also describes papers in the collections of Ryga's literary agents, arranged similarly. Title list and general index. — *LMcD*

Wiebe

BC78   University of Calgary. Libraries. - **The Rudy Wiebe Papers, First Accession: An Inventory of the Archive at the University of Calgary Libraries** / comp., Jean F. Tener, Sandra Mortensen, Marlys Chevrefils; ed., Jean F. Tener, Apollonia Steele; biocritical essay, J.M. Kertzer. - Calgary, AB: Univ. of Calgary Pr., 1986. - xxxiv, 328 p.; map. - (Canadian archival inventory series. Literary papers, no. 4).

Class Numbers:
    National Library of Canada Z8972.36
  OCLC 14937275
  LCCN 93-129288

• Begins with an overview of the background and literary career of Wiebe, whose works frequently examine Prairie and Mennonite themes. Correspondence, from 1959 to 1974, constitutes approximately half the 1,843 items; letters are arranged by correspondent, with summaries. The remainder of the collection is organized in series: early works, 1953-60; anthologies, 1970-74; novels, 1960-73, with related correspondence, galleys, proofs, and reviews; plays, 1975; and short stories, 1955-74. The final series consists of interviews and miscellaneous items. Title and name indexes; letter indexes, by correspondent and date. — *LMcD*

BD : Art and Architecture

Scope Includes all aspects of art (painting, sculpture, print-making, illustration, photography), architecture, and crafts.

United States

BD1   Dawdy, Doris Ostrander. - **Artists of the American West : A Biographical Dictionary**. - Chicago, IL : Sage Books, [1974]-c1985. - 3 v.

> Class Numbers:
>   Library of Congress N6536
> ISBN 0804006075 (v. 1)   0804003521 (v. 2)
>   0804008515 (v. 3)
> OCLC 1118680
> LCCN 72-91919
> Notes:
>   Includes bibliographies; index
>   Vol. 3 has imprint: Athens, OH: Swallow Pr., 1985
>   Vol. 3 has subtitle:
>   *A Biographical Dictionary of Artists Born Before 1900*

• Includes 4,100 painters, illustrators, or printmakers born before 1900 who worked west of the 95th meridian. Several hundred women artists have entries. Sources include *American Art Annual*, art directories, art periodicals, and the Inventory of American Painting and vertical files at the Smithsonian Institution. Entries vary greatly in length, but most include locations of works, years of residence at specific places, trips, exhibits, and citations to sources, and many are followed by a biographical sketch. Each volume has a bibliography, and since v. 2 and 3 are supplements, each has its own alphabetical sequence, but the index in v. 3 covers all three volumes. — *JD*

BD2   Ewers, John Canfield. - **Artists of the Old West**. - Garden City, NY : Doubleday, 1965. - 240 p. ; ill. (some col.), ports. (some col.).

> Class Numbers:
>   Library of Congress N6525
> LCCN 65-20054
> Notes:
>   Includes bibliographical references (p. 237-240)

• Ewers's book has chapters about 22 artists of the Old West, including George Catlin, Karl Bodmer, Alfred Jacob Miller, George Caleb Bingham, Albert Bierstadt, Frederic Remington, and Charles M. Russell; others are lesser-known. Reproductions of drawings and paintings dominate

the volume. Reproduction quality is not high, but many illustrations are in color. Of particular note, the chapter on artists of the Indian Wars of the Great Plains includes Remington and Theodore Davis. Rounding out the book is a short selective bibliography, but there is no index. — *MB*

BD3   Fees, Paul. - **Frontier America : Art and Treasures of the Old West from the Buffalo Bill Historical Center** / text and captions by Paul Fees and Sarah E. Boehme. - New York : The Buffalo Bill Historical Center in association with H.N. Abrams, 1988. - 128 p. ; ill. (some col.).

> Class Numbers:
>   Library of Congress N8214.5.U6
> ISBN 0810909480   093161824X (pbk.)
> OCLC 16873164
> LCCN 87-72421
> Notes:
>   Bibliography: p. 124-125; index

• The Buffalo Bill Historical Center (Cody, WY) is devoted to collections that chronicle the history and iconography of the American frontier. Fees (the Center's Curator) and Boehme (Whitney Gallery of Western Art) supply essays on the art, sculptures, and artifacts that helped shape a unique American identity during westward expansion. Bibliography of 23 reference works; illustrations include maps, paintings, and photographs. — *GK*

BD4   Joslyn Art Museum. - **Legacy of the West** / by David C. Hunt ; with a contribution by Marsha V. Gallagher. - Omaha, NE : Center for Western Studies, Joslyn Art Museum ; distr. by Univ. of Nebraska Pr., 1982. - 157 p. ; ill. (some col.).

> Class Numbers:
>   Library of Congress N8214.5.U6
> ISBN 0936364114   0936364084 (pbk.)
> OCLC 8533322
> LCCN 82-10109
> Notes:
>   Bibliography: p. 156; index
> Catalog of the collection of Western U.S. art, including
>   that of Native Americans, in the Joslyn   Art Museum
> Partially funded by InterNorth Art Foundation

• An exhibition catalog, *Legacy* is also a reference work that provides biographies of all the artists represented in the Joslyn's extensive collection of 19th-century art (it also includes a few 20th-century artists) depicting the trans-Mississippi West. Many of them lived or worked on the Great Plains, producing both art works and historical records. They included draftsmen and cartographers working for surveys or transcontinental railroads, correspondents for Eastern magazines or newspapers, some who accompanied early explorers, some who regarded themselves as naturalists or ethnographers, and artists trained in

European traditions. Entries cover the artists' lives, significant works, critical assessment, awards, exhibitions, and representation in collections. Since, as the foreword records, the artists inadvertently recorded their own cultural views, romanticizing and commercializing the West, *Legacy* acts as a resource for prevailing 19th-century views of the West. A separate section covers the many works of art depicting the West that were reproduced as prints or engravings. Ethnographic entries describe Indian clothing, basketry, and pottery. Excellent foreword; black-and-white and color reproductions. —*JD*

BD5   Kovinick, Phil. - **An Encyclopedia of Women Artists of the American West** / [by] Phil Kovinick and Marian Yoshiki-Kovinick ; foreword by William H. Goetzmann. - Austin, TX : Univ. of Texas Pr., c1998. - xxxv, 405 p. ; ill. - (American studies series).

Class Numbers:
    Library of Congress N8214.5.U6
ISBN 0292790635
OCLC 36621704
LCCN 97-3160
Notes:
    Includes bibliographical references (p. [393]-405)

• Many of the 1,000 women artists covered are from the Great Plains, or found the region a rich source of inspiration. The subjects are painters, sculptors, and graphic artists who had by 1980 produced works depicting the West, which the authors define as the 17 westernmost states. They come from the U.S. or elsewhere, some well-known and others lesser-known, both self-taught artists and professionals whose works have been exhibited, reproduced, or owned by important collections or museums. Entries appear in two sequences, both alphabetical; the first provides personal and professional information, selected lists of exhibitions, galleries currently showing their work, and references, and the second supplies briefer information about additional artists. The authors planned the encyclopedia as a starting point for considering male and female views of the West and for gender differences in portrayals of the West's diverse population. The early works complement women's diaries and letters that describe life of the early settlers. Includes numerous black-and-white reproductions and an extensive bibliography that cites easily accessible books and articles, archives, manuscripts, and ephemeral materials. Despite its inconvenient double entries, a unique contribution to the study of art of the American West. —*JD*

Site List 5
Arts Councils

Arts council Internet sites offer calendars of events, information about artists, directories, research links, and links to local arts organizations. In the U.S., arts councils generally deal with visual and performing arts, and Centers for the Book with written and book arts; in Canada, all arts activities fall within the scope of the arts councils. Internet sites for the National Endowment for the Arts (http://www.nea.gov) and the Canada Council for the Arts (http://www.canadacouncil.ca) offer links and directory information for affiliated arts councils.

UNITED STATES

Colorado Council on the Arts
    http://www.coloarts.state.co.us

Kansas Arts Commission
    http://arts.state.ks.us

Montana Arts Council
    http://www.art.state.mt.us

Nebraska Arts Council
    http://www.nebraskaartscouncil.org

New Mexico Arts
    http://www.nmarts.org

North Dakota Council on the Arts
    http://www.state.nd./us/arts

Oklahoma Arts Council
    http://www.state.ok.us/~arts

South Dakota Arts Council
    http://www.artscouncil.sd.gov

Texas Commission on the Arts TCAnet
    http://www.arts.state.tx.us

Wyoming Arts Council
    http://wyoarts.state.wy.us

CANADA

Alberta Foundation for the Arts
    http://www.cd.gov.ab.ca/all_about_us/
        commissions/arts

Manitoba Arts Council
    http://www.artscouncil.mb.ca

Saskatchewan Arts Board
    http://www.artsboard.sk.ca

BD6   Samuels, Peggy. - **The Illustrated Biographical Encyclopedia of Artists of the American West** / [by] Peggy and Harold Samuels. - Garden City, NY : Doubleday, 1976. - xxvi, 549 p. ; [40] leaves of plates, ill.

> Class Numbers:
>> Library of Congress N8214.5.U6
>
> ISBN 0385017308
> OCLC 2283728
> LCCN 76-2816
> Notes:
>> Includes bibliographical references (p. xv-xxvi)
>> Reprinted under title: *Samuels' Encyclopedia of Artists of the American West*. [Secaucus, NJ]: Castle Publ., 1985

• Supplies entries for more than 1,500 artists (principally painters) working in Canada or the U.S. by 1950, all of whom lived in the West at one time and created works with Western subjects. Many lived and worked west of the Rockies, but some depicted the Plains in a variety of genres and media. The authors arrange artists in nine categories: explorer artists, railway survey artists, post-Civil War correspondents, panoramic landscapists, pioneer artists, myth-makers (magazine artists, Remington, Russell), Taos sophisticates, cowboy artists, modernists. Plains artists include Karl Bodmer, who accompanied Prince Maximilian's 1833-34 Missouri River expedition, sketching and painting inhabitants and landscapes; Colorado artist Henry Farny, prolific illustrator for the 19th-century *Harper's Weekly*, whose drawings of Sitting Bull and the Ghost Dance were widely copied; and Eliza Pratt Greatorex, one of Colorado's first women professional artists. Entries include personal information, describe works, evaluate artists, and cite other biographical works. Intended for collectors, the encyclopedia gives sale prices. There are few entries for women or Indian artists. Includes reproductions of 300 works. — *JD*

Nebraska

BD7   Bucklin, Clarissa, ed. - **Nebraska Art and Artists**. - Lincoln, NE : School of Fine Arts, Univ. of Nebraska, [c1932]. - 82 p. ; ill. (incl. ports.).

> Class Numbers:
>> Library of Congress N6530.N2
>
> OCLC 6570019
> LCCN 32-34672

• This first published reference work on Nebraska artists supplies biographical information for 200 artists. The first two chapters provide brief art histories and biographical sketches for early deceased artists and for living artists. Some sketches are long, particularly those on early artists, and include partial lists of works. The following chapters describe four focal points of Nebraska art in the late 1800s and early 1900s: early art teachers at the Univ. of Nebraska, the state capitol building, the Joslyn Art Museum, and the Univ. of Nebraska School of Fine Arts. Final chapters cover art organizations, art in public schools, and art programs in colleges and universities. Index by artists' names and topics. The chapter on early artists by Martha Turner was later republished as *Early Artists in Nebraska*. — *JD*

BD8   Gustafson, Sharon L. - **Early Nebraska Women Artists : (1880-1950)**. - [Lincoln, NE : Univ. of Nebraska], 2000. - 55 leaves ; [13] leaves of plates. ill. (some col.).

> OCLC 45797987
> Notes:
>> Includes bibliographical references
>> Thesis (M.A.) — Univ. of Nebraska–Lincoln, 2000

• Gustafson's resource for Nebraska history, art history, and women's studies presents biographies of 12 women artists in Nebraska. Well-researched, concisely written, and heavily cited biographies provide personal details, critics' comments, commissions, exhibits, and current locations of works, and include Gustafson's appraisals of the artists' work. During compilation she consulted primary and secondary sources–articles, interviews, museum files, exhibition catalogs, letters, school records. An appendix reproduces a representative painting or mural by each artist. One of the few sources that focuses on early Nebraska artists. — *JD*

BD9   **Nebraska Arts Council [Internet Site]**. - Omaha, NE : Nebraska Arts Council, 2000?. - http://www.nebraskaartscouncil.org/

> Access Date: July 2005
> Fees: None

• Nebraska's dispersed rural population and numerous community groups make it difficult to identify local artists and art organizations. This Internet site makes an excellent starting point, offering a Nebraska Artists Directory that covers "all disciplines and fields of creative expression" (contact information, biographies, and summaries of works for some 150 artists, including a women's a capella vocal trio, an African dancer-drummer, a Native American appliqué specialist, a painter of historic sites), a directory of 50 town, county, and regional arts councils (with links to Internet sites), and "Resources" (links to arts societies, galleries, theaters, and museums). Also keeps an online calendar of arts and cultural events. — JD

BD10   Norwood, Tom. - **Contemporary Nebraska Art & Artists**. - [Omaha, NE : UNO Duplicating Services], 1977, c1978. - ca. 200 leaves ; ill.

Class Numbers:
    Library of Congress N6530.N2
OCLC 4036076
LCCN 78-103037
Notes:
    Research project funded by Committee for the
    Improvement of Instruction, Univ. of Nebraska-Omaha

• For 80 Nebraska artists, includes a black-and-white photo of the artist, a statement by the artist, preferred medium, education, exhibitions, awards and recognitions, and black-and-white reproductions of selected works. Selected by surveying Nebraska school and higher education personnel for names of local artists; those included represent several ethnic groups and work in a variety of media and genres. One of the few sources about Nebraska artists before the 1990s when arts information began to be disseminated over the Internet and by the Nebraska Arts Council. — *JD*

North Dakota

BD11 Barr, Paul Everett, 1892-1953. - **North Dakota Artists**. - [Grand Forks, ND] : Univ. of North Dakota Library, 1954. - 64 p. ; ill., ports. - (University of North Dakota. Library. Studies, 1).

Class Numbers:
    Library of Congress N6530.N9
LCCN 54-63075

• Forty-seven sculptors, illustrators, and painters, amateurs and professionals, who spent at least part of their lives in North Dakota are covered in this charming, earnest book. Many were also art educators, and some are regional artists, like John D. Allen, who specialized in Plains scenes. A few are prominent figures (Emile Walter accepted numerous international commissions). One little-known painter who traded or gave away his works, Thorarin Snowfield, was recently rediscovered and his works exhibited for the first time in 2004. Narratives of 200-400 words give personal information, art studies, artistic themes and influences, commissions, awards, exhibitions, and major works. Half the entries include a photograph of the artist's work or the artist at work. Sources of information are not given. Updated biographies of some of the artists can be found in *North Dakota Visual Artist Archive* (**BD12**), which used Barr's book as one of its sources. — *JD*

BD12 **North Dakota Visual Artist Archive [Internet Site]**. - Bismarck, ND : North Dakota Council on the Arts, 2000?-   . - http://www.state.nd.us/artist_archive/archive_home.htm

    Access Date: Feb. 2006
    Fees: None

• An official North Dakota state government site, NDVAA operates both to promote the artists themselves and as a historical register. Biographies of just over 100 artists (the site does not say, you have to count) can be browsed by artist's name from an alphabetic grid, time period, or by subject terms that cover media, schools, and related fields (music, literature). The time periods are: contemporary (currently living and working in the state); 1889 to the present (since statehood); before 1889; and "Just Passing Through" (travelers and brief residents). Media include glass, metal, painting, and wood; schools include abstract/experimental and traditional/folk; and related fields include dance and literature. Biographies supply personal history, training, artistic themes, genres, accomplishments, bibliographies, and lists of additional sources. Many entries have photographs of the artist or of works, and contact information is given for contemporary artists. Professional artists may register for inclusion. — *JD*

South Dakota

BD13 MacIntyre, Ron, comp. and ed. - **The Arts in South Dakota : A Selective, Annotated Bibliography** / comp. and ed. by Ron MacIntyre, Rebecca L. Bell. - Sioux Falls, SD : Augustana College, Center for Western Studies, 1988. - 282 p.

Class Numbers:
    Library of Congress NX510.S8
OCLC 18766642

• MacIntyre (Director, American Film and Video Association) offers a selected annotated bibliography of 1,103 entries. As part of the celebrations of the state's centennial (1989) this compilation was funded by the South Dakota Arts Council and the South Dakota Committee on the Humanities. The compilers defined South Dakota artists as individuals who were natives of the state, resided in South Dakota for one year or produced work related to the state, and made a significant contribution to the arts in South Dakota. The first section deals with general materials and with visual, literary, music, and performing arts, media, Native American arts, and education related to the arts. The second covers Dakota/Lakota resources for the visual arts, literature (bibliographies, anthologies, nonfiction, fiction, criticism, language), and music and dance. An appendix lists availability codes for holdings in South Dakota and out-of-state libraries. Indexes by title, author, and subject. — *GK*

BD14 **South Dakota Arts Council Directories [Internet Site]**. - Pierre, SD : South Dakota Arts Council, 2000?-   . - http://www.artscouncil.sd.gov/directories.htm

Access Date: Feb. 2006
Notes:
    Published annually in print, 1900s–
    Fees: None

• The Council's site focuses on nonprofit organizations in the arts, not individual artists. It lists art centers and galleries, dance organizations, literary societies, choral organizations, theater groups, Indian organizations, visual arts and crafts groups, municipal bands, community concert programs, and service organizations. Information is provided by the nonprofits themselves. Entries provide directory information (including e-mail addresses) and links to Internet sites. The Directories are accessed from a Council page that also links to an Arts Festival Directory and a Powwow schedule. — *JD*

BD15   South Dakota Memorial Art Center. - **Index of South Dakota Artists** / Joseph Stuart, ed. ; comp. and ed. by staff of the South Dakota Memorial Art Center of South Dakota State Univ., Brookings, 1972-1974. - Brookings, SD : South Dakota Memorial Art Center, [1974]. - 1 v. (loose-leaf).

    Class Numbers:
        Library of Congress N6530.S68
        OCLC 1093337
        LCCN 74-8832
    Notes:
        Includes bibliography

• A biographical directory of about 400 amateur and professional artists who were born in South Dakota, lived there a year or more, or contributed substantially to the state's art history. Information was drawn from questionnaires, interviews, published sources, and archival records. The brief biographies include birth and death dates, art study and training, works available in public collections, exhibitions, publications, and recognitions. Many entries are incomplete, and for any artist, only four exhibitions or recognitions may be listed. Artists vary from Ralph Blakelock, a self-taught artist whose works are found in major collections across the U.S., to Amos Bad Heart Bull, a late 19th-century tribal historian whose graphic work was published as *A Pictographic History of the Oglala Sioux* (Lincoln, NE: Univ. of Nebraska Pr., 1967) and to several later artists whose only showings were at state fairs. Lists the sources used to research deceased artists. The loose-leaf format allows easy updating, with one artist per page, but makes the book unwieldy. A unique compilation. — *JD*

Texas

BD16   Amon Carter Museum of Western Art. - **An American Collection : Works from the Amon Carter**

Museum / Patricia Junker [et al.] authors ; Will Gillham, general ed. - New York : Hudson Hills Pr. in association with the Amon Carter Museum ; distr. in U.S. : Lanham, MD : National Book Network, 2001. - 287 p. ; ill. (some col.).

    Class Numbers:
        Library of Congress N6510
        ISBN 1555951988
        LCCN 2001-24472
    Notes:
        Includes bibliographical references; index

• A chronological survey of the major works in the collection, including photographs, lithographs, paintings, and sculpture. Major works by Charles Russell, Frederic Remington, Karl Bohmer, Charles Dias, and Peter Rindisbacher are pictured, but the catalog surveys the entire range of American art. Two pages are devoted to each work, one page of description and analysis, the other the illustration. The introductory essay describes how Amon Carter's collection of Russells and Remingtons became the foundation for a major museum of American art. — *MS*

BD17   Cohen, Rebecca S. - **Art Guide Texas : Museums, Art Centers, Alternative Spaces, and Nonprofit Galleries**. - Austin, TX : Univ. of Texas Pr., 2004. - 464 p. ; ill.

    Class Numbers:
        Library of Congress N511.T4
        ISBN 0292712308
        LCCN 2003-25803
    Notes:
        Includes bibliographical references (p. [439]-441); index
        Table of contents: http://www.loc.gov/catdir/toc/
            ecip0411/2003025803.html

• Entries are organized regionally; materials relevant to the Prairies-Plains region will be found in the sections for North Central Texas, South Texas, Central Texas, Panhandle and Plains, and West Texas. Institutions included range from the Kimbell Art Museum in Fort Worth to the Buddy Holly Center in Lubbock. Entries provide location and contact information, admission fees, information about parking and access for the disabled, a brief history of the institution and a description of its notable holdings. Photographs of one or two notable holdings accompany the entries. Photographs of the museum building are provided for those institutions whose buildings are deemed architecturally significant. Quotations interspersed throughout the book are documented in endnotes. — *MS*

BD18   Fisk, Frances Battaile. - **A History of Texas Artists and Sculptors**. - Abilene, TX : F.B. Fisk, c1928, 1986.

    Class Numbers:
        Library of Congress N6530.T4

OCLC 2594008

LCCN 29-1015

Notes:

Reprinted in facsimile in 1986 by Morrison Books with a new table of contents and new index

• Limiting entries to Texas residents who worked between 1888 and the post-World War I era, Fisk provides information on over 300 primarily non-Native American painters and sculptors of portraits, landscapes, and historical events. The work begins with an introduction to early, middle, and late periods in Texas art history, arranging sketches by city or region, subdivided by period and subject matter and interspersed with explanatory text. Based on interviews with the artists, the entries are designed to inspire rather than evaluate. The new index by name in the reprint edition is a valuable addition. — *JD*

BD19   Grauer, Paula L., 1958-   , comp. - **Dictionary of Texas Artists, 1800-1945** / comp. by Paula L. Grauer and Michael R. Grauer. - College Station, TX : Texas A&M Univ., 1999. - 240 p. ; ill. (some col.). - (West Texas A&M Univ. series, 3).

Class Numbers:

Library of Congress N6530.T4

ISBN 0890968616

OCLC 40396670

LCCN 98-51603

Notes:

Includes bibliographical references (p. [229]-240)

• The compilers offer biographical sketches (some very brief) of about 2,000 artists who lived and exhibited in Texas before 1946. Interest in Texas artists grew in the last quarter of the 19th century, leading to the many state and local exhibitions that are the focus of this work. Heavily abbreviated entries give primary media, city of residence, birth date, birthplace, art studies, Texas exhibition venues and dates, locations of works, and sources. Many entries list only the artist's medium and exhibitions. A general list of sources, organized by material type, includes archival files, publications, correspondence, and exhibition catalogs. Tables show the artists' years of participation in 22 Texas art exhibits held 1945 or earlier. The 157 color plates of paintings in an appendix show primarily works by lesser-known artists. One of the few biographical reference works about Texas artists, this "dictionary" lacks detailed information, reflecting the large number of artists and the paucity of documentation. — *JD*

BD20   Powers, John E., 1935-   . - **Texas Painters, Sculptors & Graphic Artists : A Biographical Dictionary of Artists in Texas before 1942** / [by] John and Deborah Powers ; foreword by Ron Tyler. - Austin, TX : Woodmont Books, 2000. - 606 p.

Class Numbers:

Library of Congress N6530.T4

ISBN 0966962206

OCLC 44105253

LCCN 00-701390

• Identified from city directories, census documents, archival records, interviews, and published sources, the artists covered worked in Texas before World War II and either showed in formal exhibitions, had formal training, or advertised themselves as artists. Some produced works of historical or critical interest; many are classified as amateurs. Entries vary widely in length and information; some simply note an exhibition or residency. Others give alternate names, birth and death dates, residences, occupations, and media. Summary sketches of better-known artists include education and training, accomplishments, significant events, and excerpts or summaries of critical judgments. Sketches may be followed by lists of exhibitions, murals and collections, and professional art affiliations. The authors emphasize the Texas connections of very well-known artists like Frederic Remington. References pertaining to individual artists are cited in full in the entry, others in short form with full citation in an appendix. Other appendixes describe existing and defunct Texas art education institutions and Texas museums, art associations, and exhibitions. — *JD*

CANADA

See also Morcos, **Dictionnaire des artistes et des auteurs francophones de l'Ouest canadien, BC58**

Alberta

BD21   Baker, Suzanne Devonshire. - **Artists of Alberta**. - Edmonton, AB : Univ. of Alberta Pr., 1980. - 97 p. ; ill. (some col.).

Class Numbers:

Library of Congress N6546.A4

ISBN 0888640676

OCLC 6640394

LCCN 80-506356

Notes:

Electronic book: http://www.netLibrary.com/urlapi.asp?
action=summary&v=1&bookid=131086

• Handbook of 95 artists in the fields of painting, sculpture, printmaking, weaving, and mixed media; photography is excluded. Each artist receives a single page for biographical sketch, awards, exhibitions, summary of work, and contact information. The inclusion of a representative piece, chosen by the artist and usually in color, gives a sense of individual style and makes the book more than simply a directory. Not arranged alphabetically. — *LMcD*

Manitoba

BD22 Manitoba Society of Artists. - **The Manitoba Society of Artists : Artists Directory, a Directory of MSA Members from 1902-2003** / [research and data entry by Jaime Stoppler ; project manager and editor, Les W. Dewar]. – Winnipeg, MB : Manitoba Society of Artists, 2003. - 585 p.

    Class Numbers:
        National Library of Canada N55 C3
    ISBN 0973399007
    OCLC 54372108
    Notes:
        Includes bibliographical references and index

• Profiles of approximately 560 artists. Biographical information typically includes last known address, place and date of birth and death, and education, and summarizes professional affiliations, awards, commissions, and related professional activities. Entries note artistic medium used as well as a brief description of work, in many cases supplied by the artist. Indicates dealers and agents who have represented the artist. Selected exhibitions, divided between group/juried and solo, are listed in reverse chronological order and give title, sponsoring institution and location of each. Entries conclude with a bibliography of publications and reviews, also by date in reverse order. A very useful source covering a century of Manitoba art. — *LMcD*

Saskatchewan

BD23 **Biographical Dictionary of Moose Jaw Artists**. - Moose Jaw, SK : Moose Jaw Museum & Art Gallery, 2005. - 1 v. (loose-leaf) : ill. (some col.).

    Class Numbers:
        Library of Congress N6547 M663
    ISBN 0968400892
    OCLC 62129896
    Notes:
        Includes bibliographical references and index

• Handbook of artists who were either born in Moose Jaw, SK, or spent a major part of their artistic career there. Profiles include a biographical sketch, lists of solo and group exhibitions, awards, writings, selected works in collections, illustrations, works cited, and selected bibliography. Elaborates on the information found in *Biographical Dictionary of Saskatchewan Artists* (**BD24**). Periodic revi-

sions and additions are planned. In its design and presentation, the book is itself a work of art. — *LMcD*

BD24 Newman, Marketa, 1918-   , ed. - **Biographical Dictionary of Saskatchewan Artists** / comp. and ed. by Marketa Newman ; with the assistance of Eva Jana Newman. - Saskatoon, SK : Fifth House Pub., 1990-1994. - 2 v.

    Class Numbers:
        Library of Congress N6546.S2
        National Library of Canada N6546 S3
    ISBN 0920079660 (v. 10)   1895618452 (v. 2)
    OCLC 22279799
    LCCN 92-222851
    Notes:
        Contents: v. 1, Women Artists; v.2, Men Artists

• Newman (retired Fine Arts librarian, Univ. of Saskatchewan) covers 130 female and 189 male artists, either born in the province between 1872 and 1950 or with a significant role there. Painters, printmakers, sculptors, and installation artists are included; fiber artists, photographers, and ceramists are not. The biographical and professional information is conveniently organized in the manner of a résumé. Details include gallery dealers representing the artist, media and style, individual and collective exhibitions, major collections containing works, commissions, and selected bibliographies. A very useful source for identifying noteworthy figures in Saskatchewan art. — *LMcD*

Illustration

BD25 Dykes, Jeff, 1900–   . - **Fifty Great Western Illustrators : A Bibliographic Checklist**. - [Flagstaff, AZ] : Northland Pr., [1975] 1996. - 457 p. ; ill. (some col.).

    Class Numbers:
        Library of Congress N8214.5.U6   Z5965.W45
    OCLC 1601790
    LCCN 73-79780

• The 50 artists with whom Dykes is concerned worked from the early 19th century to the late 20th. Although all are known for Western themes, the checklist cites many kinds of illustrations; the entry for South Dakotan Harvey Dunn, for example, includes a cookbook, an edition of *A Tale of Two Cities*, and an image of a World War I sniper, besides Prairie illustrations. Entries, arranged alphabetically by artist, list books, pamphlets, separates, and dust jackets, and catalogs of museum exhibitions and gallery shows (a category sought by scholars but difficult to identify). Magazine illustrations and reprints are excluded. Books and articles about the artists are listed separately. Dykes based the checklist in part on his own collection, intending it for other collectors, but librarians, art historians, book historians, and historians of the West and the Plains will also find it useful. For the benefit of collectors, entries provide thorough physical descriptions of bindings, endpapers, editions, frontispieces, illustrations (for which page numbers are given), and one or two reproductions. — *JD*

Photography

BD26   Palmquist, Peter E. - **Pioneer Photographers from the Mississippi to the Continental Divide : A Biographical Dictionary, 1839-1865** / [by] Peter E. Palmquist, Thomas R. Kailbourn ; foreword by Martha A. Sandweiss. - Stanford, CA : Stanford Univ. Pr., 2005. - 742 p. ; ill.

> Class Numbers:
> Library of Congress TR139
> ISBN 0804740577   9780804740579
> OCLC 56334078
> LCCN 2004-19262
> Notes:
> Includes bibliographical references (p. 728-742)
> Table of contents: http://www.loc.gov/catdir/toc/ ecip0421/ 2004019262.html

• Palmquist and Kailbourn provide biographical sketches for a very large number of daguerrotypists, ambrotypists, and photographers, suppliers to the photographic trade, and persons active in trades or professions linked to photography, all of whom practiced their art, trade, or craft in the region between the Mississippi River and the Rocky Mountains, Mexico to Canada. The compilers define the region they cover as the Dakotas, Minnesota, Iowa, Nebraska, Missouri, Kansas, Arkansas, Oklahoma, Louisiana, Texas, Manitoba, Saskatchewan, and Mexico with the exception of Baja California. All the photographers and others had to have begun working in the region before Jan. 1, 1866, although the compilers attempt to give full coverage to post-1865 work where possible. Photographers range from the likes of Albert Bierstadt (who had photographic studios in Kansas, Nebraska, and Wyoming before turning his attention to painting and to the mountains) to obscure back-alley photographers who are mentioned in the directories, census records, or newspapers the contributors consulted. The biographies are often brief, sometimes a single sentence, but others run several columns, depending on the amount of information unearthed. Sketches give name, dates, specialty, where the practitioner was active, and source notes. Appendixes list photographic partnerships, companies, and galleries; panoramas, stereopticons, and other public presentations; women; workers known only as "artist"; and, highly important for Prairies-Plains research, geographic distribution. Reproductions of photographs are scattered throughout the biographies, many of them portraits, showing the subjects

staring into the camera, faces expressionless and unsmiling, as was the custom before fast film made the toothpaste smile possible and the influence of Hollywood stills made it mandatory. A fascinating glimpse into a trade that grew up with the West. — *RB*

BD27   Pearce-Moses, Richard, comp. - **Photographic Collections in Texas : A Union Guide**. - College Station, TX : publ. for the Texas Historical Foundation by Texas A&M Pr., 1987. - 381 p.

> Class Numbers:
> Library of Congress TR12
> ISBN 0890963517 (pbk.)
> LCCN 87-9979

• A union catalog of collections of photographs on a wide range of topics held by libraries in Texas. Arranged alphabetically by depository (of which the largest is the Harry Ransom Humanities Research Center at the University of Texas at Austin), the catalog is divided into abstracted collections (those which provided detailed information about their collections) and unabstracted collections (those which did not). A list called simply "Collections" arranges collections by the town or city where they are located. Indexes by place, personal name, photographer, and subject can help locate Texas Plains people, locales, and topics. In the abstracted section, the catalog gives for each depository: address and contact, purpose, hours, assistance, reproduction requirements, finding aids, bibliography (publications that reproduce materials from the collection), scope, geographic coverage, subjects, people represented in the collection, photographers, and record groups. — *RB*

ARCHITECTURE

General Works

BD28   Noble, Allen George, 1930- . - **Wood, Brick, and Stone : The North American Settlement Landscape** / drawings by M. Margaret Geib. - Amherst, MA : Univ. of Massachusetts Pr., 1984. - 2 v. ; ill.

> Class Numbers:
> Library of Congress NA703
> ISBN 0870234102 (v. 1)0870234110 (v. 2)
> LCCN 83-24110
> Notes:
> Contents: v. 1, Houses; v. 2, Barns and Farm Structures
> Electronic book: http://www.netLibrary.com/urlapi.asp? action=summary&v=1&bookid=35286
> Includes bibliographies; indexes

• An interesting set that studies the settlement landscape of

North America, Colonial times to the 1980s. Volume 1 supplies an overview and considers housing; v. 2 covers rural America, discussing barns, silos, and outbuildings. A section treats fencing, hedges, and walls. The final section, on settlement landscape, discusses cultural groups who immigrated to America and the building styles they brought with them. Each main section offers maps, photographs, drawings, and floor plans for many of the buildings. Of interest to Prairies-Plains researchers will be the sod houses, barns, outbuildings, fences, and cultural designs that dotted the region. — *JB*

UNITED STATES

BD29 Blumenson, John J.G., 1942–   . - **Identifying American Architecture : A Pictorial Guide to Styles and Terms, 1600-1945** / foreword by Nikolaus Pevsner ; with photos from the Historic American Buildings Survey ; commentary on the photos by David Paine. - Nashville, TN : American Association for State and Local History ; New York : Norton, 1981. - 118 p. ; ill.

Class Numbers:

Library of Congress NA705
ISBN 0393014282 (Norton)   0910050503 (pbk.)
LCCN 80-28103
Notes:
     Bibliography; index

• Blumenson's slim volume organizes architectural styles, such as Dutch Colonial, Italianate, and Bungalow, by related motif rather than chronological or geographical factors. Geography and time period are nonetheless important. Blumenson shows that American architecture was a continuation of European patterns: Spanish Colonial began on the West Coast and moved east, and English Colonial began on the East Coast and moved west. Alterations and combinations of these styles and others, often nearly unrecognizable, can be found in the Great Plains today. Each style is illustrated by two to four photographs of buildings (most are homes but some are public buildings). Entries supply a brief description, dates of popularity, and a list of common features keyed to the photographs. "Pictorial Glossary of Terms" illustrates types of orders (columns), roofs, chimneys, gables, porches, porticos, entrances, doors, windows, wall finishes, and moldings. Portions and subtypes are defined and keyed to photographs. Much information is packed into this field guide for tourists, travelers,

Site List 6
Offices of Historic Preservation

In the United States, historic preservation offices offer local histories, images, and registers of historic sites and buildings, and information about standards, projects, and grants. Offices are distinct units, often connected to state historical societies, park services, or state museums; all are accessible from the National Council of State Historic Preservation Offices, http://www.ncshpo.org/stateinfolist/. Canadian offices vary more widely in structure.

United States

Colorado Office of Archaeology and Historic Preservation. [Colorado Historical Society]
     http://coloradohistory-oahp.org

Kansas Historic Preservation Office
     http://www.kshs.org/resource/shpohome.htm

Montana State Historic Preservation Office
     http://www.montanahistoricalsociety.com/shpo

Nebraska State Historic Preservation Office
     http://www.nebraskahistory.org/histpres

New Mexico Historic Preservation Division
     http://www.nmhistoricpreservation.org

North Dakota Historic Preservation
     http://www.state.nd.us/hist/ahp.htm

Oklahoma State Historic Preservation Office
     http://www.ok-history.mus.ok.us/shpo/shpom.htm

South Dakota Historic Preservation Office
     http://www.sdhistory.org/HP/histpres.htm

Texas Historical Commission
     http://www.thc.state.tx.us

Wyoming State Historic Preservation Office
     http://wyoshpo.state.wy.us

Canada

Alberta Historical Resources Foundation
     http://www.cd.gov.ab.ca/preserving/heritage/ahrf

Manitoba Historical Society Historic Preservation Committee
     http://www.mhs.mb.ca

Saskatchewan Culture Youth and Recreation Heritage Resources Branch
     http://www.cyr.gov.sh.ca/heritage.html

students, and other nonprofessionals. Index of terms; bibliography. Most photographs are taken from the Library of Congress' Historic American Building Survey but are unidentified. — *JD*

BD30 Longstreth, Richard W. - **The Buildings of Main Street : A Guide to American Commercial Architecture**. - Updated ed. - Walnut Creek, CA : AltaMira Pr., 2000. - 154 p. ; ill. - (American Association for State and Local History book series).

> Class Numbers:
> Library of Congress NA6212
> ISBN 0742502791
> OCLC 44510458
> LCCN 00-22384
> Notes:
> Includes bibliographical references (p. 135-145); index
> Originally published: Washington, D.C. : Preservation Pr., 1987

• A typology of American commercial building façades beginning in the 19th century when distinctive commercial styles developed and commerce centered on Main Street. Longstreth believes that main streets everywhere share the same elements; regional differences lie in materials, motifs, and frequency of building types. Well-preserved main streets in the Plains states can thus be used to study local and national history, building construction, economics, and city planning. The typology, developed to support preservation efforts, is based on structure of the façade. Two broad categories encompass ten types, six characterized by division of the façade into horizontal zones, and four featuring an arrangement of major elements, such as columns and vaulted openings. An 11th type has neither zones nor major design elements. The 11 types show variations in scale and decoration. Entries for each type explain the primary characteristics, origin, development and decorative elements. The text is keyed to photographs of designed and vernacular buildings, chiefly retail stores, banks, offices, hotels, and theaters. Buildings peripheral in style or location, such as railroad stations, gas stations, and motels, are excluded. Captions give building name, date of completion, architect, and location. An epilogue discusses postwar design changes. Appendixes include a glossary; contemporary and period sources for further reading; preservation, building trade, and other organizations; and an index of places, building names, architects, and building uses. — *JD*

BD31 Short, Charles Wilkins, 1884-1954. - **Public Buildings : A Survey of Architecture of Projects Constructed by Federal and Other Governmental Bodies between the Years 1933 and 1939 with the Assistance of the Public Works Administration** / by C.W. Short, R. Stanley-Brown. - Washington, DC : Public Works Administration ; U.S. Govt.

Print. Off., 1939. - xxiii, 697 p. ; ill.

> Class Numbers:
> Library of Congress NA4298
> Government Document FW 5.2:P 96/2
> LCCN 40-26196
> Notes:
> Index
> Reprinted: New York : Da Capo Pr., 1986; ISBN 0306802651 (pbk.)

• Chosen for their architectural or engineering interest from over 15,000 federal and nonfederal projects financed with federal funds and substantially completed by the end of 1938, 620 projects from the building boom are described. Plains projects include the "Sonotorium," an open air theater in Kearney, NE; the Municipal Auditorium in Oklahoma City; and the Alcova Dam in Wyoming. Projects are arranged in 24 categories by type (e.g., libraries, elementary schools, jails and penal institutions, sewage-disposal plants, dams, post offices, housing projects). Each project entry has a black-and-white photograph, a blueprint, and a description that gives name, location, purpose, building materials, dimensions, completion date, and cost. A self-congratulatory introduction provides useful information on the policies and accomplishments of the PWA and the architectural qualities of the buildings. Statistics on number, costs, labor, and types of projects are included. Indexed by city, state, and building type. — *JD*

BD32 Upton, Dell, ed. - **America's Architectural Roots : Ethnic Groups that Built America**. - New York : Preservation Pr., 1986. - 193 p. ; ill. - (Building watchers series).

> Class Numbers:
> Library of Congress NA705
> ISBN 0891331239 (pbk.)
> LCCN 86-25165
> Notes:
> Bibliography: p. 169-176; index
> Table of contents: http://www.loc.gov/catdir/toc/onix02/95046054.html

• Upton shows the ways ethnicity was expressed in American architecture through the early 20th century, focusing on 22 immigrant groups who reproduced their native buildings and adapted their cultural traditions to new resources, climates, and landscapes. Three sections, all alphabetically arranged, cover different periods of immigration. The first, covering Native Americans and Native Hawaiians, includes the grass thatched houses, earth lodges, hide tepees, and cypress-palmetto leaf houses of the Plains Indians. The second deals with groups who immigrated in great numbers before the Revolutionary War. The third treats groups who immigrated after the Revolution, mostly between the Civil War and World War I, and includes the styles brought to the Plains by Scandinavians, Czechs, and Germans from Russia. Entries have drawings, photographs, and detailed descriptions of immigrants, architectural traditions, and individual buildings. The introduction discusses the methodology used to classify people and architectural traditions. Both a reading list and a list of additional information sources (e.g., historical preservation offices, historical societies, archives) are categorized by ethnic group. The size and shape of the book show it is intended as a field guide, but it is a good beginning resource for researchers in anthropology, sociology, architectural history, and social history. — JD

Colorado

BD33　Guide to Colorado's Historic Architecture and Engineering [Internet Site]. - Denver, CO : Colorado Historical Society. Office of Archaeology and Historic Preservation, 2003. - http://www.coloradohistory-oahp.org/guides/architecture/archindex.htm

> OCLC 52075363
> Access Date: Feb. 2006
> Notes:
> > Originally publ. as: *A Guide to Colorado Architecture* / written and prepared by Sarah J. Pearce with contributions by Merrill A. Wilson. [Denver, CO]: State Historical Society of Colorado, 1983
> > This 2nd ed. revised and expanded with contributions by Thaddeus Gearhart, Chris Geddes, Lyle Hansen, Dale Heckendorn, and Holly Wilson
> Fees: None

• Designed to provide standard terminology for surveyors for the Colorado Inventory of Cultural Resources (access to CICR is available at the Office of Archaeology and Historic Preservation). Entries are pdf files that describe traditional Colorado materials (adobe, log, sod), styles (craftsman, Queen Anne, rustic), forms (basement, ranch, early high rise), and special use (gas stations, barns, bridges). Entries give history and description of the type of structure including subtypes and a numbered list of common elements. Photographs of unidentified buildings show the common elements in place. The guide includes suggested readings; hard copy is available from the Society. It will be useful to writers, students, and researchers in identifying and describing Colorado buildings and common architectural features. — JD

BD34　Historical Guide to Colorado Architects [Internet Site]. - Denver, CO : Colorado Historical Society. Office of Archaeology and Historic Preservation, 2000s–　. - http://www.coloradohistory-oahp.org/guides/architects/architectindex.htm

> OCLC 50413055

Access Date: Feb. 2006
Fees: None

• Includes 45 professional architects, landscape architects, engineers, and designers who practiced in Colorado after 1860. Entries, alphabetical by name, are not searchable. Biographical sketches, which include birth and death dates, dates of practice, dates with specific firms, and bibliographies of sources, vary in length. Sketches also give lists of accredited buildings, structures, and other sites that include locations, dates, and assessment (i.e., presence in a historic register or district). Information on accredited buildings is usually drawn from agency files and nominations for historic registers. The URL may not be recognized, but the site can be reached through the Colorado Office of Archaeology and Historic Preservation site (http://www.coloradohistory-oahp.org/); see Site List 6, Offices of Historic Preservation. — JD

BD35　Noel, Thomas Jacob. - Buildings of Colorado. - New York : Oxford Univ. Pr., 1997. - 669 p. ; ill. - (Buildings of the United States).

> Class Numbers:
> > Library of Congress NA730.C6
> ISBN 0195090764
> LCCN 97-12674
> Notes:
> > Includes bibliographical references (p. 605-611); index

• Colorado is the only Plains state covered in this important series, which has never been completed. The Colorado volume features public buildings, and a few significant private ones, representative of Colorado's varied architecture. The state is divided into four regions based on major river basins—South Platte, Arkansas, Rio Grande, and Colorado—subdivided by county and community. Larger cities are subdivided by neighborhood. Ghost towns are included. Introductions to each region and county give brief histories, architectural summaries, and detailed maps. Community entries give date of first post office, altitude, history, and a map. Sites in each community are listed in walking or driving tour order. Building entries give a site number keyed to the maps, current name, earlier names, completion date, architects or builders, any designation in the National Register of Historic Places or National Register District, a description, and sometimes a photograph. Includes a bibliography, a glossary with lengthy definitions, and a through index by place, person, and building. — JD

Kansas

BD36　Grant, H. Roger, 1943-　. - Kansas Depots. - Topeka, KS : Kansas State Historical Society, 1990. - 117 p. ill.

Class Numbers:
   Library of Congress TF302.K2
   ISBN 087726097
   LCCN 90-61325
   Notes:
      Index

• Railroad lines had a role in settling the Plains, and the locations of lines determined prosperity. As depots became centers of activity, depot architecture developed. According to Grant, early Plains depots, unlike those in other parts of the U.S., were cheap, simple, wooden, and standardized. In the bigger cities, railway lines later erected elaborate depots in distinctive styles. Grant presents both types. Following an excellent introduction to Plains depot and railroad history, he lists depots by railway–Santa Fe, Missouri Pacific, Union Pacific, Rock Island, Frisco, Katy, and Chicago, Burlington & Quincy–evaluating each railway's depot history and style, and illustrating the text with photographs, drawings, and blueprints. Indexes by city name and topic. —*JD*

BD37   Sachs, David H. - **Guide to Kansas Architecture** / [by] David H. Sachs & George Ehrlich. - Lawrence, KS : Univ. Pr. of Kansas, 1996. - 349 p. ill.

   Class Numbers:
      Library of Congress NA730.K2
      ISBN 0700607773
      LCCN 95-49204
      Notes:
         Includes bibliographical references (p. 333-336); index

• Intending to give a representative picture of Kansas architecture, the authors select churches, barns, businesses, public buildings, architect-designed homes, vernacular homes, bridges, cemeteries, and other structures, all considered to have architectural, historical, or cultural merit. They were chosen from the National Register of Historic Places, the Kansas State Register, architectural publications, architectural awards, the authors' files, and recommendations by archivists, preservationists, historians, and others. A well-written introduction discusses the historical and environmental factors that affect Kansas architecture and gives an overview of Kansas architects and architectural trends. Entries are organized by seven geographical regions, then by county and city, each introduced with a summary of development and a map. Each entry is assigned an alphanumeric code keyed to the map, a photograph, construction dates, architects, address, and architectural style. The text gives a brief description of the building, its importance, history of ownership, and use. A selected bibliography is divided into local Kansas references, general Kansas references, and general architectural references. Two indexes, by architect and builder and by style, place, and type of structure. —*JD*

Nebraska

BD38   Nebraska Historic Buildings Survey [Internet Site]. - Lincoln, NE : Nebraska State Historical Society, 2000s–   . - http://www.nebraskahistory.org/histpres/nehbs.htm

   Access Date: Dec. 2005
   Fees: None

• Part of the Society's Internet site, NHBS catalogs historical buildings in the state, both those extant and those no longer standing. The site has two sections, "Thematic Surveys" (which has only a single entry, "Nebraska Historic Highway Survey") and "County Survey Reports," a thorough review and catalog of historic buildings in each county, with descriptions of historic buildings and many photographs. Entries for most counties are not up and running (only 14 at present out of 93), but what the site offers will be useful to students of Nebraska history and more tangentially to students of Plains history. — *RB*

Oklahoma

BD39   Oklahoma State Univ. School of Architecture. - **Oklahoma Landmarks : A Selection of Noteworthy Structures** / prepared by the School of Architecture, Oklahoma State Univ. - Stillwater, OK : Dept. of Publ. and Printing, Oklahoma State Univ., 1981. - 1 v. (unpaged) ; ill., map.

   Class Numbers:
      Library of Congress F695
      LCCN 67-65736
      Notes:
         "Exhibition prepared by F. Cuthbert Salmon, Cecil D. Elliott [and] Coy V. Howard; photography by James R. White [et al.] . . . Text by Cecil D. Elliott."

• One hundred fifty residences and public buildings were chosen to represent a full range of times and places. All were considered to be "authentic and complete" and to be of historical or architectural interest. They include Native American homes and ritual structures of grass, wood and skin; sod and wood homes of the first European settlers; early public buildings with a Southern style; Victorian, craftsman, cottage and modern styles built as the state prospered; and two buildings designed by Frank Lloyd Wright, a rarity in the Plains states. The entries are arranged county by county with the address, a brief description, and the name of the architect. An outline map of the counties is useful for travelers. A separate section with photographs of 65 of the buildings organized in chronological order by date of construction provides a visual overview of development. Though some structures may no longer exist and others may have been discovered, this remains a useful resource on state and architectural history. — *JD*

South Dakota

BD40   Erpestad, David. - **Building South Dakota : A Historical Survey of the State's Architecture to 1945** / by David Erpestad and David Wood. - Pierre, SD : South Dakota State Historical Society Pr., 1997. - 246 p. ; ill. - (Historical preservation series, v. 1).

Class Numbers:
    Library of Congress NA730.S9
    ISBN 0962262129
    LCCN 97-7336
    Notes:
        "Published in celebration of the pioneering work of the State Historical Preservation Office and the 25th anniversary of the South Dakota Humanities Council."
        Includes bibliographical references (p. 215-228); index

• Erpestad (historic restoration architect) and Wood (professional writer, both Minneapolis), in a work funded by the National Park Service, trace South Dakota's early architectural heritage. Chapters describe Native American shelters, fur trading posts, military forts, homes, churches, schools, parks, and industrial and commercial buildings. Includes 325 color and black-and-white photographs. — *GK*

BD41   Erpestad, David. - **A Guide to Building Records in South Dakota** / [by] David Erpestad, Carolyn Torma, David Wood. - 1984 ed. - Vermillion, SD : Historical Preservation Center ; Sioux Falls, SD : Siouxland Heritage Museum, 1984. - 39 p.

Class Numbers:
    Library of Congress F646   Z1335
    LCCN 85-621131
    Notes:
        Includes bibliographical references (p. 11-32)

• Erpestad (historic restoration architect), Wood (professional writer, both Minneapolis), and Torma (Historical Preservation Center, Vermillion, SD) provide a guide to help engineers, curators, and restoration specialists find information on professionally designed buildings in South Dakota. The title contains general works and publications about South Dakota architecture. One section reprints an index of 500 names attributed to early structures in the state. The last two chapters list the locations of archives or libraries that hold book or manuscript collections for researchers interested in architectural history. — *GK*

Texas

BD42   Kelsey, Mavis Parrott, 1912- . - **The Courthouses of Texas : A Guide** / by Mavis P. Kelsey Sr. and Donald H. Dyal ; photographs by Frank Thrower. - 2nd ed. - College Station, TX : Texas A&M Univ. Pr., 2007. - 334 p. ; col. ill. - (TAM travel guides).

Class Numbers:
    Library of Congress NA4472.T4
    ISBN 1585445495   9781585445493
    OCLC 70230661
    LCCN 2006-21197
    Notes:
        Includes bibliographical references (p. 313-315) ; index
        Table of contents: http://www.loc.gov/catdir/toc/ ecip0616/2006021197.html

• Each of Texas' 254 county courthouses is represented by a full-page entry with a color photograph, history, description, location, and colorful notes. New photographs and other material document recent restorations and update the original guide (1993). Kelsey's introductory "Personal Tour" highlights the intertwining stories of counties and courthouses. Appendixes include a list of county seats and counties, along with essays on the naming of Texas counties, the lives of those honored by county names, and the naming of county seats. Subject and name index. A guidebook, coffee table book and history text for Texas historians, travelers, and students of public architecture. — *JD*

Wyoming

BD43   Starr, Eileen F., 1953– . - **Architecture in the Cowboy State, 1849-1940 : A Guide** / with foreword by David Kathka ; photographs by Richard Collier ; drawings by Jamie Wells and Herbert E. Dawson. - Glendo, WY : High Plains Pr., 1992. - 199 p. ; ill.

Class Numbers:
    Library of Congress NA730.W8
    ISBN 093127107X (pbk.)
    LCCN 92-4701
    Notes:
        Includes bibliographical references (p. 190-195); index

• Written to encourage preservation, Starr's work examines Wyoming structures as architecture and as representations of social history, exploring these themes in opening chapters on the real versus mythical Western building and on Wyoming architectural style as the confluence of landscape and culture. Specific buildings illustrate two separate analyses of Wyoming architecture: by design and construction (architect-designed, manufactured, and folk) and by theme (agriculture, commercial, government, military, railroad, religious, residential, and tourism). Buildings chosen are those that have changed little, hence are easily photographed. Only exteriors are examined. Distinctive buildings include extravagant oil boom homes, farm buildings by Scandinavian stonemasons, wagons used as shelter for sheepherders, public projects of the WPA and CCC, and false front commercial buildings of the gold rush era. A separate section profiles architects and architectural firms. Instructions for the systematic description of structures, a glossary of terms, diagrams of common Wyoming architectural elements, suggested readings, and a minimal index end the work. Profusely illustrated with photographs and drawings. — *JD*

CANADA

Alberta

BD44 White, Anthony G. - **Canadian Architecture, Alberta : A Selected Bibliography**. - Monticello, IL. : Vance Bibliographies, 1990. - 8 p. - (Architecture Series. Bibliography, A 2293).

Class Numbers:
Library of Congress Z5942
National Library of Canada Z5944 C3
ISBN 0792004434
OCLC 15806906
LCCN 90-196753

• Brief listing of about 115 items, mostly articles, with some general books included. White also compiled the related *Architecture of Calgary, Alberta, Canada: A Selected Bibliography* (Monticello, IL: Vance Bibliographies, 1987), 50 items in the same format. Neither work has a subject index. — *LMcD*

Manitoba

BD45 Wade, Jill, 1942– , comp. - **Manitoba Architecture to 1940 : A Bibliography**. - Winnipeg, MB : Univ. of Manitoba Pr., 1976. - 109 p. ; [8] leaves of plates, ill.

Class Numbers:
Library of Congress Z5944.C3   NA746.M36

ISBN 0887551165
OCLC 5754084
LCCN 80-457437
Notes:
Includes indexes

• A historical approach to the architecture of Manitoba consisting of 747 items. Books are arranged by author or title, but articles are listed chronologically. A separate section lists special materials such as building plans and photographic collections. Some entries indicate specific buildings and their architects. Separate indexes for architect, building, and subject. Buildings can be searched by architect, name, place, type, or date. Twenty-seven black-and-white plates of noteworthy structures. Partially updated by Anthony G. White's Canadian Architecture, Manitoba: A Selected Bibliography (Monticello, IL: Vance Bibliographies, 1990.) — *LMcD*

Saskatchewan

BD46 White, Anthony G. - **Canadian Architecture, Saskatchewan Province : a Selected Bibliography**. - Monticello, IL : Vance Bibliographies, 1990 1996. - 5 p. - (Architecture series. Bibliography, A-2314).

Class Numbers:
Library of Congress Z5942
National Library of Canada Z5944 C3
ISBN 0792004647
OCLC 21144855
LCCN 90-194850

* An author list of approximately 60 items, some of which are rather general. The brief introduction gives a geographical and cultural context for the work. Similar in approach to the compiler's bibliographies on the architecture of Alberta (**BD44**) and Manitoba (mentioned at **BD45**). — *LMcD*

BE : Performing Arts

Scope   Lists works having to do with music, theater, film, and radio and television.

MUSIC

General Works

BE1   The Handbook of Texas Music / editorial board, Roy R. Barkley [et al.]. - Austin, TX : Texas State Historical Association in cooperation with the Center for Studies in Texas History at the Univ. of Texas at Austin, 2003. - 393 p. ; ill.

> Class Numbers:
> Library of Congress ML106.U4
> ISBN 0876100932
> LCCN 2003-12756
> Notes:
> Includes bibliographical references; indexes

• A handbook that covers all things musical in Texas—musicians born in Texas, music organizations, music industry personalities. Hence it has entries for Blind Lemon Jefferson, Bob Wills, Selena, the Dallas Opera, and Norman Petty, but it also includes musicians who have spent portions of their careers in the state, and institutions or places connected to music—Clifton Chenier (Louisiana Cajun in Houston), Gruene Hall (German dance hall), and Willie Nelson's Fourth of July Picnic. Entries are arranged alphabetically. Only deceased musicians have biographical articles, but many living musicians are discussed in topical articles; all are easy to locate in the subject index. Articles are signed, vary in length, and include brief bibliographies. Roster of contributors. — *JB*

BE2   Kallmann, Helmut, ed. - **Encyclopedia of Music in Canada** / ed. by Helmut Kallmann and Gilles Potvin ; Robin Elliott (English style), Mark Miller (Jazz and English-language pop music), associate eds. - 2nd ed. - Toronto, ON ; Buffalo, NY : Univ. of Toronto Pr., 1992. - 1524 p. ; ill.

> Class Numbers:
> National Library of Canada ML106 C3

> OCLC 27725769
> LCCN 93-109483
> Notes:
> 1st ed.: Toronto, Ont.; Buffalo, NY: Univ. of Toronto Pr., 1981
> Electronic book: http://www.collectionscanada.ca/emc/index-e.html

• Covers all facets of Canadian music. Although the Prairies do not receive collective treatment, among the 3,800 signed articles are articles on the musical history of individual prairie cities. Performers, composers, orchestras, choirs, festivals, and all manner of organizations are included. Entries frequently include both bibliographies and discographies. A revision of the second edition is in progress at the *Historica* Internet site (http://thecanadianencyclopedia.com) and contains more than 4,000 entries. The subject index is skeletal but the full text search capability substantially improves the usefulness of the encyclopedia for locating Prairie content. — *LMcD*

BE3   The New Grove Dictionary of American Music / ed. by H. Wiley Hitchcock and Stanley Sadie. - New York : Grove's Dictionaries of Music, 1986. - 4 v. ; ill.

> Class Numbers:
> Library of Congress ML101.U6
> ISBN 0943818362
> LCCN 86-404
> Notes:
> Includes bibliographies

• Hitchcock and Sadie celebrate the musical scene in North America, emphasizing classical music but including popular, jazz, Broadway, and numerous other means of musical expression, especially ethnomusicology. Locating a Prairies-Plains musical presence in a work of this size that is devoted to music of all kinds can challenge researchers; but the editors include entries for ethnomusicology, for European-American music (European traditions practiced by North American immigrants such as Scandinavians), "Indians, American" (with a section for the Plains), individual peoples (e.g., Sioux), composers whose work has gained identification with Plains subjects (Virgil Thomson, Copland), musical life in individual cities (Omaha, Tulsa), composer-musicologist Thurlow Lieurance, the polka (and Lawrence Welk). The search is not made easier by the absence of any index, but entries are arranged alphabetically and cross-references are ample. Most articles end with bibliographies that for major figures or topics can be very full, often listing compositions as well as publications. As with all the Sadie-Grove collaborations, scholarship is impeccable and the bibliographies and cross-reference structure can lead in unexpected directions. Nevertheless, use for Prairies-Plains research will depend on initial work in other sources. — *RB*

Ethnomusicology

BE4   Burr, Ramiro. - **The Billboard Guide to Tejano and Regional Mexican Music**. - New York : Billboard Books, 1999. – 256 p. ; ill.

> ISBN 0823076911
> LCCN 8-51910
> Notes:
>> Includes bibliographies; index

• *Tejano* music, rooted in the traditional Mexican rancheras, polkas, and cumbias, updates the sound with blues, pop, and country. This volume provides introductory essays on the history, cultural influence, and industry of the music. The principal part consists of biographies of individual performers and groups, covering well-known musicians such as Rubin Ramos (pioneer of *Tejano* music), Mariachi Cuarteto Coculense (first recorded Mariachi group), Flaco Jimenez, less familiar names (Los Lobos, Tish Hinojosa, Selena), and local favorites–e.g., the Hometown Boys. The last section gives a "Tex-Mex Chronology" of highlights in the industry movement, top ten lists, and glossary. Regrettably, coverage stops with 1999, so does not include current crossover groups such as the Los Lonely Boys. For researchers studying the influences of culture groups in the southern Plains. — *JB*

BE5   **The Garland Encyclopedia of World Music** / advisory eds., Bruno Nettl and Ruth M. Stone ; founding eds., James Porter and Timothy Rice. - New York : Garland, 1998-2002. - 10 v. ; ill., maps ; 9 sound discs.

> Class Numbers:
>> Library of Congress ML100
> ISBN 0824060350 (v. 1)0824049470 (v. 2)
>> 0824049446 (v. 3)   0824060407   (v. 4)
>> 0824049462 (v. 5)   0824060423 (v. 6)
>> 0824060415 (v. 7)   0824060342 (v. 8)
>> 0824060385 (v. 9)   0815310846 (v. 10)
> LCCN 97-9671
> Notes:
>> Includes bibliographical references, discographies, filmographies, indexes

• Of the ten volumes in this set, which attempts to cover music practiced by all the peoples of the world, the most useful for Prairies-Plains research will be volumes 3 (United States and Canada) and 10 (general perspectives and reference sources). The emphasis in all ten volumes rests on ethnomusicology. Volume 3 has three sections (as do all the volumes): a summary, "The United States and Canada as a Musical Area," "Music in Social and Cultural Contexts," and the largest section, "Musical Cultures and Regions." Part 2 offers subsections on country and western music and intercultural traditions in the Prairie provinces of Canada, and part 3 offers an entire section on music of American Indians and First Nations, with subsections for Plains, bands (i.e., peoples), and Prairies (Canada again). The editors consciously refrained from an alphabetical arrangement, preferring volumes that concentrate on music in a region of the world, with articles written by experts. Volume 10 supplies general regional summaries, a glossary, a bibliography regionally arranged, and a very full index for the set of names, subjects, and titles, where additional approaches to Prairies-Plains interests may be found (e.g., names of states and provinces, "oral tradition and transmission," "singing," "Plains Indian groups," "Dakota Indian nation," "dance and movement"). A very important work. — *RB*

Folk

BE6   Reuss, Richard A., comp. - **A Woody Guthrie Bibliography, 1912-1967**. - [New York : Guthrie Children's Trust Fund], 1968. - 94 leaves.

> Class Numbers:
>> Library of Congress ML134.G969
> OCLC 432772
> LCCN 68-4501

• Reiss's annotated bibliography of materials by and about Guthrie (he tries to include "every known item in print relating to...Guthrie") begins with publications of the 1920s and concludes with 1968 obituaries. Annotations are brief and nonevaluative. Reiss excludes items about other members of the Guthrie family, passing references in discussions of the folk song movement, Guthrie songs in song compilations, and most record reviews. Entries include articles in newspapers, magazines, and journals; books; performance reviews; and lesser-known publications. The compiler warns of the need to separate the man from the myth, but includes pieces that helped create the myth. Author index. — *JB*

Country

BE7   Fry, Philip L. - **Texas Country Singers** / by Philip L. Fry and James Ward Lee. - Fort Worth, TX : TCU Pr., 2008. - 96 p. ; ill.

> Class Numbers:
>> Library of Congress ML400
> ISBN 9780875653655
> LCCN 2007-38863
> Notes:

• Consists of 25 biographical sketches of about 1,000 words each. All the subjects were born in Texas; collectively, their lives coincide with the history of country music. Modern country-pop, rockabilly, or purely Western singers are excluded, as are individuals who may have sung on occasion, but were more instrumentalist than singer (Bob Wills) or more movie star than singer (Dale Evans). Approximately half the musicians covered were born in West or Central Texas. — *MS*

BE8 Stambler, Irwin. - **Country Music : The Encyclopedia** / [by] Irwin Stambler & Grelun Landon ; contributors, Alice Seidman and Lyndon Stambler. - New York : St. Martin's Pr., 1997. - 708 p. ; ill.

Class Numbers:
  Library of Congress ML102.C7
  ISBN 0312151217 0312264879
  LCCN 96-43043
  Notes:
    Includes videography and discography (p. 569-600), bibliography (p. 633-638); indexes
    Rev. ed. of country music entries from: *Encyclopedia of Folk, Country & Western Music* (2nd ed., 1983; **BE9**)

• Strictly biographical, this encyclopedia covers performers but not organizations, events, or topics related to country music. Entries, arranged alphabetically by surname, are relatively substantive, providing information about the life and work of many performers. A handful of black-and-white photos are clustered in four sections of plates rather than with the entries. Supplementary material includes an awards section that gives, besides industry recognitions such as the Grammys, gold and platinum awards arranged by date, and a short bibliography. Indexes of artists, albums, and song titles, and a general index. Artists associated with the Prairies-Plains region are not separately identified, but Stambler's encyclopedia can provide information about Prairies-Plains country music figures who have been identified elsewhere. — *MB*

BE9 Stambler, Irwin. - **The Encyclopedia of Folk, Country, & Western Music** / [by] Irwin Stambler and Grelun Landon. – 2nd ed. - New York : St. Martin's Pr., 1983. - 902 [i.e., 912] p. ; [56] p. of plates, ill., ports.

Class Numbers:
  Library of Congress ML102.F66
  ISBN 0312248180
  LCCN 82-5702
  OCLC 8430828
  Notes:
    1st ed., 1969
    Includes bibliographical references (p. 897-902)

• If any musical style can be held characteristic of the Prairies-Plains region, it is country and western. Stambler's encyclopedia, now ancient by country and western stan-

dards, is more collective biography, since the overwhelming number of entries is concerned with performers and group members. The alphabetical entries, some fairly long, give specialties (Sam Hinton is singer, guitarist, educator, marine biologist), birthplace and date, and a career summary. Some Prairies-Plains use can be found for the book as it stands by scanning entries for birthplace where Plains place-names are common, especially for Texas (although many performers moved away from the Plains at an early age); but the work is best used to read up on country and western performers after they have been identified elsewhere. Several lists of awards (e.g., Country Music Hall of Fame), alphabetical list of performers, bibliography, but no index. — *RB*

THEATRE

BE10 Lynch, Richard Chigley, 1932– . - **Musicals! : A Complete Selection Guide for Local Productions**. - Chicago, IL : American Library Association, 1994. - 404 p.

Class Numbers:
  Library of Congress ML19
  ISBN 0838906273
  LCCN 93-27387
  Notes:
    Indexes
    Previous ed. (1984) had subtitle: *A Directory of Musical Properties Available for Production*

• Alphabetical listing of approximately 500 musicals available for staging by amateur theatrical groups. Entries contain date of original New York production, authorship credits (writer, music, lyrics), licensing agent, recordings, original cast and their parts, number of male and female roles, and songs. Plot summaries indicate location, time period, and occasional production notes. *Oklahoma!, Annie Get Your Gun*, and *Calamity Jane* are well-known musicals with Plains settings or themes but the guide identifies a few more obscure works such as *Wildcat* (oil prospecting in the Southwest in 1912) and *The Will Rogers Follies*. Appendixes list licensing agents and music publishers. Indexes of composers, lyricists, and librettists, as well as songs. Although aimed at the practical needs of local groups, the guide also serves as a useful directory of major shows. — *LMcD*

BE11 Nielsen, Alan. - **An Historical Survey of Opera Houses and Legitimate Theatres Built in the State of Nebraska between 1865 and 1917** / project director, Tice L. Miller. - [Lincoln, NE : s.n.], 1978. - 2 v.

OCLC 4235021
Notes:
  Bibliography at the end of v. 2
  Funded by the Center for Great Plains Studies,

College of Arts and Sciences, Univ. of Nebraska-Lincoln

• Drawn primarily from the annual *Nebraska Gazetteer and Business Directory*, Nielsen's survey lists theaters by town with each name change listed separately. Establishment dates are approximate since they are stated (inexplicably and annoyingly) using only the first three digits (189, 191). Buildings built as movie theaters are excluded. No attempt was made to determine current existence or use. The surprisingly rich theater life of rural Nebraska is demonstrated by a study in greater depth of theaters in one town, Chadron, which boasted three rival opera houses by the late 1800s. This unique compilation is a beginning place for theater and architectural researchers. — *JD*

BE12   Zivanovic, Judith Kay, 1938-   . - **Opera Houses of the Midwest** / eds., Judith K. Zivanovic [et al.]. – [Manhattan, KS?] : Mid-America Theatre Conference, 1988. - 115 p. ; ill.

Class Numbers:
   Library of Congress PN22173.M52
Notes:
   Includes bibliographies

• Identifies and describes opera houses in four states: Iowa, Nebraska, and South and North Dakota. Entries are arranged by state, then alphabetically by county; a short essay by the contributor introduces each section. A few entries have small photos. Each entry gives the city and location of the opera house, provides historical background (e.g., date of construction), and a physical description of the facility. Entries for each of the states have different contributors, causing lack of consistency in the format and content of entries. Many entries provide minimal information. Since there is no index, the arrangement by county psresents a barrier to users who know the city, but not the county (e.g., Red Cloud, in Webster County, Nebraska). At the end are five short bibliographies: general, and one for each of the four states. Except for the title page, the book is reproduced from typescript, which does not help readability. — *MB*

FILM

Westerns

BE13   Adams, Les, 1934-   . - **Shoot-Em-Ups : The Complete Reference Guide to Westerns of the Sound Era** / [by] Les Adams & Buck Rainey. - New Rochelle, NY : Arlington House Publ., 1978. - 633 p. ; ill.

Class Numbers:
   Library of Congress PN1995.9.W4

ISBN 0870003933
OCLC 3627647
LCCN 78-656
Notes:
   Index

BE13a   Rainey, Buck. - **The Shoot-Em-Ups Ride Again : A Supplement to Shoot-Em-Ups.** - Metuchen, NJ : Scarecrow Pr., 1990. - 309 p. ; ill.

Class Numbers:
   Library of Congress PN1995.9.W4
ISBN 081082132X
OCLC 21330659
LCCN 90-34151
Notes:
   Index

• Rainey and Adams's *Shoot-Em-Ups* arranges about 3,400 films chronologically, from "The Silent Years, 1903-1927" through "The Continental Westerns, 1962-1977." Each section begins with a narrative history of the period's Westerns, then lists films by year, supplying for each its title, studio, release date, running time, cast, director, screenplay, story, and producer. Both it and the sequel are shamelessly overwritten ("I have branded and corralled a number of films grazing on the western periphery ..." [*Shoot-Em-Ups Ride Again*, p. ix]), but both titles list an astonishing number of films (the sequel has 3,000 more), not a few relating to the Prairies-Plains region. Covering 1928-1990, the sequel has five chapters. Chapter 1 arranges films released 1978-1990 alphabetically, giving title, studio, release date, running time, cast, director, screenwriter, and producers. Chapter 2 lists films released 1928-1978 that were not included in *Shoot-Em-Ups,* chapter 3 supplies additional data for 1,500 films listed in the earlier book (but without repeating its entries), chapter 4 lists TV Western series 1948-1990, and chapter 5 full-length Westerns made for TV. Readers may want to avoid the narrative text that begins each chapter ("... the Western has the tenacity of a bull buffalo in heat"), and the sequel's usefulness would have been enhanced had it reprinted information from the original; but fans of the genre will find the lists of films useful (the index lists all the titles). Plains Westerns are not separately identified, nor does the compiler give locales of individual films, so some prior knowledge is required, although searching the index under "Plains," "Oklahoma," "Dakota," or the like turns up some titles. — *RB*

BE14   Buscombe, Edward, ed. - **The BFI Companion to the Western**. - Rev. ed. - London : Andre Deutsch, 1993. - 432 p. ; ill. (some col.), facsims. (some col.), maps, ports.

Class Numbers:
   Library of Congress PN1995.9.W4
ISBN 0689119623
LCCN 94-170417

Notes:
1st ed.: New York: Atheneum, 1988
Bibliography: p. 429-430; index
Publ. in association with British Film Instiute

• The British Film Institute, who can always be counted on to publish sensibly about film, here present a companion that provides context not only for Westerns but for Prairies-Plains as well. A history, not too long, summarizes the place Westerns have occupied in film and the vital signs of the genre; a guide to Western films provides some basic data (directors, cast) and plot summaries for a selected roster of films; a list of filmmakers discusses producers and directors, omitting actors (who are often discussed in the films they worked in); "TV Westerns" treats rather dismissively the genre as practiced for the small screen (*Gunsmoke* and a cloud of dust); and sums up with a two-page bibliography. The best part, however, is a "Cultural and Historical Dictionary" that in a fairly long list of topics covers subjects important not only for Westerns but for Prairies-Plains as well: places (Abilene, Black Hills, Dodge City), people (Butch Cassidy, Jesse Chisholm, Earp, Fred Harvey), Indians (Cheyenne, Crazy Horse, smoke signals), and a host of background topics (agriculture, barbers, costume, landscape, oil, train robbery), writing about all of them knowledgeably and with flair, usually not at great length. Vastly entertaining and informative, useful to any Plains student and to any library. — *RB*

BE15　Fagen, Herb, comp. - **The Encyclopedia of Westerns** / foreword by Tom Selleck ; preface by Dale Robertson. - New York : Checkmark Books, c2003. - xx, 618 p. ; ill.

Class Numbers:
Library of Congress PN1995.9.W4
ISBN 0816044562
LCCN 2002026355
Notes:
Includes bibliographical references (p. 542-543); i
index

• Since the Western is the film genre most closely identified with the Plains, any reference work treating the genre has potential use. Fagen's compilation lists films alphabetically, adding a brief bibliography, some stills, and an index of names and titles. It does not identify films by region (ignoring, for example, that *Days of Heaven* was placed in the Texas Panhandle but filmed in Alberta), and Fagen's appraisals of films (he wrote all the entries) are idiosyncratic. Useful to acquire basic information about individual films. — *RB*

BE16　Key, M. David, comp. - **Hollywood and the American West : A Selective Bibliography** / M. David Key

and Angela Thomas, comps. - Albuquerque, NM : Center for the American West, Dept. of History, Univ. of New Mexico, 2001. - 84 leaves. - (University of New Mexico. Center for the American West. Occasional papers, 22).

Class Numbers:
Library of Congress PN1995.9.W4
OCLC 49606739
Notes:
Includes bibliographical references

• The compilers assembled this bibliography to fit the needs of a mythical student engaged in writing a 20-page paper about Western films. It therefore is confined to secondary works, and is arranged in sections for movie watchers and moviemakers. It opens with a section for general bibliography, then has six sections about the audience and nine about people who make Westerns. The 800 entries have no annotations, and there is no index. Films with Plains settings will undoubtedly be discussed, there is no avoiding it; but they must be extracted by scanning the entries. — *RB*

BE17　Nachbar, John G. - **Western Films : An Annotated Critical Bibliography**. - New York : Garland Publ., 1975. - 98 p. - (Garland Reference Library of the Humanities, v. 17).

Class Numbers:
Library of Congress PN1995.9.W4 Z5784.M9
ISBN 0824010868 9780824010867
OCLC 1255036
LCCN 75-6696
Notes:
Indexes

• Nachbar organizes his bibliography of serious studies on western movies by category: reference sources, pre-1950 criticism, specific films, actors, directors, history, theory, audience, comparative works, and educational use. Within each, books and articles are listed separately. The subject index includes film titles. Identifying those with a Plains connection is not readily done, however, and is largely a matter of guesswork (e.g., *Red River*, about the first cattle drive on the Chisholm Trail) and testing assumptions (e.g., *High Plains Drifter* or *Oklahoma Raiders*). Nachbar, with Jackie R. Donath and Chris Foran, also produced Western *Films 2* (NY: Garland Publ., 1988; 308 p.), covering 1974 through 1987. — *LMcD*

BE18　**The Overlook Film Encyclopedia : The Western** / ed. by Phil Hardy ; ill. from the Kobal Collection. - Woodstock, NY : Overlook Pr., 1994. - 416 p. ; ill.

Class Numbers:
Library of Congress PN1995.9.W4
ISBN 0879515171

OCLC 28413733
LCCN 93-24439
Notes:
   Includes bibliographical references; index
   Rev. ed. of: *The Western*. 2nd rev. updated ed. (1991)

• Large in format, this volume is lavishly illustrated throughout, with an additional color photo spread in the center. The contents are arranged chronologically by decades: the 1930s are categorized as the rise of the series Western, the 1940s is subtitled "Resurgence of the Genre," the 1950s focus on Indians and psychopaths, the 1960s addresses the genre's international elements, the 1970s are called "Western in Transition," and the last section is subtitled "The Eighties and Beyond." Comparatively few Westerns were released after 1980. Films are listed by year of release, then alphabetically by title, providing title, studio, color or black-and-white, running time, and personnel (producer, director, writers, and cast). Most descriptions are a paragraph in length. Appendixes include a list of top video rentals, top box office grosses (adjusted for inflation), best paid stars, various critics' top ten picks, Academy Awards for westerns, Westerns based on novels, and a selective bibliography. A title index concludes the volume. A subject index would have been useful. — MB

BE19   **Shooting Stars : Heroes and Heroines of Western Film** / ed. by Archie P. McDonald. - Bloomington, IN : Indiana Univ. Pr., 1987. - 265 p. ; ill.

   Class Numbers:
      Library of Congress PN1995.9.W4
   ISBN 0253366852
   LCCN 85-45988
   Notes:
      Includes bibliographies

• The first ten essays describe the life and work of famous Western actors, beginning with silent film star William S. Hart and continuing to the recent past. The final two essays are topical, dealing with women in Westerns and with television as a new medium. Each chapter is illustrated with several black-and-white photos and is followed by notes. An appendix, which escaped the table of contents, lists TV Westerns, 1948-1985, arranged by title. It provides inclusive dates, network, and audience (adult or juvenile). There is no general bibliography and no index by subject or title. — *MB*

Film Noir

BE20   Silver, Alain, 1947–   , ed. - **Film Noir : An Encyclopedic Reference to the American Style** / ed. by Alain Silver and Elizabeth Ward ; co-editors, Carl Macek

and Robert Porfirio ; co-editor 3rd ed., James Ursini. - 3rd ed., rev. and expanded - Woodstock, NY : Overlook Pr., 1992. - 479 p. ; ill.

   Class Numbers:
      Library of Congress PN1995.9.F54
   ISBN 0879514795
   L CCN 93-236035
   Notes:
      Includes bibliographical references (p. 444-446);
         index

• An appendix dealing with Westerns which can be classified as Film Noir enables readers to identify a number of films which could be relevant to the study of the Prairies-Plains region. Other appendixes identify gangster, comedy, and period films. The greater part of the book is an alphabetical listing of films. Each of the entries, several hundred in number, lists the cast and crew, release date, and running time and includes a short description. A few entries have black-and-white illustrations. — *MB*

Multicultural Films

BE21   Welsch, Janice R. - **Multicultural Films : A Reference Guide** / [by] Janice R. Welsch and J.Q. Adams. - Westport, CT : Greenwood Pr., 2005. - 231 p. ; ill.

   Class Numbers:
      Library of Congress PN1995.9.M56
   ISBN 0313319758
   OCLC 56590707
   LCCN 2004-22529
   Notes:
      Includes bibliographical references (p. [215]-219);
         index
      Review by C. Hendershott: *Choice* 43.2 (Oct. 2005):
         review 43-0662
      Table of contents: http://www.loc.gov/catdir/toc/
         ecip051/2004022529.html

• The authors cover several broad ethnic groups, including black Americans, Middle Eastern Americans, Asian Americans, European Americans, Latino Americans, and Native Americans. Depending on the category, the number of films discussed ranges from six to 24. Although most of the films were released between 1970 and 2003, a handful predate that period. The most relevant section for Plains studies is that for Native Americans. The information for each film includes director, distributor, length, rating, and type (e.g., documentary). For each film, the authors provide narrative commentary of about one page and a list of sources. Notable Plains movies include *In the Spirit of Crazy Horse*, *Incident at Oglala*, *Lakota Woman*, and *Skins*. The final section, "Intercultural Films," includes one or two pertinent titles as well. Useful index to films by theme; brief bibliography; index. — *MB*

Blacks

BE22   Sampson, Henry T., 1934-   . - **Blacks in Black and White : A Source Book on Black Films**. - 2nd ed. - Metuchen, NJ : Scarecrow Pr., 1995. - 735 p. ; ill.

> Class Numbers:
> Library of Congress PN1995.9.N4
> ISBN 0810826054
> LCCN 93-1965
> Notes:
> Index

• A few items in this volume will interest Prairies-Plains students, and the index helps find them–for example, entries that relate to the Kansas City Monarchs baseball team and Prairie View University in Texas. The overall arrangement provides an overview of black cast films, a chronological synopses of films (1910-1950), and biographies of black actors and actresses. Appendixes include an alphabetical list of black films produced before 1960, corporations specializing in black film, theaters catering to black audiences (1910-1950), and film credits for featured players. — *MB*

Actors

Note   Some other actors (e.g., Fatty Arbuckle, Montgomery Clift) were born in the Prairies-Plains region but left at very early ages, never to return, so are omitted.

BE23   Rollins, Peter C. - **Will Rogers : A Bio-Bibliography**. - Westport, CT : Greenwood Pr., 1984. - 282 p. ; ports. - (Popular culture bio-bibliographies).

> Class Numbers:

> Library of Congress PN2287.R74 Z8754.5
> ISBN 0313226334
> LCCN 83-10696

• Rollins begins with a brief illustrated summary of the life of humorist Rogers (1879-1935), continuing with a more extensive essay on the reasons for his popularity. A bibliographic essay on primary and secondary sources leads into the checklist of works by and about Rogers. The secondary bibliography is arranged alphabetically by author in sections organized by material type: books, articles, dissertations, films, and recordings. A chronology of Rogers's life is set alongside a chronology of world events. The book ends with a record of archival materials and a detailed index. — *MB*

BE24   Sweeney, Kevin. - **Henry Fonda : A Bio-Bibliography**. - New York : Greenwood Pr., 1992. - 278 p. ; port. - (Bio-bibliographies in the performing arts, 25).

> Class Numbers:
> Library of Congress PN2287.F558
> ISBN 0313265712
> LCCN 91-47057
> Notes:
> Index

• Sweeney's book reviews the life and work of Nebraskan Fonda, who was born in Grand Island and spent his boyhood in Omaha. The book begins with a brief biography and chronology. The annotated bibliography cites books and magazine articles (the latter listed alphabetically by magazine title). The filmography provides production information, cast, and plot summary. Information about Fonda's work in live theater, television, and radio includes production dates, cast, description, and other information appropriate to the medium. There are lists of awards and nominations and a short list of videos (as of 1991). Films by his children, Peter and Jane, are listed. Detailed index. The book was offset from typescript. — *MB*

BF : RECREATION AND SPORTS

RECREATION

Bibliographies

BF1 Research Bibliography : The Development of Parks and Playgrounds in Selected Canadian Prairie Cities, 1880-1930. - Wolfville, NS : School of Recreation and Physical Education, Acadia University, 1989. - 49 leaves.

> Class Numbers:
> Library of Congress GV433.C3
> OCLC 29201425

• Expanded from the compiler's doctoral thesis (Univ. of Alberta, 1988), the bibliography contains sections on urban history, urban development, policy development, urban reform, and civic boosterism. Chapters on planning, parks and recreation, and individual cities (Calgary, Edmonton, Regina, Saskatoon, Winnipeg) are divided between primary sources (chiefly from four municipal planning journals, 1905-1930) and secondary material (books, theses, articles). Although a relative minority of the citations deal specifically with parks and playgrounds in the five cities, the work is useful for Prairie urban history. — *LMcD*

Parks and Camping

BF2 Clancy, Michael T., 1956- . - A User's Guide to Saskatchewan Parks / [by] Michael T. Clancy & Anna Clancy. - Regina, SK : Canadian Plains Research Center, Univ. of Regina, 2006. - 443 p. ; [16] p. of plates, ill. (some col.), maps, ports. - (Discover Saskatchewan series, 5 ; ISSN 1484-1800).

> Class Numbers:
> National Library of Canada FC3513
> ISBN 0889771987
> OCLC 69785849
> Notes:
> Index

• A hands-on guide to the regional, provincial, and national parks of Saskatchewan. Organized by geographic area, the directory covers regional parks in two or three pages and gives longer treatment to the other levels of parks. The location and description of each is followed by an indication of amenities such as campsites, recreational facilities, services, and contact information. Lists parks recommended for activities such as birding, cowboy poetry and rodeos, and star-gazing. Based on first-hand visits to every park, the guide refutes stereotypical notions of the province as an area bereft of natural and historical interest; the small black-and-white photographs, however, do not quite do justice to the landscape. Comprehensive in coverage and filled with practical detail. — *LMcD*

Hunting and Fishing

BF3 Bauer, Erwin A. - Big Game of North America / text by Erwin A. Bauer ; photographs by Erwin and Peggy Bauer. - Stillwater, MN : Voyageur Pr., 1997. - 160 p. ; col. ill.

> Class Numbers:
> Library of Congress QL715
> ISBN 0896583368
> OCLC 35450367
> LCCN 96-35224
> Notes:
> Contents: Horned animals; Antlered animals; Large cats; Bears
> Includes bibliographical references (p. 155); index
> Previous ed.: *Erwin Bauer's Horned and Antlered Game.* New York: Outdoor Life Books, distr. by Stackpole Books, 1986

• The chapters that will interest Prairies-Plains researchers are those on white-tailed deer, mule and black-tailed deer, pronghorn, and bison. Topics covered include range and population, habitat, distinguishing physical features, reproduction ecology, and predators. Many photographs in color; appendix of national refuges and parks. — *JB*

BF4 National Survey of Fishing, Hunting, and Wildlife-Associated Recreation. - [1st] (1980)- . Washington, DC : U.S. Dept. of the Interior, Fish and Wildlife Service, 1980- . Irregular.

> Class Numbers:
> Library of Congress SK41
> Government Document I 49.98
> OCLC 9101960
> LCCN 83-640464 82-600262
> Notes:
> After 1996, no longer distributed in printed form to depository libraries
> Also issued in CD-ROM version
> Complemented by: *Net Economic Values for Bass and Trout Fishing, Deer Hunting, and Wildlife*

Watching
Earlier title: *National Survey of Hunting, Fishing, and Wildlife-Associated Recreation*;
ISSN 0191-6947
Some issues available at Census Bureau Internet site: http://www.census.gov/prod/www/abs/fishing.html
Current access via PURL: http://purl.access.gpo.gov/GPO/LPS4428 (requires Adobe Acrobat)
Supplement: *Fishing, Hunting, and Wildlife-Associated Recreation Trends*
Usually quinquennially ; occasionally issued at six-year intervals

• "Used for estimating the economic impact of wildlife-related recreation for each state; for estimating the value of wildlife resources lost due to pollution or disease; for use in critical habitat analysis of threatened species; and for preparing environmental impact statements, budgets, and legislative proposals," the survey is based on household surveys conducted by the Census Bureau. It consists of a national and 50 state reports on the number of anglers, hunters, and wildlife observers by type of activity; trips and days spent on activities; expenditures (including equipment and transportation) by type of activity; number of persons and days of participation by animals sought; and demographic characteristics of participants (including age, income, race, education, and sex). Addenda to the core reports include topics such as "Participation and Expenditure Patterns of African-American, Hispanic, and Female Hunters" and "Private and Public Land Use By Hunters." All reports are separate pdf files, but hard copy is available from the Fish and Wildlife Service; datasets are available for ftp. Reports for 1996 and 1991 are also available at the Internet site. An excellent business start-up and marketing tool as well. The 2006 survey issued in spring 2007. — *JD*

BF5   Snook, Michael, 1948-   . - **Fishing Saskatchewan: An Angler's Guide to Provincial Waters.** - Regina, SK : Canadian Plains Research Center, 2004. - 240 p. ; ill. (some col.), maps. - (Discover Saskatchewan series, 4 ; ISSN 1484-1800).

Class Numbers:
Library of Congress SH572
ISBN 0889771669
OCLC 53822328
LCCN 2004-381191
Notes:
Includes bibliographical references (p. 227-229) ; index

• Although not often thought a fisherman's paradise, Saskatchewan has more than 100,000 lakes and, reportedly, some of the best freshwater fishing in the world. Snook provides a practical guide to exploring this bounty. Chapters cover fish species, fish stocking, various kinds of fishing (commercial, fly, ice, and competitive), and conservation. He identifies recommended locations, both popular and more secluded, in the southern, central, and northern regions and indicates the facilities and species found at each. Appendixes provide information of value to visiting and local anglers: travel contacts, clubs and tournaments, gear lists, and tackle shops. Vintage photographs add a nostalgic touch. A useful resource for both seasoned and novice fishermen. — *LMcD*

SPORTS

Bibliographies

BF6   Burianyk, Kathy. - **A Saskatchewan Sport Bibliography** / Greg Unger, ed. - Regina, SK : Saskatchewan Sports Hall of Fame and Museum, 1994. - 175 p.

Class Numbers:
National Library of Canada Z7515 S37
ISBN 0969631863 (pbk.)
OCLC 35934472

• 1,045 entries arranged by sport, archery to wrestling. Lists archival and secondary materials separately under each sport, lightly annotated. Appendixes describe the sports holdings of 42 Saskatchewan museums and list 400 local history books, with a note of the specific sports included in each. The *SportDiscus* database (Sport Information Resource Centre; http://www.sirc.ca/products/sportdiscus.cfm) covers more recent material. —*LMcD*

Collective Biographies

BF7   **Saskatchewan Sports : Lives Past and Present** / volume ed., Holden Stoffel ; series ed., Brian Mlazgar. - Regina, SK : Univ. of Regina, Canadian Plains Research Center, 2007. - 138 p. ; ports. - (Saskatchewan Lives Past and Present Series, 18).

Class Numbers:
National Library of Canada GV585.3
ISBN 0889771677 (pbk.) 9780889771673 (pbk.)
OCLC 81601253
Notes:
Includes bibliographical references

• Short accounts of 241 athletes associated with Saskatchewan by virtue of birth, career, or contributions to sport. Entries provide biographical background and emphasize accomplishments; many have photos and suggestions for further reading. As might be expected, winter sports–especially hockey–predominate but 35 different sports are represented. Surprisingly there is no index by sport, making it difficult to identify individuals associated with a particular game or league such as swimming or the NFL. Both the internationally famous such as Gordie Howe and the lesser known but regionally significant are included. An informative addition to provincial cultural history. — *LMcD*

Baseball

BF8   Porter, David L., 1941-   , ed. - **Biographical Dictionary of American Sports : Baseball**. - New York : Greenwood Pr., 1987. - 713 p.

> Class Numbers:
>   Library of Congress GV865.A1
> ISBN 0313237719
> LCCN 86-12091
> Notes:
>   Includes bibliographies ; index

• Entries are arranged alphabetically by players' names. Appendixes list players by position played, Negro League players, Hall of Fame members, and by birthplace, which could assist in identifying players associated with the Prairies-Plains region (more than 80 players listed were born in the region). There is a complete index of names and a roster of contributors. Each of the player entries provides name and nickname(s), date and place of birth and death, playing history, and a brief bibliography. — *MB*

Basketball

BF9   Douchant, Mike, 1951-   . - **Encyclopedia of College Basketball** / foreword, "Hoop Heaven," by Dick Vitale. - New York : Gale Research, 1995. - 615 p. ; ill., maps.

> Class Numbers:
>   Library of Congress GV885.7
> ISBN 0810396408
> OCLC 31074948

LCCN 94-35209
Notes:
    Includes bibliographical references; index

• Douchant covers the history of the sport, beginning in 1891 and extending to the 1990s. A register of players lists NCAA greats. Other directories list coaches, women's basketball, small colleges, Olympics, conferences, NCAA schools, awards, records, statistics. The most applicable sections are the conference and school directories, which can provide information about basketball in the Prairies-Plains region, including basketball powerhouse Kansas University. Information about specific schools includes team logo, contact information (address and phone), enrollment, team colors, tournament appearances, and all-time leading players. — *MB*

BF10   Porter, David L., 1941-   , ed. - **Biographical Dictionary of American Sports : Basketball and Other Indoor Sports**. - New York : Greenwood Pr., 1989. - xxv, 801 p.

> Class Numbers:
>   Library of Congress GV697.A1
> ISBN 0313262616
> LCCN 88-17776
> Notes:
>   Includes bibliographical references ; index

• Arranged by sport (basketball, bowling, boxing, diving, figure skating, gymnastics, ice hockey, swimming, weight lifting, wrestling, and miscellaneous), Porter's work offers several appendixes. One lists athletes by place of birth, which could help identify athletes from the Prairies-Plains region (about 50 are listed). Another lists sports figures in a single alphabet and identifies their specific sport. Other appendixes include women athletes by sport, major halls of fame, sports associations (e.g., the defnct Big 8 Conference), and periodicals about sports. Detailed index of names and organizations. Each of the personal entries provides name and nickname(s), date and place of birth and death, the subject's athletic history, and a short bibliography. — *MB*

C   Social Sciences

CA : EDUCATION

Scope   The education of the young, kindergarten through undergraduate colleges, and of adults, graduate school through distance education.

Site List 7
EDUCATION : State Agencies and Directories

Some directories in education appear in print as serials, usually published annually, some as Internet sites. Those listed here are those issued by state or provincial departments of education; other directories of education are issued by commercial enterprises, including Google. Some include statistics; some list only schools in the state, others list officers and employees of the state board of education; some split the directory function into several categories, issuing them separately. The home page of the official state or provincial agency charged with administering public education is often a source of directorial and statistical information, and of numerous other kinds of information (news releases, publications, standards), so is often a useful starting place for research in education-related topics.

UNITED STATES

Colorado
Print: *Colorado Education & Library Directory*. 1990-1991- . Annual.
Online: *Colorado Education and Library Directory*.
    http://www.cde.sate.co.us/edulibdir/directory.htm
State agency: Colorado Department of Education.
    http://www.cde.state.co.us/

Kansas
Print: K*ansas Educational Directory*. 1969-1970- Annual.
Online: Kansas State Department of Education.
    http://ksbe.ks.us/ [Also state education agency]

Montana
Print: *Montana Educational Directory*. [1968/1969?]- . Annual.
State agency: Montana Office of Public Instruction.
    http://www.opi.state.mt.us/

Nebraska
Print: *Nebraska Education Directory*. [1890s]- . Annual.
Online: *Nebraska Education Directory*.
    http://www.nde.state.ne.us/
State agency: Nebraska Department of Education.
    http://www.nde.state.ne.us/

New Mexico
Print: New Mexico. Dept. of Education.
New Mexico Educational Directory. 1929/30-1961/62. Annual.

State agency: New Mexico Public Education Department.
    http://www.ped.sttae.nm.us/

North Dakota
Print: *North Dakota Educational Directory*. [1900s]- . Annual.
Online: North Dakota. Dept. of Public Instruction.
    Education Directory.
    http://www.dpi.state.nd.us/resource/directory/index.shtm
State agency: North Dakota Department of Public Instruction.
    http://www.dpi.state.nd.us/

Oklahoma
Print: *Oklahoma Directory of Education*. 1999/2000- . [Annual?]
Online: *Oklahoma Directory of Education*.
    http://www.sd.state.ok.us/
State agency: Oklahoma State Department of Education.
    http://www.sde.state.ok.us/

South Dakota
Print: South Dakota. Div. of Education. *Educational Directory*. 1990- . Annual.
State agency: South Dakota Department of Education.
    http://doe.sd.gov/

Texas
Online: *AskTED* [Texas Education Agency].
    http:///asted.tea.state.tx.us/ State agency: Texas Education Agency.
    http://www.tea.state.tx.us/

Wyoming
Print: *Wyoming Education Directory*. 1964-1996. Annual.
State agency: Wyoming Department of Education Home Page.
    http://www.k12.wy.us/

CANADA
Alberta
Provincial agency: Alberta Education.
    http://ednet.edc.gov.ab.ca/

Manitob
Provincial agency: Manitoba Education.
    http://www.edu.gov.mb.ca/

Saskatchewan
Provincial agency: Saskatchewan Learning.
    http://www.sasked.gov.sk.ca/

CB : ANTHROPOLOGY

Scope   Lists works that cover study of other cultures, especially non-Western cultures, using methods and principles of either physical or social anthropology. Includes the related discipline of archaeology.

General Works

CB1   **Encyclopedia of World Cultures** / David Levinson, ed.-in-chief. - Boston, MA : G.K. Hall, 1991-1996. - 10 v. ; maps.

> Class Numbers:
> Library of Congress GN307
> ISBN 081688840X (set)
> OCLC 22492614
> LCCN 90-49123
> Notes:
> Includes bibliographical references, filmographies; indexes

• The most authoritative and readable compilation on world cultures, written by anthropologists but used by students, officials, teachers, and travelers. Volume 1 covers North America, defined as Canada, the U.S., and Greenland. Following an introduction to the region and maps of culture locations, culture summaries describe selected Native peoples and unassimilated "folk cultures" such as the Amish. Immigrant groups in North America are described in the volumes covering their places of origin; migratory patterns are noted. Entries vary in length and cover orientation (identification, location, demography, linguistic affiliation), history and cultural relations, settlements, economy, kinship, marriage and family, sociopolitical organization, and religion and expressive culture. Entries include ethnonyms (variant names for the culture) and bibliographies. A filmography and glossary end each volume. Appendixes vary to suit each region. The North America appendix lists extinct Native American cultures. Each volume is indexed by ethnonyms; volume 10 has cumulative indexes. Because names of groups vary with time, language, transcription, and the relationship of the namer to the culture, ethnonyms are an invaluable feature, providing search terms for additional research. — *JD*

CB2   MacKenzie, John M., ed. - **Peoples, Nations, and Cultures : An A-Z of the Peoples of the World, Past and Present**. - London : Weidenfeld & Nicolson, 2005. - 672 p. ; maps.

> Class Numbers:

> Library of Congress GN316
> ISBN 0304365505
> OCLC 58547960
> Notes:
> Index
> Review by M. Cedar Face: *Choice* 43.2 (Oct. 2005): review 43-0689

• Attempts to account for the cultural place of identifiable groups around the world. The first section, "The Americas," offers brief summary essays for many Indian peoples–e.g., Sioux, Comanche, Metis, Assiniboine, Wichita–as well as Americans and Canadians, but provides no mechanism for identifying peoples by region. Although the compiler (St. Andrews Univ., UK) supplies occasional outline maps to show the approximate location inhabited by individual peoples, he provides no other scholarly aids except an index of entries, an aid with little use, since entries are arranged alphabetically in each section. There are no notes, no acknowledgment of sources, not a shred of bibliography. Perhaps of some use in placing peoples in international or national context, or in identifying and locating them. — *RB*

Anthropologists

CB3   Babcock, Barbara A., 1943- . - **Daughters of the Desert : Women Anthropologists and the Native American Southwest, 1880-1980: An Illustrated Catalogue** / [by] Barbara A. Babcock [and] Nancy J. Parezo. - Albuquerque, NM : Univ. of New Mexico Pr., 1988. - 241 p. ; ill., ports.

> Class Numbers:
> Library of Congress E78.S7
> ISBN 0826310834 (pbk.) 0826310877
> OCLC 17551876
> LCCN 88-2979
> Notes:
> Includes bibliographical references (p. 227-241); index

• Babcock (English, Univ. of Arizona) and Parezo (Curator of Ethnology, Arizona State Musuem) describe the accomplishments of 45 women in studying and interpreting the American Southwest. Based on a museum exhibit, the work is part of a larger project that includes oral histories, a conference, and a book of essays. Women featured are pioneers, anthropologists, ethnologists, archaeologists, museum founders, writers, photographers, an architect, and a jeweler. A photograph of each subject (their entries are arranged alphabetically) is followed by biographical information, research, education, and professional activities. A full map of Arizona, New Mexico, and northern Mexico shows the location of 26 Native American groups. Selected Southwest bibliography. — *GK*

FOLKLORE AND FOLKLIFE

UNITED STATES

CB4   Bronner, Simon J. - **Encyclopedia of American Folklife**. - Armonk, NY : M.E. Sharpe, 2006. - 4 v.; ill.

> Class Numbers:
> Library of Congress GR105
> ISBN 07655680521   9780765680525
> OCLC 62282052
> LCCN 2005-32119
> Notes:
> Includes bibliographical references; indexes
> Table of contents: http://www.loc.gov/catdir/toc/
> ecip063/2005032119.html

• This encyclopedia covers a broad range of folklife topics, "defined socially as tradition-centered communities, locations, or groups, and culturally as the skills, symbols, identities, and customs that characterize such groups" (Introd.). Some topics relate to the past and some to the present, some are widespread and some distinctly regional. Topics relevant to the Plains include: Amish in Nebraska; barns; branding; cowboys; Germans in the Great Plains; Great Plains Indians; the Great Plains Region; powwowing; saddles and saddle making; Texas; Tulsa; and many more. Lengthy entries cover social, geographic, and historical backgrounds; prominent ideas and traditions; importance in contemporary life; demographic data; and sources of further information. Terms relevant to the discipline of folklife studies, such as "symbol and structure" and "ethnography and fieldwork," are also included. A table of contents, classified topic finder, general index, cultural group index, and a geographical index are replicated in all four volumes. Little coverage of Native American traditions. — *JD*

CB5   Brunvand, Jan Harold. - **American Folklore : An Encyclopedia**. - New York : Garland Publ., 1996. - 794 p. ; ill. - (Garland reference library of the humanities, v. 1551).

> Class Numbers:
> Library of Congress GR101.A54
> ISBN 0815307519
> LCCN 95-53734
> Notes:
> Includes bibliographical references; index

• Brunvand (syndicated columnist and urban legends specialist) and a team of 200 scholars present a general reference work on folk culture in the U.S. and Canada. Entries, arranged alphabetically, cover ethnic, racial, regional, and religious groups; each ends with a brief bibliography. Nineteen topical essays treat the history of folklore and various approaches to the discipline. The work contains regional folklore entries on the Midwest, Great Plains, Southwest, and Rocky Mountains. Entries on ethnic groups include American Indian, German, Hungarian, Scandinavian, and Slavic. Cross-references; 200 illustrations. — *GK*

CB6   Dorson, Richard Mercer, 1916- , ed. - **Handbook of American Folklore** / Inta Gale Carpenter, associate ed. ; Elizabeth Peterson, Angela Maniak, assistant eds.; introd. by W. Edson Richmond. - Bloomington, IN : Indiana Univ.Pr., 1983. - 584 p. ; ill.

> Class Numbers:
> Library of Congress GR105
> ISBN 0253327067
> LCCN 82-47574
> Notes:
> Bibliography: p. 541-563; index

• Dorson (history and folkore, Indiana Univ.) and his colleagues have assembled a guidebook for scholars and students about the emerging discipline of folklore. Dorson provides the introductory essays for each section. Topics explored by 60 scholars include family folklore, American cultural myths, folk craftsmen, folk healers, and performers. The volume has four parts: topics of research, interpretation of research, methods of research, and presentation of research. Among articles of interest to Plains researchers are those that address Native Americans, westward movement, Mormons, and the Southwest. Annotated bibliography, illustrations, and tables. — *GK*

CB7   Haywood, Charles, 1904- . - **A Bibliography of North American Folklore and Folksong**. - 2nd rev. ed. - New York : Dover Publ., 1961. - 2 v. (xxx, 1301 p.) ; maps (on lining papers).

> Class Numbers:
> Library of Congress Z5984.U5
> LCCN 62-3483
> Notes:
> Contents: v. 1, The American People North of Mexico,
> Including Canada; v. 2, The American Indians North of
> Mexico, Including the Eskimos

• Haywood (music, Queens College) provides a revision of the first edition (New York: Greenberg, [1951]), expanding the table of contents and correcting errors, misprints, and misspellings. Like the first, this edition lists approximately 40,000 items with a cutoff date of 1948. Vol. 1 begins with a general bibliography on folklore and folk music consisting of ballads, songs, dances, and sung games, followed by a regional bibliography arranged by state, subdivided by periodicals, general studies, collections, witchcraft, general studies, collections, proverbs, riddles, speech, and place-names, an ethnic bibliography for French-Canadians, Jews, Germans, Russians, and Spanish, and finally an occupational bibliography with listings for cowboys, lumberjacks, and miners. Vol. 2 is concerned with Native Americans, arranged first by culture, then subdivided by tribe. The subject sections are similar to those found in the first volume. Key to abbreviations; index supplement of composers, arrangers, and performers. — *GK*

CB8   Mood, Terry Ann, 1945- . - **American Regional Folklore : A Sourcebook and Research Guide**. - Santa

Barbara, CA : ABC-CLIO, 2004. - 476 p. ; maps.

Class Numbers:
    Library of Congress GR105.34
    ISBN 1576076202
    OCLC 55746532
    LCCN 2004-14737
    Notes:
        Includes bibliographical references; index

• Mood (Auraria Library, Univ. of Colorado, Denver) sets out to help American folklore researchers locate resources. In Part 1, she introduces readers to techniques and sources in folklore research—searching the Internet, libraries, periodical indexes, national databases, journals, vocabulary, retrieving information, and government publications. Part 2 divides the U.S. into eight geographic regions, each with an outline map highlighting states of the region. Each section opens with an essay written by a folklore scholar, followed by an annotated bibliography, literary authors, list of museums, journals in folklore, and selected Internet sites. Chapters 4-7 cover the Midwest, Southwest, West, and Northwest, from which Plains researchers will have to extract resources for their region. This was an opportunity for the compiler to lift her gaze beyond state boundaries and describe resources by physiographic region; she can probably see the Plains out her office window. — *GK*

CB9   Sackett, S.J., ed. - **Kansas Folklore** / ed. by S.J. Sackett and William E. Koch. - Lincoln, NE : Univ. of Nebraska Pr., 1961. - 251 p. ; ill.

Class Numbers:
    Library of Congress GR110.K2
    LCCN 61-11628
    Notes:
        Bibliography: p. 245-249
        Includes music (unaccompanied) for the folksongs and
            ballads, and some of the dances

• A dozen chapters by nine contributors (including the editors) covering such topics as folktales, legends, superstitions, proverbs, dialect, folk verse, folk song, dances, games, customs, and recipes. A two-part appendix analyzes motifs of folktales and legends. Includes a brief bibliography of Kansas folklore and a title index of songs. Songs provide both words and music. —*MB*

CB10   Slatta, Richard W. - **The Mythical West : An Encyclopedia of Legend, Lore, and Popular Culture**. - Santa Barbara, CA : ABC-CLIO, 2001. - 446 p. ; ill.

Class Numbers:
    Library of Congress GR109
    ISBN 1576071510
    OCLC 47018405
    LCCN 2001-2784
    Notes:

Includes bibliographical references (p. 405-424); index

• Slatta (history, North Carolina State Univ.) provides a comprehensive encyclopedia on Western lore and American history. He bases entry selections on occurrences in Internet sites of people, places, and events in Western mythology. Many figures (Wild Bill Hickok, Custer, Larry McMurtry) are omitted to avoid duplicating entries in previous ABC-CLIO publications. Entries, arranged alphabetically, end with two or three citations for further reading. "Mythical West" list of Internet sites; bibliography; roster of contributors. —*GK*

CB11   Tully, Marjorie F. - **An Annotated Bibliography of Spanish Folklore in New Mexico and Southern Colorado** / [by] Marjorie F. Tully and Juan B. Rael. - New York : Arno Pr., 1977. - 124 p. - (International Folklore).

Class Numbers:
    Library of Congress GR104   Z5984.U6
    ISBN 0405101325
    OCLC 2893941
    LCCN 77-70628
    Notes:
        A revision and enlargement by J.B. Rael of M.F. Tully's
            unpublished master's thesis, "An Annotated Bibliography of Spanish Folklore in New Mexico"
        Reprint of the 1950 ed. publ.: Albuquerque, NM : Univ. of
            New Mexico Press, issued as University of New Mexico Publications in Language and Literature, 3

• Lightly annotated author bibliography of an estimated 700 items, chiefly articles and books but also including unpublished manuscripts collected by the New Mexico Writers' Project. Citations frequently note the existence of book reviews. The compilers cast a wide net across their territory and include not only expected sforms such as folk songs, folk tales, superstitions, and related literature, but also architecture, religion, music, and other areas. The subject index identifies Indian tribes, geographical locations, and specific topics. Useful though considerably dated (nothing after 1948); for later coverage, consider sources such as the folklore sections of *Modern Language Association International Bibliography* (**BC6**), *HAPI, Hispanic American Periodicals Index*, or its Internet counterpart, *HAPI Online*. — *LMcD*

CANADA

CB12   Alberta Folklore and Local History Collection. - **A Guide to the Alberta Folklore and Local History Collection** / ed. by Erika Banski and Fern Russell ; comp. by Joel MacKeen. - Edmonton, AB : Univ. of Alberta Libraries, 2001. - 159 p.

Class Numbers:
    Library of Congress F1078
    National Library of Canada Z1392

OCLC 46951522

LCCN 2002-483167

Notes:

Electronic book: http://folklore.library.ualberta.ca/

• Inventory of a 1940s project to collect examples of folklore, pioneer reminiscences, and local history of the province. Homesteading, ranching, and railroads are among the many areas represented. The collection contains a mélange of biographies, radio scripts, submissions to creative writing competitions, school yearbooks, articles, photographs, and assorted items. Organized in series by format, with geographic and subject indexes. Much of the collection is available online at http://folklore.library.ualberta.ca, where it can be searched by author, genre, geographic name, contributor, publication, and title. — LMcD

CB13 Fowke, Edith Fulton, 1913-   . - **Folklore of Canada**. - Toronto, ON : McClelland and Stewart, 1976. - 349 p. ; ill.

Class Numbers:

Library of Congress GR113

ISBN 0771032021

LCCN 77-356393

Notes:

Bibliography: p. 314-333; indexes

• This anthology presents a cross-section of the various kinds of Canadian folklore. The organization is by groups: native peoples, French Canadians, Anglo-Canadians, and other groups, e.g., Ukrainian and Yiddish. Content is varied, including songs, square dance calls, jokes, riddles, tall tales, anecdotes, and legends. Scores are provided for a handful of songs. A number of the chapters are relevant to Prairies-Plains study, e.g., "Autograph Versers from Saskatchewan" and "Ukrainian-Canadian Folktales." Following all the chapters is a sources and notes section arranged in the same order as the chapters. Eighteen relevant periodicals are cited. The bibliography is alphabetical in categories for "Reference," "General," "Native Peoples," "Canadiens," "Anglo-Canadians," "Canadian Mosaic," and "Material Folk Culture." There are five indexes: tale types, motifs, contributors, informants, and general index of topics. — MB

Material Culture

CB14 Graham, Joe Stanley, comp. - **Hispanic-American Material Culture : An Annotated Directory of Collections, Sites, Archives, and Festivals in the United States**. - New York : Greenwood Pr., 1989. - xxiv, 257 p. 24 cm. - (Material Culture Directories, 2 ; ISSN 0743-7528).

Class Numbers:

Library of Congress E184 S75

ISBN 0313247897

OCLC 19323859

LCCN 89-1922

Notes:

Bibliography: p. [237]-245

• Four chapters feature state-by-state listings of resources on material culture produced from the mid-16th century to the 1980s. Chapter 1, the most extensive, is a directory of artifact collections in 181 museums, historical societies, and other public and private organizations, with brief descriptions of content and accessibility. Artifacts include textiles, furniture, dishes, toys, tools, religious objects, buildings, and more. Other chapters list sites named on the National Register of Historic Places, folklore archives, and cultural festivals. Hispanic populations of all types are considered, but the majority of resources relate to the cultures of Mexican Americans in New Mexico and Texas. Colorado, New Mexico, Texas, Kansas, and Wyoming are represented in at least one chapter. Bibliography and index by topic and type of artifact. Though dated and not comprehensive, the book identifies possible resources for follow-up. — JD

Festivals

CB15 Roy, Christian, 1963-   . - **Traditional Festivals : A Multicultural Encyclopedia**. - Santa Barbara, CA : ABC-CLIO, 2005. - 2 v. (548 p.) ; ill.

Class Numbers:

Library of Congress GT3925

ISBN 1576070891

LCCN 2005-10444

Notes:

Electronic book: http://www.netLibrary.com/urlapi.asp?
action=summary&v=1&bookid=138286

Includes bibliographical references; index

Table of contents: http://www.loc.gov/catdir/toc/
ecip0511/2005010444.html

• Roy (Laval Univ.) covers festivals celebrated throughout the world, many religious in origin, but some secular. Entries are well-written and intended for educated adults rather than specialists, but explore various aspects of the observances and offer helpful section headings. Entries end with brief lists of readings. Plains students will find helpful introductions to powwows, Shalako (Zuni), and the Sun Dance. The second volume supplies an index and tables of the dates of occurrence of various festivals throughout the 21st century. — RB

Proverbs

CB16 Glazer, Mark, comp. - **A Dictionary of Mexican American Proverbs**. - New York : Greenwood Pr., 1987. - xxii, 347 p.

Class Numbers:
Library of Congress PN6426.3.T4
ISBN 031325854
LCCN 87-23721
Notes:
Bibliography: p. xvii-xx; indexes

• The first systematic dictionary of Mexican American proverbs in current usage, based on research conducted in the Lower Rio Grande Valley of Texas and archived in the Rio Grande Folklore Archive. It contains 986 proverbs with doubles and variations raising the number to 3,485. Interestingly, a fifth of the total consists of variations on only 16 proverbs, the most common translating as "Tell me with whom you walk and I will tell you who you are." Each is listed alphabetically in Spanish by an underlined keyword followed by a listing of variations and an English translation or interpretation. Entries are enhanced with contextual information on usage and references to previous publications of the same or similar proverbs. The frequency of male and female informants is reported for each. A statistical analysis of topics is found in the introduction and tabular summary data on the informants and the form for recording oral interviews in an appendix. Indexed by topic in separate Spanish and English indexes. — *JD, JB*

CB17 Mieder, Wolfgang, ed. - **A Dictionary of American Proverbs** / Wolfgang Mieder, ed.-in-chief ; Stewart A. Kingsbury, Kelsie B. Harder, eds. - New York ; Oxford, UK : Oxford Univ. Pr., 1997, 1992. - 710 p.

Class Numbers:
Library of Congress PN6426.D53
ISBN 0195053990 0195111338 (pbk.)
LCCN 91-15508
Notes:
Bibliography: p. 691-710

• Mieder (German and Russian, Univ. of Vermont) edits a comprehensive collection of 15,000 proverbs used in American speech. His work is the result of field research conducted under the direction of Margaret M. Bryant, head of the Committee on Proverbial Sayings of the American Dialect Society, 1945-1985. The proverbs are listed in alphabetical order by the most significant keyword followed by common phrases (e.g., blame; 1. "Avoid that which you blame in others. 2. When fools make mistakes, they blame it on Providence" [p. 55]). Further information includes variants, informants' comments, recorded regional distribution, history, and cross-references. Midwestern and Western states where proverbs are commonly heard include Arizona, California, Kansas, Nebraska, North Dakota, South Dakota, Oklahoma, and Wyoming. There is no index that would allow easy identification of proverb origins by state. List of abbreviations; 20-page bibliography. — *GK*

Archaeology

CB18 **Annotated Bibliography of Saskatchewan Archaeology and Prehistory** / ed. by Tim E.H. Jones ; with contributions by Dennis C. Joyes, David L. Kelly and Henry T. Epp. - Saskatoon, SK : Saskatchewan Archaeological Society, 1988. - 196 p.

Class Numbers:
National Library of Canada Z1395 A67
OCLC 20439895
Notes:
Electronic book: http://www.ourroots.ca/e/toc.asp?
id=2577

• Author listing of an estimated 1,050 items, including unpublished reports. The detailed index identifies individual archaeological sites, pictographs, petroglyphs, objects such as stone axes and iron ware, and a variety of elements in the province's prehistory. Concise annotations. — *LMcD*

CB19 Bell, Robert Eugene, 1914- . - **Oklahoma Archaeology : An Annotated Bibliography**. - Norman, OK : Univ. of Oklahoma Pr., 1978. - 155 p. - (A Stovall Museum publication).

Class Numbers:
Library of Congress Z1208.U5
ISBN 0806114975
OCLC 4364968
LCCN 78-113267
Notes:
1st ed., 1969
Index

• The compiler claims most items in this bibliography "report archaeological discoveries, excavation reports, area surveys, or interpretive accounts." It is arranged alphabetically by author, with no indexes, rendering the contents almost completely inaccessible. — *MB*

CB20 Bell, Robert Eugene, 1914- . - **Oklahoma Indian Artifacts** / by Robert E. Bell and George Lynn Cross. - Norman, OK : Stovall Museum, [1980]. - 114 p. ; ill. - (Contributions from the Stovall Museum, Univ. of Oklahoma, 4).

Class Numbers:
Library of Congress E78.O45
LCCN 80-624089

• A field guide for identifying Indian artifacts dating from Paleo-Indian times through the 18th century, all commonly found in Oklahoma. Rare artifacts, such as effigy pipes and monolithic axes, are not included. Artifacts are organized first by material (chipped stone; pecked, ground and polished stone; bone; shell; clay; or metal), then by function. Descriptions cover uses, age, locations, makers, materials, and fabrication techniques. Each type is illustrated with clear drawings of several specimens from the collections of the University of Oklahoma. A scholar's work that makes identification easy for professional archaeologists and amateurs. —*JD*

CB21   Hardy, Kenneth J. - **Calgary Archaeology, 1959-1980 : A Select, Annotated Bibliography**. - Calgary, AB : K.J. Hardy, 1982. - 57 leaves.

Class Numbers:
Library of Congress Z1392.C24
National Library of Canada FC3697.39
OCLC 10057680
Notes:
Non-thesis project submitted to the Faculty of Library Science, Univ. of Alberta

• Chronological listing of 92 inventories and excavations conducted in an area of southwestern Alberta centered on Calgary. Most are unpublished reports located at the Archaeological Survey of Alberta in Edmonton. Author, title, and keyword indexes. Intended as a preliminary guide for archaeologists and interested amateurs. — *LMcD*

CB22   Simons, Helen, comp. - **Archeological Bibliography for the Northern Panhandle Region of Texas**. - Austin, TX : Texas Historical Commission, 1988. - 225 p. ; [2] leaves of plates, ill., maps. - (Office of the State Archeologist, special report, 30).

Class Numbers:
Library of Congress F392.P168
Government Document Texas H2000.7 Sp31 no. 30
OCLC 18597958
LCCN 88-622923

• Covers the 20 northernmost counties. Materials are presented in two main sections: an archaeological bibliography, accompanied by keyword, county, and regional indexes; and two bibliographies, one covering enthnohistory, the other the environment. Materials are organized alphabetically by author within each section. The appendix consists of a bibliography of bibliographies and a general index, along with a summary of the methodology used to identify resources listed in the publication. — *MS*

CB23   Turner, Ellen Sue, 1924-   . - **A Field Guide to Stone Artifacts of Texas Indians** / [by] Ellen Sue Turner

and Thomas R. Hester ; ill. by Kathy Roemer ; foreword by Harry J. Shafer. - Houston, TX : Gulf Publ. Co., 1999. - 395 p. ; ill. - (Gulf Publishing field guide series).

Class Numbers:
Library of Congress E78.T4
ISBN 0891230513
LCCN 99-18245
Notes:
Includes bibliographical references (p. 338-395)
Reprint. Originally publ.: Austin, TX: Texas Monthly Pr., 1985

• An archaeological study of stone artifacts made and used by Indians in the prehistory of Texas. Artifacts are divided into three categories: projectile points, chipped stone artifacts, and ground, pecked, and polished stone artifacts. In the projectile point section, artifacts are listed by conventional names, often derived from the name of the place where they were discovered; in the other sections, names describe their use or the number of flaked surfaces (biface, uniface). Most artifacts occupy a page that includes line drawings and a small distribution map. Appendixes pay homage to the social network of archaeology (archaeological societies, groups to contact); the work ends with a 58-page bibliography, but no index. Many artifacts were discovered in the Prairies-Plains regions of Texas: lower Pecos, Central, North Central, Llano Estacado, and Panhandle. — *RB*

CB24   Zimmerman, Karen P. - **Sources for South Dakota Prehistory** / by Karen P. Zimmerman and Larry J. Zimmerman. - Vermillion, SD : Univ. of South Dakota Archaeology Laboratory, 1981. - 51 p. ; map. - (South Dakota Archaeological Society. Special publication, 5).

Class Numbers:
Library of Congress Z1208.S62
LCCN 81-14751

• The Zimmermans (archaeology and library, Univ. of South Dakota) list 611 sources on South Dakota prehistory in alphabetical order by primary author. The intended audience is researchers and contractors coming into the state to conduct field work. A map indicates archaeological regions of South Dakota; the authors list the recorded sites by county. The bibliography is divided into general works, source listings by authors, and source listings by geographic regions. — *GK*

CC : ETHNOLOGY

Scope Lists works concerned with non-Native groups that have emigrated to the United States or Canada, settled in the Prairies-Plains region, and retain a degree of the culture or language of their home countries, allowing them to be identified as separate cultural groups. This section also makes room for Native peoples–American Indians and Canadian First Nations, and for general works about ethnography.

ETHNOGRAPHY

CC1   eHRAF Collection of Ethnography [Internet Site]. - [New Haven, CT] : Human Relations Area Files Inc., 1997- . - http://www.yale.edu/hraf

> OCLC 58781211
> Access Date: Jan. 1980
> Fees: Subscription

• Makes accessible full-text excerpts from anthropology books, articles, and manuscripts at the paragraph level according to *Outline of Cultural Materials* and *Outline of World Cultures*, classifications developed by George Peter Murdock. Begun in the 1930s, offered in paper in 1949, converted to microfiche in the late 1950s and available only in electronic format since 1994, the collection is used to research particular culture groups or to make comparisons across cultures. Currently, *eHRAF* is incomplete; each annual installment contains about 40 percent new material, the remainder converted from the microfiche version. Some older files will not be converted. North American cultures include Great Plains Pawnee, Blackfoot, Assiniboine, Chicanos, Chipewyan, and Arab Canadians. Since HRAF continues to convert older microfiche documents to electronic format, with North American cultures receiving high priority, Great Plains researchers will see *eHRAF* grow in usefulness. HRAF also produces *eHRAF Collection of Archaeology*, which at present does not cover the Great Plains. — *JD*

CC2   Harvard Encyclopedia of American Ethnic Groups / Stephan Thernstrom, ed. ; Ann Orlov, managing ed. ; Oscar Handlin, consulting ed. - Cambridge, MA : Belknap Pr. of Harvard Univ., 1980. - xxv, 1076 p.

> Class Numbers:
>   Library of Congress E184.A1

> ISBN 0674375122
> LCCN 80-17756
> Notes:
>   Includes bibliographies

• Thernstrom and Handlin (both history, Harvard Univ.) and Orlov (freelance writer) present a comprehensive review of 100 ethnic groups that live in the U.S. and Canada. The scholarly thematic essays interpret economic, educational, religious, political, discrimination, and policy issues. Groups and definitions in this volume that pertain to Prairies-Plains include American Indians, Czechs, Germans, Hispanics, Hungarians, Hutterites, Mexicans, Mormons, Norwegians, Slovaks, and Swedes. Contains 87 maps; 29 thematic essays; 116 tables; two appendixes (size of ethnic groups and Census information). — *GK*

CC3   Murdock, George Peter, 1897- . - Ethnographic Bibliography of North America / [by] George Peter Murdock and Timothy J. O'Leary, with the assistance of John Beierle [et al.]. - New Haven, CT : Human Relations Area Files, 1975. - 5 v. ; maps. - (Behavior science bibliographies).

> Class Numbers:
>   Library of Congress E77   Z1209.2.N67
> ISBN 0875362052
> LCCN 75-17091

• Murdock's standard reference set cites 40,000 publications, 1959-1972, having to do with 277 native peoples found in North America (the U.S. and Canada). Citations, arranged alphabetically by author, include book or journal title, subtitle, title of article, publisher information, year/volume of publication, inclusive page numbers. Each volume includes a distribution map of ethnic groups, an introductory essay about geographic characteristics of the region, and a brief history of the ethnic groups. Prairies-Plains researchers should consult volume 1, which cites general reference works on the Plains, Midwest, and Southwest; section 10 of volume 4, concerned with the Midwest (e.g., Fox, Menomini, Potawatomi, Shawnee); and volume 5, treating the Plains (e.g., Arapaho, Blackfoot, Cheyenne, Comanche, Kansas, Kiowa, Mandan, Omaha, Pawnee, Ponca, Siouans) and Southwest (e.g., Acoma, Hopi, Jicarilla, Mescalero, Taos). Murdock (anthropology, Yale and Univ. of Pittsburgh) was associated with Human Relations Area Files. — *GK*

UNITED STATES

General Works
See also **Upton, America's Architectural Roots, BD32**

CC4   The Greenwood Encyclopedia of Multiethnic American Literature / ed. by Emmanuel S. Nelson. - Westport, CT : Greenwood Pr., 2005. - 5 v.

> Class Numbers:
>> Library of Congress P153.M56
>> ISBN 031333059X (set) 0313330603 (v.1)
>>   0313330611 (v. 2) 031333062X (v. 3)
>>   0313330638 (v. 4) 0313330646 (v. 5)
>> OCLC 60839325
>> LCCN 2005-18960
>> Notes:
>>> Includes bibliographical references (p. [2372]-2379) ; index
>>> Review by P.M. Adams: *Choice* 43.8 (Apr. 2006): review 43-4376
>>> Table of contents: http://www.loc.gov/catdir/toc/ecip0515/2005018960.html

• Nelson (English, SUNY Cortland) edits a comprehensive reference set concerned with the flourishing field of ethnic and multicultural literature. The volumes contain 1,100 alphabetical entries, 1,000 of them devoted to individual authors. The ethnic groups covered are Native Americans and Americans whose ancestry is Mexican, Czech, German, Slovak/Slovene, Norwegian, and Polish. Among topics covered in the work are the American Indian Movement, immigration, and multiculturalism. General sources are cited after each entry, and the "Guide to Related Topics" lists significant authors categorized by ethnic group. Includes photographs of authors and a roster of scholarly contributors. — *GK*

CC5   Inglehart, Babette F. - The Image of Pluralism in American Literature : An Annotated Bibliography on the American Experience of European Ethnic Groups / by Babette F. Inglehart and Anthony R. Mangione. - New York : Institute of Pluralism and Group Identity of the American Jewish Committee, 1974. - 73 p.

> Class Numbers:
>> Library of Congress PS173.M54; Z1225
>> LCCN 75-308114

• Inglehart (Chicago State Univ.) and Mangione (Brooklyn College) present a selective bibliography of 400 items intended to help teachers and students understand the immigrant experience. The entries, heavily weighted toward fiction, cover only European immigrants, since the editors believe other ethnic groups are adequately treated by other sources. A subject index, arranged by social experiences of immigrant groups (politics, acculturation, generational conflict), cites only titles of works and entry numbers. Since no geographic approach is provided (most entries deal with New York and Chicago), titles relating to Prairies-Plains (chiefly well-known writers such as Cather, Ostenso, Rølvaag) must be dug out by scanning entire sections. — *RB*

CC6   Levinson, David, 1947-   , ed. - American Immigrant Cultures : Builders of a Nation / ed. by David Levinson, Melvin Ember. - New York : Macmillan Reference USA, 1997. - 2 v. ; ill., maps.

> Class Numbers:
>> Library of Congress E184.A1
>> ISBN 0028972082 0028972139 (v. 2) 0028972147 (v. 1)
>> LCCN 97-17477
>> Notes:
>>> Includes bibliographical references; index

• Edited by two well-known anthropologists presently or formerly associated with Human Relations Area Files, *American Immigrant Cultures* attempts to account for the impact 161 immigrant groups have had on the culture and society of the U.S. (Indigenous groups are considered in Levinson's *Encyclopedia of World Cultures*, **CB1**.) For each group, the editors discuss its place of origin, the immigration patterns the group followed, and the history of its integration into American society, or its attempts to resist assimilation. Articles usually run several pages, incorporate illustrations, and end with bibliographies; they are arranged alphabetically by group name. Appendixes include outline maps of portions of the world showing approximate region of origin for all groups, a table showing numbers of persons who reported one or two specific ancestries in the 1990 Census, and numbers of persons of specific ancestry residing in each state of the U.S., also from the 1990 census. The index allows the set to be used by Prairies-Plains researchers, since it lists for each state immigrants who have settled or had influence there; all Plains states are represented. — *RB*

CC7   Nebraska Curriculum Development Center. - Broken Hoops and Plains People : A Catalogue of Ethnic Resources in the Humanities : Nebraska and Surrounding Areas / writers, Galen Buller [et al.] ; photographer, Roger Rejda. - Lincoln, NE : Nebraska Curriculum Development Center, 1976. - xxiii, 438 p. ; [32] leaves of plates, ill.

> Class Numbers:
>> Library of Congress F675.A1
>> LCCN 78-620647
>> Notes:
>>> Bibliography: p. [417]-438

• The title might make one expect this work to be concerned chiefly with Plains Indians, but in fact the 11 chapters cover a wide variety of ethnic groups in Nebraska: Indians, Chicanos, blacks, Czechs, Russian Germans, Scandinavians, Jews, Italians, Irish, Dutch, and Japanese. Chapters were written by specialists, nearly all faculty at the University of Nebraska. Each chapter begins with a well-chosen selection of black-and-white photos. Most sections contain bibliographic references and useful demographic data. Ten bibliographies at the back of the book, arranged by ethnic group (omitting the Japanese) vary in arrangement. — *MB*

CC8   Santa Barbara (CA). County Board of Education. - **The Emerging Minorities in America : A Resource Guide for Teachers**. - Santa Barbara, CA : ABC-Clio, 1972. - 256 p.

    Class Numbers:
        Library of Congress E184.A1
    ISBN 0874360927
    OCLC 827230
    LCCN 72-77550
    Notes:
        Includes bibliographies
        Prepared for the Santa Barbara County Board of
            Education

• For each of four ethnic groups (black Americans, Asian Americans, Indians, and Mexican Americans), discussion focuses on historical perspectives, biographical summaries, a bibliography of sources used, and other references. In the case of Asian Americans the first three sections are further subdivided into Japanese, Chinese, and Filipino. The sections most likely to interest Prairies-Plains students are those on Indians and Mexican Americans, which provide biographies of such persons as Black Elk, Crazy Horse, Vine Deloria, Red Cloud, Carlos Rivera, and Lee Trevino. Appendix A identifies persons mentioned by historical period and appendix B by profession. There is no index. In keeping with the subtitle, there is a brief introductory section on teaching strategies. Now somewhat dated. — *MB*

CC9   Sherman, William Charles, 1927-   . - **Prairie Mosaic : An Ethnic Atlas of Rural North Dakota**. - Fargo, ND : North Dakota Institute for Regional Studies, 1983. - 152 p. ; ill. ; 29 cm.

    Class Numbers:
        Library of Congress F645.A1
    ISBN 091104227X
    OCLC 9697508
    LCCN 82-61305
    Notes:
        Bibliography: p. [120]-122; index

• Sherman (sociology, North Dakota State Univ.) provides commentary on the settlement patterns, community life, and statistical characteristics of a number of ethic groups who settled in North Dakota. The locations and counties of these nationalities (Scandinavians, Bohemians, Irish, Polish, Swedes, Germans, Hutterite, and French) is traced until 1965. The data are shown on double-page maps that divide the state into six regions (Northwest, Southwest, Southcentral, Northcentral, Southeast, and Northeast). A bibliographic essay contains information on historical applicability and contemporary reliability. Five tables: "County Totals of North Dakota's Largest National Groups," "Population Density of Rural North Dakota," "Parallel Landownership Studies," "Land Owned by People

of Norwegian Descent, 1913-14," "Ethnic Settlement Areas in North Dakota as of 1965." — **GK**

CC10   Svoboda, Joseph G., comp. - **Preliminary Guide to Ethnic Resource Materials in Great Plains Repositories** / comp. by Joseph G. Svoboda and David G. Dunning. - Lincoln, NE : Univ. Libraries and Center for Great Plains Studies, Univ. of Nebraska-Lincoln, 1978. - 48 p.

    Class Numbers:
        Library of Congress F596.3.A1
    LCCN 80-622842

• Svoboda (formerly archivist, Univ. Libraries, Univ. of Nebraska–Lincoln) identifies reference materials having to do with 27 ethnic groups. The compilers define ethnic resources as materials (manuscript collections or newspapers) of organizations or individuals that pertain to a specific ethnic group. Within each ethnic group, resources are organized by state, then by institution. — *MB*

Blacks

CC11   Abajian, James de T. - **Blacks and Their Contributions to the American West : A Bibliography and Union List of Library Holdings through 1970** / comp. for the Friends of the San Francisco Public Library. - Boston, MA : G.K. Hall, 1974. - xxii, 487 p.

    Class Numbers:
        Library of Congress Z1361.N39
    ISBN 0816111391
    OCLC 902971
    LCCN 74-8695
    Notes:
        In cooperation with the American Library
            Association

• Heavily weighted toward California, Abajian's bibliography includes works by and about blacks in Montana, Wyoming, New Mexico, and Colorado. Beginning with the early settlement period and extending through the Civil Rights and Black Power eras, it cites over 4,000 published monographs and serials held by surveyed public and academic libraries, as well as articles in scholarly and black journals, but excludes archival materials and articles in general popular magazines. Organized by topics, including art and architecture, black movements and racial dissent, cookbooks and food, education, journalism, literature, ranch life, and slavery and antislavery. Entries include brief annotations and holding libraries. Sections on bibliographies and finding aids, directories and Census records, and black periodicals are especially useful, as is a state-by-state list of newspapers, many owned by blacks. Indexed by authors, topics, and place-names. — *JD*

CC12 Curtis, Nancy C. - **Black Heritage Sites : An African American Odyssey and Finder's Guide**. - Chicago, IL : American Library Association, 1996. - 677 p. ; ill.

> Class Numbers:
> Library of Congress E159
> ISBN 0838906435 1565844327
> OCLC 32087153
> LCCN 95-5788
> Notes:
> Includes bibliographical references ; index

• Curtis's travel guide to major landmarks in black American history throughout the U.S. and Canada is divided into geographic regions, covering the Midwest, Southwest, and West in parts 3-5. The author provides a historical introductory overview, and the sites appear by state in alphabetical order. Information includes addresses, telephone numbers, fees, illustrations, and sources consulted. — *GK*

CC13 Glasrud, Bruce A., comp. - **African Americans in the West : A Bibliography of Secondary Sources** / with contributions by Laurie Champion, William H. Leckie, Tasha B. Stewart ; ed. by Sheron Smith-Savage. - Alpine, TX : Sul Ross State Univ., Center for Big Bend Studies, 1998. - 192 p. ; ill. - (Sul Ross State University. Center for Big Bend Studies. Occasional papers, 2).

> Class Numbers:
> Library of Congress E185.925
> Government Documents Texas Z S900.7 OC1 No.2
> ISBN 0964762935 9780964762930
> OCLC 39475498
> LCCN 98-222377
> Notes:
> Includes bibliographical references; index

• Intended for graduate students, Glasrud's bibliography concentrates on secondary sources "to enable students to discover ... what has been written on a topic prior to undertaking their own research" (Preface). He arranges the bibliography in four sections: a general section, seven chronological chapters, ten chapters for states or regions, and four topical chapters. Entries are alphabetical by author in each chapter; there are no annotations, but entries supply all the needed elements. For Prairies-Plains students and researchers, the most useful sections are likely to be chapters 5, "Cowboys," 7, "Buffalo Soldiers," 11, "Dakotas, Colorado, Wyoming, Nebraska, Montana," 13, "Indian Territory/Oklahoma," 14, "Kansas and the Exodusters," and 20, "Women." Chapter 22 lists films. Author index. — *RB*

CC14 Gordon, Jacob U. - **Narratives of African Americans in Kansas, 1870-1992 : Beyond the Exodust Movement**. - Lewiston, NY : E. Mellen Pr., 1993. - 302 p. ; ill.

> Class Numbers:
> Library of Congress E185.96
> ISBN 0773493506 9780773493506
> OCLC 28633613
> LCCN 93-30605
> Notes:
> Includes bibliographical references (p. [301]-302)

• Of this volume's two parts, the first, by far the larger, contains 35 narratives by black Americans with connections to Kansas. The narratives vary widely in format depending on the author. They are chiefly reminiscences by older black Americans, most born in the first 20 years of the 20th century. Best known among them is photographer Gordon Parks. The second part consists of 88 brief biographical sketches of "Black Role Models," where Parks is again included. Some black athletes are included (e.g., Gale Sayers), but others are conspicuous by their absence (e.g., Wilt Chamberlain). The volume concludes with information on black history collections at the University of Kansas and brief entries on black state legislators. A center section of full-page photos enhances the book's usefulness. — *MB*

CC15 Hudson, J. Blaine. - **Encyclopedia of the Underground Railroad**. - Jefferson, NC : McFarland, 2006. - 308 p. ; ill., maps.

> Class Numbers:
> Library of Congress E450
> ISBN 0786424591 9780786424597
> OCLC 62895801
> LCCN 2005-37582
> Notes:
> Includes bibliographical references (p. 288-300); index
> Table of contents: http://www.loc.gov/catdir/toc/ecip066/2005037582.html

• Canada may have proved the safest place for fugitive slaves, but the rest of the Great Plains played a role in the underground railroad. Entries in Hudson's encyclopedia describe underground railroad sites in Colorado, Nebraska, and Kansas; "Friends of the Fugitive" such as John Brown in Kansas and John Boulwar in Nebraska; the significance of events such as the Kansas-Nebraska Act; and fugitive slave migrations into and across the Plains territories. Appendixes consist of "Selected Friends of the Fugitive by Last Name," "Selected Friends of the Fugitive by State (and Canada)," "Selected Underground Railroad Sites by State (and Canada)," "National Park Service Underground Railroad Sites," "Bibliography of Slave Autobiographies," and "Selected Antislavery and Underground Railroad Songs." An extensive bibliography covers black American newspapers, government documents, document collections, and unpublished documents as well as published secondary sources. Topical index includes states. — *JD*

CC16 Junne, George H. - **The Black American West : A Bibliography**. - Greeley, CO : Univ. of Northern Colorado, Africana Studies Dept., [1998?]. - 228 p. - (University of Northern Colorado. Dept. of Africana Studies. Occasional papers series, 2).

Class Numbers:
Library of Congress E185.925
OCLC 41464298

• Recognizing the West's shifting borders and early occupation, this bibliography of 5,000 entries broadly defines it in terms of time and space. The bibliographic entries are equally broad and include scholarly and popular books and journals in all fields. It is organized by topical chapters: general Black western history; art and artists; James Beckwourth and Edward Rose (explorers); Black and Native American relationships; Black towns, black women, environmental issues; Estevanico (explorer) and Spanish explorations; health; Kansas-Nebraska Act; Ku Klux Klan; George McJunkin (cowboy); Bill Pickett (cowboy); and York (explorer). Additional sections cover twenty states including Colorado, Kansas, Nebraska, New Mexico, North Dakota, Oklahoma, South Dakota and Texas. Each section is divided into articles and books. Books include speeches, pamphlets, and government documents. A few entries are briefly annotated. Works include "Negroes and the Creek Nation" published in *Southern Workman* in 1908; Slave *Narratives of the Federal Writers' Project* collected from 1936-1938; *The Negro Cowboy*, a watershed title from 1965; and "Black Soldiers at Fort Hays, Kansas, 1867-1869" published in *Great Plains Quarterly* in 1997. The work includes a bibliography of related bibliographies and an author index. — *JD*

CC17 Junne, George H. - **Blacks in the American West and Beyond–America, Canada, and Mexico : A Selectively Annotated Bibliography**. - Westport, CT : Greenwood Pr., 2000. - 686 p. - (Bibliographies and Indexes in Afro-American and African Studies, 40 ; ISSN 0742-6925).

Class Numbers:
Library of Congress E185.925; Z1361.N39
ISBN 0313312087 9780313312083
0313065055(electronic bk.)
9780313065057 (electronic bk.)
OCLC 43333625
LCCN 00-20764
Notes:
Electronic book: http://www.netLibrary.com/urlapi.asp?
action=summary&v=1&bookid=152369
Indexes

• Junne lists several thousand works examining the history and experience of blacks in a range of areas, both jurisdictionally and thematically. Organization is topical (general history, Kansas-Nebraska Act, Ku Klux Klan, etc.) and geographical by state. Within each category entries are separately arranged by publication type: articles, books, theses, and other publications; article citations do not indicate pagination. The relatively few annotations are rarely more than a phrase in length. Coverage appears uneven: art and music are treated but literature is not. Black newspapers are identified under each state. All Plains states are included but the states smaller in population (e.g., the Dakotas) are covered in two or three pages. Despite the western focus suggested by the title, the Canadian portion oddly includes sections on the eastern provinces of Ontario, Quebec and Nova Scotia. Author and subject indexes, although the latter is not detailed. Useful to update earlier works such as *Blacks and Their Contributions to the American West* (**CC11**). —*LMcD*

CC18 Polk, Donna Mays, 1943-   . - **Black Men and Women of Nebraska** / photographed by John Spence. - Lincoln, NE : Nebraska Black History Preservation Society, 1981. - 62 p. ; ports.

Class Numbers:
Library of Congress E185.93.N5
OCLC 8582523
Notes:
Bibliography: p. 56-61

• Biographies and portraits of 28 Nebraskans who are historical and contemporary figures with regional or national reputations in a variety of fields. They include Mildred Brown, founder and publisher of the *Omaha Star*; Bertha Calloway, founder and curator of the Great Plains Black Museum; Ernie Chambers, an eloquent and powerful state legislator since 1970; Johnny Rodgers, Nebraska's most famous college football player; and Matthew Oliver Ricketts, a 19th-century physician and legislator who was the first African American to graduate from a Nebraska university. Primary and secondary sources are listed in an appendix. An updated and more complete edition is needed. —*JD*

Europeans

CC19 **Danes in America** / tr. by Ninna Engskow ; ed. by John W. Nielsen. - Blair, NE : Lur Publ., Danish Immigrant Archive, Dana College, 2000-2001. - 2 v. ; ill., ports., maps.

ISBN 093069712X
OCLC 50408988
Notes:
Contents: v. 1, Danish-American Lutheranism from 1860 to 1908 / Peder Kjølhede, Per Sorensen Vig, Ivar Marius Hansen; foreword by Peter l. Petersen; tr. by Edward Hansen and Inga Larsen; v. 2, Kansas and Nebraska / tr. by Ninna Engskow, ed. by John W. Nielsen
Includes bibliographical references; indexes
Originally publ.: *Danske i Amerika*, 1899

• The second volume will interest Prairies-Plains researchers. The editor notes that in the Danish original, the selections were rather random with some areas getting excellent coverage and others none at all (e.g., Omaha). The shorter of the two parts, which concerns Danes in Kansas, has two essays on Danish settlers in Marshall and Lincoln counties and includes brief biographical sketches with photos of the subjects. There is a single page of population data. The Nebraska coverage is more extensive, with more than a dozen essays on pioneer life and settlements in several counties, including Cass, Lancaster, and Washington. This section is also illustrated with photos from the original publication. There are two good indexes, for persons and places. A valuable historical resource. — *MB*

CC20 Jerabek, Esther, 1897-1979. - **Czechs and Slovaks in North America : A Bibliography**. - New York : Czechoslovak Society of Arts & Sciences in America, 1976. - 448 p.

> Class Numbers:
> Library of Congress E184.B67   Z1361.C94
> LCCN 77-155955

* A *tour d'horizon* of immigrant Czech and Slovak history and culture from the 1600s to the late 20th century, the 7,600 titles in this bibliography also reflect the major influx of immigrants to the Great Plains in the mid-19th century. Many titles are in Czech or Slovak, though most are published by U.S. presses. The entries are unannotated and organized by broad topics such as education, music, immigration, literature, journalism, and law. Bibliographies, reference books, dictionaries, directories, and periodicals and newspapers are in separate sections. The latter section is particularly useful, giving periodical publisher, place, frequency, dates of publication, and brief histories of mergers and title changes, followed by an index of previous titles. Many materials, uncataloged at the time the bibliography was published, have found their way into WorldCat. Extensive index of names, places, and subjects. — *JD*

CC21 Rife, Janet Warkentin. - **Germans and German-Russians in Nebraska : A Research Guide to Nebraska Ethnic Studies**. - Lincoln, NE : Center for Great Plains Studies : Nebraska Curriculum Development Center, 1980. - - (Nebraska ethnic resources series).

> Class Numbers:
> Library of Congress F675.G3 ; Z1307
> ISBN 0938932012 (pbk.) 9780938932017 (pbk.)
> OCLC 7378899
> LCCN 80-70961

• In the Plains states, successive influxes of German immigrants arrived from the eastern states and directly from Germany beginning in the early 1800s. The numbers swelled in the 1870s when Germans resident in Russia for decades also began emigrating to North and South America in large numbers, driven by Russian social conditions and government policies. The guide begins with a bibliography of books, journals, brochures, booklets, theses, and unpublished works, with detailed annotations and holdings information for Nebraska libraries. Then come descriptions of museums, music groups, newspapers, church records, communities, events, organizations, institutions, collections of personal papers, photograph collections, tape collections, and resource people. Appendixes describe naturalization, land, tax, census, probate and military records. The growing number of people researching Germans from Russia will locate many of the items Rife lists in the library of the American Historical Society of Germans from Russia in Lincoln, NE, and will want to update the book at the AHSGR Internet site, http://www.ahsgr.org/. — *JD*

CC22 Thompson, Harry Floyd, 1953- , comp. - **Guide to Collections Relating to South Dakota Norwegian-Americans** / comp. by Harry F. Thompson, with the assistance of Arthur R. Huseboe and Paul B. Olson ; additional assistance by Carol Riswold and D. Joy Harris. - Sioux Falls, SD : Center for Western Studies, Augustana College, 1991. - 65 p.

> Class Numbers:
> Library of Congress F660.S2 Z1335
> ISBN 0931170508
> OCLC 23692986
> LCCN 91-3761
> Notes:
> Index

• A quick reference guide to collections relating to South Dakota Norwegian Americans located in 55 institutions. The guide has a table of contents, a ten-page introduction, an alphabetical list of collections with annotations, and a personal name index. Thompson is director of the Center for Western Studies, Augustana College. Since many institutions failed to return questionnaires describing their holdings, the guide is not comprehensive. — *GK*

Latinos/Latinas

Note Includes persons or groups claiming heritage from countries of the Iberian peninsula, from Mexico, from Latin America, or from Spanish-speaking islands of the Caribbean.

CC23 Beers, Henry Putney. - **Spanish & Mexican Records of the American Southwest : A Bibliographical Guide to Archive and Manuscript Sources**. - Tucson, AZ : Univ. of Arizona Pr., 1979. - 493 p. ; ill.

> 0816506736
> Class Numbers:
> Library of Congress F799; Z1251.S8

ISBN 0816505322 (pbk.)
OCLC 4804700
LCCN 79-4313
Notes:
Includes bibliographical references (p. 385-454); index

• Beers compiles information from finding aids for archival and manuscript repositories throughout the U.S., clarifying complex records produced by two governments over three centuries. The first four parts cover the records of four states: New Mexico, Texas, California, and Arizona. Following a summary of the state's history and government, each part describes and gives locations for provincial records, legislative records, archival reproductions, documentary publications, manuscript collections, land records, local jurisdiction records, and ecclesiastical records. Part five has a bibliography of bibliographies; manuscript and archive collections; published material from manuscripts and archives; other published primary sources; guides, inventories and catalogs; and secondary publications. Appendixes include a list of repositories, a documentary list of California archives, files in the Office of the U.S. Surveyor General, and files in the Spanish Archives of the Land Office in San Francisco. Thoroughly indexed by name, agency, region, collection, and type of material. Essential for researchers seeking primary records on the Southwest. — *JD*

CC24 Glasrud, Bruce A. - **Bibliophiling Tejano Scholarship : Secondary Sources on Hispanic Texans** / [comp. by] Bruce A. Glasrud and Arnoldo De León. - Alpine, TX : Sul Ross State Univ., Center for Big Bend Studies, 2003. - 471 p. ; ill. - (Center for Big Bend Studies occasional papers, 8).

Class Numbers:
Government Document Texas Z S900.7 OC1 no. 8
ISBN 097077091X

• A unique volume that surveys the world of Tejano culture–works that focus on Texas in setting or theme and have as subjects people of Mexican descent. Entries cite books, articles, dissertations, and other publications, and are arranged by three areas: general reference, historic time periods, and topics. The historic period covers 1716 to the present and the topical section covers, e.g., economics, education, family, folklore, music, religion, and demographics. A thorough review of Tejano culture, which is set in part in the southern Great Plains. — *JB*

CC25 Meier, Matt S. - **Bibliography of Mexican American History.** - Westport, CT : Greenwood Pr., 1984. - 500 p.

Class Numbers:
Library of Congress E184.M5 Z1361.M4
ISBN 031323776X

OCLC 10019924
LCCN 83-18585
Notes:
Indexes

• Meier (Santa Clara Univ.) compiles a comprehensive bibliography of primary and secondary sources in the growing field of Chicano studies for scholars, researchers, and students. The work has 4,372 entries with brief annotations in 12 chapters: general works; Colonial period; Mexican period; Guadalupe Hidalgo to 1900; 1900 to World War II; World War II to 1980s; labor, immigration, and border region; civil rights and politics; culture; bibliographies and guides; collections, archives, and libraries; and journals. Within each topical section, the sources are further subdivided by books, theses/dissertations, and periodicals. Author and subject index. — *GK*

CC26 Meier, Matt S. - **Dictionary of Mexican American History** / [by] Matt S. Meier and Feliciano Rivera. - Westport, CT : Greenwood Pr., 1981. - 498 p. ; ill.

Class Numbers:
Library of Congress E184.M5
ISBN 0313212031
OCLC 6863125
LCCN 80-24750
Notes:
Includes bibliographical references (p. [377]-383);
index

• Meier (Santa Clara Univ.) and Rivera concentrate in their encyclopedia on the exploration, opening, and development of the Southwest from the Texas Revolution in 1835 to the emergence of Mexican Americans in the 1980s. The work is arranged alphabetically by keywords, phrases, organizations, and individuals. Organizations are listed by their full names followed by the acronym in parentheses while individuals are listed by last name, first name, followed by birth and death dates. The appendixes include a bibliography, chronology of historical events, text of the Treaty of Guadalupe Hidalgo (1848), glossary of Chicano terms, Mexican American journals, tables of census, education, employment, and immigration, statistical figures, and maps. Cross-references; roster of 28 contributors from academic institutions. — *GK*

CC27 Meier, Matt S. - **Mexican American Biographies : A Historical Dictionary, 1836-1987.** - New York : Greenwood Pr., 1988. - 270 p.

Class Numbers:
Library of Congress E184.M5
ISBN 0313245215
OCLC 15792206
LCCN 87-12025

Notes:
Includes bibliographies; indexes

• Biographies of 270 *prominentes* in education, arts, religion, law, publishing, medicine, sports, and other fields focus on their public and professional lives. Most became prominent in the 20th century, although some are historical figures dating as far back as the Texas Revolution. Averaging about 300 words, entries are based on published sources and information provided by the subjects. Suggestions for additional reading are noted. The majority of subjects are from the Great Plains–132 from Texas or New Mexico and ten from Colorado, Kansas, or Nebraska. Appendixes list biographies by field of professional activity and by state. Subject and name index. — *JD*

CC28 Simons, Helen, ed. - **A Guide to Hispanic Texas** / ed. by Helen Simons and Cathryn A. Hoyt; comp. with the assistance of Ann Perry and Deborah Smith. - 1st abridged edition - Austin, TX : Univ. of Texas Pr., 1996. - 347 p. : ill., maps.

Class Numbers:
Library of Congress F387
ISBN 0292777094
OCLC 34192922
Notes:
Abridged edition of Simons and Hoyt's *Hispanic Texas: A Historical Guide*. Austin, TX: Univ. of Texas Pr., 1992

• "An introduction to the best-known expressions of Hispanic heritage in Texas," the abridged edition operates as a travel guide, eliminating the scholarly essays featured in the first edition. It divides Texas into seven regions, each centered around a major visitor center, to facilitate planning of tours and day trips. Each region is introduced with a history followed by an annotated list of information centers; historic sites; notable architecture; museums, libraries and cultural centers; public art; festivals and events; and scenic drives in each city and its vicinity. Annotations give exact location, description, history, and significance. Extensive references and an index by place, feature, and topic. Illustrated with maps and black-and-white photographs. — *JD*

CC29 Vigil, Maurilio E., 1941- . - **Los Patrones : Profiles of Hispanic Political Leaders in New Mexico History**. - Washington, DC : Univ. Pr. of America, 1980. - 169 p.

Class Numbers:
Library of Congress F805.S75
ISBN 0819109622 0819109630 (pbk.)
LCCN 79-6813
Notes:
Includes bibliographical references

• Hispanic perspectives on 26 Hispanic political leaders cover

three time periods: the Mexican and American occupation, 1812-1850; the territorial period, 1850-1911; and statehood, 1911 onward. Each period is introduced with a historical sketch followed by biographies of varying lengths and source notes that include newspaper articles and other primary documents. Subjects range from Antonio Jose Martinez (priest, educator, public servant, publisher, and folk hero of the occupation) to Donaciano Vigil (second governor during the U.S. occupation), Jose Manuel Gallegos (controversial Catholic priest), and Joseph Montoya (U.S. Senator and member of the panel investigating Watergate). The biographies, which emphasize their subjects' careers and roles in shaping the region, are good sources for readers beginning research and seeking wider views of well-known events. No index. — *JD, JB*

CANADA

French

CC30 Anderson, Alan B., 1939- . - **Guide des sources bibliographiques des communautés francophones de la Saskatchewan = Guide to Bibliographic Sources on Francophone Communities in Saskatchewan**. - Saskatoon, SK : Research Unit for French-Canadian Studies = Unité de recherches pour les études canadiennes-françaises, Univ. of Saskatchewan, 1987. - 15, 10 p. - (Research report / Research Unit for French-Canadian Studies, University of Saskatchewan, 13).

Class Numbers:
National Library of Canada Z1392 S27
OCLC 49142779
Notes:
Index
Preliminary text in French and English
Publ. by Societé historique de la Saskatchewan

• Sections on the French, Belgian, and Métis elements of the Saskatchewan population are organized by type of publication: books, community histories listed by place, reports, theses, articles, etc. Useful in combination with *Guide des sources historiques des francophones aux Archives de la Saskatchewan* (**DB162**). — *LMcD*

CC31 Atlas des francophones de l'Ouest / [Rose Heinekey [et al.] ; Armand Bédard, directeur]. - [s.l.] : [s.n.], 1979. - 124 p. ; ill., folded maps, folded plates ; 41 cm.

Class Numbers:
Library of Congress G 1151 E6
OCLC 8159517
Notes:

Includes bibliographical references, glossary and
  filmography
Printed in Winnipeg by Hignell Printing

• An atlas that examines aspects of the social, economic, and historic situation of the French population of the Prairie provinces and, to a lesser extent, British Columbia. Maps, tables, and graphs illustrate elements such as demography, urban population, migration, education, assimilation, and various types of cultural organizations. Intended for school use. — *LMcD*

CC32 Dorge, Lionel. - **Introduction à l'étude des Franco-Manitobains : essai historique et bibliographique.** - Saint-Boniface, MB : Société historique de Saint-Boniface, 1973. - 298 p.

Class Numbers:
  Library of Congress Z1392.M35
OCLC 1094259
LCCN 74-183310

• The first section (p. 1-78) reprints and updates *Histoire du groupe français au Manitoba*, a 1938 essay by Antoine d'Eschambault on the history of the French community in Manitoba. The remainder consists of a bibliography of 2,885 items in French or English on Franco-Manitobans, arranged by subject. Sections treat topics such as Métis, religion, education, agriculture, politics, culture, and literature. A well-organized listing of a century of writing on a historically significant element of the province's population. — *LMcD*

CC33 Gagné, Peter J. - **French-Canadians of the West : A Biographical Dictionary of French-Canadians and French Métis of the Western United States and Canada.** - [Pawtucket, RI] : Quintin Publ., 2000. - 3 v. ; ill.

Class Numbers:
  National Library of Canada FC 3250
OCLC 46371017
Notes:
  Also available as CD-ROM
  Based on a translation of *Dictionnaire historique des Canadiens et des Métis français de l'Ouest*, by A.G. Morice, first published in 1908

• Biographical accounts of 650 noteworthy figures of the 19th century and earlier; clerics, explorers, trappers, and settlers constitute a significant proportion of those profiled. The translation incorporates new information and adds a glossary, time line of significant events, and updated bibliography. Each volume has a combined index of all biographies in the entire set. — *LMcD*

CC34 Lapointe, Richard. - **La Saskatchewan de A à Z.** - [Régina, SK] : Société historique de la Saskatchewan, 1987. - 376 p. : ill., maps, ports.

Class Numbers:
  Library of Congress F1072
  National Library of Canada FC3511
ISBN 0920895018
OCLC 20130251
LCCN 88-130071
Notes:
  Includes bibliographical references; index

• Collected items, arranged alphabetically, on aspects of the social and cultural history of the French community in Saskatchewan. Also available in *Musée Virtuel Francophone de la Saskatchewan* (http://www.societehisto.com/Musee/) on the Internet site of Société historique de la Saskatchewan. — *LMcD*

Germans

See also **Anderson, German, Mennonite and Hutterite Communities in Saskatchewan, BA9**

CC35 Mardon, Ernest G., 1928- . - **Alberta Ethnic German Politicians** / Ernest George Mardon, Austin Albert Mardon. - Edmonton, AB : RTAJ Fry Pr., 1990. - 56 p.

Class Numbers:
  National Library of Canada FC3700
ISBN 1895385245 (pbk.) 1895385261
OCLC 23052280
Notes:
  Includes bibliographical references and index

• Politicians, aspiring as well as actual, are the focus: 108 biographical sketches of candidates in territorial, provincial, and federal elections, 1882-1990. The work documents an ethnic dimension of the political history of Alberta. — *LMcD*

CC36 Prokop, Manfred, 1942- , comp. - **Annotated Bibliography of the Cultural History of the German-Speaking Community in Alberta, 1882-2000 : A Project of the German-Canadian Association of Alberta.** - Edmonton, AB : German-Canadian Association of Alberta, 2000. - 707 p.
Class Numbers:
  Library of Congress F1080   Z1392.A4
ISBN 0968787606
OCLC 50002428
LCCN 2002-391256
Notes:

"Published in cooperation with the financial support of the Alberta Historical Resources Foundation and the German-Canadian Association of Alberta."

Electronic book: http://www.ualberta.ca/~german/altahistory

Updated by supplements: 1997-2003 (81 p.) and 2004 (78 p.), and 2005-2007 (67 p.)

• The cultural focus of this exhaustive bibliography extends beyond typical areas such as art, literature, music, and religion to encompass the historical, political, business, and social elements of German life in Alberta. Austrians, Swiss, and other German-speaking groups are included; there is substantial coverage of both Mennonites (350 items) and Hutterites (700 items). Arrangement is by format (e.g., photos, book chapters, books, theses, letters, journal articles); approximately three-quarters of the 7,200 items are newspaper articles. Locations and call numbers are given for all but the last category. The keyword index is structured hierarchically at the front of the book and alphabetically at the back, identifying topics as diverse as elections, hiking, and naturalization. The online version consolidates the updates and provides for searching by field, date, and type of publication. A major contribution to the study of ethnic groups in Alberta. — *LMcD*

Ukrainians

CC37 Kaye, Vladimir J., 1896-   , ed. and comp. - **Dictionary of Ukrainian Canadian Biography : Pioneer Settlers of Manitoba, 1891-1900** / foreword by W.L. Morton. - Toronto, ON : Ukrainian Canadian Research Foundation, 1975. - xxv, 249 p. ; maps.

Class Numbers:
  Library of Congress F1065.U4
OCLC 2838261
LCCN 76-488836
Notes:
  Includes bibliographical references (p. [xxiii]-xxv) and index

• A meticulously researched compilation of information on the first wave of Ukrainian settlement. Slightly more than 1000 pioneers are listed, the majority originating from Borshchiv and Zalishchyk (Galicia) and Zastavna and Kitsman (Bukovina). Entries are grouped by Manitoba district: Dauphin, Stuartburn, Pleasant Home, and Mountain Road. Biographical information includes variant names, year and place of birth and death of settler and spouse, names and ages of children on landing, name of ship and landing date in Halifax or Quebec, place of settlement. Index of names. Based on archival sources including homestead grant registers, naturalization records and sailing records, supplemented by newspaper obituary notices. Useful for genealogical research and demographic studies of settlement patterns. — *LMcD*

CC38 Kaye, Vladimir J., 1896- , ed. and comp. - **Dictionary of Ukrainian Canadian Biography of Pioneer Settlers of Alberta, 1891-1900** / foreword by W.L. Morton ; preface by Isodore Goresky]. - Edmonton, AB : Ukrainian Pioneers' Association of Alberta, 1984. - 360 p. ; maps.

Class Numbers:
  Library of Congress F1080.U5
  National Library of Canada FC3700 U5
OCLC 11918310
LCCN 84-231420
Notes:
  Includes bibliographical references (p. 15-16)

• Brief biographies of 660 early Ukrainian settlers, based chiefly on homestead records in the Public Archives of Canada, ship passenger lists, and naturalization records. Index numbers in the official records are provided to facilitate identification of the original sources. Obituary notices from Ukrainian and English newspapers supplied additional detail. An addendum (p. 345-356) gives further information from interviews with descendants, cross-referenced to the main sequence. The numerous spelling variations of surnames are given as recorded on government forms. —*LMcD*

CD: Indians

Scope. Works about Indians, both those in the United States and First Nations in Canada, are entered under three general headings: General Works, Peoples, and Topics. Titles having to do with Indian languages will be found in BB, Languages; Linguistics, and with religion in BA, Religion.

General Works

Guides

CD1   The Cambridge History of the Native Peoples of the Americas. - Cambridge, UK; New York: Cambridge Univ. Pr., 1996-2000. - 3 v. in 6; ill., maps.

> Class Numbers:
> Library of Congress E77
> ISBN 0521344409 (v. 1)   0521352057 (v. 2)
> 0521333938 (v. 3)
> OCLC 33359444
> LCCN 95-46096
> Notes:
> Contents: v. 1, North America / ed. by Bruce G. Trigger, Wilcomb E. Washburn (2 v.); v. 2, Mesoamerica / ed. by Richard E.W. Adams, Murdo J. MacLeod (2 v.); v. 3, South America / ed. by Frank Saloman, Stuart B. Schwartz (2 v.)
> Includes bibliographical references; indexes
> Publisher description: http://www.loc.gov/catdir/ description/cam027/95046096.html
> Sample text: http://www.loc.gov/catdir/samples/cam031/ 95046096.html
> Table of contents: http://www.loc.gov/catdir/toc/cam026/ 95046096.html

• The two parts of volume 1, edited by Trigger (McGill Univ.) and Washburn (Smithsonian Institution), cover the history of native peoples north of the Rio Grande. Articles that will interest Prairies-Plains researchers include Michael Green on expansion of European colonization to the Mississippi Valley; Loretta Fowler on the arrival of the horse on the Great Plains; Frederick Hoxie on the reservation period (1880-1910); Howard Lamar on European settlement of the Southwest and California to the 1880s; and Linda Cordell and Bruce Smith on indigenous farmers. Includes maps and illustrations. — *GK*

CD2   Deloria, Philip Joseph. - **A Companion to American Indian History** / ed. by Philip J. Deloria and Neal Salisbury. - Malden, MA: Blackwell Publ., 2002. - 513 p.; maps. - (Blackwell companions to American history, 4).

> Class Numbers:
> Library of Congress E77
> ISBN 0631209751
> LCCN 2001-18461
> Notes:
> Includes bibliographical references (p. [475]-494); index

• Deloria and Salisbury's scholarly collection of 25 essays in five parts–"Contacts," "Native Practice and Belief," "Language, Identity, and Expression," "Exchange and Social Relations," and "Governmental Relations"–provides a state-of-the-art review of current thinking about Native American history and its place in the global indigenous world. Contributors, Native and non-Native, are all established or cutting-edge scholars in this field. Each essay stands alone, supported by its own extensive bibliography on its topic, and the volume is enhanced with a general 20-page bibliography of additional titles, and a 20-page index. Although a seminal work for the future of American Indian/Native American studies, and therefore recommended for all libraries, there is no access by region or tribe, other than superficially in the index. — *LM*

CD3   Hirschfelder, Arlene B. - **Guide to Research on North American Indians** / [by] Arlene B. Hirschfelder, Mary Gloyne Byler, Michael A. Dorris. - Chicago, IL: American Library Association, 1983. - 330 p.; map.

> Class Numbers:
> Library of Congress Z1209.2.N67
> ISBN 0838903533
> LCCN 82-22787
> Notes:
> Indexes

• Noted, prolific scholar Hirschfelder, author of numerous reference works and guides to literature on Native America, provides with coauthors Byler and Dorris a compilation of 1,100 books, articles, government documents, and other written materials arranged in 27 topical sections grouped under four broad areas: "Introductory Material," "History and Historical Sources," "Economic and Social Aspects," and "Religion, Arts, and Literature." Coverage for the U.S. and Canada includes works published up to 1982. Each chapter begins with a substantial narrative bibliographic survey, overview keyed to the titles in the section, which are alphabetical by author or editor and accompanied by excellent weighty annotations. Each chapter is subdivided geographically, making identification of Plains materials easy. Written from a librarian's perspective, this work is an excellent reference source. A new edition is needed to cover materials published over the past 25 years. Highly recommended. — *LM*

CD4   Hoebel, E. Adamson. - **The Plains Indians: A Critical Bibliography**. - Bloomington, IN: publ. for the Newberry Library [by] Indiana Univ. Pr., 1977. - 75 p. -

(Newberry Library. Center for the History of the American Indian. Bibliographical series).

Class Numbers:
    Library of Congress E78.G73   Z1209.2.G7
    ISBN 025334509X   9780253345097
    OCLC 3275660
    LCCN 77-6914

• One of a series on Indians of various regions, Hoebel's bibliography is a guide to reliable, published, Native and non-Native sources on individual peoples, to culture areas defined by outside researchers, and to significant issues. The work begins with two brief lists of highly recommended works, one for beginners and one for a basic library collection. At the center is a critical bibliographical essay that succinctly and expertly analyzes the extent and quality of research and documentation on Plains Indians in general–habitat, prehistory, early contacts, and tribal culture. Although much research has been done since its publication, the essay is still recommended reading for students of Plains Indians. It is followed by a 205-item bibliography of books and articles mentioned in the essay. Works for secondary school students are marked. For both scholars and students. —*JD*

CD5   Library of Congress. - **Many Nations: A Library of Congress Resource Guide for the Study of Indian and Alaska Native Peoples of the United States** / ed. by Patrick Frazier and the Publishing Office. - Washington, DC: Library of Congress, 1996. - xx, 334 p.; ill. (some col.), maps (some col.). - (Library of Congress resource guide).

Class Numbers:
    Library of Congress Z1209.2.U5
    ISBN 0844409049
    LCCN 96-42503
    Notes:
        Includes bibliographical references; index

• Because of the unique government-to-government relationship between the federal government and the Native peoples of the U.S., the Library of Congress holds the most comprehensive collection of materials on American Indians. *Many Nations* is a handbook to locating and using these resources. It covers the entire country, so Plains peoples are only part of the work's coverage. The guide is organized by Library of Congress divisions: General Collections, Special Collections, the Manuscript Division, The Law Library of Congress, Prints and Photographs Division, Geography and Map Division, Motion Picture, Broadcasting and Recorded Sound Division, and the American Folklife Center. Identifying works about Prairies-Plains can be accomplished using the 25-page index, where researchers can look for materials on specific tribes and events. A guide to an essential collection, but some work is required to narrow the focus to the region. — *LM*

CD6   **Native American Sites [Internet Site]** / maintained by Lisa Mitten. - Middletown, CT: Lisa Mitten,

1995-   . - http://www.nativeculturelinks.com/indians.html

Access Date: Jan. 2006
Fees: None
Notes:
    Site is also "Home of the American Indian Library Association Web Page."

• A gateway site that intends to list all publicly accessible sites for Indian peoples on the Internet. Periodically updated, the most recent date of revision at date of access was Dec. 3, 2005. The site provides links to several hundred sites, arranged by topic–individual Native nations, Native organizations and urban centers, education (including colleges and Native studies programs), languages, the mascot issue (which cites printed and electronic sources concerning Indian names and objects used as rallying symbols, chiefly by athletic teams), media, powwows and festivals, music and arts organizations and individuals, Indians in the military, businesses, and general Indian-oriented sites. There is no search engine, but the site arrangement is straightforward and longer sections provide alphabetic browsing grids. Links to Plains Indians are numerous (e.g., to Mandan, Lakota-Dakota, Comanche, Cherokee, Wichita). Any gateway can only be as good as the sources to which it provides links, and some in *Native American Sites* simply record institutional presence without leading to further information; but this site is conscientiously maintained and is an excellent place to find what the Internet offers for Indian studies. Mitten is Social Sciences Editor at *Choice*. — *RB*

CD7   Thompson, William Norman. - **Native American Issues: A Reference Handbook**. - Santa Barbara, CA: ABC-CLIO, 2005. - xx, 329 p. - (Contemporary world issues).

Class Numbers:
    Library of Congress E98
    ISBN 1851097414   1851097465 (electronic bk.)
    OCLC 58546164
    LCCN 2005-7570
    Notes:
        Includes bibliographical references (p. 245-284); index
        Review by M. Cedar Face: *Choice* 43.7 (Mar 2006): review 43-3798
        Table of contents: http://www.loc.gov/catdir/toc/ecip059/2005007570.html

• Thompson, who teaches public administration and is a noted authority on gambling, builds his handbook "around one unifying concept or idea: sovereignty" (p. xi) that is key to that new enterprise. About a third of the work deals with contemporary sovereignty issues in the U.S. (land claims, water rights, hunting and fishing rights, religious freedom, gambling, political jurisdiction), and adds a 20-page section on Canadian First Nations issues. Other chapters follow standard reference tracks—chronology, biographical sketches (historical and contemporary), court cases and legislation, "Points of View" (quotes by Native spokespeople and U.S. presidents), a directory of print and nonprint resources. Neither the glossary nor index is searchable by tribe, hence, although most issues discussed are relevant to Prairies-Plains concerns, state or tribal information cannot be retrieved. Primarily an introduction to the issues for general study by undergraduates. — *LM, MB*

Bibliographies

CD8 Bibliography of Native North Americans [Internet Site] / Human Relations Area Files; ed. by George Murdock and M. Marlene Martin. - Ipswich, MA: EBSCO Publishing, 1990s-   . - http://www.ebsco.com

> OCLC 64549342
> Access Date: Mar. 2006
> Notes:
>> Printed counterparts: George Peter Murdock, *Ethnographic Bibliography of North America*, 4th ed. (CC3);
>> M. Marlene Martin, *Ethnographic Bibliography of North Americans*, 4th ed. and Supplement, 1973-1987
>> Review by P. Aguilar: *Choice* 43.8 (Apr. 2006): review 43-4395
> Fees: Subscription

• Murdock and Martin offer the broadest possible coverage for topics related to Native North Americans. Like the printed counterparts (8 v.), the online version includes books, articles, chapters, and government publications dating from the 16th century to the present on the culture, history, and contemporary lives of U.S. and Canadian Native Americans. Topics include laws, language, material culture, folklore, education, and economy. The printed version was conveniently organized by broad geographic areas (e.g., Plains, Southwest) and subdivided by tribe. The online version lacks the broad geographic search but has added narrow geographic terms, abstracts, and subject headings. Pdf and html full text are available for some articles. New records are added regularly. A classic for both applied and academic researchers interested in historical events and contemporary issues. —*JD*

CD9 Hodge, William H., 1932-   . - A Bibliography of Contemporary North American Indians: Selected and Partially Annotated with Study Guides. - New York: Interland Publ., 1976. - 310 p.

> Class Numbers:
>> Library of Congress E77   Z1209.2.N67
> ISBN 0879891025
> LCCN 75-21675
> Notes:
>> Indexes

• Hodge (anthropology, Univ. of Wisconsin) offers a bibliography somewhat unique in its focus on "contemporary" Native peoples, which Hodge considers "contemporary" to be roughly 1875 to the "future." It is a "study guide" with "a very general and loose kind of organization where ease of presentation is stressed at the expense of an inclusive, but less satisfactory classification system" (p. xv). Hodge intends that his work complement similar bibliographies, so concentrates on unpublished state, federal, and tribal government papers and reports, works that have not been widely circulated, works of relevance to contemporary (at the time) theoretical social science questions, or works that focus on "current Indian activity" (p. vi). Consequently, he relies heavily on scholarly journal articles; he writes brief, selective annotations. Hodge begins with two thorough prefatory study guides to explain how his book is structured. He arranges the 2,594 titles within the complex subject arrangement alphabetically by author and editor. The 28 subject categories include , e.g., "Other Bibliographies and Resources," "Population Dynamics," "Stability and Change in Culture," "City Living," "Formal Education," "Health-Disease-Poverty," "Canadian Government Documents," and "Maps," as well as directory-like categories such as "Current Newspapers, Newsletters, Magazines," "Arts and Crafts-Supplies," and "Some Museums Having Display/Publications Concerned with American Indians–Prehistory, History, and Contemporary Periods." An index provides some access by tribe and region, where a quick count by tribe and state yields about 345 titles relevant to Prairies-Plains. Useful, with references to sources not easily found in other bibliographies; difficult arrangement. — *LM*

CD10 Hoxie, Frederick E., 1947-   . - Native Americans: An Annotated Bibliography / [by] Frederick E. Hoxie and Harvey Markowitz. - Pasadena, CA: Salem Pr., 1991. - 325 p. - (Magill bibliographies).

> Class Numbers:
>> Library of Congress E77   Z1209.2.N67
> ISBN 0893566705
> LCCN 91-16427
> Notes:
>> Index

• Comprehensive and well-organized, this bibliography by noted scholars Hoxie and Markowitz takes a more distinctly anthropological approach than many similar titles. Covering the entire U.S., the book begins with a thorough introduction setting out the work's scope. Two brief sections describe general studies and references and history, but the bulk of the work is organized by culture areas, including a large section on the Plains. Each cultural section has standard subsections for general studies and references, archaeology, folklore, sacred narrative, religious beliefs and practice, subsistence and land use, family and society, material culture and the arts, tribal life, biography and autobiography, and contemporary life across Native

America. All entries are annotated in fine detail, and there is an index of proper names. A solid work. — *LM*

CD11 Indians of the United States and Canada: A Bibliography / Dwight L. Smith, ed.; John C. Ewers, introd. - Santa Barbara, CA: ABC-Clio, 1974-1983 - 2 v. - (Clio bibliography series, v. 3, 9).

> Class Numbers:
> Library of Congress E77   Z1209.2.N67
> ISBN 0874361249 (v. 1)0874361494 (v. 2)
> LCCN 73-87156
> Notes:
> Indexes

• Entries are drawn from *America: History and Life* (AHL) (**DA12, DA12a**), and keep the AHL entry format. Volume 1 covers 1954-1972 and contains 1,687 annotated citations, volume 2 an additional 3,218 citations from AHL 1973-1978, reflecting the huge output of writing on Native Americans in that period. Entries are arranged in broad chronological sections (pre-Columbian, tribal history to 1900, 20th century), and within each section, by culture area or region, then by tribe. "Great Plains Area" is the relevant section, consisting of about 443 entries in volume 1, and another 648 for the five years in volume 2. Entries in each subsection are arranged alphabetically by author or editor. Kept up to date by the AHL database. — *LM*

CD12 Jett, Stephen C., 1938- , comp. - A Bibliography of North American Geographers' Works on Native Americans North of Mexico, 1917-1991 / in cooperation with the American Indian Specialty Group, Association of American Geographers. - Lawrence, KS: Haskell Indian Nations Univ., 1994. - 82 p. - (Haskell Indian Nations University studies in the geography of the American Indian, 1; Association of American Geographers. American Indian Specialty Group. Publication, 2).

> Class Numbers:
> Library of Congress E77   Z1209.2N67
> OCLC 33209856
> LCCN 95-167784
> Notes:
> Includes preface by Daniel R. Wildcat ... and an appendix of abstracts of papers on American Indians presented at the 1993 and 1994 annual meetings of the Association of American Geographers, ed. by Michael Caron

• Jett's very specific work of roughly 550 titles includes "books, monographs, articles, and reports" on North America north of Mexico written by "geographers or geographical writers presently or formerly resident in the United States or Canada" (p. ix). Titles chosen for inclusion were written after 1971, to supplement Alvar W. Carlson's "A Bibliography of the Geographical Literature on the American Indian, 1920-

1971," *The Professional Geographer* 24.3 (Aug. 1972): 258-263. Consequently, the topics of the entries in the current work often have less to do with Native ideas about geography than the fact that their authors are geographers. No index or contents list provides access to the entries other than the alphabetical author arrangement of the bibliography. Appendix: "Recent Geographical Research on American Indians: Abstracts of Papers on American Indians Presented at the 1993 and 1994 (89th and 90th) Annual Meetings o the Association American Geographers." Of limited use. — *LM*

CD13 Perkins, David, comp. - Native Americans of North America: A Bibliography Based on Collections in the Libraries of California State University, Northridge / comp. by David Perkins and Norman Tanis. - Metuchen, NJ: Scarecrow Pr., 1975. - 558 p.; ill.

> Class Numbers:
> Library of Congress Z1209.2.N67
> OCLC 1866132
> Notes:
> Reprint.
> Originally publ.: Northridge, CA: California State Univ., 1975

• Perkins and Tanis's bibliography (over 3,400 titles) reflects the holdings on Native Americans in the library collections of CSU Northridge. The collection's nucleus was a large collection of books donated by a faculty member. This bibliography was seen as a step in supporting the then-developing discipline of Native American studies. Entries are numbered and topically arranged, with the large subjects of anthropology and archaeology subdivided by four broad geographical groupings: general, eastern U.S. and Canada, western U.S. and Canada, and Mexico and Central America. History is further divided by region, of which "Trans-Mississippi Region" and "Rocky Mountains, Southwest" are relevant for Plains studies. Besides the other topical sections (e.g., "Indian Wars," "Language," "Technology"), a section lists "Tribes (A-Z)" for titles that deal solely with one tribe. This section contains about 1,000 titles, and includes entries for Prairies-Plains tribes such as Shoshoni, Osage, Kiowa, and Dakota. An author-title index refers to the accession numbers in the main list. A very thorough and comprehensive resource, useful for Plains studies. — *LM*

CD14 Stensland, Anna Lee, 1922- . - Literature by and about the American Indian: An Annotated Bibliography. - [Urbana, IL]: National Council of Teachers of English, 1979. - 382 p.

> Class Numbers:
> Library of Congress Z1209
> ISBN 0814129846
> LCCN 79-18073
> Notes:
> 1st ed, 1973

• Stensland's classic bibliography describes and evaluates literature for young people about American Indians. Intended for classrooms and school libraries, the book features an excellent introductory section, "Books by and about the American Indian," which includes a discussion of stereotypes in children's literature and the criteria used to select titles for this book. The bibliography itself focuses on fiction and biography, but also contains sections for myths and oratory, drama, history, anthropology, modern life, and music and arts. Stensland also provides study guides for nine selected books, four of which, *Indian Boyhood, Black Elk Speaks* (Lakota/Dakota), *Indians: A Play* (Buffalo Bill and Plains Indians), and *House Made of Dawn* (Kiowa) deal with Plains peoples. There are title and author indexes, but no way to identify specific books on Plains and Prairies peoples. — *LM*

CD15 Tate, Michael L. - **The Indians of Texas: An Annotated Research Bibliography**. - Metuchen, NJ: Scarecrow Pr., 1986. - 514 p.; maps. - (Native American bibliography series, 9).

> Class Numbers:
> Library of Congress Z1209.2.U52
> ISBN 0801018523
> OCLC 12557377
> LCCN 85-19674
> Notes:
> Indexes

• Tate's work is divided into "The Tribal Arrangement ..." and "The Chronological Arrangement of Indian-White Relations." Some entries are annotated. Bibliographic sections in the chronological arrangement include, besides the usual historical and Indian-white conflict topics, titles on buffalo hunters, peyote, and the Native American Church, several lists for tribes in Western Oklahoma, urban Indians of Texas and Oklahoma, and juvenile fiction and nonfiction on Texas Indians. The tribal arrangement groups peoples by region or origin, and there is a section for "The Plains Peoples," with Comanche and Kiowa getting their own sections. Useful. — *LM*

CD16 Thomas Gilcrease Institute of American History and Art, Tulsa, OK. Library. - **The Gilcrease-Hargrett Catalogue of Imprints** / comp. by Lester Hargrett. - Norman, OK: Univ. of Oklahoma Pr., 1972. - xviii, 400 p.

> Class Numbers:
> Library of Congress Z1209.2U5
> ISBN 0806110201
> LCCN 72-859

• The Thomas Gilcrease Institute is noted for its collection of Western Americana, particularly manuscripts. This cata-

log reflects the holdings purchased from Lester Hargrett in 1946. Hargrett collected American Indian history, particularly for the South and Southeast; consequently, the catalog focuses on the Five Civilized Tribes, but it is organized by tribe, then by date, and lists materials for a number of Plains tribes (e.g., Arapaho, Caddo, Cheyenne, "Colorado Indians," Dakota, Sioux). The catalog also includes titles on Western history in general. The rarity of many of these materials and the detailed descriptions Hargrett provides warrant this title's inclusion in this bibliography. — *LM*

CD17 Weist, Katherine M. - **An Annotated Bibliography of Northern Plains Ethnography** / by Katherine M. Weist and Susan R. Sharrock; with the assistance of Mavis Loscheider, Ira Lax, John Taylor. - Missoula, MT: Dept. of Anthropology, Univ. of Montana, [1985]. - 299 p.; map. - (Contributions to anthropology / Dept. of Anthropology, Univ. of Montana, v. 8).

> Class Numbers:
> Library of Congress E78.G73; Z1209.2.G7
> ISBN 091629207X 0195111338 (pbk.)
> LCCN 85237614

• Author list of primary sources on the native peoples occupying an area from the North Platte River to the Saskatchewan River, and from the Missouri River to the Rockies. An introductory unannotated section covers secondary ethnographic works arranged by tribe as well as historic works on general Indian and regional history, tribal histories, fur trade, Indian agents and missionaries, and the U.S. Army. The bibliography consists of works written by first-hand observers such as explorers and traders from 1690 to 1880 or based on such material, and published or reprinted before 1974. Entries include time period, place and summary. The index contains tribes, authors, geographic locations, and subjects; its usefulness would have been increased by including the numerous "other subjects" portion that concludes each entry. An important tool, nonetheless, for studying aboriginal life in an extensive area of the Prairies-Plains. – *LMcD*

CD18 White, Philip M. - **American Indian Studies: A Bibliographic Guide**. - Englewood, CO: Libraries Unlimited, 1995. - 163 p.

> Class Numbers:
> Library of Congress E77   Z1209
> ISBN 1563082438
> OCLC 31243460
> LCCN 94-24345
> Notes:
> Indexes

• White's guide is concerned with Indian nations throughout the U.S., therefore includes nations identified with the

Great Plains (e.g., Sioux, Omaha). Most entries have annotations and are divided into chapters by form of publication: guides to the literature, directories, encyclopedias, bibliographies of bibliographies, periodical indexes and databases, American Indian publications, biographical sources, dissertations and theses, government publications, and archival materials. Entries provide bibliographic descriptions that include price, LCCN, and ISBN or ISSN. A useful appendix extracts the subject headings for "Indians of North America" from the 1991 edition of *Library of Congress Subject Headings*. Indexes of subjects and authors/titles. — *MB*

CD19 White, Philip M., comp. - **Bibliography of Native American Bibliographies**. - Westport, CT: Praeger Publishers, 2004. - 241 p. - (Bibliographies and indexes in ethnic studies; no.11).

Class Numbers:
Library of Congress Z1209.2
ISBN 0313319413
LCCN 2004043771

• White (librarian and American Indian studies, San Diego State Univ.) provides a service whose time has come with this bibliography of Native bibliographies. His collection of 843 titles, up to date through 2003, is arranged by a detailed and somewhat serendipitous list of topics–e.g., "Aged," "California Indians," "Captivities," "Ghost Dance," "Métis of Canada," "Religion & Mythology," "Osage Indians," "Suicide"–many listing only a single title. All entries are annotated, and White includes Web sites when he determined them to be both bibliographic in nature and stable. He excludes online databases, periodical indexes, annual reviews, most library book catalogs, most guides to special collections and archives, and specialized encyclopedias that "simply provide listings of materials" (p. xv-xvi). An index lists authors, editors, tribes, people, and subjects, as well as *see* and *see also* references. Attempts to identify Plains entries via the index is not much more revealing than using the lengthy table of contents, which includes regional bibliographies for Arapaho Indians (three titles), Cheyenne (one), Colorado (one), Ghost Dance (one), and South Dakota (two). To be sure, many of the broader subject bibliographies will include references to Plains peoples as well. An excellent, solid work reflecting new formats for research. Highly recommended. — *LM*

Manuscripts; Archives

CD20 Hill, Edward E. - **Guide to Records in the National Archives of the United States Relating to American Indians**. - Washington, DC: National Archives and Records Service, 1981. - 467 p.; front., [16] p.of plates.

Class Numbers:
Library of Congress Z1209.2.U5

ISBN 0911033134
LCCN 81-22357
Notes:
Index

• The federal government is the primary repository for records pertaining to the Native peoples of the US. In the new American republic (1789), the War Department was given principal responsibility for the implementation of policies between the Indian nations and the federal government. In 1849, that responsibility was transferred to the new Interior Department's Bureau of Indian Affairs (BIA), where it remains to this day. This responsibility has been supplemented over the past century by various "Indian programs" in many of the departments (e.g., Labor, Education, Health and Human Services) in the executive branch. In addition, the National Archives holds records pertaining to American Indians from various short-term commissions, committees, and other not-so-obvious federal agencies.

§   This guide does an excellent job cataloging and explaining how these records are organized, how they may be accessed, and their relevance to research on Indians. The work is organized by government department and archival record group. Some record groups clearly pertain to Prairies-Plains regions, states, or BIA area offices, other record groups will contain materials relevant to the particular group or the time frame involved. Examples of such entries in this work include Records of the Board of Indian Commissioners; Records of the Indian Arts and Crafts Board; Records of the National Park Service; Records of the Office of the Secretary of War; Records for the Departments of Dakota, Kansas, the Missouri, Texas, and the Western Division, all in the Records of the United States Army Continental Commands, 1821-1920; Records of the Supreme Court of the United States; Records of the National Council on Indian Opportunity; Records of the Bureau of the Budget; Records of the Indian Claims Commission; Records of the Civilian Conservation Corps; and Records of the Smithsonian Institution. An essential work. — *LM*

CD21 Rose, LaVera, comp. - **Guide to American Indian Research in South Dakota**. - [Pierre, SD?: s.n.], 2000. - ca. 200 p.; maps.

Class Numbers:
Library of Congress E99.D1
OCLC 45658405

• Archivist Rose provides a guide to collections housed in the South Dakota State Archives in Pierre regarding the Lakota, Nakota, and Dakota peoples. The guide's first section offers general information concerning political organization, a land cession map, addresses of reservations, Bureau of Indian Affairs realty offices, tribal colleges, and other facilities located in South Dakota, out of state, or on the Internet. The second section lists resources in the Archives, arranged by government agency. The manuscript collection lists papers alphabetically by organization or individual; maps are listed alphabetically by reservation, then by date and map numbers. Information about newspapers can be accessed via the online library catalog. The Archives also maintains a vertical file containing miscellaneous topical and biographical materials. — *GK*

CD22 Svoboda, Joseph G., comp. - **A Guide to American Indian Resource Materials in Great Plains Repositories**. - Lincoln, NE: Center for Great Plains Studies, Univ. of Nebraska-Lincoln, 1983. - 401 p.

> Class Numbers:
> Library of Congress E78.G73
> OCLC 9810335
> Notes:
> Index

• Svoboda's guide describes sources in repositories in ten states of the U.S. and three provinces of Canada. Most are unpublished—manuscripts, diaries, correspondence, photographs, oral history transcripts—but some newspaper and magazine articles are included. Manuscripts include anthropological field notes and personal histories of tribal members; official records include mission, military, medical, court, Indian school, Indian agency, and tribal enrollment records. Entries, each a paragraph long, are arranged by state or province, city, and name of collection, and are packed with information, including important proper names and places, historical context, and evaluative notes. The guide covers all Indian tribes, not just those living in the Great Plains, but no repositories are listed outside the Great Plains. Repositories that failed to respond to Svoboda's questionnaire are omitted. Indexes cover names, tribes, locations, subjects, and newspaper titles, although subject indexing is sketchy. Invaluable for identifying resources held by 94 dispersed institutions. — *JD*

Encyclopedias

CD23 **Encyclopedia of the Great Plains Indians** / David J. Wishart, ed. - Lincoln, NE: Univ. of Nebraska Pr., 2007. - 254 p.; ill.
> Class Numbers:
> Library of Congress E78.G73
> ISBN 0803298625 (pbk.)   9780803298620 (pbk.)
> LCCN 2006-20334
> Notes:
> Includes bibliographical references; index

• The core of this spin-off consists of the essay that introduces the Native American chapter in *Encyclopedia of the*

Great Plains (**AA4**) and reprints 123 entries about Indians originally published there. Twenty-three new entries, all written by a single contributor, Charles Vollan (history, South Dakota State Univ.), focus primarily on contemporary Plains Indians. Most entries are biographies (of, e.g., Suanne Big Crow, a Lakota basketball star; Ella Deloria, a Yankton Sioux anthropologist and writer who worked with Franz Boas; and Silverhorn, a Kiowa artist). Others are topical essays on such matters as Indian-owned and operated casinos. Although the new entries round out the coverage of Indians, the new work lacks the context provided by the depth and range of the original encyclopedia. Entries are arranged alphabetically, with suggested readings for most entries and a general index; new photographs. — *JD*

CD24 Foster, William C., 1928-   . - **Historic Native Peoples of Texas** / foreword by Alston V. Thoms. - Austin, TX: Univ. of Texas Pr., 2008. - 366 p.; ill., maps.

> Class Numbers:
> Library of Congress E78 T4
> ISBN 9780292717923   9780292717930 (pbk.)
> OCLC 177063313
> LCCN 2007-43191
> Notes:
> Contents: Between the Lower Brazos and the Lower Colorado Rivers – Between the Lower Colorado and the San Antonio Rivers – The Central Texas Coast – South Texas – The Texas Trans-Pecos – The Texas Southern Plains – Northeast Texas – The Upper Texas Coast – Conclusions.

• An impressive and unique work that can be read as history text or consulted for reference, this "ethnohistory" encapsulates the first-person accounts of 40 members of 25 Spanish and several French expeditions into the area that is now Texas. In summarizing and citing the accounts, beginning with Cabeza de Vaca of the Narváez Expedition of 1528 and ending in 1722, it provides new access to information on the indigenous people, landscape, and climate of a multicultural, well-situated, and fluctuating region. According to the introduction, the accounts, as nearly as possible, describe the Indians in the pre-exploration state; show the impact of the first explorations as seen in the commentaries of the later ones; and provide comparisons with contemporary peoples and conditions. Following a summary of the prehistory of Texas, chapters address eight geographic "study areas" with maps, detailed yet anecdotal summaries of expeditions to the region, lists of diaries and other documentary sources for expeditions, and sightings of Indian tribes noted in each commentary. Appendixes include "Selected Animals Reported" and "Selected Trees and Other Plants Reported." Notes, bibliography, and index. For historians, anthropologists, and general readers. — *JD*

CD25 Fowler, Loretta, 1944-   . - **The Columbia Guide**

to **American Indians of the Great Plains**. - New York: Columbia Univ. Pr., 2003. - 283 p.; ill., maps. - (Columbia guides to American Indian history and culture).

> Class Numbers:
> > Library of Congress E78.G73
>
> ISBN 0231117000
> LCCN 2002-73708
> Notes:
> > Includes bibliographical references (p. 222-263); index
> > Review by N.C. Greenberg: Choice 41.8 (Apr. 2004): review 41-4398

• A highly useful work that provides five overview chapters of Plains peoples' history and culture, followed by an alphabetical "Peoples, Places, and Events" encyclopedia whose entries amplify highlighted terms from the first five chapters. This is followed by a chronology that begins with a dozen or so broad pre-1492 entries and ends in 1990. Part 4, "Resources," includes a guide to doing research on Plains Indians, followed by a lengthy bibliography of general works on Plains archaeology, published primary sources, general and comprehensive studies, and 23 tribal studies, ending with selected literary works, video and film, and Internet resources. A solid resource. — *LM*

CD26   **Handbook of North American Indians** / William C. Sturtevant, general ed. - Washington, DC: Smithsonian Inst.; U.S. Govt. Print. Off., 1978-   (In progress). - v. 4-13, 15, 17 in 13 v.

> Class Numbers:
> > Library of Congress E77.H25
> > Government Document SI1.20/2:
>
> ISBN 0160504007 (v. 13)
> LCCN 77017162
> Notes:
> > Contents: v.4, History of Indian-White relations; v. 5, Arctic; v. 6, Subarctic; v. 7, Northwest coast; v. 8, California; v. 9-10, Southwest; v. 11, Great Basin; v. 12, Plateau; v. 13, Plains (2 v.); v. 15, Northeast; v. 17, Languages
> > Review (v. 13) by David Wishart: *Great Plains Quarterly* 22.3 (summer 2002): 217-220
> > Review (v. 13) by Lisa Mitten: *Choice* 39 (Jun. 2002): review 39-5560

• A substantial work dealing with the Indians of the North American continent, this anthropological monument has only recently resumed after publication had been suspended. Luckily, the region chosen for publication of the latest volume (v. 13) covers the Plains, defined with some precision in the introductory matter; it is substantially the region covered by the present bibliography. The two physical volumes that make up v. 13 cover "the traditional cultures and histories of the Native peoples indigenous to the Plains region of the US and Canada" (L. Mitten, *Choice*), treating

individual tribes in 35 chapters; archaeology, prehistory, history, and languages in another 23 chapters; and special topics (music, art, ceremonies, tribal traditions, archives) in nine more. A bibliography of 200 pages, an index of 70, and a detailed illustration list add to the luster of this incomparable set. Also of interest to students of the Prairies-Plains region are volumes 4, "History of Indian-White Relations," and 17, "Languages." Anthropologists, Plains scholars and Indian specialists will watch for the appearance of other volumes, supposedly 20 when the set is complete. — *RB*

CD27   Hodge, Frederick Webb, 1864- , ed. - **Handbook of American Indians North of Mexico**. - Washington, DC: [U.S.] Govt. Print. Off., 1907-1910. - 2 v.; ill., ports. - (Smithsonian Institution. Bureau of American Ethnology. Bulletin, 30).

> Class Numbers:
> > Library of Congress E77
>
> LCCN 07-35198
> Notes:
> > Bibliography: v. 2, p. 1179-1221

CD28   Hoxie, Frederick E., 1947- , ed. - **Encyclopedia of North American Indians**. - Boston, MA: Houghton Mifflin, 1996. - 756 p.; ill., maps.

> Class Numbers:
> > Library of Congress E76.2
>
> ISBN 0395669219
> LCCN 96-21411
> Notes:
> > Indexes

• Noted historian Hoxie's authoritative if selective 447 entries divide roughly equally among four types of entries for the U.S. and Canada: individual tribes, biographies, thematic cultural topics, and "definitions for terms and events that are frequently mentioned and often misunderstood" (p. ix). Hoxie seeks to "introduce, to teach, and to invite further inquiry." The contributor list is a veritable who's who of some 300 Native and non-Native scholars and experts, lending great credibility and authority to the work. Most entries are signed, and lengthier entries cite further readings; most run several pages, give tribal affiliations when logical. Relevant, captioned photos appear throughout the text, as do maps. A contributor index and a general index round out the work. There is no separate bibliography. The general index provides some access by tribe, but does not list every instance of a tribe's appearance in the articles. A sampling of relevant entries includes "Prairie Tribes," "Murie, James R.," "Plenty Coups," "Herding and Ranching" (i.e., Indian livestock activities), "Fishing and

Hunting Rights," "Indian-White relations in Canada, 1763 to the Present," "Hand Game," and "Santee Normal Training School." A solid work that requires some effort to identify entries relevant to the region. — *LM*

CD29 Johnson, Michael G., 1932- . - **The Native Tribes of North America: A Concise Encyclopedia** / with color plates by Richard Hook. - New York: Macmillan; Toronto, ON: Maxwell Macmillan Canada, 1993. - 210 p.; ill (some col.), maps.

Class Numbers:
Library of Congress E76.2
ISBN 0028971892
OCLC 28801140
LCCN 93-23429
Notes:
Includes bibliographical references (p. 201-205); index

• A popular work from England whose author "has been fascinated with the North American Indians since childhood, with a particular fervor for costume, especially beadwork, and an ongoing interest in the demographics of tribes." That obsession shows: a series of color plates illustrate a kaleidoscope of "costumes," headdresses, house types, and modes of transportation, and the text is generally accurate, with a welcome emphasis on population figures throughout history. Glossary of random words, bibliography, and an index of tribes and linguistic groups. The latter, along with the culture area arrangement of the encyclopedia itself, makes identifying Prairies-Plains topics a snap. — *LM*

CD30 Keoke, Emory Dean. - **Encyclopedia of American Indian Contributions to the World: 15,000 Years of Inventions and Innovations** / [by] Emory Dean Keoke and Kay Marie Porterfield. - New York: Facts on File, 2002. - 384 p.; ill., maps. - (Facts on File library of American history).

Class Numbers:
Library of Congress E54.5
ISBN 0816040524
OCLC 45068567
LCCN 00-49034
Notes:
Includes bibliographical references (p. 340-343); index

• Acknowledging the difficulties of researching technological history, establishing dates, and assigning "credit" for inventions, the authors attempt a broad picture of pre-contact technologies throughout the Americas. Organized alphabetically, entries include estimated date ranges, summaries of current knowledge, and sources for further reading. Great Plains technologies include fish decoys, tobacco pipes, diuretics, wrenches, and double cropping. Appendixes include tribes by geographical culture area,

maps, a glossary, a chronology, a bibliography, entries by tribe and linguistic group, entries by geographical culture area, and a subject index. A starting place rather than a scholarly work. — *JD*

CD31 Klein, Barry T. - **Reference Encyclopedia of the American Indian**. - 11th ed. - Nyack, NY: Todd Publ., 2005. - 777 p.

Class Numbers:
Library of Congress E76.2
ISBN 0915344777
Notes:
Includes bibliographical references (p. 355-528)

• The 11th edition of a work first published in 1967 is a landmark, comprehensive, kaleidoscopic resource for identifying nearly anything about the contemporary Native American social and cultural world. Klein has compiled this work since its inception, and until recently, it was the only resource of its type. Primarily a directory of reservations, tribal offices and museums, Indian educational resources (all levels and all types—financial aid, college courses, BIA schools, tribal colleges, etc.), media outlets, casinos, and medical providers, to mention a few of the many categories, the work also offers a Canadian section with similar information, an extensive bibliography for all formats of materials, and a Native "Who's Who" biographical section running about 250 pages. What is unclear is how often fact-checking and updating of information occurs (about which the brief introduction is silent other than to say that editor Klein should be contacted about changes and additions—a not altogether reliable updating method). For example, both entries checked in the biography section were woefully out of date, by over five years. However, the work's sheer scope makes the work valuable, since it gathers a huge amount of scattered information that by itself can make readers aware of the depth of the contemporary Native world. Although only some of the 50 directory sections lend themselves to easy identification of Plains and Prairies resources, all libraries should have a recent edition. An essential resource. — *LM*

CD32 Markowitz, Harvey, ed. - **American Indians**. - Pasadena, CA: Salem Pr., 1995. - 3 v. (xxii, 953 p.); ill., maps.

Class Numbers:
Library of Congress E76.2
ISBN 0893567574 (set)
LCCN 94-47633
Notes:
Includes bibliographical references; index (in v. 3)

• Although comprehensive, this set is a curious mixture. Markowitz (D'Arcy McNickle Center for the History of the American Indian, Newberry Library) provides no introductory material or scope notes. The 1,129 articles (mostly unsigned) were contributed by about 170 academics and some independent scholars. A publisher's note (less than two pages), the only prefatory material, states that the goal was "to assemble articles on a wide range of American Indian topics–including personages, tribes, organizations, historical events, cultural traditions, and contemporary issues" (p. v) in articles between 200 and 3,000 words. The result is a jumble. Articles longer than 1,000 words conclude with a bibliography, those longer than 2,000 words with annotated bibliographies. Articles are in alphabetical order across the three volumes. Articles relevant to Plains studies include "Allotment System," "Arapaho," "Arts and Crafts–Plains," "Big Foot," "Earthlodge," "Fort Laramie Treaty of 1868," "Grass, John," "Prehistory–Plains," "Medicine Wheels," "Rosebud Creek, Battle of," "Wounded Knee Massacre," "Wounded Knee Occupation." Each volume concludes with a "List of Entries by Category" that covers the entire set and that includes "Archaeological Sites," "Ceremonies, Dances, and Festivals," "Beliefs and Religion," "Historical Events," "Organizations," "Personages," and an alphabetical list of "Tribes." Volume three concludes with several directory-like sections: "Educational Institutions and Programs" (tribal colleges are excluded), "Festivals and Pow-wows," "Museums, Archives, and Libraries," and "Organizations, Agencies, and Societies." All groupings are "selected"; that none are inclusive limits their usefulness. Other miscellaneous appendixes (also selective) in v. 3 include "Populations of U.S. Reservations," "Reservations: United States," "Reserves and Bands: Canada," "Time Line," "Tribes by Culture Area," "Glossary," "Mediagraphy," and "Bibliography." Volume 3 ends with an index to the set. The appendixes, "List of Entries," and index provide access points to identify material on Plains and Prairies peoples. —*LM*

CD33 Native America in the Twentieth Century: An Encyclopedia / ed. by Mary B. Davis; assistant eds., Joan Berman, Mary E. Graham, Lisa A. Mitten. - New York: Garland, 1994. - xxxvii, 787 p.; ill., maps. - (Garland reference library of social science, v. 452).

Class Numbers:
  Library of Congress E76.2
  ISBN 0824048466
  LCCN 94-768
  Notes:
    Includes bibliographical references; index

• Entries include summaries of the histories and contemporary lives of Native nations; overviews of broad aspects of Native American life, such as art, economic development, health, and religion; and detailed articles on specific topics, such as quillwork, gaming, traditional medicine, and sacred sites. Canadian peoples and individual biographies are not included. Each entry includes cross-references and further readings. Illustrated with tables, photographs, and simple, clear maps of land claims, reservations, and other areas. For Great Plains researchers, a detailed index provides access to articles by geographical locations, peoples, topics, and organizations. The expert contributors, many of native heritage, convey the essentials. —*JD*

CD34 Pritzker, Barry M. - Native Americans: An Encyclopedia of History, Culture, and Peoples. - Santa Barbara, CA: ABC-CLIO, 1998. - 2 v. (868 p.); ill., maps.

Class Numbers:
  Library of Congress E77
  ISBN 087436867   1851095543 (electronic bk.)
  OCLC 39322558
  LCCN 98-21718
  Notes:
    Contents;
    v. 1, Southwest, California, Northwest Coast, Great Basin, Plateau;
    v. 2, Great Plains, Southeast, Northeast Woodlands, Subarctic, Arctic
    Electronic book: http://www.netLibrary.com/urlapi. asp?action=summary&v=1&bookid=83361
    Includes bibliographical references (p. 803-805); index

• Focusing on Indian societies currently resident in the U.S., Pritzker's work emphasizes the dynamics of traditional and contemporary Indian cultures and their contributions to the broader society. Entries for Indian peoples are organized by ten geographical regions, 28 in the Great Plains section. New Mexico is covered in the Southwest section. Each region opens with an introduction, then entries briefly cover three types of information: general (alternate names, location, population, language), historical (history, religion, government, customs, dwellings, diet, key technology, trade, notable arts, transportation, dress, war and weapons) and contemporary (government/reservations, economy, legal status, daily life). Discussion of mythology is omitted as "too elusive" for the brief entries, and information about precontact life is limited. Only a few extinct peoples are included. At the end of volume 2 are a glossary, a bibliography by chapter, data sheets on Canadian reserves and bands by territory and Alaska Native villages by language, and a list of Alaska Native Corporations. Indexes by peoples, reservation, organization, and publication name. —*JD*

CD35 Yenne, Bill, 1949- . - The Encyclopedia of North American Indian Tribes: A Comprehensive Study of Tribes from the Abitibi to the Zuni. - New York: Crescent Books; distr. Avenel, NJ: Outlet Book, c1986. – 191 p.; ill. (some col.), maps (some col.)

Class Numbers:
  Library of Congress E76.2

ISBN 0517604698
LCCN 85-31409

• Very brief descriptions of tribes, giving minimal information about geographic region, linguistic group, dwelling type, subsistence type, and a cursory historical note. A map of linguistic families indicates major Plains tribes; other maps show reservations (1880 and 1980), and Indian Territory over time. Heavily illustrated with contemporary and 19th-century photographs and paintings that threaten to overwhelm the text. "Comprehensive" in the subtitle misses the mark; entries tend to be superficial. Considerably more useful in both organization and content is Pritzker's *Native Americans*: (**CD34**), but eclipsing both in depth and authoritativeness is *Plains*, (v. 13, pts. 1 and 2, of *Handbook of North American Indians* [**CD26**]), which examines 34 peoples of the Prairies-Plains (prehistory, history, culture), and has detailed bibliographies and index. — *LMcD, MB*

Atlases

CD36 Prucha, Francis Paul. - **Atlas of American Indian Affairs**. - Lincoln, NE: Univ. of Nebraska Pr., 1990. - 1 atlas (1912 p.); ill., maps; 31 cm.

    Class Numbers:
      Library of Congress G1210.E1
    ISBN 080326891
    LCCN 90-675000
    Notes:
      Includes bibliographical references; index
      Scales differ

• Noted historian Prucha's standard work surveys Indian population trends, land cessions, and reservations across the U.S. Although he focuses on the 20th century, maps include those based on the U.S. Census (1890-1980), Indian land cessions 1784-1889, reservation maps by regional state groupings, and maps of Indian agencies, schools, and hospitals. Special maps focus on Oklahoma and Indian Territory, Alaska, the Army, and the Indian frontier. Much of the work, which features black-and-white line drawings of varying detail and explanatory captions, but little text, focuses on the Plains region. Very useful. — *LM*

CD37 Waldman, Carl, 1947-   . - **Atlas of the North American Indian** / ill. by Molly Braun. - New York: Facts on File, 2000. - 1 atlas (385 p.); ill., maps; 28 cm.

    Class Numbers:
      Library of Congress G1106.E1
    ISBN 0816039747   0806139755 (pbk.)
    LCCN 2001-622016; 99-23678
    Notes:
      Includes bibliographical references (p. 365-369); index
      Scales differ

• Waldman divides his atlas into seven sections. The second treats ancient civilizations (Maya, Anasazi); "Indian Lifeways" is concerned with culture, art, clothing, transportation, religion, language; "Indians and Explorers" with interaction between the two groups; "Indian Wars" with the Colonial period, Canadian Indian Wars, and the West (including the Great Plains and mountain West); and the final section with contemporary issues, including Native-American gaming laws and activities. Of special interest to Plains studies are the historical sections, including Indian Wars and land cessions. Several useful appendixes include a chronology, 35,000 BCE to the present; a roster of nations with languages and locations; a list of contemporary nations, listed by state; major place-names of Indian origin; museums and organizations, arranged geographically. A glossary, bibliography, and index complete the volume. Abundant black-and-white maps, line drawings, and photos are helpful additions to the cultural sections. — *MB*

Chronologies

CD38 **Chronology of Native North American History: From Pre-Columbian Times to the Present** / Duane Champagne, ed. - Detroit, MI: Gale Research, c1994. - lxxv, 574 p.; ill., maps.

    Class Numbers:
      Library of Congress E77.C555
    ISBN 0810391953
    LCCN 94-18455
    Notes:
      Includes bibliographical references (p. 533-540); index

• Intending to cover "many issues and topics that affected Native peoples, were important to Native peoples, and which influenced U.S. and Canadian society" (p. xi), this chronology's ten chapters emphasize 20th-century events. Chapter 1 covers Native North American history from 50,000 BCE to 1499; chapters 2-6 cover the following centuries, through 1899; chapter 7 provides information for 1900-1959; and the final three chapters each cover a decade, up to the publication date 1994. Each chapter arranges information by year, then by events that occurred over the course of the year, or for which no exact date is known, then by month and day in that year. Topics vary widely from entry to entry. "1875 – Fort Marion, Florida" is followed by "1875 – Navajo Rug Making," which, while reflecting the wide variety of events taking place simultaneously throughout the U.S. and Canada makes a chaotic arrangement. Following the chronology itself are appendixes for "American Indian Orators," "Documents of History," "Excerpts from Significant Legal Cases," "General Bibliography," an extensive but cranky six-page "Illustrations Credits," and a detailed index. The latter runs just under 30 pages, and provides the only tribal or regional access to the work. The work contains solid information, and for browsing through U.S. and Canadian history it can be quite enlightening, but it is not easy to use to identify specific information.

§ Similar in intent is *Chronology of American Indian History: The Trail of the Wind* by Liz Sonneborn (New York: Facts on File, 2001; 442 p.), an eclectic mix of facts, historic events, and contemporary developments. A single brief chapter covers prehistory to first European contact. Succeeding chapters cover progressively smaller time periods, with the number of items under each year generally increasing through the latter part of the 20th century. The index lists individual tribes, identifying a limited measure of Plains content — *LM, LMcD*

CD39 Nies, Judith, 1941- . - **Native American History: A Chronology of the Vast Achievements of a Culture and their Links to World Events**. - New York: Ballantine Books, 1996. - 420 p.; ill., maps.

> Class Numbers:
> Library of Congress E77
> ISBN 0345393503
> LCCN 96-32659
> Notes:
> Includes bibliographical references (p. 403-405); index

• Using parallel timelines to place Native American history in the national and international context, Nies reveals levels of cultural development and suggests connections among events. Examples: the first record of London as a city was 603, the same time that Mississipians built a large center in what is now Spiro, OK; in 1862 the Homestead Act opened land to settlement at the same time the Santee Sioux Uprising began, leading to the dispersal of surviving Santee to Canada and reservations. Present-day U.S. and Mexico from 28,000 BCE to the 1990s are covered in eight chapters, each introduced by Native American perspectives on the era. The index includes states and tribes as well as people and events. The timeline is easy to scan for Great Plains entries. A unique work. — *JD*

Collective Biographies

CD40 Barrett, Carole A. - **American Indian Biographies** / ed. by Carole Barrett, Harvey Markowitz; project ed., R. Kent Rasmussen. - Pasadena, CA: Salem Pr., 2005. - 623 p.; ill., maps. - (Magill's choice).

> Class Numbers:
> Library of Congress E98
> ISBN 1587652331
> LCCN 2004-28872

> Notes:
> Essays reprinted from other Salem Press publications:
> *American Indian Biographies* (1999);
> *Dictionary of World Biography, Great Lives from History: The Renaissance & Early Modern Era, 1454-1600* (2005);
> *American Ethnic Writers* (2000).
> Includes bibliographical references; index
> Review by J.R. Burch Jr.: *Choice* 43.1 (Sep. 2005): review 43-0001

• Biographical profiles of almost 400 individuals, some well-known in a variety of occupations and accomplishments e.g., Olympians (Jim Thorpe), revolutionaries (Louis Riel), politicians (Charles Curtis), writers (Vine Deloria), and humorists (Will Rogers). Persons selected are those the publisher believes had "the greatest impact on popular culture" (p. xi), by which they mean individuals familiar to white rather than Native society. Sketches give basic factual information, tribal background, and a brief life; some have bibliographies. An index of tribal affiliations identifies members of individual Plains tribes, and culture area maps list tribes. Also included are lists of persons by birth years and variant names, and a timeline of historical events. A 12-page subject index lists primarily individuals, so supplies little regional help. Tribal entries include four Arapaho, one Assiniboine, four Blackfoot, two Blood, 14 Cheyenne, five Comanche, seven Crow, three Osage, two Ponce, and an impressive 57 Lakota.

§ A comparable work that overlaps considerably, *American Indian Portraits* (Detroit, MI: Macmillan Reference, 2000; 359 p.) has fewer but longer profiles; about half its 150 entries are derived from *Encyclopedia of the American West* (**DA44**). Intended for elementary and high school students. — *LMcD, LM*

CD41 Brumble, H. David. - **An Annotated Bibliography of American Indian and Eskimo Autobiographies**. - Lincoln, NE: Univ. of Nebraska Pr., 1981. - 177 p.

> Class Numbers:
> Library of Congress E89   Z1209
> ISBN 0803211759
> LCCN 80-23449
> Notes:
> Indexes

• A library staple since its publication, Brumble's unique compilation (he teaches English at the Univ. of Pittsburgh) offers more than 500 fully annotated entries for autobiographies (no biographies). Entries are alphabetical by subjects' names, and the work includes an index of editors, anthropologists, ghosts, and amanuenses, and others by tribe and by subject, allowing one to identify Plains peoples. Essential. — *LM*

CD41a Brumble, H. David. - **American Indian**

Autobiography. - Berkeley, CA: Univ. of Califoria Pr., 1988. - 278 p.; ill.

> Class Numbers:
> Library of Congress E89.5
> ISBN 0520062450
> LCCN 88-14425
> OCLC 17983328
> Notes:
> Bibliography: p. 259-270; indexes

• Unlike its predecessor, this work, also confined to Indians north of Mexico, consists of extended chapters that discuss various aspects and practitioners of the autobiographical art (in chapters, e.g., on preliterate traditions; editors, ghosts, and amanuenses; Eastman; and Momaday). Following the text are a section of notes, a list of autobiographies discussed in the text and others mentioned (with lengthy annotations for the latter), a bibliography of sources, and two indexes, of Indian names and of other names and subjects. Brumble's two useful works are best consulted together. — *RB*

CD42 Dockstader, Frederick J. - **Great North American Indians: Profiles in Life and Leadership**. - New York: Van Nostrand Reinhold, 1977. - 386 p.; ill. - (A Norback book).

> Class Numbers:
> Library of Congress E89
> ISBN 0442021488
> LCCN 77-23733
> Notes:
> Bibliography: p. 355-369; index

• Anthropologist Dockstader presents 300 brief biographical sketches of Native North American leaders. Entries treat historical persons of significance to Indian people, "rather than the evaluation of a career from the White point of view" (p. 5), and contain birth and death dates and portraits, where available. The work includes an extensive bibliography of works consulted, a chronology of entries organized by date of birth, a very useful tribal listing in which entries are organized by their tribal affiliation, and a thorough index of individuals, Indian and non-Indian. Dockstader reports he relied heavily on Hodge's *Handbook of American Indians North of Mexico* (**CD27**) for information about many of the people in this volume. About 100 (a third) of the entries are for people from tribes of the Plains or Prairies, making this an essential reference title for the region. — *LM*

CD43 **Indian Lives: Essays on Nineteenth- and Twentieth-Century Native American Leaders** / ed. by L.G. Moses and Raymond Wilson. - Albuquerque, NM: Univ. of New Mexico Pr., 1985. - 227 p.; ports.

> Class Numbers:

> Library of Congress E89
> ISBN 0826308147   0826308155 (pbk.)
> LCCN 85-1188
> Notes:
> Bibliography: p. [215]-216; index

• The biographies of eight national leaders who maintained their Indian identity range from the first Indian woman to be a doctor to a vice-president of the U.S. Four of the eight are from tribes in the Great Plains: Susan LaFlesche Picotte, Henry Chee Dodge, Charles Curtis, and Luther Standing Bear. Based on primary and secondary documents, the heavily cited entries are 20-30 pages long. The "essays on sources" that supplement the notes at the end of each entry are a model for future reference works. They give the locations of major primary sources, describe and rate primary and secondary sources, discuss the applications of the sources to the entries, and advise future researchers. Portraits and an index by topics and proper names. —*JD*

CD44 McKenney, Thomas Loraine, 1785-1859. - **The Indian Tribes of North America: With Biographical Sketches and Anecdotes of the Principal Chiefs** / [by] Thomas L. McKenney and James Hall. - New ed., ed. by Frederick Webb Hodge. - Edinburgh [UK]: J. Grant, 1933-1934. - 3 v.; col. fronts., ports. (part col.), folded maps.

> Class Numbers:
> Library of Congress E77
> OCLC 1535976
> LCCN 35-1659
> Notes:
> "An Essay on the History of the North American Indians," by James Hall: v. 3, p. 83-345
> First ed., Philadelphia, PA, 1836-1844, had title: History of the Indian Tribes of North America
> Vol. 2 ed. by Frederick Webb Hodge and David J. Bushnell Jr.
> Vol. 3 contains introd. by H.J. Braunholtz

• Hodge and Bushnell's revision of the first ed. (which was prepared under the auspices of the War Department) provides in v. 1-2 biographical sketches of prominent American Indians prior to 1840 of the Seneca, Sioux, Sauk, Osage, Chippeway, Choctaw, Cherokee, Shawnee, Oto, Winnebago, Pawnee, Creek, Delaware, Mandan, Yuchi, Fox, Iowa, Potawatomi, Seminole, and Ottawa peoples. Volume 3 contains two essays, "Indian Tribes of North America," and "An Essay on the History of the North American Indian," and two folded maps showing the locations of peoples in 1833 and the status of reservations as of 1906. Includes 123 full-page color plates. — *GK*

CD45 **Notable Native Americans** / Sharon Malinowski, editor; George H.J. Abrams, consulting ed. & author of foreword. - Detroit, MI: Gale Research, 1995. - xliv, 492 p.

Class Numbers:
    Library of Congress E89
ISBN 0810396386
OCLC 31172957
LCCN 94-36202
Notes:
    Includes bibliographical references; index

• Of the more than 265 individuals profiled, about 30 percent are historical personages and about 70 percent are from the 20th century. An all-Indian advisory board of a dozen Native faculty members reviewed the 1,400 candidates and made recommendations. Seneca anthropologist and consulting editor George Abrams contributed an eight-page introduction about the issue of American Indian identity. The biographical and bibliographical entries run about two pages each, and include dates, role or notable achievement, alternate names, and selected references, besides the biographical sketch. At the front, a list of entries by name serves as a quick table of contents, and gives tribal affiliation and role, allowing one to identify quickly entries on Plains tribal individuals. There is also a list of entries grouped by tribal group or name, and another rather unfocused list organized by occupation or tribal role (e.g., activist, administrator, jewelry designer, military figure, fisherman, religious figure), although some of the latter categories are confusing (both "religious figure" and "spiritual leader"; "activist," "resistance leader," "warrior"). There are no scope notes to help novices. A concluding 13-page subject index, primarily of names and organizations, is not helpful in identifying entries relevant to Plains studies. Using the "entries by tribal groups/names" table reveals that about 97 of the 265 subjects are Plains individuals, making this a useful work on this region. — *LM*

CD46   North American Indian Biographical Database [Internet Site]. - Alexandria, VA: Alexander Street Pr., 2005 –   . - http://www.alexanderstreet.com/products/ibio.htm

    Access Date: Nov. 2005
    Notes:
        Available through outright purchase or subscription

• Covering North American Indians and Canadian First Peoples from first encounters in the 17th century through Indians living in the urbanized 21st century, this site when complete will offer more than 100,000 pages drawn from published and unpublished sources and from oral history interviews. It includes full-text autobiographies, biographies, reference works, manuscripts, and oral histories. Entries provide links to related materials. Numerous photographs accompany entries, and some important visual sources (e.g., Edward Curtis's *The North American Indians*) are reproduced in their entirety. For Plains students, the source emphasizes the Ojibwa, Cheyenne, and Sioux, and numerous individuals such as Sacajawea, Black Elk, and

Dennis Banks. Members of the editorial board are H. David Brumble, Arlene B. Hirschfelder, and Lotsee Patterson (Univ. of Oklahoma).

§   **Searching Alexander Street sites**. Alexander Street sites emphasize full-text reproduction of published materials, inclusion of unpublished and oral materials, and integration of source materials under broad categories. A table of contents at each site has sections for "Guides" (sample searches), "All Works" (an alphabetical list by title of all the base documents), and searching by individuals, peoples, places, environment, subjects, documents, year, events, images, and audio/video. A search window allows keyword searching, and advanced search allows Boolean searching, limitation by primary or secondary material, and high specificity as to nature of corporate authorship; document type, content, and date; dates; locations; peoples concerned in historical events; and even (should a reader happen to know it) the document number in the database. —*JB*

CD47 O'Brien, Lynn Woods. - **Plains Indian Autobiographies**. - Boise, ID: Boise State College, 1973. - 48 p. - (Boise State College western writers series, 10).

    Class Numbers:
        Library of Congress E78.G73   Z1209.2.U52
    ISBN 0884300099
    LCCN 73-8339
    Notes:
        Bibliography: p. 45-48

• Because the written word and the life story are not Plains Indian forms of expression, the author defines autobiographies as written, oral, dramatic, and pictographic retellings of specific events, activities, and spiritual visions. Following a 40-page introduction to the forms, purposes, and renderings of Indian autobiographies, a bibliography lists 58 published sources containing stories told to others, memoirs, and pictographic narratives. Many are coup stories and most take place in the 19th century. The author points out that the stories told to anthropologists, missionaries, soldiers, historians, and others may tell us more about the recorder than the teller. The works in "Western Writers Series" are intended as introductions to regional literatures and their most important sources. The skimpiness of this list calls attention to the need for a more comprehensive one that indexes the many autobiographies in periodicals, archives, private collections, and museums. —*JD*

CD48 Saskatchewan First Nations: Lives Past and Present / volume ed., Christian Thompson. - Regina, SK: Canadian Plains Research Center, Univ. of Regina, 2004. - xxiv, 151 p.; ill. - (Lives past and present).

    Class Numbers:
        National Library of Canada E78.S2
    ISBN 0889771618 (pbk.)
    OCLC 56329261

LCCN 2004-463256

Notes:

    Includes bibliographical references

• Short biographies of approximately 125 Saskatchewan aboriginal people, ranging from historically important figures to contemporary notables in a variety of fields. Emphasizes the contributions of First Nations people to the cultural, political, and economic life of the province. Relatively few historical chiefs are included, since they will be the subject of a future volume, as will the Métis. The introductory essay reviews native political development, education, health care, media, and sports. A convenient source illustrating the diversity of Saskatchewan indigenous life. — *LMcD*

CD49 Waldman, Carl, 1947- . - **Biographical Dictionary of American Indian History to 1900**. - Rev. ed. - New York: Facts on File, 2001. - 506 p.; ill.

    Class Numbers:

      Library of Congress E89

    ISBN 0816042527   0816043535 (pbk.)

    LCCN 00-49027

    Notes:

      Includes bibliographical references (p. 432-436)

      Rev. ed. of: *Who Was Who in Native American*

        History (**CD50**)

• Despite its title, this work includes at least as many non-Indians as Indians, something Waldman admits in his preface. He intends to include figures who were "an integral part of the Native American story" (p. v) through the 19th century, hence includes many anthropologists, generals, photographers, writers, and explorers to the likely exclusion of indigenous notables. In spite of that, many entries are indeed relevant to the history of the Plains, although the book's time frame begins with an entry for Columbus and includes individuals to the end of the 20th century, but almost no pre-Columbian figures. For Waldman, "American Indian history" means Indian-white history; e.g., he includes Deganawidah of the Iroquois, but not White Buffalo Calf Woman of the Lakota or Sweet Medicine of the Cheyenne. — *LM*

CD50 Waldman, Carl, 1947- . - **Who Was Who in Native American History: Indians and Non-Indians from Early Contacts through 1900**. - New York: Facts on File, 1990. - 410 p.; ill.

    Class Numbers:

      Library of Congress E89

    ISBN 0816017972

    LCCN 89-35088

• Waldman provides entries on historical figures "from early

contacts between Indians and whites through the end of the 19th century" (p. iv), in the U.S. and Canada. Entries are alphabetical by name and provide alternate names and spellings, tribal affiliation, birth and death dates, and role or function when relevant and available. Most entries are a paragraph or two long; some reach two to three columns. Cross-references to individuals who have their own encyclopedia entries are printed in capitals. Appendixes by tribe (oddly, not birth tribe but "historically relevant tribe"–an odd construct) and "non-Indians listed by their most relevant contributions to Native American history" (p. 406, such as "Explorers & Traders," "Frontier Painters and Photographers," and "Officials, Agents, & Reformers"), another unusual approach. Plains tribes are well-represented. No index. — *LM*

Directories

CD51 Estell, Kenneth. - **Native Americans Information Directory**. - 2nd ed. - Detroit, MI: Gale Research, 1998. - 372 p.

    Class Numbers:

      Library of Congress E76.2

    ISBN 0810391163

• In need of an update but convenient as a combined directory of tribal communities, agencies and organizations, library collections, museums, research centers, education and studies programs, financial aid and grant programs, awards, publishers, print and broadcast media, and Internet sites. American Indian, Canadian Aboriginal Native, and general entries are listed separately. Entries, largely drawn from other Gale directories, are annotated and indexed by the standard Gale master name and keyword index. — *JD*

CD52 Spencer, Velva-Lu, comp. - **Regional Directory of Native American Resources** / comp. by Velva-Lu Spencer and Charles L. Woodard; ed. by Jack W. Marken. - [Brookings, SD]: South Dakota State Univ., 1994. - 1 v. (loose-leaf).

    Class Numbers:

      Library of Congress E78.S63

    OCLC 31212318

• Spencer (Native American advisor) and Woodard (English, South Dakota State Univ.) provide a directory for teachers of regional Native American materials and speakers. The work has four parts: (1) "Human Resources," including contact information (names, profession, title, address, phone number, areas of specialization, speaking topics, cultural background) for individuals and organizations; (2) "Audiovisual Resources," films, cassette tapes, or slides found in the collections at SDSU, State Library, South Dakota Humanities Council, Featherstone, and

Great Plains Writers' Conference; (3) "Printed Resources," arranged by author, divided into topics (contemporary literary criticism, legends and myths, bibliographies, biographies, dictionaries, education, fiction, health, history, sociology, juvenile literature, music, visual arts, crafts, oratory, periodicals, politics, religion, and women); (4) "College and University Courses and Programs," descriptions of classes at Augustana College, Black Hills State Univ., Cheyenne River Community College, Dakota Wesleyan Univ., Northern State Univ., Oglala Lakota College, Sinte Gleska Univ., Sisseton-Wahpeton Community College, SDSU, and Univ. of South Dakota. — *GK*

Oral History Aids

CD53 American Indian Research Project. - **Oyate iyechinka woglakapi: An Oral History Collection**. - Vermillion [SD]: [American Indian Research Project], 1970-   . - [1] v. (In progress).

> Class Numbers:
>   Library of Congress Z1209
> OCLC 138620
> LCCN 76-635149
> Notes:
>   List of taped interviews with Plains Indians and non-Indians working actively with them.
>   Housed in the Library of the Univ. of South Dakota, Vermillion
>   Text in English

• Part of a four-volume set of catalogs of oral history interviews gathered by the American Indian Research Project at the University of South Dakota that was funded by a Doris Duke Foundation grant. The interviews, conducted in South Dakota, Nebraska, Montana, Minnesota, and Canada, are ongoing. Entries are arranged by last name and provide subject headings and the catalog numbers of tapes. Peoples included are Chippewa, Sioux, and Winnebago; other topics include music, art, legend, and religious ceremonies. — *GK*

Almanacs

CD54 Champagne, Duane. - **The Native North American Almanac: A Reference Work on Native North Americans in the United States and Canada**. - 2nd ed. - Detroit, MI: Gale Research, 2001. - xxvii, 1472 p.; ill., maps, ports.

> Class Numbers:
>   Library of Congress E77
> National Library of Canada E77

ISBN 0787616559   9780787616557
OCLC 48062774

• Concerned with traditional and contemporary Canadian First Nations people and United States Native Americans, this comprehensive work consists of signed essays, annotated directory information, and nearly 500 concise biographies of prominent Native Americans. Section headings include: "Chronology," "Major Culture Areas" (e.g., Northern Plains Indians; Oklahoma Indians; Indians of the Plateau, Great Basin, and Rocky Mountains; Aboriginal Peoples in Canada), "Native North American Languages," "Law and Legislation," "Urbanization and Non-Reservation Populations," "Religion," "Literature," "Health," "Education," "Economy," and "Prominent Native North Americans." A glossary of terms relevant to Native issues and a bibliography (more than 40 p.) conclude the work. Well-captioned, informative, and relevant illustrations, and a thorough index. An essential work. — *LM*

CD55 Healy, Donald T. - **Native American Flags** / [by] Donald T. Healy and Peter J. Orenski; foreword by Carl Waldman. - Norman, OK: Univ. of Oklahoma Pr., 2003. - xxii, 325 p.; ill.

> Class Numbers:
>   Library of Congress E98.M34
> ISBN 0806135565 (pbk.)
> LCCN 2003-47397
> Notes:
>   Includes bibliographical references; index
>   Revision of an article: Donald T. Healy, "Flags of the Native Peoples of the United States," *Raven : A Journal of Vexillology* 3/4 (1996-97): 1-242

• A guide to the flags of 187 tribes and a small number of intertribal organizations, arranged alphabetically. Each account consists of a brief tribal history, location on a map of the U.S., black-and-white illustration, description of the flag, and significance and symbolism of its components. In the absence of additional information, a few tribes such as the Prairie Band of Potawatomi Indians of Kansas have only a thumbnail sketch. A section of plates displays the flags in full color. The flags convey a surprising amount of information and visually represent historical and cultural elements important to each group. Some of the content is available at Healy's Internet site (http://users.aol.com/Donh523/). — *LMcD*

CD56 Hirschfelder, Arlene B. - **The Native American Almanac: A Portrait of Native America Today** / [by] Arlene Hirschfelder, Martha Kreipe de Montaño. - New York: Prentice Hall General Reference, 1993. - 341 p.; ill.

> Class Numbers:

Library of Congress E77
ISBN 0671850121
LCCN 93-1057
Notes:
　Includes bibliographical references (p. 315-327); index

• Respected author Hirschfelder and National Museum of the American Indian librarian Kreipe de Montaño provide a highly readable "portrait that emphasizes Native American experiences, achievement, and point of view" (p. x). They say it is "not designed to be an encyclopedic compendium"; instead, their wide-ranging work is "not designed to be an encyclopedic compendium" but to provide both snapshot and overview of contemporary Native perspectives on issues important to Indian people. Following a brief but thorough historical overview of Indian-White relations, sections explore Native perspectives such as "Native America Today" (population, tribes, and reservations), Supreme Court decisions, the Bureau of Indian Affairs and the Indian Health Service, tribal governments, languages, education, religion, games and sports, artists, film and video, economic issues, and a very useful section on Native military service. The work concludes with appendixes of directories and listings of tribes by state, reservations by state, a chronology of Indian treaties, Native landmarks, and a general chronology of Indian history. A 15-page bibliography is keyed to each text section, and there is a thorough index. All these resources offer access points by tribe and state, making identification of information relevant to Prairies-Plains easy to locate. Many black-and-white illustrations and abundant tables, lists, and charts. A solid work for all libraries. — *LM*

Guidebooks

CD57 Webber, Bert. - **Indians along the Oregon Trail: The Tribes of Nebraska, Wyoming, Idaho, Oregon, and Washington Identified**. - Medford, OR: Webb Research Group, 1992. - 208 p.; ill.

Class Numbers:
　Library of Congress E78.W5
ISBN 093673860X
OCLC 24872524
LCCN 91-39448
Notes:
　Includes bibliographical references; index

• Webber (a research photojournalist) identifies tribes associated with the states along the Oregon Trail, with an eye to identifying facts not found in earlier encyclopedias. In the introduction, Webber discusses Indian origins, physical characteristics, health issues, variations of tribal names, and the establishment and objectives of the Bureau of Indian Affairs. For Nebraska, Wyoming, Idaho, Oregon, and

Washington, Webber provides information pertaining to history, geographical location, tribal name changes, and highways near the original trail. Maps, illustrations, and two appendixes: unique subjects and Indian population as of January 1987. — *GK*

PEOPLES

Arapaho

CD58 Salzmann, Zdenek, comp. - **The Arapaho Indians: A Research Guide and Bibliography**. - New York: Greenwood, 1988. - vii, 113 p. - (Bibliographies and indexes in anthropology).

Class Numbers:
　Library of Congress Z1210.A67
ISBN 0313253544
LCCN 87-32274

• Salzmann's tightly-structured bibliography attempts to "provide a comprehensive and reliable listing of sources concerning all aspects of the Arapaho people and their culture–both in the past and the present" (p. 17). A topical subject index provides secondary access to the over 700 items in the bibliography proper, but Salzmann also includes a list of government publications concerning the Arapaho divided into separate listings for the Serial Set, CIS *U.S. Serial Set Index*, CIS *U.S. Congressional Committee Hearings Index*, USGPO listings, and *U.S. Statutes at Large*. Rounding out the information for these little-known people in this densely-packed volume is a directory of archives with holdings on the Arapaho, a list of Arapaho holdings at the Thomas Gilcrease Institute, and a list of museums with holdings of Arapaho cultural material. An amazing amount of information (unfortunately, in tiny computer print) in barely 100 pages. — *LM*

Blackfoot (Siksika)

CD59 Dempsey, Hugh Aylmer, 1929-　. - **Bibliography of the Blackfoot** / [by] Hugh A. Dempsey and Lindsay Moir. - Metuchen, NJ: Scarecrow Pr., 1989. - 245 p. - (Native American bibliography series, 13).

Class Numbers:
　Library of Congress Z1210.S59
ISBN 0810822113   0810847620 (pbk.)
LCCN 89-6444
Notes:
　Indexes

• Dempsey, a noted historian of the Blackfoot and other Canadian Plains peoples, and librarian Moir (both at the

Glenbow Museum) offer a bibliography on the three tribes of the Blackfoot people—Blood, Blackfoot, and Piegan—that covers the literature on the Blackfoot in both Alberta and Montana, where they are found in about equal numbers. The 1,828 titles were published through 1986, and are grouped alphabetically by main entry within 24 categories that include both types of works ("Journals and Newspapers," "Fiction and Poetry," "Legends and Folklore," "Literature—Collections and Stories") and topics ("Archaeology and Anthropology," "Education," "History," "Military and Police," "Treaties"). Entries include a large number of Canadian titles, and are taken from "books, monographs, reports, and articles in periodicals, magazines, and the native press" (p. vii). Among works excluded are titles on the fur trade and exploration that refer to the Blackfoot in passing, and newspaper articles and stories in the non-Native press. About half the entries contain one- or two-sentence annotations, mostly descriptive. A very useful 84-page author index ties all an author's works together. A much briefer general index is largely unhelpful. A very thorough work on this important Plains people, and a good addition to a useful series. — *LM*

Cherokee

CD60   Conley, Robert J. - **A Cherokee Encyclopedia**. - Albuquerque, NM: Univ. of New Mexico Pr., 2007. - 312 p.; ill.

LCCN 2007-38318

• Conley (author and Cherokee activist) provides an alphabetical encyclopedia to the various Cherokee nations, of which three survive: the Cherokee Nation and United Keetoowah Band, both of Oklahoma, and the Eastern Band of Cherokees of the southeastern U.S., centered in North Carolina. Most entries briefly treat individual Cherokee, but some run several pages (Ada-gal'kala, Wilma Mankiller, John Ross). There are discussions as well of aspects of Cherokee culture and institutions. Conley briskly dismisses several white figures who were instrumental in the disgraceful robbery of Cherokee land and their removal to Oklahoma. A rambling six-page bibliographic essay ends the book. — *RB*

Cheyenne

CD61   Powell, Peter, 1928-   . - **The Cheyennes, Maheoo's People: A Critical Bibliography**. - Bloomington, IN: publ. for the Newberry Library [by] Indiana Univ. Pr., 1980. - 123 p. - (Newberry Library. Center for the History of the American Indian. Bibliographical series).

Class Numbers:
    Library of Congress E99.C53   Z1210.C49

ISBN 0253304164 (pbk.)
OCLC 6891160
LCCN 80-8033
Notes:
    Index

• Lists of recommended titles follow a brief introduction and some maps of the area inhabited by the Cheyenne—a five-item list recommended for beginners and a list of 21 books for basic library collections. The remainder of the volume is divided about equally between a bibliographic essay and a list of 241 references to books, dissertations, journal articles, and government publications. The essay is organized by chapters on primary works, holy traditions and ceremonies, archaeology, language, art, Christian missions, U.S. government relations, tribal government, and the "struggle to preserve the Cheyenne way," the latter by far the longest section. — *MB*

Dakota/Lakota

CD62   Hardorff, Richard G. - **The Oglala Lakota Crazy Horse: A Preliminary Genealogical Study and an Annotated List of Primary Sources** / foreword by John M. Carroll. - Mattituck, NY: J.M. Carroll & Co., 1985. - 59 p.; [5] p. of plates, ill., ports.

Class Numbers:
    Library of Congress E90.C82
ISBN 0848800192
Notes:
    Bibliography: p. [47]-59

• Introduced, surprisingly, with a lengthy, heavily researched biography of the army private who bayoneted Crazy Horse at Fort Robinson, NE (Sept. 1877), Hardorff's work is nevertheless a good starting place for those studying either Crazy Horse or Sioux-government relations in the mid-19th century. The genealogy is a description of what is known, unknown, and uncertain about Crazy Horse's lineage and family, accompanied by a simple chart. Divided into manuscripts, articles, newspapers, books, and photographs and other material, the bibliography gives detailed descriptions and evaluations of content. Little information is provided concerning the research methods used to compile the bibliography or its completeness. — *JD*

CD63   Hoover, Herbert T. - **The Sioux: A Critical Bibliography**. - Bloomington, IN: publ. for the Newberry Library [by] Indiana Univ. Pr., 1979. - 78 p. - (Newberry Library. Center for the History of the American Indian. Bibliographical series).

Class Numbers:
    Library of Congress E99.D1   Z1210.D3
ISBN 0253349729
LCCN 79-2167

Notes:

Includes bibliographical references (p. xv-xvi); index

• Follows a topical organization, beginning with 20 recommended works and a bibliographic essay which occupies about half the volume. In this essay each of the items in the bibliography which follows is either discussed or mentioned. The broad categories into which the 213 numbered items are arranged are: general histories, autobiographies and biographies, battles and wars, observations and influences of non-Indian groups, special Sioux groups, and culture. Some items are marked with an asterisk to denote their suitability for secondary school students. Most of the items are books, but a number of journal articles and government publications are included as well. — *MB*

CD64   Hoover, Herbert T. - **The Sioux and Other Native American Cultures of the Dakotas: An Annotated Bibliography** / comp. by Herbert T. Hoover and Karen P. Zimmerman; editorial assistant for computer operations, Christopher J. Hoover. - Westport, CT: Greenwood Pr., 1993. - xx, 265 p. - (Bibliographies and indexes in anthropology, 8; ISSN 0742-6884).

Class Numbers:

Library of Congress E99.D1   Z1210.D3

ISBN 0313290938

OCLC 28213494

LCCN 93-25004

Notes:

Indexes

• This bibliography, a companion to *South Dakota History: An Annotated Bibliography*, also compiled by Hoover and Zimmerman (**DB76**), shares its index and continues its numbering of entries, beginning with 3181. The present volume is arranged by broad topics (the largest cover prehistory, religion, and traditional Sioux culture), and within topics alphabetically by main entry. Among the smaller divisions are the Sioux federation outside the U.S. and reference materials. A reasonably detailed chronology precedes the bibliographic entries; following them are detailed author and subject indexes to the two volumes, with entries for the volume in hand in boldface. Annotations are usually brief and descriptive rather than evaluative. — *MB*

CD65   Lakota-Dakota Comprehensive Bibliography [Internet Site] / comp. by Raymond A. Bucko. - Omaha, NE: Creighton Univ., 2000?-   . - http://puffin.creighton.edu/lakota/biblio_total.html

Access Date: Jan. 2006

Fees: None

• Bucko (S.J., anthropology, Creighton Univ.) has compiled a bibliography with 4,361 entries (last updated Aug. 2,

2005) that is "a comprehensive bibliography of primarily scholarly works on the Lakota and Dakota. I first compiled this bibliography while working on my dissertation and have...[added] materials from other research projects as well as entries contributed by other scholars." Entries are in a single list, alphabetical by author (anonymous works by date or title), with formats not differentiated. Readers need to know, for example, that a publisher identified as "Indian House" is a music label. Although it is easy to scroll through the list, and word searching using the browser's "Find" function is simple, the font is the same throughout, making it mind-numbing to scan. But the list is comprehensive as claimed, and includes most formats (government publications, monographs, articles, ERIC documents, sound recordings, photographs, materials in languages other than English, chapters in books, newspaper articles, book reviews), but omitting Internet pages, although they are linked in the parent page, *Lakota na Dakota Wowapi Oti Kin = Lakota Dakota Information Home Page*, http://puffin.creighton.edu/lakota/. Entries range in date from about 1835 to 2006. Comprehensive but difficult to use. — *LM*

CD66   Marken, Jack W. - **Bibliography of the Sioux** / by Jack W. Marken and Herbert T. Hoover. - Metuchen, NJ: Scarecrow Pr., 1980. - 370 p. - (Native American bibliography series, 1).

Class Numbers:

Library of Congress E99.D1   Z1210.D3

ISBN 0810813564

LCCN 80-20106

Notes:

Indexes

• The 3,367 numbered entries in this bibliography are arranged in 33 categories, chiefly topical ("Arts and Culture," "Education," "History," "Religion"), but some based on the form of publication ("Bibliographies," "Journals," "Theses"). The topical headings are likely to be more useful for most readers. In each category, entries are alphabetical by author; most provide only basic bibliographic information. Annotations, when they appear, are never longer than two sentences. Journal titles are abbreviated; a key to abbreviations is at the front. There are lengthy personal name and briefer subject indexes, the latter focusing more on place-names and treaties than topics. — *MB*

Displaced Peoples

CD67   Unrau, William E., 1929-   . - **The Emigrant Indians of Kansas: A Critical Bibliography**. - Bloomington, IN: publ. for the Newberry Library [by] Indiana Univ. Pr., 1979. - 78 p.; [1] leaf of plates, maps. - (Newberry Library Center for the History of the American Indian bibliographical series).

Class Numbers:
    Library of Congress E78.K18   Z1209.2.U52
    ISBN 0253368162
    OCLC 4983585
    LCCN 79-2169
    Notes:
        Index

• Unrau's bibliographic essay pulls together 187 titles on the various Iroquoian and Algonquian tribes from the Eastern U.S. who passed through or remained in Kansas during the forced migrations of these peoples. Consequently, while the location is certainly the Plains, the peoples are mostly woodlands Indians who now make their homes in this region, and the works discussed deal largely with the Eastern U.S. Unrau's chronological essay has chapter headings such as "Historical Setting and Cultural Identification," "Removal to the Kansas 'Desert'," "Role of the Missionaries," and "Expulsion from Kansas." Many of these peoples ended up in Oklahoma. A unique work covering a little-known but important aspect of the region's history. — LM

First Nations

CD68   Aboriginal Canada Portal = Portail des autochtones au Canada [Internet Site]. - [Ottawa, ON]: Government of Canada, 2001- . - http://www.aboriginal-canada.gc.ca/

Class Numbers:
    Library of Congress E78.C2
    OCLC 56331615
    Access Date: June 2006
    Notes:
        Review by J.L. Brudvig: *Choice* 43.9 (June 2006):
            review 43-6086
    Fees: None

• ACP provides centralized access to a wide range of information for, by, and about Canadian aboriginal peoples, supplying information about government programs and services, contacts, native groups, bands, communities, and businesses. It is a cooperative project of the federal government and six national organizations, including the Assembly of First Nations, Congress of Aboriginal Peoples, and the Métis National Council. Major areas include economic development, claims and treaties, education, employment, environment, health and social services, housing, justice, language and culture, policy and research, subdivided as appropriate. Under each, links to federal government agencies are followed by other sources of information. The portal is also arranged by province and territory, making systematic examination of Prairie resources straightforward.

Each jurisdiction has the same basic subject arrangement, modified where necessary. The Aboriginal Communities section under each province is particularly useful in listing First Nations reserves and Métis communities, giving homepages, profiles from Indian and Northern Affairs Canada, and statistical profiles and mapping from Statistics Canada. Resources for particular demographic populations are clearly identified: elders, women, youth, and children. Other features include a virtual tour of aboriginal Canada, arranged by province, region, and individual community, as well as aboriginal news items from daily newspapers. The advanced search option includes Boolean options and limits by topic and geographic region. A well-organized portal offering more than 16,000 links to Canadian government and aboriginal sites, a large number of which concern First Nations peoples in the Prairie provinces. — LMcD

CD69   Atlas of Urban Aboriginal Peoples [Internet Site]. - [Saskatoon, SK: Univ. of Saskatchewan], 1988. - http://gismap.usask.ca/website/Web%5Fatlas/AOUAP/

Access Date: May 2006
Notes:
    "The Atlas is part of the research on Aboriginal people and cities associated with the Canada Research Chair on Identity and Diversity: The Aboriginal Experience held by Dr. Evelyn J. Peters at the University of Saskatchewan"
    Includes glossary and bibliography
Fees: None

• Using Statistics Canada Census data, the atlas details changes in native settlement patterns in selected Prairie cities, 1971-2001: Calgary and Edmonton, AB; Prince Albert, Regina, and Saskatoon, SK; and Winnipeg, MB. Data are mapped at the level of census tract and enumeration/dissemination area; maps show city rather than Census Metropolitan Area boundaries. The map viewer is ArcIMS software, with detailed instructions on using it. A useful tool graphically illustrating demographic shifts in Prairie cities. — LMcD

CD70   Barnett, Don C. - Research Related to Native Peoples at the University of Saskatchewan, 1912-1983 / [by] Don C. Barnett and Aldrich J. Dyer. - [Saskatoon, SK]: Univ. of Saskatchewan, 1983. - 163 p.

Class Numbers:
    Library of Congress E78.S2
    OCLC 12693561
    LCCN 84-206057

• Detailed abstracts, arranged by author, of theses dealing with Indians, Métis, and Inuit. Each gives a description of the study, research design, findings, and conclusion.

Education, anthropology, and history are the largest areas of study. The final chapter analyzes the theses by department, date, particular peoples (Cree being the most widely examined), geographic area, type, and subject. — *LMcD*

CD71 Hill, Yvonne B., 1954- . - **Alberta District, Indian Agency Enumerations**. - Lethbridge, AB: Ancestor Answers, 1998. - 224 p.; map. - (Ancestor Answers's Canadian 1901 Census series).

> Class Numbers:
> Library of Congress CS88.A46
> National Library of Canada E98
> ISBN 1894215133
> OCLC 43973164
> LCCN 99-491973

• Transcription of 1901 Census of the eight Indian agencies in preprovincial Alberta, listed in the order in which they are found in the Census record. Some agencies include related boarding schools, bands, and reserves. Records indicate name, sex, relationship to head, marital status, age, nation (Blackfoot, Sarcee, Stoney, etc.), birthplace, and religion. Name index. — *LMcD*

CD72 [Profiles of Saskatchewan Indian Bands]. – Ottawa, ON: Indian and Northern Affairs Canada, 1995. - [142] p.; maps.
> Notes:
> Two-page leaflets, each treating a specific band and issued separately, collected with a binding title supplied by the Regina Public Library Prairie History Room

• Brief descriptions of 70 bands indicating location, history, language, economy, governmental representation, band government, membership, community services, education, and address. — *LMcD*

CD73 Provincial Archives of Alberta. Historical Resources Library. - **Native Peoples of Alberta: A Bibliographic Guide**. - [Edmonton, AB]: Alberta Culture and Multiculturalism, Historical Resources Division, 1988. - 36 p.; ill.

> Class Numbers:
> Library of Congress E78.A34
> National Library of Canada Z1209.2 C32
> ISBN 0919411150
> OCLC 20671347
> LCCN 89-105764

• A brief guide to indigenous Alberta, organized by type of material: bibliographies, periodicals, indexes, theses, series, museum catalogs, travel narratives, and language studies. A subject section focuses on Métis, women, and treaties; surprisingly few studies of individual First Nations. Listing of specialized libraries and archives. Although based on a single collection, the guide is sufficiently general to serve as an introduction to sources on Alberta native history. — *LMcD*

Metis

CD74 Arora, Ved Parkash. - **Louis Riel: A Bibliography**. - Rev. 2nd ed. - Regina, SK: Saskatchewan Library Association with the co-operation of Saskatchewan Library, 1985. - 193 p.

> Class Numbers:
> Library of Congress F1060.9.R529   Z8745.3
> National Library of Canada COP.SA.2.1986-7
> ISBN 0919059139
> OCLC 16050424
> LCCN 86-213883
> Notes:
> 1st ed. publ. 1972
> Electronic book: http://www.ourroots.ca/f/toc.aspx?id= 2759

• Arora's bibliography brings together over 1,600 items, in a variety of formats, on the charismatic and still controversial Métis leader and principal figure in the Red River Rebellion of 1869-1870 in Manitoba and the North-West Rebellion of 1885 in Saskatchewan. Many deal with the general history of the Métis as well as the broader politics of the time. Arranged by author or title; index of titles and secondary authors. A very useful source for a significant period of 19th-century Prairie history. — *LMcD*

CD75 Metis Legacy: A Metis Historiography and Annotated Bibliography / ed. by Lawrence J. Barkwell, Leah Dorion, Darren R. Préfontaine. - Winnipeg, MB: Pemmican Publ., 2001. - 512 p.; ill. (some col.), ports. (some col.).

> Class Numbers:
> Library of Congress E99.M47
> National Library of Canada Z1209.2
> ISBN 189471704X   1894717031 (pbk.)
> OCLC 46627958
> LCCN 2002-405509
> Notes:
> "A Millennium Project of the Louis Riel Institute of the Manitoba Metis Federation, Winnipeg, Manitoba [and] Gabriel Dumont Institute of Métis Studies and Applied Research, Saskatoon, Saskatchewan"–T.p. verso
> Includes index

• The initial chapter tracing the evolution of Metis studies is followed by chapters treating historical and cultural issues including identity, ethnography, music, language, and art. Numerous photographs illustrate material culture, particularly clothing. The extensive bibliography (p. 273-494), arranged alphabetically by author, constitutes approximately half the book; there is a separate bibliography of audiovisual material. An earlier version of the bibliography, unannotated, appeared in the editors' *Resources for Métis Researchers* (Winnipeg, MB: Louis Riel Institute of the Manitoba Metis Federation, 1999). The most current and comprehensive reference work available. — LMcD

Omaha

CD76   Tate, Michael L. - **The Upstream People: An Annotated Research Bibliography of the Omaha Tribe**. - Metuchen, NJ: Scarecrow Pr., 1991. - 504 p.; maps. - (Native American bibliography series, 14).

> Class Numbers:
> Library of Congress E99.O4   Z1210.O45
> ISBN 0810823721
> LCCN 90-24533
> Notes:
> Index

• Tate's fully-annotated bibliography containing 1,836 entries for these often-neglected Missouri River people seeks to "spark new interest" and "provide a body of raw material for further research among academicians, the public at large, and the Omahas themselves" (p. ix). His arrangement of entries is somewhat over-specific. Entries are divided among 32 chapters, allowing, perhaps, for a very Omaha-centric arrangement, but making the work awkward to use. No entries are duplicated, so reliance on the index is a must. Entries from books, scholarly articles, and theses and dissertations are spread among chapters such as "Children and Family Life," "Mormon Relations," "Omaha Personalities," "Half-Breed Tract," and "John G. Neihardt and the Omahas." Tate also includes many government publications and provides special chapters for newspaper articles and archival collections. Thorough and highly useful. — *LM*

Osage

CD77   Wilson, Terry P. - **Bibliography of the Osage**. - Metuchen, NJ: Scarecrow Pr., 1985. - 162 p. - (Native American bibliography series, 6).

> Class Numbers:
> Library of Congress Z1210.O8
> ISBN 0810818051
> OCLC 11815724
> LCCN 85-2087

> Notes:
> Indexes

• Wilson begins with a historical introduction, then organizes his occasionally annotated bibliography of almost 700 titles into three sections: archaeology, anthropology, culture; history before 1871; and history after 1871. Entries are alphabetical by author in each section. Seventy titles appear in more than one location. Includes theses and dissertations in addition to books and articles; author and subject indexes. A useful resource for this neglected people. — *LM*

Pawnee

CD78   Blaine, Martha Royce. - **The Pawnees: A Critical Bibliography**. – Bloomington, IN: Indiana Univ. Pr., 1980. - 110 p.

> Class Numbers:
> Library of Congress E99.P3
> ISBN 0253315026
> LCCN 80-8034

• Following the introduction is a map of Pawnee distribution, ca. 1800, and a list of three dozen recommended titles. A bibliographic essay comprises about half the volume and the 274-item bibliography the other half. The essay is organized as follows: Spanish and French colonial period, explorers after the Louisiana Purchase, military affairs: depredations and hostilities, traders and trappers, missionaries and teachers, United States relations, archaeology, and cultural studies, which in turn is subdivided into art, religion and traditions, language, marriage and kinship, social organization, and music. Entries include references to books, government documents, and journal articles. Each entry has a cross- reference to the page where it is mentioned or discussed in the bibliographic essay. — *MB*

CD79   Boughter, Judith A., 1940-   . - **The Pawnee Nation: An Annotated Research Bibliography**. - Lanham, MD: Scarecrow Pr., 2004. - xxii, 305 p. - (Native American bibliography series, 28).

> Class Numbers:
> Library of Congress E99.P3   Z1210.P38
> ISBN 0810849909
> OCLC 53796759
> LCCN 2003-25415
> Notes:
> Includes bibliographical references; indexes
> Review by M. Cedar Face: *Choice* 42.3 (Nov. 2004): review 42-1308
> Table of contents: http://www.loc.gov/catdir/toc/ ecip0411/2003025415.html

• Boughter (history, Univ. of Nebraska) organizes 1,306 titles on the Pawnee people originally of northern Kansas and much of Nebraska, and now of Oklahoma, into 27 detailed cultural and historical categories of Pawnee history and culture. Beginning chapters are culturally thematic, historical chapters more or less chronological. Categories include "Bibliographies, Indexes, and Guides," "Language and Linguistic Studies," "Music and Dance," "White Contact to 1806," "The Pike-Pawnee Village," "Nebraska Reservation Period (1859-1875)," "Pawnee Personalities," and "Graves Protection and Repatriation." Almost all titles are annotated, and include works published from the first explorers' reports on the Shawnee in the early 19th century through contemporary works into the beginning of the 21st century. Subject and author-editor indexes. Another first-rate, essential reference source from this Scarecrow series. — *LM*

CD80 Pawnee Nation of Oklahoma [Internet Site]. - Pawnee, OK: Pawnee Nation of Oklahoma, 2000?- . - http://www.pawneenation.org/

Access Date: Aug. 2006
Fees: None

• Tribal Internet sites vary greatly in sophistication, content, and target audience. All are created primarily to serve their constituencies, so supply information about local tribal government activities and services, but many also provide historical and cultural background information for the tribe. The *Pawnee Nation of Oklahoma* site holds to both goals. Emphasizing tribal activities, it features 14 sections of governmental information (many with subsections) that include "Administrative Departments," "Commissions," "Constitution of the Pawnee Nation," "Education & Training," "Environmental Conservation & Safety," "Law Enforcement," and "Job Announcements." Of more general interest to nontribal members are issues of the tribal newsletter, "Chaticks si Chaticks," for the current and past year, and a "History" section. The latter, however, is sparsely populated, consisting of a list of books about the Pawnee with links to ordering them from *Amazon.com*, the Pawnee Nation flag, and a 25-image "Photographical Tour" that failed to run. Other sections are still under construction or are empty, such as "Gift Shop," "Directory," and "Tribal Development Coporation." Like many Internet pages for dynamic organizations, one needs to check back often to keep abreast of additions and enhancements. Useful for the information it contains. — *LM*

Potawatomi

CD81 Edmunds, Russell David, 1939-   . - **Kinsmen through Time: An Annotated Bibliography of Potawatomi History**. - Metuchen, NJ: Scarecrow Pr., 1987. - 217 p. - (Native American bibliography series, 12).

Class Numbers:

Library of Congress Z1210.P67
ISBN 081082020X
OCLC 16227621
LCCN 87-16679
Notes:
Index

• The Potawatomi, like many former eastern woodlands tribes (especially the Shawnee, whose transcontinental journey they parallel), have a long history of interaction with non-Indians that ranges from the Great Lakes regions to the central and southern Plains, where they settled ultimately in the former Indian Territory. Current reservations are found in Oklahoma, Kansas, Michigan, and Wisconsin. Significant communities still exist in their old homelands and along their exodus route, in Indiana, Texas, and Ontario. Cherokee historian Edmunds's bibliography consists of 1,092 predominantly historical entries. Anthropological works are included when useful for historical research. Entries are alphabetical by author, within six broad chronological periods. Earlier periods contain entries for the Potawatomi before they reached the Prairies-Plains region. Most relevant for Plains studies are chapters 4-6 ("Removal Period," "Kansas, Oklahoma, and the Midwest: Postremoval Period, 1847-1900," and "Twentieth Century"), which contain over half the total entries. A special feature of the index, mostly names, is the inclusion of Potawatomi family names, a gift for Potawatomi genealogists. A key regional work. — *LM*

Topics

Archaeology
See **Oklahoma Indian Artifacts, CB20**.

Art

Guides

CD82 Lovett, John R., 1952- , comp. - **Guide to Native American Ledger Drawings and Photographs in United States Museums, Libraries, and Archives** / comp. by John R. Lovett Jr. and Donald L. Dewitt. - Westport, CT: Greenwood Pr., 1998. - 135 p.; ill.

Class Numbers:
Library of Congress E98.A7
ISBN 0313306931
LCCN 98-41033
Notes:
Includes bibliographical references (p. [97]-119); index

• Ledger drawings, unique both as an art form and as a

visual history of life on the Great Plains in the 19th and 20th centuries, developed as Plains Indians used materials (ledger books, stationery, inks, and watercolors) obtained from immigrants to the Plains to set down the images traditionally drawn on buffalo hides. Besides commemorating warriors' coup counts, the drawings depict important events, village life, and customs. Many of these highly prized drawings are now in museums, libraries, and archives. Lovett's guide has three sections. The first, a directory of institutions holding ledger drawings arranged by state and city, includes in its entries directory information and details about the collections, including artists and tribal affiliations, volume (number of drawings held) and media, dates drawn, themes and geographical locations, published descriptions of drawings, and comments on special collection names or locations. Second is an annotated bibliography of books and articles related to specific drawings, collections, artists, or ledger art in general. Cross-references point to entries in the directory. Third is an index by subjects, tribal affiliations, and artists cited in either the directory or the bibliography. Fifteen ledger drawings are reproduced in black-and-white. Even the titles are evocative: "The Rescue of Hairy Hand at the Wagon Box Fight," "Cheyenne Camp Scene" by Soaring Eagle, and a Silverhorn drawing, "Saynday, the Kiowa Trickster." —*JD*

Bibliographies

CD83 Dawdy, Doris Ostrander. - **Annotated Bibliography of American Indian Painting**. - New York: Museum of the American Indian, Heye Foundation, 1968. - 27 p. - (Contributions from the Museum of the American Indian, Heye Foundation, v. 21 pt. 2).

> Class Numbers:
>   Library of Congress E51   Z1209
>   OCLC 50619
>   LCCN 78-8195

• Documents the first 50 years' use of canvas, oils, and other traditional European materials by contemporary Indian painters, beginning in the Southwest around 1910 and reaching the Plains by 1918. Some painters used indigenous subject matter and rendering techniques, others turned to abstraction and other international styles. Most publications indexed are articles, but Dawdy includes books, occasional papers, newspapers, government publications, and theses as well. A few entries cite commonly available titles (*Newsweek*, *Art News*) but many cite less well-indexed titles like *Smoke Signals*, *New Mexico Sun Trails*, and *Indians at Work*. Annotations are brief but list names of artists. An index by artists' names would have been useful, but the bibliography is brief and easily scanned. —*JD*

Catalogs

CD84 Philbrook Museum of Art. - **Visions and Voices: Native American Painting from the Philbrook Museum of Art** / ed. by Lydia L. Wyckoff. - Albuquerque, NM: distr. by the Univ. of New Mexico Pr.; Tulsa, OK: Philbrook Museum of Art, 1998. - 304 p.; ill. (some col.).

> Class Numbers:
>   Library of Congress ND238.A4
>   ISBN 0866590129   0866590137 (pbk.)
>   OCLC 35991964
>   LCCN 97-142894
>   Notes:
>   Contents:
>   Visions and Voices: A Collective History of
>   Native American Painting / Lydia L. Wyckoff;
>   Bacone College and the Philbrook Indian Annals /
>   Ruthe Blalock Jones; Marla Redcorn and Adrea
>   Rogers-Henry
>   Includes bibliographical references (p. 299-300); index

• Wyckoff's history of Native American art profiles Native American painters who entered the Philbrook's national juried competitions, 1946-1979, and are represented in its renowned Native American painting collection. Profiles consist of high quality reproductions of artworks and excerpts from interviews and correspondence with the artists, friends, relatives, and colleagues. The excerpts are personal, touching on private lives, artistic development, specific paintings, and Indian art in general, but they do not provide detailed biographical information or critical evaluations. The artworks reflect both paths of 20th-century Indian art: traditional Native American painting styles and non-Native styles with Native American themes. Bibliography of cited references and an index by name and organization. —*JD*

Indexes

CD85 **Great Plains Indian Illustration Index** / ed. by John Van Balen. - Jefferson, NC: McFarland & Co., 2004. - 399 p.

> Class Numbers:
>   Library of Congress E78.G73
>   ISBN 0786416149   9780786416141
>   OCLC 52738691
>   LCCN 2003-20699
>   Notes:
>   Bibliography: p. 391-399
>   Review by J. Drueke: *Choice* 41.10 (June 2004): review
>   41-5674
>   Table of contents: http://www.loc.gov/catdir/toc/ecip049/

2003020699.html

• Van Balen's index to photographs, drawings, maps, and other illustrations in 340 monographs published 1911-2002 focuses on 44 Great Plains tribes but includes tribes resettled in Indian territory, tribes from other geographic regions, traders, Indian agents, missionaries, and others. Illustrations include works by well-known non-Indian artists (e.g., Karl Bodmer, George Catlin, Edward Curtis); photos of material culture such as clothing, weapons, and dwellings; group and individual portraits; maps of archaeological sites; contemporary Native American art; events such as the Ghost Dance and naming ceremonies; and village and domestic life. Entries, organized by personal name and topic, give brief description, type of illustration, date of work, artist, and source. The works indexed, primarily modern trade, university, historical society, and state agency publications, are limited in number and scope, but the index is useful in locating illustrations and bringing similar art works together. — *JD*

CD86 Harding, Anne Dinsdale, 1917-   , comp. - **Bibliography of Articles and Papers on North American Indian Art** / comp. by Miss Anne Harding and Miss Patricia Bolling ... under the direction of Dr. Otto Klineberg in cooperation with Dr. George Vaillant and Dr. W.D. Strong. - [Washington, DC: Dept. of the Interior, Indian Arts and Crafts Board, 1938]. - 365 p.; map.

> Class Numbers:
> Library of Congress Z1209
> OCLC 1371749 (reprint)   444589 (preliminary ed.)
> LCCN 39-26510
> Notes:
> Preliminary mimeographed ed.
> Reprinted: New York: Kraus, 1969

• Based on the American Museum of Natural History collections, the bibliography lists articles in periodicals published by museums and universities, a class of publications notoriously difficult to identify. It includes articles on ceremonial, decorative, and utilitarian objects of Plains Indian nations. Part 1, the bibliography, is arranged alphabetically by author, with annotations coded for type of article (analytical, descriptive, historical, technical, theoretical) and illustrations (drawings, color plates, photographs, none). Parts 2-4 are indexes to Part 1, citing authors and dates only (full bibliographic details are found only in Part 1). Part 2 lists only general articles on Indian art or on specific crafts. Part 3 will be of most interest to Plains researchers, since it indexes articles by nine cultural areas developed by anthropologist Clark Wissler, then by tribe. Wissler's culture area map places most of the Great Plains region in his Plains culture area. Part 4 indexes specific crafts. A final section lists the publications from which articles are drawn. — *JD*

Collective Biographies

CD87 King, Jeanne Snodgrass. - **American Indian Painters: A Biographical Directory**. - New York: Museum of the American Indian, Heye Foundation, 1968. – 269 p. - (Contributions from the Museum of the American Indian, Heye Foundation, v. 21 pt. 1).

> Class Numbers:
> Library of Congress E51
> OCLC 51958
> LCCN 67-27949
> Notes:
> Bibliography: p. 264-269

• Like Dawdy's *Annotated Bibliography of American Indian Painting* (**CD83**), King's directory focuses on contemporary painters using European materials and methods. The 1,187 painters, many of whom were born or lived on the Plains, worked between the early 20th century and 1966 with a variety of inks, paints, pencils, canvases, and papers in styles varying from pictographic to abstract. Artists are listed alphabetically by most commonly used names and spellings with cross-references from alternate forms. Entries give tribal affiliations, alternate names, birth and death dates and places, marriages and children, education, exhibitions, military service, careers, honors, books illustrated, works published, exhibitions, awards, collections holding works, and addresses. Brief anecdotes and quotations by the artists add color to some entries. Sources include exhibition catalogs and personal contact with the artists; 157 museums and 973 private collections are listed as holding the artists' works. Appendixes include index by tribe; key to abbreviations for exhibitions, schools, and collections; and a bibliography. — *JD*

CD88 Lester, Patrick David, 1939- . - **The Biographical Directory of Native American Painters**. - Tulsa, OK: SIR Publ.; distr. Norman, OK: Univ. of Oklahoma Pr., 1995. - 701 p.; ill.

> Class Numbers:
> Library of Congress ND203
> ISBN 0806199369   0964070634 (limited ed.)
> OCLC 34721611
> LCCN 95-69012
> Notes:
> Bibliography: p. 687-701; index

• A greatly expanded edition of King's *American Indian Painters* (**CD87**), Lester's work includes the 1,187 contemporary painters listed in the original edition, updating hundreds of them and expanding the list to more than 3,000 artists. New painters are included if they consider themselves Indians and are actively pursuing painting careers.

Information was gathered using survey forms. Entries differ from those in the previous work in some significant ways. References to artists' spouses and children, private collections, private galleries, and specific biographical publications have been dropped. Official tribal preferences are used for tribal affiliations unless the artist preferred a particular reservation or regional division. Entries now include occupations, media, and commissions. Anecdotes are drawn from the original edition and other works. The work ends with a tribal index, a list of abbreviations, and an updated bibliography of books and exhibition catalogs. — *JD*

CD89 Matuz, Roger, ed. - **St. James Guide to Native North American Artists** / preface by Rick Hill; introd. by W. Jackson Rushing. - Detroit, MI: St. James Pr., 1998. - xxxii, 691 p.; ill.

> Class Numbers:
> Library of Congress E98.A7
> ISBN 1558622217
> OCLC 37341203
> LCCN 97-18453
> Notes:
> Includes bibliographical references (p. 649-651); index

• *St. James* covers more than 350 artists active in the 20th century in a variety of media, both artists producing work rooted in European traditions and artists using traditional tribal motifs and materials. To some degree, most works incorporate Native American cultural elements or contemporary issues. Plains researchers will find discussions of Lakota symbolism in Colleen Cutshall's paintings, Cherokee women's traditions reflected in Dana Tiger's work, and elements of traditional Chippewa beadwork in Alex Janvier's abstract paintings. Artists were omitted if information was scarce or if tribal affiliation could not be established. Entries are alphabetical by the name most frequently used to sign artworks. Entries give brief information about variant names, tribal affiliation, media, education, career, awards, current address, individual exhibitions, group exhibitions, collections, and publications by and about the artist. Comments by the artist precede personal histories, cultural influences, artistic themes, and scholarly criticisms. Some entries have photographs of the artists or their work. Selective bibliography of general works on Native American art or artists; indexes by name, tribe, state or province, and medium. — *JD*

CD90 Reno, Dawn E. - **Contemporary Native American Artists.** - Brooklyn, NY: Alliance Publ.; distr. by National Book Network Inc., c1995. - 230 p.; ill.

> Class Numbers:
> Library of Congress E98.A7
> ISBN 0964150964
> OCLC 33155282

LCCN 96-198398
> Notes:
> Includes bibliographical references

• Reno briefly describes more than 1,000 artists working in pottery, textiles, painting, sculpture, carving, basketry, beadwork, jewelry, dollmaking, and other arts and crafts. Entries, arranged alphabetically by artist, include tribal affiliation, birth and death dates, location, alternate names, media, art education, awards, agent representation, and a brief statement about the artist or the artist's work. Indexes by media, gallery or representation, and tribe; brief bibliography of books and articles. Useful to collectors and researchers. — *JD*

CD91 Schaaf, Gregory, 1953- . – **American Indian Art Series.** – Santa Fe, NM : CIAC Pr., 1998- .

> **LCCN 98-87933**

Hopi-Tewa Pottery: 500 Artist Biographies, ca. 1800-Present ... / ed. by Richard M. Howard. – 2004. – 199 p. ; ill. (some col.), genealogical tables, ports. – (American Indian Art Series, v. 1).
> Class Numbers:
> Library of Congress E99.H7
> ISBN 0966694805   9780966694802
> OCLC 55637910
> Notes:
> Includes bibliographical references (p. 194-199)

Pueblo Indian Pottery : 750 Artist Biographies, ca. 1800-Present ... / designed by Angie Yan. – 2000. – 295 p. ; ill. (some col.), genealogical tables. - (American Indian Art Series, v. 2).
> Class Numbers:
> Library of Congress E99.P9
> ISBN 0966694813   9780966694819
> OCLC 43470641
> Notes:
> Includes bibliographical references (p. 290-295)

American Indian Textiles : 2,000 Artist Biographies, ca. 1800-Present... / with assistance by Angie Yan Schaaf. – 2000. – 317 p. ; ill. (some col.), ports. – (American Indian Art Series, v. 3).
> Class Numbers:
> Library of Congress E98.T35
> ISBN 0966694848   9780966694840
> OCLC 45568121
> Notes:
> Includes bibliographical references (p. 315-317)

Southern Pueblo Pottery : 2,000 Artist Biographies, c. 1800-Present ... / with assistance by Angie Yan Schaaf. – 2002. – 342 p. ; ill. (some col.), genealogical tables. – (American

Indian Art Series, v. 4).

    Class Numbers:

      Library of Congress E98.P48

      OCLC 48624322

    Notes:

      Bibliographical references (p. 339-342)

American Indian Jewelry I : 1,200 Artist Biographies, ca. 1800-Present / assisted by Angie Yan Schaaf. – 2003. – 342 p. ; ill. (some col.). – (American Indian Art Series, v. 5).

    Class Numbers:

      Library of Congress E98.P48

      ISBN 0966694872   9780966694871

      OCLC 51929348

    Notes:

      Includes bibliographical references (p. 341-342)

American Indian Baskets I : 1,500 Artist Biographies, ca. 1770-Present / foreword by John Kania ; assisted by Angie Yan Schaaf. – 2006. – 342 p. ; ill. (some col.), ports (some col.). – (American Indian Art Series, v. 6

    Class Numbers:

      Library of Congress E98.B3

      ISBN 0977665208   9780977665204

      OCLC 70225399

    Notes:

      Includes bibliographical references (p. 337-342); index

• Expected to reach 20 volumes, this set will provide brief biographies of an estimated 30,000 past and contemporary Indian artists. Volumes as of spring 2007 are listed above; the forthcoming *Baskets II* will focus on Plains Indians, and future sets will cover paintings, carvings, beadwork, and other art forms. The entire set will interest Plains researchers since artists in many regions were influenced by traditions, techniques, and trade items of Plains people. Following an introduction to forms and techniques, the entries, of varying completeness, give alternate names, general descriptions of artwork, photos of the artists, and black-and-white reproductions of their works. Additional fields give residence, birth date, lifespan, family, galleries, teachers, students, awards, demonstrations, exhibitions, collections, values, favorite designs, and biographical databases. Appendixes in the various volumes include types, designs, terminology, media, hallmarks, and signatures; family trees; bibliographies; and indexes. A fine set with unique information, beautiful design, and high quality production. —*JD*

Directories

CD92 **North Dakota Native American Arts and Crafts: A Source Directory**. - [Bismarck, ND: North Dakota Indian Arts Association; North Dakota Economic Development Commission], 1988. - 65 p.; photos.

    Class Numbers:

      Library of Congress E78

      OCLC 18337942

• Intended to promote sales and tourism, the directory profiles 21 individual artists and 11 Indian-owned and operated private, cooperative, and tribal enterprises producing sculptures, quilts, baskets, beadwork, and other arts and crafts. Although the directory information is outdated, the work remains useful for identifying artists and outlets and for the artists' statements about their work. Many of the artists do not appear in a more contemporary Internet resource, *North Dakota Visual Artist Archive* (http://www.state.nd.us/arts/artist_archive/archive_home. htm, **BD12**). Entries are organized by reservation, as are a mailing list and an artist index. Includes a brief list of North Dakota arts and crafts organizations. — JD

CLOTHING

CD93 Paterek, Josephine. - **Encyclopedia of American Indian Costume**. - Denver, CO: ABC-CLIO, 1994. - 516 p.; ill.

    Class Numbers:

      Library of Congress E98.C8

      ISBN 0874366852

      OCLC 29254783

      LCCN 93-39337

    Notes:

      Includes bibliographical references (p. 473-485); index

• Of Paterek's ten chapters, only the third ("Plains") is relevant to Prairies-Plains research. The chapter's map covers the area east of the Rockies, extending from Texas to northern Alberta. "Plains" categorizes peoples of the region into 51 groups, of which 17 are covered in some detail. Each section provides information on men's basic dress, women's basic dress, footwear, headgear, outerwear, accessories, jewelry, armor, hair styles, garment decoration, and face and body embellishment. The book is illustrated (essential in such a volume) with black-and-white drawings and period photos. Color illustrations are absent, despite their availability. Appendixes include a glossary and "Clothing Arts of the American Indians," which discusses such topics as dyeing, tanning, and the use of quills and feathers. The book ends with an extensive bibliography arranged by region and an excellent index. — *MB*

CRAFTS

See also **North Dakota Native American Arts and Crafts: A Source Directory, CD92**

CD94 Porter, Frank W., 1947-   , comp. - **Native**

American Basketry: An Annotated Bibliography. - New York: Greenwood Pr., 1988. - 249 p. - (Art reference collection, 10; ISSN 0193-6867).

Class Numbers:
  Library of Congress E59.B3   Z1209.2.N67
  ISBN 0313253633
  OCLC 17413718
  LCCN 87-37570
  Notes:
    Indexes

• Information about Plains Indian baskets is as rare as the baskets themselves. During the 1800s to early 1900s, when traditional basket making was at its height for other tribes, Plains Indians made containers from leather, which was more readily available and more integral to their culture. A few baskets found at archaeological sites have uncertain origins; those found elsewhere may be recent. The bibliography's 23 entries on Plains basketry are a meager fraction of the 1,100 total entries, but they constitute a fairly comprehensive list that would be difficult to enlarge. Entries include books, articles, dissertations, master's theses, and government documents. The introduction provides a cogent explanation of the cultural meaning and decline of basket making. Subject and author indexes. — JD

DANCE

CD95 Laubin, Reginald. - **Indian Dances of North America** / [by] Reginald and Gladys Laubin; with paintings, drawings and photos by the authors; foreword by Louis R. Bruce. - Norman, OK: Univ. of Oklahoma Pr., 1977. - xxxviii, 538 p.; [16] leaves of plates, ill. - (The civilization of the American Indian series, [v. 141]).

Class Numbers:
  Library of Congress E98.D2
  ISBN 0585194521 (electronic bk.)
  LCCN 77-2099
  Notes:
    Electronic book: http://www.netLibrary.com/urlapi.asp?
      action=summary&v=1&bookid=15484
    Includes bibliographical references; index

• Although not arranged in reference format, this seminal resource for Native American dance focuses on traditional dancing across the U.S., but concentrates on the northern Plains and, to a lesser extent, the eastern woodlands. Heavily illustrated, it is based on the Laubins' personal experience with Native dancers and celebrations as well as thorough research in the anthropological literature. Written before the growth in contemporary powwow dancing, the work does not reflect this common contemporary intertribal dance form, although most of the dances it describes are still performed in nonpublic forums. Others may appear as

demonstration dances or local competitions at regional powwows. The index is extensive, offering some access to regional information, but generally, readers must identify from other sources what dances or type of dance they will find of interest. Index entries particularly relevant to Plains peoples include "Sun Dance," "Buffalo Dance," "Grass Dance," "Round Dance," "Victory Dance," "Oklahoma State," "Pine Ridge Reservation," "Plains Region," "Standing Rock Reservation," and "Warrior Societies." There is also an index entry for "Indian tribes," with individual listings for Arapaho, Arikara, Assiniboine, Blackfoot, Cheyenne, Crow, Hidatsa, Kiowa, Sioux, etc. An important work all libraries should have. — LM

EUROPEAN CONTACT

CD96 Early Encounters in North America [Internet Site]. - Alexandria, VA: Alexander Street Pr., 2001– . - http://www.alexanderstreet.com/

Access Date: Jan. 2006
Notes:
  Available through outright purchase or subscription
  Fees: Subscription

• A full-text database covering interactions between Indians and Europeans. Sources selected cover the years 1534-1860, include descriptions of North America (either natural features or interactions among cultural groups), and reproduce the entire text except for indexes; the editors exclude materials exclusively about Latin America, the Northwest Passage, or the Arctic (but include them if they are part of a larger work). Materials about interactions between Plains Indians and Europeans are plentiful. Numerous illustrations accompany the text, but browsing is less convenient than in other Alexander Street sites. The editorial board consists of Raymond A. Bucko (Creighton Univ.), Michael Edmonds (Wisconsin Historical Society) and Daniel R. Mandell (Truman State Univ.). The Alexander Street search engine is described at **CD46**. — JB

FOLKLORE

CD97 Native American Folklore, 1879-1979: An Annotated Bibliography / comp. by William M. Clements and Frances M. Malpezzi. - Athens, OH: Ohio Univ. Pr., 1984. - xxiii, 247 p.

Class Numbers:
  Library of Congress E98.F6 Z1209
  ISBN 0804008310
  OCLC 13330041
  LCCN 83-6672

• Intended to guide readers through the staggering amount of collected Native American "folklore" (i.e., oral literature) and the scattered books and journal articles written about Native folklore during the century specified, this work covers "books and articles which treat oral narratives, songs, chants, prayers, formulas, orations, proverbs, riddles, word play, music, dances, games, and ceremonials" (p. xiii). The compilers group nearly 5,500 entries by tribe within region following a section, "General Works" (about 800 titles) that includes articles and papers on collections, theory, and commentary. An index by subject and another by author, editor, and translator conclude the work. Entries have brief, one- to four-line descriptive annotations. The regional arrangement makes finding works on Plains peoples simple. There are 697 entries for Plains spread across 20 tribes and a general category. The Midwest group contains another 391 titles, which include some Prairie peoples (Ojibwa, Osage, Potawatomi, Quapaw, Winnebago). — *LM*

GHOST DANCE

CD98 Osterreich, Shelley Anne, comp. - **The American Indian Ghost Dance, 1870 and 1890: An Annotated Bibliography**. - New York: Greenwood Pr., 1991. - 96 p. - (Bibliographies and indexes in American history, 19).

> Class Numbers:
> Library of Congress E98.D2
> LCCN 91-7957

• A selective annotated index of just 110 items, which allows substantial description of each entry. Items are arranged in seven general categories (e.g., history, religion, biography, anthropology, music), then alphabetically by author. Indexes of authors, journals, and subjects round out the volume. Entries include a number of books, but most cite journal articles. Entries survey more than a century of scholarship on the topic, and are typically 200-300 words in length. Indexes of authors, journal titles, and subjects. The brevity of the subject index makes it less useful than one might hope. — *MB*

HEALTH AND MEDICINE

See also Moerman, **Native American Ethnobotany, EC127**

CD99 Gray, Sharon A. - **Health of Native People of North America: A Bibliography and Guide to Resources**. - Lanham, MD: Scarecrow Pr., 1996. - 393 p. - (Native American bibliography series, 20).

> Class Numbers:
> Library of Congress RA448.5.I5   Z6661
> ISBN 0810831708
> OCLC 34321261

LCCN 96-11844

• Gray covers works published between 1970 and about 1995 concerning Native peoples' contemporary health issues in the U.S. and Canada. Some Canadian publications in French are included. The focus is contemporary, although Gray includes works on traditional medicine and ethnobotany, but excludes works of archaeology, fiction, and reprints, as well as most government publications. Gray explains the latter omission was caused by the "sheer volume" of work on this topic produced by the U.S. and Canadian governments, but sagely warns that most works on "minority health" fail to encompass Native American and First Nations peoples. SUNY Buffalo professor Edward Starr provides a 30-page introductory overview of "Health Care Systems in Indian Country" to set the book's framework. The annotated entries are spread over nine additional chapters organized by format, e.g., "Bibliographies"; "Electronic Resources, Indexes, and Abstracting Publications"; "Books and Book Chapters"; "Dissertations/Theses." In the subject index, devoted mainly to topics, tribal entries are rare. Although it is comprehensive and thorough, identifying titles by region or tribe in this work is nearly impossible. — *LM*

CD100 Lyon, William S. - **Encyclopedia of Native American Healing**. - Santa Barbara, CA: ABC-CLIO, 1996. - xxxv, 373 p.; ill., maps.

> Class Numbers:
> Library of Congress E98.M4
> National Library of Canada E98
> ISBN 0874368529   058503088X (electronic bk.)
> OCLC 34984233
> LCCN 96-26860
> Notes:
> Electronic book: http://www.netLibrary.com/urlapi.
>   asp?action=summary&v=1&bookid=1284
> Includes bibliographical references (p. 335-351); index

• Not a New Age survey of trendy healing ceremonies, this serious work by anthropologist Lyon seeks to be "the first scholarly work to survey the mystery powers of Native American shamans with respect to healing" (p. xiv). Entries, alphabetically arranged, range in length from a single sentence to several pages. Each entry contains a tribal and regional affiliation, making browsing for Plains-relevant entries fairly easy, and refers as well to the extensive 16-page bibliography. *See* and *see also* references are abundant, an essential feature, since Lyon uses Native language terms as the entry points to many of his cross-references to maintain the cultural integrity of the information. He provides coverage of individuals, Native shamanic terminology, ceremonies and rituals, accessories, and paraphernalia. An extensive index allows searching by tribe and anthropological region (but not state), making identification of entries relevant to Plains studies easy. Other index entries include individual names and "key concepts germane to Native American healing" (p. xvii). For example, the index entry "Plains" points to 95 separate page numbers or page ranges, 32 for "Lakota," four for "Pawnee," three for "Comanche," and 17 for "Cheyenne." Obviously, tribal coverage intensity will vary widely for various tribes, reflecting the degree to which these peoples have been willing to share religious information with the anthropologists, missionaries, etc., seeking it. An excellent, essential work for Plains studies. — *LM*

HISTORY

CD101   Prucha, Francis Paul. - **A Bibliographical Guide to the History of Indian-White Relations in the United States.** – Chicago, IL: Univ. of Chicago Pr., 1977. - 454 p.

> Class Numbers:
> Library of Congress Z1209.2.U5
> ISBN 0226684768   0226684776 (pbk.)
> OCLC 2213250
> LCCN 76-16045
> Notes:
> A publication of the Center for the History of the
> American Indian of the Newberry Library
> Index

• Prucha divides this extensive bibliography into two parts: a brief "Guides to Sources," which gives an overview of general research sources for Indian history, and a much larger "Classified Bibliography of Published Works." The classified bibliography has 13 chapters covering various elements of Indian-white relations, including Indian policy, treaties and councils, military relations, Indian education, and Indian health. Chapter 16, "Indians and Indian Groups," is divided into regions and then features a few representative tribes. "Indians of the Plains" within this section contains 279 entries. Prucha warns that none of the entries is repeated, and advises use of the extensive index to locate entries of interest. — *LM*

LAW

CD102   Cohen, Felix S., 1907-1953. - **Cohen's Handbook of Federal Indian Law.** - 2005 ed. - Newark, NJ: LexisNexis, 2005. - xxxviii, 647 p.

> Class Numbers:
> Library of Congress KF8205
> ISBN 0327164441
> OCLC 61228600

• Federal Indian law mediates among tribal, state, and U.S.

law. Cohen's legal classic, first published in 1941, brings together treaties, statutes, court cases and regulations and provides a masterful analysis of tribal culture and the rights of Native Americans. It virtually created the field of Indian law. The goal of the first new edition in 23 years (this time under the guidance of law school dean Nell Jessup Newton, Univ. of Connecticut) is the same as that of the original: to protect and promote Indian nations, legal traditions, and land. Rich, substantive introductory chapters cover federal policy, legal interpretations, Indian tribes, Indians and Indian Country, tribal governments, tribal/federal relationships, tribal/state relationships, and jurisdiction. Topical chapters treat taxation, criminal jurisdiction, environmental regulation, child welfare, gaming, liquor, civil rights, property, natural resources, hunting, fishing and gathering rights, water rights, cultural resources, economic development, and government services. The text heavily references and indexes the U.S. Constitution, *U.S. Code*, and *Code of Federal Regulations*; state constitutions, statutes, and regulations; tribal codes; and other legal sources. Although nearly everything in Cohen has relevance for Prairies-Plains concerns, the table of cases can be browsed to find case names involving specific tribes, and the table of statutes can be accessed by state. A necessity for scholarly and legal collections, Cohen presents complex material clearly. The previous editions, the original 1941 edition, the revisionist 1958 edition that stressed federal power, and the 1988 ed. are still of interest to legal scholars. — *JD, LM*

CD103   The Encyclopedia of Native American Legal Tradition / ed. by Bruce Elliott Johansen; foreword by Charles Riley Cloud. - Westport, CT: Greenwood Pr., 1998. - 410 p.

> Class Numbers;
> Library of Congress KF8204
> ISBN 0313301670
> LCCN 97-21994

• Because this volume concerns itself with all Indian law, only occasional entries relate to Indians of the Prairies and Plains. Many entries (they are arranged alphabetically) conclude with a short list of recommended readings. Entries not written by the editor are signed. Court cases (e.g., Cherokee Nation v. Hitchcock) are interfiled with subjects such as "Cheyenne Political and Legal Traditions" (where a variety of treaties can be found). There are few illustrations. Substantial bibliography; subject index; roster of 13 contributors. — *MB*

CD104   Grossman, Mark. - **The ABC-CLIO Companion to the Native American Rights Movement.** - Santa Barbara, CA: ABC-CLIO, 1996. - 498 p.; ill. - (ABC-CLIO companions to key issues in American history and life).

Class Numbers:
    Library of Congress KF8203.36
ISBN 0874368227
LCCN 96-36782
Notes:
    Includes bibliographical references (p. 455-483); index

• Features alphabetically arranged brief-entry articles across a wide spectrum of time and space, covering legal cases, Indian activist organizations, government legislation, and Native and non-Native individuals that had an impact on Indian civil rights. Selection criteria are unclear. Extensive coverage of legal cases. Usefulness for Prairies-Plains study is limited. — *LM*

CD105   Indian Affairs: Laws and Treaties [Internet Site]. - Stillwater, OK: Oklahoma State Univ. Library Electronic   Publishing   Center,   1999-2003.   - http://digital.library.okstate.edu/kappler/

    Class Numbers:
        Library of Congress KF8203
    OCLC 44288939
    Access Date: Mar. 2006
    Notes:
        Produced with support from Coca-Cola Foundation and
            AMIGOS Bibliographic Council
    Fees: None

• The digitized version of Charles J. Kappler's classic seven-volume compilation of U.S. treaties, laws, and executive orders relating to Indians (*Indian Affairs: Laws and Treaties* offers pages both as digitized text and JPEG image files. The original tables of contents and indexes to each volume link to text pages, and the entire text can be searched by keyword. No subject terms have been added to account for preferred names, alternate spellings, or changes in terminology. This site completes the set of federally recognized agreements with Indians by linking to the seven early British and two U.S. treaties not found in Kappler, separately digitized by the Univ. of Nebraska-Lincoln University   Libraries,   (http://libr.unl.edu:8888/etext. treaties/). The Oklahoma State site is elegantly designed, with links to page images and easy access to Kappler's extensive margin notes. Important for jurists, lawyers, researchers, teachers, and students. — *JD*

LITERATURE

Guides

CD106   Lundquist, Suzanne Evertsen. - **Native American Literatures: An Introduction**. - New York: Continuum, 2004. - 315 p. - (Continuum studies in genre).

Class Numbers:
    Library of Congress PS163.I52
ISBN 0826415989   0826415997 (pbk.)
LCCN 2004-14784
Notes:
    Includes bibliographical references; index
    Table of contents: http://www.loc.gov/catdir/toc/
        ecip0419/2004014784.html

• Lundquist presents an overview of and introduction to Native American literatures and issues unique to this field. More a monograph or handbook than a reference work, the book includes chapters on "How to Read Native American Literatures," "Themes in Native American Literatures," "The Best and Best Known," "Key Questions," and "Who Are the Major Critics in the Field, and What are Their Arguments?" Tangentially reference in nature is chapter eight, "Selected Further Readings, Reference Works and Research Tools," consisting of 20 titles, and a glossary. There is no way to identify Plains and Prairies titles. Of use to doctoral students preparing for comprehensive exams, but not recommended for regional study. – LM

CD107   Ruoff, A. LaVonne Brown. - **American Indian Literatures: An Introduction, Bibliographic Review, and Selected Bibliography.** - New York: Modern Language Association of America, 1990. - 200 p.

Class Numbers:
    Library of Congress PM155
ISBN 0873521919   0873521927
LCCN 90-13438
Notes:
    Includes bibliographical references (p. [146]-189); index

• Ruoff's relatively slim volume includes an introduction to American Indian literatures, a bibliographic essay, and a selected bibliography. She concentrates on Indians in what is now the U.S., but includes groups that overlap with Canada or Mexico (e.g., Yaqui, Ojibwa, Iroquois). The book considers both oral and written literatures; discussion of the oral tradition occupies nearly a quarter of the volume, followed by an extensive review of the written literature. The bibliographic essay covers research guides, anthologies, scholarship, criticism (both general and author-specific), and related topics, e.g., ethnohistory. The selected bibliography is organized along the same lines as the review, adding references to periodicals and nonprint media. The book includes a three-page chronology of important dates in American Indian history (1500-1989) and a brief index of proper names. — *MB*

Bibliographies

CD108   Beam, Joan, 1947- . - **The Native American in**

Long Fiction: An Annotated Bibliography / by Joan Beam and Barbara Branstad. - Lanham, MD: Scarecrow Pr., 1996. - 359 p. - (Native American bibliography series, 18).

Class Numbers:
        Library of Congress PS374.I49   Z1231
    ISBN 0810830167
    OCLC 32086802
    LCCN 95-5635
    Notes:
        Includes bibliographical references; indexes

• Librarians Beam and Branstad attempt to "identify and annotate all long fictional works by and about Native Americans written during the past 100 years" (p. v) from a Native perspective. Short stories, folktales, poems, myths, and personal narratives are excluded, as well as works about prehistoric times. The geographic focus is the contiguous U.S., omitting novels portraying Native peoples of Canada and Mexico, and even Alaska and Hawai'i. The authors include all genres of adult fiction, as well as a "representative sample" of young adult fiction (but no children's books or juvenile literature). The bibliography cites about 400 novels, all critically annotated with a brief synopsis and commentary on literary style or historical accuracy. Entries, alphabetical by author, follow the bibliographic citation with comment on the work's time period and tribe and place portrayed, then with a list of citations to additional reviews. Six very useful indexes follow the bibliography: titles, dates, tribes, historical persons, historical events, and literary genre. Plains tribes are well-represented in the tribal index, especially the Sioux, always a favorite of novelists. A list of "Novels Not Included" gives reasons for omission (e.g., they fell outside the bibliography's geographic scope, were written for juveniles or from a non-Native viewpoint, or were "poorly written" [p. 345]). The work concludes with a bibliography of sources used to identify Native authors and works about them. Very thorough and thoughtfully compiled. — *LM*

CD108a   Beam, Joan, 1947-   . - **The Native American in Long Fiction: An Annotated Bibliography: Supplement, 1995-2002** / Joan Beam and Barbara Branstad. - Lanham, MD: Scarecrow Pr., 2003. - xx, 304 p. - (Native American bibliography series, 27).

Class Numbers:
        Library of Congress PS374.I49 Z1231
    ISBN 0810848414
    OCLC 52085914
    LCCN 2003008245
    Notes:
        Includes bibliographical references; indexes

• Beam and Branstad extend their 1996 title with this supplement, nearly as large as the original (364 titles), but covering only a tenth of the time frame, reflecting the huge output of fiction about and by American Indians over the intervening period, and including the emergence of not a few new Native novelists. The format for this supplement follows that of the original work, with the same caveats and exclusions, and features the same six thorough topical indexes and the list of "Novels Not Included." New appendixes include a "Best Books" list of the authors' favorites, and an update to the resources list of the original volume. Very highly recommended. — *LM*

CD109   Littlefield, Daniel F. - **A Bibliography of Native American Writers, 1772-1924** / by Daniel F. Littlefield Jr. and James W. Parins. - Metuchen, NJ: Scarecrow Pr., 1981. - 343 p. - (Native American bibliography series, 2).

Class Numbers:
        Library of Congress E77   Z1209.2.U5
    ISBN 0810814633
    LCCN 81-9138
    Notes:
        Indexes

• Littlefield and Parins cover writing by Native Americans from Colonial times to 1924, the year Indians were granted citizenship. The 4,000 entries, none of which are annotated, are arranged alphabetically by author and identify tribal affiliation. Entries are consecutively numbered using a code that incorporates genre (e.g., 3907F indicates a work of fiction). Part 2, a briefer list, is a bibliography of writers known only by pen names, and Part 3 contains biographies of the writers, some quite brief. Indexes of subjects and writers by tribal affiliation. — *MB*

CD109a   Littlefield, Daniel F. - **A Biobibliography of Native American Writers, 1772-1924: A Supplement** / by Daniel F. Littlefield Jr. and James W. Parins. - Metuchen, NJ: Scarecrow Pr., 1985. - 339 p. - (Native American bibliography series, 5).

Class Numbers:
        Library of Congress E77   Z1205.2.U5
    ISBN 0810818027
    LCCN 85-2045
    Notes:
        Index

• Follows the format and content of the earlier work, adding additional authors and titles. The two volumes together have entries for nearly 1,200 Native writers (250 in the 1981 volume, an additional 942 in the Supplement), making it the most comprehensive bibliography of its kind at the time of publication. The Supplement cross-references the first volume. New to the Supplement are annotations and a list of periodicals cited. "Index of Writers by Tribal Affiliation" provides easy access to writers from Plains and Prairies tribes, as does the 1981 volume. A quick count by tribe lists about 500 authors from regional tribes. An essential reference work. — *LM*

Indexes

CD110   The Native American in Short Fiction in the *Saturday Evening Post*: **An Annotated Bibliography** / Peter G. Beidler, Harry J. Brown, Marion F. Egge. - Lanham, MD: Scarecrow Pr., 2001. - xiii, 315 p. - (Native American bibliography series, 25).

> Class Numbers:
> Library of Congress Z1231
> ISBN 0810838796
> LCCN 00-046360

• The authors "focus on the Indian in the short fiction from [the *Saturday Evening Post*], giving detailed summaries of the plots, including dialogue from the characters, to show how American Indians were presented by story writers" (p. xi). The 265 stories considered expand on the titles in chapter 7 of Beidler and Egge's *The Native American in the* Saturday Evening Post (2000), which is much wider in scope but lacks the detailed summaries of fictional works Beidler et al. feature. The short fiction the authors describe was published in the magazine between 1897 and 1968. In some stories, Indians were peripheral characters making brief appearances; in others, they are the main characters. Indexes by author, subject, and tribe, the latter highly useful for identifying Plains tribes. A sample of the tribal index reveals 17 stories with Arapaho characters, two with Assinibione, one with Arikaree, 49 with Blackfeet, etc., showing high representation of works relevant for this region. A unique resource for Prairies-Plains studies. — *LM*

Encyclopedias

CD111   The Cambridge Companion to Native American Literature / ed. by Joy Porter and Kenneth M. Roemer. - New York: Cambridge Univ. Pr., 2005. - 365 p. - (Cambridge companions to literature).

> Class Numbers:
> Library of Congress PS153.I52
> ISBN 0521822831   0521529794 (pbk.)
> OCLC 60321214
> LCCN 2005-44298
> Notes:
> Includes bibliographical references; index

• Besides essays on Indian themes and writers, the work has several illustrations and a half dozen maps, the latter reproduced from Jack Utter's *American Indians: Answers to Today's Questions*. There are extensive notes on each of the 18 contributors, a solid index, and a selective reading list of just under two dozen items. The book has a sturdy library binding, as might be expected of a Cambridge Companion. A very useful volume. — *MB*

CD112   Dictionary of Native American Literature / Andrew Wiget, ed. - New York: Garland, 1994. - 598 p. - (Garland reference library of the humanities, v. 1815).

> Class Numbers:
> Library of Congress PM155
> ISBN 0815315600
> LCCN 94-3811
> Notes:
> Contents:
> Electronic book: http://www.netLibrary.com/urlapi.asp?
>   action=summary&v=1&bookid=38853
> Includes bibliographical references; index
> Reprinted: Handbook of Native American Literature.
>   New York; London: Garland, 1996

• A compilation of essays by more than 50 contributors. Three main sections cover oral literature, written works before 1967, and works since that date. Essays in the first section (oral literature) are organized geographically, while the second and third sections are subdivided both thematically and by specific authors. The date for the break between sections was determined by the publication of N. Scott Momaday's *House Made of Dawn*, the first Native American book to earn the Pulitzer Prize. Essays are signed, give the writer's institutional affiliation, and conclude with substantial lists of primary and secondary sources. Extremely detailed index. An excellent overview of Native American literature up to 1994. A second edition would be welcome.— *MB*

Collective Biographies

CD113   Hirschfelder, Arlene B., comp. - **American Indian and Eskimo Authors: A Comprehensive Bibliography**. - New York: Association on American Indian Affairs; [distr. by Interbook, Inc.], [1973]. - 99 p.

> Class Numbers:
> Library of Congress Z1209
> LCCN 73-82109

• An early work by prolific and respected author Hirschfelder, this list of Native and Eskimo authors was among the first attempts to identify the creators of Native literary works. "It contains almost 400 titles written or narrated by nearly 300 Indian or Eskimo authors representing more than 100 tribes" [p. iii]. The author list supplies tribal affiliation and works written or narrated. A tribal index at the beginning lists writers by tribe. For Plains purposes, there are two listings for Arapaho, three for Assiniboine and for Blackfeet, seven for Cheyenne, 20 for Chippewa, five for Cree, six for Crow, one for Fox, three for Gros Ventre, one for Hidatsa, three for Kiowa, one for Kiowa-Apache, three for Menominee, two for Omaha, three for Osage, five for Paiute, one for Pawnee and for Ponca, two for Sauk and Fox, one for Shoshone, 25 for Sioux, three for

Winnebago. A basic, useful work. — *LM*

CD114   Native American Writers of the United States / ed. by Kenneth M. Roemer. - Detroit, MI: Gale Research, 1997. - xxi, 414 p.; ill. - (Dictionary of literary biography, v. 175).

> Class Numbers:
> Library of Congress PS153.I52
> ISBN 0810399385
> OCLC 36084574
> LCCN 96-52414
> Notes:
> Includes bibliographical references (p. 337-341); index

• Authors selected must live or have lived in the U.S. and have written primarily in English. Notable exceptions are Canadian First Nations authors George C. Copway (Ojibwa) and E. Pauline Johnson (Mohawk), whom Roemer included not only because of their impact in the U.S., but, admirably, in recognition of the irrelevance of political boundaries that artificially bisect Native peoples. An essential, though highly selective, reference for any library, 11 of the 43 authors featured here are from Plains tribes: Dakota/Lakota authors Ella and Vine Deloria, Charles A. Eastman, Elizabeth Cook-Lynn, and Zitkala-Sa; Kiowas N. Scott Momaday and Hanay Geiogamah; Lance Henson (Cheyenne); Francis La Flesche (Omaha); John Joseph Mathews (Osage); and Ray A. Young Bear (Meskwaki). Entries, which range between three and 16 pages, feature selected bibliographies of the author's works and conclude with references to books, articles, and interviews about the writer and his or her work. No index other than a cumulative name index for the entire series, and no way to easily identify tribal affiliation. — *LM*

CD115   Native North American Literature: Biographical and Critical Information on Native Writers and Orators from the United States and Canada from Historical Times to the Present / Janet Witalec, editor; Jeffery Chapman, Christopher Giroux, associate eds. - New York: Gale, 1994. - 706 p.; ill., maps.

> Class Numbers:
> Library of Congress PS508.I5
> ISBN 0810398982
> LCCN 94-32397
> Notes:
> Includes bibliographical references; indexes

• Of this volume's two parts, the first deals with oral literature and includes chapters about Black Elk, Sitting Bull, and Lame Deer (Sioux), along with Indians from regions other than the Plains. The second, written literature, is more extensive and includes chapters on Plains writers Paula Gunn Allen, Jim Barnes, Gertrude Bonnin, Mary Brave Bird, Elizabeth Cook-Lynn, Ella Deloria, Charles

Eastman, Louise Erdrich, Francis La Flesche, Luther Standing Bear, Hyemeyohsts Storm, and Will Rogers, among others. Several Métis writers are included. Each entry includes an introduction, list of major works, samples of criticism, and sources for further study. Some have a photo. Indexes by tribe, genre, and title. Maps of tribal distribution and reservations. — *MB*

Music

CD116   Keeling, Richard. - North American Indian Music: A Guide to Published Sources and Selected Recordings. - New York: Garland, 1997. - xlix, 420 p. - (Garland library of music ethnology, v. 5; Garland reference library of the humanities, v. 1440).

> Class Numbers:
> Library of Congress ML128.F75
> ISBN 081502320
> LCCN 96-41847

• Ethnomusicologist Keeling cites and annotates 1,497 sources for North American Indian and Alaska Native music published or produced between 1535 and 1995, and includes Mexico. He cites works on dance, ritual, and "other aspects of religion or culture related to music" (p. vii) , as well as "select 'classic' recordings." A 40-page introduction outlines the historical study of Native American music in the academic world. Ten culture area chapters ("regional bibliographies") provide titles and substantial annotations organized by author. The Plains chapter contains 174 entries, but Keeling warns that readers should also consult the bibliographies for adjacent regions, as well as the "General or Inter-Regional" chapter. Indexes of authors, tribes and languages, and subjects. — *LM*

CD117   Wright-McLeod, Brian, 1958-   . - The Encyclopedia of Native Music: More than a Century of Recordings from Wax Cylinder to the Internet / ill. with photographs and album covers. - Tucson, AZ: Univ. of Arizona Pr., 2005. - 464 p.; ill.

> Class Numbers:
> Library of Congress ML156.4.I5
> ISBN 0816524475   0816524483 (pbk.)
> OCLC 56880467
> LCCN 2004-23862
> Notes:
> Includes bibliographical references; index
> Includes discographies
> Review by A. Patrice: *Choice* 43.2 (Oct. 2005):
>   review 43-0663
> Table of contents: http://www.loc.gov/catdir/toc/
>   ecip052/2004023862.html

• Wright-McLeod (Dakota-Anishinabe music journalist and radio personality) provides a seminal work on Native

American music, a body of work neglected in studies of American music. His encyclopedia concentrates on indigenous musical artists across various genres of Native American traditional and contemporary music. Excluded are Latin America and Mexico, Hawai'i, and the Pacific Rim, each of which have massive and complex musical traditions of their own. Entries are organized in seven sections: "Arctic/Circumpolar," "Chicken Scratch," "Contemporary Music" (with many subsections), "Flute Music," "Peyote Ritual Music," "Powwow Music," and "Traditional/Archival Music." The work also has a bibliography and a minimally useful index by artist. In "Contemporary Music," each entry includes the performer's tribal identity, musical style (rock, folk, rap, blues, etc.), brief description, and discography. Other sections simply list an artist's or group's name, the members of the group, and a discography. Unfortunately, regional artists cannot be easily identified except by browsing the entries, looking for specific tribal affiliations. Of the seven sections, all but "Arctic/ Circumpolar" and "Chicken Scratch" (a genre found in the Southwest U.S.) will be relevant to Prairies-Plains research. An excellent work that belongs in all libraries, although ease of use for this region could have been better. — *LM*

Mythology

CD118 Bastian, Dawn E. - **Handbook of Native American Mythology** / by Dawn E. Bastian and Judy K. Mitchell. - Santa Barbara, CA: ABC-CLIO, 2004. - 297 p.; ill. - (Handbooks of world mythology).

> Class Numbers:
> Library of Congress E98.R3
> ISBN 1851095330
> LCCN 2004-9634
> Notes:
> Includes bibliographical references (p. 257-270); index
> Table of contents: http://www.loc.gov/catdir/toc/ ecip0417/2004009634.html

• Written for general readers, Bastian's introductory work provides a sampling of the mythologies "of cultures found in native North America, including the region from north of Mexico to the Arctic Circle" (p. x). An introduction presents an overview of the culture areas of Native America and mentions the sources for and importance of Native American mythology. A brief chapter, "Time in Native Cultures," precedes the greater part of the work, a sampling of 90 seemingly randomly chosen topics on "Deities, Themes, and Concepts." An entry may be general, running several pages, and discussing the term in various Native cultures (e.g., "Corn," "Owl," "Gamblers and Gambling," "Seasons, Origin of") or very specific, pertaining to one tribe (e.g., "Skeleton House" [Hopi], "How Bluebird Got

Its Color" [Pima], or "Blood Clot" [Ute]). A useful "Annotated Print and Nonprint Resources" list follows the entries, but even these have little direct relevance to Native mythology. There are also a "Reference List" and glossary, but the latter, includes arbitrarily chosen terms, some relevant others puzzling ("narwhal," "Klamath River," "Medicine Bundle," "Saguaro Cactus," and "Sun Dance."). The index is as quirky as the rest of the work. Although one can look up "Plains," the information it leads to is ephemeral. — *LM*

CD119 Dixon-Kennedy, Mike, 1958- . - **Native American Myth & Legend: An A-Z of People and Places**. - London: Blandford, 1996. - 288 p.; maps.

> Class Numbers:
> Library of Congress E98.F6
> ISBN 0713726237
> Notes:
> Includes bibliographical references (p. 287-288)

• Dixon-Kennedy's encyclopedia, heavily focused on Central and South America, reflects a basic lack of understanding about Native peoples and their beliefs, a common flaw in works about Indians by British writers. Uninformed comments in the introduction such as "many of the native American peoples have over the centuries either been totally or very nearly wiped out" (p. 4); missing entries basic to Native mythologies (White Buffalo Calf Woman, Changing Woman, and even Wakan Tanka are all absent); inclusion of non-Indians (Christopher Columbus) and African references (Haitian deities and voodoo abound); a very brief and outdated bibliography (at least half the titles predate 1970); and the lack of any index make this work of little use to most libraries, including collections focusing on the Plains. — *LM*

Politics

CD120 Pritzker, Barry. - **Native America Today: A Guide to Community Politics and Culture**. - Santa Barbara, CA: ABC-CLIO, 1999. - xx, 453 p.; ill., map.

> Class Numbers:
> Library of Congress E98.T77
> ISBN 1576070778
> OCLC 42771369
> LCCN 99-52306
> Notes:
> Includes bibliographical references (p. 397-399); index

• Broad and somewhat random, this overview of contemporary Indian issues touches only tangentially on the Plains. Thirteen "contemporary issues" articles (e.g., "Gaming,"

"Identity," "Media," "Arts and Crafts") each present brief case studies of three different tribes. Inclusion of Prairies-Plains peoples is by chance. "Contemporary Profiles" offers overviews of 32 individual nations, most outside the Prairies-Plains region. Relevant tribes covered are Cree, Dakota, Menominee, Metis, and Osage. — *LM*

Publications

CD121   Littlefield, Daniel F. - **American Indian and Alaska Native Newspapers and Periodicals** / [by] Daniel F. Littlefield Jr. and James W. Parins. - Westport, CT: Greenwood Pr., 1984-1986. - 3 v. - (Historical guides to the world's periodicals and newspapers).

> Class Numbers:
> Library of Congress PN4883
> ISBN 0313234264 (v. 1)   0313234272 (v. 2)
>   0313234265 (set)
> LCCN 83-1483
> Notes:
>   Contents:
>   v. [1], 1826-1924;
>   v. 2, 1925-1970;
>   v. 3, 1971-1985
>   Includes bibliographies; index

• A unique and essential reference title that lists all newspapers and periodicals the editors could identify that were "edited or published by American Indians or Alaska Natives and whose primary purpose was to publish information about contemporary Indians or Alaska Natives" in the U.S. The editors exclude "ethnohistorical, archaeological, or historical subjects and those published in Canada or Mexico." Entries, arranged alphabetically by title, feature a narrative history and background for the publication that varies from a single paragraph to several pages, followed by "Information Sources" (bibliography, index sources, and location sources, where known). Full publication history concludes each entry, as well as holdings information–critical for locating these often rare titles. Finding aids include appendixes by tribe and location (state), making identification of titles for the region easy. Each volume has a full index. Titles were identified from collections all over the U.S. Usefulness for Plains studies is undeniable. An outstanding work. — *LM*

Religion

See **BA, Religion**

Treaties

See also **Indian Affairs: Laws and Treaties, CD105**

CD122   **Documents of American Indian Diplomacy: Treaties, Agreements, and Conventions, 1775-1979** / [comp. by] Vine Deloria Jr. and Raymond J. DeMallie; with a foreword by Daniel K. Inouye. - Norman, OK: Univ. of Oklahoma Pr., c1999. - 2 v.; (1540 p.). - (Legal history of North America, v. 4).

> LCCN 98045365
> Notes:
>   Includes bibliographical references (p. [1496]-1500); index

• The only compilation that includes not just the 375 treaties in Kappler (**CD105, CD123**) that are generally defined as valid and recognized, but others that "comprehensively cover the diplomatic engagements of Indian tribes." Though many are in the U.S. Serial Set they are difficult to identify. They include treaties with foreign nations; railroad agreements; settlement acts; treaties with the Republic of Texas, the Confederate States and the Russian American Company; treaties between Indian nations and intertribal compacts; Pre-Revolutionary, Revolutionary War, and Articles of Confederation treaties; unratified treaties and treaties rejected by the Indian nations or the Senate; and foreign treaties affecting Indian nations. Organized by type of agreement or treaty, entries include texts of treaties with names of signatories, texts of accompanying documentation, and sources. Texts are transcriptions, not facsimiles. A bibliography in volume 2 includes government publications of the U.S. and other countries, unpublished papers, compilations of legal documents, and published works. A cumulative index in volume 2 is by names of tribes, bands, government entities, and other parties to agreements. A supplement to Kappler, the work informs discussions on the legal status of specific agreements and depicts the historical context of current Indian law. A standard for students, historians, and legal experts. — *JD*

CD123   **Indian Treaties, 1778-1883** / comp. and ed. by Charles J. Kappler; with a new foreword by Brantley Blue. - New York: Interland Publ., 1972. - 1099p.; ill.

> Class Numbers:
> Library of Congress KF8203
> ISBN 0879890258
> OCLC 391564
> LCCN 72-75770
> Notes:
>   Reprint of: *Indian Affairs: Laws and Treaties*, v. 2.
>   Washington, DC: U.S. Govt. Print. Off., 1904.

• The reprint from Kappler's two-volume original, itself an essential reference work for the Prairies-Plains region, contains the "Treaties" volume. Libraries that own the original do not need this reprint, but all libraries supporting interest in the Prairies and Plains should have some version (there have been several reprints). An essential compilation of legal documents still governing much of the region's peoples. See also **CD105**. — *LM*

Urbanization

CD124   Kastes, Wade G. - **The Future of Aboriginal Urbanization in Prairie Cities: Select Annotated Bibliography and Literature Review on Urban Aboriginal Issues in the Prairie Provinces**. - Winnipeg, MB: Institute of Urban Studies, 1993. - 135 leaves. - (Bibliographica [University of Winnipeg. Institute of Urban Studies], 5).

> Class Numbers:
>   Library of Congress E78.P7   Z1209.2.C2
>   National Library of Canada Z1209.2
> ISBN 0920213979
> OCLC 33282365
> LCCN 94-211203
> Notes:
>   Includes index

• Cites 121 publications examining a range of social, health, economic, and political problems confronting urban natives. The literature review consolidates findings in areas such as demography, migration, child care, and housing. — *LMcD*

Wars

CD125   Axelrod, Alan, 1952-   . - **Chronicle of the Indian Wars: From Colonial Times to Wounded Knee**. - New York: Prentice Hall General Reference, 1993. - 280 p.; ill., maps.

> Class Numbers:
>   Library of Congress E81 .A9
> ISBN 0671846507
> LCCN 92-20827
> Notes:
>   Includes bibliographical references (p. 269-273); index

• Contains 27 chronological chapters describing conflicts between Native Americans and European Americans over a span of about 400 years in the area now occupied by the continental U.S. The book "reflects Euro-American concerns," so the wars are named accordingly. Well-illustrated with black-and-white drawings, maps, and photographs. Numerous sidebars supply biographical sketches of key figures, such as Kit Carson and Red Cloud. A brief summary chronology follows the essays, as do a bibliography and detailed subject index. — *MB*

CD126   Dillon, Richard H. - **North American Indian Wars**. - New York: Facts on File, 1983. - 256 p.; ill. (some col.).

> Class Numbers:
>   Library of Congress E81

ISBN 0871966417
OCLC 8475379
LCCN 82-7348
Notes:
    Index

• The "Indian" wars are so named to identify the opponents of the victorious side–whites, especially the U.S. Army. Dillon arranges his book chronologically. The first three chapters do not apply to the Prairies-Plains region, but beginning with chapter 4, "Manifest Destiny, 1816-1849" and continuing to "Custer and Thereafter, 1876-1891" the remainder of the book relates directly to Prairies-Plains history. An abundance of old photos and colorful paintings, many of them full-page or double-page spreads, overwhelm the text. Colorful maps vividly illustrate the locations of battles, forts, and campaigns. A brief chronology and charts of Indian populations (1890, 1980) follow the subject index. — *MB*

CD127   Hedren, Paul L. - **Traveler's Guide to the Great Sioux War: The Battlefields, Forts, and Related Sites of America's Greatest Indian War**. - Helena, MT: Montana Historical Society Pr., 1996. - 126 p.; ill., maps.

> Class Numbers:
>   Library of Congress E83.876
> ISBN 0917298381 (pbk.)   091729839X (spec. ed.)
> OCLC 33865959
> LCCN 95-43026
> Notes:
>   Includes bibliographical references (p. 121-122); index

• Presents the chronological history of the Great Sioux War, 1876-81, in a narrative interrupted by 54 numbered "Getting There" sidebars describing sites important to the war and providing driving directions to each location. The sidebar numbers are keyed to several maps showing locations of the sites. One or two black-and-white photos on nearly every page show landscapes, landmarks, buildings, and key persons. A brief bibliography and subject index end the volume. — *MB*

CD128   Hoig, Stan. - **A Travel Guide to the Plains Indian Wars**. - Albuquerque, NM: Univ. of New Mexico Pr., 2006. - 217 p.; ill., maps.

> Class Numbers:
>   Library of Congress E83.866
> ISBN 0826339344 (pbk.)
> LCCN 2005-28715
> Notes:
>   Index
>   Table of contents: http://www.loc.gov/catdir/toc/
>   ecip061/2005028715.html

• Part 1, a history of the wars, has eight brief chapters, each ending with an excellent list of books for further reading. These chapters emphasize names, events, and places, and incorporate the points of view of individuals and groups on both sides. Part 2 is a state-by-state guide to the "historical remains" of the wars in nine Plains states: Colorado, Kansas, Montana, Nebraska, North Dakota, Oklahoma, South Dakota, Texas, and Wyoming. Remains include battle sites, fort sites, other sites, museums, and trails. Entries describe the historical importance and current state of the sites and point out relevant collections in the museums. Clear, well-chosen illustrations, maps, and diagrams. Subject index. Both practical and scholarly, handy for visiting researchers and tourists. — *JD*

CD129   Kessel, William B., ed. - **Encyclopedia of Native American Wars and Warfare** / general eds., William B. Kessel, Robert Wooster. - New York: Facts on File, 2005. - 398 p.; ill., maps. - (Facts on File library of American history).

> Class Numbers:
> Library of Congress E81
> ISBN 0816033374   081606430X (pbk.)
> LCCN 00-56200
> Notes:
> Includes bibliographical references (p. 369-376); index
> Review by M. Brunsdale: *Choice* 43.1 (Sep. 2005):
>   review 43-0062

• Kessel and Wooster's encyclopedic overview of warfare between Indian nations and various European and American armies "attempts to identify the key people, places, and events" (p. xiii) of armed conflict, 1492 to the late 1800s. Over 600 entries, arranged alphabetically, vary in length; some list further readings. Cross-references in the text to other entries are printed in small capitals, and there are a few other cross-references. Entries are unsigned, but the editors wrote many of them, and eight contributors are thanked in the preface. The work includes introductory essays on "American Indians Prior to 1492," "Warfare Terminology," "Armies of Empire: Colonial, State, Federal, and Imperial Forces in the Indian Wars," "War and Warfare," and "War and Warfare: Another View" before the actual entries begin. An appendix lists Indian tribes by culture area (although entries do not exist for all the tribes listed, nor are they all referenced in the index), followed by a chronology, a selected bibliography, and a detailed index. Because of the long time frame covered, many entries treat events outside the Plains region; there is no way to identify events by region, but since wars between Indians and the Army ground to their end on the Plains, readers can be assured Plains conflicts are covered. Useful but not essential. — *LM*

CD130   McDermott, John D. - **A Guide to the Indian Wars of the West**. - Lincoln, NE: Univ. of Nebraska Pr.,

1998. - 205 p.

> Class Numbers:
> Library of Congress E81
> ISBN 080328246X
> OCLC 38602472
> LCCN 98-16048
> Notes:
> Includes bibliographical references

• Part 1 provides context–information on treaties, Indian culture, the U.S. Army, and the Indian Wars in literature and the arts. The second part, covering places to visit, is arranged by state. Relevant sections for study of Prairies and Plains occupy p. 136-193, divided into Southern Plains (Colorado, Kansas, Missouri, and Oklahoma) and Northern Plains (Minnesota, Montana, Nebraska, North Dakota, South Dakota, and Wyoming). For each state, sections are included as applicable on historic sites, battlefields, museums, and Indian heritage sites. Where possible, phone numbers and hours of operation are provided. Includes a handful of black-and-white photos, ten tables of data, and a list of 50 basic books for further research. No index. — *MB*

CD131   Michno, Gregory F., 1948- . - **Encyclopedia of Indian Wars: Western Battles and Skirmishes, 1850-1890**. - Missoula, MT: Mountain Pr. Publ. Co., 2003. - xxxv, 429 p.; ill., maps.

> Class Numbers:
> Library of Congress E83.863
> ISBN 0878424687
> LCCN 2003-8753
> Notes:
> Includes bibliographical references (p. 394-410); indexes
> Review by Lance Janda: *Great Plains Quarterly* 24.3
>   (summer 2004): 202-203
> Table of contents: http://www.loc.gov/catdir/toc/ecip042/
>   2003008753.html

• Michno lists some 600 battles and skirmishes between Indians and European-Americans in chronological order, beginning with a battle in New Mexico on April 6, 1850, and ending with the massacre at Wounded Knee, SD, on December 29, 1890. The description of each battle, following the date, name and location, ranges from a short paragraph to several hundred words and includes key personnel, a description of the battle, and casualty counts on both sides. Preceding the list of battles, 21 maps (chiefly of the Prairies-Plains region) show locations of the battles. Other maps show Rocky Mountain and West Coast states. Supplementary information includes statistical data on casualties. Extensive notes and bibliography; illustrations of persons and places. Prairies-Plains researchers will find useful the index of battles arranged by state and location. An index of Indian peoples precedes the general index. — *MB*

CD132   Nunnally, Michael L. - **American Indian Wars: A Chronology of Confrontations between Native Peoples and Settlers and the United States Military, 1500s-1901.** - Jefferson, NC: McFarland, 2007. - 171 p.

Class Numbers:
Library of Congress E81
ISBN 0786429364   9780786429363
OCLC 79004000
LCCN 2007-1912
Notes:
Includes bibliographical references; index
Table of contents: http://www.loc.gov/catdir/toc/ecip078/2007001912.html

• Nunnally lists military engagements, skirmishes, hostile encounters, and conflicts gleaned from 154 sources that include 112 books and articles and 43 Internet sites. Besides the chronology, listing events by year, there is an index. Entries simply give factual accounts, each citing a source in the bibliography. Text in italics provides background and historical information, and some entries feature brief quotations from the source materials. Some cite historical marker locations. A paragraph or two introduces each century's list, setting a historical framework, and many years open with a note about key historical events. As the Indian wars progress (if that is the appropriate verb) from east to west, the incidence of confrontation between Native peoples and settlers increases. Every year in this 400-year span has an entry; some include only a brief historical note, while others, especially during the period between the Civil War and the end of the 19th century (the period of greatest relevance for Prairies-Plains study) may show several pages of incidents. For 1860, Nunnally notes, "Fort Belmont is established in Kansas," followed by 14 incidents throughout the year (e.g., "April 1860 - Texas - A Comanche party kills fifteen-year-old James Hamby, an employee on the Thomas Lambshead farm new at the Comanche reservation. Source: 17"). A curious work that collects many minor and major incidents in Native-settler conflict. — *LM*

CD133   Rajtar, Steve, 1951-   . - **Indian War Sites: A Guidebook to Battlefields, Monuments, and Memorials, State by State with Canada and Mexico.** - Jefferson, NC: McFarland, 1999. - 330 p.

Class Numbers:
Library of Congress E81
ISBN 0786401427 (ill. casebound)   0786407107
LCCN 99-25893
Notes:
Includes bibliographical references (p. 289-299); index

• The subtitle describes this book's content. It is arranged by state (all 50 are included, as well as Canada and Mexico), so searches can easily be limited to specific Prairies-Plains states. Within state sections, battles are organized chrono-

logically. Each entry provides name of battle, date, location, a brief description, and relevant resources (indicated by cross-reference numbers pointing to the 425-item bibliography). At the front, a detailed chronology arranged by the date of the event provides the name of the larger conflict, the entry number (e.g., NE3), and the name of the battle. At the end are a detailed alphabetical index of battles and place-names and an index of persons, both referring to entry identifiers (e.g., MT16) rather than page numbers. A polished publication with great usefulness to historical researchers. — *MB*

Women

CD134   Bataille, Gretchen M. - **American Indian Women: A Guide to Research** / [by] Gretchen M. Bataille, Kathleen M. Sands; ed. assistant, Catherine Udall. - New York: Garland, 1991. - 423 p. - (Garland reference library of social science, v. 515; Women's history and culture, v. 4).

Class Numbers:
Library of Congress E98.W8   Z1209.2.N67
ISBN 0824047990
LCCN 91-2961
Notes:
Index

• A thoroughly annotated research guide by Bataille, a noted author or coauthor of many works on Native American literature, and Sands, Southwestern and Western literature professor, that cites 1,573 titles on Native women in the U.S. and Canada. The authors supply thorough descriptive annotations for all titles. They exclude popular fiction, depictions of Native women in travel journals, and titles written for children and young adults. Entries are arranged in eight broad categories, and are listed alphabetically in each category, title entries first (initial articles are observed in alphabetizing), then authors. The categories are: "Bibliographies and Reference Works," "Ethnography, Cultural History, and Social Roles," "Politics and Law," "Health, Education, and Employment," "Visual and Performing Arts," " Literature and Criticism," "Autobiography, Biography, and Interviews," and "Film and Video." A 36-page index allows identification of titles by tribe and narrower topics. Index entries identified as directly for Plains and Prairies tribes total over 150 titles, with many entries for people, authors, and topics highly relevant as well. A solid, necessary, and scholarly resource. — *LM*

CD135   Bataille, Gretchen M., 1944-   , ed. - **Native American Women: A Biographical Dictionary** / Gretchen M. Bataille, Laurie Lisa, eds. - 2nd ed. - New York: Routledge, 2001. - 396 p.; ill.

Class Numbers:
Library of Congress E98.W8

ISBN 0415930200
LCCN 2001-19749
Notes:
    1st ed. publ.: New York: Garland, 1993
    Includes bibliographical references (p. 345-351); index

• Bataille and Lisa present brief biographical sketches, arranged alphabetically, of Native American women in Canada and the U.S. from contact to the date of the work's publication in an expansion and revision of the first edition (1993). Entries cover many professions and roles, and many of the names will be refreshingly unfamiliar to readers. All entries are signed, and most provide references. Appendixes include a substantial selected bibliography, a descriptive list of contributors and editors (itself a miniature biographical dictionary, since many of the contributors are Native scholars), a list of entries by specialization, a list of entries by decade of birth, and, most useful for identifying regional women, a list by state/province of birth, and another by tribal affiliation. An index of names and organizations ends the work. A quick count by state/province turns up over 100 Prairies-Plains names; the count by tribe about the same. A good resource. — *LM*

CD136   Sonneborn, Liz. - **A to Z of Native American Women**. - New York: Facts on File, 1998. - 228 p.; ill. - (Encyclopedia of women; Facts on File library of American history).

Class Numbers:
    Library of Congress E98.W8
ISBN 0816035806
LCCN 97-36674
Notes:
    Includes bibliographical references (p. 213-214); index

• The 100 biographies of Native American women selected for this work were "chosen to represent a variety of tribes, regions, chronological periods, and fields" (p. xi) and represent women who have influenced both Native and non-Native society. The women range in time from Pocahontas to contemporary Ojibwa environmental activist and Green Party vice-presidential candidate (1996 and 2000 elections) Winona LaDuke. Entries include dates, tribe, and role. Some cite further readings; there are a few cross-references, photos, and illustrations. Finding aids include a 37-title "Recommended Sources on Native American Women Studies," "Entries by Area of Activity," "Entries by Tribe," and "Entries by Year of Birth." Index entries are mostly to personal and organizational names. "Entries by Tribe" is the key tool for Prairies-Plains studies; about a third of the biographical sketches portray women from regional tribes. The usual women are included. Libraries with other works on Native women can probably skip this, but it is useful if nothing else is available. — *LM*

CE : STATISTICS

Scope   Lists compilations of statistics, usually in tabular form, reporting current or historical counts for population, economic measures, education, health, births and deaths, and like measures.

UNITED STATES

CE1 Historical Statistics of the United States : Earliest Times to the Present / [by] Susan B. Carter [et al.]. - Millennial ed. - New York : Cambridge Univ. Pr., 2006. – 5 v. ; ill.

> Class Numbers:
> Library of Congress HA202.H57
> ISBN 0521584965 (v.1) 0521585406 (v. 2)
>   0521817900 (v. 3)   0521853893 (v. 4)
>   0521853907 (v. 5)   0521817919 (set)
> OCLC 61757927
> LCCN 2005-27089
> Notes:
> Includes bibliographical references ; index
> Rev. update of: *Historical Statistics of the United States,*
>   *Colonial Times to 1970.*   Bicentennial ed.
>   Washington, DC: U.S. Dept. of Commerce, Bureau of
>   the Census, 1975

CE1a   Historical Statistics of the United States : Earliest Times to the Present [Internet site] / [by] Susan B. Carter [et al.] – Millennial ed. online - New York : Cambridge Univ. Pr, 2006. – http://hsus.cambridge.org/HSUSWeb/

> ISBN 0511132972
> Notes:
> Includes bibliographical references ; index
> Table of contents: http://www.loc.gov/catdir/toc/
>   ecop061/2005027089.htm
> Fees: Purchase; pay-per-view

• While the edition statement may seem a piece of marketing hyberbole, the publisher does not exaggerate in calling this work a "monumental work of collaborative scholarship." Though privately issued, it is the "approved successor" to the three previous editions published by the Census Bureau. With added years, new topics, and enhanced coverage, the first update since 1975 includes 37,339 data series from more than 1,000 public and private sources. Tables arranged by state, territory, and local area can be used to establish demographic, economic, and other changes in the Plains over long periods. Volume 1 covers population statistics; volume 2, work and welfare; volume 3, economic structure and performance; volume 4, economic

sectors; and volume 5, governance and international relations. Chapter introductions, a new feature, give quantitative histories of topics, guides to sources, and assessments of data reliability. Tables are elegantly formatted, series well footnoted, sources clearly cited, and data collection methodologies heavily documented. Cumulative index in volume 5.

§   The online version allows users to graph data, create custom tables, and download data to spreadsheets, but its high functionality comes at a high price. — *JD*

Nebraska

CE2   The Nebraska Databook [Internet Site]. - Lincoln, NE : Nebraska Dept. of Economic Development, 2000?- . - http://info.neded.org/databook.php

> Access Date : Feb. 2006
> Notes:
> 1998-2001, issued to depository libraries on microfiche by
>   the Nebraska Library Commission as
>   Nebraska government publication E1500 S002–
> Title varies: 1970-1990/1991, published in print as
>   *Nebraska Statistical Handbook*
> Fees: None

• Tables and charts, organized by 20 categories that include agriculture, crime, energy, finance, business, and tourism, provide data on demographic, social, physical, and economic life of the state. A "Maps" section offers maps of traffic flow, employment, and population, and geologic and geographical maps of registered water wells, watersheds, water depth, soil types, earthquakes, and river discharge. "People" has biographical sketches of famous Nebraskans, and "History" describes state symbols, the capitol building, and the Great Seal of the State of Nebraska. Data, gathered from a variety of state and federal agencies, and from nongovernmental organizations, are updated with varying frequency. Many tables give historical comparisons, but data are not archived. — *JD*

CE2a   Nebraska Statistical Handbook. - [190? ed. (190?) - 1990/91 ed. (1991)]. Lincoln, NE : Nebraska Dept. of Economic Development, 1900s-1991. Annual.

> Class Numbers:
> Library of Congress HA491
> Government Document Nebraska E1500 S001
> sLCCN 73-622040
> Notes:
> Continued by Nebraska Databook, http://info.neded.
>   org/databook.php (above)
> 1998-2001, issued to depository libraries on microfiche
>   by the Nebraska Library Commission as Nebraska
>   government publication E1500 S002–

• NSH's tables and charts supply data about the state's demographic, social, physical, and economic life. Tables are organized by topics that include agriculture, crime, energy, finance, business, and tourism. Each topical section begins with a summary of reporting changes, statistical trends, and significant national rankings. Sources shown for tables and charts indicate that the information has been gathered from a variety of federal and state agencies and private organizations. Many tables provide comparative historical statistics. —*JD*

Site List 8
Statistical Sources

The 2008 *Statistical Abstract of the United States* (http://www.census.gov/compendia/statab/st_abstracts.html) publishes a bibliography of state statistical abstracts that provides links to abstracts that are online. For states that lack official abstracts, the bibliography lists other sources of statistical abstracts that cover a variety of topics. The list below of state statistical sources is drawn from that bibliography, supplemented here with other useful titles. Besides state sources, the U,S, Census Bureau's *American FactFinder* (http://factfinder.census.gov) is a comprehensive source of Census information that covers the Plains states. The Bureau's *State and County QuickFacts* (http://quickfacts.census.gov/qfd/index.html) offers easier but more limited access to Census data.

UNITED STATES

Colorado
Online: *Colorado by the Numbers.*
http://www.colorado.edu/libraries/govpubs/online.htm
    University of Colorado. University Libraries.
      Continually updated. Contains some historical data.
    Colorado Data Book.
        http://www.state.co.us/oed/business-development/
          colorado-dat-book.cfm
      Colorado. Office of Economic Development and
        International Trade.
      Continually updated. Contains some historical data.
      Colorado State Demography Office.
        http://156.108.28.187/dlg/demog/index.html
      Colorado. Division of Local Government. State
        Demography Office.
      Continually updated in pdf and Excel formats. Contains
      some historical data.

Kansas
Online: *Kansas Statistical Abstract.*
http://www.ipsr.ku.edu/ksdata/ksah/ksa34.shtml
    Publ. online only, 2001-present in pdf format.
    Pdfs, 1965-2000, available online.
    Kansas Data Archive.
      http://www.ipsr.ku.edu/ksdata/#ksa
    Archival data, 1890-present, not included in Kansas
    Statistical Abstract.
Print: *Kansas Statistical Abstract.* 1900s-2000. Publ. by
    various agencies.

Montana
Online: *Census and Economic Information Center.*
http://ceic.commerce.state.mt.us/
    Montana. Dept. of Commerce. Census and Economic
    Information Center.

Continually updated. Contains some historical data.
Part of Montana government site mt.gov.

Nebraska
Online: *Nebraska Databook.*
http://www.neded.org/content/view/ 22/698/
    Nebraska. Dept. of Economic Development.
    Online only. Continually updated. Internet site data
    archived by Nebraska Library Commission.
Print: *Nebraska Statistical Handbook.* 1970-1990/1991.
    Annual.

New Mexico
Online: *Bureau of Business and Economic Research.* http://www.unm.edu/~bber/
    University of New Mexico. Bureau of Business and
    Economic Research.
    Continually updated. Contains some historical data.

North Dakota
Online: *North Dakota Statistical Abstract.*
http://www.business/und.edu/abstract.cfm
    University of North Dakota. Bureau of Business and
    Economic Research.
    Online only, 1991-present.
    Continually updated. Contains some historical data.
Print: *Statistical Abstract of North Dakota.* 1979-1990. Annual.

Oklahoma
Online: *Oklahoma's Advantage.*
http://www.okcommece.gov/
    Oklahoma. Dept. of Commerce.
    Continually updated. Contains some historical data.

South Dakota
Online: *South Dakota State Data Center.*
http://www.usd.edu/sdsdc/
    University of South Dakota. Business Research Bureau.
    South Dakota State Data Center.
    Continually updated. Contains some historical data.
Print: *South Dakota Community Abstracts.* 1900s-present.
    Annual.
CD-ROM: *South Dakota Community Abstracts.* 2003-present.

Texas
Online: *Texas Almanac.*
"http://texasalamnac.com" http://texasalmanac.com
    Dallas Morning News.
      Current edition online in html. Contains some archival
      data.
    Texas Data Center and Office of the State Demographer.

continued on following page

CE3   Nebraska ... Vital Statistics Report. - / Nebraska Health & Human Services System, Dept. of Regulation and Licensure [and] Dept. of Finance & Support. - Lincoln, NE : Dept. of Regulation & Licensure, 1997-   .

continued from previous page

> http://txsdc.tusa.edu
> University of Texas at San Antonio.
> Continually updated.
> *Texas Fact Book.*
> http://www.lbb.state.tx.us/
> Texas. Legislative Budget Board.
> Current edition online in pdf.
> Print: *Texas Almanac.* 1857-present. See DB101.
> *Texas Fact Book.* 1978-present.
> University of Texas. Bureau of Business Research.
>
> *Wyoming*
> Online: *Equality State Almanac.*
> http://eadiv.state.wy.us/Almanac/ Almanac.html
> Wyoming. Dept. of Administration and Information.
> Economic Analysis Division.
> Current edition online in pdf.
> Print: *Equality State Almanac.* 1993-present. Annual.
>
> Canada
>
> *Alberta*
> Online: *Statistics and Publications.*
> http://www.finance.gov.ab.ca/publications/statistics/
> index.html
> Alberta Finance and Enterprise.
> Contains some historical data.
> Print: *Alberta Statistical Review.* 1972-1992.
> Frequency varies.
>
> *Manitoba*
> Online: *Province of Manitoba.*
> http://www.gov.mb.ca/
> *Province of Manitoba.*
> No print equivalent. Contains some historical data.
> Print: *Manitoba Statistical Review.* 1973-1980 ; 1983-1986.
> Formerly *Manitoba Digest of Statistics.*
> Bureau of Statistics.
>
> *Saskatchewan*
> Online: *Saskatchewan Bureau of Statistics.*
> http://www.stats.gov.sk.ca/
> Saskatchewan Bureau of Statistics.
> Current statistics available only online.
> Includes pdf files of *Economic Review* (annual),
> *Labour Force*
> *Survey* (annual), and *Statistical Review* (monthly), all
> back to 2000.
> Includes searchable database of *Provincial Economic*
> *Accounts* back to 1951.

Annual.

> Class Numbers:
> Library of Congress HA494
> Govrnment Document Nebraska H6810 S0001
> LCCN 98-641481
> Notes:
> Title varies: 1985-1995, publ. [Lincoln, NE : Dept.
> of Health, Bureau of Vital Statistics] under title:
> *Vital Statistics Report*

• Presents in tables, graphs, and maps about 60,000 state vital records filed during the calendar year. Three sections cover births, deaths, and marriage and divorce. Data from the Nebraska Birth Defects Registry is included in the births section. Each section opens with statistical highlights of the year and includes such specific topics as births by method of delivery, deaths by cause and county of residence, divorces by duration of marriage. Some tables include historical information, some as far back as 1940. Maps showing numbers and rates by county are available for some data. Data are published for individual towns with population of 2,500 or more. The current report is available in pdf format at the *Nebraska Health and Human Services* Internet site (http://www.hhs.state.ne.us/ced/vs.htm), which offers a separate statistical report on abortions. A resource for researchers, businesses, human service providers, and general readers. — *JD*

Oklahoma

CE4   Statistical Abstract of Oklahoma. - [1st] (1972)-   . Norman, OK : Bureau for Business and Economic Research, College of Business Administration, Univ. of Oklahoma, 1972-   . Annual.

> Class Numbers:
> Library of Congress HA581
> OCLC 3436814
> LCCN 79-642515
> Notes:
> Preceding title: *Oklahoma Data Book*, ISSN 0078-4354
> Vols. for 1975- issued by Center for Economic and
> Management Research, Univ. of Oklahoma
> Vols. for 1978- include "...Guide to Statistical Sources."

• A summary of Oklahoma statistics for such topics as agriculture, communications, education, population, and vital statistics and health. Published annually, with data presented in tabular form. No indexes. An Internet site (http://www.utulsa.edu/govdocs/oklahoma.htm) carries similar information but not in tabular form. — *RB*

South Dakota

CE5   A Graphic Summary of South Dakota / New Community Project, Dept. of Rural Sociology, South Dakota State Univ. - [Brookings, SD] : Dept. of Rural

Sociology, South Dakota State Univ., 2001. - 14 v. ; maps, charts.

Class Numbers:
Library of Congress HA635
Government Document South Dakota ED 550:N 421
OCLC 48646333
Notes:
Chiefly tables and maps
Combines population counts from the 2000 Census with data from the Bureau of Economic Analysis and includes data from the *Census of Agriculture*, 1997
Some vols. available over the Internet: http://purl.sdln.net/sds/ed550-n421/1

• Staff at the Department of Rural Sociology, South Dakota State Univ., have compiled population data for the state based on the 2000 decennial Census. The work's 13 parts are arranged by county into three geographic regions: West (four sections), South (four sections), and North (five sections). For each county, the work provides statistics, maps, and graphs representing percentage changes in population. The tabulated information includes historical data, percentage of males versus females by age ranges, number of farms and households, median income, employment figures, school districts, births, deaths, divorce rates, airports, hospitals, taxable sales, and building permits. — *GK*

Texas

CE6   Texans for Public Justice. - **The State of the Lone Star State : How Life in Texas Measures Up** / eds. Paul Robbins & Andrew Wheat. - Austin, TX : Texans for Public Justice, 2000. - 155 p.

Class Numbers:
Library of Congress HN60
OCLC 46698927

• Robbins and Wheat compiled for Texans for Public Justice this report that rates the state of Texas against the rest of the U.S. in the following broad categories: environment, education, human services, economy, public safety, and democracy, each divided into subtopics. The front matter describes the methodology used, and the conclusion provides a table of all 150 indicators. The area of greatest interest to Plains researchers will be environment, which includes subcategories for water quality, water planning, animal manure, energy use, and open space protection. — *JB*

Wyoming

CE7   Jordan, Roy A., 1928-   . - **Wyoming : A Source Book** / [by] Roy A. Jordan and S. Brett DeBoer. - Niwot, CO : Univ. Pr. of Colorado, 1996. - 351 p. ; ill., maps.

Class Numbers:
Library of Congress F761
ISBN 0870814249 (pbk.)
058503673X (electronic bk.) 9780870814242 (pbk.)
9780585036731 (electronic bk.)
OCLC 33161462   42330402 (electronic bk.)
LCCN 95-40937
Notes:
Electronic book: http://www.netLibrary.com/urlapi.asp?action=summary&v=1&bookid=178
Includes bibliographical references (p. 321-339); index

• Based in large part on state and federal publications, the source book pulls together statistics on land, water, environmental protection, population, American Indians, government and politics, economy, minerals, agriculture, life and health, social services, marriage and divorce, crime, education, highways, conservation and wildlife, and miscellaneous topics. Some information sources, such as Census figures, are common; others, such as Indian health and mineral sites, are elusive. Information is presented in large, easy-to-read graphs and charts with explanatory text. Most charts give data for the 1980s and 1990s while the accompanying text provides a deeper historical context. Useful for general reading, identifying trends, and making comparisons over time. Excellent bibliography. Indexed by names, places, topics, and agencies. — *JD*

Indians

CE8   **Statistical Record of Native North Americans** / Marlita A. Reddy, ed. - Detroit, MI : Gale, 1993. - lxvi, 1661 p.

ISBN 0810389630
OCLC 28257149
Notes:
Includes bibliographical references (p. 1457-1464) ; index
• This massive work compiles statistical data from many federal and state agencies, tribal governments, associations, and other organizations, much of it, the publisher claims, not previously available in published format. Statistics, based on the 1980 U.S. Census, compare Native Americans with other racial and ethnic groups, or compare various reservations, tribes, cities, Standard Metropolitan Statistical Areas, regions, etc. Coverage encompasses "20th century estimates of pre-European contact populations to population projections for 2040" (p. xliii). All information is strictly numerical; other than an introduction and a very useful "Guide to Chapters and Contents," there is no textual material. Eleven thematic chapters reflect the type of information gathered by the U.S. Census Bureau: "History," "Demographics," "The Family," "Education, Culture and Tradition," "Health and Health Care," "Social and Economic Conditions," "Business and Industry," "Land and Water Management," "Government Relations," and "Law

and Law Enforcement." An especially welcome addition is chapter 12 (more than 300 p.), which covers Canada with tables addressing the same topics as the U.S. information, although in less detail. The Canadian information comes from the 1986 Canadian Census; like the 1990 U.S. Census, 1990 Canadian Census results were unavailable at the time this book was published. Providing a final entry to the data is a massive, thorough, 196-page keyword index of over 3,000 entries that make it possible to locate statistics by tribe, state, town, county, reservation, and just about any other entry point one could desire. Essential. — *LM*

CE9 Stuart, Paul, 1943- . - **Nations within a Nation : Historical Statistics of American Indians**. - Westport, CT : Greenwood Pr., 1987. - 251 p.

Class Numbers:
Library of Congress E77
ISBN 0313238138
LCCN 86-33618
Notes:
Bibliography: p. [233]-241

• Stuart intends this collection as a "beginning point for most investigations" (p. 1). Coverage is strongest for the 20th century, because he held suspect data and statistics for earlier periods. His major sources, as might be expected, are the U.S. Census and "publications of federal government agencies such as the Bureau of Indian Affairs and the Indian Health Service" (p. 2), while he gleaned other data from congressional investigations and reports of federal agencies. Consequently, tribal-specific statistics are mostly missing, making it difficult to locate data for Plains Indians. Eight thematic chapters offer narrative overviews of the data for that topic, followed by raw numbers presented in tables and charts. All the chapters are relevant for Plains studies ("Land Base and Climate," "Population," "Removal, Relocation, and Urbanization," "Vital Statistics and Health," "Government Activities," "Health Care and Education." "Employment, Earnings, and Income," "Indian Resources and Economic Development"), but extracting data specific to the Plains is difficult. Some topics, presented regionally, best lend themselves to Plains studies. — *LM*

CF : Economics and Business

Scope   Works treating the economic and business climate and history of the Prairies-Plains region, including manufacturing, mining, banking, energy, transportation.

General Works

CF1   Hoover's Texas 500 : A Guide to the Top Texas Companies. -. -3rd ed. - . Austin, TX : Hoover's Business Press, 2002-   . Annual.

> Class Numbers:
> Library of Congress HG4057.T4
> LCCN 2004-209703

• The 3rd edition describes the 500 largest private and public companies in Texas. Nonprofit institutions such as universities are included. The 100 largest companies are profiled in two pages accompanied by sidebars containing data about current and historical financial circumstances, number of employees, officers, and competitors. The remaining 400 companies are described in a paragraph apiece, along with data about current finances, officers, number of employees, and competitors. Indexes refer to industries, headquarters locations, companies, and people. Includes essays on the economic outlook, and key Texas companies, and provides ranked lists of companies by sales, growth over one year, and number of employees. — *MS*

CF2   Nebraska Economic Development Information Online [Internet Site]. - Columbus, NE : Nebraska Public Power District, Economic Development Dept., 1995-   . - http://sites.nppd.com/nediindex.htm

> Access Date: Jan. 2006
> Fees: None

• Nebraska is the only U.S. state without private power companies; electricity is generated and delivered by government entities called public power districts, which have been in operation since 1933. Central to their mission since the earliest days of rural electrification has been economic development of rural areas. Largest of the current four districts, NPPD produces *NEDI Online,* an up-to-date source of economic and demographic information intended for communities, business firms, and site selectors. It profiles the state's 536 communities, assessing them according to 17 standards commonly used to evaluate business locations. The site offers information not readily available in Census

or community sources, covering labor force, transportation, utilities, tax structure, recreational facilities, educational facilities, municipal services, housing, health facilities, commercial facilities, manufacturing, employers, and industrial buildings. The site provides the capability to search for commercial building and industrial sites, with maps, images, and links to demographics for any community or areas in a radius of 15, 30, and 50 miles. Older data are not archived. Update frequency varies with community. — *JD*

Directories

CF3   The [State] Business Directory. - Omaha, NE : American Directory Publ. Co., 1983-   . - Annual.

> *Colorado.* – [1st] (1987-88)-
> Class Numbers:
> Library of Congress HF3161.C6
> OCLC 15875386
> LCCN 88-656099

> *Kansas.* – [1st] (1983-84)-
> Class Numbers:
> Library of Congress HF5065.K2
> LCCN 86-642761

> *Montana.* – [1st] (1989-90)-
> Class Numbers:
> Library of Congress HF5065.M9
> LCCN 80-648452

> *Nebraska.* – [v.1] (2001)-
> Class Numbers:
> Library of Congress HF5065.N2.N4
> OCLC 53864748
> LCCN HF5065.N2

> *New Mexico.* – [1st] (1990-91?)-
> Class Numbers:
> Library of Congress HF5065.N6
> LCCN 90-644070

> *North Dakota.* – [1st] (1987-88)-
> Class Numbers:
> Library of Congress HF5065.N9
> LCCN 89-656206

> *Oklahoma.* – (1987)-   .
> Class Numbers:
> Library of Congress HF5065.O5
> LCCN 88-641140

> *South Dakota.* – [1st] (1987-88)-
> Class Numbers:
> Library of Congress HF5065.S8
> OCLC 16393779
> LCCN 87-649163

Notes:
Preceding title: *Dakotas Business Directory*

Texas. - [1st] (1991/92) - [Final] (1998/1999).
Class Numbers:
Library of Congress HF5065.T4
LCCN 91-644015

Wyoming. – 2004 ed. (2004)-
Class Numbers:
Library of Congress HF5065.W8
OCLC 53394461

Notes:
Preceding title: *Wyoming Business-to-Business Sales & Marketing Directory*

• State business directories from this publisher have sections for business by city, businesses by yellow pages category, major employers (more than 100 employees), publicly traded companies, and manufacturers with more than ten employees by city and by Standard Industrial Classification. Information is gathered from telephone yellow and white pages, annual reports, filings with the Security and Exchange Commission, newspapers, and magazines. Useful to business professionals, sales executives, and potential job seekers. Entries give firm name, address, telephone, owner or manager, credit rating code, number of employees, SIC, years in business, and estimated sales. — *GK, JD*

Atlases

CF4   **Economic Atlas of Nebraska** / project director, Merlin P. Lawson ; ed. by Richard E. Lonsdale ; cartographer, John D. Magill. - Lincoln, NE : Univ. of Nebraska Pr., 1977. - 165 p. ; ill. (some col.), maps (some col.).

Class Numbers:
Library of Congress G1451.G1
ISBN 0803209118
OCLC 2680871
LCCN 76-30887

• One of three atlases produced by the Nebraska Atlas Project (the others treat agriculture and climate, **G8** and **EA25**), this atlas combines maps and graphs with narrative analysis to portray Nebraska's economy—the overall picture, eight economic sectors, and regional variations. An introductory chapter on economic history portrays economic health of the state, using data on income level and distribution, taxation and expenditures in the public sector, and the labor force. Other chapters treat economic sectors: agriculture; mining; construction; manufacturing; transportation and public utilities; trade and services; finance, insurance, and real estate; and government. For each sector,

regional variations are shown in maps, highlighting the interplay between geography and economy. Historical statistics are supplied in tables and accompanying text. A convenient source for baselines for analyzing more recent changes. — *JD*

Banking

CF5   **Banks and S&Ls of Nebraska**. -   [s.l.] : Sheshunoff & Co., 1998–   . Annual.

Notes:
Supplement, *National and Statewide Bank Performance Standards*, discontinued after 1989
Title history: *Banks of Nebraska*, 1985-1997; *Banks and S&Ls of Nebraska*, 1998–

• A directory and financial analysis of banks and savings and loan institutions in Nebraska. An introductory section covers "Comprehensive Overview," "Balance Sheet Analysis," "Income Statement Analysis," and "Competitive Overview." An index of specific banks is arranged alphabetically by city of headquarters. Information includes assets, income, detailed analysis of balance sheets and income statements, five-year performance reviews, and capital adequacy. — *MB*

Energy

CF6   **A Dictionary for the Oil and Gas Industry**. - Austin, TX : Petroleum Extension Service, Continuing & Extended Education, Univ. of Texas at Austin, 2005. - 317 p. ; ill.

Class Numbers:
Library of Congress TN865
ISBN 0886982138 (pbk.)
LCCN 2005-17112
Notes:
Based on *A Dictionary for the Petroleum Industry*, 3rd ed. rev.

• Consists of three sections: the list of terms, abbreviations, SI (metric) Units. Defines 11,000 terms and lists 700 abbreviations and their meanings. Covers technical, legal, geological, and meteorological terms, professional associations, and government agencies. Concludes with tables and lists of metric measures and their English equivalent. — *MS*

CF7   **Keystone Coal Industry Manual**. - [1st] (1969)–

. New York : McGraw-Hill, 1969–   . Annual.

    Class Numbers:
        Library of Congress TN805.A4
    LCCN 72-622648; sn 93-33801
    Notes:

Affiliated with *Coal; Coal Age* (Overland Park, KS)
Also available on CD-ROM
Preceding title: *Keystone Coal Buyers Manual;* ISSN
    0450-1772
Publisher varies: Chicago, IL : Maclean Hunter Publ. Co.

Site List 9
Manufacturers

State agencies, often with nonprofit partners, produce printed and online manufacturing directories for most Plains states, as do private publishers like Harris Infosource and Manufacturers' News, and national sources like the free *ThomasNet* (http://www.thomasnet.com). Official state online directories may be Internet sites or pdf versions of printed directories. Although the Internet sites are updated regularly, deleted data may be available through state libraries or other agencies that archive official Internet sites. This list excludes state databases of registered corporations that are used to search for "business entities" and their records. Printed directories below show only latest title, issuing agency, and frequency listed by WorldCat or other sources.

Colorado
Print: *Directory of Colorado Manufacturers*. Biennial,
    1900s-2002.
    Bureau of Business Research, Univ. of Colorado-
    Boulder with Colorado Development Council

Kansas
Print: *A Directory of Kansas Manufacturers and Their*
    Products. Annual, 1957-   .
    Research Division, Kansas Industrial
    Development Div.

Montana
Online: *Montana Manufacturer's Information System*.
http://www.nmis.umt.edu/
Produced by partnership of educational and state agencies
Print: *Montana Manufacturers Directory*. Irregular, 1963- .
    Montana Dept. of Commerce, Small Business
    Development Div.

Nebraska
Online: *Nebraska Manufacturers Directory*. (pdf, current
    issue only) http://pio.neded.org.manufacture
    Nebraska Dept. of Economic Development
Print: *Nebraska Directory of Manufacturers*. Biennial,
    1946-   .
    Nebraska Dept. of Economic Development

New Mexico
Print: *Directory of New Mexico Manufacturers*. Biennial,
    1955-2003.
    New Mexico State Univ., Center for Economic
    Development Research and Assistance

North Dakota
Online: *North Dakota: A New State of Business*.
    http://www.growingnd.com
    North Dakota Dept. of Commerce
Print: *Directory of North Dakota Manufacturers and*
    Food Processors. Biennial, 1983-   .
    North Dakota Dept. of Economic Development and
    Finance

Oklahoma
Online: *Oklahoma Business Directory*. http://www.ok.
    gov/businessdir/businessdir.php
    State of Oklahoma
Print: *Oklahoma Directory of Manufacturers and*
    Processors. Annual, 1900s-   .
    Oklahoma Dept. of Commerce, Research and
    Planning Div.

South Dakota
Online: *South Dakota Manufacturers and Processors*
    Directory.
    http://www.sdgreatprofits.com/asp/goods.asp
    Governor's Office of Economic Development
Print: *South Dakota Manufacturer's Directory. Annual,*
    1975-   .
    Governor's Office of Economic Development

Texas
Print: *Directory of Texas Manufacturers*. Annual, 1932-
1999.
    Univ. of Texas, Bureau of Business Research

Wyoming
Online: *All Wyoming Business Directory*.
    http://allwyoming.uwyo.edu/wyoBusinesses
Manufacturing-Works, university and business partner
    ship
Print: *Wyoming Directory of Mining and Manufacturing*.
Irregular, 1956?-   .
    Wyoming Dept. of Commerce, Div. of Economic
    and Community Development

; Primedia

• Wyoming is by far the largest coal producer in the country, the Powder River Basin in Wyoming and Montana is the largest coal reserve in the U.S., six of the 12 largest coal producers are located in the Plains states, and two additional Plains states produce coal. This major coal industry source for the U.S. and Canada offers extensive directory and statistical information about the Plains. Besides listing mines, mining companies, transporters, associations, consultants, financial services, sales companies, and other coal-related businesses, it includes consumer data, coal industry statistics, technology updates, and coal geology reports. A "Mine Matrix" presents commonly sought information in a simple format. Index. — JD

CF8   Nebraska Energy Statistics / Nebraska Energy Office. - [1st] (1900s)-   . Lincoln, NE : Nebraska Energy Office, 1900s-   . - Annual.

    Class Numbers:
        Library of Congress H9502.U53
        Government Document Nebraska E5700 S004-
    OCLC 29623952
    LCCN 94-660626
    Notes:
        Issued 1960-1997 to depository libraries on microfiche

• Detailed tables of Nebraska energy consumption and costs. Sections on prices of diesel fuel and gasoline for metropolitan areas and the entire state (with comparative figures for the previous day, a month earlier, and a year earlier); wholesale and residential costs of heating oil and propane; Nebraska rankings for electricity rates, ethanol production, natural gas residential prices, total energy consumption, wind generation capacity; state totals of consumption and expenditure by fuel type, by sector, and per capita; state profiles of energy, electricity, petroleum, and renewable energy. Links lead to sites on renewable resources, and to some archival data (a rarity in state agency sites). Convenient features include a glossary, 90-day weather forecast, conversion tables, and calculators. — JD

Fur Trade

See The Mountain Men and the Fur Trade of the Far West, DA86

Manufacturing

CF9   Directory of Canadian Manufacturers : Western. - Mississauga, ON : Dun & Bradstreet Canada, 1999-   . Annual.

    Class Numbers:
        Library of Congress HF3223

OCLC 41164350
LCCN 99-41597
Notes:
    Also available on CD-ROM

• Alphabetical directory of 15,000 companies in the Prairies, British Columbia, Yukon, and the Northwest Territories. Entries give legal name, contact information, parent company and subsidiaries, number of employees, sales and main sales territory, year started, line of business, and executive names and titles. Additional sections list businesses by sales volume, location (by province, then city), and Standard Industrial Classification code. — LMcD

Media

See also Gale Directory of Publications and Broadcast Media, AB1

CF10   Clark, Robert A., 1948-   . - The Arthur H. Clark Company : An American Century, 1902-2002 / by Robert A. Clark and Patrick J. Brunet. - Spokane, WA : Arthur H. Clark Co., 2001. - 300 p.

    Class Numbers:
        Library of Congress Z473.A69
    ISBN 0870623192
    LCCN 2002-34763

• Following a section of background about Arthur H. Clark and his book company, the book consists of a bibliography of titles published and reprinted by the company, which specialized in studies relating to the history of the trans-Mississippi West. Entries, arranged alphabetically by author, provide physical description of the title, including material and color of binding, number of copies in the press run, series, and price. The Clark imprints are integral to the study of the West (and of the Prairies-Plains region), including titles on medical aspects of the Lewis and Clark Expedition, repeal of the Missouri Compromise, the frontier of northwest Texas, the Comanche barrier in the southern Plains, and Fort Custer on the Bighorn. — JB

Mining

See also O'Harra, A Bibliography of the Geology and Mining Interests of the Black Hills Region, EA13

CF11   The Mining West : A Bibliography & Guide to the History & Literature of Mining in the American & Canadian West / ed. by Richard E. Lingenfelter. - Lanham, MD : Scarecrow Pr., 2003. - 2 v.

    Class Numbers:

Library of Congress TN22
OCLC 51326096
LCCN 2002-114094

• Lingenfelter's massive compilation cites more than 20,000 titles, but each section begins with a bibliographical essay that helpfully points out the core works. The general section on Western mining is subdivided into segments treating history, description, law, economics, literature, and reference works. The metallurgy section deals with prospecting, technology, assaying and processing, and equipment catalogs. The regional portion is arranged by state, province, and territory, each subdivided by history, description, literature, and reference works. Among the Plains jurisdictions covered are New Mexico, West Texas, Colorado, Montana, the Dakotas, and the Prairie provinces. Journal articles, manuscripts, geological and mineralogical studies, and reports from individual mining companies are excluded. The regional organization works well, for the most part, but the lack of indexes makes it difficult to locate material on specific subjects. — *LMcD*

CF12   Nestor, Sandy. - **Silver and Gold Mining Camps of the Old West : A State by State American Encyclopedia**. - Jefferson, NC : McFarland, 2007. - 269 p. ; ill.

Class Numbers:
Library of Congress TN413.A5
ISBN 0786428137 9780786428137
OCLC 74965131

Site List 10
Business Directories and Statistics

An absorbing interest in the environment provided for business enterprises and the success they enjoy lies near the heart of every state and provincial government, in the Prairies-Plains region as elsewhere. Business research tends to center around finding out what firms are currently active, where they are located, who runs them, and reports of their financial performance.

Nearly all the official government sites listed in "Official Government Sites" Site List 11, p. 00 have a component that concentrates on the seedbed provided for businesses. At Colorado.gov, for example, the site's table of contents has sections for "Economic Base," "Population and Demographics," "Employment and Training," "Technology Sectors," and "Taxes" (first entry in the last category is "Colorado Business Taxes"). Some states offer separate statistics sites (Nebraska's, called *Statistics about Nebraska*, has sections for agriculture, business and economy, census data, etc.), and some provinces provide business service centers (Saskatchewan Business Service Centre, with links to business-related sites).

The search for online state business statistics is complicated by shifting state agencies, splitting of responsibility among multiple agencies, and confusing state government Internet sites. Paths to statistics pages are sometimes lengthy or unmarked; change is frequent. The current trend appears to be the creation of a comprehensive "data center" within an Office of Economic Development. Archived data is rare. In the list below, when a statistics page has a lengthy URL, the path from a higher level page is given.

Commercial firms also supply business sites that report business activity, give addresses and rosters, and compile statistics. Among these in the U.S. are One Source, Harris InfoSource, Go Leads, AOL Yellowpages, Hoovers, and BizHwy.com; in Canada, Canadian Business Information and Hinton Business Directory. Some are free, but most require subscription. Sites for all Prairies-Plains states or provinces sponsored by these enterprises can easily be found on the Internet. Examples below show some of the range of choices available.

UNITED STATES
Colorado
Statistics:
Labor Market Information. Dept. of Labor and Employment. http://www.coworkforce.com/LMI/

Colorado Tax Statistics. Dept. of Revenue. http://www.revenue.state.co.us/Stats_Dir/wrap.asp?incl=taxstats
State Demography. Division of Local Government. http://dola.colorado.gov/dlg/demog/index.html

Colorado Data Book (pdf file). CO Office of Economic Development and International Trade. http://www.state.co.us/oed/business-development/colorado-data-book.cfm
Colorado by the Numbers. University of Colorado. http://www.colorado.edu/libraries/govpubs/online.htm

Directory:
Colorado Food and Agricultural Directory. CO Dept. of Agriculture. http://www.ag.state.co.us/mkt/default.asp
Kansas
Statistics:
Research and Data Center. *Labor Market Information*. KS Dept. of Labor. http://www.dol.ks.gov/lmis/research.html
Kansas Data Book (pdf file) http://kdoch.state.ks.us/KDOCHdocs/BD/databook_all.pdf

Directory:

continued on following page

LCCN 2006-36399

Notes:

Covers Alaska, Arizona, California, Colorado, Idaho, Montana, Nevada, New Mexico, Oregon, Utah, Washington, and Wyoming

Includes bibliographical references (p.253-259); index

Table of contents: http://www.loc.gov/catdir/toc/ecip074/2006036399.html

• Nestor (independent writer, Medford, OR) documents the history of silver and gold mining in the Western states. Chapters, organized by state, have entries that supply location, names of miners who worked a specific site, buildings at mine sites, year of discovery, and ore value. The book includes a glossary of mining terms, one appendix–a copy of "The Miner's Ten Commandments" (1853)–and a bibliography that cites sources under each state in alphabetical order. — *GK*

Transportation

CF13   Atlas of Alberta Railways [Internet Site]. - [Edmonton, AB] : Univ. of Alberta Pr., 2005. - http://railways-atlas.tapor.ualberta.ca/cocoon/atlas/

OCLC 62873375

Access Date: May 2006

---

continued from previousg page

Kansas Business Directory [ResourceLinks.net]

http://www.resourcelinks.net/indexks.htm

Montana

Statistics:

Research and Analysis Bureau. MT Dept. of Labor & Industry.

http://www.ourfactsyourfuture.org

Census and Economic Information Center. MT Dept. of Commerce.

http://ceic.mt.gov

Directory:

Montana Means Business. [click on "Searchable Database"] Governor's Office of Economic Development.

http://business.mt.gov

Montana Business.

http://www.businessmt.com/

Nebraska

Statistics:

Research and Databook. NE Department of Economic Development.

http://www.neded.org/content/view/22/697

Statistics about Nebraska. Univ. of NE-Kearney. Government Documents Dept. [A gateway]

http://www.unk.edu/acad/library/gov_doc/nebraska/index.php?id=12695

Directory:

Nebraska Business Directory. [Automated Systems Inc.]

http://www.asiweb.com/community/business-directory/index.asp

New Mexico

Statistics:

Data Center. New Mexico Economic Development Department.

http://ww1.edd.state.nm.us/index.php?/data

Directory:

New Mexico Business Directory. [Procure@Pro]

http://directory.procureapro.com/b2directory/NM/

North Dakota

Statistics:

Division of Economic Development and Finance. [click on "Data Center"] ND Dept. of Commerce.

http://www.growingnd.com

Directory:

North Dakota Business Directory. [USA Business]

http://www.externalhardrive.com/business/usa/northdakota.html

Oklahoma

Statistics:

Oklahoma's Advantage. [click on "Data & Research"] OK Dept. of Commerce.

http://www.okcommerce.gov

Directory:

OK Yellow Pages. [Superior Business Network].

http://www.sbn.com/newstates/

South Dakota

Statistics:

SD Governor's Office of Economic Development [click on "Demographics and Statistics"]

http://www.sdreadytowork.com

Directory:

South Dakota Business Directory. [Zeezo]

http://south-dakota.zeezo.com/

Texas

Statistics:

Texas Business and Industry Data Center.

http://www.bidc.state.tx.us

Directory:

Texas Business Directory: Businesses in Texas. [BizHwy.com]

http://texas.bizhwy.com/

Wyoming

Statistics:

Economic Analysis Division.Dept. of Administration &

continued on following page

Notes:
Geoffrey Lester, author and cartographer [et al.]
Fees: None

• The site uses the structure of railroads to organize a wide variety of material documenting the history of railways in the province. "Tracks" are divided between main lines such as Canadian Pacific, Canadian National, Grand Trunk Pacific, and their branches, and small local lines. Each has a historical account with references, maps, and supporting items. The "Sidings" section is organized by format and provides photographs, charts, news clippings, poems, statutes, correspondence, reports, tables, book excerpts, diagrams, and illustrations. The almost 225 maps, using the Flash interface with Zoomifyer viewer, were created specifically for the atlas. They deliver even more than is suggested by the title of the site. In addition to the expected railway maps, there are numerous topographic, climatic, territorial, and economic maps. The Prairie branch line network section, for example, includes maps of agriculture in the 1920s for Manitoba and Saskatchewan. As well as long-abandoned lines, a section maps incorporated lines that were never built. A pre-railroad unit provides context for the coming of the railways with sections on early transportation routes, the land grant system, initial settlement, early planners, and the physical geography of Alberta. A "Railway Mania" section covers topics such as town layout, railway finances, timetables, and related industries. Fully searchable with results returned in relevance order. An intriguing site bringing together a multitude of resources of interest to Prairie historians and railway fans alike. — *LMcD*

---

continued from previousg page

Information.
http://eadiv.state.wy.us/
Directory:
The 100% Wyoming Business Directory.
http://allwyomin.uwyo.edu/

CANADA
Alberta

Statistics:
Alberta Statistics. Alberta Economics and Public Finance.
http://www.finance.gov.ab.ca/aboutalberta/index.html
Directory:
Hinton Alberta Business Directory.
http://www.hintonbusinessdirectory.com/
Manitoba

Statistics:
MB Business Facts. Manitoba Business Information Service.
http://www.gov.mb.ca/iedm/invest/busfacts
Directory:
Manitoba Companies. Manitoba Business Information Service.
http://db.itm.gov.mb.ca/MBIS/MCD.nsf/if?readform&ID=CompaniesHome

Manitoba Business Directory. [Classifieds 1000]
http://directory.classifieds1000.com/Manitoba/biusiness
Saskatchewan

Statistics:
Industry and Resources.
http://www.ir.gov.sk.ca
Directory:
Saskatchewan Provincial Directory Towns, Cities and Businesses
http://www.shopsaskatchewan.com/

CF14   Encyclopedia of North American Railroads / ed. by William D. Middleton, George M. Smerk & Roberta L. Diehl. - Bloomington, IN : Indiana Univ. Pr. ; [distr. by] Chesham : Combined Academic, 2007. - 1281 p. ; ill.

Class Numbers:
Library of Congress TF22
ISBN 0253349163 9780253349163
OCLC 85689613
LCCN 2007-297216
Notes:
Reviewed by M. Nilsen: *Choice* 45.2 (Oct. 2007): Review 45-0617

• Consists of more than 500 entries, most with bibliographies, covering all aspects of railroading. Illustrations and photographs are interspersed throughout the text. Five introductory essays cover the development of North American railroads, a social history of railroads, technology and operating practice in the 19th and 20th centuries, and the feasibility of rebuilding the rail system. The appendix consists of statistics relating to railroads, 43 pages of maps, a glossary, and a bibliography of 130 of the most notable railroad books. Contributors are scholars and enthusiasts. Material on railroading in the Prairies-Plains region, spread throughout the book, can be found by browsing the entries or searching the extensive subject index. — *MS*

CF15   Stover, John F. - The Routledge Historical Atlas of the American Railroads / Mark C. Carnes, series ed. - New York : Routledge, 1999. - 1 atlas (144 p.) ; ill. (some col.), col. maps ; 26 cm. - (Routledge atlases of American history).

Class Numbers:
Library of Congress G1201.P3
ISBN 0415921341 0415921406 (pbk.)
LCCN 99-27356
Notes:
Includes bibliographical references; index

Scales differ

• Stover (an authority on railroad history) and Carnes (history, Barnard College) trace the emergence and development of American railroads from the early 19th to the late 20th centuries. The histories of 25 major lines are used to address issues such as engineering, legal structures, and how the railroads standardized time across the country.

Contents of interest include the Grange, the growth of railroads in the 1880s-1890s, and federal land grants. Western lines that receive attention are four Chicago lines; Illinois Central; Missouri Pacific; Missouri, Kansas, and Texas; Denver and Rio Grande Western. — *GK*

CG : POLITICAL SCIENCE

Scope. Includes works having to do with government, politics, political parties, elected officials, elections, constitutions, law, criminal justice, and like matters.

GENERAL WORKS

Encyclopedias

CG1   Erwin, James L., 1974-   . - **Declarations of Independence: Encyclopedia of American Autonomous and Secessionist Movements**. - Westport, CT: Greenwood Pr., 2007. - 240 p.

> Class Numbers:
>   Library of Congress E183
> ISBN 0313332673   9780313332678
> OCLC 71004171
> LCCN 2006-26198
> Notes:
>   Includes bibliographical references (p. [225]-235); index
>   Table of contents: http://www.loc.gov/catdir/toc/
>   ecip0619/20066026198.html

• Erwin's encyclopedia explores 86 American groups that sought separate political existence as nations or states. It includes no local or communal and few Native American movements. Those in the Great Plains region include the Cherokee Nation, North Dakota, Lincoln Territory (South Dakota), South Nebraska, West Kansas, and Texas. Each entry has further readings. Includes a chronological listing; a bibliography of books, articles and Internet sites; and an index of movements, names and locations. More popular than scholarly, it will spur interest and provide starting points for research. — *JD*

Collective Biographies

CG2   **Biographical Dictionary of the American Left** / ed. by Bernard K. Johnpoll and Harvey Klehr. - Westport, CT: Greenwood Pr., 1986. - 493 p.

> Class Numbers:
>   Library of Congress HC84.A2
> ISBN 0313242003
> LCCN 85-27252
> Notes:
>   Index

• Although only 12 of the activists profiled are from Plains states, the many voices of the American Left have long been influential in the region. In the early 20th century, for example, the Socialist Party was active in Oklahoma and the Nonpartisan League with farmers in North Dakota. Covering key leaders in such organizations, entries include general biographical information, other names, year of immigration to the U.S., religious and ethnic background, occupation, father's occupation, political affiliation, major roles in the radical movement, an assessment of contributions, and sources. Appendixes give chronology of key events, entries listed by major radical party affiliation, entries by place of birth, entries by date of birth, a list of those who abandoned the radical movement, and entries by ethnic origin. Indexed by personal, organization, and publication names. Access points do not greatly aid the Great Plains researcher, so previous research will be useful and browsing may be required. A good companion to *Farmers' Organizations* (**G14**) and *The Nonpartisan League, 1915-1922* (**CG49**). — *JD*

CG3   Jones, Nancy Baker. - **Capitol Women: Texas Female Legislators, 1923-1999** / [by] Nancy Baker Jones and Ruthe Winegarten. - Austin, TX: Univ. of Texas Pr., 2000. - 328 p.; ill.

> ISBN 0292740638 (pbk.)
> LCCN 99-44225
> Notes:
>   Book review (H-Net):
>   http//www.h-net.org/review/hrev-a0c6a3.aa
>   Includes bibliographical references
>   Table of contents:
>   http://www.loc.gov/catdir/toc/ fy0609/99044225.html

• *Capitol Women* consists of four essays, 58 biographies, 28 brief "snapshots," appendixes of statistical analysis, and a lengthy bibliography. Essays cover project interviews, historical overviews of women and the Texas political scene, and the basics of the Texas legislature. Each of the biographies contains a portrait of the subject, brief biographical data, and a 4- to 5-page biography of the woman's background and her contributions to Texas government; the snapshots contain portraits and brief biographical information of women who held seats in the legislature at the time of printing. Appendixes list the number of women in each legislative session and give a chronology of events relating to women in Texas government. Useful for biographical data about women politicians from the Plains counties. — *JB*

Atlases

CG4   **Atlas of American Politics, 1960-2000** / [by] J. Clark Archer [et al.]. - Washington, DC: CQ Pr., a division of Congressional Quarterly Inc., 2002. - 1 atlas (242 p.); col. maps; 29 cm.

Class Numbers:
    Library of Congress G1201.F1
ISBN 156802665X
LCCN 2001-18267 ; 2001-5996
Notes:
    Includes bibliographical references; index
    Scale not given

• Using over 200 maps, the atlas examines the relationships of federal, state, and local governments to geography, which is both the organizing principle of government and the source of its diversity. Most are choropleth maps, which use color and shading to show the value of one or more variables. Eight chapters cover contemporary government and politics, presidential elections, Congress, executive branch, judiciary, political culture of the states, foreign policy, and social and economic policy. Maps include Native American population, church adherents, state origins of major Supreme Court cases, methods of capital punishment, firearms injury death rates, spending on education and prisons, popular presidential votes by county, presidential campaign stops, and federally owned land. The chapter on political culture compares state recall provisions, selection of judges, term limits, gubernatorial powers, length of constitutions, party affiliations of elected officials, tax collection, state aid, lottery proceeds, and minority elected officials. An aid to analyzing contemporary differences among Plains states, as well differences among regions and relationships to the federal government. The accompanying interpretive text is footnoted and map sources cited. Indexed by topic, proper name, and region. — *JD*

UNITED STATES

Kansas

CG5   Wilder, Bessie E., 1887-1968. - **Bibliography of the Official Publications of Kansas, 1854-1958.** - [Lawrence, KS]: Governmental Research Center, Univ. of Kansas, 1965. – 1 v.

Class Numbers:
    Library of Congress Z1285
OCLC 3935848
LCCN 65-63730
Notes:
    Contents: Territorial and state publications

• Valuable because it lists early publications, including those issued during the period of the Kansas Territory. Entries are arranged alphabetically by issuing agency, then by date. Notes give information concerning the agency, contents, and occasionally excerpts from laws bearing on the publica-

tion of specific items or series. Holdings are shown for seven depository libraries. Entries are very full, providing title-page transcriptions. A brief supplementary section lists "Kansas Public Documents," which seems to be a binder's title for collections of documents that will be of general interest to the public. — *RB*

Nebraska

CG6   Miewald, Robert D. - **Nebraska Government: Sources and Literature** / [by] Robert Miewald and Robert Sittig. - [Lincoln, NE]: Government Research Institute, Dept. of Political Science, Univ. of Nebraska-Lincoln, 1983. - 41 leaves. - (Nebraska research reports, 5).

Class Numbers:
    Library of Congress JK6616; Z7165.U6
OCLC 11234583
LCCN 84-621214

• Complementing Miewald's *Nebraska Government & Politics* (**CG7**), this bibliography includes scholarly and popular articles, government publications, master's theses, doctoral dissertations, books, and pamphlets. The authors note both the paucity of existing literature and its distortion– most scholarly works study the unicameral legislature, Nebraska's most famous and distinctive feature, ignoring equally important elements. The introduction summarizes the information available in three areas: "Documents and Sources" covers information found in Nebraska libraries, historical resources, and general reference works; "Institutions of Government" describes resources that document the state constitution and the three branches of government; and a third summary treats research institutions and data sources. The bibliography is arranged by broad categories but has no annotations. The authors intend the bibliography both to disseminate information and to form the basis for future research. A revised edition is needed. —*JD*

CG7   Miewald, Robert D., ed. - **Nebraska Government & Politics**. - Lincoln, NE: Univ. of Nebraska Pr., 1984. - 230 p.; ill.

Class Numbers:
    Library of Congress JK6616
ISBN 0803230788   0803280037 (pbk.)
OCLC 9324584
LCCN 83-3684
Notes:
    Bibliography: p. [207]-226; index

• Although not arranged in a format that resembles other reference sources, this book belongs in every Nebraska reference collection. The primary historical, descriptive work about Nebraska's unicameral legislature and other unique features of

Nebraska government, it presents behind-the-scenes stories of state agencies that are known to most readers only through directories and agency Internet sites. Brief chapters on aspects of state government (the constitution, the governor and other elected executives, the legislature, the judiciary, the bureaucracy, the citizens, tax and budget structure, local government, intergovernmental relations) form an encyclopedia of state government functions. The complex development of the government through accident, design, politics, and social pressure is analyzed by an astute group of University of Nebraska political scientists. A bibliography emphasizing the postwar years cites books, government publications, articles, master's theses, doctoral dissertations, and surveys conducted by the University's Bureau of Sociological Research. An updated version that will include the last 20 years is badly needed, but this title is still vital and in print. — *JD*

CG8   Boards and Commissions in Nebraska / Nebraska. Legislature. Legislative Research Div. - [1st] (1990s)- . Lincoln, NE: Nebraska Legislature; Legislative Research Div., 1990s- . Annual.

    Class Numbers:
        Library of Congress JK6630
        OCLC 41208174
        LCCN 99-103974
• Nebraska currently has over 228 statutory boards with a

variety of significant responsibilities such as overseeing programs, conducting studies, regulating professional licenses, and advising state agencies. They include the Nebraska Ethanol Board, Interrelated Water Review Board, Commission on Indian Affairs, and Rural Health Advisory Commission. Compiled and updated annually, this document describes new boards, lists repealed boards, and summarizes legislative actions affecting boards. Tables show each board, the statute that created it; whether members must be confirmed by the legislature; any termination date for the board; whether the statute allows for expenses; and any maximum per diem rate allowed by statute. It is a handy reference used primarily to locate enabling statutes. The latest issue is available online through the official Internet site *Legislative Audit and Research Office* at http://www.unicam. state.ne.us/web/public/legresearch. — *JD*

CG9   Nebraska Blue Book. - Lincoln, NE: Nebraska Legislative Council, 1899– . Annual.

    Class Numbers:
        Library of Congress JK6630
        Government Document Nebraska L3000 D001
    LCCN 99-1456
    Notes:
        Online version: http://www.unicam.state.ne.us/bluebook/
        Title and issuing agency vary.

Site List 11

Official Government Sites

Official Internet sites maintained by state or provincial governments offer directories, statistics, facts, histories, images, tourism guides, laws, online services, state publications, and links to state agencies, local governments, and other organizations.

United States

Colorado: Colorado.gov
http://www.colorado.gov

Kansas: Kansas.gov
http://www.accesskansas.org

Montana: mt.gov
http://mt.gov

Nebraska: Nebraska.gov
http://www.nebraska.gov

New Mexico: Welcome to New Mexico
http://www.state.nm.us

North Dakota: nd.gov
http://www.nd.gov

Oklahoma: ok.gov
http://www.oklahoma.gov

South Dakota: sd.gov
http://www.state.sd.us

Texas: TexasOnline
http://www.texasonline.com

Wyoming: Wyoming Welcomes You
http://wyoming.gov

Canada

Alberta: Government of Alberta
http://www.gov.ab.ca

Manitoba: Province of Manitoba
http://www.gov.mb.ca

Saskatchewan: Government of Saskatchewan
http://www.gov.sk.ca

CG9a Nebraska Blue Book Online [Internet Site] /
Nebraska. Office of Unicameral Legislature. - Lincoln,
NE: Nebraska Office of Unicameral Legislature, 199?–   .
http://www.unicam.state.ne.us/bluebook/

Access Date: Jan. 2005
Notes:
    Includes table of contents; index
Fees: None

• The official reference manual and directory of the State of
Nebraska, *Blue Book* provides information about the structure and operation of the federal, state, and local governments in Nebraska, augmented by sections on history, politics, geography, education, economy, climate, people, and
culture. It includes tribal/sovereign governments, explanation of Nebraska's unique unicameral legislature, and
extended descriptions of the activities of government agencies. It links to online sites for official manuals of other
states. *Blue Book* is published biennially, but the online version is the most recently released version; earlier numbers
are available in printed form. — *JD*

CG10 Nebraska Legislature Online [Internet Site]. -
Lincoln, NE: Nebraska Unicameral Legislature, 199?-   . -
http://www.unicam.state.ne.us/index.htm

Access Date: Jan. 2005
Fees: None

• The Nebraska Legislature's motto, "The salvation of the
state is watchfulness in the citizen," appears in the title logo
of this site, which provides numerous venues for citizens to
keep watch over the legislature (or as it likes to call itself,
the "Unicameral"). Searches for bills or documents by number or keyword, committee hearing schedule, session calendar, daily legislative agenda, Senators' voting records, and a
list of registered lobbyists make this a working site for state
officials, lobbyists, and citizens. Other services include
"BillTracker" (e-mail updates about bills), "UniCAM Live!"
(video streaming of current action on the floor), and
"Unicameral Update Online" (brief news updates of actions in
committee and on the floor). The site supplies a thorough
description of the legislature's unusual structure and operation,
a searchable database of current Nebraska statutes, the
Nebraska Constitution, and an online version of *Nebraska Blue
Book* (**CG9a**), the official state manual. — *JD*

CG11 Nebraska State Government Directory /
Nebraska Div. of Communications. - 1977-   . [Lincoln,
NE: Nebraska Div. of Communications], 1977-   .
Biennial.

Class Numbers:
    Library of Congress JK6630
OCLC 5819882

LCCN 80-60231
Notes:
    Preceding title: *Nebraska Capitol Directory*

• Both an in-house tool and a public document, this comprehensive directory of state government can be a more
convenient source of contact information than the state
government Internet site. The first section lists state legislators with districts, e-mail addresses, capitol phones, home
addresses, and home phones. The second section is an
alphabetical list of departments, boards, commissions and
their subunits, with locations, URLs, personnel and e-mail
addresses. The third section is an alphabetical list of all personnel, with departments, e-mail addresses, and telephone
numbers. It includes the faculty and staff of the state colleges, but not the University of Nebraska campuses. — *JD*

North Dakota

**CG12 Bird, J.W. - North Dakota Government &
Politics: A Selected Annotated Bibliography** / prepared by
J.W. Bird, Wilbur Stolt, Dan Rylance. - Bismarck, ND:
State Library Commission, 1975. - 23 p. - (North Dakota
library notes, v. 6 no. 6).

Class Numbers:
    Library of Congress JKI6146; Z7165.U6;
    Z732.N9 N925 v. 6 no. 6

• Bird and Rylance (both Univ. of North Dakota) and Stolt
(teacher, Manvel, ND) provide an annotated bibliography
of 139 records on North Dakota government and politics.
The work's two parts deal with the territorial period, 1861-
1889, and with the state from admission in 1890 through
the late 20th century. There are six subject subdivisions–
general, government, isolationism, populism, progressivism,
and Nonpartisan League. — *GK*

CG13 North Dakota Blue Book. - 1st-   . [Bismarck,
ND, etc.]: North Dakota Dept. of State [publisher varies],
1887-   . Biennial.

OCLC 1760600

• First published as a legislative guide for Dakota Territory
(1887), *Blue Book*, now in its 29th edition, provides a variety of information relating to the state. Sections include
writers, poets, and artists; North Dakota almanac; federal-
state relationships; judicial branch; executive branch; legislative branch; tribal-state relationships; elections; education; water resources; agriculture; and commerce, each
offering brief history and statistics related to the topic. The
opening section ("Notable Contributors to the Arts") supplies brief biographies and work samples. The almanac sec-

tion provides general statistics, description of the capitol grounds with its sculptures, and recipients of the Rough Rider awards given to outstanding North Dakota citizens. Tribal-state relationships profiles past and present tribal leaders. *Blue Book* includes color and black-and-white photographs, maps, and a fairly comprehensive index. Useful as a ready reference for North Dakota government and statistics. — *JB*

CG14 University of North Dakota. Bureau of Governmental Affairs. - **The Structure of North Dakota State Government: A Compendium of North Dakota State Agencies, Boards, Commissions & Institutions.** - Bismarck, ND: North Dakota State Library, 1981. - 1 v. (various pagings).

> Class Numbers:
>   Library of Congress JK6431
>   OCLC 8975761
>   LCCN 82-622148
>   Notes:
>   Index

• This directory provides descriptions of North Dakota state government agencies, councils, boards, and commissions. State agencies, including the Edible Bean and Potato councils, are listed in alphabetical order. Each entry contains the legislative code, statute, or constitutional article that created the agency, major responsibilities, and components of that body. Two appendixes: Repeal, major revision, or name changes of state agencies after 1979; and State agencies created since 1979. — *GK*

South Dakota

CG15 Clem, Alan L., 1929-   , comp. - **A Bibliography of South Dakota Government and Politics** / comp. by Alan L. Clem and George M. Platt. - Vermillion, SD: Governmental Research Bureau, Univ. of South Dakota, 1965. - 80 p.; map. - (University of South Dakota. Governmental Research Bureau. Report, 53).

> Class Numbers:
>   Library of Congress KFS3421.Z9 S6
>   LCCN 65-63014
>   Notes:
>   Supplements: L.M. Carlson, *Bibliography on South Dakota Government*, 1951

• Clem and Platt (government, Univ. of South Dakota) provide a bibliography of materials related to South Dakota government for use by public officials, teachers, students, and researchers. Their work primarily indexes entries from two sources, publications by the Government Research Bureau and articles in *South Dakota Journal of County*

Government, 1952-1964. The bibliography is arranged in 20 subject categories, subarranged by author or title. Categories are: "Constitution," "Intergovernmental Relations," "Citizenship," "Elections," "Legislative Bodies," "Judicial Bodies," "Administration of State, County, or Municipal Government," "Personnel," "Taxes," "Fiscal Planning," "Agriculture," "Natural Resources," "Education," "Health," "Transportation," "Law Enforcement," "Business," and "Public Utilities." Three appendixes list South Dakota newspapers, printed periodicals (a selected list), and state offices and agencies. — *GK*

CG16 **An Index of South Dakota State Government Publications** / [by] John N. Olsgaard, Connie Meyer. - [1st] (1975/76)-   . Vermillion, SD: I.D. Weeks Library, Univ. of South Dakota, 1978-   . Quarterly.

> Class Numbers:
>   Library of Congress Z1223.5.S62
>   OCLC 4825409
>   Notes:
>   1978 cumulation comp. with assistance of Connie Meyer
>   1979 vol. publ. as: *A Cumulative Index of South Dakota State Government Publications, 1975- 1979*
>   Supplement: *Index of South Dakota State Government Publications. Serials Supplement.* ISSN 0277-5069

• Indexes South Dakota government publications issued monthly by the State Library, 1975-1979. Olsgaard (librarian, Univ. of South Dakota) arranges the volume in three sections. First comes a bibliography that lists the entry with a bibliographic code number, author, title, full corporate author, South Dakota document number, year published, volume, and issue number; second is an author index; and the final part is a keyword index that lists title, author name, and significant searchable words. The compiler suggests that users go to the keyword index first, find the bibliographic code number, then proceed to the bibliography section. — *GK*

Texas

CG17 **Texas Legislative Handbook.** - [1st] (1900s)–   . Dallas, TX: Legislative Handbook, 1900s-   . Biennial.

> Class Numbers:
>   Library of Congress JK4830
>   OCLC 4721222
>   LCCN 79-643346
>   Notes:
>   Some issues also called *Legislative Roster with Committees*

• A pocket-sized directory designed for use during the biennial legislative session. Lists legislators, Capitol contact information, and committee assignments. Includes a map of the Capitol complex, maps showing House and Senate districts, a flow chart of the legislative process, a Senate seating chart, telephone numbers for executive officers and agencies, and permanent and session-specific committees. — *MS*

CG18   Texas Legislature Online [Internet Site]. - Austin, TX: Texas State Legislature, 2000s-   . - http://www.capitol.state.tx.us/

    Access Date: June 2007
    Fees: None

• A site that intends to supply information about the Legislature and the procedure used to introduce, argue, amend, and vote on pending legislation. The houses in the Texas Legislature mirror those in the federal government (the House has a Speaker, but in the Senate the Lieutenant Governor presides). Users can search for members of both houses, find committee assignments and committee meetings, scan calendars, read journals, follow the progress of individual bills, and read state statutes and the Texas Constitution. The site provides tutorials on following bills and how bills become law. Useful in finding addresses for individual members and following current legislation. Both House and Senate provide pages for children. — *RB*

Wyoming

CG19   Harmon, Robert Bartlett, 1932-   . - Government and Politics in Wyoming: An Information Source Survey. - Monticello, IL: Vance Bibliographies, 1980. - 16 p. - (Public administration series. Bibliography, P-556).

    Class Numbers:
        Library of Congress Z7164.A2 P83

• A very brief bibliography that cites about 60 sources, relying heavily on Wyoming state government publications, that provide information about state government and politics (collections, branches of state government, constitution). No index. —*RB*

C A N A D A

Alberta

CG20   Alberta Premiers of the Twentieth Century / ed. by Bradford J. Rennie. - Regina, SK: Canadian Plains Research Center, Univ. of Regina, 2004. - 298 p.; ill. - (TBS; 10).

    Class Numbers:
        National Library of Canada FC3655

ISBN 0889771510
OCLC 55473537
Notes:
    Includes bibliographical references; index

• Essays, the majority written by historians and political scientists, examining the careers of each of the 12 men who have occupied the office of premier. Superficially similar, Alberta and Saskatchewan have had very different political histories; the book provides a useful counterpoint to the volume treating the latter province (**CG29**). — *LMcD*

CG21   Mardon, Ernest George, 1928-   . - The Men of the Dawn: District of Alberta Politicians, North West Territories 1882-1905; Politicians from the North West Territories of the District of Alberta and Candidates for the First Alberta General Election / [by] Ernest George Mardon, Austin Albert Mardon. - Edmonton, AB: Shoestring Pr., 1991. - 160 p.

    Class Numbers:
        Library of Congress F1078
        National Library of Canada FC3217.1 A1
    ISBN 1895385229 1895385164 (pbk.)
        9781895385229 9781895385168 (pbk.)
    OCLC 23052284
    Notes:
        Bibliography: p. 154

• Brief biographical accounts of territorial Alberta politicians; a somewhat amateurish production, with blank time charts, maps, and legislative appendixes. — *LMcD*

CG22   McDougall, D. B., 1938-   . - Premiers of the Northwest Territories and Alberta, 1897-1991. - Edmonton, AB: Alberta Legislature Library, 1991. - 62 p.; col. ill.

    Class Numbers:
        Library of Congress F1060.3
    OCLC 25872777
    LCCN 91-212959
    Notes:
        Includes bibliographical references (p. 61-62)

• Biographical summaries of the single territorial premier (1897-1905) and his 11 successors after Alberta became a province in 1905. — *LMcD*

CG23   Mardon, Ernest G., 1928-   . - Alberta Election Results 1882-1992 / by Ernest Mardon and Austin Mardon. - [Edmonton, AB?]: Documentary Heritage Society of Alberta in association with Alberta Community Development, 1993. - 205 p.

    Class Numbers:

Library of Congress JL339 A15
OCLC 28715298

• Arranged by constituency, giving candidates, parties, and results for each election. Results for the District of Alberta, Northwest Territories, 1882-1905, are in an appendix. Lacks a name index. Useful statistical source for the electoral history of Alberta, both provincial and federal. Companion to the authors' *Who's Who in Alberta Politics, 1882-1970* (**CG27**) and *Alberta Mormon Politicians* (**CG25**). — *LMcD*

CG24   Mardon, Ernest G., 1928- . - **Alberta Judicial Biographical Dictionary** / Ernest G. Mardon & Austin A. Mardon. – Edmonton, AB: RTAJ Fry Pr., 1990. - 132 leaves.

Class Numbers:
National Library of Canada KE396 A4
ISBN 1895385121 (pbk.) 1895385148
OCLC 23052291

• An introductory essay, almost a civics lesson, outlines the structure of Canada's government and court systems. Lists of various court levels and their justices follow in chronological order. Biographies of judges from Alberta's inception in 1905 to 1990 are grouped by prime minister making the appointment, rather than listed in a more customary alphabetical order. A contribution to Prairie legal history. — *LMcD*

CG25   Mardon, Ernest G., 1928- . - **Alberta Mormon Politicians** / [by] Ernest G. Mardon and Austin A. Mardon; introd. by Brigham Y. Card. - Edmonton, AB: Fisher House Publ., 1992. - 76 p.; map, ports.

Class Numbers:
Library of Congress F1080.M67
National Library of Canada FC3700 M8
ISBN 0969530902 (pbk.) 0969530903
    0969530904 (leather)
OCLC 24909895
Notes:
Includes bibliographical references and index
Originally published under title: *Alberta Ethnic Mormon Politicians, 1880s-1990s*

• Biographies of 80 candidates in provincial and federal elections, 1882-1991. Election results, by electoral district and date, are included. A brief overview of Mormon history in Alberta provides a background for this record of political involvement by a distinctive religious minority. — *LMcD*

CG26   Mardon, Ernest G. - **French Canadians in the**

Political Life of the Province of Alberta: 1891-2005 / [by] Ernest G. Mardon, Austin Mardon & Allyson V. Riobar. - Edmonton, AB: Institut pour le patrimoine de la francophonie de l'Ouest canadien, 2007. - 117 p.: ill., ports.

Class Numbers:
National Library of Canada FC3700.5
ISBN 9781551952123
OCLC 85737524
Notes:
Includes bibliographical references and index.

• Biographical notes, arranged by surname, of Alberta Francophone members of the Canadian Parliament (federal) and Alberta Legislature (provincial); unsuccessful candidates are also included. Appendixes identify senators, members of Parliament and members of the Legislative Assembly, and list election results from constituencies having a sizable Francophone population. A companion piece to the authors' similar works on Alberta politicians of German and Mormon background. —*LMcD*

CG27   Mardon, Ernest G. - **Who's Who in Alberta Politics, 1882-1970** / Ernest George Mardon, Austin Albert Mardon, May Mardon. - Edmonton, AB: Golden Meteorite Pr., 2001. - 1024 p.

Class Numbers:
National Library of Canada FC3674.1
ISBN 1894573935
OCLC 47365513

• Biographical sketches, usually a single paragraph, of provincial and federal legislators. Appendixes list lieutenant-governors, premiers, senators, members of Parliament, and holders of other offices. Companion volume to the authors' *Alberta Election Results 1882-1992* (**CG23**). —*LMcD*

CG28   Powell, Karen L. - **Reference Guide to Alberta Government Committees, 1905-1980**. - Edmonton, AB: Alberta Legislative Library, Cooperative Government Library Services, 1982. - ca. 150 p.

Class Numbers:
Library of Congress JL333.3 C6
National Library of Canada COP.AL.4439
OCLC 15965252
Notes:
Includes bibliography and index

• Checklist of departmental and interdepartmental committees, arranged by first word in the name; legislative committees are not included. Entries provide appointment information, purpose, membership, and citations of reports issued. — *LMcD*

Saskatchewan

CG29 Barnhart, Gordon, ed. - **Saskatchewan Premiers of the Twentieth Century**. - Regina, SK: Univ. of Regina, Canadian Plains Research Center, 2004. - 418 p.; ill. - (TBS; 8).

> Class Numbers:
>   National Library of Canada FC3505
>   ISBN 0889771642
>   OCLC 53307265

• Chapter-length biographies, with critical assessment of accomplishments and legacy, of the first 13 leaders of the provincial government. A useful addition to the study of Saskatchewan politics. — *LMcD*

CG30 **Directory of Members of Parliament and Federal Elections for the North-West Territories and Saskatchewan, 1887-1966**. - [Rev.ed.] - Regina, SK: Saskatchewan Archives Board, 1967. - 64 p.; maps.

> Class Numbers:
>   Library of Congress JL307
>   OCLC 13948249
>   Notes:
>   Electronic book: http://www.saskarchives.com/web/
>   services-gov-directory.html
>   First ed. prepared by staff of the Saskatchewan Archives
>   under the direction of Lewis H. Thomas; E. C. Morgan
>   did revisions for the Revised ed.

• Senators and MPs for the two jurisdictions are listed alphabetically with dates of birth and death, term of office and party affiliation. MPs are also given by election, sub-arranged by electoral district. Election results by district and date indicate candidates, party, and number of votes. Maps illustrate changes in electoral boundaries. The History of "Federal Ridings Since 1867" section of the Parliament of Canada Internet site (http://www.parl.gc.ca/) updates the information and provides searching by province, district, candidate, and election. It also outlines the evolution of individual electoral districts, giving candidates, their occupations, and vote totals in each election. — *LMcD*

CG31 Quiring, Brett, ed. - **Saskatchewan Politicians: Lives Past and Present**. - Regina, SK: Canadian Plains Research Center, Univ. of Regina, 2004. - 249 p.; ill. - (The Saskatchewan Lives Past and Present Series).

> Class Numbers:
>   Library of Congress F1070.8
>   National Library of Canada FC3505
>   ISBN 0889771650
>   OCLC 59402931
>   LCCN 2005-362065

• Biographical profiles of some 275 provincial and federal politicians, from territorial days to the present; municipal politicians are excluded. Premiers, lieutenant-governors, federal cabinet ministers, noteworthy members of the Legislative Assembly, members of Parliament, senators, and party activists are well represented. The brief sketches summarize individuals' careers and accomplishments; many entries conclude with suggestions for further reading. Usefully presents a composite picture of Saskatchewan politics. — *LMcD*

CG32 **Saskatchewan. Legislative Assembly. - Guide to the Records of Royal and Special Commissions and Committees of Inquiry Appointed by the Province of Saskatchewan Revised to December 31, 1968**. - [Regina, SK?: s.n.], 1968. - 103, 7 leaves.

> Class Numbers:
>   Library of Congress JL302
>   OCLC 61539737

• Directory of official inquiries on matters of public concern, 1906-1968, arranged chronologically, indicating for each the purpose, membership, and resulting reports. Among predictably weighty affairs such as education, rural land assessment, and judicial reform are oddities such as a 1915 commission on the South Carolina system of liquor dispensaries. The guide brings together details on a sometimes elusive form of government document. Subject index. — *LMcD*

CG33 Saskatchewan Archives Board. - **Saskatchewan Executive and Legislative Directory, 1905-1970**. - Regina, SK: Saskatchewan Archives Board, 1971. - 171 p.; maps.

> Class Numbers:
>   Library of Congress JL307.A2
>   OCLC 539171
>   LCCN 72-187400
>   Notes:
>   Electronic book: http://www.saskarchives.com/web/
>   services-gov-directory.html
>   First ed. publ. 1954 under title: *Directory of Saskatchewan
>   Ministries, Members of the Legislative Assembly and
>   Elections, 1905-53*
>   *Supplement*, publ. 1978, covered 1964-1977

• Information about members of the Executive Council and Legislative Assembly, deputy ministers, and candidates in provincial elections. Not a biographical directory but a listing of holders of various offices. Election results by electoral district, with maps showing the evolution of boundaries. The online version extends the coverage to 2000. — *LMcD*

CG34 **Saskatchewan Municipal Directory**. - [1st] (1958)-   . Regina, SK: Saskatchewan Municipal Government, 1958-   . Irregular.

Class Numbers:
Library of Congress JS1721.S3
National Library of Canada JS1721
OCLC 2441690
LCCN 70-12510; cn 75-33484
Notes:
Electronic book: http://www.municipal.gov.sk.ca/
Issued variously by Dept. of Municipal Affairs;
Sakatchewan Municipal Affairs; Saskatchewan Urban
Affairs; and Saskatchewan Rural Development
Preceding title: *Municipal Directory*

• Provides contact data, property assessment figures, population, officials, and other information for communities of various sizes, from northern hamlets to cities, as well as rural municipalities. It also lists staff from relevant provincial departments, municipal associations, and health districts. —*LMcD*

CG35 Whiteway, Kenneth. - **Biographical Directory of the Judges of Saskatchewan** / comp. by Ken Whiteway and Jim Ridgway. - Saskatoon, SK: Univ. of Saskatchewan Libraries, 1991. - 42 leaves.

Class Numbers:
Library of Congress KE 396

• Directory of the Saskatchewan judiciary as of 1990. Outlines the court system with the names of judges at each level. Biographies, compiled from surveys, follow alphabetically. — *LMcD*

CONSTITUTIONS

CG36 **Reference Guides to the State Constitutions of the United States** / G. Alan Tarr, series ed. - Westport, CT: Greenwood Pr., 1990- .

OCLC 28231138
Notes:
Publisher projects publication of volumes for all states of
the U.S. (In progress.)
Title is general series title; individual volumes publ. for
Prairies-Plains states are: no. 5, James E. Leahy, *The
North Dakota State Constitution.* Westport, CT:
Praeger, 2004. ISBN 0313311439; no. 9, Dale A.
Oesterie, Richard B. Collins, *The Colorado State
Constitution.* Westport, CT: Greenwood Pr., 2002.
ISBN 0313308497; no. 10, Danny M. Adkinson, Lisa
McNair Palmer, *The Oklahoma State Constitution.*
Greenwood Pr., 2001. ISBN 0313275076; no. 11, Larry
M. Elison, Fritz Snyder, *The Montana State
Constitution.* Greenwood Pr., 2000. ISBN
0313273464; no. 17, Janice C. May, *The Texas State
Constitution.* Greenwood, 1996. ISBN 0313266379;
no. 20, Chuck Smith, *The New Mexico State
Constitution.* Greenwood Pr., 1996. ISBN
0313295484; no. 33, Robert D. Miewald, Peter J.
Longo, *The Nebraska State Constitution.* Greenwood

Pr., 1993. ISBN 0313279470; no. 35, Robert S. Keiter,
Tim Newcomb, *The Wyoming State Constitution.*
Greenwood Pr., 1992. ISBN 0313272476; no. 37,
Francis H. Heller, *The Kansas State Constitution.*
Greenwood Pr., 1992. ISBN 0313264732

• Of the ten Prairies-Plains states, only the volume on South Dakota awaits publication. The standard series format begins with a constitutional history followed by the text of the constitution with section-by-section expert commentary that explains the provisions, their origins, and their subsequent interpretations in the courts. A bibliographic essay gives background reading on the state, sources on the constitution, and a detailed bibliography organized by constitution section. Includes footnotes on the commentary, a table of cases cited, and a subject index. A unique and exceedingly useful series of interest to scholars, students, lawmakers, activists, and legal analysts. A summary volume and a cumulative index volume are planned. —*JD*

CRIMINOLOGY; LAW ENFORCEMENT

CG37 Anderson, Ken, 1952- . - **Crime in Texas: Your Complete Guide to the Criminal Justice System**. - Rev. ed. - Austin, TX: Univ. of Texas Pr., 2005. - 208 p.

Class Numbers:
Library of Congress HV9955.T4
ISBN 0292706197 (pbk.)
LCCN 2004-16473
Notes:
Index
Table of contents: http://www.loc.gov/catdir/toc/
ecip0420/2004016473.html

• Organized in six chapters: the system, police, prosecutors, and judges; criminal procedures; criminal law; criminal punishment; victims' rights; and juvenile system. Includes a history of the Texas criminal justice system, a table of crimes and punishment with the applicable section of the criminal justice code, a glossary, and index. Anderson is a judge, former district attorney, and victims' rights advocate. —*MS*

CG38 **Crime in Nebraska [Internet Site]**. - Lincoln, NE: Nebraska Commission on Law Enforcement and Criminal Justice, 1995- . - http://www.ncc.state.ne.us/documents/stats_report_and_research.htm

Class Numbers:
Library of Congress HV7277
OCLC 38141050
Access Date: Jan. 2006
Notes:
Annual

Available in printed form, 1971–
Fees: None

• Compiles crime statistics in compliance with federal statutes as part of the National Uniform Crime Reporting program. One hundred sixty-four law enforcement agencies in Nebraska (sheriff departments, police departments, Nebraska State Patrol, two campus police departments, State Fire Marshal's Office) provide data on numbers of crimes, arrests, and citations. The Commission Internet site links to pdf files of crime reports produced annually in print: a preliminary report, a list by reporting agency, and a final report. Tables include hate crimes by type, burglaries by place of occurrence, and murder by age, sex, and race. Includes for some data a crime index measuring the extent, fluctuation, and distribution of crime, and a crime rate. Definitions of crimes and analyses of data accompany the tables. Time lag for publishing or posting final data is two to three years. Printed reports, produced since 1971, are distributed on microfiche to Nebraska depository libraries. — *JD*

CG39 Nebraska Criminal Justice Directory / Nebraska Commission on Law Enforcement and Criminal Justice. - [1st] (May 1986)-   . Lincoln, NE: Nebraska Commission on Law Enforcement and Criminal Justice, 1986-   . Annual.

Class Numbers:
Library of Congress HV9955.N2
Government Document Nebraska L2500 D002
OCLC 17820461
LCCN 88-648612

• Developed to foster communications among law enforcement personnel, the Directory attempts to list comprehensively criminal justice personnel throughout the state— local, state, county, and federal field offices. Its eight sections cover law enforcement offices and personnel, corrections facilities, the judicial system, criminal justice education, representatives in the Nebraska Legislature and U.S. Congress, victims' programs, criminal justice organizations, and criminal justice Internet sites. Among categories that often prove elusive are campus police departments, tribal courts, mediation centers, county and city jails, criminal justice degree programs, law enforcement training centers, domestic violence and sexual assault programs, and railroad security offices. Gives only directory information (address, telephone, fax, e-mail, etc.). — *JD*

ELECTIONS

CG40 Congressional Quarterly Inc. - **Presidential Elections, 1789-2004**. - Washington, DC: CQ Pr., 2005. - 277 p.; ill., maps.

Class Numbers:

Library of Congress JK524
ISBN 1568029837
OCLC 62557724
Notes:
New edition published the year following each presidential election.

• Statistics include state-by-state electoral votes for president, popular vote for president 1824 and quadrennially thereafter, and primary returns 1912 and quadrennially thereafter. Background information covers the electoral college; presidential primaries; nominating conventions; and biographies of all presidential and vice-presidential candidates. A variety of tables and sidebars cover topics such as party nominees for each election, major platform fights at party conventions, political party rules, and convention keynote speakers. Minor candidates are included. Bibliography and index by name and topic. A convenient source for tracking Great Plains voting records over time and a good companion to *Historical Atlas of Political Parties in the United States Congress, 1789-1989* (**CG51**). — JD

ELECTED OFFICIALS

CG41 Kallenbach, Joseph E., 1903-   . - **American State Governors, 1776-1976** / by Joseph E. Kallenbach and Jessamine S. Kallenbach. - Dobbs Ferry, NY: Oceana Publ., 1977-1982. - 3 v.

Class Numbers:
Library of Congress JK2447
ISBN 0379006650
OCLC 2655614
LCCN 76-51519
Notes:
Bibliography: v. 3, p. 611-629; index
Contents: v. 1, Electoral and Personal Data; v. 2, Biographical Data, Alabama – Montana; v. 3, Biographical Data, Nebraska – Wyoming

• Kallenbach (political science emeritus, Univ. of Michigan) presents a reference set about governors of states in the U.S. in observance of the country's 1976 bicentennial. Vol. 1 supplies addresses and electoral and personal data for each state, including the name of the governor, political party, period of incumbency, and the number of votes, analyzed by candidate and party. Vols. 2 and 3 include brief biographical sketches for each governor, listed under state by terms of office. Sources consulted and cumulative index in v. 3. — *GK*

CG42 Oyos, Lynwood. - **Over a Century of Leadership: South Dakota Territorial and State Governors**. - Sioux Falls, SD: Center for Western Studies, Augustana College, 1987. - xx, 224 p.; ports.

Class Numbers:

Library of Congress JK6551
ISBN 0931170346
LCCN 87-71833
Notes:
"1861-1987, A Retrospective." (Cover)
Includes bibliographical references (p. 223-224)
Revision and expansion of: Charles Dalthrop, South
    Dakota Governors, 1953

• Oyos (history, Augustana College) provides biographical sketches of governors of South Dakota who held office between 1889 and 1987, expanding the coverage of Dalthrop's book and adding Dakota territorial governors, 1861-1889. Sketches range in length from three to six pages and supply photographs of all the subjects. The bibliography lists no periodical articles, only books. — GK

CG43   Pressler, Larry, 1942-   . - **U.S. Senators from the Prairie.** - Vermillion, SD: Dakota Pr., 1982. - 196 p.; ill.

Class Numbers:
    Library of Congress E747
ISBN 0882490338 0882490346 (pbk.)
OCLC 6914717
LCCN 80-25220
Notes:
    Bibliography: p. 189-192; index

• Pressler (former South Dakota senator) presents biographical sketches of 23 senators from the state of South Dakota. The work is an analysis of their role in national and state politics. Each portrait provides personal background information (date of birth, death, education, spouses, children, and military service), a brief description of their political accomplishments, and excerpts from important speeches. Foreword comments by William O. Farber (political science emeritus, Univ. of South Dakota), George McGovern, and Howard Baker, Jr. (U.S. senators). Illustrations, charts, bibliography. — *GK*

CG44   Sharp, Nancy Weatherly. - **American Legislative Leaders in the Midwest, 1911-1994** / Nancy Weatherly Sharp and James Roger Sharp, eds.; Gina Petonito and Kevin G. Atwater, assistant eds.; Charles F. Ritter and Jon L. Wakelyn, advisory eds. - Westport, CT: Greenwood Pr., 1997. - 358 p.

Class Numbers:
    Library of Congress F350.5
ISBN 0313302146
LCCN 96-53519
Notes:
    Includes bibliographical references (p. [249]-257); index

• The greater part of this volume is an alphabetical listing of legislative leaders in Midwestern states. Numerous appen-

dixes list, e.g., political party, gender, education, and occupation, and there is a name index to entries. Each biographical entry provides personal dates, educational background, record of public service, and additional sources for biographical information. Each entry is signed; a roster of contributors gives organizational affiliations. — *MB*

CG45   Socolofsky, Homer Edward, 1922-   . - **Kansas Governors.** - Lawrence, KS: Univ. Pr. of Kansas, c1990. - 255 p.; ill., maps.

Class Numbers:
    Library of Congress F680 .S63 1990
ISBN 0700604219
LCCN 89-29123
Notes:
    Includes bibliographical references (p. 235-241); index
    Review by R.S. La Forte: *Choice* 28 (Oct. 1990): review
      28-1166

• A biographical dictionary of all Kansas territorial governors, acting governors, and governors of the state from territorial formation (1854) through 1989. An interesting introductory section provides contextual material (e.g., birthplaces of the governors, election data, and a table showing comparative information about the governors' backgrounds– educational level, religious affiliation, age at inauguration). Biographical entries start with essential biographical information: birth, education, family, death (where applicable), term of service. Each entry has a formal photograph and one or more additional illustrations. Entries are typically several pages in length and close with references. The volume ends with notes, an extensive bibliography, and a good subject index. — *MB*

FOREIGN RELATIONS

CG46   Valk, Barbara G. - **BorderLine: A Bibliography of the United States-Mexico Borderlands** / [by] Barbara G. Valk, with Ana María Cobos [et al.]. - Riverside, CA: UC MEXUS, Univ. of California Consortium on Mexico and the United States; Los Angeles, CA: UCLA Latin American Center Publications, 1992. - xxii, 711 p. - (UCLA Latin American Center Publications. Reference series, v. 12).

Class Numbers:
    Library of Congress Z1251.M44
ISBN 0879031123
LCCN 88-4565
Notes:
    Index

• Although the Prairies-Plains region touches the U.S.-Mexican border only along the Rio Grande east of Big Bend, this work, concentrating on the entire border region, deserves inclusion for its completeness and for numerous occasions in which it dwells on subjects of Prairies-Plains interest. Its nearly 9,000 entries cover all aspects of the international boundary (including U.S. states of Texas, New Mexico, Arizona, and California, and Mexican states of Baja California Norte, Sonora, Chihuahua, Coahuila, Nuevo León, and Tamaulipas), arranging entries (most without annotations) under 26 topics (e.g., "Biotic Characteristics," "Urbanization," "Emigration and Immigration," "Literature and the Arts"). These topics are subdivided, sometimes with subheadings and always by "U.S. Borderlands" and "Mexican Borderlands," both sub-arranged by state. No subject bearing on these states and on the friction caused by their proximity is ignored. Entries, the editor claims, follow MARC cataloging rules, but more important is that they observe strict consistency and provide all needed elements for all the formats cataloged (books, serials, articles, government publications, etc.). Entries in many sections touch on Prairies-Plains interests, especially for Texas and New Mexico. Index of names. Thorough and exhaustive. — *RB*

LAW

CG47 Gardner, Linda, 1940-   , comp. - **The Texas Supreme Court: An Index of Selected Sources on the Court and its Members, 1836-1981** / with a historical postscript by Joe R. Greenhill. - [Austin, TX]: Tarlton Law Library, Univ. of Texas School of Law, 1983. - 146 p. - (Tarlton Law Library legal bibliography series, 25).

Class Numbers:
Library of Congress KFT1712.A1
ISBN 0935630082 (pbk.)
OCLC 9873345
LCCN 83-623519

• Begins with two pages of citations to books, newspaper articles, and journal articles about the Supreme Court, then offers bibliographies for all the justices, 1836-1981, arranged alphabetically. No index nor table of contents, but neither is needed in a bibliography whose arrangement is so simple. Journal articles are commonly grouped by journal title, and cite only volume and page. The compilers report some quirks in the Court's history – e.g., two justices appointed by the military governor just after the conclusion of the Civil War resigned the day they were appointed, and the only three women justices, all appointed in 1925 to hear a case involving Woodmen of the World, gained appointment because they could not possibly be members of that organization. —*RB*

CG48 Jorgensen, Delores A. - **South Dakota Legal Documents: A Selective Bibliography**. - [Chicago, IL]:

American Association of Law Libraries, 1988. - 35 p. - (American Association of Law Libraries. Occasional papers series, 3-34).

Class Numbers:
Library of Congress KF1.S2; KFS3001
OCLC 25298944
Notes:
American Association of Law Libraries. Annual Meeting (81st: Atlanta, GA, June 26-29, 1988)

• Jorgensen (Law Library, Univ. of South Dakota) offers a selective list of sources related to South Dakota law and state government. Entries are listed alphabetically or chronologically under six categories (general reference, state constitution, legislation, judiciary, administrative, and miscellaneous). Four appendixes: state depository libraries for government documents, unified judicial system, court structure, and chart of South Dakota government. — *GK*

POLITICAL PARTIES

CG49 Coleman, Patrick K., 1952-   , comp. - **The Nonpartisan League, 1915-22: An Annotated Bibliography** / comp. by Patrick K. Coleman and Charles R. Lamb. - St. Paul, MN: Minnesota Historical Society Pr., 1985. - 86 p.; ill.

Class Numbers:
Library of Congress HD1485.N4 Z5075.U5
ISBN 0873511891
OCLC 12558377
LCCN 85-21480
Notes:
Index

• The Nonpartisan League, an agrarian protest organization, rose in North Dakota in 1915 and disbanded in 1922. This bibliography is limited to works relevant to the NPL. It covers books, articles, pamphlets, periodicals, court cases, government publications, archival and manuscript collections, doctoral dissertations, master's theses, and other unpublished items. Each of the 1,010 items is numbered; 131 are books, 302 are journal articles. The annotations are rarely more than a single sentence or a few words in length. Many items are noted "not seen by compilers." A few photos and line drawings add visual interest. The subject and name index is extensive. Reproduced from typescript. — *MB*

CG50 George, John, 1936-   . - **American Extremists: Militias, Supremacists, Klansmen, Communists & Others** / [by] John George & Laird Wilcox. - Amherst, NY: Prometheus Books, 1996, 1992. - 443 p.; [8] p. of plates, ill.

Class Numbers:

Library of Congress HS2325
ISBN 1573920584
LCCN 96-16425
Notes:
    Includes bibliographical references; index
    Originally publ. 1992 with subtitle: *Nazis, Communists, Klansmen, and Others on the Fringe*

• George (political science, Univ. of Central Oklahoma) and Wilcox (founder of the Wilcox Collection of Contemporary Political Movements, Univ. of Kansas) examine radical extremist movements in the U.S. They explain why these groups exist, who become members, and what the groups are trying to accomplish. Of interest are sections on Robert Bolivar DePugh and the Minutemen, a rightist paramilitary organization centered in Kansas City, MO; Gerald L.K. Smith and the Christian Nationalist Crusade, an anti-Semitic, racist organization in Eureka Springs, AR; and formless antigovernment militias that attract such persons as Timothy McVeigh and Terry Nichols, who destroyed the Murrah Federal Building in Oklahoma City. The work also covers Bureau of Alcohol, Tobacco, and Firearms clashes with Randy Weaver in Ruby Ridge, ID and the Branch Davidians in Waco, TX. — *GK*

CG51   Martis, Kenneth C. - **The Historical Atlas of Political Parties in the United States Congress, 1789-1989** / Kenneth C. Martis, author and ed.; Ruth Anderson Rowles and Gyula Pauer, cartographers. - London: Collier Macmillan; New York: Macmillan, 1989. - 1 atlas (518 p.); col. maps; 34 x 46 cm.

Class Numbers:
    Library of Congress G1201.F9
ISBN 0029201705
OCLC 18520389
LCCN 88-675270
Notes:
    Includes bibliographies; index
    Scale: 1:12,225,000

• Part 1 consists of introductory essays on political parties, congressional elections, party information sources, and data analysis and mapping. Parts 2-4 have maps and tables analyzing the party affiliations of members of the 1st-100th Congresses. For each Congress, a map of the U.S. uses color coding to show the political affiliations of the House members from each district. A smaller map shows party affiliations in the Senate and pie charts show the percentage of House and Senate members from each party. Congressional membership lists with party affiliations accompany each map. Tables show each member's party affiliation according to standard reference sources and according to the author's "final political affiliation," which he based on voting records. The maps make it easy to track changes in political representation in the Plains over time and make comparisons with other states and the U.S. as a whole; the tables both allow tracking the political affiliations and records of individual members of Congress and cross-reference the maps. — *JD*

CH : WOMEN

Scope Includes titles confined to women or treating women in their roles as wives, mothers, and homemakers. Works about or including women that focus on their occupations, professions, or other social roles (e.g., women anthropologists, writers, artists) are entered by subject.

General Works
See also **Prophetic Sisterhood, BA8**

CH1 North American Women's Letters and Diaries [Internet Site]. - Alexandria, VA : Alexander Street Pr., 2001- . - http://www.alexanderstreet.com/products/nwld.htm

> Access Date: Jan. 2006
> Notes:
> Fees: Subscription or outright purhase

• Materials reproduced in this full-text database consist of 150,000 pages of letters and diaries published between the 1700s and 1950s. Texts chosen had to be written by women residing in North America and to have been published before 1950 but written contemporaneously. As might be expected, materials written by men are excluded. Some entries include images from original documents. Letters and diaries by women living on the Plains are well represented, especially female homesteaders and pioneer Plains residents. An extremely important resource for researchers seeking resources about women and life on the Plains. The Alexander Street search engine is described at **CD46**. —*JB*

CH2 Fairbanks, Carol, 1935- . - **Farm Women on the Prairie Frontier : A Sourcebook for Canada and the United States** / by Carol Fairbanks and Sara Brooks Sundberg. - Metuchen, NJ : Scarecrow Pr., 1983. - 237 p. ; ill.

> Class Numbers:
> Library of Congress HQ1438.A17
> ISBN 0810816253
> OCLC 9394273
> LCCN 83-4498
> Notes:
> Index

• Fairbanks's book supplies four literature reviews and annotated bibliographies. The reviews treat early agricultural settlement of the North American grasslands, pioneer women on the Prairies, farm women on the Canadian frontier, and the fictional perspective of farm women on the Prairie frontier. Each is followed by footnotes and by the annotated bibliographies, which average 30-40 words and address history and background, women's nonfiction, women's fiction, and literary backgrounds. The sections on fiction and nonfiction are subdivided into U.S. and Canada. Because the reviews and the bibliographies are organized differently, and the only index is by subject, it is difficult to determine congruence between the essays and the bibliographies. A few botanical line drawings, a dozen woodcuts, and a map add visual interest. — *MB, JB*

UNITED STATES

CH3 Clinton, Catherine, 1952- . - **The Columbia Guide to American Women in the Nineteenth Century** / [by] Catherine Clinton, Christine Lunardini. - New York : Columbia Univ. Pr., 2000. - 331 p. - (Columbia guides to American history and culture).

> Class Numbers:
> Library of Congress HQ1418
> ISBN 0231109202
> LCCN 98-50373
> Notes:
> Book review (H-net): http://www.h-net.org/review/
> hrev-a0c3e2-aa
> Includes bibliographical references (p. 277-282) ;
> index

• *Columbia Guide* is arranged in four sections, each of which can be used independently. Part 1, the longest, consists of essays describing all aspects of the status and role of women in the U.S. in the 19th century: a general overview, division of labor, education, church, law, Indians, immigrants, culture, gender roles, reproduction, suffrage. The last essay in the section covers the status of women at the beginning of the 20th century. Part 2 provides biographic entries about notable individual American women, arranged alphabetically with cross-references, that include events, organizations, and groups that had impact on women and that women affected. Part 3 is an annotated chronology of events during the century. Part 4, an extensive bibliography, the book's most useful section, covers monographs, periodicals, and archival collections, most with brief annotations. It has a classed arrangement, beginning with topics (one of which, "Westward Migration," will interest Plains students), then groups bibliographies and reference works, general histories, biographies and similar works, journals and archives, electronic resources, and novels and films. The index has entries for "American Indians" and "Westward Migration." The editors focus closely on such matters as gender issues, suffrage, the women's movement, and women's roles, rather than on regional issues; although it surveys the field carefully, Plains students will find limited application to their interests. —*JB*

CH4 Encyclopedia of Women in the American West / ed. by Gordon Morris Bakken and Brenda Farrington. - Thousand Oaks, CA : Sage, c2003. - xxiii, 381 p. ; ill.

Class Numbers:
Library of Congress HQ1438.W45
ISBN 076192356X   9780761923565
OCLC 51921848
LCCN 2003006729
Notes:
Includes bibliographical references (p. 341-362) ; index
Table of contents: http://www.loc.gov/catdir/toc/
ecip041/2003006729.html

• Devoted to women of the trans-Mississippi West, Bakken and Farrington's encyclopedia includes women from all occupations, most of them well-known in history or at present. The editors also supply topical articles about notable events, organizations, and cultural influences (e.g., Asian women, cowgirls, suffrage, education). Entries vary in length, are alphabetically arranged, signed, and provide suggested readings. Appendixes include a chronology, a list of women's organizations, and a guide to research in women's history. The front matter includes a list of entries. The Plains researcher will find the likes of Elinore Pruitt Stewart (homesteader), Libby Custer (military wife), Margaret Greever (temperance leader), Jeannette Rankin (politician), Delphine Red Shirt (Lakota author), Linda Hasselstrom (rancher author) and many others among the entries. —*JB*

CH5 A History of Women in the United States : State-by-State Reference / Doris L. Weatherford, ed. - Danbury, CT : Grolier Academic Reference, 2004. - 4 v. ; ill., maps.

Class Numbers:
Library of Congress HQ1410
ISBN 071725805X (set)
OCLC 52631499
LCCN 2003-49299
Notes:
Contents: v. 1, Alabama-Illinois; v. 2, Indiana-Nebraska; v. 3, Nevada-South Dakota; v. 4. Tennessee-Wyoming; appendixes

• Following introductory essays on women in specific eras, the history of American feminism, race and ethnicity, and cultural representations of women, entries for each state offer histories of women that include prehistory, Native people, and immigrant ethnic groups; sidebars and special features on particular events, people or trends; time lines of key state and national events; biographies of prominent women; historical sites; and resources that include further readings, Internet sites, and organizations. Each state entry includes a quotation from a woman's work, a statistical chart, maps, and excerpts from primary documents. Appendixes in volume 4 consist of an expanded timeline,

primary documents of national interest, and additional statistics. Bibliography and an index by name, place, and topic. Nicely designed and readable, a good starting place for students and others beginning research on women in the Great Plains. —*JD*

CH6 Notable American Women, 1607-1950 : A Biographical Dictionary / Edward T. James, ed. ; Janet Wilson James, associate ed. ; Paul S. Boyer, assistant ed. - Cambridge, MA : Belknap Pr. of Harvard Univ. Pr., 1971. - 3 v.

Class Numbers:
Library of Congress CT3260.N57
ISBN 0674627318 0674627342
OCLC 167545
LCCN 76-152274
Notes:
Contents: [v. 1] A-F ; [v. 2] G-O ; [v. 3] P-Z
Prepared under the auspices of Radcliffe College

CH6a Notable American Women : The Modern Period : A Biographical Dictionary / ed. by Barbara Sicherman, Carol Hurd Green, with Ilene Kantrov, Harriette Walker. - Cambridge, MA : Belknap Pr. of Harvard Univ. Pr., c1980. - xxii, 773 p. ; [16] p. of plates, ports.

Class Numbers:
Library of Congress CT3260.N573
ISBN 0674627326
LCCN 83-12948

CH6b Notable American Women : A Biographical Dictionary Completing the Twentieth Century / Susan Ware, ed. ; Stacy Braukman, assistant ed. - Cambridge, MA : Belknap Pr., 2004. - xxx, 729 p.

Class Numbers:
Library of Congress CT3260.N5725
ISBN 067401488X
LCCN 2004-48859
Notes:
Includes bibliographical references; index
Prepared under the auspices of the Radcliffe Institute for Advanced Study, Harvard Univ.

• The basic set attracted immense attention when it was released in 1971, and was recognized at once as the first collective biography of American women to take advantage of scholarship about women, to be prepared by editors and contributors who were themselves scholars, and to be very broad in scope, including, besides expected professions, abolitionists, classicists, educators of the handicapped, and prison reformers. With its supplementary volumes, it has gained recognition as the preeminent biographical source for American women. The basic set and the supplements each provide lengthy introductions that provide an overview of the status and roles of women, the time period covered, social and cultural influences, and guidelines for inclusion. The five volumes provide biographies of women from all parts of the U.S., all ethnicities, all areas of creativity, and all professional fields. Entries, all signed, are arranged alphabetically in all five volumes, and run from several paragraphs to several columns. Entry headings list the subject's name, birth and death dates, and field of contribution. End notes are often extensive and include bibliographic citations. The fourth volume includes women who died between 1951 and 1975, the fifth volume those who died between 1976 and 1999. Both the basic set and the supplements end with lists of women by profession, occupation, specialty, or field of notoriety, but provide nothing to help identify women from the Plains or any other region. A good source for well-written, informed biographical sketches of well-known women (e.g., Cather, Sacajawea, Carry Nation, Louise Pound, Wilder, Dorothy Canfield Fisher, Olive Beech, Angie Debo) but for lesser-known women, researchers will need to rely on collective biographies that are state-oriented. —*JB*

TRANS-MISSISSIPPI WEST

CH7   Butruille, Susan G. - **Women's Voices from the Oregon Trail : The Times that Tried Women's Souls, and a Guide to Women's History along the Oregon Trail** / artwork by Kathleen Peterson ; photographs by author unless otherwise noted. - Boise, ID : Tamarack Books, 1993. - 251 p. ; ill., maps.

Class Numbers:
Library of Congress F597
ISBN 0963483900
LCCN 93-161624
Notes:
Includes bibliographical references (p. 235-241); index

• To approximate the viewpoint of women who traveled the Oregon Trail, Butruille and her mother retraced the trail of wagon trains bound for the Pacific Coast in the 1800s. The first of two sections reprints excerpts from diaries and journals and includes quotations, song lyrics, poems, cooking directions, and the like, retelling what the women faced traveling in covered wagons across territory that was unfamiliar and perhaps dangerous. The second section is a state-by-state guide to museums, historical markers, statues, buildings, organizations, and natural areas that help give life to the history of the Oregon Trail venture. Photos and drawings throughout the book. —*JB*

CH8   Patterson-Black, Sheryll. - **Western Women in History & Literature** / [by] Sheryll & Gene Patterson-Black. - Crawford, NE : Cottonwood Pr., 1978. - [142] p.

Class Numbers:
Library of Congress Z7964.W4
OCLC 4180991

• A bibliography of primary works of women writers, publishers and printers that covers the region west of the Missouri and Mississippi rivers from pre-Anglo times through World War II. Introductory essays are followed by unannotated lists by material type: bibliographies including early imprints; archival sources in museums and historical societies; biographies including oral histories; personal statements including letters, diaries, journals, autobiographies, and memoirs; literary works including criticisms, novels and pulps, short stories, poetry, essays, drama, and juvenile fiction. Works published by the Smithsonian Bureau of Ethnology are included. Though far from complete, it identifies important and elusive material. Both the topic and the types of material listed have become of increasing interest since this work was published in 1978. —*JD*

CH9   Riley, Glenda, 1938-   , ed. - **By Grit & Grace : Eleven Women Who Shaped the West** / ed. by Glenda Riley and Richard W. Etulain. - Golden, CO : Fulcrum Publ., 1997. - 226 p. ; ill. - (Notable westerners).

Class Numbers:
Library of Congress F596
ISBN 1555912591 (pbk.)
LCCN 97-25057
Notes:
Includes bibliographical references; index

• Many of the women profiled are associated with the far West rather than with the Prairies-Plains region. Those of interest for Plains study include Jessie Frémont (for at least part of her life), Calamity Jane (née Martha Canary), Annie Oakley, Elinore Stewart, and the Omaha Indian sisters Suzette and Susan LaFlesche. Each chapter provides narrative text, a small selection of illustrations, and an annotated list of recommended reading. Preceding the index, a roster of contributors includes their academic credentials. A scholarly work, consistent with the reputation of editor Etulain. — *MB*

SOCIAL HISTORY

CH10   **"This Shall Be the Land for Women" : The Struggle for Western Women's Suffrage [Internet Site].** - Boulder, CO : Women of the West Museum, [2004?]. - http://www.autry-museum.org/explore/exhibits/suffrage/suff_resource.htm

Access Date : July 2006
Notes:
Exhibit at Museum of the American West, Los Angeles, CA, Jan. 2002; formerly called Autry Museum of Western Heritage
Exhibit producer: Selma Thomas; exhibit curator, Marcia Goldstein
Fees: None

• Materials intended to support an exhibition (viewing dates not disclosed) about women's efforts to obtain the vote in states west of the Missouri Basin. The site includes a timeline, 1776-1975, that lists failures as well as successes, a section of biographical sketches of 17 women important in the Western suffrage movement, and an "Activities" page (contests and quizzes). Most important is "Resources," a bibliography that lists materials about the suffrage struggle that includes books, parts of books, periodical articles, and primary sources, the latter usually citing collections of papers and their depository. There is no search engine, but the arrangement is simple, beginning with a general section followed by sections for individual states, arranged alphabetically. Although the region covered stretches from the eastern border of Texas to the Pacific (excluding Alaska but including Hawai'i), the bibliography has sections for Colorado, Kansas, Montana, Nebraska, New Mexico, North Dakota, Oklahoma, South Dakota, Texas, and Wyoming. Three items among the primary sources are cited by title without further elaboration (e.g., *The New Northwest*). — *JB*

CH11   Women and Social Movements in the United States, 1600-2000 [Internet Site]. - Alexandria, VA : Alexander Street Pr., 2004-   . - http://www.alexander street.com/

> Access Date : Jan. 2006
> Notes:
> > Available through outright purchase or subscription
> > Fees: None

• Currently reproducing more than 23,000 pages of documents (with additional images and links to Internet sites) pertaining to women and their involvement in social movements in the U.S., this site covers the period 1600-2000. It treats a wide variety of topics, early women's clubs to current controversies over abortion. Among the social currents sweeping the U.S. during these years were suffrage (perhaps the most enduring and influential struggle), prohibition, and the right of choice. Prohibition may be found in nearly 800 documents (though poor Carry Nation has only one mention), Plains nearly 80 (but many are not the Great Plains), and such topics as Kate O'Hare and populism. Includes many documents not otherwise available on the Internet. The site includes a dictionary of social movements and organizations, a chronology of women's history in the U.S., and "Teaching Tools," giving teachers ideas and lesson plans based on documents at the site. Kathryn Kish Sklar and Thomas Dublin (both SUNY Binghamton) lead an editorial board of 30 contributors. The Alexander Street search engine is described at **CD46**. — *JB*

Colorado

CH12   Varnell, Jeanne. - Women of Consequence : The

Colorado Women's Hall of Fame / foreword by M.L. Hanson. - Boulder, CO : Johnson Books, 1999. - 321 p. ; ill.

> Class Numbers:
> > Library of Congress CT3260
> > ISBN 1555662137 1555662145 (pbk.) 9781555662134
> > > 9781555662141 (pbk.)   0585196575 (electronic bk.)
> > > 9780585196572 (electronic bk.)
> > OCLC 41601236   44958174 (electronic bk.)
> > LCCN 99-35597
> Notes:
> > Electronic book: http://www.netLibrary.com/urlapi.asp?
> > > action=summary&v=1&bookid=17076
> > Includes bibliographical references (p. 287-318); index

• Instituted by the Colorado Federation of Business and Professional Women, the Colorado Women's Hall of Fame began inducting women leaders in 1984. Varnell has compiled biographical sketches of the inductees, most of which are three to four pages long. Photographs are grouped in a section of plates, with notes and bibliography at the end of book. Not all the women are natives of Colorado, but all have lived there and contributed to the state's development. — *JB*

Montana

CH13   Olsen, Lauri. - Whispers on the Wind : Stories of Women from Montana's History. - [S.l.] : Timberline Pr., 2001. - 158 p.

> Class Numbers:
> > Library of Congress F730
> > OCLC 47970296
> Notes:
> > Includes bibliographical references; index

• Covering an assortment of women, this volume was designed to tell the stories of Montana women of little fame or notoriety. They represent many aspects of life, 1800s-2000. Most entries run two to three pages. No photographs, but there are references and an index. — *JB*

CH14   Shirley, Gayle Corbett. - More than Petticoats : Remarkable Montana Women. - Helena, MT : Falcon Pr., 1995. - 142 p.

> Class Numbers:
> > Library of Congress CT3260
> > ISBN 1560443634
> > LCCN 95-32881
> Notes:
> > Includes bibliographical references (p. 129-137); index

• Shirley provides information on 14 women who contributed to Montana's history and who could challenge the stereotypes of women as "madonnas of the prairies," enterprising floozies, or spinster schoolmarms. She limits subjects to women born before 1900, presenting a cross-section of fields and ethnicities–a Crow healer, teacher, Indian advocate, religious leader, doctor, photographer, business owners, artists, bronc rider, and representative. A photograph of each woman accompanies the selection, and a bibliography lists primary and secondary sources. — *GK, JB*

North Dakota

CH15 Svore, Hedvig Clausen, 1885-   . - **Mothers of North Dakota : Pioneers, Educators, Home Builders, Church Workers, and Civic Leaders, Mothers All** / [by] Hedvig Clausen Svore, Lorraine Moline Martinson, Ardeith Juven Richter. - [2nd ed.] - [Bismarck, ND : North Dakota Mothers Association], 1978-1998. - 2 v. (257, 192 p.) ; facsim., ill., ports.

Class Numbers:
Library of Congress F635
OCLC 4309882 (v. 1)   41410767 (v. 2)
Notes:
Vol. 1 is photocopy of ed. publ.: Bismarck, ND : *Bismarck Tribune*, 1963, with pt. 2 added
Vol. 1, called 2nd ed., comp. by Hedvig Clausen Svore, Eva Voris Case, Anne Bucklin

• Published by the North Dakota Mothers Association, this volume extends coverage of the earlier editions through 1998. It provides for each Mother of the Year and Merit Mother a brief biography and a photograph, and also supplies a list of Mothers of the Year since 1945, "The Mother's Pledge," a selection of poetry, and the history of the Association. Index. —*JB*

CH16 Witteman, Barbara. - **Prairie in Her Heart : Pioneer Women of North Dakota.** - Chicago, IL : Arcadia Publ., 2001. - 128 p. ; ill., ports. - (Voices of America).

Class Numbers:
Library of Congress F635
ISBN 0738518654 9780738518657
OCLC 17653015

• Drawing from a variety of original sources–WPA interviews; Homemakers Extension Council Oral History Project; the Hultstrand and Pazandak photograph collections (both at North Dakota State Univ., Fargo); and county museum collections and archives–Witteman's book relates how women of the late 19th and early 20th centuries conducted their lives on the Prairie and were influenced by it. Photographs and quotations from interviews are scattered throughout the text. Some of the topical chapters

include homes, food, daily routines, and special occasions–e.g., threshing, community holiday celebrations. The index lists all persons cited in the text. — *JB*

South Dakota

CH17 **South Dakota Women, 1850-1919 : A Bibliography.** - [Pierre, SD : s.n.], 1975. - [23] p. ; ill.

Class Numbers:
Library of Congress HQ1438.S6 Z7964.U5
LCCN 76-621272
Notes:
Compiled by the South Dakota Historical Society in conjunction with the South Dakota Commission on the Status of Women

• A bibliography consisting of 144 annotated records compiled from books and pamphlets about women in South Dakota, 1850-1919 (first white settlement to ratify the suffrage amendment). Intended for general research, the bibliography includes books and pamphlets but excludes periodicals and county histories. Entries are arranged in three sections (bibliographies, nonfiction, and fiction), each arranged alphabetically by author. Annotations run 30 to 70 words; 18 photographs depict topics or life on the Prairie. Includes well-known women like Libby Custer, Calamity Jane, and Laura Ingalls Wilder, and lesser-known figures such as Laura Bower Van Nuys, Mary Reddick Waterman, and Sarah Wood Ward. The editors promise new editions, but none have appeared. Gives library locations. — *GK, JB*

Texas

CH18 Beaird, Miriam G., ed. - **Notable Women of the Southwest : A Pictorial Biographical Encyclopedia of the Leading Women of New Mexico, Oklahoma, and Arizona.** - Dallas, TX : W.T. Tardy, 1938. - 384 p. ; ill., ports.

Class Numbers:
Library of Congress F786
OCLC 1187198
LCCN 39-12316

• Published in 1938, Beaird's volume covers notable women of the time who resided in Texas, New Mexico, Oklahoma, and Arizona. Arranged alphabetically, entries contain brief biographies and photographs. Inclusion is based on the contributions women have made to their community, profession, and society. No indexes. —*JB*

CH19   Notable Women of Texas. - Irving, TX : Emerson Publ., 1984. - 647 p.

Class Numbers:
   Library of Congress CT3260
   OCLC 11842137
   LCCN 84-234581

• In a who's who format, *Notable Women* offers biographical sketches of women from all fields recognized for their contributions to society, their professions, and their communities. Entries give name, occupation, place and date of birth, family members, education, activities and affiliations, accomplishments, and current address. Entries are alphabetical; a guide assists in reading entries. Only living women are included. A new edition, planned for 1986, has yet to appear. — *JB*

CH20   Snapp, Elizabeth, ed. - Read All About Her! : Texas Women's History : A Working Bibliography / comp. and ed. by Elizabeth Snapp, Harry F. Snapp. - Denton, TX : Texas Woman's Univ. Pr., 1995. - 1070 p.

Class Numbers:
   Library of Congress HQ1438.T4
   ISBN 0960748830
   OCLC 32712597

• The Snapps' thousand pages cite resources about women and their place in Texas history. Entries are alphabetical by authors, titles, and subjects. Subjects can include personal names, place-names, institutions, historical journals, and organizations as well as topics. Some entries have brief annotations, but many do not. The front matter includes a key to subject and *see also* entries. Entries are not regionally sensitive; Prairies-Plains readers will need to use other resources to identify topics or persons of interest before using *Read All About Her!* — *JB*

CH21   Winegarten, Ruthe, ed. - Bibliography [Texas Women's History Project] / Ruthe Winegarten, ed. ; Mary Beth Rogers, project director. - Austin, TX : Texas Foundation for Women's Resources, 1980. - 349 p. ; 10 plates (incl. front.).

Class Numbers:
   Library of Congress Z1229.W8
   OCLC 6106179

• Winegarten's bibliography, designed to "recognize the contributions of Texas women to the development of their state," was published under the auspices of the Texas Foundation for Women's Resources. Introductory material provides editor's notes and an abbreviation key for depository locations. Entries are not annotated. Chapters cover topics: diaries, education, health, legal rights, life cycles, lit-

erature, pioneers, politics, religion, work. Other chapters include reference aids and ethnic groups. An appendix describes the Foundation. Author index. — *JB*

Wyoming

CH22   Beach, Cora May, 1878-   . - Women of Wyoming : Including a Short History of Some of the Early Activities of Women of Our State, Together with Biographies of Those Women Who Were Our Early Pioneers as well as of Women Who Have Been Prominent in Public Affairs and in Civic Organizations and Service Work. - Casper, WY : [S.E. Boyer & Co., 1927]. - [1] v. ; ill., ports.

• As the subtitle notes, this work covers women in the broad sweep of Wyoming history to the year of its publication. The entries are randomly arranged, but can be easily located in the index. The style resembles that found in high school composition assignments from an earlier era, but the entries provide useful information in spite of that. Entries are fairly long, include portraits, and vary in scope from Wyoming first ladies to the first Wyoming woman to serve on a jury. For many of the subjects, this will be the only source of information. — *JB*

CH23   First Ladies of Wyoming, 1869-1990 / ed. by Mabel E. Brown. - [Cheyenne, WY] : Wyoming Arts Council ; [Cheyenne, WY] : Wyoming Commission for Women (Wyoming Council on Women's Issues), 1990. - 160 p. ; ill.

Class Numbers:
   Library of Congress F760.F57
   LCCN 91-162532
Notes:
   Includes bibliographical references

• Published as the official Centennial project of the Wyoming Commission on Women's Issues, Brown's title covers all the state's first ladies, 1869-1990. Entries, by a roster of writers, vary in length from two or three pages to nine or ten. All include photographs of both the First Lady and the Governor and a bibliography; many also have photographs of homes, families, and special occasions. The last chapter is devoted to the Governor's Mansion Museum (the original mansion, 1905-1976). Includes information that might be hard to find. — *JB*

CANADA

General Works

CH24   Jackel, Susan. - Canadian Prairie Women's

History : A Bibliographic Survey. - Ottawa, ON : CRIAW/ICREF, 1987. - 31 p. - (CRIAW papers ; no. 14).

Class Numbers:
National Library of Canada Z7964 C3
ISBN 0919653146
OCLC 20647063
Notes:
Includes bibliographical references
Includes: "Women and Men in Western American History" by Susan Armitage

• Brief overview of works published for the most part in the 1970s to mid-1980s, pointing out trends and gaps in Prairie feminist historiography. Approximately 70 titles are mentioned in the text or endnotes. — *LMcD*

Alberta

CH25 Sanderson, Kay. - **200 Remarkable Alberta Women** / Elda Hauschildt, ed. - Calgary, AB : Famous Five Foundation, [1999] - 101 p. ; ports.

Class Numbers:
Library of Congress CT3270
National Library of Canada HQ1459 A4
ISBN 0968583202
OCLC 48958779
LCCN 00-303384
Notes:
At head of title: The Kay Sanderson Collection
Biographies and portraits of 200 Alberta women, 1800-1980, to accompany the photo exhibit

• Intriguing accounts of a diverse group of women who significantly influenced the development of Alberta as educators, missionaries, politicians, and activists, among other occupations, roughly from 1860 to the late 1990s. Profiles are only half a page long, but capture the spirit of these extraordinary individuals; postage-size photographs. Arranged by period: 1800-1875, 1876-1900, 1901-2000. — *LMcD*

CH26 Dryden, Jean E. - **Some Sources for Women's History at the Provincial Archives of Alberta.** - [Edmonton, AB] : Alberta Culture, Historical Resources Division, 1980. - 198 p. ; ill. - (Occasional paper [Provincial Archives of Alberta], no. 2).

Class Numbers:
Library of Congress HQ1453
National Library of Canada Z7964
OCLC 7736775
LCCN 81-107371

• Guide to archival collections documenting the experiences of women in Alberta. Arranged by personal and family

papers, organizations, and churches (Anglican, United Church of Canada, Oblates of Mary Immaculate). Personal and organizational entries contain a biographical or historical note, indication of size, inventory availability, and collection description. Guides to the archives of the United Church (**BA23**) and Oblates (**BA22**) in Alberta provide additional information. — *LMcD*

Manitoba

CH27 Kinnear, Mary, 1942- . - **Planting the Garden : An Annotated Archival Bibliography of the History of Women in Manitoba** / [by] Mary Kinnear, Vera Fast. - Winnipeg, MB : Univ. of Manitoba Pr., 1987. - 314 p.

Class Numbers:
Library of Congress HQ1459.M25
ISBN 0887551408
OCLC 17228844
LCCN 87-168172

• A guide to more than 1,400 collections in 65 Manitoba archives. Arranged in three broad categories with subdivisions: "Identity" (biography, autobiography, local history, early settlement, native life, immigration); "Work and Activities" (agriculture, business, education, health, social services); "Mentality, Faith and Reform" (religion, art, literature, music). An appendix lists photographic collections. Entries indicate format, physical extent, and restrictions. The detailed index clearly identifies archival resources dealing with almost any facet of women's history in Manitoba. — *LMcD*

CH28 **Extraordinary Ordinary Women : Manitoba Women & Their Stories** / [ed., Colleen Armstrong]. - [Winnipeg, MB] : Manitoba Clubs of the Canadian Federation of University Women, 2000. - 95 p. ; ill., ports.

Class Numbers:
National Library of Canada FC3355
ISBN 0968788049
OCLC 46628029
Notes:
Includes bibliographical references

• Biographical accounts, uniformly two pages in length, of 42 women who significantly contributed to Manitoba in areas as diverse as prospecting and forensic pathology. The biographies are grouped thematically: fur trade, farm, arts, health care, commerce, education, wartime, labor force, community builders, and activists. Similar to *200 Remarkable Alberta Women* (**CH25**) in its intent to recognize noteworthy but largely neglected women. — *LMcD*

CH29 **Femmes de chez nous.** - Saint-Boniface [MB] : Éditions du Blé pour la Société historique de Saint-

Boniface et la Ligue féminine du Manitoba, 1985. - 125 p. : ill., ports. - (Cahiers d'histoire de la Société historique de Saint-Boniface ; 4).

Class Numbers:
    Library of Congress F1061.8
    National Library of Canada FC3400.5
    ISBN 0920640516
    OCLC 16180600
    Notes:
        Includes index

• Short biographical accounts of 100 francophone women in Manitoba. In its purpose of recognizing the contributions of neglected pioneers of the late 19th and early 20th centuries, it resembles *Extraordinary Ordinary Women: Manitoba Women & Their Stories* (**CH28**). — *LMcD*

CH30   Out from the Shadows : A Bibliography of the History of Women in Manitoba / researched and comp. by Pam Atnikov [et al.]. - [Winnipeg, MB] : Manitoba Human Rights Commission, 1975. - 64 p.

Class Numbers:
    Library of Congress HQ1459.M25   Z7964.C36
    OCLC 2424012
    LCCN 76-369651

• Many of the works listed are not histories in the conventional sense but the materials from which history can be fashioned: e.g., Census reports, studies of particular industries with a substantial female workforce, studies of the role of women in education. Organized in sections treating legal status, politics, employment, social and cultural situation, and bibliographies. Arranged by author; the social-cultural area, however, is grouped by time period. Very briefly annotated. — *LMcD*

Saskatchewan

CH31   Notable Saskatchewan Women : 1905-1980. - Regina, SK : Saskatchewan Labour, Women's Division, 1980. - 36 p. ; ill.

Class Numbers:
    National Library of Canada FC3505
    OCLC 15890409
    Notes:
        Bibliography: p. 33-36; index
        Electronic book: http://www.ourroots.ca/e/toc.
          aspx?id=4436

• Very brief accounts, arranged alphabetically, of 80 women who made significant contributions to the province as pio-

neers, politicians, teachers, etc. Comparable to Manitoba's *Extraordinary Ordinary Women* (**CH28**) and *200 Remarkable Alberta Women* (**CH25**). — *LMcD*

CH32   Powell, Barbara Pezalla. - Piecing the Quilt : Sources for Women's History in the Saskatchewan Archives Board / by Barbara Powell and Myrna Williams. - Regina, SK : Canadian Plains Research Center, University of Regina, 1996. - 177 p. - (Canadian plains reference works, 1).

Class Numbers:
    Library of Congress CD3645.S2
    National Library of Canada Z7964
    ISBN 0889770905
    OCLC 35275219
    LCCN 97-200421
    Notes:
        Index

• A guide to 1,435 collections in the Saskatchewan provincial archives containing material by or about women. Collections range from single items to voluminous institutional records. Material listed includes manuscripts, audiotapes, photographs, minutes of women's organizations and printed publications. Family histories, community histories and most clippings, unless related to women whose papers are in the archives, are excluded. Arrangement is by collection name, usually personal or organizational. Entries provide location number, dates, extent, finding aid number, and brief annotations. Index of women's names found within entries. Lack of both subject index and topical structure requires either sustained reading or inspired browsing on the part of the user. Useful for identifying primary sources on the history of Prairie women. — *LMcD*

CH33   Savage, Candace Sherk. - Foremothers : Personalities and Issues from the History of Women in Saskatchewan. - [s.l. : s.n.], 1975. - 99 p.

Class Numbers:
    Library of Congress HQ1455.A3
    OCLC 3966342
    LCCN 77-374402
    Notes:
        Bibliography: p. 92-97; index

• The 21 individuals profiled represent women pioneering in a variety of fields as journalists, politicians, and judges, among others. Controversies alluded to in the title involve concerns such as birth control, suffrage, and property laws. Considerable overlap with *Notable Saskatchewan Women : 1905-1980* (**CH31**). — *LMcD*

CI : Geography ; Landscape

Scope Includes works devoted to the geography, physiography, or landscape of the United States or Canada, national atlases of either country, or maps and cartography in general, to the extent those works are concerned with the Prairies-Plains region.

Bibliographies

CI1 Conzen, Michael P. [comp.]. - **A Scholar's Guide to Geographical Writing on the American and Canadian Past** / [by] Michael P. Conzen, Thomas A. Rumney, Graeme Wynn. - Chicago, IL : Univ. of Chicago Pr., 1993. - 741 p. ; ill., maps.

  Class Numbers:
    Library of Congress E179.5 Z1247
  ISBN 0226115690 (pbk.)
  LCCN 92-23520
  Notes:
    Indexes

• Thought out with great care, intensely scholarly, and breathtakingly complete, *Scholar's Guide* cites works of historical geography bearing on the U.S. and Canada published 1850-1990, excluding most working papers, discussion papers, technical reports, book reviews, review essays, and editorials. It offers just over 10,000 entries in three categories: general sources, Canada, and the U.S. The general section has subsections for bibliographies, methodological statements, "Benchmark Scholars," and atlases and map series, while the Canada and U.S. sections begin with general works about the region, followed by sectional divisions. For Canada, the Prairie provinces are grouped but include British Columbia and Yukon Territory, and for the U.S., the Great Plains is limited to North and South Dakota, Nebraska, Kansas, and Oklahoma (New Mexico, Colorado, Wyoming and Montana are with the Mountain West, Texas with the South). Introductory essays survey historical geographical writing about the U.S. (by Conzen) and Canada (by Wynn), and supply a careful description of the book's organization by all three compilers. The latter will be required reading for all researchers. Three appendixes following the introductory essays supply an outline map of North America that shows the geographic regions used in the bibliography, a list of serials, and a table of gaps in topical coverage of North American historical geography. Citations are carefully complete, and there are indexes of names and subjects. The authors (Conzen, Univ. of Chicago; Rumney, SUNY Plattsburgh; Wynn, Univ. of

British Columbia) provide a landmark work that attends to scholarly concerns but will be useful to many levels of readers. — *RB*

Catalogs

CI2 **Checklist of Printed Maps of the Middle West to 1900** / Robert W. Karrow Jr., general ed. - Boston, MA : G.K. Hall, 1981-1983. - 14 v. in 12 ; maps.

  Class Numbers:
    Library of Congress GA408 Z6027.U5
  ISBN 0816103453 (v. 1)
  OCLC 7378345
  LCCN 81-131746
  Notes:
    Contents: v. 1, North Central States Region / comp. by Patricia A. Moore; v. 2, Ohio / comp. by Stephen Gutgesell, James F. Monteith, Arlene J. Peterson; v. 3, Indiana / comp. by Thomas Rumer; v. 4, Illinois / comp. by David A. Cobb; v. 5. Michigan / comp. by LeRoy Barnett; v. 6, Wisconsin / comp. by Michael J. Fox and Elizabeth Singer Maule; v. 7, Minnesota / comp. by Nancy Erickson; v. 8, Iowa / comp. by Diana J. Fox; v. 9, Missouri / comp. by Randolph K. Tibbits; v. 10 & 11, North Dakota and South Dakota / comp. by Eileen H. Dopson (1 v.); v. 12 & 13, Nebraska / comp. by Helen Brooks; Kansas/ comp. by Ann Hagedorn (1 v.); v. 14, Subject, Author, and Title Index
  Includes bibliographies; indexes
  Vol. 14 has imprint: Chicago, IL: Newberry Library

• This set covers the North Central states region, bounded on the east by Ohio, on the south by Kansas and Missouri, on the north by the Canadian border, and on the west by the western border of the four states, North Dakota to Kansas. The checklist includes over 25,000 entries in 11 separate volumes, each including maps of states showing political and physical features–e.g., towns, rivers. Entries, photoreproductions of typescript catalog cards, are alphabetically arranged in each volume. Each entry, where possible, identifies the author, title, imprint, physical description, scale, and notes, and gives locations of copies. Subject, author, and title indexes are in v. 14. State volumes lack their own indexing, making them awkward to use. — *MB*

CI3 Texas State Library. - **Maps of Texas, 1527-1900 : The Map Collection of the Texas State Archives** / comp. by James M. Day, assisted by Ann B. Dunlap, Mike Smyers, Kenneth Parker. - Austin, TX : Pemberton Pr., 1964. - 178 p.

  Class Numbers:
    Library of Congress GA452 Z6027.A5
  LCCN 80-135806
  Notes:

Earlier ed. publ. under title: *The Map Collection of the Texas State Archives, 1527-1900*
Index

• An annotated list of Texas maps dated 1527-1900 held in the Texas State Archives. Entries indicate the time period, title or created title, and archive file number. Brief descriptions include publisher where known and scale. Detailed index. — *JB*

CI4   Van Balen, John Adrianus, 1947-   , comp. -
Historical Maps in the Richardson Archives : I.D. Weeks Library, University of South Dakota : An Annotated List. - Vermillion, SD : I.D. Weeks Library, Univ. of South Dakota, 1982. - 106 p. ; maps.

> Class Numbers:
> Library of Congress G3200
> Notes:
> Originally publ.: 1978

• Van Balen (library science, Univ. of South Dakota) offers a catalog of 218 maps that span the 18th and 19th centuries and are held in Special Collections and Archives at the University of South Dakota library. Arrangement is chronological by year of publication, then alphabetical by map title. Annotations provide physical descriptions and note changes in various editions of the maps. The book reproduces sections of some maps. Indexes of titles, place-names, and authors. This version updates the 1978 edition, which listed 143 maps. — *GK*

Dictionaries

CI5   **Home Ground : Language for an American Landscape** / Barry Lopez, ed. ; Debra Gwartney, managing ed. - San Antonio, TX : Trinity Univ. Pr., 2006. - xxiv, 449 p. ; ill.

> Class Numbers:
> Library of Congress G108.E5
> ISBN 1595340246 9781595340245
> LCCN 2006-19942
> Notes:
> Includes bibliographical references (p. 401-405); index
> Review by C.W. Bruns: *Choice* 44.9 (Apr. 2007): review 44-4222
> Table of contents: http://www.loc.gov/catdir/toc/ecip0615/2006019942.html

• A collection of brief essays describing terms applied to features of landscape toward which people living in various parts of the world (but especially North America) have developed a deep emotional attachment. Many of the terms apply to the Prairies-Plains landscape: "aquifer," "breaks,"

"chop hills," "lek," "plain" itself, "section," "shelterbelt," "staked plain," "tableland." But it would be a mistake to visit this compilation to learn what most dictionaries provide—etymology, pronunciation, part of speech, usage, lexical meaning. Instead it presents reactions by a group of writers (among them Linda Hogan, Barbara Kingsolver, Jon Krakauer, Larry Woiwode) to terms that refer to parts of the world they love. Fascinating to browse, even though it does not restrict its scope to the Prairies-Plains region. —*RB*

Atlases, National

CI6   Canada Centre for Mapping. National Atlas Information Service. - **The National Atlas of Canada** / produced by the National Atlas Information Service, Geographical Services Division, Canada Centre for Mapping, Energy, Mines, and Resources Canada. - 5th ed. - Ottawa, ON : Energy, Mines and Resources Canada, 1978-1995. - 1 atlas (9 p.) ; col. folded maps ; 46 x 40 cm.

> Class Numbers:
> Library of Congress G3400
> LCCN 91-680536
> Notes:
> Earlier sheets prepared by Geographical Services Division, Geographical Services Directorate, and Surveys and Mapping Branch Electronic book: http://atlas.nrcan.gc.ca/site/english/maps/archives/5thedition#historical
> Issued also in French: *L'Atlas national du Canada*
> Scale 1:7,500,000; 1 cm. to 75 km.
> Some sheets include text, index, ancillary maps, graphs, and statistical data

• Consists of a boxed set of 93 maps, issued separately over several years, treating a variety of physical, environmental, social, economic, and historical subjects. The atlas displays elements at a national level, with the Prairies one of the regions mapped. — *LMcD*

CI7   **Color Landform Atlas of the United States [Internet Site]** / Ray Sterner - [Baltimore, MD] : Johns Hopkins University. Applied Physics Laboratory, 1995-. - http://fermi.jhuapl.edu/states/states.html

> Access Date: May 2008
> Fees: Some uses

• For each state, *Color Landform Atlas* offers a topographic map with color shading, a topographic map with black-and-white shading, a map of county boundaries superimposed over a topographic map, a National Oceanic and Atmospheric Administration weather satellite image, an 1895 map from an early Rand McNally atlas, and a map of counties for high quality images using a PostScript Printer. Maps for the Plains states highlight the variety of landforms found in the Plains and the distinctiveness of each. Links to other map sites such as *Roadside America*, *EPA Watershed Information*, and *USGS Biological Resources* are especially useful. Readers who want to use maps or images for projects are asked to contact the site creator and owner for permission. Minimum fees may be charged for some uses. — *JD*

CI8 United States. Geological Survey. - **The National Atlas of the United States of America** / [Arch C. Gerlach, ed.]. - Washington, DC : United States [Geological Survey], 1970. – 1 atlas (xiii, 417 p.)

> Class Numbers:
> Library of Congress G1200
> LCCN 79-654043
> Notes:
> Raster image version: http://hdl.loc.gov/loc.gmd/
> g3701gm.gct00013
> Scales vary
> Six transparent overlays in envelope
> Signed by William T. Pecora, Under Secretary of Interior;
> W.A. Radlinski, Associate Director, U.S.G.S.; Arch C.
> Gerlach, Chief Geographer; and William B. Over-
> street, Chief, National Atlas Project

• The officially sanctioned atlas of the United States, prepared with the cooperation of more than 80 federal agencies beginning in 1954, intended to be useful to a broad audience of "decision makers in government and business, planners, research scholars, and others needing to visualize country-wide distributional patterns and relationships between environmental phenomena and human activities" (Introd., p. vii). Its 765 maps for the most part show a wide range of physical, historical, sociocultural, and administrative factors drawn to standard outline maps of the continental U.S., with Alaska and Hawaii shown in insets. But the atlas opens with sectional maps that show places, major roads and rail lines, and physical features such as rivers and mountain ranges (this part includes Prairies-Plains regional maps, divided into Northern, Central, and Southern Plains states, and southern Texas), and ends with a section of world maps. Subject maps include topics of interest to Plains students such as physiographic divisions, soils, sunshine, precipitation, temperature, and water (including ground water). Historical maps include three pages of Indian tribes, cultures, and languages, and six maps of exploration and settlement by period from pre-1675 through 1890. An index of maps by subject precedes the atlas proper, and an index of place-names follows it, giving not only map numbers and coordinates, but latitude and longitude. The introduction speaks of future editions of the *Atlas*, but none has been issued, leaving this edition sadly out of date. It nevertheless has considerable content of interest to Plains studies. — *RB*

Atlases, Regional

CI9 Conservation and Survey Division : Statewide Digital Data Bases [Internet Site]. - [Lincoln, NE] : Univ. of Nebraska-Lincoln, Conservation and Survey Div. (CSD), School of Natural Resources, 2000?- . - http://csd.unl.edu/general/gis-datasets.asp

> OCLC 44207355
> Access Date: Jan. 2006
> Notes:
> [In cooperation with] Center for Advanced Land
> Management Information Technologies (CALMIT)
> Fees: None

• CALMIT and CSD, divisions of the University of Nebraska-Lincoln, offer a set of spatial databases for Geographic Information System mapping. The databases contain primarily vector data related to state conservation and natural resources and exclude data with less than statewide coverage. Databases are listed in a table of contents and are described in brief records. The latter display a thumbnail and description of the mapped data, links to the metadata, data in ARC/INFO export format, and larger map images in JPEG format. Data descriptions cover source, methodology, scale, date, related data, and planned updates. Among topics are active mineral operations, bedrock geology, center pivot irrigation systems, railroads, depth to water, slope, land use and land cover, streams, ranges and townships, and native vegetation. Useful for researchers and practitioners. — *JD*

CI10 DeLorme (Firm). - [**Atlases and Gazetteers of the States**]. - Yarmouth, ME : DeLorme, 1900s- .

> Notes:
> Detailed topographic maps emphasize outdoor recreation
> Relief shown by contours, spot heights, and shading
> Scales vary with size and topography of state
> Contents:
> *Colorado Atlas & Gazetteer.* - 7th ed. - 2004. - 1 atlas
> (104 p.)
> Class Numbers:
> Library of Congress G1500
> ISBN 0899332889
> OCLC 57180417
> *Kansas Atlas & Gazetteer.* - 2006. – 1 atlas (80 p.)
> Class Numbers:
> Library of Congress G1455
> ISBN 0899333427
> OCLC 80016041
> *Montana Atlas & Gazetteer.* - 2001. - 1 atlas (96 p.).
> Class Numbers:
> Library of Congress G1470
> ISBN 0899333397
> OCLC 47645138
> *Nebraska Atlas & Gazetteer.* - 3rd ed. – 2005 - 1 atlas

(80 p.).
Call Numbers;
    Library of Congress G1450
ISBN 0899333281
OCLC 60130397
New Mexico Atlas & Gazetteer. – 2003 - 1 atlas (72 p.).
Class Numbers:
    Library of Congress G1505
ISBN 0899333176
OCLC 54013296
North Dakota Atlas & Gazetteer. - 2005. - 1 atlas
    (64 p.).
Class Numbers:
    Library of Congress G1440
OCLC 62394223
Oklahoma Atlas & Gazetteer. - 2006. - 1 atlas (68 p.).
ISBN 0899332838
OCLC 70963094
South Dakota Atlas & Gazetteer. - 2004. - 1 atlas
    (72 p.).
Class Numbers:
    Library of Congress G1445
ISBN 0899333303
OCLC 61048587
Texas Atlas & Gazetteer. - 6th ed. - 2005. - 1 atlas
    (168 p.).
Class Numbers:
    Library of Congress G1370
ISBN 0899333206
OCLC 65198444
LCCN 2007-627150
Wyoming Atlas & Gazetteer. - 2006. - 1 atlas (72 p.).
OCLC 76950945

• Besides topographical maps, DeLorme atlases list features
(e.g., attractions, scenic drives, historic sites and districts)
and provide charts that show locations of state parks and
recreation areas, campgrounds, national lands, wildlife
viewing areas, natural features, hunting areas, bicycle
routes, and areas for fishing, boating, or hiking. Maps show
roads, trails, railroads (active and abandoned), power lines,
and settled areas. The combination of features and contour lines
is useful, allowing, for example, bicyclists to determine difficulty of trails, and showing terrain near historic sites. Serious
researchers and some travelers will need supplementary sources,
but the DeLorme maps have large scale and will be found useful by a wide variety of readers. —*JD, GK*

CI11   Virtual Nebraska [Internet Site] / Consortium for
the Application of Space Data to Education (CASDE). -
[Lincoln, NE] : Consortium for the Application of Space
Data to Education, 1995- . - http://casde.unl.edu/

Access Date: Jan. 2006
Notes:
    Co-sponsored by Jet Propulsion Laboratory (Pasadena,

CA), Univ. of Nebraska-Lincoln, and Univ. of
Nebraska-Omaha
Fees: None

• *Virtual Nebraska* is an online archive of satellite imagery,
space shuttle photographs, color infrared photographs of
towns and landscapes, vegetation, airport images, digital
elevation models, and image processing tools, all relating to
Nebraska. Since it was developed for classroom use at the
K-12 level, the site and its highly technical data are easy to
understand and use, especially with such user aids as tutorials and a glossary. Among the educational modules is
"Historical Nebraska," which contains histories and early
photos of 600 Nebraska communities digitized from a book
series, "Nebraska... Our Towns." Despite its educational
emphasis, the site will interest practitioners in engineering,
architecture, history, city planning, business, and agriculture. Image files have been reduced in size for Internet
delivery; most exceed 50K. Readers may acquire posters of
images on the site and original data on CD-ROM or ftp;
fees are charged for these items. —*JD*

Atlases, Historical

CI12   Atlas of Ancient America / by Michael Coe, Dean
Snow, and Elizabeth Benson. - New York : Facts on File,
1986. - 240 p. ; col. ill.

Class Numbers:
    Library of Congress E61
ISBN 0816011990
OCLC 11518017
LCCN 84-25999
Notes:
    Bibliography: p. 226-227; index
    Originally publ.: Oxford (UK): Equinox, c1986

• An encyclopedia of archaeological sites in the Western
Hemisphere, Greenland to Tierra del Fuego, that describes
the Indian cultures that inhabited the Hemisphere, and
their remains, before the advent of Europeans. Intended for
a general audience, the style does not fight shy of technical
terminology, but can be easily understood by educated
adults. The authors, while clearly familiar with the archaeological literature, are not identified (Coe's specialty is the
Maya). Splendid photographs (many in color) constitute
the book's principal appeal, and maps in color are plentiful.
The section on the Great Plains is brief (4 p.), in part
because early sites there are scattered and lack the magnif-
icence of those in the Southwest, never mind those in
Mexico and South America. Useful principally to provide
background concerning pre-European cultures in the
Americas. —*RB*

CI13 Hoehn, R. Philip, 1941- . - **Union List of Sanborn Fire Insurance Maps Held by Institutions in the United States and Canada** / foreword by Walter W. Ristow. - Santa Cruz, CA : Western Association of Map Libraries, 1976-1977. - 2 v. - (Western Association of Map Libraries. Occasional paper, 2-3).

Class Numbers:
Library of Congress HG9771   Z6026.I7
LCCN 76-6129
Notes:
Includes bibliographical references (v. 2, p. 200-201)
Vol. 2 by W.S. Peterson-Hunt and E.L. Woodruff; with
suppl. and corrigenda to v. 1 by R.P. Hoehn

• Lists Sanborn fire insurance maps held by libraries and other institutions in the U.S. and Canada, indicating the institutions that hold copies. The Library of Congress and California State Univ., Northridge, are omitted, since their holdings are listed elsewhere (for LC's holdings, see below). Participating institutions are listed in the front matter. The list is arranged alphabetically by state, then by city or town. — *RB*

CI13a Library of Congress. Geography and Map Division. Reference and Bibliography Section. - **Fire Insurance Maps in the Library of Congress : Plans of North American Cities and Towns Produced by the Sanborn Map Company** / introd. by Walter W. Ristow. - Washington, DC : Library of Congress, 1981. - 2 v. (773 p.) ; ill., maps (some col.).

Class Numbers:
Library of Congress Z6026.I7
ISBN 0844403377
LCCN 80-607938
Notes:
Indexes

• Lists maps originally compiled by the Sanborn Map Company (Pelham, NY) that depicted some 12,000 cities and towns in the United States and that were intended to assist agents of fire insurance firms in determining risks associated with writing fire insurance for individual buildings. Sanborn began publishing the maps in 1867 and continued into the late 20th century. Many of the maps no longer represent the situation on the ground in U.S. cities and towns, so do not serve for insurance purposes, but they are a rich source for civic history. Maps for many locations were revised frequently, making them highly valuable in tracing town histories. Maps are arranged alphabetically by state, then city. All ten Plains states have place in the checklist, and although the front matter claims maps for towns in Canada, only five towns are covered, none in the Prairie provinces. Indexes of counties and of cities and towns. —*RB*

CI13b **Digital Sanborn Maps, 1867-1970 [Internet Site]**. - Ann Arbor, MI : ProQuest Information and Learning Co., 2001. - http://sanborn.umi.com/

Access Date: Sep. 2006
Fees: Subscription

• Over 660,000 maps of over 12,000 towns, on a scale of 50 feet to an inch, were digitized from the black-and-white microfilm files, reproduced in turn from the original printed color maps in the Library of Congress. Sanborn maps show building outlines and heights, construction materials, locations of doors and windows, street and sidewalk widths, street names and numbers, pipelines, railroads, wells, dumps, machinery, and other features. Additions and corrections were issued at intervals so that seven to eight maps may have been issued for a particular city over time. The maps use shading, but the loss of color in the microfilm and digital versions makes the maps more difficult to read and appreciate. The Library of Congress also owns a set of printed maps in which revisions were pasted over the original map, as the Sanborn Company intended. Such maps, in which a city's growth and development can be "read" in the varied thicknesses of pasted paper, are often still available at state historical societies or city planning offices. An excellent resource for urban planners, historians, and genealogists. —*JD*

CI14 Paullin, Charles Oscar, 1868 or 1869-1944. - **Atlas of the Historical Geography of the United States** / by Charles O. Paullin ; ed. by John K. Wright. - Westport, CT : Greenwood Pr., 1975. - 162 p. ; 688 maps (part col.) on 166 plates (part double) 37 cm. - (Carnegie Institution of Washington. Publication, 401).

Class Numbers:
Library of Congress G1201.S1
ISBN 0837182085
OCLC 2014398
LCCN 75-14058
Notes:
Reprint of the 1932 ed. publ. jointly by Carnegie
Institution of Washington and the American
Geographical Society of New York

• The first historical atlas of the U.S., this compilation by Paullin and a host of colleagues offers nearly 700 maps, a very detailed supporting text, and a thorough index. Its interest turns principally on its reproductions of early maps of portions of the North American continent and on its newly drawn maps that show various aspects of U.S. history through about 1930; any pretense of being up to date has long disappeared. Some maps will interest Prairies-Plains students (the 1810 Clark map of the Missouri River route between St. Louis and the mouth of the Columbia, Indian tribes and linguistic stocks, average annual rainfall, American exploration 1803-1852, western boundary of the Louisiana Purchase) but any of its maps will need to be reconciled with those based on more recent data. Of interest to historians and cartographers. —*RB*

D   History

DA: HISTORY, GENERAL

Scope. Includes works that cover the histories of North America, the United States, or Canada in their entirety and during all periods, but in which the Prairies-Plains region is recognized and has a defined place. The section also includes histories of the trans-Mississippi West, in which Prairies-Plains may be presumed to have a part, and histories that cover exploration in the region.

General Works

DA1   Cooke, Jacob Ernest, 1924–   , ed. - **Encyclopedia of the North American Colonies** / ed.-in-chief, Jacob Ernest Cooke;   associate eds., W.J. Eccles . . . [et al.]; special consultants, Mathé Allain . . .[et al.]. - New York: C. Scribner's Sons;   Toronto, Ont.: Maxwell Macmillan Canada;   New York: Maxwell Macmillan International, 1993. - 3 v.; maps.

> Class Numbers:
>   Library of Congress E45
>   ISBN 0684192691 (set)
>   LCCN 93-7609
>   Notes:
>   Book review (H-Net): http://www.h-net.org/review/
>   hrev-a0a3w5-aa
>   Includes bibliographical references; index

• Cooke (Lafayette College) and his colleagues offer a comprehensive encyclopedia about the European conquest and colonization of Canada and the U.S. The 274 topical essays, which range in length from 1,000 to 15,000 words, were written by 193 contributors from such fields as cultural anthropology, archaeology, folklore, history, theology, fine arts, and linguistics. The impact of frontier colonization on the Spanish borderlands and the subjugation of Native Americans are extensively covered. Thirty-two maps; chronology; cross-references; annotated bibliography; subject index. — *GK*

DA2   Kuehl, Warren F., 1924-   . - **Dissertations in History: An Index to Dissertations Completed in History Departments of United States and Canadian Universities.** - [Lexington, KY]: Univ. of Kentucky Pr., 1965-1972. - 2v.

> Class Numbers:
>   Library of Congress Z6201
>   ISBN 0813112648 (v. 2)
>   OCLC 5209325

LCCN 65-11832

> Notes:
>   Contents: [v. 1]. 1873-1960; v. 2, 1961-June 1970.
>   Supplement: Warren F. Kuehl, *Dissertations in History, 1970-June 1980*. Santa Barbara, CA: ABC-CLIO, 1985.
>   No more published

• An author list to dissertations accepted for the PhD degree written under "formally organized departments of history" (v. 1, p. ix) at institutions in the U.S. and Canada. The compilers make no attempt to identify dissertations on historical topics written outside departments of history. The first volume lists 7,659 dissertations, the second 5,884; entries are assigned sequential numbers that incorporate alphabetical letters (e.g., M95). Entries give author, title, university, and year. An index in each volume lists persons, places, and topics, referring to the sequential numbers. Dissertations relevant to Plains studies must be coaxed out of the index ("Great Plains," names of states, "Indians," names of peoples, "Buffalo"). The supplement, covering 1970-1980, adds 9,905 titles and abandons the alphanumeric scheme in favor of straight numbers, making an author index necessary to supplement the general index. Important for history graduate students settling on a dissertation topic. — *RB*

UNITED STATES

Guides

DA3   Billington, Ray Allen, 1903-   . - **Westward Expansion: A History of the American Frontier** / [by] Ray Allen Billington [and] Martin Ridge. - 5th ed. - Norman, OK: Univ. of Oklahoma Pr.; New York: Macmillan, 1982. - 892 p.; maps.

> Class Numbers:
>   Library of Congress E179.5
>   ISBN 0826319815
>   LCCN 2001-1518
>   Notes:
>   1st ed.: New York: Macmillan, 1949
>   A 6th ed., Albuquerque, NM: Univ. of New Mexico Pr., 2001, is an abridgment
>   Includes bibliographical references (p. 699-858)

• A standard history of the expansion to the West by white settlers into territory occupied by Indians, from the first settlements on the Eastern seaboard to the settlement of the Plains between the mid-19th century and its end. Billington and his successor Ridge consciously attempt to enlarge on Turner's frontier thesis, stressing the role of ordinary citizens in expansion and settlement and the geographic continuity in settlement that lay at the heart of Turner's hypothesis. The book deserves inclusion here on the strength of its bibliography (150 pages in the 5th edition), a long bibliographic essay that follows the arrangement of the book's 35 chapters and embodies at numerous points capsule appraisals of the titles it cites. There is no index, but Plains material can be easily isolated in chapters and sections in the bibliography on "The West and Slavery," "The Transportation Frontier," "The Indian Barrier," "The Ranchers' Frontier," " Opening the Plains," "The Farmers' Frontier," and "The Agrarian Revolt." A classic treatment, old but useful. — *RB*

DA4   Carman, Harry James. - **A Guide to the Principal Sources for American Civilization, 1800-1900, in the City of New York: Printed Materials** / by Harry J. Carman and Arthur W. Thompson. - New York: Columbia Univ. Pr., 1962. - xlvi, 630 p.

> Class Numbers:
>   Library of Congress Z1236
> OCLC 1267238
> LCCN 62-10450
> Notes:
>   Chronological successor to: *A Guide to the Principal Sources for Early American History (1600-1800) in the City of New York* / by E.B. Greene
>   For manuscript materials, see **DA13**

• Carman and Thompson list 19th-century printed materials held in depositories and major libraries in New York City. Topics include politics, architecture, boundary controversies, cookery, travel, economic institutions, education, ethnic groups, fine arts, foreign affairs, immigrants, social sciences, law, technology, libraries, literature, medicine, military science, music, newspapers, personal records, philosophy, pictorial files, public records, reform, religion, science, societies, sports, theater, and vital statistics. Materials regarding the Great Plains and the West are listed by state under each subject classification. Key to abbreviations; directory of the principal libraries and depositories. — *GK*

DA5   **Harvard Guide to American History** / Frank Freidel, ed., with the assistance of Richard K. Showman. - Rev. ed. - Cambridge, MA: Belknap Pr. of Harvard Univ. Pr., 1974. - 2 v. (xxx, 1290 p.).

> Class Numbers:
>   Library of Congress Z1236
> ISBN 0674375556 (pbk.)   0674375602
> LCCN 72-81272
> Notes:
>   Editions for 1954 and 1967 by O. Handlin and others

• One might expect that the Harvard Department of

History would be dismissive toward the Prairies-Plains region, since it lies west of the Alleghenies, but in fact *Harvard Guide* treats Prairies-Plains evenhandedly, reporting a decent share of the books and articles that had appeared by the time of its publication. Under Section 12, "Regional, State, and Local Histories," citations to Prairies-Plains items are divided about equally between "Middle West" and "West" (Prairies-Plains has no subsection of its own), and under subsection 12.3, "State and Local History," publications concerning all 13 of the Prairies-Plains states and provinces may be found (although for some states the list is embarrassingly brief). In Section 13, "Westward Expansion and the Frontier," citations relating to Prairies-Plains are scattered through several subsections, including "General," "Exploration," "Regional Studies: Middle West," "Regional Studies: Great Plains" (the only recognition the editors award the Plains as a region), and "Spanish Borderlands." "Topical Studies" (also in Section 13) lists Prairies-Plains publications under subheadings "Military Frontier," "Law Enforcement," "Pioneer Life," "Trails," "The Western Hero" (only four citations), "Cowboys and Cattle Raising," "Buffalo," "Government Policy and the Territories," and "Frontier Mining: Other Gold Rushes." Finally, a section on "Historiography" (Section 13 again) offers a long subsection, "Turner Thesis," and another, "Comparative Frontiers," that covers Canadian Prairie provinces and probably occurs in the section on historiography for want of any better place to put it. These are rather small parts of *Harvard Guide*, and publications of interest to Plains students no doubt occur elsewhere in the two volumes, but digging them out requires scanning pages of closely set type under headings one hopes will yield some result. There are no annotations to help searchers. If an argument were needed concerning the benefits of electronic databases, one need only consider the comparative ease with which a well-designed computer-based file could turn up individual items on a topic of interest from a file the size of *Harvard Guide*. Despite its age, *Harvard Guide* will still serve students well. Not only is it a selection by specialists from a very large corpus of publications, it is arranged by a classification scheme that puts the discipline in order and tells readers at any moment where they are in the subject. — *RB*

DA6   Library of Congress. General Reference and Bibliography Division. - **A Guide to the Study of the United States of America: Representative Books Reflecting the Development of American Life and Thought** ... / prepared under the direction of Roy P. Basler, by D.H. Mugridge and B.P. McCrum . - Washington, DC: [Library of Congress. General Reference and Bibliography Division], 1960. - 1193 p.

> Class Numbers:
>   Library of Congress Z1215
> ISBN 0844401641 (v. 2)
> OCLC 248042

Notes:
> Supplement: *A Guide to the United States of America, Supplement 1956-1965: Representative Books Reflecting the Development of American Life and Thought* / prep. under the direction of Roy P. Basler, by Oliver H. Orr Jr. and staff of the Bibliography and Reference Correspondence Div. Washington, DC: Library of Congress, 1977. 526 p.

• Although intended to select titles "that reflect the development of life and thought in the United States," this well-known bibliography is equally a guide to the life and thought of the era in which it was compiled. The nearly 6,500 extensively annotated entries are organized into chapters on such topics as language, the American Indian, intellectual history, medicine and public health, religion, law and justice, and books and libraries. An appendix includes selected readings for American studies courses. The thorough index provides access to works on Great Plains individuals, places, peoples, and topics. Still a useful, highly cited source for American history. — *JD*

DA7   Parish, Peter J., ed. - **Reader's Guide to American History**. - London; Chicago, IL: Fitzroy Dearborn Publ., 1997. - xxxv, 880 p.

> Class Numbers:
> Library of Congress E178   Z1236
> ISBN 1884964222
> LCCN 98-101338
> Notes:
> > Includes bibliographical references; indexes

• Parish's historiographical approach to events, issues, and individuals that shaped American history concentrates on political, economic, and social scholarship. Entries, alphabetically arranged, cite references to major books or articles used as sources. Subjects of interest to Prairies-Plains study include immigration, Native Americans, German Americans, Scandinavian Americans, and populism, along with geographical essays on the Midwest, Great Plains, and Southwest. Thematic list of entries by category, cross-references, booklist index, and notes on contributors. — *GK*

DA8   Prucha, Francis Paul. - **Handbook for Research in American History: A Guide to Bibliographies and Other Reference Works**. - 2nd ed., rev. - Lincoln, NE: Univ. of Nebraska Pr., 1994. - 214 p.

> Class Numbers:
> Library of Congress E178   Z1236
> ISBN 0803237014
> LCCN 93-4240
> Notes:
> > Index

• Prucha (history, Marquette Univ.) surveys reference materials for research in U.S. history, arranging materials by form of publication (e.g., "General Bibliographies," "Oral History Materials," "Dictionaries and Encyclopedias") or by source ("The National Archives"). The 1,000 titles he cites are numbered, but citations and sequential numbers are buried in a narrative text that conveys their relationships and stitches them together, which makes digging out individual titles an annoyance readers might have been spared. Most of the titles related to Prairies-Plains are found in chapter 15, "Local, State, and Regional Materials"; most of those will be found in the present bibliography. Students of U.S. history, whatever their interest, should examine Prucha's sturdy book as a means of situating themselves in the literature of the discipline. — *RB*

Bibliographies

DA9   History Resource Center, U.S. [Internet Site]. - [Farmington Hills, MI]: Gale Group, c2002–   . - http://infotrac.galegroup.com/

> LCCN 2002-556418
> Access Date: Mar. 2006
> Fees: Subscription

• HRCUS provides access to more than 1,000 primary source documents, some 30,000 articles from various Gale publications, and citations to journal articles, including full text from over 65 journals, covering themes, events, personalities, and eras in U.S. history from pre-Colonial times to the present. Because the database is so large, it holds a great deal of information relevant to the study of the Prairies-Plains region. It offers basic search, free-form subject search, person search (by name) or, using Boolean operators, by nationality, profession, birth/death dates, birthplace, and gender. The search engine allows choice of free text or controlled vocabulary searching, but the results when subject terms are entered in the basic search box vary widely and unpredictably. For example, "Sacagawea" and "Sacajawea" yield completely different records, with the latter the preferred spelling. "Crazy Horse" in the person index gets different results than "Crazy Horse" in the subject index. Advanced search allows Boolean operators in searching full text, keyword, subject, person, title, headline, source, author, or time period. Search results are displayed by data type: reference materials, periodical articles, primary sources, maps, and multimedia (including audio and video clips of historic speeches and events). The database also features an interesting "mouse over" chronology bar (1492-present). — *MB*

DA10   **Writings on American History**. – [1st] (1902) -

[Final] (1989/90.) - Millwood, NY [etc.]: KTO Pr. [etc.], 1902-1989/90. Annual.

Class Numbers:
  Library of Congress AS32.A5; Z1236.L331
OCLC 1770230
LCCN 04-8590
Notes:
  Carnegie Institution of Washington. Publication, 38
  Cumulative index: 1902-1940. 1 v.
  Cumulative index: Writings on American History.
    Indexes. Comp. by Grace G. Griffin (with Dorothy M.
    Louraine), 1906- ; Katherine M. Tate, 1933-1934;
    Margaret K. Patterson, 1937/1938 –. Card file, 3 x 5, in
    two segments, 1906-1935 and 1936- . Held by Local
    History and Genealogy Reading Room, Library of
    Congress
  Earlier information in: *The Literature of American
    History* and its supplements
  No bibliographies issued for 1904-1905, 1941-1947
  Publisher varies: v. for 1909-1911 reprinted from *Annual
    Report* of the American Historical Association; 1918-
    1929 as supplement to the *Report*; 1930-1931, 1935 –
    as v. 2 of the *Report*; 1932 as v. 3 of the *Report*; 1933-
    1934 as the complete *Report*; 1948-1949 by the Library
    of Congress; 1950 by the National Historical Publica-
    tions Commission; [1973/1974–1977/1978] by the
    American Historical Association
  Some vols. issued in the congressional series as House doc-
    uments
  Some years issued in multiple vols.
  Supplementary vols.: Grace Gardner Griffin, Writings on
    American History, 1909-1911: A Bibliography of
    Books and Articles on United States and Canadian
    History. Washington, DC: [American Historical
    Association], 1911-1913. 2 v. – *Writings on American
    History, 1962- 1973: A Subject Bibliography of Books
    and Monographs: Based on a Compilation by James
    R. Masterson*. Washington, DC: American Historical
    Association; White Plains, NY: Kraus International
    Publ., 1985. 10 v.;
  Suspended 1962-1972; a 4 v. set covering 1962-1972 publ.
    1976

• For many years, *Writings* was the American Historical Association's principal means of recording historical scholarship relating to the North American continent. Beginning in 1902 and continuing with various interruptions and suspensions until the issue for 1989/90, it was then abandoned, perhaps because of competition from other publishers or from electronic sites; *Writings* is not available in electronic form. From the beginning, it was arranged by a subject classification that went through a number of revisions, finally settling into four categories: "General," "Chronological," "Geographical," and "Subjects." The general section has divisions for matters of concern to historians (historiography, teaching). The chronological section has divisions for various colonizers of North America (British, French, Spanish, other), and beginning with a division for 19th century, is arranged by

recognizable temporal divisions (Civil War, industrialism, World War I, New Deal) to the present. Any of these divisions will have potential for Prairies-Plains study. The geographical section has a division "Great Plains and Rocky Mountain States" that covers Idaho, Montana, Colorado, Wyoming, the Dakotas, Nebraska, Kansas, Nevada, and Utah; Texas, Oklahoma, and New Mexico are considered Southwest. In the subjects section, a number of subdivisions will yield Prairies-Plains material: "Agriculture," "Transportation," "Exploration," "Weather," "Flora and Fauna," "Literature," "Popular Culture," "Rural History," "Immigration and Settlement," "History of the American Indian," various ethnic groups. There is no other subject access, although each volume has an author index. Entries give all necessary bibliographic details, without annotations. Researchers may like to save Writings until a project nears its end, then use it to be certain no item of interest has been missed; even then, it means poring over many volumes. The attractions of *Writings* for researchers in American (or Plains) history are the care with which it was compiled and its reach back to materials published at the beginning of the 20th century. — *RB*

Catalogs

DA11   Harvard University Library. - **American History**. - Cambridge, MA: Distr. by Harvard Univ. Pr., 1967. - 5 v. - (Harvard University. Library. Widener Library shelflist, no. 9-13).

Class Numbers:
  Library of Congress Z1236
LCCN 67-30955
Notes:
  Contents: v. 1, Classification schedule and classified listing
    by call number US 1-10796; v. 2, Classified listing by
    call number US 10805-42629; v. 3, Alphabetical listing
    by author or title A-L; v. 4, Alphabetical listing by
    author or title M-Z; v. 5, Chronological listing by date
    of publication

• The "Widener Library Shelflists" were among the early library publications produced with the assistance of computerized processing (in this case, punched cards). They generated much interest in the library world, and were seen as important sources in building library collections, since the shelflist format could be compared with comparative ease with books at the shelf. (A shelflist is a set of records arranged in the same order as books on the shelf, by classification.) The *American History* shelflist is arranged by the classification used at the Harvard libraries; a typical class number begins with the designation "US" followed by a set of numbers that represent class divisions. Volume 1 supplies the classification schedule, then lists, continuing into volume 2, records in class order that give, item for item, all books and other materials that sat on the Harvard shelves, supplying for each entry author, title, place, and publication date. Volumes 3 and 4 consist of author and title indexes to the entries in volumes 1-2, and volume 5 is an index by date of publication. Several parts of the classification may be helpful to students or collection building staff working on Prairies-Plains topics: American Indians at US 10200-10566; Kansas at US 28505-28996, Nebraska at US 29005-29496, Oklahoma at US 30005-30496, the Dakotas at US 31005-31996. The remaining Prairies-Plains states can be easily found in the classification summary, and in the classified lists by call number that follow. To be sure, this shelflist is now 40 years old, so lacks the utility it once had, even at the Harvard libraries; nevertheless, it provides a useful benchmark for libraries trying to appraise their collections, so can be helpful even to libraries that lack Harvard's resources. These days, libraries have access to files that can be more easily manipulated and compared with local holdings, but for pre-1965 publications, the Widener shelflists stand as a useful record of publication. — *RB*

Indexes

DA12   America: History and Life. - v. 26 no. 1 (1989)- . Santa Barbara, CA: ABC-CLIO, 1989- . Quarterly.

Class Numbers:
   Library of Congress Z1236
   OCLC 19247941
   LCCN 89-659058 sn 89-44080
   Notes:
      Also available on CD-ROM
      Also publ.: *Five-Year Index*, covering v. 1-5 (1964-1969)–v. 26-30 (1989-1993), 6 v., quinquennial
      Publishing history: v. 0 (1972) covers periodical literature publ. 1954 until the issuance of v. 1 (1964); v. 1 (1964)–v. 5 (1969) publ. in 1 v.; v. 6 (1969)–v. 10 (1973); split into pt. A, Article Abstracts and Citations, v. 11 no. 1 (1974)–v. 25 no. 3 (1988), 3 nos. per year; pt. B, Index to Book Reviews, v. 11 no. 1 (1975)–v. 25 no. 2 (1988). semiannual; pt. C, American History Bibliography, Books, Articles and Dissertations, v. 11 (1974)–v. 25 (1988), annual; pt. D, Annual Index, v. 11 (1974)–v. 25 (1988), annual; sections A-D merged to form *America: History and Life*, v. 26 no. 1 (1989)–

DA12a   America: History and Life [Internet Site]. - Santa Barbara, CA: ABC-CLIO Information Services, 2001- . - http://sb1.abc-clio.com/

Class Numbers:
   Library of Congress E171   Z1236
   LCCN 2001-561909
   Access Date: Oct. 2005
   Notes:
      Coverage: Prehistory to the present
      HTML source code title: ABC-CLIO history online

Indexes periodicals published 1964–
Updated three times yearly
Fees: Subscription

• A standard, highly useful index to periodicals in American and Canadian history, AHL offers (as of Oct. 2005) 490,000 entries, 1954 to the present, drawn from 1,700 journals, supplemented by 6,000 entries for book reviews. About 16,000 records are added to the database annually. The Advisory Board includes such noted historians as James M. McPherson (Princeton), William Leuchtenburg (North Carolina–Chapel Hill), Lawrence S. Kaplan (Georgetown), and Nancy Hewitt (Rutgers). The source will prove very useful to scholars and students researching Prairies and Plains topics. It provides ample citations to articles about the ten Plains states and three Canadian Prairie provinces (e.g., 1,736 records for Manitoba, 1,329 for Saskatchewan, and 1,958 for Alberta) and about specific locations (Black Hills, 110 records). Using AHL emphasizes the limitations of LC subject headings in searching: a "Great Plains" search produces 1,873 records, while "Middle West" produces only 110; but "Midwest" (not an official LC subject heading) produces 960. AHL provides entries for regional and state journals, many of which are not available in electronic format, either individually or in various journal collection archive sites. An "Advanced Search" feature allows users to search by keyword, subject term, author or editor, title, language, document type, journal, publication date, period of coverage, and entry number. Searches can be limited to articles, book/media reviews, collections, and dissertations. Adding a second keyword box and the ability to limit searches by geographic region would be significant improvements. — *GK*

§   Using AHL in its printed form requires patience and the willingness to confront a battery of printed volumes that have taken up residence on library shelves. The editors at ABC-CLIO took time to arrive at the present state of the publication, which is issued every year in four quarterly volumes that index periodical articles, list reviews, and cite dissertations, and a fifth volume that indexes the quarterly issues in elaborate detail. The citations are complete but are arranged in a sequence used only by AHL: author, title, journal, date (printed in italic so it appears to be part of the title), issue, inclusive pages. Citations to articles all have abstracts (reviews do not) which are signed by the preparer, or end with "J" (copied from the journal abstract) or "S" (prepared by ABC-CLIO staff). The quarterly issues are arranged by a classification that emphasizes period divisions but includes topical sections as well, and has regional sections, one of which is "Western States" that sweeps up all the Prairies-Plains states except Oklahoma and Texas, which are listed with "South Central or Gulf States." Indians have a section with the initial class, "North America." Since each quarterly issue begins the classification afresh, the index volume is essential. Not many researchers will choose the printed version of AHL over its electronic counterpart, but everyone should visit the printed version at least once in order to get the classification sequence in mind: it sets everything in context, not only for AHL, whichever version is used, but for the study of American history for all periods. It presents the discipline in an order worked out by historians (with advice from librarians)—a service whose value cannot be overstated. —*RB*

Manuscripts; Archives

DA13 Carman, Harry J. - **A Guide to the Principal Sources for American Civilization, 1800-1900, in the City of New York: Manuscripts** / by Harry J. Carman and Arthur W. Thompson. - New York: Columbia Univ. Pr., 1960. - 453 p.

Class Numbers:
    Library of Congress Z1236
    LCCN 60-6935
    Notes:

Site List 12
Historical Records Surveys

Between 1935 and 1942, the Historical Records Survey of the Work Projects Administration, in partnership with state agencies, surveyed research resources in American history available in each state. Four major series were compiled, as well as indexes of school, church, military, cemetery, and other records. Work was slow, and in many cases by the time WPA disbanded, only preliminary editions had appeared or the work remained unpublished. Although the records they cite may have met a variety of fates, the state surveys remain useful in identifying primary documents. Published in short press runs, the surveys were distributed to selected libraries and depositories in each state; many are not listed in WorldCat. The original files and microfilm copies were deposited with the state partners, often the state historical society, where they constitute a little-known resource valuable to researchers. Many indexes of interest to genealogists can be found on the Internet.

Two titles provide comprehensive bibliographies:

Sargent B. Child and Dorothy P. Holmes, *Checklist of Historical Records Survey Publications: Bibliography of Research Projects Reports* (**DA14**).

Loretta L. Hefner, *The WPA Historical Records Survey: A Guide to the Unpublished Inventories, Indexes and Transcripts* (**DA15**).

Major Surveys

Inventory of the County Archives of [state]. Issued in separate volumes for each county, identifying unique and specialized local documents. Volumes summarize county history; government organization and records system; housing, care, and accessibility of records; and histories and functions of local government agencies. Documents cited include insanity records, financial ledgers, court cases, and water rights records. Inventories were completed for some counties in all Prairies-Plains states.

Inventory of Federal Archives in the States: [state]. Describe federal archives in federal offices, field offices, and other agencies in each state. Issued in series: Series I discussed administration of the survey and location, condition, and content of archives; Series I-XVII covered executive departments or major units of federal government. In each series, no. 1 introduces organization and records of the agency, reserving subsequent numbers for records available in individual states. Records include correspondence, lawsuits, blueprints, immigration inves-tigations, and work assignments. Inventories were published for all Prairies-Plains states.

Guide to Depositories of Manuscript Collections in the United States: [state]. Least complete of the surveys, guides inventoried manuscripts and archives in libraries, historical societies, museums, and other organizations in the states, including papers of early settlers, meeting notes, and business records. Only Nebraska published a guide, issued as a preliminary edition.

"American Imprints Inventory" series. [State titles vary.] HRS planned to publish checklists of titles printed or published in each state to the time of statehood. According to the American Memory project, when work ceased in 1942 HRS had on hand about 15 million slip records of books, pamphlets, and broadsides; 49 checklists had been published from the slips. Now held by Rutgers Univ., the slips continue to be used by researchers. Prairies-Plains titles are:

No. 10, *Check List of Kansas Imprints, 1854-1876.*
No. 18, *Check List of Wyoming Imprints, 1866-1890.*
No. 25, *Check List of New Mexico Imprints and Publications, 1784-1876.*
No. 26, *Check List of Nebraska Non-Documentary Imprints, 1847-1876.*
No. 47, *Check List of Texas Imprints, 1848-1860.*
No. 48, *Check List of Texas Imprints, 1861-1876.*

No. 27, *Check List of Nebraska Documentary Imprints*, although listed in both WorldCat and the Library of Congress catalog, was apparently never published.

Continues (in part): *A Guide to the Principal Sources for Early American History (1600-1800) in the City of New York* / by E.B. Greene
    For printed materials, see **DA4**

• Carman and Thompson list 19th-century manuscripts held in depositories and major libraries in New York. Topics include politics, architecture, boundary controversies, cookery, travel, economic institutions, education, ethnic groups, fine arts, foreign affairs, immigrants, social sciences, legal, technology, libraries, literature, medicine, military, music, newspapers, personal records, philosophy, pictorial, public records, reform, religion, science, societies, sports, theatre, and vital statistics. Manuscripts regarding the Great Plains and the West are listed by state under each subject classification that include major entries for Colorado, Kansas, Missouri, Montana, Nebraska, New Mexico, the Dakotas, and Wyoming. Key to abbreviations and directory of principal libraries. — *GK*

DA14 Child, Sargent Burrage, 1900- . - **Check List of Historical Records Survey Publications: Bibliography of Research Projects Reports** / prepared by Sargent B. Child and Dorothy P. Holmes. – Baltimore, MD: Genealogical Publ. Co., 1969. - 110 p.

   Class Numbers:
      Library of Congress Z1236
   OCLC 47927
   Notes:
      Reprint. Originally publ.: Washington, DC: Federal
         Works Agency. Work Projects Administration.
         Div. of Service Projects, 1943. (WPA technical series.
         Research and records bibliography, 7).

• In 1936, the Historical Records Survey began surveying each state's resources in American history. Surveys were coordinated with various state agencies, often the state historical society or state library. HRS produced four major surveys for each state: *Guide to Depositories of Manuscript Collections in the United States:* [state]; *Inventory of the County Archives of* [state]; *Inventory of Federal Archives in the States:* [state]; and "American Imprints Inventory" series. HRS also indexed school, military, and other records that interest genealogists. Though about 1,800 volumes were ultimately published, many titles in the series were not completed when the WPA disbanded in 1942. In this final list of HRS publications 1936-1943, entries are arranged by state and series. Appendix 1 lists records microfilmed as part of the survey projects; Appendix 2 is a bibliography of articles and papers about the HRS; Appendix 3 lists the manuals used by the surveyors; Appendix 4 is a bibliography of state reports and summaries; and Appendix 5 lists the state depositories holding the remaining unpublished material, estimated by the authors to be eight to ten times the amount of the published material. Essential for those trying to identify and locate HRS titles. — *JD*

DA15 Hefner, Loretta L., comp. - **The WPA Historical

198

Records Survey: A Guide to the Unpublished Inventories, Indexes and Transcripts. - Chicago, IL: Society of American Archivists, 1980. - vi, 42 p. 28 cm.

   Class Numbers:
      Library of Congress E173 Z1236
   ISBN 0931828252 (pbk.)
   OCLC 7381769
   LCCN 80-51489
   Notes:
      Microfiche (90 frames) in pocket
      Supported in part by a grant from the National
         Endowment for the Humanities

• Historical Records Survey, a project of the WPA, conducted in 1936-1942 a series of massive inventories of public records and state imprints. By the time it disbanded, HRS had produced about 1,800 publications and a mass of unpublished inventory records. The inventories were sent to repositories (often historical societies or land-grant universities) in each of the participating states. Hefner surveyed the repositories nearly 40 years later to find out which series were still available to researchers and which had been lost, discarded, or moved to another location. Her findings, organized by state, summarize each state's activities, give directory information for the current repository, note collection size, and list inventory series for which records exist. An appendix provides a matrix of repositories and series holdings. The microfiche contains a list of agencies surveyed by HRS and copies of inventory forms. — *JD*

Encyclopedias

DA16 **Dictionary of American History** / Stanley I. Kutler, ed.-in-chief. - 3rd ed. - New York: Charles Scribner's Sons, c2003. - 10 v.; ill., maps.

   Class Numbers:
      Library of Congress E174
   ISBN 0684805332 (set)
   LCCN 2002-12433
   Notes:
      1st ed., ed. by James Truslow Adams, New York:
         Scribner, 1940 (6 v.); 2nd ed., ed. by Adams,
         New York: Scribner, 1976 (6 v.) and Supplement,
         ed. by Robert H. Ferrell and Joan Hoff, 1996 (2 v.)
      Contents: v. 1-8, A-Z; v. 9, Archival maps and primary
         sources; v. 10, Contributors, learning guide, index

• Since publication of the 1st ed., DAH has been the leading encyclopedia for history of the U.S. This edition, although longer than its predecessor by 20 percent, has 2,000 fewer articles, the effect of consolidating smaller articles (which the preceding edition favored) into longer articles on more general topics. Some articles were retained but brought up to date to reflect recent research, some thoroughly revised, some replaced, some new (these changes are summarized in the preface, p. xvi-xvii). Illustrations are included for the first time. This edition also includes maps drawn contemporaneously with the events they portray, and a selection of primary documents, both in v. 10. The roster of contributors includes those whose articles have been carried over from the previous edition, gives for others their affiliations, and lists the articles written by all of them. The index is thorough and planned for easy consultation, with subheadings in a vertical stack below the entry instead of in paragraph form. For Plains students, the index will be essential, since subjects having to do with Prairies-Plains are scattered throughout the eight volumes of text. Some topics central to Plains studies are treated dismissively ("Lewis and Clark Expedition" has a column and a half and a map not wholly accurate). The editor claims to depart from emphasis on political and military history to the extent of including social, cultural, and economic forces that affect politics and giving greater emphasis to diversity–ethnic groups, socioeconomic classes, and women. But while generous coverage is given Pike, William Jennings Bryan, Frémont, Powell, and John Brown (all deserved), there is no mention of Sandoz, Cather, Wright Morris, Inge, or Angie Debo, or of aquifers or ground water. No reference work can be perfect, but DAH will continue to be a starting point for research in Plains history. — *RB*

DA17 **Encyclopedia of American History** / Gary B. Nash, general ed. - New York: Facts on File, 2003. - 11 v.; ill., maps.

Class Numbers:
Library of Congress E174 .E53
ISBN 081604371X (set)
OCLC 48074033
LCCN 2001-51278
Notes:
Contents: v. 1, Three Worlds Meet; v. 2, Colonization and Settlement; v. 3, Revolution and New Nation; v. 4, Expansion and Reform; v. 5, Civil War and Reconstruction; v. 6, The Development of the Industrial United States; v. 7, The Emergence of Modern America; v. 8, The Great Depression and World War II; v. 9, Postwar United States; v. 10, Contemporary United States; v. 11, Comprehensive Index
Includes bibliographical references; indexes

• Nash (history, UCLA) intends this set for a collegiate and pre-collegiate audience, and bases its unusual structure on the recommendations in *The National Standards for United States History*, rev. ed. (Los Angeles, CA: National Center for History in the Schools, 1996; Nash is Director of the Center). Nash follows the recommendations of *Standards* to divide U.S. history into sections according to the periods shown in the Contents note above and to choose major

topics, arranging topical articles alphabetically within each volume. Every volume lists the articles it contains, supplies a chronology, reprints key primary documents, and has an index to the volume. A number of longer articles appear in several volumes, so students can follow the development of important themes through various periods; some of these treat black Americans, business, family life, agriculture, immigration, Native Americans, and women. Volume 11 has a roster of editors and an index for the entire set. The volumes with content of greatest interest for Prairies-Plains study are 1, 3, 4, and 6, but the index is the best guide for Plains-related topics. Although the set devotes only two pages to "Great Plains" and two more to "Great Plains Indians," it has entries for Powell, Wilder, Bryan, McGovern, Chivington, Custer (of course), and the Lewis and Clark Expedition, but neglects aquifers, Angie Debo, Warren Buffett, and Earp. Cather is mentioned in a single sentence in one of the longer articles on literature, and Wounded Knee (1890) is mentioned only in a chronology. The writing gives the impression of breathless haste, and is pitched at the chosen audience, so will have limited interest for scholars. This set and the latest edition of *Dictionary of American History* (**DA16**) appeared within a week of one another in 2003. DAH is the more thorough work, with broader coverage and better bibliographies, and is intended to appeal to university students and scholars, so remains the encyclopedia of choice. — *RB*

DA18 Morris, Richard Brandon, 1904- . - **Encyclopedia of American History** / ed. by Richard B. Morris and Jeffrey B. Morris. - New York: HarperCollins, 1996. - 1278 p.; ill., maps.

Class Numbers:
Library of Congress E174.5
ISBN 0062700553
OCLC 34281392
LCCN 96-11191
Notes:
Index

• Arranged chronologically rather than topically, the Morrises' encyclopedia begins with a "basic" chronology that arranges entries by broad period (colonies and empire 1624-1775, Revolution, national and antebellum periods 1789-1860, Civil War, U.S. during World War II, etc.), beginning with a very brief 12-page summary of "Original Peopling of the Americas." This is followed by a topical chronology covering such topics as national expansion, population and immigration, important Supreme Court decisions, economy, science and invention, thought and culture, and mass media. A section of brief biographies includes among its 450 entries one Plains writer (Cather) and one Indian (Tecumseh). A brief final section ("Structure of the Federal Government") lists the presidents and their cabinets and Supreme Court justices. It is discouraging to search this book for any recognition of the existence of Prairies-Plains as a region. The landmark Lewis and Clark Expedition is dismissed in half a column, and Wounded Knee (called a "battle") in a sentence. Any chronology depends on its index to lead readers to topics, but of 12 index entries under "Great Plains," the two searched had nothing about the Plains on the pages cited. The Morrises' book may be helpful in establishing the sequence of events in U.S. history, but will be of little other use to Prairies-Plains students. — *RB*

DA19   The Oxford Companion to United States History / ed.-in-chief, Paul S. Boyer; eds., Melvyn Dubofsky [et al.]. - Oxford, UK; New York: Oxford Univ. Pr., 2001. - xliv, 940 p.; ill., maps.

> Class Numbers:
>   Library of Congress E174
> ISBN 0195082095
> OCLC 44426920
> LCCN 00-55801
> Notes:
>   Book review (H-net):
>   http://www.h-net.org/review/hrev-a0c0i3-aa
>   Includes bibliographical references; index
>   Also available at Oxford's Internet site:
>   http://www.oxfordreference.com/

• Boyer (history, Univ. of Wisconsin-Madison) with five associate editors presents an encyclopedia of 1,570 topical entries, signed and alphabetically arranged, that vary in length from 250 to 6,000 words. Longer essays for topics on the Prairies-Plains region include the West, expansionism, Indian history and culture, rural life, race and ethnicity, agriculture 1890-1920, livestock industry, and railroads, while shorter pieces cover German-Americans, Populist Party, Farmers Alliance Movement, Kansas-Nebraska Act, Battle of the Little Bighorn, Cherokee cases, Bureau of Indian Affairs, and the Rocky Mountains. Some legendary figures the work considers are Sitting Bull, Geronimo, Crazy Horse, Davy Crockett, and Jesse James. Roster of contributors; 26 maps. — *GK*

DA20   The Reader's Companion to American History / Eric Foner and John A. Garraty, eds. - Boston, MA: Houghton-Mifflin, 1991. - xxii, 1226 p.; maps.

> Class Numbers:
>   Library of Congress E174
> ISBN 0395513723 0585130833 (electronic bk.)
> OCLC 23766809
> LCCN 91-19508
> Notes:
>   Electronic book:
>   http://www.netLibrary.com/urlapi.asp?action=
>   summary&v=1&bookid=6785
>   Includes bibliographical references; indexes

Sponsored by the Society of American Historians

• Foner and Garraty (history, Columbia University) edit 1,000 alphabetical entries by 400 scholars, authors, and journalists that deal with major issues, events, and individuals that shaped American history. Entries of interest pertaining to Western history include agriculture, Granger movement, Brown v. Board of Education, William Jennings Bryan, Buffalo Bill Cody, Missouri Compromise, Compromise of 1850, cowboys, Dwight Eisenhower, Homestead Act, homesteading, immigration, Geronimo, Lewis and Clark expedition, Mormons, migration (Oregon Trail and Dust Bowl), railroads, Frederick Jackson Turner, Kansas-Nebraska Act, Indians, Chief Joseph, Gadsden Purchase, Gold Rush, and Zitkala-Sa. Roster of contributors. — *GK*

Atlases

DA21   The American Heritage Pictorial Atlas of United States History / by the editors of *American Heritage*. - New York: American Heritage Publ. Co.; book trade distr. by McGraw-Hill Book Co., 1966. - 424 p.; ill. (part col.), maps (part col.).

> Class Numbers:
>   Library of Congress G1201.S1
> OCLC 244933
> LCCN 66-29

• Intended to appeal to beginning students, *American Heritage* is filled with contemporary illustrations and with maps, some contemporary, some drawn for this atlas. Its maps cover topics of concern to Prairies-Plains researchers–the Louisiana Purchase, Indian cessions of land 1610-1850, routes to the West, government explorations and surveys 1849-1860, frontier and Indian wars 1860-1890, Indian reservations, cattle trails and the open range, railroad land grants, and the insensitively titled "Breaking Indian Resistance." Maps are accompanied by text that has space only for rude summary. Useful to help visualize national development for students new to U.S. or Plains studies. — *RB*

DA22   Atlas of American History / W. Kirk Reynolds, ed. . - 2nd rev. ed. - New York: Scribner, 1984. - 306 p.; maps; 29 cm.

> Class Numbers:
>   Library of Congress G1201.S1
> ISBN 068484112
> OCLC 11620514
> LCCN 84-675413
> Notes:
>   Based on the original ed., ed. by James Truslow Adams and

the rev. ed., ed. by Kenneth T. Jackson
Index

• The 253 maps include all 147 from the original edition, which emphasized the 18th and 19th century and focused on boundary disputes, battles, routes to the West, and American Indians, and some from the revised edition, emphasizing tribal groups, transportation, economic development, human rights, immigration, and 20th-century developments. Maps have been corrected and revised as needed. They are grouped chronologically, from America at the time of discovery by Europeans to the U.S. as a world power in 1977, with a separate section on economic and social development. Plains maps include "Trans-Mississippi French and Spanish 1600-1750"; "Indian Land Cessions 1784-1798"; "Indian Territory and the Southern Plains, 1817-1860"; "The Kansas-Missouri Border, 1854-1859"; "Cow Country, Railroads and Indian Troubles, 1865-1885"; "Sioux-Cheyenne Country 1865-1890"; "Woman's Suffrage 1869-1920"; "Indian Territory and the State of Oklahoma, 1883-1907"; "Sources of Immigration 1820-1975"; "Black Migration 1890-1980"; and "Hazardous Waste, 1983." The clearly drawn outline maps aid in understanding and teaching Plains history and life and, when used in combination with the location index, show the evolution of the region. A standard based on authoritative sources. —JD

DA23   Gilbert, Martin. - **Routledge Atlas of American History**. - 5th ed. - London; New York: Routledge, 2006. - 156 p.; 26 cm.

Class Numbers:
Library of Congress G1201 S1
ISBN 0415359023 0415359031 (pbk.)
9780415359023 9780415359030
OCLC 57281014
Notes:
4th ed., 2002
Scales vary.

• Augmented by inset tables and facts, the 156 maps cover politics, military events, social history, transportation, and economics from early Native American settlements to the beginning of the 21st century. Organized chronologically, maps include "Indian Peoples before 1492"; "Texas Independence 1836-1845"; "Indian Reservations 1788-1894"; "Public Lands and Railway Grants 1796-1890"; "Indian Lands Lost 1850-1890"; "Farming in 1920"; "Hazardous Waste Sites 1990"; and "Urbanization of the United States by 2000." Though more up-to-date and international in scope than *Atlas of American History* (**DA22**), Gilbert's atlas also complements Reynolds's coverage of 18th- and 19th-century Plains history and life. The clear, detailed, single-page maps can be easily copied for teaching and class assignments. No index. —JD

DA24   Texas Historic Sites Atlas [Internet Site]. - Austin, TX: Texas Historical Commission, 2000?-. - http://atlas.thc.state.tx.us/Index.asp

Access Date: May 2008
Fees: None

• Sponsored by the Texas Historical Commission, this site features over 300,000 entries for historic sites in Texas—official Texas historical markers, National Register of Historic Places properties, museums, courthouses, cemeteries, military sites, sawmills, and neighborhood surveys. From the home page, users are invited to enter the atlas, which leads to the preferred search method, by county. Counties are listed alphabetically, but are not keyed to a Texas map to indicate their location in the state. Other search types include keyword, map address, address, historic site designation, and site name. Searches can be limited by type of site, and in keyword search, cities, towns, and names of sites may be found. Sites located in a search are listed in alphabetical order in the left-hand column; entries for individual sites supply a site description (sometimes with a photograph) and a location map with zoom capabilities. Maps are somewhat indistinct, and zooming in does not provide greater clarity, only an enlargement of the basic map. County data, formatted for Excel, can be downloaded to the site. The site links to *Texas Beyond History*, a companion site on Texas archaeology (http://www.texasbeyondhistory.net/). —JB, RB

Oral History Aids

DA25   **Directory of Oral History Programs in the United States** / ed. by Patsy A. Cook. - Sanford, NC: Microfilming Corp. of America, 1982. - 138 p.

Class Numbers:
Library of Congress Z1236
ISBN 066700680X
LCCN 82-236695

• Cook, in cooperation with the Oral History Association, presents a directory of oral history programs in the United States. Oral history programs provide recordings of the recollections of individuals, adding an aural dimension to traditional written sources used in research. Entries are arranged by state and city and include the institution, the name of the program, director's name, address, cooperating institutions, principal topics, major collections, collection size, and general information (duplication services, interlibrary loan availability, hours of operation). Indexes of directors, programs, and subjects. — GK

Almanacs; Yearbooks

DA26   **Profiles of America**. - Millerton, NY: Grey House Publ., 2003. - 4 v.; ill., maps.

Class Numbers:
    Library of Congress HT123
    ISBN 1891482807 (set)
    OCLC 52458060
    LCCN 2003-269991
    Notes:
        Indexes
        Subtitle on cover: *Facts, Figures & Statistics for Every
            Populated Place in the United States*

• Organized by region, then alphabetically by state. Each state's entry begins with an outline county map that identifies Metropolitan Statistical Areas and primary cities, followed by an alphabetical place index (cities, counties, postal areas). Entries for each county include physical description, climatic data, population, religious affiliation, economic data, income, taxes, education, housing, health, elections, parks, and official contact information. Major community information adds history, school districts with phone numbers, church demographics, colleges and universities with enrollments and contact information, hospitals, newspapers, airports, and crime rates. Originally published in 1995, this 2003 update provides sources for the information, most of which is derived from 2000 census data. The work provides a total of 39,141 community profiles in all 50 states, made useful by the condensation of census data. Volume 4 contains a master index. All the Prairies-Plains states are included in volume 2 ("Western Region") except for Texas, classed in volume 1 ("Southern Region"). — *MB*

DA27   Worldmark Encyclopedia of the States. - 6th ed. - Detroit, MI: Gale Research, 2004. - 859 p.; ill., maps.

Class Numbers:
    Library of Congress E156
    ISBN 0787673382 0787677744 (electronic bk.)
    OCLC 451445522
    Notes:
        1st ed., 1981
        Formerly publ. by Worldmark Pr. Ltd.
        Includes bibliographical references
        States arranged alphabetically, including U.S. Caribbean
            and Pacific dependencies, but omitting District of
            Columbia

• A state-by-state compendium of information drawn from government and private sources that covers all the states of the U.S., its territories and dependencies, and adds a section on the United States itself. For each state, it shows (in black-and-white) the state seal and flag (flags are shown in color on the back endpapers); an outline map of the state that shows county lines, cities, rivers, interstate highways, and points of interest (e.g., grasslands, wildlife refuges); and disposes briefly at the beginning of some common characteristics (e.g., origin of state name, date of admission to the union, motto, state bird, legal holidays). For each

state, the editors then supply information in no fewer than 50 categories (topography, religions, history, state government, industry, social welfare, arts, famous citizens), ending with a bibliography, sometimes fairly long. The front endpapers show a map of the U.S. in color that serves to locate individual states. All the Plains states are included. Useful in gaining a factual picture of individual states. — *RB*

SOCIAL HISTORY

DA28   American Family History: A Historical Bibliography. - Santa Barbara, CA: ABC-Clio Information Services, 1984. - 282 p. - (ABC-Clio research guides).

Class Numbers:
    Library of Congress HQ535
    ISBN 0874363802
    OCLC 10532913
    LCCN 84-2955
    Notes:
        Indexes

• Editors at ABC-Clio drew the records in this research guide from the company's American history database. Its 1,167 abstracts cover 1973-1982 and use an author index and a subject profile index (ABC-SPIndex) to ensure accuracy in headings and cross-references. The book has four chapters: "Family in Historical Perspective," "Family and Social Institutions," "Familial Roles," and "Individual Family History." To find entries related to the Midwest or the Plains, readers must search each individual state or ethnic group. The most productive headings in the index are "Western Reserve," "Western States," and "Westward Movement," which yield ten records; only one is found under "Great Plains." — *GK*

DA29   Encyclopedia of American Social History / Mary Kupiec Cayton, Elliott J. Gorn, Peter W. Williams, eds. - Toronto, Ont.: Maxwell Macmillan Canada; New York: Maxwell Macmillan International; New York: Scribner, 1993. - 3 v. (xix, 2653 p.); ill.

Class Numbers:
    Library of Congress HN57
    ISBN 0684192462 (set)
    OCLC 25628823
    LCCN 92-10577
    Notes:
        Includes bibliographical references; index

• This set's 14 parts contain 169 essays by 174 contributors, the majority of whom are recognized scholars. Volume 1, focusing on methodology, includes articles on social change, identity, contexts, and methods, while volume 3 is devoted to specific themes such as popular culture, family history, social problems, social protest, science, medicine, technology, and education. Volume 2 will particularly interest readers researching the American West and Prairies-Plains; its part 5, "Ethnic and Racial Subcultures," includes essays on American Indians, Germans, Scandinavians, and Central and Eastern Europeans. Part 6, "Regionalism," has essays about the Upper Midwest, Great Plains, Southwest, Mormon Region, and Mountain West, and part 7, "Space and Place," includes articles on the natural environment of the West, the frontier, and rural life. Each essay is followed by a bibliography. — *GK*

TRANS-MISSSIPPI WEST

Bibliographies

See also Winther, **A Classified Bibliography of the Periodical Literature of the Trans-Mississippi West, AB12**

DA30 Adams, Ramon F. - **Burs Under the Saddle: A Second Look at Books and Histories of the West**. - Norman, OK: Univ. of Oklahoma Pr., 1964. - 182 p.

Class Numbers:
Library of Congress Z1251.W5
OCLC 514079

• This volume is much more specific in content than either the title or subtitle suggest. The very thorough subject index reveals the bibliography's scope: most entries are the names of outlaws. Since the volume's 424 numbered entries, arranged alphabetically, cover nearly 600 pages, each can be quite extensive. Entries are arranged alphabetically by main entry. Adams points out inaccuracies where necessary (e.g., he declares one biography of Calamity Jane fictional). — *MB*

DA30a Adams, Ramon F. - **More Burs Under the Saddle: Books and Histories of the West** / by Ramon F. Adams; foreword by Wayne Gard. - Norman, OK: Univ. of Oklahoma Pr., 1979. - 182 p.

Class Numbers:
Library of Congress F596   Z1251.W5
ISBN 080611469X
LCCN 77-18606

• Adams, a noted bibliographer and lexicographer, describes 233 titles having to do with the American West. His aim is to distinguish fact from fiction in books and pamphlets treating the American West that were published after 1964

(when the first ed. was published). Adams points out errors found in the publications he lists. Entries are arranged by author. The foreword is by Wayne Gard (retired editor, *Dallas Morning News*). — *GK*

DA31 Etulain, Richard W., comp. - **The American West, Comparative Perspectives: A Bibliography**. - Albuquerque, NM: Center for the American West, Dept. of History, Univ. of New Mexico, 1996. - 69 leaves. - (University of New Mexico. Center for the American West. Occasional papers, 12).

Class Numbers:
Library of Congress F591
OCLC 36831768

• Etulain (history emeritus, Univ. of New Mexico) compiles a bibliography of books, essays, and dissertations comparing the American West with foreign countries (Canada, Europe, Australasia, Latin America, and Africa), cultures, and regions. The 700 entries are not annotated; master's theses, newspapers, and popular magazines are excluded. The work's eight sections cover bibliographies and references, general comparative books and essays, American West and other U.S. regions; the remaining chapters are concerned with other countries. — *GK*

DA32 Etulain, Richard W., ed. - **The American West in the Twentieth Century: A Bibliography** / Richard W. Etulain, ed.; with Pat Devejian, Jon Hunner, Jacqueline Etulain Partch. - Norman, OK: Univ. of Oklahoma Pr., c1994. - 456 p.

Class Numbers:
Library of Congress F595   Z1251.W5
ISBN 0806126582
LCCN 94-16520
Notes:
"Published in cooperation with the Center for the American West, University of New Mexico."

• Etulain (history emeritus, Univ. of New Mexico) provides a classed bibliography of the trans-Mississippi West in the 20th century. He arranges 8,187 numbered entries in 12 general categories (e.g., reference, historiography, regional history, environment, public policy, cultural and intellectual history), some subdivided (economic history has subsections for agriculture and ranching, business, forestry and fishing, labor, land, mining, transportation, and water). Entries are as complete as is necessary to allow items to be located in libraries, although dissertations give only university and year, omitting microfilm numbers; citations to periodical articles give inclusive pagination. In every section or subsection, entries are arranged alphabetically by author or other entry, even in sections ("Regional and State Histories") that would benefit from topical arrangement. The index lists only names and refers to entry numbers. The editor attempts to include publications through 1992, emphasizing recent work, and lists 1993 publications only as they came to his attention during final compilation. He excludes master's theses, government publications, personal memoirs, and nonscholarly sources. Readers concerned with the Plains will need to dredge work about the region out of sections that treat the entire Western U.S. Some fruitful sections include "Bibliographies and Reference Works," "Regional and State Histories," "Indians," "Agriculture and Ranching," "Land," "Water," "Conservation and Preservation," "Public Policy History," and all the subcategories under "Cultural and Intellectual History." A well-thought out bibliography, with a useful classification of topics. — *MB, RB*

DA33   Smith, Dwight L., ed. - **The American and Canadian West: A Bibliography** / introd. [by] Ray A. Billington. - Santa Barbara, CA: ABC-Clio, 1979. - 558 p. - (Clio bibliography series, 6).

> Class Numbers:
>   Library of Congress F591   Z1251.W5
> ISBN 0874362725
> LCCN 78-24478

• Consists of 4,157 entries (all periodical articles) selected from *America: History and Life* (DA12) for the years 1964-1973. Entries are complete (but not in MLA format) and all have abstracts that are signed (but the contributors are not identified) and that vary as to length. There is no list of journals from which articles were drawn. Coverage begins with "prehistory" and ends with 1945, and scope is confined to the trans-Mississippi West in the United States and to Canada west of the Ontario-Manitoba border. Indians are omitted, since another volume in this series covers that subject, as are for the most part articles about states bordering the west bank of the Mississippi. Among the sections that will interest Prairies-Plains students are "Exploration and Travel," "The Indian Wars," "Agriculture," "Railroads," "Water," "Pioneer Life," "The Great Plains States" (p. 201-223, which must be supplemented by Rocky Mountain states immediately following), and "The Prairie Provinces." An extremely full subject index (200 p.) repays exploration, and there is an author index as well. A promised second volume drawn from the next five years' publication of AHL has never appeared. — *RB*

DA34   University Microfilms International. - **Western Americana: An Annotated Bibliography to the Microfiche Collection of 1012 Books and Documents of the 18th, 19th, and Early 20th Century**. - Ann Arbor, MI: Univ. Microfilms International, 1976. - 107 p.

> Class Numbers:
>   Library of Congress F591   Z1251.W5
> ISBN 0835701263

OCLC 2728674
LCCN 76-25022
Notes:
   Indexes

• Divided into 22 subject areas, this work indexes University Microfilms' microfiche collection of   books and other publications focusing on Western Americana based on materials from 46 cooperating libraries. Entries are arranged alphabetically within each subject grouping, providing a full bibliographic description of each work, volume number, and location number in boldface. Topics include the frontier thesis, fur trade, trails, Mormons, ethnic influences, politics, Native Americans, agriculture, extractive industries, women, transportation, urban development, land, water issues, conservation, travel accounts, memoirs, and regional, state, and local histories. Author and title indexes. — *GK*

DA35   Wallace, William Swilling. - **Bibliography of Published Bibliographies on the History of the Eleven Western States, 1941-1947: A Partial Supplement to the** *Writings on American History*. - Albuquerque, NM: [s.n.], 1954. - 224-233 p.

> Class Numbers:
>   Library of Congress Z1251.W5
> OCLC 6787087
> LCCN 55-62545

• The 115 numbered items in Wallace's slim volume are arranged alphabetically by main entry (usually author), and include books, bibliographies in journals, and U.S. government publications. Wallace intended to fill a gap left by *Writings on American History* (**DA10**). — *MB*

Catalogs

DA36   Dippie, Brian W. - **West-Fever** / introd. by James H. Nottage. - Los Angeles, CA: Autry Museum of Western Heritage;   Seattle, WA: in association with the Univ. of Washington Pr., 1998. - 128 p.; col. ill.

> Class Numbers:
>   Library of Congress F591
> ISBN 0295977353 1882880064 (pbk.)
>   1882880072 (softcover) 1882880080 (limited)
> LCCN 98-13528
> Notes:
>   Includes bibliographical references (p. 118-128)

• Dippie (history, Univ. of Victoria, B.C.) uses an essay format focusing on artist Charles M. Russell to describe the mythic stature and realities of the American West. The work commemorates the Autry Museum's tenth anniversary. The catalog features 118 color illustrations of the 40,000 objects found in the Museum's collections, among them paintings, sculptures, guns, swords, quilts, maps, and movie memorabilia; extensive notes. — *GK*

DA37 Newberry Library. - **A Catalogue of the Everett D. Graff Collection of Western Americana** / comp. by Colton Storm. - Chicago, IL: publ. for the Newberry Library by the Univ. of Chicago Pr., 1968. - xxv, 854 p.; port.

Class Numbers:
Library of Congress Z1251.W5
LCCN 66-20577
Notes:
Supplemented by: Brenda Berkman, comp., *Index to Maps in the Catalog of the Everett D. Graff Collection of Western Americana* / ed. by Robert W. Karnow Jr. Chicago, IL: Hermon Dunlap Smith Center for the History of Cartography at The Newberry Library, 1972. 17 p. Often tipped into copies of the *Catalogue*

• An author list of 4,801 entries, principally for books, broadsides, maps, and manuscripts held in the Graff Collection. Entries provide detailed bibliographic descriptions intended to give a sense of the appearance of the entry's title page, and are often followed by explanatory notes, including citations to source bibliographies, a list of which is provided (p. xix-xxv). A thorough index is useful in locating entries that bear on Prairies-Plains topics. There are none for "Great Plains," but for Great American Desert there are three, Plains five, Chivington two, Indians about 630, Indian campaigns about 108, Indian captivities about 65, Zebulon Pike eight, Frémont 25, agriculture four, farming 23, numerous entries for all Plains states and territories, for both Lewis and Clark and the Lewis and Clark Expedition, railroads, ranching, etc. The compiler's introduction twice makes the point that this compilation does not attempt to be a bibliography of the history of Western development, but is only a catalog of a specific collection. Storm also notes the special strengths of the Collection: overland travel, early exploration, the fur trade, freighting, the cattle industry, early town, county, and state histories, and records left by early settlers. Thorough and highly useful. — *RB*

Manuscripts; Archives

DA38 Augustana College (Sioux Falls, SD). Center for Western Studies. - **The Archives and Manuscripts Collections of the Center for Western Studies** / comp. and ed. by Harry F. Thompson. - Sioux Falls, SD: Center for Western Studies, Augustana College, 1984. - 30 p.

Class Numbers:
Library of Congress CD519.S55
ISBN 0931170249
OCLC 12549642
LCCN 84-72272
Notes:
Index

• Thompson (Director, Center for Western Studies, Augustana College) provides a descriptive guide of 68 major collections and 102 smaller collections found in the Center Archives. The Center collects materials that pertain to the Upper Great Plains region (North Dakota, South Dakota, Iowa, Nebraska, Wyoming, and Montana). Larger religious manuscript collections include American Lutheran College, South Dakota District, and the Episcopal Diocese of South Dakota. Center collections donated by individuals, organizations, or societies are listed in alphabetical order. — *GK*

DA39 Guide to Manuscripts in the Western History Collections of the University of Oklahoma / comp. by Kristina L. Southwell; foreword by David L. Boren; introd. by Donald J. Pisani and Donald L. Dewitt. - Norman, OK: Univ. of Oklahoma Pr., 2002. - xxiii, 439 p.; ill.

Class Numbers:
Library of Congress F694   Z1325
ISBN 0806134739 (pbk.)
LCCN 2002-28637
Notes:
Index

• Southwell (Univ. of Oklahoma), to celebrate the Diamond Jubilee of the Western History Collections, offers this catalog of the Collection's manuscript holdings. The manuscript division has custody of 11,000 linear feet of primary materials, 1,500 sound recordings, 300 Native American collections, 1,000 microform series, papers of seven governors and of noted Oklahoma authors, diaries, and business-related materials. Southwell's 1,535 entries, arranged alphabetically by collection title, include biographical data, type of materials, number of volumes, collection summary, and finding aids. Ten illustrations. — *GK*

DA40 Southwell, Kristina L., comp. - **Guide to Photographs in the Western History Collections of the University of Oklahoma** / foreword by David L. Boren; introd. by Donald J. Pisani and Donald L. DeWitt. - Norman, OK: Univ. of Oklahoma Pr., 2002. - xxiii, 190 p.; ill.

Class Numbers:
 Library of Congress F695
 ISBN 0806134747 0806181737 (electronic bk.)
  9780806181738 (electronic bk.)
 OCLC 50291117   62097000 (electronic bk.)
 LCCN 2002-28638
 Notes:
  Electronic book: http://www.netLibrary.com/urlapi.asp?
   action=summary&v=1&bookid=136744
  Index

• Lists by collection name photographs held at the Western History Collections. Entries indicate number of items in the collection, brief description of content, and whether a finding aid is available. Index of personal names, subjects, and place-names. Includes reproductions of ten photographs (a sod house, false-front stores in Guthrie, the Hole in the Wall Gang). — *RB*

DA41 Yale University. Library. Collection of Western Americana. - **A Catalogue of Manuscripts in the Collection of Western Americana Founded by William Robertson Coe: Yale University Library** / comp. by Mary C. Withington. - New Haven, CT: Yale Univ. Pr., 1952. - 398 p.; front. (port.).

 LCCN 52-5370
 Notes:
  See also *A Catalogue of the Frederick W. & Carrie S. Beinecke Collection of Western Americana* (**DA42**)

• A catalog arranged by author or catch title of manuscripts and manuscript groups collected by Coe and deposited in the Yale University Library. The index lists primarily names, but enables readers to find entries by subject (e.g., "Overland Journeys," "Indians," "Arkansas River," "Lewis and Clark Expedition," names of states). — *RB*

DA42 Yale University. Library. Collection of Western Americana. - **A Catalogue of the Frederick W. & Carrie S. Beinecke Collection of Western Americana** / comp. by Jeanne M. Goddard and Charles Kritzler; ed. with introd. by Archibald Hanna. - New Haven, CT: Yale Univ. Pr., 1965. - 1 v.; facsims., port.

 Class Numbers:
  Library of Congress Z1251.W5
 OCLC 557771
 LCCN 65-12542
 Notes:
  Contents: v. 1, Manuscripts
  No more published

• A catalog of manuscripts and manuscript groups collected by the Beineckes and deposited in the Yale University

Library. Its 285 entries are arranged by author or catch title, and the index (which lists mostly names) allows retrieval by topic (e.g., "Missions," "Missouri River," "Bison"). Little relating to Prairies-Plains. — *RB*

Encyclopedias

DA43 **Encyclopedia of Immigration and Migration in the American West** / eds., Gordon Morris Bakken, Alexandra Kindell. - Thousand Oaks, CA: Sage Publ., 2006. - 2 v. (xxix, 848 p.); ill., maps.

 Class Numbers:
  Library of Congress HB1965
 ISBN 1412905508 1412939577 (electronic bk.)
  9781412905503 9781412939577 (electronic bk.)
 OCLC 61478720 84386267 (electronic bk.)
 LCCN 2005-25714
 Notes:
  Available through Gale Virtual Reference Library
  Includes bibliographical references; index

• Chronicling movements of people into the Plains and Far West from the 16th century to the present, the editors' encyclopedia examines both the motivations and effects of that movement and highlights the diversity of Western people and cultures. It does not provide comprehensive coverage of Western immigration and migration, but the entries are varied, lengthy, and written by experts, and can be read easily by all audiences. Major areas of coverage are American Indian tribes (including forced migrations); biographies; cities and towns; economic change and war; racial and ethnic groups; immigration laws and policies; libraries; natural resources (events and laws); and Western trails. The entries, with suggested readings, include war brides in Montana; Okies; Route 66; the Trail of Tears; the Homestead Act; and Czechs and Swedes in Saunders County, Nebraska. An appendix of research guides, written by librarians, is a primer on researching ethnic and racial groups, using government information, and searching Census records. A master bibliography is duplicated in both volumes and a cumulative subject index is in volume 2. — *JD*

DA44 **Encyclopedia of the American West** / Charles Phillips and Alan Axelrod, eds. - New York: Macmillan Reference USA; London [etc.]: Simon & Schuster and Prentice Hall International, 1996. - 4 v. (1935 p.).

 Class Numbers:
  Library of Congress F591.E485
 ISBN 0028974956
 LCCN 96-1685

• The four volumes of Phillips and Axelrod's set certainly look like an encyclopedia: articles vary in length to reflect the editors' estimate of topical importance; biographical entries are numerous; an index runs more than a hundred pages; an appendix classes biographical entries by profession; although there is no general bibliography, nearly every article ends with suggested readings, usually listing recent studies; articles are signed and arranged alphabetically. As reviews point out, maps are pitiful; they are included only for states, and consist of a half-page black-and-white physical map of the continental United States west of the Mississippi with the state outlined in black and only the capital city located (separate maps for Alaska and Hawaii show no cities at all). A roster of contributors lists their academic affiliation and the articles they wrote for the encyclopedia. A few contributors show no affiliation, and several are identified only by a corporate name ("Raven Group," "Turner Publishing," "Zenda, Inc."). Editor Axelrod wrote 124 of the articles, Phillips 168, and assistant editors Patricia Hogan 145 and Candace Floyd 48. The qualifications of these heaviest contributors are not revealed. The bibliographies have occasional errors, chiefly misspellings of authors' names, and imprints cite place and date, but never publisher, which is a source of annoyance in trying to verify citations in other sources.

None of this is fatal, and an estimate of the set has to rest not on credentials but on how useful it will be to students and scholars. The subject matter is broad in scope, and although the style is accessible to any educated reader, no attempt is made to simplify any subject. The bibliographies, although brief, are for the most part up to date. Illustrations, all black-and-white photographs or reproductions, are well-chosen and do for the text what illustrations are meant to do—they provide a different way of understanding the topics. The editors show affection for cities and towns and for individual American Indians, providing numerous entries for both. Instead of devoting entries to individual historians (although there are some of those) the set gives its attention to schools of Western history—to "Arid-lands Thesis," "Borderlands Theory," "New Western History," "Safety-Valve Theory." Among the topics that will interest students of the Prairies and Plains are "Cactus," "Dude Ranching," "Gun Fighters," "Harvey Girls," "Homesteading," "Ogallala Aquifer," "Oklahoma Land Rush," "School Life on the Frontier," "Tumbleweed," and "Windmills." Some omissions are inevitable: Thomas Hart Benton, the Missouri senator, has his own article, but his namesake the painter is mentioned only in passing in the article on Missouri. John Steuart Curry is omitted altogether. The principal rival is *The New Encyclopedia of the American West*, ed. by Howard R. Lamar (**DA45**). Both take as their subject the entire trans-Mississippi West, so both contain considerable material that is outside the Prairies-Plains scope. The two encyclopedias show some overlap in subject matter (it would be surprising if they did not), but each contains material the other omits. Either fulfills the purposes of a subject encyclopedia—to provide a starting place for research, to answer questions of fact, and to make a context for the subject. Most libraries will want both. — *RB*

DA45   The New Encyclopedia of the American West / ed. by Howard R. Lamar. - New Haven, CT: Yale Univ. Pr., 1998. - 1324 p.

Class Numbers:
  Library of Congress F591
ISBN 0300070888
LCCN 98-6231
Notes:
  Rev. ed. of: *The Reader's Encyclopedia of the American West*, also ed. by Lamar. New York: Crowell, c1977.

• The standard encyclopedia of Western history, which the editor interprets in a broad sense to include not just the trans-Mississippi West, but the western edge of white settlement (the "frontier") from the earliest contact, and relations between colonies and the mother countries. In some 2,400 entries and 600 illustrations and maps, the work covers the frontier stage of all 50 states (with separate entries for each), biographies, events, physiography (landforms and water, chiefly rivers), migration, transportation, discoverers and explorers, folklore and fiction (including films and theme parks), art and artists (including photography), minorities, and women. More than 300 contributors wrote the entries; many were revised (often by Lamar himself) from the 1977 version. Entries are signed and arranged alphabetically, with cross-references printed in small capitals, and the editor attempts to show how cross-references make possible the assembly of various articles relating to a general topic (an example is provided for Texas, p. v), but there is no list of entries arranged by category. A brief chronology precedes the entries, and the volume ends with a roster of contributors (many very prominent in the field, not a few of them former students of Lamar's) and an index confined to names of persons. Most entries are followed by brief short-title bibliographies, but there is no general bibliography. The style is clear, aimed at educated adults through advanced students. The work includes many persons and topics of interest to Plains students, making this an excellent place to begin reading. Many topics are covered at greater depth than might be expected in a single-volume encyclopedia (e.g., "New Mexico Missions," "Vegetation," "Railroads," "Protestant Churches"). — *RB*

DA46   Rodriguez, Junius P. - The Louisiana Purchase: A Historical and Geographical Encyclopedia. - Santa Barbara, CA: ABC-CLIO, 2002. - xxxv, 513 p.; ill., maps.

Class Numbers:
  Library of Congress E333
ISBN 157607188
OCLC 48784568
LCCN 2002-3228
Notes:
  Includes bibliographical references (p. 473-488); index

• Rodriguez arranges entries alphabetically, adding a very useful table of contents that includes all the entry headings (but fails to mention that some entries are only *see* references). The contributors (there are more than 50) are listed with their institutional affiliations. The 300 entries are signed and list additional sources of information. There are only six maps and a handful of other illustrations. Supplementary material includes a detailed chronology (1492-2002), and key documents, e.g., the Treaty of Luneville, 1801. The extensive bibliography collects the resources mentioned in the entries. — *MB*

DA47   Roth, Mitchel P., 1953–   . - **Issues of Westward Expansion**. - Westport, CT: Greenwood Pr., 2002. - xxi, 292 p. - (Major issues in American history).

> Class Numbers:
> Library of Congress E179.5
> ISBN 0313311676
> OCLC 48613200
> LCCN 2001-58640
> Notes:
> Includes bibliographical references; index
> Table of contents: http://www.loc.gov/catdir/toc/fy034/2001058640.html

• Roth (criminal justice, Sam Houston State Univ.) explores 13 issues in Western expansion, 1800-1900, arranging them in chronological order. Each entry contains a narrative overview, primary accounts in the form of diaries, memoirs, and documents, followed by a selected annotated bibliography. Topics include the Lewis and Clark expedition, Indian removal, Texas annexation, Mormon settlement, Homestead Act, transcontinental railroad, Sand Creek Massacre, Little Bighorn, Yellowstone National Park, Chinese exclusion, Wounded Knee, and the Dust Bowl. Chronology of events, 1536-1992. — *GK*

DA48   Schweikart, Larry. - **The American West** / [by] Larry Schweikart, Bradley J. Birzer. - Hoboken, NJ: John Wiley & Sons, c2003. - xxiv, 542 p.; ill., maps.

> Class Numbers:
> Library of Congress F591
> LCCN 2002-32395
> Notes:
> Includes bibliographical references (p. 519-542)
> Table of contents: http://www.loc.gov/catdir/toc/wiley031/2002032395.html

• The compilers (history, Univ. of Dayton, OH, and Hillsdale College, MI) arrange their encyclopedia chronologically, pre-Columbian period to the present. They include ample extracts from diaries, letters, and newspaper accounts. The book's five sections cover periods in the history of the West and include such topics as Pueblo uprisings, the Louisiana Purchase, and the Lewis and Clark Expedition. Narrative entries (e.g., on the Pony Express, buffalo soldiers, Cochise, Colt firearms, Barry Goldwater) are informative and well-written. The entries are supported by 80 illustrations, photographs, line drawings, and maps. — *GK*

DA49   Utley, Robert Marshall, 1929-   , ed. - **Encyclopedia of the American West**. - New York: Wings Books, 1997. - 496 p.; ill., maps, ports.

> Class Numbers:
> Library of Congress F591
> ISBN 0517149885 9780517149881
> OCLC 34474877
> LCCN 96-14687
> Notes:
> Includes bibliographical references (p. 491-496)

• Utley arranges articles in his encyclopedia alphabetically. Many are illustrated with black-and-white photographs or line drawings, and 11 full-page maps follow the text, each focusing on a specific topic–e.g., mining sites, rail systems, Indian reservations. Sample entries: "Lewis and Clark Expedition," "Bat Masterson," "Danish Settlers," "Annie Oakley," "Pony Express," "Carry Nation." The entry "Sioux Indians" is cross-referenced from "Dakota," but not from the commonly used "Lakota." There is no subject index, although one would have improved accessibility. Extensive bibliography. — *MB*

Atlases

DA50   Beck, Warren A. - **Historical Atlas of the American West** / by Warren A. Beck and Ynez D. Haase. - Norman, OK: Univ. of Oklahoma Pr., c1989. - xlii, 78 (i.e., 156) p; maps; 32 cm.

> Class Numbers:
> Library of Congress G1381.S1
> ISBN 0806121939 0806124563 (pbk.)
> OCLC 18907112
> LCCN 88-40540
> Notes:
> Includes bibliography; index

• Beck (a historian) and Haase (a cartographer), authors of two previous atlases for California (1974) and New Mexico (1969), define the West geographically as the six states through which the 100th meridian runs and eleven more between those states and the Pacific coast. They cover a vast array of topics and periods—early explorations, climate, flora, cattle trails, territorial expansion, conflicts, Indian land tenure, mineral and agricultural deposits, railroads, military installations, POW camps during World War II. The 78 maps, illustrations, and tables are accompanied by a single page of succinct explanatory text. Population patterns and demographics are not treated. Advisors include such prominent scholars as Ray Billington, Gordon Bakken, and John Francis Bannon. — *GK*

DA51 Ridge, Martin. - **Atlas of American Frontiers**. - Chicago, IL: Rand, McNally, c1993. - 191 p.; ill. (some col.), col. maps ; 36 cm.

> Class Numbers:
> Library of Congress E179.5
> ISBN 0528834932
> LCCN 92-4647
> Notes:
> Indexes

• Of this atlas' six sections, the first four cover the frontier and are organized chronologically by topic. Twenty topics constitute Section 3, "The Frontier Across the Mississippi." The two pages devoted to each topic consist of a map, an illustration (usually a reproduction of a contemporary line drawing), and a present-day landscape photograph. Six transportation maps of the entire United States, all reproductions of maps originally published between the 1770s and the 1920s, comprise Section 5, and Section 6 consists of reference maps and includes maps of the Northern and Southern Great Plains. Map and subject indexes. — *MS*

Chronologies

DA52 Bowman, John Stewart, 1931-   . - **The World Almanac of the American West** / introduction, Alvin M. Josephy, Jr.; general ed., John S. Bowman. - New York: World Almanac: distr. in the U.S. by Ballantine Books, 1986. - 368 p.; [16] p. of color plates, ill.

> Class Numbers:
> Library of Congress F591
> ISBN 0345337204 0866872731
> LCCN 85-52319

• Calling itself an "almanac," Bowman's compilation is in fact a chronology that begins August 3rd, 1492 and ends in August 1985. Entries are brief, each given an identifier in boldface ("Exploration," "Westward Movement," "Indians"); many are short on specifics ("Indians: President Hayes issues a warning to illegal settlers, ranchers, and trespassers who have been stealing lands in Indian Territory"). The numerous illustrations, the work's best feature, are acknowledged only in a one-page list of credits on the last page, but the text provides no acknowledgements of any kind, and there is no sign of a bibliography. Sidebars flesh out the text somewhat, and some treat Prairies-Plains concerns ("Water and the West," "The Frontier Thesis," "Populism in the West," "The Indians' Last Stand"), but are scattered without relation to surrounding text, and there is no list to help locate them. The index lists only four entries under "Great Plains," although there are far more than that; some entries are heavily posted; and entries beginning "Indian" or "Indians" are interfiled without regard for alphabetic sequence.

Useful, as is any chronology, for getting the sequence of events straight, but now 20 years old and in need of revision. — *RB*

DA53 Flanagan, Mike. - **The Old West: Day by Day**. - New York: Facts on File, c1995. - 498 p.; ill.

> Class Numbers:
> Library of Congress F591
> ISBN 0816026890
> LCCN 94004663
> Notes:
> Includes bibliographical references (p. 463-465); indexes
> Updated and enl. ed. of the author's *Days of the West*, c1987

• Flanagan's chronology contains 15,000 entries that focus on the trans-Mississippi West, 1848-1890. Among the topics treated are major battles, historical figures, territorial expansion, cowboys, and patterns of settlement. Chronologies of important historical events and important personalities appear in sidebars; illustrations are found throughout. Useful for checking facts and dates. — *GK*

DA54 Zeman, Scott C. - **Chronology of the American West: From 23,000 B.C.E. through the Twentieth Century** / foreword by Peter Iverson. - Santa Barbara, CA: ABC-CLIO, c2002. - 381 p.; ill.

> Class Numbers:
> Library of Congress F591
> ISBN 157607207X
> LCCN 2002003372
> Notes:
> Includes bibliographical references (p. 339-365); index

• Zeman (history, New Mexico Tech Univ.) examines the history of the American West from the period of earliest human habitation to the close of the 20th century, from early Paleo-Indian civilizations through such recent events as Salt Lake City's bid to host the Olympics and the Columbine High School shootings. To describe a region still evolving, Zeman combines social, political, and cultural events. He divides history of the West into four periods: "Native West" (2,000 BCE-1500 CE), "Imperial West" (1500-1840), "Incorporated West" (1841-1932) and "Contested West" (1933-2001). Sidebars provide insight into key topics—e.g., bison, Native Americans, black Americans, immigrants, water rights.— *GK*

Collective Biographies

DA55 Etulain, Richard W., ed. - **Western Lives: A Biographical History of the American West**. - Albuquerque, NM: Univ. of New Mexico Pr., 2004. - 454 p.; ill., maps.

Class Numbers:
   Library of Congress F590.5
ISBN 0826334725
LCCN 2004-9061
Notes:
   Includes bibliographical references; index
   Publ. in cooperation with the Univ. of New Mexico
      Center for the Southwest
   Review by L. Graves: *Choice* 42.11 (July 2005): review
      42-6718
   Review by Richmond L. Clow: *Great Plains Quarterly*
      25.4 (fall 2005): 266-267
   Table of contents: http://www.loc.gov/catdir/toc/
      ecip0417/2004009061.html

• Etulain (history emeritus, Univ. of New Mexico) edits 15 bibliographical scholarly essays on notable Westerners. The work is divided into three time frames and is intended for undergraduates or general readers. The first five essays cover the early period of contact between Spanish colonizers, Indians, and Europeans to the mid-19th century; the second set pertains to 1850-1900, focusing on Mormons, miners, ranchers, Native Americans, and California Hispanics; and the final five essays deal with influential Western figures in the 20th century. Etulain winds everything up with a bibliographic essay, "The American West." Each contributor appends a section of useful sources; 17 maps, 48 illustrations. — *GK*

Guidebooks

DA56   Ruth, Kent. - **Landmarks of the West: A Guide to Historic Sites**. - Lincoln, NE: Univ. of Nebraska Pr., 1986. - 309 p.; ill.

   Class Numbers:
      Library of Congress F595.3
   ISBN 0803238754 0803289197 (pbk.)
   LCCN 85-29014
   Notes
      Rev. ed. of the author's *Great Day in the West*, c1963

• Ruth describes 150 significant sites of the trans-Mississippi West. Revisions to the 1963 edition are minimal. Each chapter treats sites found in a single state. A page of description accompanies each map, illustration, or photograph. Intended for casual readers or travelers, the book has weaknesses: some sites need fuller description, and nearly a third of the book is devoted to historic forts. — *GK*

Historiographic Aids

DA57   Historians of the American Frontier: A Bio-Bibliographical Sourcebook / ed. by John R. Wunder. -

New York: Greenwood Pr., 1988 - 814 p.

   Class Numbers:
      Library of Congress E175.45
   ISBN 0313248990
   OCLC 17650402
   LCCN 88-5637
   Notes:
      Includes bibliographies

• Wunder (history, Univ. of Nebraska-Lincoln) edits a collective biobibliography of 57 scholars who wrote about the American frontier. Chapters, written by academic colleagues, have four sections: biography, themes, analysis, and bibliography. All the subjects are deceased, and all made significant contributions to the early history of agriculture, land policy, railroads, Native American studies, political science, anthropology, ethnohistory, or geography in the trans-Appalachia or trans-Mississippi region. Roster of contributors. — *GK*

DA58   Mattson, Vernon E. - **Frederick Jackson Turner: A Reference Guide** / [by] Vernon E. Mattson and William E. Marion. - Boston, MA: G.K. Hall, 1985. - xxxiii, 302 p. - (A reference guide to literature).

   Class Numbers:
      Library of Congress E175.5 Z8893.9
   ISBN 0816179972
   OCLC 11496745
   LCCN 84-25266
   Notes:
      Includes bibliographies; index

• Turner's most enduring contribution to American historiography was his "frontier thesis" of westward expansion. Briefly stated, it holds that the draw of relatively unlimited quantities of inexpensive land and the accompanying social process of adapting to new forms of settlement played a pivotal role in the evolution of the American national character. The annotated bibliography charts the response, both positive and negative, to Turner's still controversial ideas over the course of nearly a century. Arranged chronologically, entries begin with an 1895 article by Woodrow Wilson and end with a book published, appropriately, by the Huntington Library, where Turner's papers are housed. Although the editors emphasize secondary writings, they include a list of writings by Turner (p. xxix-xxxiii), also in order by date. A major source for an important historian whose work continues to influence the interpretation of Plains history. — *LMcD*

THE FRONTIER

See also Snodgrass, **Encyclopedia of Frontier Literature, BC12**; Billington, **Westward Expansion, DA3**

DA59 Hubach, Robert Rogers, 1916- . - **Early Midwestern Travel Narratives: An Annotated Bibliography, 1634-1850**. - Detroit, MI: Wayne State Univ. Pr., 1961. - 149 p.

Class Numbers:
  Library of Congress Z1251.W5
  LCCN 60-15110
  Notes:
    Index

• The area of coverage defined as the Midwest stretches from the western boundary of Pennsylvania west, and north from the Ohio River and the northern boundaries of Oklahoma and Arkansas to the border with Canada, hence includes considerable territory outside Prairies and Plains. The narratives, divided chronologically among 14 chapters, include those by early French explorers, those from the Colonial and Revolutionary War eras, and those by writers with literary reputations, such as Washington Irving, Francis Parkman, and Walt Whitman. Each chapter contains both a narrative overview of the topics included and an annotated bibliography. A notes section precedes the subject index. — MB

DA60 Paul, Rodman Wilson, 1912- . - **The Frontier and the American West** / comp. by Rodman W. Paul and Richard W. Etulain. - Arlington Heights, IL: AHM Pub. Corp., c1977. - 168 p. - (Goldentree bibliographies in American history).

Class Numbers:
  Library of Congress Z1251 W5
  ISBN 088295542X 0882955659 (pbk.)
  LCCN 76-11622

• Since the "Goldentree Bibliographies" are intended primarily for undergraduates, teachers, and librarians rather than advanced researchers, Rodman and Etulain's volume is deliberately selective rather than comprehensive. Entries are arranged under 54 categories (e.g., "Indians," "Fur Trade and Trappers," "Explorers and Scientists," "Agriculture," "Labor," "Ethnic Groups," "Politics," "Literature," "Religion," "Cattle and Sheep," "Irrigation, Reclamation, and Water Supply," "Land and Land Policy in the West," "The Great Trails," "Western Characteristics") with no more than 100 unannotated entries per category. The editors provide an extensive author index, but no subject index. — MB

DA61 Tuska, Jon, ed. - **The Frontier Experience: A Reader's Guide to the Life and Literature of the American West** / ed. by Jon Tuska and Vicki Piekarski with Paul J. Blanding. - Jefferson, NC: McFarland, c1984. - 434 p.

Class Numbers:

Library of Congress Z1251 W5 F76
  ISBN 0899501184
  LCCN 84-4261

• Calling their work a "reader's guide," the editors provide extensive essays on topics, as well as lists of recommended readings and films. Essays are signed, several by the editors, some by invited contributors. The work is arranged in broad divisions of people, land, and literature, each subdivided into categories, e.g., gunfighters, cowboys, pioneers, the fur trade, the overland trail, artists, and films. Each category supplies a narrative essay on the topic, an annotated list of key reference materials, and brief lists of suggested fiction and films. Name and title indexes, but no subject index. — MB

The Wild West: Myth and Reality

Scope. The West, especially that part occupied by Prairies and Plains, holds a place in the imagination of every American (a place occupied in the imagination of Canadians by the Royal Canadian Mounted Police). It is the West populated by gunslingers, firm-jawed lawmen, brave pioneers migrating in covered wagons, farmers and cattlemen at sixguns drawn, and cowhands fresh from the Chisholm Trail roaming the streets of cattle towns spoiling for a fight. The picture is almost entirely fictional, but has been nurtured carefully by generations of mass media, from dime novels to radio, movies, and television. The reference literature devoted to that period (it lasted perhaps thirty years and was far less blood-soaked than the myth would have us believe) focuses on the imaginative rendering of the West, so is concerned with gunplay, faceoffs on Front Street, and Cleaning Up Dodge.

DA62 Adams, Ramon Frederick, 1889-1976, comp. - **Six-Guns and Saddle Leather: A Bibliography of Books and Pamphlets on Western Outlaws and Gunmen**. - [Norman, OK]: Univ. of Oklahoma Pr., 1969. - xxv, 808 p.

Class Numbers:
  Library of Congress Z1251.W5
  ISBN 0806108495
  OCLC 51015
  LCCN 69-16729

• The compiler includes four types of authors: writers of dime novels or "penny dreadfuls," publications notable for their inaccuracies; the old-timers who pen carelessly written and edited memoirs; "rocking chair historians"; and serious historical scholars. He then arranges the 1,132 numbered entries in one alphabetical list. For each entry, he includes author, title, place of publication, publisher, date, binding, in-print status as of 1954 (e.g., OP, scarce, In Print), then supplies detailed descriptive information, including pagination, size, illustrations, series, and bibliography (the descriptive data appears to have been drawn directly from catalog records). Adams annotates each entry, adding comments on the value of the item. Scattered through the volume are reproductions of title pages from selected items. Extremely detailed subject index. — *MB*

DA63 Breihan, Carl W., 1915- . - **Lawmen and Robbers**. - Caldwell, ID: Caxton Printers, 1986. - 128 p.; ill.

> Class Numbers:
> Library of Congress F596
> ISBN 0870043188
> OCLC 12695539
> LCCN 85-25447
> Notes:
> Bibliography: p. 125-128

• Heavily illustrated, this volume covers Black Bart, Judge Parker, Butch Cassidy, and nine others. Persons of interest to Prairies-Plains study include Jim Courtright of Texas, and Bill Doolin and Al Jennings, who gained notoriety in Oklahoma and Kansas. A brief bibliography cites other books of interest, but there is no subject index. — *MB*

DA64 Chamberlain, Kathleen P., comp. - **Wild Westerners: A Bibliography**. - Albuquerque, NM: Center for the American West, Dept. of History, Univ. of New Mexico, 1998. - 67 leaves. - (Univ. of New Mexico. Center for the American West. Occasional papers, 16).

> Class Numbers:
> Library of Congress F591
> OCLC 39912024

• Brief unannotated bibliographies, prepared by graduate students at the Univ. of New Mexico, concerning nine of the "best-known men and women of the Old West"–Custer, Geronimo, Belle Starr, Billy the Kid–all historical figures whose nature and comparative importance have disappeared behind decades of tale-telling and moviemaking. No index. — *RB*

DA65 Cusic, Don. - **Cowboys and the Wild West: An A-Z Guide from the Chisholm Trail to the Silver Screen**. - New York: Facts on File, c1994. - 356 p.; ports.

> Class Numbers:
> Library of Congress F596
> ISBN 0816027838 0816030308 (pbk.)
> LCCN 93045584
> Notes:
> Includes bibliographical references (p. 319-330); index

• The scope of Cusic's book is broad, including working cowboys and those appearing in various forms of popular culture, outlaws, lawmen, American Indian tribes, and songs. Entries for cowboys in film and on television are thorough and well written. Factual and geographic errors may be found throughout the book: North Platte is not in North Dakota but Nebraska (p. 243); Deadwood is not in Colorado but South Dakota (p.188). Cusic provides a good index for a book that will be useful for general readers. — *GK*

DA66 DeArment, Robert K., 1925- . - **Deadly Dozen: Twelve Forgotten Gunfighters of the Old West**. - Norman, OK: Univ. of Oklahoma Pr., 2003. - 266 p.; ill.

> Class Numbers:
> Library of Congress F596
> ISBN 080613559X
> LCCN 2003-44797
> Notes:
> Contents: John Bull; Pat Desmond; Mart Duggan; Milt Yarberry; Dan Tucker; George Goodell; Bill Standifer; Charley Perry; Barkey Riggs; Dan Bogan; Dave Kemp; Jeff Kidder
> Includes bibliographical references (p. 239-253); index

• DeArment (western history writer, Sylvania, OH) addresses the careers of 12 little-known Western gunfighters. These men had varied backgrounds; some were European immigrants while others had earned college degrees. Many were married with families, and ten of them wore badges while oftentimes stretching the boundaries of the law. The author uses court records and newspaper accounts to recount their lives without resorting to glorification. Eight illustrations; bibliography. — *GK*

DA67 Horan, James David, 1914- . - **The Authentic Wild West**. - New York: Crown Publ., 1976-1980. - 3 v.; ill.

> Class Numbers:
> Library of Congress F594
> ISBN 0517526808 (v. 1)
> LCCN 76-10758
> Notes:
> Bibliography: v. [1], p. 302-308; v. [2], p. 304-309; v. [3], p. 303-306; index
> Contents: v. [1], The Gunfighters; v. [2], The Outlaws; v. [3], The Lawmen

• Using newspapers, official records, letters and first-person accounts, Horan attempts to portray the authentic lives, rather than the myths, of the gunfighters, outlaws, and lawmen who roamed the West from the end of the Civil War to the 1880s. Written in a lively anecdotal style with lengthy excerpts from primary documents, the 30- to 100-page biographies of individuals and gangs convey the 19th-century public and media fascination that bred the myths. Presented as entertainment rather than scholarship, the text is nonetheless based on primary sources, provides little-known and new information, and acknowledges the difficulty of discovering the "truth" about these well-documented figures. Profusely illustrated with photographs and facsimile documents. The source notes and the bibliography of books, manuscripts, memoirs, journals, letters, tape recordings, and official documents make good starting places for researchers. Name index. — *JD*

DA68   Lamb, Frank Bruce, 1913-   . - **The Wild Bunch: A Selected Critical Annotated Bibliography of the Literature**. - Worland, WY: High Plains Publ. Co., 1993. - 163 p.; ill.

> Class Numbers:
>   Library of Congress F595   Z1251.W5
> ISBN 1891019055
> OCLC 29389963
> LCCN 93-77747
> Notes:
>   Index

• The Wild Bunch roamed the Great Plains at the turn of the century, becoming part of Western mythology. The outlaws are familiar, even romantic, figures in Plains history: Harry Longabaugh (name spelling varies but better known as the Sundance Kid), Will Carver, Ben Kilpatrick, Harvey Logan (Kid Curry), and Robert Leroy Parker (Butch Cassidy). The books and pamphlets in the bibliography are histories, biographies, memoirs, and travel guides that treat the gang or its members briefly or at length. Other major sources, such as newspaper articles and archival materials, are excluded. Annotations are extensive, analyzing the anomalies, inaccuracies and disagreements in the accounts. They are lessons in discernment and discrimination in using historical sources. Illustrated with photos of people and places. Indexed by people and locations. — *JD*

DA69   Miller, Nyle H. - **Why the West Was Wild: A Contemporary Look at the Antics of Some Highly Publicized Kansas Cowtown Personalities** / by Nyle H. Miller and Joseph W. Snell. - Topeka, KS: Kansas State Historical Society, 1963. - 685 p.; ill., ports., maps, facsims.

> Class Numbers:
>   Library of Congress F680
> LCCN 63-63480
> Notes:
>   Bibliographical footnotes
>   Much of the material originally published in *The Kansas Historical Quarterly*, 1960-1962.

• Profiles 57 lawmen and other colorful figures in Abilene, Newton, Ellsworth, Wichita, Dodge City, Caldwell, and Hays, drawing from newspaper articles, letters, and other primary sources that are reprinted in full and connected by the author's narrative. They portray the "stage and plot," as well as the characters, of the booming Kansas cowtowns, 1867-1886. Characters range from the heavily mythologized "Doc" Holliday to the locally infamous "Rowdy Joe" Lowe, a Wichita brothel owner. An appendix lists 250 less well-documented peace officers by office held and location. Illustrated with photographs, posters, maps, city views, and drawings, and indexed by names, places, and topics. — *JD*

DA70   O'Neal, Bill, 1942-   . - **Encyclopedia of Western Gunfighters**. - Norman, OK: Univ. of Oklahoma Pr., 1979. - 386 p.; ports.

> Class Numbers:
>   Library of Congress F596
> ISBN 0806115084
> OCLC 4593264
> LCCN 78-21380
> Notes:
>   Bibliography: p. 349-360; index
>   Electronic book: http://www.netLibrary.com/urlapi.asp?
>   action=summary&v-1&bookid=15335

• O'Neal (history emeritus, Panola College) provides brief biographical sketches of 255 gunfighters with the intention of separating fact from fiction with regard to Western gunfighters. They are listed alphabetically in entries that include nicknames, birth and death dates, and known gunfights. Where available, photographs accompany the entries. Tables list previous occupations, number of gunfights, and deaths that can be attributed to each gunfighter. O'Neal relies heavily on primary materials–memoirs and newspaper accounts. A standard reference work for aficionados of Western history, but as documents continue to surface, it will require revision, expansion, and updating. — *GK*

DA71   Patterson, Richard M., 1934-   . - **Historical Atlas of the Outlaw West**. - Boulder, CO: Johnson Books, c1985. - 232 p.; ill., maps, ports.

> Class Numbers:
>   Library of Congress F595
> ISBN 093472897 (pbk.)
> LCCN 84082543
> Notes:
>   Bibliography: p. [222]-225; index

• Patterson (senior editor at a legal publishing house, Bargersville, IN) relates stories of outlaws and desperados of the West. Chapters are subdivided alphabetically by state and provide narratives, photographs, facsimiles of 19th-century maps, locations of ghost towns, hideouts of famous criminals. The bibliography cites chiefly secondary literature from magazines. Useful for general readers, but of no interest to scholars. — *GK*

DA72 Rainey, Buck. - **Western Gunslingers in Fact and on Film: Hollywood's Famous Lawmen and Outlaws**. - Jefferson, NC: McFarland, 1998. - 341 p.; ill.

> Class Numbers:
> Library of Congress PN1995.9.W4
> ISBN 0786403969
> LCCN 97-41807
> Notes:
> Includes bibliographical references (p. 265-304); index

• Although it is concerned with only five individuals and two groups, Rainey's book provides some background about men and a woman who lived by the gun in the late 19th-century West, most of them spending time and wasting bullets in parts of the Prairies-Plains region. The individuals are Billy the Kid, Belle Starr, Earp, Hickok, and Masterson, the groups the James-Younger and Dalton-Doolin gangs. Each of the seven sections opens with a biographical sketch of individual or gang, supported by such evidence as exists, then reviews the movies in which each was a central figure. The movie lists provide title, studio, date, running time, director, cast, and plot summary. The book ends with a long bibliography and an index principally of names. Since the biographies reproduce contemporary photographs and the filmographies include studio stills, it can be seen how far the moviemakers stray from the facts. — *RB*

DA73 Schoenberger, Dale T. - **The Gunfighters** / by Dale T. Schoenberger ; ill. by Ernest L. Reedstrom. - Caldwell, ID: Caxton Printers, 1971. - 207 p.; ill.

> Class Numbers:
> Library of Congress F594
> ISBN 0870042076
> LCCN 70-123583
> Notes:
> Bibliography: p. [187]-198

• Schoenberger (writer, St. Louis, MO) traces the lives of seven notorious western gunfighters–Wyatt Earp, Doc Holliday, Bat Masterson, Clay Allison, Ben Thompson, Luke Short, and Wild Bill Hickok. The author's purpose is to distinguish between legend and reality that surrounds these men. His research includes primary and secondary sources compiled from newspaper accounts, correspondence, interviews, and National Archives materials. Numerous illustrations. — *GK*

DA74 Tuska, Jon. - **Billy the Kid: A Bio-Bibliography**. - Westport, CT: Greenwood Pr., 1983. - 235 p.; ill. - (Popular culture bio-bibliographies).

> Class Numbers:
> Library of Congress F786.B54
> ISBN 0313232660

> LCCN 83-5709
> Notes:
> Includes bibliographies; index
> Reprinted as: *Billy the Kid: A Handbook*. Lincoln, NE:
> Univ. of Nebraska Pr., 1986

• The first half of Tuska's book is a biography of the almost mythical 19th-century outlaw; Tuska's later *Billy the Kid: His Life and Legend* (Albuquerque, NM: Univ. of New Mexico Pr., 1994; 295 p.) provides a more extensive treatment. Much of the rest of the work consists of a debunking of representations of Billy the Kid in various media. Separate bibliographical essays examine, and idiosyncratically critique, his portrayal in biographies and general books, fiction, and film; chapters conclude with bibliographies. Includes a chronology of Billy the Kid and his contemporaries. Of limited usefulness. — *LMcD*

CANADA

Bibliographies

DA75 Artibise, Alan F.J. - **Western Canada since 1870: A Select Bibliography and Guide**. - Vancouver, BC: Univ. of British Columbia Pr., 1978. - 294 p.; ill.

> Class Numbers:
> Library of Congress F1060Z1392.N7
> ISBN 0774800909 0774800917 (pbk.)
> OCLC 4028034
> LCCN 78-320314
> Notes:
> Includes indexes

• Approximately three-quarters of the 3,663 items examine aspects of the Prairies. The initial chapter consists of sections on general works, immigration, Indians and ethnic groups, government and politics, railways, agriculture, economics, education and socio-cultural development, and urban development. The same structure applies to the individual provinces. Separate chapters deal with the Riel Rebellions and the Northwest Territories to 1905. Includes a brief guide, "Western Canadian Studies." Although the subject index is inadequate (a mere three pages), this is an important reference source, carefully selected. *America: History and Life* and the general databases *CBCA* (Canadian Business and Current Affairs) and *CPI.Q.* (Canadian Periodical Index) cover later material. — *LMcD*

DA76 **Canadian Studies: A Guide to the Resources [Internet Site]** / John D. Blackwell. - Antigonish, NS: International Council of Canadian Studies, 1998-   . - http://www.iccs-ciec.ca/blackwell.html

> Access Date: Nov. 2005
> Notes:

Latest update: 20 January 2005
Fees: None

• By default, a portion of this database relates to the Canadian Prairies. It originated as a bibliographic essay published in *Choice* (1997) and has been updated since then, but the original version is still noted on the home page, along with the names of the authors and links to their credentials. The site covers all aspects of Canadian culture, history, and literature including the Prairie provinces; its links generally lead to government or academic sites. In making the transition from print, the authors failed to take advantage of the opportunities the new medium offers; it is simply a linear version in one very long page of the text published in *Choice*. Since it has several sections, navigation could have been enhanced by breaking it up into a number of shorter pages linked to a single screen table of contents page. Visual interest could have been improved with the use of a few illustrations. — *MB*

DA77   Martin, Shirley A., ed. - **Louis Riel and the Rebellions in the Northwest: An Annotated Bibliography of Material in Special Collections, University of Saskatchewan Library** / comp. and ed. by Shirley Martin and Glen Makahonuk. - [Saskatoon, SK]: University of Saskatchewan, 1985. - 145 p.

Class Numbers:
   National Library of Canada FC3214
   OCLC 56246935
   Notes:
      Includes author, title and subject indexes (p. 109-145)

• One element of the University's impressive holdings in Prairie history is highlighted by this bibliography. The largest section consists of separate sequences of books on the Red River Rebellion (1869-1870), the North-West Rebellion (1885), and Louis Riel, the central figure, each subdivided into contemporary and modern works. The same topical division is used for the manuscript collections (correspondence, clippings, photographs, personal papers), arranged by record number. The *Northwest Resistance* Internet site (http://library.usask.ca/northwest/contents.html) provides a database that can be searched and browsed by author, title, and subject; some items have been digitized. Other features include a chronology and biographies of major participants. The annotations, archival content, and detailed indexes nicely complement Arora's *Louis Riel: A Bibliography* (**CD74**), published the same year. — *LMcD*

DA78   **Peel's Bibliography of the Canadian Prairies to 1953** / based upon the work of Bruce Braden Peel; Ernie B. Ingles, N. Merrill Distad, editors & compilers; Linda M. Distad, associate ed.; Tom Williams, Richard Spafford, associate contributors; Darcy A. Sharman, Lorraine N. Strilesky, editorial & research assistants. - Toronto, ON: Univ. of Toronto Pr., 2003. - xxviii, 899 p.; [8] p. of plates, ill. (chiefly col.), ports.

Class Numbers:
   Library of Congress Z1392.P7
   National Library of Canada Z1365
   ISBN 0802048250
   OCLC 54400435
   LCCN 2004-296053

• Long a foundation for Western Canadian studies, *Peel* appears in a much-anticipated new edition that builds on the many strengths of its predecessor. With more than 7,400 entries (a growth of 60 percent over the second edition) and an additional 1,100 titles included in annotations, it remains the definitive reference work on the region. All aspects of the Prairies are represented (beginning with an 1816 printing of the 1670 charter of the Hudson's Bay Company) but not all publications. Most federal and provincial documents, later travel accounts only peripherally describing the prairies, newspapers and most journals, and works by Prairie writers on other than Prairie subjects, are excluded, but works of literature with a clearly Prairie setting are included. Arrangement is chronological by content, conveying evolving context, and alphabetical within year. Separate indexes of subjects (1,825 proper names and topical headings), titles, authors (many with biographical notes), languages, and pseudonyms. Handy chart of second edition entry numbers and third edition equivalents. Many titles in the former were reproduced in the series *Peel Bibliography on Microfiche* (Ottawa: National Library of Canada, 1976-1979).
§   *Peel's Prairie Provinces* Internet site (http://peel.library.ualberta.ca), developed by the University of Alberta Libraries, enhances the value of the bibliography by providing a searchable version as well as an ongoing project to digitize texts of the works (as of September 2006, approximately 4,000 titles are full text). "Quick Search" has all fields, Peel number, title, author, and subject options; "Advanced Search" offers additional fields such as publication date, activity date, language, Boolean, and sorting. Eventually the database will extend the scope by including post-1953 publications. Essential. — *LMcD*

DA79   **A Selective Bibliography of Canadiana of the Prairie Provinces: Publications Relating to Western Canada by English, French, Icelandic, Mennonite, and Ukrainian Authors** / [A.F. Jamieson, ed.]. – Winnipeg, MB: Winnipeg Public Library, 1949 [1997]. - 33 p.

Class Numbers:
   Library of Congress Z1392

OCLC 25453281

• An ethnic approach to the region. In addition to standard works, the brief bibliography usefully includes titles outside the scope of *Peel* (**DA78**) because of format (e.g., Icelandic periodicals published in Manitoba) or content (literary works by prairie writers, but without a Prairie setting). — *LMcD*

Manuscripts; Archives

DA80   Spry, Irene M. - **The Records of the Department of the Interior and Research Concerning Canada's Western Frontier of Settlement** / [by] Irene M. Spry and Bennett McCardle. - Regina, SK: Canadian Plains Research Center, Univ. of Regina, 1993. - 198 p., [32] p. of plates; ill., maps. - (Canadian plains studies, 24; ISSN 0317-6290).

   Class Numbers:
      Library of Congress CD3638.5
   ISBN 0889770611
   OCLC 29030012
   LCCN 94-186726
   Notes:
      Includes bibliographical references and index

• Begins with a literature review on Western settlement and land management, and a summary of the importance of records of the Dept. of Interior (1870-1936), the agency responsible for developing the West by surveying and disposing of homestead lands, issuing Métis scrip, and grant-ing ranching leases and mining licenses. Interior also oversaw other functions and agencies vital to the Prairies such as immigration, Indian Affairs, and the Royal Canadian Mounted Police. The majority of the book is a guide to surviving records, listed by administrative body. Given the complexity of location and organization, "Research Strategy: Suggestions for Users" (p. 36-38) is recommended reading. Appendixes provide additional detail on the transfer of federal records to the provinces, a list of Dominion Land Agencies 1873-1930, and a guide to legislation affecting Prairie settlement. Useful for identifying primary sources in areas such as resource management, settlement patterns, native land claims, and genealogy. — *LMcD*

Atlases

DA81   Matthews, Geoffrey J. - **Historical Atlas of Canada** / Geoffrey J. Matthews, cartographer/designer. - Toronto, ON ; Buffalo, NY : Univ. of Toronto Pr., 1987-1993. - 1 atlas (3 v.) ; col. ill., col. maps ; 38 cm.

   Class Numbers:
      Library of Congress G1116.S1
   ISBN 0802024955 (v. 1)   0802034470 (v. 2) 0802034489 (v. 3)

OCLC 18188779
LCCN 88-155090 ; 91-149828
Notes:
   Bibliography: v. 1, p. [179]-198 ; v. 2, p. [153]-184 ; v. 3, p. [163]-197
   Contents: v. 1, From the Beginning to 1800 / R. Cole Harris, ed. ; v. 2, The Land Transformed, 1800-1891 / R. Louis Gentilcore, ed. ; v. 3, Addressing the Twentieth Century, 1891-1961 / Donald Kerr, ed.
   Scales differ

• Traces the social, political, and economic development of Canada, from prehistory to 1961, in a series of visually beautiful plates. Typically the plates consist of one or two principal distribution maps, accompanied by charts, graphs, photographs, and illustrative examples. The set emphasizes changing trends in ordinary life over the centuries. Coverage of the West in volume 1 ends in 1821, with the merger of the Hudson's Bay Company and the North West Company. Volume 2, covering most of the 19th century, devotes almost half its 58 plates to Western settlement and economic development. Specifically Prairie themes include the fur trade Northwest to 1870, native reserves, dispersal of the Métis in Manitoba, and homesteading and agriculture from 1872 to 1891. Volume three is divided between "The Great Transformation 1891-1929" and "Crisis and Response 1929-1961," covering the Depression, World War II and postwar prosperity. Among the regionally focused plates are those concerned with settling the Prairies, Prairie agriculture, Winnipeg, and the dust bowl period. *Concise Historical Atlas of Canada* (Toronto: Univ. of Toronto Pr., 1998; 180 p.) contains a selection of 67 plates, with some new essays. *Historical Atlas of Canada Online Learning Project* (http://historicalatlas.ca/website/hacolp/) provides interactive maps; a work in progress, it is currently about 15 percent complete. The full atlas presents a great deal of information in a very appealing fashion, effectively dispelling lingering myths about the blandness of Canadian history. — *LMcD*

EXPLORATION

Bibliographies

DA82   Schmeckebier, Laurence Frederick, 1877-1959. - **Catalogue and Index of the Hayden, King, Powell, and Wheeler Surveys**. - Washington, DC: [U.S.] Govt. Print. Off., 1904. - 208 p. - (U.S. Geological Survey. Bulletin, 222; U.S. Geological Survey. Subject series: G, Miscellaneous, 26).

   Class Numbers:
      Library of Congress QE75   Z6034.U49

Notes:
 Collective titles of the surveys: *United States Geological and Geographical Survey of the Territories* (Hayden); *United States Geological Exploration of the Fortieth Parallel* (King); *United States Geographical and Geological Survey of the Rocky Mountain Region* (Powell); *United States Geographical Surveys West of the Hundredth Meridian* (Wheeler)
 Subtitle: *Namely, Geological and Geographical Survey of the Territories, Geological Exploration of the Fortieth Parallel, Geographical and Geological Surveys of the Rocky Mountain Region, Geographical Surveys West of the One Hundredth Meridian*

• Schmeckebier (editorial division, U.S. Geological Survey) compiled this catalog and index of the publications issued as the result of the four great early surveys of U.S. lands and territories in the trans-Mississippi West, conducted 1867-1879 (the formative years of the Geological Survey) under the leadership of F.V. Hayden, Clarence King, J.W. Powell, and G.M. Wheeler. The catalog occupies p. 9-65, and simply gives bibliographic descriptions of the publications issued by each of the surveys, including annual reports, all other publications, and maps. The very detailed index (p. 67-208) refers to the survey publications by a system of abbreviations for which the code is given at the beginning, and shows that the surveyors were interested not only in the geology of the West, but among other matters in plants and animals, minerals, the prospects for agriculture, and Indian languages and ethnography. Although the surveys covered vast stretches of the West, the index refers on nearly every page to Great Plains topics (hymenoptera collected in Kansas, comparative vocabulary of Indian languages, cretaceous rocks of the Upper Missouri region). Essential for students of exploration of the West, including the Plains. — *RB*

DA83 Thomas, Marcia L., 1950-   . - **John Wesley Powell: An Annotated Bibliography**. - Westport, CT: Praeger, 2004. - xxvi, 256 p.; port. - (Bibliographies and indexes in American history, 49; ISSN 0742-6828).

 Class Numbers:
  Library of Congress F788.P68   Z8709.5
 ISBN 0313319421
 LCCN 2004-42286
 Notes:
  Includes bibliographical references; index
  Review by J. Drueke: *Choice* 42.8 (Apr. 2005): review 42-4405

• In the only comprehensive bibliography of Powell, Thomas cites a thousand items by and about him. Soldier, explorer, teacher, anthropologist, geologist, and environmentalist, Powell directed both the U.S. Geological Survey and the Smithsonian Institution's Bureau of Ethnology. He wrote extensively on Western exploration, American Indians, geology, and natural resources. His writings on conservation of water resources, the scientific classification of land, and government regulation of land use are particularly relevant today in the Plains, where these topics are the focus of public policy discussions. Powell, who often created bibliographic confusion by publishing his work in several venues, was most prolific as a writer of government reports. The bibliography includes Powell's articles, monographs, congressional testimony, archival records, manuscripts, forewords, and speeches. Entries are organized by type of work and indexed by subject, author, and title. Works about Powell and his associates include journals and letters of his expedition teams, dissertations, and Internet resources. — *JD*

DA84 Wagner, Henry Raup, 1982-1957. - **The Plains & the Rockies: A Critical Bibliography of Exploration, Adventure, and Travel in the American West, 1800-1865** / [by] Henry R. Wagner & Charles L. Camp. - 4th ed. / rev., enl., and ed. by Robert H. Becker - San Francisco, CA: J. Howell-Books, 1982. - xx, 745 p.

 Class Numbers:
  Library of Congress F591   Z1251.W5
 ISBN 0910760111
 LCCN 81-86051
 Notes:
  1st ed.: Henry R. Wagner's *The Plains and the Rockies; A Bibliography of Original Narratives of Travel and Adventure, 1800-1865*. San Francisco, CA: Grabhorn Pr., 1937
  Includes bibliographical references (p. [xvi]-xx); index

• Compiled by a mining executive and continued by a paleontologist, this work is of first importance for the history of the West, which by definition includes the Prairies and Plains region. It cites 1,800 separate issues of 690 individual works covering the West (Mexico to the Arctic Circle, the Missouri River to the Cascades and Sierra Nevada) published 1801-1865. Entries provide full descriptive cataloging, transcribing title pages in great detail and collating both signatures and pagination. Annotations cover content, significance, and publishing history. Libraries holding copies are noted, as are item numbers in the *National Union Catalog*. Items are numbered consecutively; the index, which lists primarily names and titles, refers to item numbers. Of particular interest, because of its elaborate descriptions, to collectors building personal libraries, but highly useful to students and scholars in identifying early accounts of exploration in the West. — *RB*

DA84a White, David A., 1927-   . - **Plains & Rockies, 1800-1865: One Hundred Twenty Proposed Additions to the Wagner-Kemp and Becker Bibliography of Travel and Adventure in the American West: with 33 Selected Reprints** / comp. and annotated by David A. White. - Spokane, WA: Arthur H. Clark Co., 2001. - 544 p.; ill., maps.

Class Numbers:

    Library of Congress F591

ISBN 0870623117

LCCN 2001-42464

Notes:

    "A supplemental volume to the series *News of the Plains and Rockies.*"

    Includes bibliographical references; index

• Cites 120 additions to those listed in Henry R. Wagner's *The Plains & the Rockies*, ranging from Samuel Mitchell's periodical *The Medical Repository* (1801-1821) to Alfred Sully's "A Wasted Sioux-Hunting Campaign to Devils Lake" (1865). Like the sources cited by Wagner, those White cites are concerned with early exploration by whites of the region between the Mississippi River and the Sierra Nevada and Cascade ranges, and between Mexico and the Arctic Circle. White provides careful title-page transcriptions and notes which comment on the importance and content of the source, supply details of publication, and add notes and bibliographies. White's additions are drawn from his *News of the Plains and Rockies 1803-1865* (Spokane, WA: Arthur H. Clark Co., 1996-2001. 8 v.). He arranges entries chronologically and in a second section reprints 33 of the briefer items. Appendixes provide tables of item numbers and authors in the 1953 and 1982 editions of Wagner and similar tables for White's own list. Thorough index of names, titles, place-names, and topics. A useful addition to Wagner with which Plains students should be familiar. — *RB*

Encyclopedias

DA85 Howgego, Raymond John. - **Encyclopedia of Exploration to 1800: A Comprehensive Reference Guide to the History and Literature of Exploration, Travel and Colonization from the Earliest Times to the Year 1800.** - Sydney, N.S.W. : Hordern House, c2003. - 1168 p.; ill.

Class Numbers:

    Library of Congress G200

ISBN 1875567364

Notes:

    Includes bibliographical references; indexes

DA85a Howgego, Raymond John. - **Encyclopedia of Exploration, 1800 to 1850: A Comprehensive Reference Guide to the History and Literature of Exploration, Travel and Colonization between the Years 1800 and 1850.** - Sydney, N.S.W. : Hordern House, 2004. - 690 p.

ISBN 1875567399 1875567445 (set)

OCLC 56889569

Notes:

    Includes bibliographical references; indexes

• An elaborate, curious, and fascinating set, written by a single British researcher not affiliated with any academic institution, who was trained in physics. His encyclopedia is concerned with exploration in all parts of the world, and devotes most of its articles to individual explorers, although it also supplies entries for places explored (e.g., Missouri River). All articles end with bibliographies, some very full, many divided into early accounts and later studies (often listed as "Bibliography 1" and "Bibliography 2"). Expeditions involving groups of explorers are commonly entered under the name of the leader (although Lewis and Clark have separate entries), with members of the group mentioned in the article about the leader. Separate expeditions (e.g., by Pike, Frémont) get separate entries. The second volume will be more useful for Plains studies than the first, which has entries for the likes of Coronado and la Verendrye. Not supremely convenient to use: there are indexes in both volumes for ships and for names, but the only geographic access is in brief indications of places or regions explored that appear at the head of each entry, for which there is no index. Few readers interested in exploration will care once they begin reading, since articles are packed with fascinating facts about the expeditions and explorers, and are written in highly literate style. Unusual entries show Howgego's sensitivity to the varied curiosities of readers (e.g., "Fictitious Voyages" in v. 1). A third volume (2006) covers 1850-1940 but is concerned with exploration of oceans, islands, and polar regions, so will be of little use in Prairies-Plains research. — *RB*

Collective Biographies

DA86 **The Mountain Men and the Fur Trade of the Far West** / biographical sketches of the participants by scholars of the subject and with introductions by the editor; under editorial supervision of LeRoy R. Hafen. - Glendale, CA: A.H. Clark Co., 1965-1972. - 10 v.; ill., map, ports.

Class Numbers:

    Library of Congress F592

ISBN 0870620959 (v. 8)   0870621009 (v. 10)

LCCN 64-7629

Notes:

    Vol. 10: Bibliography & Index

• Provides biographical sketches of about 300 men engaged in the trans-Mississippi fur trade in the first half of the 19th century. Entries are arranged alphabetically in each volume. Volume 1 provides a summary history of the fur trade, and v. 10 the index to the set, a detailed bibliography, information on the illustrations and contributors, and an especially detailed subject index that should prove very useful. The bibliography has three parts: archival materials; newspaper articles; and books, journal articles, and theses. Among the notable subjects are George Drouillard from the Lewis and Clark Expedition, Kit Carson, and Peter Sarpy. – MB

§ A selection of the more important biographies has been reprinted as:

DA86a Hafen, Le Roy Reuben, 1893– . - **Mountain Men and Fur Traders of the Far West: Eighteen Biographical Sketches** / selected with an introd. by Harvey L. Carter. - Lincoln, NE: Univ. of Nebraska Pr., 1982, 1965. - 401 p.; ill.

> Class Numbers:
> Library of Congress F592
> ISBN 0803272103 (set)
> LCCN 81-21803
> Notes:
> Includes bibliographical references; index

• Biographical sketches, written by scholars, of 18 fur traders and trappers who explored the American West in the late 19th century. The essays include footnotes for source materials and one map. — *GK*

Atlases

DA87 Goetzmann, William H. - **The Atlas of North American Exploration: From the Norse Voyages to the Race to the Pole** / [by] William Goetzmann and Glyndwr Williams; [cartographic director, Malcolm Swanston; maps created by Isabelle Lewis and Jacqueline Land]. - New York: Prentice Hall General Reference, 1992. - 224 p.; ill. (chiefly col.), col. maps; 29 cm.; scales vary.

> Class Numbers:
> Library of Congress G1106.S12
> ISBN 0132971283
> LCCN 92-8573
> Notes:
> Bibliography: p. 203-209; index

• Goetzmann and Williams cover all the early explorations of the North American continent, but the relevant portion for Prairies-Plains study will be "Jeffersonian Pathfinders," 1792-1820. The entry for each expedition provides background narrative and a map. Maps show the route of a particular track of exploration and provide a legend that shows settlements, trading posts, encounters with Indians, military skirmishes, and territories claimed by various European countries and by the U.S. The Jeffersonian section covers early explorers of the Missouri River, the Lewis and Clark Corps of Discovery, Spanish travels from the southwest, and the expeditions of Pike and Long. The authors include an entry for the Palliser-Hinds survey of the Canadian Prairies. Most maps and illustrations are in color. — *JB*

DA88 Hayes, Derek, 1947- . - **America Discovered: A Historical Atlas of North American Exploration**. - Vancouver, B.C.; Berkeley, CA: Douglas & McIntyre; distr. in U.S., [Emeryville, CA]: Publishers Group West, 2004. - 224 p.; ill. (some col.), maps (some col.), ports.; 33 cm.

> Class Numbers:
> Library of Congress G1106.S12
> National Library of Canada G1106 S12
> ISBN 1553650492 9781553650492
> OCLC 55596419
> Notes:
> Includes bibliographical references; index
> Review by B. Osborne: *Choice* 43.5 (Jan. 2006): review 43-2582

• A fascinating compilation of facsimiles of early maps of the North American continent that shows the developing realization explorers acquired of the shape and extent of the continent. Maps are arranged in roughly chronological order, grouped by evocative titles ("A Northern Passage" [the search for a water passage to China and the Spice Islands], "Seeking Furs and Lost Souls" [trappers and missionaries], "Internal Parts of Louisiana" [Lewis and Clark], "Exploring a Prairie" [Canadian surveys], "The Great Western Surveys" [King, Wheeler, Powell, Hayden]). Discussion of maps is swept into highly literate descriptions of exploration, but a "Map Catalog" (p. 210-217) provides full and accurate citations, including sources from which facsimiles were drawn. Brief bibliography; index. Worth the time of any student of cartography, the exploration of North America, or the settlement of the continent, including the Plains. — *RB*

DA89 Hulbert, Archer Butler, 1873-1933, ed. - **The Crown Collection of American Maps, Series IV: The American Transcontinental Trails**. - Colorado Springs, CO: Stewart Commission on Western History, 1925-1928. - 6v.; maps; 30 cm.

> Class Numbers:
> Library of Congress G1381.P25
> LCCN map 66-742
> Notes:
> Consists of blue prints or blue line prints of manuscript maps and notes
> Contents: v. 1, The Platte River Routes; v. 2, North and South Platte Routes; v. 3, The Oregon Trail in Idaho and Oregon; v. 4, The California Trail, Fort Hall to Placerville, with Branch to Salt Lake City; v. 5, The Santa Fé Trail (Raton Mountain Route); v. 6, The Santa Fé-California Trail
> Includes bibliographical references

• A fascinating collection of map reproductions for the major Western migration trails (reproduced by the blueprint process–white on blue) issued as a resource for teaching history. Introductions and notes that accompany the maps are written in longhand; a brief bibliography cites publications relating to migrations that followed the trails. Interesting for Prairies-Plains study are volumes 1-2 that cover the Kansas, Nebraska, Colorado, and Wyoming portions of the North and South Platte routes of the Oregon Trail, and volume 5 that depicts the Kansas and Nebraska sections of the Santa Fe Trail. Absorbing background detail about the trails headed West. — *JB*

DA90   The Settling of North America: The Atlas of the Great Migrations into North America from the Ice Age to the Present / ed. by Helen Hornbeck Tanner; associate eds., Janice Reiff [et al.]. - New York; [UK]: Macmillan, c1995. - 208 p.; ill. (some col.), maps, ports. (some col.); 32 cm.

> ISBN 0026162725
> LCCN 95-37756

• Maps in this atlas show waves of migration, while portraits, letters, poems, and songs personalize individual migrations. It is divided into eight periods, the first reaching back 16,000 years. In all eight, maps show significant migrations to and across the Plains. Each section begins with a timeline of events in six parts of the world that sent migrants to North America, and the accompanying text analyzes the reasons for migration, settlement patterns, and cultural effects. Besides patterns of movement and population strongholds, maps show natural resources, lifeways, industries, and trade networks. Maps of the Plains include the trade routes that moved metals, cloth, and shells through the Plains; Native migration onto the Plains into areas of Spanish and French control, 1515-1818; the spread of horses; and areas of Scandinavian settlement between 1865 and 1915. Bibliography and subject index. — *JD*

DA91   Wexler, Alan. - Atlas of Westward Expansion / [by] Alan Wexler; maps and pen-and-ink drawings by Molly Braun; Carl Waldman, editorial consultant. - [New York]: Facts on File, 1995. - 240 p.; ill., maps (some col.); 29 cm.

> Class Numbers:
>   Library of Congress G1201.S1
> ISBN 0816026602
> LCCN 94-756
> Notes:
>   Includes bibliographical references (p. 225-227)
>   Mainly covers the period 1754-1917
>   Scale not given

• Covers westward expansion from 1754 to 1900. While not

all chapters pertain to the Prairies-Plains region, the majority do. Each of the eight chapters covers a range of years, six to 40, and each is divided into subtopics. Relevant sections discuss the exploration of the region, including the Lewis and Clark Expedition, the Plains Indian wars, and settlement of the region by homesteaders. Approximately 100 maps are distributed throughout; a list follows the table of contents. There are also a number of interesting, helpful black-and-white illustrations and photos. Appendix B offers a useful chronology of U.S. territorial expansion, 1750-1917. Rounding out the volume are a solid bibliography and a detailed index. — *MB*

LEWIS AND CLARK EXPEDITION

DA92   Appleman, Roy Edgar. - Lewis and Clark: Historic Places Associated with their Transcontinental Exploration (1804-06). - Washington, DC: U.S. National Park Service; [for sale by the Supt. of Docs., U.S. Govt. Print. Off.], 1975. - 429 p. - (The National survey of historic sites and buildings, v. 13).

> Class Numbers:
>   Library of Congress F592.7
>   Government Document I 29.2:H 62/9/V.13
> LCCN 73-20144
> Notes:
>   Bibliography: p. 379-381

• Appleman devotes the first 250 pages of his book to "Historical Background" before turning his attention to the presumed focus of the book, historic sites along the route followed by Lewis and Clark between St. Louis and Fort Clatsop on the Pacific Coast. The entries for specific historic sites are organized unhelpfully by state (arranged alphabetically) rather than by their sequence along the Lewis-Clark route. Appleman supplies excellent maps and some absorbing present-day photographs to accompany contemporary drawings. An especially telling shot shows the trickle that remains of the Great Falls of the Missouri when the flood gates of Cochrane Dam upstream are closed. Notes; list of 15 titles for further reading; index. — *RB*

DA93   Before Lewis and Clark: Documents Illustrating the History of the Missouri, 1785-1804 / ed. with introductory narrative by A.P.Nasatir; introd. by James P. Ronda. - Norman, OK: Univ. of Oklahoma Pr., 2002. – xxv, 854 p.; ill., maps. - (St. Louis Historical Documents Foundation. Joseph Desloge Fund. Publication, 3).

> Class Numbers:
>   Library of Congress F598
> ISBN 0806134674
> LCCN 2002-66844
> Notes:
>   Bibliographical footnotes

Reprint. Originally publ. in 2 v.: St. Louis, MO: St. Louis Historical Documents Foundation, 1952

• Reprints hundreds of documents, chiefly letters or drafts of letters, translated into English, from the 20 years before Lewis and Clark embarked on their expedition of discovery. All are related to explorations intended to reach the headwaters of the Missouri River. Also includes, but in lesser numbers, various legal documents, such as agreements between parties, petitions, and promissory notes. Ronda's introduction gives as the collection's major themes "geographic discovery, scientific curiosity, personal power, national rivalries, and cultural conflicts" (p. xvi). Documents are arranged chronologically, the first chapter covering 1785-1793, and subsequent chapters each devoted to a single year. Nearly all the entries contain copious explanatory footnotes, note the original language, and cite supporting literature. There are a handful of illustrations. The index at the end of the second volume is thorough, running some 70 pages. An important compilation. — *MB*

DA94   Clarke, Charles G. - **The Men of the Lewis and Clark Expedition: A Biographical Roster of the Fifty-One Members and a Composite Diary of Their Activities from All the Known Sources** / introd. to the Bison Books ed. by Dayton Duncan. - Lincoln, NE: Univ. of Nebraska Pr., 2002, 1970. - 351 p.; ill., fold. map, ports. (part col.). - (Western frontiersman series, 14).

Class Numbers:
Library of Congress F592.7
ISBN 0803264194
LCCN 76-116914
Notes:
Bibliography: p. [333]-337; index
Originally publ.: Glendale, CA: A.H. Clark Co., 1970

• Following the 40-page roster of the Corps, which devotes an average of one page to each member of the Expedition, is a composite diary drawn from records kept by several members and extracted from a condensed version of the journals edited by Nicholas Biddle (1814). It intends to reveal the personalities of the participants in a way earlier publications had not. The greater part of the book is a day-to-day summary of events that makes liberal use of the editorial "we." A few illustrations are scattered throughout the book. The bibliography, substantially out of date, lacks the numerous Bicentennial publications. — *MB*

DA95   Gale, Kira. - **Lewis and Clark Road Trips: Exploring the Trail across America** / campsite data by Bob Bergantino. - Omaha, NE: River Junction Pr., 2006. - 268 p.; ill. (chiefly col.), col. maps. - (Great American road trips).

Class Numbers:

Library of Congress E158
ISBN 0964931524
LCCN 2006-901711
Notes:
Further information at:
http://www.lewisandclarkroadtrips.com
Includes bibliographical references; index

• A guidebook that leaves little to chance. Not content to cover the route followed by the Corps of Discovery from Wood River Camp to Fort Clatsop, it begins in Virginia in the region of birth of both Lewis and Clark, follows them to Washington, across Pennsylvania and down the Ohio River, finally joining the expedition proper in region 4, St. Louis to Kansas City. Along the way, Gale describes points of interest, some related to the Expedition, some not (Henry Doorly Zoo and Lauritzen Gardens, both in Omaha). The book is made lively by numerous photographs and maps in color. Color-coded edge labels make it easy to find appropriate sections, and near the end comes a list of campsites along the route and in eastern parts of the Lewis-Clark country before they set paddle into the Missouri. Useful to take on trips that follow any part of the Expedition's path, but travelers who want to visit all the sites listed need to allow lots of time. — *RB*

DA96   Grossman, Elizabeth, 1957 -   . - **Adventuring along the Lewis and Clark Trail: Missouri, Illinois, Iowa, Nebraska, South Dakota, North Dakota, Montana, Idaho, Oregon, Washington**. - San Francisco, CA: Sierra Club Books, 2003. - 280 p.

Class Numbers:
Library of Congress F592.7
ISBN 1578050677
OCLC 50253144
LCCN 2002-26974
Notes:
Includes bibliographical references (p. [257]-261); index

• Designed for travelers, armchair or otherwise, Grossman's guide takes readers from Illinois to the Pacific Ocean. Since the author intends to "get readers out of their cars and into the landscape," she recommends hiking trails and canoe trips in a variety of sidebars. The book also has a number of good maps and a sprinkling of black-and-white photos. (A similar National Geographic guide is filled with color photos.) Three appendixes list status of animal species, conservation groups and tribal organizations, and public agencies, sources of maps, and miscellaneous information. The latter two are organized alphabetically by state. Brief list of recommended readings; subject index. — *MB*

DA97   Harlan, James D., 1951-   . - **Atlas of Lewis and Clark in Missouri** / [by] James D. Harlan and James Denny. - Columbia, MO: Univ. of Missouri Pr., 2003. - 138 p.; ill., maps (some col.); 31 x 44 cm.

Class Numbers:
    Library of Congress F592.7
LCCN 2003-5686
Notes:
    Includes bibliographical references (p. 133-144); index
    Review by G.J. Martin: *Choice* 41.11/12 (July/Aug. 2004)
        review 41-6734
    Table of contents: http://www.loc.gov/catdir/toc/
        ecip041/2003005686.html

• Larger than life, this atlas, although confined to the Corps of Discovery's progress through or adjacent to the state of Missouri, requires a large table for its consultation. Each of the four sections of text is preceded by a large color plate consisting of a map detailing a few miles of the Corps's progress. Accompanying each plate is a day-by-day description of the events and activities associated with the area on the map. Parts 1 and 2 (19 plates) describe the trip up the Mississippi and Missouri Rivers in 1803 and 1804 at the beginning of the expedition. Part three (4 plates) describes the return trip in 1806. Part four (4 plates) describes the "lost" Missouri River with plates showing land where the river once flowed. A variety of large, beautiful, full color illustrations and historical maps lend the atlas immediacy. Pockets inside the front and back covers each contain a large folded overview map of the entire state, one for the journey upriver, the other down. The atlas ends with a bibliography and index. — *MB*

DA98   Hartley, Alan H. - **Lewis and Clark Lexicon of Discovery**. - Pullman, WA: Washington State Univ. Pr., 2004. - xxii, 234 p.; ill.

Class Numbers:
    Library of Congress PE2970.W4
ISBN 0874222788 (pbk.)
    0874222796 (spiral-bound)
LCCN 2004-18400
Notes:
    Includes bibliographical references (p. [231]-234); index
    Table of contents: http://www.loc.gov/catdir/toc/
        ecip0421/2004018400.html

• Designed to aid study of the primary records of the expedition and to show the quirks of 19th-century vocabulary and spelling, *Lexicon* cites over 1,000 English, French-Canadian, and Native American terms used by expedition forces to describe tribes, landscape features, flora, fauna, gear, food, clothing, medicine, languages, measures, transportation, and activities. Many are obscure or obsolete or have undergone spelling shifts or changes in meaning. Excerpts from texts, most often drawn from Gary Moulton's 13-volume *Journals of the Lewis and Clark Expedition*, show spelling variations and usages in context. Both the entertainment and scholarly values are high. Highlighted

text boxes elaborate on topics such as uses of the terms "prairie" (variously spelled "preree," "prarie," "perarie") and "plains", and the technique of moving boats up the Missouri River with cords and poles. An opening essay discusses the language backgrounds of the Corps members and their reflection in the journals. Appendixes provide a classified subject index; spelling variants; abbreviations and symbols; sounds and nonstandard spellings; and a list of references. — *JD*

DA99   **Herbarium of the Lewis & Clark Expedition** / Gary E. Moulton, ed. - Lincoln, NE: Univ. of Nebraska Pr., 1999. - 357 p.; ill., maps; 32 cm.

Class Numbers:
    Library of Congress F592.4
ISBN 0803229313
LCCN 98-53495   82-8510
Notes:
    "A project of the Center for Great Plains Studies,
        University of Nebraska-Lincoln."
    227 specimens held by the Academy of Natural Sciences,
        11 by Kew Gardens, and 1 by the Charleston Museum
    Includes bibliographical references; index

• Moulton (history, Univ. of Nebraska) is editor of the definitive edition of *The Journals of the Lewis and Clark Expedition* (13 v.). This volume (v. 12 of that edition) contains the complete listing of 239 plant specimens and 177 distinct species names collected by Lewis. The specimens are arranged alphabetically by scientific name along with the repository for each plant, date of collection, reference to Frederick Pursch's *Flora Americae Septentrionalis*, and transcriptions from original labels. The majority of specimens are held at the Academy of Natural Sciences in Philadelphia. Six appendixes; illustrations of plant specimens; calendar of botanical specimens; sources cited. — *GK*

DA100   **The Literature of the Lewis and Clark Expedition: A Bibliography and Essays** / essays by Stephen Dow Beckham; bibliography by Doug Erickson, Jeremy Skinner, and Paul Merchant. - Portland, OR: Lewis & Clark College, 2003. - 315 p.; ill. (some col.), maps.

Class Numbers:
    Library of Congress Z1249.L67
ISBN 0963086618
LCCN 2002-116566
Notes:
    Includes bibliographical references (p. 287-301); index
    Review essay by Andrew R.L. Cayton: *Great Plains
        Quarterly* 24.4 (fall 2004): 283-287

• Beckham (history), Erickson and Skinner (archivists), and

Merchant (director, William Stafford Archives, all at Lewis and Clark College) provide a comprehensive bibliography of the Lewis and Clark expedition based on collections housed at the college's Aubrey R. Watzek Library. The work has seven sections: the Expedition's traveling library of maps, scientific, and technical materials (1754-1804); early congressional documents (1803-1807); Patrick Gass's journal (1802-1806); apocryphal narratives and alleged accounts of the expedition (1814-2001); 19th-century publications; 20th-century publications. Each chapter begins with a historical essay followed by annotated bibliographies that list works by year of publication. Twenty-three color plates, twelve illustrations. — *GK*

DA101 Plamondon, Martin. - **Lewis and Clark Trail Maps: A Cartographic Reconstruction**. - Pullman, WA: Washington State Univ. Pr., 2000-2004. - 3 v.; maps; 32 cm.

> Class Numbers:
> Library of Congress G1417.L4 P5
> ISBN 087422232X (v. 1)   0874222338 (v. 1 pbk.)
>   0874222427 (v. 2)   0874222435 (v. 2 pbk.)
>   0874222656 (v. 3)   0874222664 (v. 3 pbk.)
> LCCN 00-42857
> Notes:
>   Index in v. 3

• Plamondon (a professional cartographer, Clay County, WA, and chairman of the state's Lewis and Clark Trail Committee) provides in celebration of its bicentennial a meticulous reconstruction of the route followed by the Lewis and Clark Expedition (1804-1806). He bases his maps on surveys conducted by Clark during the Expedition, and on maps, notes, journals, and sketches. He includes present-day features such as highways, state and county boundaries, key geographic points, and reservoirs. Volume 1 has 153 maps for the region between the winter camp in Illinois (1803-1804) and North Dakota; volume 2, 180 maps, Fort Mandan to the Snake and Columbia rivers; and volume 3, maps from the Columbia to the Pacific Ocean. Excerpts from journal entries, an essay on frontier surveying, and indexes make this set essential for libraries, especially those supporting study of the Expedition or early exploration of the West. — *GK*

DA102 Tubbs, Stephenie Ambrose. - **The Lewis and Clark Companion: An Encyclopedic Guide to the Voyage of Discovery** / [by] Stephenie Ambrose Tubbs, with Clay Straus Jenkinson; foreword by Stephen E. Ambrose. - New York: Henry Holt, 2003. - 345 p.; ill., maps.

> Class Numbers:

> Library of Congress F592.7
> ISBN 0805067256 0805067264 (pbk.)
>   9780805067255 9780805067262 (pbk.)
> OCLC 50913607
> LCCN 2002-37992
> Notes:
>   Includes bibliographical references (p. 333-345)

• Provides entries for all aspects of the Lewis and Clark Expedition, basing articles heavily on Moulton's edition of the Lewis and Clark journals (13 v., 1983-2001). The compilers cover persons (white, black, and Indian), Expedition apparatus, places, food and medicines, Indian games, boats–few topics seem to have escaped. The compilers wrote all the articles. Appendixes list presents for Indians that the Corps carried, and Indian peoples with whom they came in contact. Bibliography of books and articles, but no index. Useful to students or scholars of the Expedition, since it clarifies many points and is so closely based on Moulton. — *RB*

DA103 Woodger, Elin. - **Encyclopedia of the Lewis and Clark Expedition** / [by] Elin Woodger and Brandon Toropov; foreword by Ned Blackhawk. - New York: Facts on File, c2004. - xxv, 438 p.; ill., maps. - (Facts on File library of American history).

> Class Numbers:
> Library of Congress F592.7
> ISBN 0816047812 0816047820 (pbk.)
> LCCN 2003-6120
> Notes:
>   Includes bibliographical references (p. 397-412); index
>   Review by J. Drueke: *Choice* 41.8 (Apr. 2004):
>   review 41-4419
>   Review by Stephen S. Witte: *Great Plains Quarterly* 26.1
>   (winter 2006): 51
>   Table of contents: http://www.loc.gov/catdir/toc/
>   ecip041/2003006120.hyml

• Covering only about 350 "salient topics," Woodger and Toropov's work creates a picture of the expedition for general readers with descriptions of flora and fauna, places, routes, equipment, transportation, food, supplies, activities, and people encountered. It provides straightforward, commonly accepted accounts rather than exploring alternative versions or contradictions among the many reports and histories. Entries, which range from a single paragraph to several pages, include occasional illustrations and a list of further print and online readings. Journal excerpts using original spellings and facsimile pages add interest and evoke the period. Entries are supplemented by an extensive bibliography of print and online sources, a chronology with route maps, a list of tribes encountered, additional maps, a classified subject list, and a subject index. — *JD*

DA104   Cordes, Kathleen A. - **America's National Historic Trails** / photographs by Jane Lammers. - Norman, OK: Univ. of Oklahoma Pr., 1999. - 370p.; col. ill., maps.

> Class Numbers:
>   Library of Congress E158
> ISBN 080613109
> LCCN 98-45075
> Notes:
>   Bibliography: p. 355-362; index

• Of the twelve national historic trails listed, six pertain to the Prairies-Plains region: Lewis and Clark National Historic Trail (NHT), Santa Fe NHT, Trail of Tears NHT, Oregon NHT, Mormon NHT, Pony Express NHT. The information for each trail includes the administering agency with address and phone number, when the trail was established, the approximate mileage, the states covered, and historical facts. There are many color photos and, for each of the trails, a map with points of interest along the way explained in the accompanying text. Supplementary material includes a good bibliography for each of the trails, and a subject index. — *MB*

DA105   Etter, Patricia A., 1932-   . - **To California on the Southern Route, 1849: A History and Annotated Bibliography** / foreword by Elliott West. - Spokane, WA: Arthur H. Clark, 1998. - 178 p.; ill., maps. - (American trails series, 18).

> Class Numbers:
>   Library of Congress F786
> ISBN 0870622706
> OCLC 39368597
> LCCN 98-35538
> Notes:
>   Includes bibliographical references (p. [167]-168); index

• Etter is concerned principally with the Gold Rush of 1849 and the overland trails that were followed to reach California, hence offers only limited information about the Prairies-Plains region. She does cover the Santa Fe Trail and its Fort Smith leg. Entry annotations run from several sentences to several paragraphs. The appendix is organized by trail. — *JB*

DA106   Heckman, Marlin L. - **Overland on the California Trail, 1846-1859: A Bibliography of Manuscript & Printed Travel Narratives** / foreword by Louis L'Amour. - Glendale, CA: A.H. Clark Co., 1984. - 159 p. - (American trails series, 13).

> LCCN 83-51609

• A list of travel narratives, alphabetical by author, consisting of 403 diaries, journals, and letters kept by men and women traveling the trails overland from the various jumping-off places on the Missouri River, via South Pass in Wyoming, to California. Both published and manuscript sources are listed. Entries supply author's name and dates, a title (often a catch title ["Diary"]), home, the company with whom the author traveled, beginning and termination, format of the narrative and its location, published form (if any), and "reference" (i.e., citations to the narrative in sources listed on p. 22-23). An index cites personal and place-names. A valuable list of personal accounts of transcontinental treks to California. — *RB*

DA107   Kimball, Stanley Buchholz. - **Historic Sites and Markers along the Mormon and Other Great Western Trails**. - Urbana, IL: Univ. of Illinois Pr., 1988. - 320 p.; ill., maps.

> Class Numbers:
>   Library of Congress F591
> ISBN 0252014553 0252014561 (pbk.)
> LCCN 87-13958
> Notes:
>   Bibliography: p. 305-307; index

• Kimball (history, Southern Illinois Univ.) provides a guide for travelers who want to retrace famous trails and routes used by pioneers in westward expansion, i.e., Mormon, Dragoon, Oregon-California, Santa Fe, Overland-Bridger, Trappers'-Cherokee, Cherry Creek, Zion's Camp, Boonslick. The work describes 550 sites or markers, giving for each site the town or city and county where it is located along with directions to the marker. Thirty maps; brief bibliography. An appendix lists museums and historical societies along Western trails. — *GK*

DA108   **North American Immigrant Letters, Diaries, and Oral Histories [Internet Site]**. - Alexandria, VA: Alexander   Street   Pr.,   2004–   .   - http://www.alexanderstreet.com/products/imld.htm

> Access Date: Nov. 2005
> Notes:
>   Available through outright purchase or subscription

• Offering full-text access to thousands of documents (including the Ellis Island Oral History interviews)—personal narratives, diaries, letters, oral histories, autobiographies, pamphlets—this database provides a first-person view of what immigration to the U.S. and Canada meant to the immigrants. Covering writings by Benjamin Franklin in the mid-1700s through the present, the greater share of the content focuses on the late 1800s through 1980. The database reproduces such visual materials as illustrations that accompany some entries and topical cartoons published in Puck. For Prairies-Plains researchers, states can be searched by name, as can immigrant groups (Danes, Irish), individuals (Marquis de Mores), and topics (floods). The editorial board consists of Joel Wurl (Univ. of Minnesota), Hasia R. Diner (NYU), Donna R. Gabaccia (Univ. of North Carolina-Charlotte), Salvador Güereña (Univ. of California–Santa Barbara), and Franklin Odo (Smithsonian Institution). The Alexander Street search engine is described at **CD46**. — *JB*

DA109   United States. National Park Service. - **National Historic Trails Auto Tour Route Interpretive Guide, Nebraska and Northeastern Colorado**. - [Salt Lake City, UT?]: National Park Service, 2006. - 61 p.; ill., map.

  OCLC 85825280

• The National Park Service marks highways as Auto Tour Routes when they lie close to pioneer and other trails that Congress has designated National Historic Trails. The first part of this guide, one of a series for each state through which the trails pass, has brief illustrated histories of four such trails: the Oregon, California, Mormon Pioneer, and Pony Express National Trails. A regional map in the pocket is keyed to the second part of the guide, which offers site-by-site driving directions for four Auto Tour Routes that parallel the trails as they cut through the center of Nebraska. Color photographs show interpretive markers and sites of interest. The book has useful information for tourists and historians, and will be welcomed by researchers in the field, who may have difficulty locating and accessing trails in strange territory. — *JD*

OREGON TRAIL

See also Webber, **Indians along the Oregon Trail, CD57**

DA110   Federal Writers' Project. - **The Oregon Trail: The Missouri River to the Pacific Ocean**. - New York: Hastings House, 1939. - 244 p.; front., plates, folded map. - (American guide series).

  Class Numbers:
    Library of Congress F880
  ISBN 0403012902
  OCLC 1284283
  LCCN 39-27221
  Notes:
    Bibliography: p. 228-230

• Published as an automobile touring guidebook, this volume now has primarily historical interest. It is arranged geographically, taking readers on a road trip across six states, Missouri to Oregon, following the route of the Oregon Trail. The part of the route relevant to the Prairies-Plains region is Section 1 (Independence, MO to Council Bluffs, IA), Sections 2-4, crossing Nebraska, and Sections 5

to 7, across Wyoming, where the Great Plains are left behind. Twenty-seven black-and-white illustrations; appendixes include a chronology of the U.S. 1837-1860 and a bibliography. The index, primarily referring to persons and locations, is quite detailed. The trek across Nebraska follows route 30, giving mileage based on this highway as of the 1930s. — *MB*

DA111   Franzwa, Gregory M. - **Maps of the Oregon Trail**. - 3rd ed. - St. Louis, MO: Patrice Pr., 1990. - 292 p.; maps; 28 cm.

  Class Numbers:
    Library of Congress G1422.O7
  ISBN 0935284826 (spiral)   0935284834 (pbk.)
  LCCN 90-39516
  Notes:
    1st ed.: 1982
    Index
    Scale: 1: 126,720

• Contains 130 contemporary maps with the route of the Oregon Trail superimposed. Each map is on the recto page with textual explanation on the verso. Some text pages also contain photos or other supplementary information. — *MB*

PLATTE RIVER ROAD

DA112   Mattes, Merrill J. - **Platte River Road Narratives: A Descriptive Bibliography of Travel over the Great Central Overland Route to Oregon, California, Utah, Colorado, Montana, and other Western States and Territories, 1812-1866** / foreword by James A Michener. - Urbana, IL: Univ. of Illinois Pr., c1988. - 632 p.; map.

  Class Numbers:
    Library of Congress F591   Z1251.W5
  ISBN 0252013425
  Notes:
    Index

• A large bibliography (2,084 entries), citing diaries, logs, journals, letters, and recollections, some published, some in manuscript, that record first-hand accounts of travel over the various trails that followed the Platte River through Nebraska into Wyoming and Colorado. Numbered entries, arranged alphabetically by writers' names, provide a bibliographic description that includes highly specific indication of where the item may be located, including the library holding the copy examined, and a five-star rating system ("of limited value" to "outstanding"). Every entry supplies a description of the traveler's itinerary (point of origin, route, destination) and many give an estimate of the usefulness of the source, including contributions it made to an understanding of the Platte River country, its Indian population, landmarks, condition of the trail, and the like. An index in tabular form gives travelers' names, year and sex of the traveler, narrative form and meaning and star rating, places of departure and arrival, Missouri River crossing point, and entry number. Mattes's preface notes that some depositories refused to lend, copy, or even provide information about items in their collections, concluding they will have "no ground for complaint when they discover that their withheld holdings are missing from this work" (p. xiii). A splendid compilation, as thorough as one might wish, of first importance to students of the Prairies-Plains region. —RB

PONY EXPRESS TRAIL

DA113 Godfrey, Anthony. - **Historic Resource Study: Pony Express National Historic Trail**. - [Washington, DC]: U.S. Dept. of the Interior, National Park Service, 1994. - 285 p.; ill., folded map.

Class Numbers:
Library of Congress HE6375.P65
OCLC 31223828
Notes:
Includes bibliographical references

• Intends to give for the National Park Service and for the public information that can be used to plan activities related to the trail and the Pony Express (actually called the Central Overland California & Pike's Peak Express Company). Of the book's nine chapters, the first three provide historical context and discuss the company, its owners, and its operations. The next five give details about each of the 184 stations along the route from St. Joseph, MO, to San Francisco. The last chapter discusses the impact of the Pony Express on subsequent events in American history. At the front is a large folded map of the entire route. Following the text is a bibliographic essay (incorrectly called an annotated bibliography), a dozen illustrations, and a select bibliography of resources, organized by type. Should prove useful to historical researchers and general readers interested in the trails of the Old West. — MB

SANTA FE TRAIL

DA114 Rittenhouse, Jack DeVere, 1912-. - **The Santa Fe Trail: A Historical Bibliography**. - Albuquerque, NM: Univ. of New Mexico Pr., [1971]. - 271 p.

Class Numbers:
Library of Congress Z1251.S8
ISBN 0826302068
LCCN 72-153936

• Rittenhouse lists 718 published items (books, articles, pamphlets, government publications, reproductions in microform, including 37 in an Addendum), providing annotations for many. Entries are alphabetical by author (anonymous titles are entered under a conventional title, e.g., "[Bent's Fort]," "[Texan-Santa Fe Expedition]"); Rittenhouse provides full bibliographic details. He omits general local and state histories, popular magazine articles, and fiction and poetry except for 11 entries he includes to steer researchers away from works "whose titles may falsely suggest serious history" (p. 28). The book begins with a summary of the history of the Trail and ends with a table of congressional publications and an index of titles, names, and place-names that excludes entries in the bibliography itself. Thorough and useful. — RB

DA115 Simmons, Marc. - **Following the Santa Fe Trail: A Guide for Modern Travelers**. - 2nd ed. - Santa Fe, NM: Ancient City Pr., c1986. - 214 p.

ISBN 0941270386 (pbk.) 0941270394
LCCN 86-71417
Notes:
Bibliography: p. 2-7

• A guide to the routes followed by the Santa Fe Trail from the vicinity of Arrow Rock, MO, on the Missouri River, through Kansas, Colorado, Oklahoma, and New Mexico to Santa Fe. Numerous maps show the route in great detail, and the text comments on monuments, historic markers, forts, geographic features, and tracks still visible of the Trail itself. Intended for modern travelers, the guide shows highways that parallel the Trail. Numerous detailed maps; bibliographies. — RB

DB : History
STATES ; PROVINCES ; TERRITORIES

Scope. Includes reference titles having to do with and confined to individual states, the territories that preceded their admission as states, and provinces. Works about specific topics within a state (e.g., architecture in Colorado) will be found with the topic.

UNITED STATES

DB1 Chronologies and Documentary Handbooks of the States. - Dobbs Ferry, NY : Oceana Publ., 1970s- .

Colorado / ed. by Mary L. Frech. - 1973. - 105 p. - (Handbooks of the States, 6).

> Class Numbers:
> Library of Congress F776
> ISBN 0379161311
> OCLC 572634
> LCCN 73-532

Kansas / Robert I. Vexler, ed. - 1978. - 145 p. - (Handbooks of the States, 16).

> Class Numbers:
> Library of Congress F681
> ISBN 0379161419
> OCLC 3844412
> LCCN 78-6554

Montana / Robert I. Vexler, ed. - 1978. - 150 p. - (Handbooks of the States, 26).

> Class Numbers:
> Library of Congress F731.5
> ISBN 0379161516
> OCLC 4056080
> LCCN 78-16163

Nebraska / Robert I. Vexler, ed. - 1978. - 148 p. - (Handbooks of the States, 27).

> Class Numbers:
> Library of Congress F666.5
> ISBN 0379161524
> OCLC 4036988
> LCCN 78-16164

New Mexico / Robert I. Vexler, ed. - 1978. - 148 p. - (Handbooks of the States, 31).

> Class Numbers:
> Library of Congress F796.5
> ISBN 0379161567
> OCLC 4469580
> LCCN 78-64403

North Dakota / Robert I. Vexler, ed. - 1978. - 148 p. - (Handbooks of the States, 34).

> Class Numbers:
> Library of Congress F636.5
> ISBN 0379161591
> LCCN 78-64411

Oklahoma / Robert I. Vexler, ed. - 1978, c1979. - 146 p. - (Handbooks of the States, 36).

> Class Numbers:
> Library of Congress F694.5
> ISBN 0379161613
> LCCN 78-26885

South Dakota / Robert I. Vexler, ed. - 1979. - 148 p. - (Handbooks of the States, 41).

> Class Numbers:
> Library of Congress F651.5
> ISBN 0379161664
> OCLC 4515968
> LCCN 78-26887

Texas / Robert I. Vexler, ed. - 1979. - 152 p. - (Handbooks of the States, 43).

> Class Numbers:
> Library of Congress F386.5
> ISBN 0379161680
> LCCN 78-26888

Wyoming / Robert I. Vexler, ed. - 1978. - 150 p. - (Handbooks of the States, 49).

> Class Numbers:
> Library of Congress F761.5
> ISBN 0379161893
> OCLC 4493941
> LCCN 78-26251

Colorado

Bibliographies

DB2   Wilcox, Virginia Lee. - **Colorado : A Selected Bibliography of its Literature, 1858-1952.** - Denver, CO : Sage Books, 1954. - 151 p.

> Class Numbers:
> Library of Congress Z1263

OCLC 1441284
LCCN 54-35636

• A bibliography of just over 1,000 publications relating to the exploration, history, and development of Colorado, 1858-1952. Wilcox (Colorado School of Mines) omits periodical and newspaper articles, manuscripts, broadsides, theses, works consisting of illustrations, works devoted only in part to Colorado, promotional publications, legal works, government publications, and transactions and reports of associations. She arranges the bibliography by author, providing an index of topics. Now desperately out of date, but useful for the period covered. — *RB*

DB3   Wynar, Bohdan S., ed. - **Colorado Bibliography** / Bohdan S. Wynar, ed. ; Roberta J. Depp, assistant ed. - Littleton, CO : publ. by Libraries Unlimited for the National Society of Colonial Dames of America in the State of Colorado, 1980. - 565 p.

　Class Numbers:
　　Library of Congress F776　　　　　Z1263
　ISBN 0872872114
　OCLC 6196638
　LCCN 80-13752
　Notes :
　　Index

• The editor judges these 9,100 books, pamphlets, theses, and dissertations about Colorado history and culture to have permanent scholarly value. Government publications, unpublished manuscripts, and promotional literature are included selectively while belles lettres, serials, and regional works without a major focus on Colorado are excluded. Entries are classified under 18 broad subject categories, such as geography, Indians, mining, economic conditions, flora and fauna, religion, and local history. Each category has a section for general works and other subdivisions specific to the subject. Entries give basic bibliographic information. The chapter on Indians, for example, is organized by tribes, subdivided by general works, social organization, and white relations. The titles include ethnographies, archaeological surveys, museum catalogs, and testimony before the Indian Claims Commission. The local history section is particularly useful, listing elusive memoirs and county histories. Subject, title, and author indexes. — *JD*

Manuscripts ; Archives

DB4   University of Colorado Libraries. Western Historical Collections. - **A Guide to Manuscript Collections** / comp. by Ellen Arguimbau [et al.] ; ed. by

Cassandra M. Volpe, John A. Brennan. - [Boulder, CO] : Western Historical Collections, Univ. of Colorado at Boulder, 1989. - 1 v. (various pagings).

　Class Numbers:　　　Library of Congress Z1263
　OCLC 34578653

• Describing the Western Historical Collections at the University of Colorado, this guide is now nearly 20 years old. It lists alphabetically items held by the collection, giving their quantitative content—e.g., "Colorado in World War I - 47 boxes," "Hotel Registers - one reel microfilm." Items are numbered ; the subject index points to item numbers rather than page numbers. — *MB*

Guidebooks

DB5   Huber, Thomas Patrick. - **Colorado Byways : A Guide through Scenic and Historic Landscapes**. - Niwot, CO : Univ. Pr. of Colorado, 1997. - 373 p. ; ill., maps.

　Class Numbers:
　　Library of Congress F774.3
　ISBN 0870814419　　　　　0870814494 (pbk.)
　　0585028613 (electronic bk.)
　LCCN 96-45882
　Notes:
　　Electronic book:
　　　http://www.netLibrary.com/urlapi.asp?
　　　　action=summary&v=1&bookid=325
　　Includes bibliographical references (p. 355-358) ;
　　　index

• Huber (geography and environmental studies, Univ. of Colorado-Colorado Springs) describes Colorado's scenic landscapes, geographic characteristics, flora, fauna, and vegetation. The work divides Colorado into six regional climax or life zones: Southwest (Alpine Loop, Trail of the Ancients, San Juan Skyway, Unaweep, West Elk Loop); North Central (Colorado River Headwaters, Flat Tops Trail, Grand Mesa); South Central (Los Caminos Antiguos, Top of the Rockies, Silver Thread, Gold Belt Tour, Frontier Pathways); Northeast (Pawnee Pioneer Trails, South Platte River Trail); and Southeast (Highway of Legends, Santa Fe Trail). South Central, Northeast, and Southeast will hold interest for Prairies-Plains readers. Fifty illustrations, 22 maps. — *GK*

Dakota Territory

DB6   Allen, Albert Henry, 1875-1953. - **Dakota Imprints**, 1858-1889. - New York : Bowker, 1947. - xxi, 221 p.

Site List 13
State and Province Historical Societies

State and provincial historical societies maintain sites that provide local history, online exhibits, collection information, research services, research links, and links to county and local societies and other local history organizations.

United States
Colorado Historical Society
    http://www.coloradohistory.org
Kansas State Historical Society
    http://www.kshs.org
Montana Historical Society
    http://www.his.state.mt.us
Nebraska State Historical Society
    http://www.nebraskahistory.org
Historical Society of New Mexico

    http://www.hsnm.org
State Historical Society of North Dakota
    http://www.state.nd.us/hist/index.html
Oklahoma Historical Society
    http://www.ok-history.mus.ok.us
South Dakota State Historical Society
    http://www.sdhistory.org
Texas State Historical Association TSHA Online
    http://www.tsha.utexas.edu
Wyoming State Historical Society
    http://wyshs.org

Canada
Historical Society of Alberta
    http://www.albertahistory.org
Manitoba Historical Society
    http://www.mhs.mb.ca
La Société historique de la Saskatchewan
    http://www.societehisto.com

Class Numbers:
    Library of Congress Z1321
OCLC 14663986
LCCN 47-31030
Notes:
    At head of title: Bibliographical Society of
    America

• With no previous inventory to draw on, Allen's work is based primarily on the incomplete files of the Federal Writers' Project's American Imprints Inventory and the files of Douglas McMurtrie, bibliographer and historian of type and printing. The bibliography lists 774 books, pamphlets, and broadsides published in Dakota Territory through 1889 (when it was divided into present-day North and South Dakota), many published by newspapers. Most titles were fugitive; single copies were found for 359. No titles printed by the many German and Norwegian newspapers were found and only one German title is included. Titles include reports of agricultural and religious societies, city directories, college catalogs, compilations of statistics, an Episcopal catechism translated into the Dakota language, protests against the forced removal of the Santee tribe, and a homesteading advertisement announcing, "Uncle Sam is rich enough to give us all a farm!" The majority are official documents (e.g., laws, court decisions, proclamations). Entries are arranged in chronological order and include summary of contents, physical description, and often, historical context. Locations for copies are given, but may no longer be valid. Appendixes include statistical summaries of printing by year and location, and indexes of authors and subjects and of printing locations, presses, and printers. — *JD*

DB7 Van Balen, John, comp. - **Dakota Place Names : Geographical Names on 18th & 19th Century Maps.** - Vermillion, SD : I.D. Weeks Library, Univ. of South Dakota, 1998. - 272 p. ; maps.

Class Numbers:
    Library of Congress F655
LCCN 98-211656
Notes:
    Cartobibliography: p. 3-17
    Includes bibliographical references (p. 18)

• Van Balen (library science, Univ. of South Dakota) compiles a finding aid to 4,700 places in the northern Great Plains, especially Dakota Territory, that are recorded in 49 maps of historical importance covering the period 1793-1889. The compiler's purpose is to index rare maps of the region for researchers seeking information about towns that no longer exist, place-names, or geographic locations. The index lists map names alphabetically. The work includes photographic reproductions of 44 complete or partial maps. — *GK*

Kansas

Bibliographies

DB8 Dary, David. - **Kanzana, 1854-1900 : A Selected Bibliography of Books, Pamphlets, and Ephemera of Kansas.** - Lawrence, KS : Allen Books ; Bryan, TX : Frontier America Corp. ; Austin, TX : Jenkins & Reese, 1986. - 294 p. ; ill. - (Contributions to bibliography, 8).

Class Numbers:
    Library of Congress F681.Z99
ISBN 0935868259
OCLC 15334507
LCCN 87-673313
Notes:
    Index

• The 275 titles Dary lists, published between the formation of Kansas Territory and the end of the 19th century, were selected for their historical value, interest to book collectors and dealers, and reflection of the "flavor" of Kansas. They include common and rare works on the Gold Rush, Civil War, homesteading, Indians, railroads, cattle trade, travel, land promotions, and local histories. Organized chronologically, the entries begin with Edward Everett Hale's *Kanzas and Nebraska*, the first book about Kansas, and end with Noble Lovely Prentis' well-used textbook, *A History of Kansas*. Of genuine scholarly interest, Dary's book is also a coffee-table bibliography that presents one well-designed entry per page along with an image of the work. Entries have complete physical descriptions, colorful annotations that often include anecdotes about the author and publishing history, references to the work in previous bibliographies, and locations of the copies inspected. Indexed by authors, publishers, printers, titles, and names of cities, towns, counties, and states mentioned in the entries. — *JD*

DB9   Socolofsky, Homer Edward, 1922- . - **Kansas History : An Annotated Bibliography** / compiled by Homer E. Socolofsky and Virgil W. Dean. - New York : Greenwood Pr., 1992. - 587 p.

Class Numbers:
    Library of Congress Z1285 S59X 1992
ISBN 0313282382
LCCN 91-46959
Notes:
    Indexes

• A very full bibliography of books and articles (and post-1970 dissertations) having to do with Kansas history. The editors (Socolofsky taught history and was university historian at Kansas State Univ., and Dean edited *Kansas History*) arrange 4,564 entries in the most useful way possible, by a classification scheme developed from the materials themselves. Its 17 sections begin with chronological divisions (prehistory, early exploration, territorial period, statehood, Kansas since 1898), followed by topical sections (agriculture, transportation, social history, historiography). Citations are carefully complete, but do not attempt to repeat citations found in previous bibliographies, which are listed in section 14, "General Histories and Reference Guides." Many entries have brief annotations. Articles are drawn from nearly 300 periodicals (listed in an appendix), and the editors include all articles

on Kansas history that appeared in three journals published by the Kansas State Historical Society. Separate indexes cover authors and subjects. No bibliography is sufficiently up to date to suit specialists, but this will be a rich source for students of the history of Kansas and of the Prairies-Plains region. — *RB*

Manuscripts ; Archives

DB10   **A Guide to Special Collections in Kansas** / ed. and comp. by Gene DeGruson [et al.] ; sponsored by the Kansas Library Network Board. - Topeka, KS : Kansas Library Network Board, 1986. - 403 p.

Class Numbers:
    Library of Congress Z732.K2
OCLC 18756683
LCCN 87-621697
Notes:
    Indexes

• Lists special collections in Kansas public libraries, museums, historical and genealogical societies, academic libraries, and a few other organizations. In two sections, academic libraries and public libraries, and other organizations. For every organization, identifiable collections are listed separately and the content of each is described with some care. The largest and most varied collections are held by the University of Kansas. Extent of collections is given in number of items (for oral history, number of tapes) or shelf measurements (for archives, linear feet). All subjects are covered, but many collections relate to Kansas or the Plains. Indexes by subject and type of material. Reproduced from typescript. — *RB*

Encyclopedias

DB11   **Kansas : A Cyclopedia of State History, Embracing Events, Institutions, Industries, Counties, Cities, Towns, Prominent Persons, etc. : With a Supplementary Volume Devoted to Selected Personal History and Reminiscence**. - Chicago, IL : Standard Publ. Co., 1912. – 3v. in 4 ; front., ill., ports.

Class Numbers:
    Library of Congress F679
OCLC 2996736
LCCN 12-15729
Notes:
    Vols. 1-2 ed. by Frank W. Blackmar

• An alphabetical compendium of 19th-century views about the state's natural history, history, economics, and politics. Includes long entries on topics of continuing interest to historians, such as the Kansas-Nebraska Act, as well as shorter entries for biographies of prominent figures, town histories, organization and business histories, flora and fauna, gubernatorial administrations, natural features, industries, Civil War and Indian conflicts, and events. While the encyclopedia focuses on European exploration, settlement, and development of the state, a lengthy piece on Indians, based on Smithsonian Bureau of Ethnology publications and government records, is included. Throughout, the influence and activism of women and women's groups is apparent. — *JD*

DB12   The Kansas Collection [Internet Site] / managed by Susan Stafford and Dick Taylor ; originated by Lynn H. Nelson. - [Lawrence, KS] : Lynn H. Nelson, 2000?-   . - http://www.kancoll.org/

> OCLC 44352634
> Access Date: May 2006
> Fees: None

• A somewhat unfocused collection of materials relating to the early years of Kansas (territory and state) that includes full text of books published from 1844 (Gregg's *Commerce of the Prairies*) through the 21st century, articles, "Research" (bibliographies), letters, diaries, reminiscences, and a random collection called "Reference Shelf" ("Cross of Gold" speech, Kansas poems by Whittier, Camp Funston 1918, and the like). Files are searchable. Some materials will interest Plains students and may be elsewhere unavailable, but the site needs to be much larger before its direction becomes clear. — *RB*

Collective Biographies

DB13   John Brown to Bob Dole : Movers and Shakers in Kansas History / ed. by Virgil W. Dean. - Lawrence, KS : Univ. Pr. of Kansas, 2006. - 408 p. ; ill.

> Class Numbers:
>   Library of Congress F680
> ISBN 070061429X
> OCLC 61278474
> LCCN 2005-22808
> Notes:
>   Includes bibliographical references (p. [343]-382) ; index
>   Table of contents:
>   http://www.loc.gov/catdir/toc/ ecip0517/
>   2005022808.html

• Twenty-seven Kansans who "made a difference," good or bad, in its history, 1854-2004, are examined in lengthy biographical essays. They include Clarina Irene Howard Nichols, a women's rights activist ; William Allen White, the best-known journalist in the Plains ; Gerald B. Winrod, the "Jayhawk Hitler" indicted for conspiring to cause insubordination in World War II ; and Wes Jackson, advocate of sustainable agriculture. Essays, written by scholars, are based on extensive research in primary and secondary sources. Portraits ; subject index. — *JD*

DB14   Smith, Patricia Douglass. - Kansas Biographical Index : County Histories / comp. by Patricia Douglass Smith. - Garden City, KS : P.D. Smith & S.C. Smith, 2001.

> Class Numbers:
>   Library of Congress F680   Z1285
> OCLC 48180293
> LCCN 2003-271204
> Notes:
>   "More than 69,000 citations from 183 volumes of
>   Kansas county histories."
>   Contents: v. 1, Surnames A-K ; v. 2, Surnames L-Z
>   Includes bibliographical references (p. ix-xxii)

DB14a   …State-Wide and Regional Histories : Citing More Than 35,500 Biographies from Sixty-Eight Volumes of Kansas Biographical Sources. - Garden City, KS : P.D. Smith & S.C. Smith, 1994. - 350 p.

> Class Numbers:
>   Library of Congress F680   F1285
> OCLC 30905818
> LCCN 94-66834

DB14b   …Town, Community & Organization Histories / comp. by Patricia Douglass Smith and Stanley Clifford Smith. - Garden City, KS : P.D. Smith & S.C. Smith, 2001. - xx, 308 p.

> Class Numbers:
>   Library of Congress F680   Z1285
> OCLC 49361345
> LCCN 2002-512608
> Notes:
>   Contains "more than 35,500 citations from 258
>   volumes of Kansas town, community and
>   organization histories."
>   Sources indexed : p. ix-xx

• All three titles consist of a numbered bibliography of books, booklets, and pamphlets, and an index of names. For *County Histories*, many titles indexed are centennial histories published from the 1960s to the 1980s, although some earlier works are included ; for *State-Wide and Regional Histories*, volumes indexed were published 1876-1976, and for *Town, Community & Organization Histories*, 1889-1996. To be indexed in *County Histories*, individuals had to be the subject of at least five biographical sketches ; for the other two, at least one vital statistic (birth, death, marriage, divorce) and two references to life activities were required. Index entries consist of name, county of residence, bibliography number, and page number in volumes where the name appears. – *MS*

Atlases

DB15 Baughman, Robert Williamson, 1907- . - **Kansas in Maps**. - Topeka, KS : Kansas State Historical Society, 1961. - 104 p. ; 37 cm.

> Class Numbers:
> > Library of Congress G1455
> > LCCN map 61-63

• An assortment of maps from a variety of sources, some in color, some black-and-white, that cover all or part of the state. There is no table of contents or index, but the arrangement is generally chronological, beginning with a map showing the distribution of Native American nations prior to the arrival of European-Americans. Early explorer maps with textual commentary come next, followed by maps of trails to the West. Thematic maps include steamboating, the Civil War, and Indian fighting. Next are railroad and land developer maps, and finally modern road and air travel maps. The text explains the selection of specific maps. More entertaining than useful, although readers may find a few nuggets of historical interest. — *MB*

DB16 Socolofsky, Homer Edward, 1922- . - **Historical Atlas of Kansas** / by Homer E. Socolofsky and Huber Self. - 2nd ed. - Norman, OK : Univ. of Oklahoma Pr., 1988. - 74 p. ; 31 cm.

> Class Numbers:
> > Library of Congress G1456 S1
> > OCLC 314217
> Notes:
> > Bibliography: p. ix-xvii

• An atlas that offers 74 specialized historical maps of Kansas or areas that include the state. Each map occupies a full page, with descriptive information on the facing page. Some maps feature natural characteristics such as flora and fauna, water resources, and landforms, but most deal with the impact of humans on the state—trails and roads, political subdivisions, battle sites, and the like. Nine regional maps show cities and towns in existence as of 1984. Several references for individual maps and an extensive place-name index follow the maps. — *MB*

Place-Names

DB17 McCoy, Sondra Van Meter. - **1001 Kansas Place Names** / [by] Sondra Van Meter McCoy and Jan

Hults ; ill. by John Gruber. - Lawrence, KS : Univ. Pr. of Kansas, c1989. - 223 p.

> Class Numbers:
> > Library of Congress F679
> > ISBN 0700603921   070060393X (pbk.)
> > LCCN 89-8885

• The compilers chose the title for effect ; it actually lists 1,068 place-names. From nearly 12,000 possible place-names, the compilers selected all 105 counties, the county seats, and all 629 incorporated places recorded in the 1980 census. They selected other names for their historical or geographic significance (e.g., Tuttle Creek Reservoir, Arkansas River). Entries include place-name, pronunciation (if necessary), county (or counties) in which the place is found, source of the name, opening and closing dates of the post office, and population. Supplementary information includes a Kansas county map and an alphabetical index of the 105 counties that lists all the place-names related to each county. Sketches scattered through the volume are decorative rather than functional. — *MB*

Chronologies

DB18 Wilder, Daniel Webster, 1832-1911. - **The Annals of Kansas**. - New York : Arno Pr., 1975. - 1196 p. - (Mid-American frontier).

> Class Numbers:
> > Library of Congress F681
> > ISBN 0405068956   9780405068959
> > OCLC 1218323
> > LCCN 75-130
> Notes:
> > Index
> > Reprint of the new ed., Topeka, KS : T.D. Thacher

• A chronology of Kansas, organized by three major periods covering early discoveries (1542-1854), territorial history (1854-1861), and statehood (1861-1885). Drawing on a variety of official, secondary and popular sources, Wilder provides a pastiche of both major and many minor events in the evolution of Kansas. He summarizes important affairs and supplies numerous election results, official appointments, constitutional documents, statistical data, and lists of Civil War military personnel. Much of the material involves events of purely local interest such as the establishment of daily mail routes between particular settlements or grasshopper invasions in a specific county. These seemingly insignificant details, however, accumulate to provide a minute account of the social, agricultural, and political concerns of Kansans. The segment covering 1854-1861 is available in *Territorial Kansas Online* (**DB20**). *The Annals of Kansas, 1886-1925*, compiled by Jennie Owen and Kirke Mechem (Topeka, KS : Kansas State Historical Society, 1954-56 ; v.1 : 1886-1910, v. 2 : 1911-1925) represents a continuation of Wilder's work. — *LMcD*

Kansas Territory

DB19   Barry, Louise. - **The Beginning of the West : Annals of the Kansas Gateway to the American West, 1540-1854**. - Topeka, KS : Kansas State Historical Society, [1972]. - 1296 p. ; ill.

>   Class Numbers:
>   Library of Congress F685 .B3
>   LCCN 78-172252
>   Notes:
>   Includes bibliographical references

• An exceedingly elaborate chronology of early Kansas history, from 1540 when Coronado's expedition to find the cities of Cibola left Compostela in Mexico, through 1854 when territorial government was established in Kansas. Many entries reprint segments of the sources used in the preparation of entries, which themselves often go into great detail, citing names of participants, sizes of military detachments, raids by Indians, itineraries of steamboats, activities of missionaries, and the like. Six sections of plates provide reproductions of maps, Catlin portraits of Indians, photographs of buildings, views of towns, etc. Full index of names and places. Many entries append bibliographies whose citations are sometimes alarmingly offhand, but there is no general bibliography. Barry was a staff member at the Kansas State Historical Society. Extremely useful for students of Prairies-Plains or Kansas history. — *RB*

DB20   **Territorial Kansas Online, 1854-1861** : A **Virtual Repository for Territorial Kansas History [Internet Site]**. - Lawrence, KS : Univ. of Kansas Libraries, 2004-   . - http://www.territorialkansasonline.org/cgiwrap/imlskto/index.php

>   Access Date: Oct. 2004
>   Fees: None

• A site covering the territorial period in Kansas history, from the Kansas-Nebraska Act (1854) through admission as a state (1861). The site offers a section for "Topics" (e.g., "Border Warfare," "National Debate about Kansas"), one for "Additional Resources" (timeline, bibliography, historic sites), tabs for "Territorial A-Z," an alphabetical list of all the topics and persons, and a map. The probable audience is secondary students, since lesson plans are provided, but such heavy reliance is placed on primary sources (contemporary accounts, letters, diaries) that the site has potential for any reader interested in this period of Kansas history. Useful, and despite its concentration on "Bleeding Kansas," light-hearted. — *RB*

Montana

Collective Biographies

DB21   Progressive Men of the State of Montana. - Chicago, IL : A.W. Bowen & Co., [1900-1905?]. - 2 v. (1886 p.) ; front., ports. - (Western Americana, 22020).

>   Class Numbers:
>   Library of Congress F730
>   OCLC 8324755   6840346 (microfiche)
>   LCCN a 15-272811
>   Notes:
>   Available in Microfiche reproduction : Ann Arbor, MI : Xerox Univ. Microfilms, 1975. 26 micro fiches, 11 x 15 cm.
>   Electronic book:
>   http://www.lib.umt.edu/gsdl/cgi-bin/

• Biographical sketches, some with photographs, of more than 2,500 individuals of importance in the history of Montana from the 1850s to 1900. The digital version prepared by the Univ. of Montana Libraries provides searching and browsing by name, county, city, occupation, and illustrations. — *LMcD*

Guidebooks
See Alt, **Roadside Geology of Montana, EA6**

Nebraska

Bibliographies

DB22   Adrian, Frederick W. - **Theses and Dissertations Dealing with Nebraska and Nebraskans**. - Lincoln, NE : Univ. of Nebraska, 1975. - 302 p. - (University of Nebraska studies - New series, 49 ; ISSN 0077-6386).

>   Class Numbers:
>   Library of Congress F666   Z1307
>   OCLC 1646547
>   LCCN 75-10049
>   Notes:
>   Indexes

• Adrian's list is far from comprehensive—*Dissertation Abstracts International* is much better for identifying doctoral dissertations about Nebraska—but is useful in finding master's theses. Organized alphabetically into 34 general topics, many subdivided. Categories include agriculture, biography, education, government, history, literature, politics, and transportation. Cites theses and dissertations about Nebraska, regardless of where accepted. Adrian canvassed libraries across the U.S. and Canada ; he includes theses accepted by 114 institutions. Entries supply author, title, degree awarded, institution, date, page length, and whether the item contains charts, maps, or illustrations. Many entries have annotations, although there are none for titles in science or education. Extensive author and subject indexes. — *MB, JD*

DB23   Gable, J. Haris, 1902-   . - **The Learned and Scientific Publications of the University of Nebraska** (1871-1926). - Lincoln, NE : Univ. of Nebraska, 1926. - 130 p. - (Bibliographical contributions from the University of Nebraska Library, 6).

> Class Numbers:
>> Library of Congress Z1009   N36   Z5055.U5N3
>> OCLC 4909942
>> LCCN 26-27257
>> Notes:
>>> Includes publications of the Geological Survey
>>> and Legislative Reference Bureau

• Cites nonadministrative monographs, series, and journals published by the University and its agricultural experiment stations, colleges, divisions, and departments. For journals, the bibliography cites individual articles. Arranged by author and series, the entries often resonate with modern audiences : Louise Pound on the literary canon, Roscoe Pound on a new school of jurists, Erwin Barbour on Nebraska bone beds, native trees, brains of criminals, beef production, a plague of Russian thistle, Shakespearean documents discovered in 1905, extermination of prairie dogs. Doctoral dissertations and occasional addresses are listed. Entries give bibliographic description and notes but no annotations. Thorough index by author, subject, series title, and organization. — *JD*

DB24   Tate, Michael L., comp. - **Nebraska History : An Annotated Bibliography**. - Westport, CT : Greenwood Pr., 1995. - xxiii, 549 p. - (Bibliographies of the States of the United States, 6).

> Class Numbers:
>> Library of Congress F666   Z1307
>> ISBN 0313282498
>> OCLC 32665055
>> LCCN 95-492

• The table of contents shows the scope of Tate's Bibliography: Nebraska's environmental diversity ; the interactions of native peoples, settlers, and developers ; dependence on agriculture and livestock ; the state's unique governmental structure ; and ongoing issues of water, land use, transportation, and communication. A chronology sets the framework for physical and human forces that the works in the bibliography discuss in greater detail—the characterization of Nebraska (and the Plains in general) as the "Great American Desert" in 1820 ; the Sioux Ghost

Dance movement of 1888-1890 ; the Kincaid Act that allowed ranches to develop in the High Plains ; the devastating blizzards of 1888 and 1949 ; the South Omaha riots of 1909 ; the abandonment of family farms beginning in the 1950s ; American Indian Movement activism in the 1970s ; and growth of minorities in the 1990s. Annotations are brief, clear, and pointed. Includes a list of local histories and a thorough subject index. — *JD*

DB25   White, John Browning. - **Nebraska History : An Annotated Bibliography: An Essay and Bibliography**. - Lincoln, NE : Nebraska State Historical Society, 1956. - 300 p. ; ports. - (Nebraska State Historical Society. Publications, v. 23).

> Class Numbers:
>> Library of Congress F661
>> LCCN 56-63172

• White's bibliography covers published materials about the region that is now the state of Nebraska during the time it was part of Nebraska Territory, 1854-67. He recounts the meagerness of early bibliographies, the lack of periodical indexes, libraries' failure to collect and preserve historical materials, and the preponderance of reminiscences and government-sponsored reports, offering his own landmark guide to primary and secondary materials. Modern online indexes of 19th-century periodicals now provide an excellent complement. The wide-ranging topics he covers include folklore, military outposts, gold rushes, freighting, Sioux Indians, currency, bison, and the Ghost Dance. He ignores some major events (e.g., the Kansas-Nebraska Act) that are part of the "larger stream" of history. Organized by format (e.g., legislative journals, government reports, laws, published diaries and letters, reminiscences, and secondary sources), his bibliography includes a thorough index. He lists territorial newspapers and maps. The useful annotations summarize each work's significance and sometimes quote specific passages. — *JD*

Government Publications

DB26   **Nebraska State Government Publications**. - [v. 20] (1992)-   . – Lincoln, NE : Nebraska Library Commission, 1993-   . Annual.

> Class Numbers:
>> Library of Congress Z1223.N4
>> Government Document Nebraska L4200 D001
>> OCLC 29338165
>> LCCN 96-659046
>> Notes:
>>> Title varies : v. 1 (1973)-v. 19 (1991), *Nebraska State*
>>> *Publications Checklist*

• Charged with providing public access to state documents, the Nebraska Publications Clearinghouse of the Nebraska Library Commission receives copies of all printed documents published by state agencies ; many are also available on microfiche at Nebraska depository libraries. For preservation and access, the Clearinghouse prints copies of some electronic publications. This bibliography lists new monograph and serial titles and all annual reports received by the Clearinghouse the previous year, compiled from its bimonthly newsletter on new documents, *What's Up, Doc?*, which includes selected federal documents. Documents are listed both alphabetically by agency and by broad subject. Documents received 1995 to the present are also listed on the NLC Internet site (http://www.nl.state.ne.us /docs/stategovpubs. html) and in 1997, the Clearinghouse began a supplementary service, *State Government Publications Online* (http:// www.nlc.state.ne.us/ docs/pilot/pilot.html) to provide ready access to all publications posted on agency Internet sites. In 2005, the Clearinghouse began to provide stable access to key documents by downloading them to its own servers. — *JD*

Encyclopedias

DB27 Nebraska.gov : **Official Web Site for the State of Nebraska [Internet Site]**. - Lincoln, NE : Nebraska@Online, 1992- . - http://www.nebraska.gov/

> Access Date: Jan. 2005
> Notes:
>> Alternate URL : http://www.state.ne.us/
>> Some services (e.g., motor vehicle or corporation record searches) require payment of subscription fee, $50.00 per year
> Technical support : techstaff@nol.org
> Fees: Free

• The official Internet site for the State, *Nebraska.gov* acts as portal to state agency, board, and commission Internet pages and is intended as a one-stop information resource for Nebraska citizens, businesses, visitors, and employees. It replicates in part information found in the biennial *Nebraska Blue Book*, but is updated continually. Among its features are access to a state staff directory, online request forms for licenses and permits, recreational information, state laws, rules and regulations, state job postings, bid opportunities, current weather, and road detours. It links to county, community, and school Internet sites. A section, "My Nebraska," offers information about state symbols, a virtual tour of the art deco/neoclassical state capitol building, and "Nebraska FAQ" (maintained by the Nebraska Library Commission). The FAQ includes, e.g., sources for state plat maps, historical newspapers, public employee salaries, and nonprofit financial statements. — *JD*

Atlases
See also **Statewide Digital Data Bases, EB18**

DB28 Bleed, Ann Salomon, ed. - **An Atlas of the Sand Hills** / Ann S. Bleed and Charles A. Flowerday, eds. - 3rd, expanded ed. - Lincoln, NE : Conservation and Survey Div., Institute of Agriculture and Natural Resources, Univ. of Nebraska-Lincoln, 1998. - 260 p. ; ill. (some col.), maps (some col.) ; 28 cm. - (Resource atlas, 5b).

> Class Numbers:
>> Library of Congress F672.S17
> ISBN 156161002X
> OCLC 19495799
> LCCN 98-24716
> Notes:
>> Includes bibliographical references ; index

• Covers climate, geology, lakes and streams, plants, insects, fishes, birds, mammals, land use, etc. The table of contents lists illustrations and tables. Illustrated extensively with attractive color photos, charts, maps, and data tables. — *MB*

DB29 NDOR Map Library [Internet Site] / Nebraska Dept. of Roads. - [Lincoln, NE] : Nebraska Department of Roads, 2000. - http://www.nebraskatransportation.org/maps/

> Access Date: May 2005
> Fees: None

• *NDOR Map Library* is part of *Trans-Portal*, the Internet site of the Nebraska Department of Roads and an official Nebraska government site (http://www.dor.state.ne.us/). It offers free pdf files of Nebraska historical maps and maps of numerous other kinds : incorporated cities, city traffic control, counties, statewide county outlines, highways, construction and detours, road classification, scenic byways, highway traffic flow, traffic volume, highway control systems, speed limits, railroads, bicycle and hiking trails, Lewis and Clark historical markers. Many maps are in color. Some county maps are available as Microstation CADD files, requiring installation of Microstation software. Some maps can be ordered by phone or e-mail for a nominal fee ; state highway maps are free. — *JD*

DB30 A Prairie Mosaic : An Atlas of Central Nebraska's Land, Culture, and Nature / eds. Steven J. Rothenberger, Susan George-Bloomfield. - Kearney, NE : Univ. of Nebraska at Kearney, 2000. - 243 p. ; ill., maps ; 28 cm.

> Class Numbers:
>> Library of Congress GB575.N2
> ISBN 0739205129
> Notes:
>> Includes bibliographical references

• The sections of this work (e.g., natural sciences, history, art and culture, economics and society) each contain about a half dozen essays by specialists. Handsomely illustrated in both color and black-and-white. There is no index, so readers must rely on the table of contents. — *MB*

DB31   Western Cartographers, comps. - **"Big Red"**
Atlas of Nebraska. - South Sioux City, NE : Western Cartographers, 1984. - 1 atlas ([128] p.) ; ill., 105 maps, ports.

> Class Numbers:
>> Library of Congress G1450
>> OCLC 18386148
>> Notes:
>>> Scales vary

• Called "Big Red" after the Nebraska football team and containing a 14-page summary of Nebraska football history, this atlas aspires to be a football resource, but its actual focus is on county maps that show section boundaries and constitute numerical history lessons. The system for establishing and numbering square mile sections, an elegant tool for the survey of public lands, rose from the Land Ordinance of 1785 and today forms the basis for land parcel legal designations familiar to historians and other researchers. Combined with geological and other maps, the section maps are state history resources, illustrating, for example, the need for the Kincaid Act (1904) that increased homestead size from 160 to 640 acres in 13 western Nebraska counties. The maps also designate farm and other buildings, railroads, roads, bridges, conservation and recreation areas, drainage systems, airports, and public utility facilities. Concise county histories accompanying each map are reprinted from *Who's Who in Nebraska* (**DB37**). Maps are arranged alphabetically by county ; there is no index of place-names. — *JD*

Place-Names

DB32   Fitzpatrick, Lilian Linder. - **Nebraska Place-Names : Including Selections from** *Origin of the Place-Names of Nebraska*. - [Lincoln, NE] : Univ. of Nebraska Pr., 1960. - 227 p.

> Class Numbers:
>> Library of Congress F664
>> OCLC 1661718
>> LCCN 60-15471
>> Notes:
>>> Bibliography: p. 148-152
>>> Part one reprints in its entirety *Fitzpatrick's Nebraska Place-Names* published in 1925 as "University of Nebraska Studies in Language, Literature and Criticism," no. 6
>>> Part two draws from chapters VIII, IX, X, and XII of John Thomas Link's *The Origin of the Place-*

Names of Nebraska printed in 1933 by authority of the State of Nebraska

• Brings together two significant, complementary titles on Nebraska place-names. Part 1 is an alphabetical list by counties and their leading place-names with concise explanations of name origins. It includes a bibliography and index by town. Part 2 offers expository and anecdotal discussions of the names of cultural and natural features. Cultural features are subdivided into trails, ranches, overland stations, and camping places ; military posts and reservations ; Indian reservations and agencies ; national forest preserves, nurseries, bird reserves, and monuments ; and state parks and other recreational grounds. Natural features are subdivided into hydrographic features and relief features. Names of natural features are further organized according to their derivation, which may be a personal name, animal life, vegetation, cultural feature, or commemorative name. No index in part 2. — *JD*

DB33   **Origin of Nebraska Place Names** / comp. by the Federal Writers' Project of the Works Progress Administration for the State of Nebraska ; sponsored by the Nebraska State Historical Society. - Lincoln, NE : [Federal Writers' Project], 1938.

> OCLC 31557957
> Notes:
>> Reproduction: Microfilm. New Haven, CT : Yale Univ. Library, 1993. 1 reel ; 35 mm.

• Using in part information gathered by the Nebraska public schools, the Federal Writers' Project compiled the name origins of 700 Nebraska towns with populations of 25 or greater in the 1930 decennial Census—half to three-fourths of existing towns. Towns were frequently named for inhabitants (railroad workers were the most common), settlement periods, ranchers, Indian tribes, Illinois towns, German towns, natural features (Pine Camp), songs (Wuaneta), poems (Rokeby), quality of the land (Superior, Surprise), and puns (Whynot). Entries supply town name, county, population, altitude, railroad, and name origin. Also included are origins of county names (often nationally prominent men) and an index of type of eponym. — *JD*

DB34   Perkey, Elton, 1911-   . - **Perkey's Nebraska Place Names**. - Rev. ed. - Lincoln, NE : J and L Lee Co., 1995. - 222 p. ; ill. - (Publications of the Nebraska State Historical Society, v. 28).

> Class Numbers:
>> Library of Congress F664
>> ISBN 0934904197 (pbk.)
>> LCCN 95-68748
>> Notes:
>>> Includes bibliographical references

(p. 203-205); index
Originally publ.: 1982

• Perkey draws primarily on Nebraska State Historical Society archives and U.S. postal records in compiling this list of territorial and state place-names and post offices. It is organized alphabetically by county, then alphabetically by place-name. Compilation required ten years, since the work includes home-based, migratory post offices, locations that functioned as railroad stations and sidings, and ghost towns and proposed towns. Entries supply population from the 1990 Census, year of peak population, dates of operation of post offices, and notes on both the origins of towns and counties and of their names. Browsing the list provides a mini-lesson in Nebraska demographic history that sharply illustrates the diversity of the state's inhabitants and settlement patterns, the effects of railroads and rivers on the economy, and dwindling population in rural areas. Includes a bibliography of atlases, books, articles, and other resources and an index of place-names cited. The 1995 edition did not update designations of railroad stations. — *MB, JD*

Collective Biographies

DB35   Baldwin, Sara Mullin, ed. - **Nebraskana : Biographical Sketches of Nebraska Men and Women of Achievement Who Have Been awarded Life Membership in the Nebraskana Society** / ed. by Sara Mullin Baldwin and Robert Morton Baldwin. - Hebron, NE : Baldwin Co., 1932. - 1374 p. ; ill. (ports.).

Class Numbers:
    Library of Congress F665
    OCLC 6359365
    LCCN 32-20116

• *Nebraskana* has several thousand biographical sketches of people granted life membership in the Nebraskana Society for their contributions to the business, civic, and social life of the state. A few honorees were nationally prominent figures such as William Jennings Bryan and Bess Streeter Aldrich, but most were state and city leaders for whom this offers their only published biography. Several hundred entries are for women, who had long played powerful roles in state settlement, politics, and business. Women such as Anna Gray Clark, teacher, sales agent for the Union Pacific, county superintendent of schools, newspaper owner, and homesteader, were not uncommon. Together, the biographies describe the numerous activities that contributed to settlement of the state and the development of communities. Entries include family histories ; school, professional and civic activities ; church affiliations ; political persuasions ; marriages and children. Full-page photographic portraits accompany a fraction of the entries. A "Nebraska Album" at the end includes 477 additional photos of men and women of distinction and one photo of "perhaps the finest pipe organ located in a private home in the middlewest." The editors believe the work's "greatest value will come in future years." *Nebraskana* is available online as part of *NEGenWeb Project Resource Center Online Library,* http : //www.rootsweb. com/~neresour/ OLLibrary /index.html. — *JD*

DB36   Sheldon, Addison Erwin, 1861-1943. - **Nebraska : The Land and the People**. - Chicago, IL : Lewis Publ. Co., 1931. - 3 v. ; ill.

Class Numbers:
Library of Congress F666
LCCN 32-3007
Notes:
    Note follows title: Nebraska biography (gratu-
        itously published) selected and prepared by
        special staff of writers
Bibliography: v. 1, p. 91-92

• Volume 1 of this uneven and idiosyncratic history of Nebraska begins with the origin of the earth, then summarizes geologic history and geography, climate and weather records, Indians in Nebraska, overland trails, Nebraska Territory, the Constitutions of 1871 and 1875, and events that affected the state. Entries are illustrated with maps, photographs, and tables of data on, e.g., motor vehicles, banks, election results, fraternal organizations, insurance coverage. There is no bibliography of sources and information is often cited poorly or not at all. Volumes 2 and 3 consist of a collection of lengthy, uncritical biographies. Although criteria for inclusion are not stated, most biographies are about men in business, law, education, or politics. Entries cover personal, professional, and civic lives with some full-page portraits. The order of entries is random and sources are not cited. An index to all three volumes by name and topic is at the beginning of volume 1. Although much of the information has lasting value, the work is now of interest for its 1931 view of Nebraska history and prehistory. — *JD*

DB37   Who's Who in Nebraska / ed. 1940-   , by John Faris. - [v. 1] (1940)-   . Lincoln, NE : Nebraska Press Association, 1940-   . Annual.

Class Numbers:
    Library of Congress F665

• The only edition of an intended annual publication provides a perspective on American life and values in 1940 with a promotional history of the state and 11,000 autobiographical sketches of "men and women who have achieved distinction in the fields of economic, civic and cultural endeavor." Entries, arranged by county, are accompanied by colorful and useful county histories. Includes a key to the numerous abbreviations in the sketches and an index by name. Online access is available through *NEGenWeb Resource Center Online Library*, http://rootsweb.com. — *JD*

Handbooks

DB38   A Legislator's Guide to Nebraska State Agencies / prepared by the Nebraska Legislative Fiscal Office. - [v. 2?] (Dec. 1982)- . [Lincoln, NE] : Nebraska. Legislature. Legislative Fiscal Office, 1982- . Biennial.

>   Class Numbers:
>   Library of Congress JK6630
>   OCLC 9473413
>   LCCN 88-641630
>   Notes:
>   Prepared for the members of ... Nebraska legislature
>   Title varies: 1977-1978 called : *A Legislative Guide to Nebraska's State Agencies*

• Prepared for each two-year legislative session, the *Guide* is designed for legislators and interested citizens. An overview of state funds begins with definitions of fund types and historical tables of expenditures, revenues, fund balances, and state income and sales tax rates. Entries for each state agency include a brief history and description, a synopsis of services, a four-year statistical summary of operations, and a four-year budget summary. Entries are organized by state agency number and indexed by agency name, agency function, state program names, and keywords. Contact information is provided for the agency director as well as for the staff people from the Executive Budget Office and the Legislative Fiscal Office who monitor the agency's operations. The guides are a convenient source for tracking revenue, budget, and program trends; and for analyzing relationships among the three. — *JD*

DB39   University of Nebraska Rural Initiative Directory [Internet Site]. - Lincoln, NE : Univ. of Nebraska Rural Initiative, 2005?- . - http://ruralinitiative. nebraska.edu/directory

>   Access Date: Jan. 2006
>   Fees: None

• Rural Initiative, one of the Univ. of Nebraska's land grant services to citizens, focuses on programs and outreach projects of the four university campuses that study or affect the economy and quality of life in nonmetropolitan Nebraska. The directory acts as a gateway site, linking to numerous rural development-related sites produced by other programs, organizations, government agencies, and businesses. Still in development, the directory and its search engine offer keyword searching of full text. Entries describe target sites, assign

categories and add keywords, and link to the Internet site. Sites cover agricultural topics (e.g., beef cattle, horticulture, agritourism, grapes and wine, drought) and other topics (e.g., golf courses, remote sensing, bioterrorism, nonprofits, entrepreneurship, habitat, telecommunications). Two supplemental files, Nebraska Rural Development Programs and Nebraska Rural Development Acronyms, are available at the *Rural Initiative* home page, http://ruralinitiative .nebraska.edu/. — *JD*

Guidebooks
See also Maher, **Roadside Geology of Nebraska, EA8**
DB40   Boye, Alan. - The Complete Roadside Guide to Nebraska : And Comprehensive Description of Items of Interest to One and All Travelers of the State, whether Native or Transplant, Sendentary [sic] or Transient .../ ...ill. by James Exten ; ...2nd ed. by Alan Boye ; prefaces by Ron Hansen and Wright Morris. - 2nd ed. - Lincoln, NE : Univ. of Nebraska Pr., 2007. - 492 p. ; ill.

>   Class Numbers:
>   Library of Congress GV1024
>   ISBN 0803259689 (pbk.)   9780803259683 (pbk.)
>   OCLC 71800661
>   Notes:
>   Includes bibliographical references (p. 455-461);
>   index
>   Originally publ.: St. Johnsbury, VT : Saltillo Pr., 1989
>   Table of contents: http://www.loc.gov/catdir/toc/
>   ecip071/2006031824.html

• A mile-by-mile guide to 33 U.S. and state highways in Nebraska, including Interstate 80, the border-to-border freeway that is the only road most visitors see. The guide describes and provides histories and local lore about towns, buildings, historic locations, landscape, and curiosities, and eloquent versions of historic and contemporary events (e.g., the Cheyenne Outbreak, 1878, in which Dull Knife's small band of northern Sioux were killed ; the growing controversy over land and water use in the Sandhills). The 28-ounce Coffeeburgers at Sioux Sundries in Harrison go unmentioned—perhaps in the next edition. The style is entertaining, the research high in quality. An excellent companion to the Federal Writers' Project Nebraska guidebook (see Site List 14 - "American Guide Series"). Bibliography of sources ; excellent index. The revised edition has over 5,000 new entries. — *JD*

DB41   Brevet's Nebraska Historical Markers and Sites. - Sioux Falls, SD : Brevet Pr., 1974. - 220 p. ; ill.

>   Class Numbers:
>   Library of Congress F667
>   ISBN 0884980200   0884980219
>   LCCN 74-79979

Notes:

Index

• Reproduces Nebraska historical markers posted along roadsides throughout the state. Organized first by three broad geographical divisions of the state, then alphabetically by county. Each entry reproduces the content of the marker, identifies its location, and has an illustration relevant to the site—sometimes a photo, sometimes a line drawing. Contains indexes of counties and illustrations, and a more extensive general index. A good traveling companion that should not go out of date ; new editions will only need to show new markers. — *MB*

DB42   Wilson, D. Ray - **Nebraska Historical Tour Guide**. - Carpentersville, IL : Crossroads Communications, 1996. - 318 p. ; ill.

Class Numbers:

Library of Congress F664.3

ISBN 0916445437 (pbk.)

Notes:

Index

Originally publ. : 1983

• Thirteen sections organized by geographical subunits (e.g., "Interstate 80 West from Omaha," "US 20 - Route to the Sandhills"). Poor quality black-and-white photos and maps throughout. Identifies area attractions for each city and town along the way. Interesting historically. — *MB*

New Mexico

Bibliographies

DB43   Hunner, John. - **A Selective Bibliography of New Mexico History**. - Albuquerque, NM : Center for the American West, Dept. of History, Univ. of New Mexico, 1992. - 157 p. - (University of New Mexico. Center for the American West. Occasional paper, 5).

Class Numbers:

Library of Congress F796   Z1315

OCLC 26517397

LCCN 93-620154

Notes:

Reproduced from typescript

• A classed bibliography of materials, arranged in five categories : "Reference Works and Bibliographies," "City, State, and Regional Histories," "Native American Era," "Hispanic American Era (1539-1846)," and "Anglo American Era (1846-Present)." The last two categories have subdivisions for environment, culture, ethnic groups, social history, public policy, government and political history, and economic history.

Hunner emphasizes post-1973 materials to avoid overlapping Swadesh's *20,000 Years of History* (**DB45**). There are no indexes, so the only means of retrieval is the classification. Hunner gives some hints about exploiting this arrangement in his preface, but it is not ease of use that led Richard Etulain (*New Mexican Lives*, **AC12**) to call this work the "most useful bibliography on the state's history." — *RB*

DB44   Saunders, Lyle. - **A Guide to Materials Bearing on Cultural Relations in New Mexico**. - Albuquerque, NM : Univ. of New Mexico Pr., 1944. - 528 p. - (New Mexico. University. School of Inter-American Affairs. Inter-Americana series. Bibliographies, 3).

Class Numbers:

Library of Congress Z1315

OCLC 1100334

LCCN 44-53707

• Saunders's preface describes his work's scope: it attempts "to list, with as much thoroughness as possible, those published and manuscript materials having some relevance to problems of cultural relations between the three main ethnic groups [Anglo, Hispanic, Indian] within the state of New Mexico." The first section is an index to the "Dictionary-Guide," the work's main section, whose entries are listed alphabetically (hence "dictionary"). The third section lists supplementary bibliographies arranged by topic: pre-Spanish period, pueblos, Spanish colonial period, Mexican period, American frontier period, Indians (general works and specific peoples), fiction, and drama. Entries are not annotated, but there are detailed subject and author indexes. The subject index allows researchers to locate such subjects as homesteading, military activities, and water supply. — *JB*

DB45   Swadesh, Frances Leon. - **20,000 Years of History : A New Mexico Bibliography** / comp. and ed. with an ethnohistorical introd. by Frances Leon Swadesh. - Santa Fe, NM : Sunstone Pr., 1973. - 128 p.

Class Numbers:

Library of Congress   Z1315

ISBN 0913270148

LCCN 73-77323

• A reading list designed for general readers, teachers, and high school and junior college students, Swadesh's bibliography focuses on the state's multicultural history and character. More than 800 entries are arranged under headings for general and background, archaeology, Spanish colonial and Mexican period, territorial period, recent history, intergroup relations, and arts and skills. Headings are subdivided by culture: specific peoples, Hispano, or Anglo. Citations to scholarly and popular books, pamphlets, articles, and government reports are very briefly annotated. Appendixes list elected and appointed governors, and museums and monuments. Useful to anyone studying or teaching native cultures, cultural change, or multiculturalism. — *JD*

DB46 Tyler, Daniel. - **Sources for New Mexican History, 1821-1848.** - Santa Fe, NM : Museum of New Mexico Pr., 1984. - 206 p. ; ill.

> Class Numbers:
>   Library of Congress F800   Z1315
> ISBN 0890131473
> OCLC 10273215
> LCCN 83-27042
> Notes:
>   Bibliography: p. 175-197 ; index

• While some of its information is dated and accessibility may have changed, this guide remains an excellent source for identifying manuscript and published sources on New Mexico 1821-1848 and for understanding their nature and scope. To help researchers locate additional material, it describes the nature of Mexican bureaucracy and the distribution channels for official documents. Materials are organized by repository with chapters covering records in New Mexico, other states, federal archives, northern Mexico, and Mexico City. Chapters include bibliographies of guides and finding aids. Extensive notes give research tips, locations of microfilm copies, and document histories. An annotated bibliography of frequently cited, printed primary sources, such as memoirs and journals, supplements the chapters. An impressively detailed work geared to scholars. — *JD*

Atlases

DB47   Historical Atlas of New Mexico / by Warren A. Beck and Ynez D. Haase. - Norman, OK : Univ. of Oklahoma Pr., 1969. - [145] p. ; 62 maps ; 31 cm.

> Class Numbers:
>   Library of Congress G1506.S1
> OCLC 7862
> LCCN 73-653153
> Notes:
>   Bibliography: p. [135]-[140]
>   Electronic book: http://www.netLibrary.com/
>   urlapi.asp?action= summary& v=1&bookid =
>   15369

• Because New Mexico's size and geography have shaped its history, Beck and Haase provide maps that depict not only geography but also concentrations of population ; routes followed by explorers, conquerors, and settlers ; frontier

posts and forts ; land systems and boundaries ; and economic development. They use place-names and spellings common to the period of each map. Maps are accompanied by brief text. Bibliography ; good index. — *JB*

DB48   Williams, Jerry L., ed. - **New Mexico in Maps.** - 2nd ed. - Albuquerque, NM : Univ. of New Mexico Pr., 1986. - 469 p. ; ill., maps ; 32 cm.

> Class Numbers:
>   Library of Congress G1505
> ISBN 0826308694   0826308708 (pbk.)
> LCCN 86-675011
> Notes:
>   Bibliography: p. 385-397
>   Greatly expanded and updated from the first edi-
>   tion published in 1979.
>   Scales differ

• Both a tour guide and a reference work, Williams's volume begins with locator maps and continues with 26 maps on the natural environment, 25 on historical landscapes, 37 on population characteristics, 18 on economic characteristics, 18 on cultural elements, and seven on government. They include flood occurrences, abandoned agricultural centers, land grants, ethnic distribution, crime rates, mineral mining, traffic flows, religious denominations, and novels of New Mexico. The title of the work is to some degree misleading. The maps are really graphic accompaniments to a remarkable historical portrait of the state presented in descriptive essays, charts, and tables. The work is ideal for teaching and for tracking trends. Selected references, map location indexes, and a subject index are included. — *JD*

Place-Names

DB49   Julyan, Robert Hixson. - **The Place Names of New Mexico.** - Rev ed., 2nd ed. - Albuquerque, NM : Univ. of New Mexico Pr., 1998. - xxviii, 385 p.
> LCCN 98-25232
> Notes:
>   Bibliography, p. xxviii

• A thorough, often elaborate discussion of the genesis of New Mexico place-names, based on research carried out by the New Mexico Writers' Project, 1936-1940. Lists post offices, mountains, bodies of water, land grants, railroad sidings, abandoned settlements, administrative areas, military sites, housing developments and subdivisions, and "just plain interesting names." Julyan focuses on name origins, ignoring, for example, the sinister associations now attached to Los Alamos ("the cottonwoods") and Roswell's numerous UFO sightings. Very useful, as place-name dictionaries go. – *RB*

Collective Biographies   *North Dakota*

DB50 Bullis, Don. - **New Mexico : A Biographical Dictionary, 1540-1980.** - Los Ranchos de Albuquerque, NM : Rio Grande Books, 2007- (In progress). - v. 1- ; ports.

> Class Numbers:
> Library of Congress F795
> ISBN 1890689602   1890689718
>   9781890689605   9781890689711
> OCLC 71270657
> LCCN 2006-928776
> Notes:
> Includes bibliographical references ; indexes

• Consists of 150-200 word entries profiling 600 individuals, living and deceased. Portraits accompany many entries. Information was derived from published books, magazine, journal and newspaper articles, interviews, and correspondence. Sources are noted following the entry. A bibliography lists only the books consulted. Two indexes : individuals listed by their profession/life work, and a names index. – *MS*

DB51 Twitchell, Ralph Emerson, 1859-1925. - **The Leading Facts of New Mexico History.** - Cedar Rapids, IA : Torch Pr., 1911-1917. - 5 v. ; fronts., ill., plates (part col.).

> Class Numbers:
> Library of Congress F796
> OCLC 3828708
> LCCN 11-23016
> Notes:
> Contains bibliographies
> Microfilmed for the series "Western Americana :
> Frontier History of the Trans-Mississippi
> West, 1550-1900," reels 545-546, no. 5473.
> Woodbridge, CT : Research Publications,
> 1975. Series now published as "Western
> American Frontier History." Detroit, MI :
> Primary Source
> Microfilm, Gale Group.

• The first two volumes are a useful compilation, though the author was accused of borrowing much of the narrative without proper attribution and the work has biases that were not uncommon at the time of writing. The reference value lies in volumes 3 and 4, which contain county histories with biographical sketches of prominent citizens. Each volume is indexed by names, places, and Indian tribes. The fifth volume, which also includes one county history, updates the narrative history through the early years of statehood and includes a useful chronology covering 1521-1917. — *JD*

Guides

DB52 Rylance, Daniel F., comp. - **Reference Guide to North Dakota History.** - Grand Forks, ND : Chester Fritz Library, Univ. of North Dakota, 1979. - 183 p.

> Class Numbers:
> Library of Congress Z1321
> OCLC 5861221
> Notes
> Includes *North Dakota Literature*, comp. by J.F.S.
> Smeall

• Rylance and Smeall (history and English, both Univ. of North Dakota) provide 35 topical headings for history and six for literature in sections for politics, women, Native Americans, climate, education, forts, religion, counties, health, business, printing, public utilities, poetry, theater, and Native literature. Their work is based on a guide published by the Minnesota Historical Society (1974), and many of their citations are found in two journals, *North Dakota History* and *North Dakota Quarterly*. The guide is useful for reference and as a finding aid, but it needs an author index. — *GK*

Manuscripts ; Archives

DB53 Gray, David P. - **Guide to the North Dakota State Archives.** - Bismarck, ND : State Historical Society of North Dakota, North Dakota Heritage Center, 1985. - 151 p. ; ill.

> Class Numbers:
> Library of Congress CD3434
> LCCN 86-620698
> Notes:
> Index

• The territorial and state government records in this guide are arranged in record groups by agency. Brief descriptions are supplied at the series level, and entries give full retrieval information. Obsolete agency names appear in the index. Some topical record groups list records from several different agencies. The table of contents provides an alphabetical listing by keyword. At the beginning of each agency grouping, an article describes the history and current status of the agency. Besides items located at the State Archives, the guide includes state-related records housed at North Dakota State University and the University of North Dakota. — *JB*

DB54 Guide to Manuscripts at the State Historical Society of North Dakota [Internet Site] / compiled by Lotte Bailey. - Bismarck, ND : State Historical Society of North Dakota, 2001. - http://ndsl.lib.state.nd.us/

Class Numbers:
    Library of Congress CD3434
    OCLC 55057719
    Access Date: May 2007
    Fees: None

• Guide to 1,756 archival collections documenting various aspects of the history and life of North Dakota. Includes records of both organizations and individuals, arranged alphabetically by collection title. Entries indicate type and extent of materials, inclusive date, availability of inventories, access restrictions, and subject headings. Collection descriptions frequently highlight useful biographical, subject, or geographic information. Thorough index. — *LMcD*

Indexes

DB55 Hager, Georgie M., comp. - **Index to the Journals of the North Dakota Historical Society, 1906-1970** : *North Dakota State Historical Society Collections*, **1906-1925** ; *North Dakota Historical Quarterly*, **1926-1944** ; *North Dakota History*, **1945-1970**. - Bismarck, ND : State Library Commission, 1973. - 121 p. - (North Dakota Library Notes, v. 4 no. 7 [Dec. 1973]).

Class Numbers:
    Library of Congress F631
    OCLC 831718

• Providing indexes by author and topic, this slim volume covers journals published by the North Dakota Historical Society, 1906-1970. Section 2 lists books reviewed, arranged by author, then by title. The appendix includes a list of all libraries that were receiving *North Dakota History* as of September 1973. — *JB*

Handbooks

DB56 North Dakota. Legislative Assembly. - **North Dakota Centennial Blue Book : 1889-1989** / [Curtis Eriksmoen, ed.]. - [Bismarck, ND?] : publ. by Legislative Authority, 1989. - 555, ci p. ; ill., ports., music.

Class Numbers:
    Library of Congress F636
    OCLC 20074974
    Notes:
        Includes bibliographical references ; index

• Chronicles the legislative, executive, and judicial branches of North Dakota government, listing 3,500 legislators and

state administrators over the past century. The work includes a brief history of the state and its counties, geography, economic staples, and famous individuals from North Dakota. The book has 14 sections—dedication, symbols and awards, history of constitution, executive and legislative office holders, structure of state government, legislative and election issues, judiciary, social and cultural, political subdivisions, economics, physical features, places of interest, bibliography, and indexes. Entries for each representative contain district number, party affiliation, time served, address, telephone numbers, birth date, occupation, and organizations. — *GK*

Atlases

See also Sherman, **Prairie Mosaic, CC9**

DB57 Hemmasi, Mohammad. - **North Dakota Thematic Atlas : Population, Social, and Economic Dimensions** / [by] Mohammad Hemmasi, Devon A. Hansen, Floyd C. Hickok. - [Grand Forks, ND] : Univ. of North Dakota, 2005. - 1 atlas (various pagings) ; 82 maps, 9 charts ; 30 cm.

Class Numbers:
    Library of Congress G1441.E24
    OCLC 57673808

• The authors collaborated to compile and print this atlas, produced as a set of looseleaf pages. The introduction claims that a CD-ROM version in color is available. Arranged according to the sections listed in the subtitle, the atlas categories cover varieties of subject matter. The opening section gives an overview of the state by counties, by general population distribution, and organized political districts. Population maps cover density, age, race, mortality, morbidity, in- and out-migration, rural population, and population centers ; the family and social section has maps for ethnicity, education, marriage, divorce, and birth ratios ; and economics topics include employment, income, health, housing, and voting. A solid review of the state, emphasizing rural demographics. — *JB*

Place-Names

DB58 Wick, Douglas A., 1947-   . - **North Dakota Place Names**. - Fargo, ND : Prairie House, 1988. - 237 p. ; ill., maps.

Class Numbers:
    Library of Congress F634
    ISBN 0911007113
    OCLC 51035730
    LCCN 89-37422

Notes:
  Includes bibliographical references (p. 235-237)

• Because areas on the Prairies and Plains are settled but often later abandoned, place-names change constantly ; a once-thriving community may now be nothing but grass and wind. Wick's volume provides a record of these places, covering place-names, historical and current, in North Dakota. Entries, alphabetically arranged, give county, township and section, history of the name and place, railroad connections (if any), and references. The last section has maps that show all county locations mentioned in the book. – *JB*

Collective Biographies

DB59   North Dakota Biography Index [Internet Site]. - Fargo, ND : North Dakota Institute for Regional Studies, North Dakota State University, 1999-   . - http://www.lib.ndsu.nodak.edu/ndirs/bio&genealogy/ndbioindex.html

  Class Numbers:
    Library of Congress Z1321
  OCLC 43423680
  Access Date: June 2006
  Notes:
    Began as a card index compiled by Allen Petersen
      of Fargo, ND
  Fees: None

• Index of more than 190,000 biographical sketches found in almost 700 publications. Searchable by name ; maiden names are in the "First Name" field. Entries typically give surname and first name, birth and death dates, and publication information. Although the database is not full text, copies of biographies are available from the Institute for a fee. North Dakota biographical dictionaries, local histories, WPA biography files, and several periodicals are indexed ; family histories and genealogies, biographical books about a single individual, and newspaper obituaries are not. Post-1980 publications are in the process of being indexed. Useful for quickly identifying sources of biographical information on a large number of North Dakotans, both living and deceased. – *LMcD*

Guidebooks

DB60   Staggs, Jason, ed. - Guide to North Dakota's Legendary Places / ed. by Jason Staggs ; Linda Olson. - Minot, ND : North Dakota Art Gallery Association, 2003. - 65 p.

  OCLC 52996482

• Designed for travelers, the guide covers state and national historic sites ; galleries, museums and studios ; music and theater venues ; historical and science museums ; refuges, zoos, and hatcheries ; state and national parks ; scenic byways ; and unique attractions. Organized by town within general regions, entries include address or location, hours, phone, URL, and brief description. Icons indicate free parking, ADA accessibility, rest rooms, food service, admission fees, shopping, camping, and lodging. Also includes a foldout map and a directory of Web sites, chambers of commerce, and convention and visitors bureaus. — *JD*

Oklahoma

Guides

DB61   Gibson, Arrell Morgan. - Oklahoma : A Students' Guide to Localized History. - New York : Bureau of Publications, Teachers College, Columbia Univ., 1965. - 36 p. - (Localized history series).

  Class Numbers:
    Library of Congress F694
  OCLC 2460944
  Notes:
    Includes bibliographical references

• A slim volume of helpful information for students of Oklahoma history. The introduction reviews why and how to pursue local history. Each chapter devotes several pages to surveying the topic, lists further readings, and suggests possible field trips. The book covers international affairs, Indian country, Oklahoma's years as a territory, economy, culture, and historical periods. No index. — *JB*

Bibliographies

DB62   Foreman, Carolyn Thomas, b. 1875. - Oklahoma Imprints, 1835-1907 : A History of Printing in Oklahoma before Statehood. - Norman, OK : Univ. of Oklahoma Pr., 1936. - xxiv, 499 p. ; front., plates, ports., maps (1 folded), facsims. (1 folded).

  Class Numbers:
    Library of Congress Z1325
  OCLC 1739061
  LCCN 36-10886
  Notes:
    Bibliography: p. [431]-436

• Foreman's bibliography covers printing and publishing in the parts of Indian Territory (unorganized land set aside for use by Indians, including those forced into relocation) and Oklahoma Territory (in the eastern part of Indian Territory) that became the state of Oklahoma in 1907. The imprints reveal a remarkable level of literacy and interest in reading by groups inhabiting both territories. Mission and other presses published tribal laws, chiefs' messages, hymns, and scriptures in Indian languages. Many newspapers were published in the Cherokee, Chickasaw, Choctaw, Osage/Peoria and Seminole Nations, and magazines in both the Indian and Oklahoma Territories. Numerous books and pamphlets published in Oklahoma Territory included session laws, legislative journals, statutes, and Supreme Court decisions. Foreman's summaries place the publications in historical context and her annotations are very thorough. Information about newspapers includes political stance, circulation figures, themes, publication schedules, and ownership. Two prolific presses, Baptist Mission and Park Hill, are covered in separate chapters. — *JD*

DB63 Hargrett, Lester, 1902-1962. - **Oklahoma Imprints, 1835-1890.** - New York : publ. for the Bibliographical Society of America [by] Bowker, 1951. - 267 p.

> Class Numbers:
> Library of Congress Z1325
> OCLC 861444
> LCCN 51-3747
> Notes:
> Bibliography: p. xvii

• Missionaries operated the first printing press in Indian Territory, shipped from Boston by the American Board of Commissioners for Foreign Missions to print materials for the tribes relocated under the Indian Removal Act of 1830. Hargrett classes later presses as tribal, military, or commercial. Of the 797 imprints from those presses he lists, no copies of 102 were known to exist and more than half were known from only one copy. Many appear in 19th-century bibliographies but Hargrett describes more than half for the first time. Unlike Foreman's similar bibliography (**DB62**), Hargrett's excludes newspapers and periodicals. Organized by year, the imprints present a lesson in the history of Indian and Oklahoma Territories. The first imprint is a broadside of the Cherokee alphabet by the Cherokee scholar Sequoya (also known as George Guess); the other 1,835 titles are scriptures and hymns translated into Indian languages. Imprints for the final year include official publications of the newly formed Oklahoma Territory and of the Indian Nations. Hargrett describes the physical pieces and their contents in detail and in many cases provides notes about the author, historical context, and printing history, and refers to earlier bibliographies, sometimes supplying corrections. Print runs are described. Appendixes include a statistical summary of publications by year; an index of places, printing presses, and printers; a chronology of Oklahoma places engaged in printing; and an index of

names, presses, titles, tribes, and publication types. Its careful scholarship makes this a fine source for scholars and book collectors. — *JD*

DB64 Oklahoma Historical Society. Library Resources Division. - **Oklahoma History : A Bibliography** / comp. by Mary Huffman with the assistance of Brian Basore. - Oklahoma City, OK : Library Resources Div., Oklahoma Historical Society, 1991. - 102 p.

> Class Numbers:
> Library of Congress F694
> ISBN 0941498646
> OCLC 27186835
> LCCN 91-623060

• Lists "manuscripts, book titles, and some microfiche titles dealing with the history of Oklahoma ... housed in the Oklahoma Historical Society Research Library," but omits journals and titles that treat single topics (e.g., petroleum industry, ranching, Indian peoples), which will be covered in separate bibliographies. Arranged by subject areas for general histories, antiquities, Indian Territory to 1907, Oklahoma Territory, statehood 1907-1991, geography, biographies, historical societies, and Oklahoma counties. In each subject, citations are arranged by the library's call number. There are no annotations and no index. Researchers familiar with Oklahoma will find this a good starting point. — *JB*

DB65 **Oklahoma Image Materials Guide** / ed. by Anne Hodges Morgan. - [Oklahoma City, OK] : Oklahoma Dept. of Libraries, 1981. - 190 p. ; [1] p. of plates, ill.

> Class Numbers:
> Library of Congress F694   Z1325
> OCLC 7322074
> LCCN 81-620001
> Notes: A publication of the Oklahoma Image Project
> which is jointly sponsored by the Oklahoma Dept.
> of Libraries and the Oklahoma
> Library Association
> Includes bibliographies ; index

• Intending to appeal to both scholars and general readers, Morgan arranges her annotated bibliography according to six major topics (natural history, Native Americans, population groups, frontier days, politics, and oil), each divided into subtopics. "Natural history" has subtopics for geography, weather, plants, and animals. In every section, printed materials precede films, and sections end with suggested readings. Annotations run 75-125 words; entries can appear in more than one section, but each is annotated only once, with *see* references from other occurrences. General index. — *JB*

Manuscripts ; Archives

DB66   Blessing, Patrick J. - **Oklahoma Records and Archives**. - [Tulsa? OK : Blessing], 1978. - 515 p. ; maps. - (University of Tulsa publication in American social history, 1).

> Class Numbers:
> Library of Congress F693   Z5313.U6
> LCCN 78-112698
> Notes:
> Reproduced from typescript

• A comprehensive catalog of records and archives in libraries and depositories in Oklahoma that will interest historians and genealogists. The compiler specifies with care the kinds of materials included: information that lists inhabitants (vital statistics, land records, city directories, telephone directories), and guides to published materials that would aid readers in putting their work in perspective. Since several publications already existed that met the second need, Blessing and his co-workers concentrated on recording locations of records and describing them; works that provide context were limited to unpublished materials—in effect, theses and dissertations. The work supplies sections for state-wide records (vital statistics, elections), records relating to minorities (Indians and blacks), an overview of county records and manuscripts, and county-by-county records, described in considerable detail. Seven appendixes list addresses of libraries and depositories in Oklahoma, and summarize laws governing record keeping for such records as vital statistics, tax assessment, and registry of deeds. No indexes, but the table of contents is thorough. Three maps show stages in the development of legal jurisdictions, from the period of Indian and Oklahoma Territory to present-day counties. Thorough and useful, but appears never to have been updated. — *RB*

DB67   Oklahoma Historical Society. Archives and Manuscripts Div. - **Microfilm Catalog 1976-1998**. - Oklahoma City, OK : Oklahoma Historical Society, Archives and Manuscripts Div., 1998. - 1 atlas (9 p. ; 27 leaves ; 150 p.) ; col. folded maps ; 46 x 40 cm.

> Class Numbers:
> Library of Congress F691
> OCLC 41949067

• This spiral-bound publication identifies holdings of the Oklahoma Historical Society as of 1998, including references to Indian pioneer history, the Five Tribes associated with the region (Cherokee, Choctaw, etc.) as well as Plains and woodland tribes such as the Kaw, Pawnee, and Otoe. It also cites Indian Territory Court Records, records of individual Oklahoma churches, and Oklahoma Historical Society archival items. There is no index, but the listing by category makes the contents relatively accessible. Sample entries: "Creek—Blacksmiths—Documents—

1867-1893"; "Pawnee—Claims vs. Government—1908-1923." — *MB*

Encyclopedias

DB68   **Encyclopedia of Oklahoma History & Culture [Internet Site]**. - Oklahoma City, OK : Oklahoma Historical Society and Oklahoma State University Library Electronic Publishing Center, 2002-. - http://digital. library.okstate.edu/encyclopedia/

> Class Numbers:
> Library of Congress F694
> LCCN 2007-619608
> Access Date: May 2008
> Notes:
> Encyclopedia staff includes Dianna Everitt, ed. ; Larry O'Dell, Linda D. Wilson, and Jon D. May, associate eds.
> Fees: None

• Drawing on the expertise of more than 500 contributors, the encyclopedia offers a scholarly panorama of the Sooner State. The project is somewhat reticent about its scope and scale and nowhere indicates the number of entries; it is clearly a work in progress, however, as many entries await content. The organization is presented in a straightforward way, without clutter: browsing by alphabetical order, chronological time frame within six large periods, and subject (twenty broad themes such as "American Indians," "Farming," "Government and Politics," and "Women"). Searching is available in both basic and advanced modes, using the familiar and intuitive Google Search. Only at the point of searching does it become apparent that the site offers more than its title would suggest: the full text of a number of journals (*Chronicles of Oklahoma*, *Oklahoma Academy of Science Proceedings*, *Oklahoma Today*, and *Oklahoma Ornithological Society Bulletin*), Indian Claims Commission decisions, Kappler's *Indian Affairs*, and other resources. The signed entries vary in length according to the importance of their subject matter and provide some illustrations, substantial bibliographic references, and a generous cross-reference structure offering suggestions for related items. Wide-ranging in its coverage of both historical (e.g., Cimarron Territory, Will Rogers, *Grapes of Wrath*) and contemporary developments, events, and people (Brad Pitt, Oklahoma City Bombing). Items are both distinctively Oklahoman (Bone-Dry Law, all-black towns) and more regional (barbed wire, Santa Fe Trail). Somewhat understated in comparison with similarly titled encyclopedias of Tennessee and Arkansas, without features such as audio and video clips, or extensive lists of links. A very useful resource for the history and culture of Oklahoma as well as selectively for the southern Plains, the encyclopedia's value will increase as it approaches completion. – *LMcD*

Atlases

DB69   Burrill, Meredith F. - **A Socio-Economic Atlas of Oklahoma.** - Stillwater, OK : Oklahoma State Univ. Agricultural Experiment Station, 1936. - 124 p. ; maps ; 28 cm.

> Class Numbers:
>> Library of Congress S103.E9
>> OCLC 7295193

• Burrill's atlas, intended to provide an economic picture of Oklahoma during the 1930s, now provides insight into a state hit hard by the Great Depression. The maps illustrate all aspects of the state's economic status, including agricultural industries, manufacturing, transportation, utilities, and mineral resources. Other maps depict the droughts that lasted 20 or 30 days in a 20-year period ; the value of farm land, buildings, and machinery; oil and gas fields in 1926 and 1935; distribution of manufactured goods such as mattresses and ice; minority, rural, and urban population distribution; bank failures; and governmental units with deficits. A section of comments following the table of contents provides guidance in interpreting the maps. — *JB*

DB70   Goins, Charles Robert. - **Historical Atlas of Oklahoma** / [by] Charles Robert Goins & Danney Goble ; cartography by Charles Robert Goins and James H. Anderson ; introd. by David L. Boren. - Norman, OK : Univ. of Oklahoma Pr., 2006. - 1 atlas (286 p.) ; ill. (some col.), col. maps ; 24 x 31 cm.

> Class Numbers:
>> Library of Congress G1366.S1
>> ISBN 0806134828   0806134836 (pbk.)
>> LCCN 2006-627733
>> Notes:
>>> Includes bibliographical references (p. 263-271); index
>>> Relief shown by shading and gradient tints
>>> Rev. and enlarged ed. of: *Historical Atlas of Oklahoma* / by John W. Morris, Charles R. Goins, and Edwin C. McReynolds. 3rd ed. 1986
>>> Review by D.S. Azzolina: *Choice* 44.9 (May 2007) : review 44-4808
>>> Scales differ

• An atlas that covers thoroughly with maps and text the natural background ("Native Oklahoma": geology, soils, precipitation, vegetation, oil and gas), the arrival of Indians and of white explorers ("Humans on the Landscape"), the territorial period ("Where the Frontier Ends" : Oklahoma Territory, Indian Territory, statehood), early years of the state ("Brand New State ..." : railroads, Tulsa race riot of 1921, crops, the Great Depression),

and present-day Oklahoma ("You're Doing Fine, Oklahoma" : sports, minorities, women). The compilers may be forgiven for placing Oklahoma at the center of the known world, but the text amplifies the maps, which sometimes are difficult to read (explorers' routes, although color-coded, use colors not always easy to distinguish). Contains a nine-page bibliography, several sections with biographical sketches of prominent Oklahomans, and an index primarily of persons and places. No topic seems to have been slighted or forgotten. Useful for students, scholars, and adult readers. — *RB*

Place-Names

DB71   Shirk, George H. - **Oklahoma Place Names** / foreword by Muriel H. Wright. - Norman, OK : Univ. of Oklahoma Pr., 1987, c1974. - 268 p. ; maps.

> Class Numbers:
>> Library of Congress F692
>> ISBN 0585277710 (electronic bk.)
>> OCLC 960809
>> Notes:
>>> Electronic book: http://www.netLibrary.com/ urlapi.asp?action=summary&v=1&bookid=15081
>>> Includes bibliographical references (p. 267-268)

• An alphabetical list of Oklahoma place-names that usually supplies the place's location within its county, including directions from some larger place, dates of operation of the post office, and source of the name. Places that no longer exist are so noted. There are no maps. List of contributors (names only) and a bibliography of 14 published items. — *MB*

Collective Biographies

DB72   Lee, Victoria. - **Distinguished Oklahomans.** - Tulsa, OK : A Touch of Heart Publ., 2003. - 317 p.

> Class Numbers:
>> Library of Congress CT255
>> ISBN 1888225238
>> OCLC 51317283
>> LCCN 2001-129315

• Biographical sketches in folksy style of distinguished Oklahomans from all occupations. Entries are a page to several pages in length and provide a photograph of the subject and a signature facsimile. Includes persons born in Oklahoma or those who moved to Oklahoma or lived several years in the state. Some personalities included : David Borne, university president; Vince Gill, musician; Rue McClanahan, actress; George Nigh, politician; Jim Shoulders, rodeo champion; Minisa Halsey, artist; Patience Swell Latting, mayor. Best for quick consultation and basic information. — *JB*

South Dakota

Bibliographies

DB73   McLaird, James D. - **Dakota Resources : A Reader's Guide to the Historical Literature of South Dakota.** - [Pierre, SD] : South Dakota State Historical Society, 1992. - p. [173]-199 ; ill.

> Class Numbers:
> Library of Congress Z1335
> Notes:Reprinted from : *South Dakota History*
> (summer 1992) : 173-199

• McLaird (history, Dakota Wesleyan Univ.) lists 100 books intended for general readers that will help them find out about South Dakota history, politics, and culture. Choosing titles that demonstrate solid research, factual content, readability, and availability, he arranges entries, all annotated, in nine categories : "General and Reference," "American Indians," "Exploration and Fur Trade," "Homesteading and Settlement," "Range and Cowboys," "Black Hills," "Sioux Wars," "Political Life," and "Twentieth Century Miscellany." — *GK*

DB74   South Dakota History : An Annotated Bibliography / comp. by Herbert T. Hoover and Karen P. Zimmerman ; editorial assistant for computer operations, Chris- topher J. Hoover. - Westport, CT : Greenwood Pr., 1993. - 521 p. - (Bibliographies of the states of the United States, 2).

> Class Numbers:
> Library of Congress Z1335
> OCLC 28181979
> LCCN 93-14048

• The 3,180 numbered entries in this substantial bibliography cite books, essays, journal articles, and dissertations. The compilers (both at the Univ. of South Dakota) begin with a chronology (pre-Columbian period to 1990), followed by a brief section, "Environment," that lists works describing the surroundings of South Dakota (geography, flora and fauna, natural history) and with sections arranged chronologically, pre-territorial history (1634-1861) through statehood, 1960-1990. They then list reference works and archival sources. Entries in the latter section fall outside the numbering scheme (except for a brief section on techniques of oral history), but describe archival holdings at South Dakota repositories and elsewhere in some detail, a feature that students of South Dakota history will find highly valuable. Author and subject indexes are very full, and refer both to this work and the authors' *The Sioux and Other Native American Cultures of the Dakotas* (**CD64**). Each section begins with brief comments about its content and arranges entries alphabetically by main entry. Because the number of items

cited is so large, the annotations noted in the subtitle are usually confined to a sentence or two. — *MB*

DB75   Writers' Program (U.S.). South Dakota. - **A Selected List of South Dakota Books** / comp. by volunteer workers of the South Dakota Writers' Project, Work Projects Administration, and of the South Dakota Library Association. - [Brookings, SD] : South Dakota Library Association, 1943. - 36 p.

> Class Numbers:
> Library of Congress Z1335
> OCLC 5863935
> LCCN 44-2647

• This booklet lists titles for general readers on South Dakota literature, culture, and history. A primary objective was to indicate which South Dakota libraries held rare or out-of-print books published prior to 1920. The work is arranged by categories: fiction, juvenile, nonfiction, poetry, description and travel, biography, Indians, history, journals and reminiscences, miscellaneous nonfiction. Books are listed by author under each category. Symbols indicate libraries that hold copies. – *GK*

DB76   South Dakota : Changing, Changeless, 1889-1989 : A Selected Annotated Bibliography / ed. by Sue Laubersheimer ; comp. by Ruth Ann Alexander [et al.]. - [Pierre, SD] : South Dakota Library Association, 1985. - 320 p.

> Class Numbers:
> Library of Congress F651   Z1335.S66
> LCCN 85-156864
> Notes:
> Indexes

• For the state centennial celebration in 1989, the South Dakota Library Association sponsored this three-part publication. Compiled by scholars at the Univ. of South Dakota and South Dakota State Univ., the first part supplies 1,200 annotated entries in four sections: "History," "Geography and Natural Resources," "Lore," and "Literature." Each part is introduced in a three- to four-page overview by the individual who compiled the entries. Entries are listed alphabetically by author, editor, or compiler. There are indexes for author/editor, title, and project theme. The second part is a subject index to part one, and the third is a supplement that serves as a guide arranged by title to additional works dealing with South Dakota found in public libraries and academic or research libraries. — *GK*

Catalogs

DB77   I.D. Weeks Library. - **Herman P. Chilson Western Americana Collection** / comp. and ed. by Bob

Carmack [et al.]. - Vermillion, SD : I.D. Weeks Library, Univ. of South Dakota, [1982]. - 504 p.

Class Numbers:
Library of Congress F651   Z1335
OCLC 11621650
LCCN 82-622739

• Carmack and his colleagues at the I.D. Weeks Library provide a catalog of books in the Herman P. Chilson Western Americana Collection. Chilson, a businessman and bibliophile from Webster, SD, donated his collection of 6,000 rare books to the library in 1980. The collection presently amounts to about 16,000 volumes, accessible through the library's online catalog. The collection's major strengths are the Great Plains, South Dakota history, Native American history, ornithology, and Western American literature. The catalog is arranged alphabetically by main entry; each entry provides full bibliographic description and LC call number. — GK

Manuscripts ; Archives

DB78   Guide to Historical Repositories in South Dakota / comp. by Kristen Anderson and Elizabeth R. Scott. - [Pierre, SD] : South Dakota State Historical Records Advisory Board, 2002. - 47 p.

Class Numbers:
Library of Congress F646
Government Document South Dakota ED 725 : R
298/2002
OCLC 50822584
Notes:
Index

• Anderson and Scott (South Dakota State Univ.) list 160 institutions that responded to a survey addressed to libraries, repositories, historical societies, museums, and archives that was intended to identify collections holding materials relating to South Dakota history. Collections are listed by city or county and repository. Subject index. — GK

Indexes

DB79   Julin, Suzanne, comp. - *South Dakota Historical Collections* Cumulative Index. - Pierre, SD : South Dakota State Historical Society, 1989. - 469 p.

Class Numbers:
Library of Congress F646
LCCN 90-620769

• In 1901, South Dakota Governor Charles N. Herreid

formed the state Department of History to collect historical information about the state and make it better known to the public. One result of this was publication of *South Dakota Historical Collections* (41 v., 1902-1982), which addressed a variety of economic, political, social, and cultural topics. This index provides access to the periodical's entire run, assisting researchers in locating historical writings about the northern Great Plains. — GK

Government Publications

DB80   Olsgaard, John N. - **A Cumulative Index of South Dakota State Government Publications, 1975-1979**. - Vermillion, SD : I.D. Weeks Library, Univ. of South Dakota, 1980. - 643 p.

Class Numbers:
Library of Congress J87.S8   Z1223.5.S62
LCCN 80-624002
Notes:
Bibliography: p. 1-312

• Olsgaard indexes nondepository South Dakota government publications held at I. D. Weeks Library at the Univ. of South Dakota. The work is arranged in three sections: a bibliography that lists the basic entry and assigns an accession number, an author index, and a keyword index that contains the first 100 characters of the title, arranged by significant words, and the accession number. Printed on green-barred computer paper, the work is bulky to use, since each section is about 200 pages long. — GK

Encyclopedias

DB81   Robinson, Doane, 1856-1946. - **Doane Robinson's Encyclopedia of South Dakota**. - Pierre, SD : [Author], 1925. - 1003 p.

Class Numbers:
Library of Congress F649
LCCN 25-20946

• Robinson's excellent early overview of South Dakota and its history is arranged alphabetically and includes place-names, important political figures, geological information, sports, Lewis and Clark, literature, and the Missouri River. A 12-page appendix of demographic information is drawn from the fourth Census of South Dakota (May 1925). — GK

Chronologies

DB82   Van Balen, John A. - **South Dakota Chronology : From Prehistoric Times to 1899**. - Vermillion, SD : I.D. Weeks Library, Univ. of South

Dakota, 1998. - 758 p.

Class Numbers:
    Library of Congress F655
LCCN 99-199864
Notes:
    Includes bibliographical references (p. 531-553) ; index

• Van Balen (library science, Univ. of South Dakota) provides a general overview of daily and yearly events in the region now called South Dakota, prehistoric era to the turn of the 20th century. He examined 450 sources in compiling the chronology. The book has four sections: chronology of prehistoric events, lists of specific events by day and year, bibliography, and subject index. Entries include Indian treaties, warfare, patterns of European settlement, founding of towns or post offices, establishment of communication and transportation networks, and birth and death dates of notable South Dakotans. — GK

Collective Biographies

DB83   The *Argus Leader* South Dakota 99 : Illustrated Profiles of 99 People Who Significantly Contributed to South Dakota's History / by the staff of the *Sioux Falls Argus Leader*. - Sioux Falls, SD : Ex Machina Publ. Co., 1989, 1988. - 273 p. ; ill.

Class Numbers:
    Library of Congress CT260
ISBN 0944287050   0944287042 (pbk.)
    0944287069 (collector's ed.)
OCLC 19555234

Site List 14
American Guide Series

Best known of the books produced by the Federal Writers' Project of the Works Progress Administration during the Depression, the *Guides* are remarkably enduring as travel guides and general reference sources. Produced in coordination with state agencies by thousands of FWP participants and volunteers, the volumes chronicle each state's history and life. Texts are based on publications, archival sources, interviews, and personal observations. Following a general series pattern, chapters cover natural setting, Indians, history, government, agriculture and the farmer, industry and labor, transportation and communication, ethnic elements, folklore and folkways, education and religion, art and music, architecture, the press, and literature. *Guides* included town portraits and road tours of scenic and historical sites; in the Plains states, many of the routes can be followed today. Appendixes include chronologies, bibliographies, and thorough indexes, illustrations, and maps. Often reprinted or reissued, the *Guides* were the subject of new attention in 2005 on the 70th anniversary of the FWP.

Colorado: A Guide to the Highest State. New York: Hastings House, 1941.
    Reprinted: *The WPA Guide to 1930s Colorado*. Lawrence, KS: Univ. Pr. of Kansas, 1987.

Kansas: A Guide to the Sunflower State. New York: Viking Pr., 1939.
    Reprinted: *The WPA Guide to 1930s Kansas*. Lawrence, KS: Univ. Pr. of Kansas, 1984.

Montana: A State Guidebook. New York: Viking Pr., 1939.
    Reprinted: *The WPA Guide to 1930s Montana*. Tucson, AZ: Univ. of Ariz. Pr., 1994.

Nebraska: A Guide to the Cornhusker State. New York: Hastings House, 1939.
    Reprinted: Lincoln, NE: Univ. of Nebraska Pr., 1979 and 2005.

New Mexico: A Guide to the Colorful State. New York: Hastings House; Albuquerque, NM: Univ. of New Mexico Pr., 1940.
    Reprinted: *The WPA Guide to 1930s New Mexico*. Tucson, AZ: Univ. of Arizona Pr., 1989.

North Dakota: A Guide to the Northern Prairie State. Fargo, ND: Knight Printing Co., 1938. 2nd ed., New York : Oxford Univ. Pr., 1950.
    Reprinted: *WPA Guide to 1930s North Dakota*. Bismarck, ND: State Historical Society of North Dakota, 1990.

Oklahoma: A Guide to the Sooner State. Norman, OK: Univ. of Oklahoma Pr., 1941.
    Reprinted: *The WPA Guide to 1930s Oklahoma*. Lawrence, KS: Univ. Pr. of Kansas, 1986.

A South Dakota Guide. Pierre, SD: State Publ. Co., 1938. 2nd ed., rev., New York: Hastings House, 1952.
    Reprinted: Pierre, SD: South Dakota State Historical Society Pr., 2005 ; reprinted: *The WPA Guide to South Dakota*. St. Paul, MN: Minnesota Historical Society Pr.,   2006.

Texas : A Guide to the Lone Star State. New York: Hastings House, 1940.
    Rev. ed.: New York: Hastings House, 1969.

Wyoming: A Guide to Its History, Highways and People. New York: Oxford Univ. Pr., 1941.
    Reprinted: Lincoln, NE: Univ. of Nebraska Pr., 1981.

LCCN 89-7713

Notes:

    Bibliography: p. 261-263

    Much of the text was originally printed in the
      Sioux Falls Argus Leader (May 1988)

• Brief biographical sketches by staff writers of the *Argus Leader* of 99 personalities who contributed to historical, political, economic, social, and cultural life at the state or national level. Fifty individuals—historians, politicians, businesspeople, journalists, educators—nominated candidates. Criteria used for inclusion were: candidates had to have been born or raised in South Dakota, made a significant contribution to the state, or for people who lived in South Dakota for a short time, that they had earned national recognition. Each sketch includes a photograph and sidebar that lists town, birth or death dates, education, and general information. — *GK*

DB84   Hoover, Herbert T., ed. - **South Dakota Leaders : From Pierre Chouteau, Jr., to Oscar Howe** / ed. by Herbert T. Hoover and Larry J. Zimmerman. - Vermillion, SD : Univ. of South Dakota Pr. ; distr. by : Lanham, MD : Univ. Publishing Associates, 1989. - xxv, 500 p. ; ill., maps.

    Class Numbers:

      Library of Congress CT260

    ISBN 0929925009   0929925033 (pbk.)

    OCLC 18715965

    LCCN 88-31942

    Notes:

      Includes bibliographical references (p. 451-476)

• Hoover and Zimmerman (history and anthropology, Univ. of South Dakota) present an anthology of chapters about 51 prominent leaders and families who made significant contributions to South Dakota history. A planning committee of academicians selected the subjects to commemorate the state's centennial. Among those profiled are artists (Harvey Dunn), novelists (Frederick Manfred), Native Americans (the Deloria family), politicians (Karl Mundt), religious leaders (Joseph Ward), women (Laura Ingalls Wilder), entrepreneurs (Seth Bullock), and ranchers (James "Scotty" Philip). Includes four maps and 86 illustrations. — *GK*

Place-Names

DB85   Writers' Program, SD. - **South Dakota Place Names.** - Enl. and rev. ed. - Vermillion, SD : Univ. of South Dakota, 1941?. - 689 p. ; maps.

    Class Numbers:

      Library of Congress F649

    LCCN 42-24078

    Notes:

      "Sponsored by the Dept. of English. Edward
        C. Ehrensperger, Head."

      Bibliography: p. 679-684 ; index

      Compiled by workers of the Writers Program of
        the Work Projects Administration in the State
        of South Dakota

      Reproduced from typescript

• A comprehensive list of place-names, arranged alphabetically, accounting for the origins of town and county names and named geographic locations. A condensed version, *South Dakota Geographic Names*, was published by Brevet Pr. (1973), ed. by Virginia Driving Hawk Sneve. — *GK*

Guidebooks

DB86   Griffith, Tom D., 1958- . - **South Dakota / photography by Paul Horsted.** - Oakland, CA : Compass American Guides, 1998. - 309 p. ; ill. (some col.), maps. - (Compass American guides).

    Class Numbers:

      Library of Congress F649.3

    ISBN 1878867474

    OCLC 37721349

    LCCN 97-38560

    Notes:

      Includes bibliographical references (p. 298-
        300) ; index

• Journalist Griffith compiles a general travel guide for visitors to South Dakota that begins with a brief history of the state followed by chapters on geographic regions, including descriptions of major cities, events, and sites of interest. The book concludes with practical information about trails, camping, caves, museums, art galleries, national parks, accommodations, book stores, and restaurants. Includes nine topical essays, nine maps, 16 literary extracts, color photographs, facts about South Dakota (capital, state flower, bird, and tree, date admitted as a state, population, five largest cities, economy, climate, geography, and famous South Dakotans), and recommended readings. — *GK*

Texas

Guides

DB87   **Texas Reference Sources : A Selective Guide [Internet Site]** / Texas Library Association. Reference Round Table ; general ed., John C. Hepner. - [Austin, TX] : Texas Library Association, 2004. - http://www.txla. org/pubs/trs/trsonline.html

Class Numbers:
Library of Congress Z1339
OCLC 56943634
Access Date: May 2007
Fees: None

• The Internet presence of *Texas Reference Sources*, like the 5th edition of the printed counterpart (2004) on which it is based, will be the preferred first stopping place for readers or library staff looking for sources that are Texas-specific. Arranged by the classification used for the 11th ed. of *Guide to Reference Books* (Chicago, IL: American Library Association, 1996), the Web site copies the entries and index from the 5th ed., providing no search enhancements—indeed, it is searchable only by either an alphabetic grid with the index entry, or by the table of contents. Annotations are usually brief and factual except for key titles like *New Handbook of Texas* (**DB96b**). Nevertheless, TRS is the most complete list of reference titles about Texas that can be found. — *RB*

Bibliographies

DB88   Cruz, Gilberto Rafael, ed. - **Texas Bibliography: A Manual on History Research Materials** / ed. and comp. by Gilberto Rafael Cruz and James Arthur Irby . - Austin, TX : Eakin Pr., 1982, c1983. - 337 p. ; ill.

Class Numbers:
Library of Congress F386
ISBN 0890153078
OCLC 9186446
LCCN 84-204100
Notes: Index

• Intended for students and scholars in history, Cruz and Irby's bibliography spends most of its entries in eight sections on periods of Texas history, "Spanish Years" through "Twentieth Century Texas," adding a section of general bibliographies, also arranged by period. At the beginning are sections of bibliography, serials, general works, and works on Indians, and the chronological sections are followed by eight topical sections (e.g., "Folklore of Texas," "Travelers' Accounts," "People in Texas" [i.e., ethnic groups], children's literature, and, this being Texas, an entire section devoted to "Texas Rangers"). An appendix lists Texas organizations, and there is an author index, but none for titles or subjects. Entries are not annotated, and the number of entries is difficult to determine, since numbering recycles at the beginning of each section to a convenient number ending in zero (jumping from 2978 at the end of part VIII to 3000 at the beginning of IX). — *RB*

DB89   **A Guide to the History of Texas** / ed. by Light Townsend Cummins and Alvin R. Bailey Jr. - New York :

Greenwood Pr., 1988. - 307 p. - (Reference guides to state history and research).

Class Numbers:
Library of Congress F386   Z1339
ISBN 0313245630
OCLC 16088381
LCCN 87-15021
Notes:
Index

• Contains 27 bibliographic essays in two sections, historical literature and archives. The first consists of contributed essays on such topics as "Texas under Spain and Mexico," "The Texas Frontier," "Native Americans in Texas History," and "Women in Texas History." The second describes 16 specific collections, including, e.g., the Benson Latin American collection at University of Texas at Austin, the Texas State Library, the Sterling Evans Library at Texas A&M, and the Houston Metropolitan Research Center at the Houston Public Library. Unhappily, the sources cited in the essays are not listed in a separate bibliography. Appendixes include a brief chronology of Texas history and a list of historical organizations in Texas. The index is extensive enough to be useful. — *MB*

DB90   Jenkins, John Holmes. - **Basic Texas Books : An Annotated Bibliography of Selected Works for a Research Library.** - Austin, TX : Texas State Historical Association, 1988. - 648 p. ; ill.

Class Numbers:
Library of Congress F386   Z1339
ISBN 0876101863
OCLC 16523651
LCCN 87-22899

• Jenkins intends to identify books general Texana libraries should own. Designed for research libraries, this book excludes fiction; works with scope larger than Texas; histories of religious denominations, counties, towns, or schools; periodicals; pamphlets; and works covering the period after 1940. The 224 items, many in Spanish, are arranged alphabetically by author, with annotations averaging 700-1,000 words in length. Each entry begins with bibliographical details about every known printing and variant, followed by a discussion of the book, including the critical reception, the author's background, representative quotations, and the book's strengths and weaknesses. Some entries include reproductions of title pages. Prairies-Plains researchers will find articles on the cattle industry, the Panhandle, and early forts and military campaigns in West Texas. The appendix is a checklist of 219 bibliographies relating to Texas, excluding articles in periodicals. Good index. — *MB, JB*

DB91   Marten, James Allen. - **Texas.** - Oxford, UK ; Santa Barbara, CA : Clio Pr., 1992. - xxiii, 229 p. ; 1 map.

- (World bibliographical series, v. 144).

> Class Numbers :
>> Library of Congress F386   Z1339
>> ISBN 185109184X   0585104891 (electronic bk.)
>> OCLC 28114876   42922712 (electronic bk.)
>> LCCN 93-215090
>> Notes:
>>> Electronic book:
>>> http://www.netLibrary.com/urlapi.asp?
>>>> action=summary& v=1&bookid=9919
>>> Indexes

• Marten (history, Marquette Univ.) lists just over 700 titles having to do with all aspects of Texas—history, politics and government, ethnic groups, economy and business, fine arts. Nearly all are secondary works and all are in English (although a handful are translations into English from other languages). In each section, entries are arranged alphabetically by author (although all the entries begin with title). All entries are annotated. Brief sections of reference works and serials conclude the bibliography, and a general index refers to authors, subjects, and titles. The audience is not specified (except by the publisher) but appears to be university students and educated adults. — *RB*

DB92   Streeter, Thomas Winthrop, 1883-1965. - **Bibliography of Texas, 1795-1845. - 2nd ed.** / rev. and enlarged by Archibald Hanna with a guide to the microfilm collection, *Texas as Province and Republic, 1795-1845* - Woodbridge, CT : Research Publ., 1983. - 576 p.

> Class Numbers:
>> Library of Congress Z1339
>> ISBN 0892350601
>> OCLC 9530902
>> Notes:
>>> 1st ed. : Cambridge, MA : Harvard Univ. Pr., 1955-1960. 3 pts. in 5 v.

• A bibliography of approximately 1,780 books, maps, and broadsides printed in or about Texas after the period covered by Henry Wagner's *The Spanish Southwest, 1542-1794: An Annotated Bibliography* (New York: Arno Pr., 1967; reprint of 1937 ed.) and before Texas was annexed by the U.S. Organized in three separate parts covering Texas imprints, Mexican imprints, and U.S. and European imprints, numbered consecutively; within each section, entries are arranged chronologically. Detailed bibliographic and historical notes indicating the significance of a work are part of most entries. Includes a brief history of Texas printing and several appendixes on Texas newspapers through 1845, unidentified public documents, government publications of Coahuila and Texas, and speeches on Texas in Congress, 1836-1845. Index of printers, presses, newspapers, editors, and publishers as well as an index of authors, titles, and subjects. Authoritative work for the pre-statehood period of Texas history. — *LMcD*

Encyclopedias

DB93   Carefoot, Jean. - **A Select Glossary of the Texas Revolution.** - [Austin, TX] : Archives Div., Texas State Library, 1986. - 74 p.

> Class Numbers:
>> Library of Congress F390
>> Government Document Texas L1900.8
>> Se48glo 1986
>> OCLC 13918317

• Compiled by the Archives Division of the Texas State Library, Carefoot's "glossary" (actually an encyclopedia) is based on *Handbook of Texas* (**DB96**) and other sources and covers the period Oct. 1835-Apr. 1836, although it sometimes steps outside that frame. The book opens with an essay on the Texas Revolution. Concise entries vary in length from 50 to 350 words. — *JB*

DB94   Dingus, Anne, 1953-   . - **The Dictionary of Texas Misinformation.** - Austin, TX : Texas Monthly Pr., 1987. - 292 p.

> Class Numbers:
>> Library of Congress F386.5
>> ISBN 0877190895
>> OCLC 16091608
>> LCCN 87-10220
>> Notes:
>>> Includes bibliographical references (p. 287-292)

• Dingus does what she can to correct common mistakes about Texas historical events, place-names, and regional terminology. Coverage includes the expected (Alamo, dust devils, town of Post) as well as less common topics (Black Bean Episode, kick over the traces, Brownsville). Entries vary in length from 50 to 600 words. Both informative and entertaining. — *JB*

DB95   The Handbook of Texas / Walter Prescott Webb, ed.-in-chief ; H. Bailey Carroll, managing ed. ; Llerena B. Friend, Mary Joe Carroll [and] Louise Nolen, ed. assistants. - Austin, TX : Texas State Historical Association, 1952-1976. - 3 v.

> Class Numbers:
>> Library of Congress F384
>> ISBN 0876110278
>> OCLC 950475
>> LCCN 53-483
>> Notes:
>>> Includes bibliographical references
>>> Vol. 3 : A Supplement, ed. by
>>>> Eldon Stephen Branda

• A reference source providing all kinds of information about Texas, with as distinguished an editor as can be imagined for Plains studies, this set was reprinted many times. Entries, arranged alphabetically with cross-references and brief bibliographies, vary in length from a few lines to several pages. It covers government, politics, education, business, and organizations, and supplies historical sketches of counties and communities. It offers biographies only for deceased persons, and covers historical periods from the earliest inhabitants to World War II, with a few topics updated to the 1950s. — *JB*

DB95a   The Handbook of Texas Online [Internet Site] / sponsored by the Texas State Historical Association and the General Libraries, Univ. of Texas–Austin. - [Austin, TX] : Texas State Historical Association, 1999 –   . - http://www.tsha.utexas.edu/handbook/ online/

> Class Numbers:
> > Library of Congress F384
> > OCLC 40987952
> Access Date: Feb. 2006
> Notes:
> > Includes bibliographical references
> > Fees: None

• HTO acts as a multidisciplinary encyclopedia covering Texas history, geography, and culture. The site may be searched by keyword and browsed, and there are ample help screens. Articles vary in length, most are signed, and many offer bibliographies. The introduction claims that the site includes 23,000 articles, covering people, places, events, historical themes, and institutions. The site provides lesson plans and guides for grades 4-7 (the grades where Texas history and geography are most often taught). Other links include media, the TSHA and its bookstore. Although the site is still, apparently, under development, it offers ample information about Texas and includes many articles for beginning Plains researchers. — *JB*

DB95b   The New Handbook of Texas / [Ron Tyler, ed. in chief ; Douglas E. Barnett, managing editor ; Roy R. Barkley, ed. Penelope C. Anderson, Mark F. Odintz, associate eds.]. - Austin, TX : Texas State Historical Association, 1996. - 6 v. ; ill. (some col.).

> Class Numbers:
> > Library of Congress F384
> > ISBN 0876111517
> > LCCN 96-12861
> Notes:
> > Includes bibliographical references

• The six volumes and more than 6,000 pages of *New Handbook* required a cast of thousands to produce—three editors-in-chief, an editorial staff whose names occupy a page of three closely-set columns, an advisory board two more pages, and cosponsors, who provided the financial backing such a project needs, two more. The encyclopedia proper ("handbook" seems out of place in a work this size) provides 23,500 entries, alphabetically arranged, written by 3,000 "volunteer" authors (meaning, probably, that they were unpaid), who sign their

articles but are otherwise unacknowledged. Of the articles, 7,200 are biographical sketches, confined to deceased persons. Coverage extends to counties, cities and other communities, topics (architecture, prostitution, religion, slavery), historic events (more than three pages for "Battle of the Alamo"), economic life (ranches, railroads). It would be surprising in a set this size if any subject had been missed, but occasionally Texas sensitivity to criticism is displayed: the article on Pantex avoids any mention of A.G. Mojtabai's *Blessed Assurance: At Home with the Bomb in Amarillo, Texas*. There is no index, but cross-references occur frequently (marked by the notation "qv"). Bibliographies are occasionally long, and often cite newspaper articles among other publications. The great care exercised in planning, selection of contributors, and development of guidelines and editorial practices are evident in the balance and fairness of the articles. Occasional black-and-white illustrations add visual context to the text, and in volume 1, the entries are preceded by 48 pages of plates in color. *New Handbook* is the successor to *Handbook of Texas*, which was edited by no less a person than Walter Prescott Webb (**DB96**). *Encyclopedia of the Great Plains* (**AA4**) required only one volume instead of six, but never mind : *New Handbook* is the best of the encyclopedias devoted to a single Prairies-Plains state, and a splendid resource for any library. — *RB*

DB96   Hatch, Thom, 1946-   . - Encyclopedia of the Alamo and the Texas Revolution. - Jefferson, NC : McFarland, 1999. - 229 p. ; ill., maps.

> Class Numbers:
> > Library of Congress F390
> > ISBN 0786405937
> > OCLC 41476868
> > LCCN 99-35608
> Notes:
> > Includes bibliographical references (p. 217-221) ;
> > index

• Hatch (freelance writer, Colorado) provides an alphabetic guide to people, places, events, politics, and documents relating to the settlement of Texas, the Revolution, and the formation of the Republic in 1836. Although the work covers major figures and issues, Hatch (who wrote all the entries) does not reveal what sources he consulted in writing them. Selected bibliography; maps. — *GK*

DB97   TexasOnline : Texas at Your Fingertips [Internet Site] / Texas Dept. of Information Resources. - Austin, TX : Texas Dept. of Information Resources, 1999- . - http://www.texasonline.com/

> Access Date: May 2008
> Notes:
> > *TexasOnline* is a public-private venture between
> > the State of Texas and BearingPoint, Inc.
> > Fees: None

• A blockbuster site, describing itself as "the official Website for the State of Texas," offering information about many aspects of the state and numerous links to other sites, especially those maintained by state agencies. The home page supplies a picture of the governor with a brief message about the site and photographs of three Texas icons: the state capitol building, bluebonnets, and, of course, the Alamo. Large sections of the site, intended for Texas residents, have to do with laws and regulations affecting such matters as driving, handguns, voting, birth certificates, and obtaining copies of documents from state agencies. The left section of the home page lists eight general topics ("Online Services," "Learning," "Government," "Emergency Preparedness"), each of which has a pulldown menu leading to specific agencies or topics. The data traditionally provided by government, directories and statistics, are available in abundance—population and demographics; colleges, universities, and K-12 schools; state officials; hospitals; etc. Texas citizens can register to vote at the site, and a button called "Where the Money Goes" leads to information about the use of tax dollars. Buttons for "Cities" and "Counties" lead to long lists of sites maintained by counties and municipalities. The home page offers a search window, but like most unorganized search devices, the sites it locates are not always relevant ; readers will have better luck following pulldowns and searching among likely sections of the site. In spite of that, a useful if enormous site. – RB

Atlases

DB98   Stephens, A. Ray. - **Historical Atlas of Texas /** by A. Ray Stephens and William M. Holmes ; Phyllis M. McCaffree, consultant. - Norman, OK ; London : Univ. of Oklahoma Pr., 1989. - 1 atlas (xxiv, 64 p., [64] p. of plates) ; 64 maps ; 32 cm.

Class Numbers:
   Library of Congress G1371.S1
ISBN 0806121580
OCLC 18415552
LCCN 88-40210
Notes:
   Bibliography: p. ix-xviii ; index
   Scales differ

• Stephens's introduction gives as the purpose of his atlas to "illustrate particular topics in Texas history with maps and accompanying brief interpretative essays." Accordingly, he begins with maps of Texas geology and physical terrain, then offers such topical maps as distribution of native plants, expeditions, Texas Revolution and Republic, the Mexican-American War, overland mail routes, cattle drives, hurricanes, oil and gas discoveries, military institutions, world wars, recreation areas, railroads, highways, education,

metropolitan areas, and political districts. An appendix lists counties with 1985 population estimates. Ten-page bibliography; index that points to map numbers. — JB

Collective Biographies

DB99   Texas Biographical Dictionary : People of All Times and All Places Who Have Been Important to the History and Life of the State. - Wilmington, DE : American Historical Publ., 1985. - 202 p. ; ports.

Class Numbers:
   Library of Congress CT262
ISBN 0937862541
OCLC 12372416
LCCN 85-18575

• A collective biography that covers persons native to Texas and transplants who have influenced Texas history and culture. In a list heavily weighted to historic figures, the unnamed editors include statesmen, war heroes, and the notorious as well as the famous. Among those included are founding father Stephen F. Austin, cattleman and trailblazer Charlie Goodnight, outlaw Sam Bass, president Lyndon Johnson, congressman Henry Gonzalez, congresswoman Barbara Jordan, folklorist J. Frank Dobie, pop musician Janis Joplin, and Hispanic leader Jose Angel Gutierrez. Entries, arranged alphabetically, vary in length from 250 to more than 1,000 words. No subject index. — JB

Almanacs

DB100 Texas Almanac. - 2000-2001 [ed.] (2001)-   . Dallas, TX : Dallas Morning News ; distr. by Texas A&M Univ. Pr. Consortium, 2001-   . - Biennial.

Class Numbers:
   Library of Congress AY311.D3
OCLC 49200209
LCCN sn 99-50104
Notes:
   Frequency varies : annual, 1857-1937
   Preceding titles : *Texas Almanac and State Industrial Guide*. Galveston, TX : A.H. Belo & Co. [etc.], 1857-1965 (ISSN 03636-4248 ; LCCN 10-3390) ; *Texas Almanac and State Industrial Guide*.[Dallas, TX] : Belo Corp., 1967-1999 (ISSN 0363-4248 ; LCCN 86-647929, sc 84-1119, sn 79-18916)
   Also available as an Internet site : http://www.texasalmanac.com/

• Useful in ready reference for all things Texas. Published continuously since 1857, *Almanac* covers a wide variety of topics, since Texas is a diverse state, as anything so big is likely to be. *Almanac* arranges information by broad topics—e.g., history, environment, weather, government, culture and the arts, crime. For each topic, it provides general information (which varies by topic), historical perspective, maps, and tables of statistics; for example, "Counties of Texas" has county profiles with statistics, colored maps, and photographs; "Business and Transportation" has brief background on current economic conditions and numerous tables on employment, cost of living, banking, highway construction, vehicle accidents, oil and gas production, and utilities. The work covers all levels of government—local, state, and federal. Detailed index. — *JB*

Wyoming

Bibliographies

DB101 Hellman, Florence S. - **Wyoming : A Bibliographical List** / comp. by Florence S. Hellman [for] Library of Congress, Div. of Bibliography. - Washington, DC : Library of Congress, Div. of Bibliography, 1936. - 50 leaves.

> Notes:
> Photostatic negative made by the New York
> Public Library from typewritten copy

• A bibliography of 1,069 entries, arranged by broad topic (history, geology, natural resources) that might provide decent guidance to publications about Wyoming up to about 1930, were it not a negative photostatic reproduction from typescript, certain to challenge the patience and the eyesight of any researcher. No index. — *RB*

DB102 Jordan, Roy A., 1928- . - **Wyoming : A Centennial Bibliography**. - Powell, WY : Northwest Community College, 1988. - 77 p.

> Class Numbers:
> Library of Congress F761
> Government Document Wyoming CK7.2:2
> OCLC 18500925

• Jordan (Northwest Community College) prepared this bibliography in order to gather sources in preparation for the observance of the Wyoming Centennial. Included are sections on the state's territorial period, Constitution and statehood process, prominent political leaders, state government, significant State Supreme Court decisions, and water and land law. The compiler also devotes several pages to primary sources found in oral histories, manuscript collections, diaries, and memoirs found in the State Archives and at the Western History Research Center, University of Wyoming. – *GK*

DB103 Malone, Rose Mary, 1902- . - **Wyomingana : Two Bibliographies**. - [Denver, CO] : Univ. of Denver Pr., 1950. - 66 p. - (University of Denver. Studies in bibliography, 1).

> Notes:"Works about Wyoming Published before
> 1939, p. 1-9" ; "Recent Books about Wyoming,"
> p. 10-66

•A slight work intended for teachers and librarians building collections of books about Wyoming. Both bibliographies are author lists, the first (about 100 titles) without annotations, the second (whose effective terminal date is the late 1940s), about 200 titles with annotations. No index. — *RB*

Manuscripts ; Archives

DB104 **Wyoming Archives Online Map Collection [Internet Site]**. - Cheyenne, WY : Wyoming State Archives, 2000?- . - http://wyoarchives.state.wy.us/maps.htm

> Access Date: Feb. 2006
> Fees: None

• The Archives' map site provides a sample of its holdings of state and territory historical maps and mineral maps. The site includes three types of historical maps: (1) maps produced by G.L. Holt in Cheyenne, 1883-1890, based on U.S. Land Office records, which document settlement and development and show ranches, trails, railroads, and telegraph lines; (2) U.S. Dept. of the Interior maps, 1876-1947, showing land offices, reservations, and military posts ; and (3) transportation and postal route maps, showing time and distance between points. The State Mineral Supervisor County Maps, prepared by the WPA in 1936-1937 and revised in the mid-1940s, show oil and gas wells, pipelines, mineral rights, railroads, and waterways. The site also links to 11 maps of historic trails and sites drawn by a retired state engineer and held by the Wyoming State Historical Society. — *JD*

Encyclopedias

DB105 **The Historical Encyclopedia of Wyoming** / Thomas S. Chamblin, ed. - Cheyenne, WY : Wyoming Historical Institute, [1970]. - 2 v. (1669 p.) ; ill., maps, ports.

> Class Numbers:
> Library of Congress F761.H5
> OCLC 153948
> Notes:
> Bibliography: p. [1662]
> Contents : v. 1, [History] ; v. 2, [Biography]

• The first volume features articles about Wyoming history ("Picturesque and Romantic Wyoming"), woman suffrage, the Supreme Court, banking, education, cattle trade, agriculture, sheep raising, Indians, and Yellowstone. A chapter is devoted to each county, a ten-page section covers cities and towns, and another nine-page section gives brief biographies (with a page of thumbnail photographs) of territorial and state governors. The heart of the set consists of fairly elaborate biographies of Wyoming luminaries, "Representative Citizens of Wyoming," that occupies the last 600 pages of volume 1 and all of volume 2. The biographies are arranged in no discernible order, and many are accompanied by full-page photographs, but an index of names makes it possible to locate biographies of individuals. The historical section includes numerous photographs and line drawings of Wyoming scenes, perhaps the set's most useful feature. — *RB*

Directories

DB106   **Wyoming State Government Directory** / Wyoming Secretary of State. - [Cheyenne, WY?] : Wyoming Secretary of State, 1996?- . Annual.

Class Numbers:
Library of Congress JK7630
Government Document Wyoming SA1.8 :
OCLC 34870381
LCCN 96-658727
Notes:
Title varies: 19??-1937?, *Official Directory of Wyoming and Election Returns for ...* (biennial) ; 1976?-1995, *Wyoming Official Directory* (annual); alternate years, 1981-1989?, *Wyoming Official Directory ... and Election Returns*

• The general information section covers executive branch elected officials, state election guidelines, public information desks, and agency and board offices and personnel. The section on the legislative branch covers state House and Senate members, district maps, and committee memberships. The section on the judicial branch covers district courts, judges, judicial agencies, and district maps. Includes lists of U.S. and county officials and tribal business councils, and directories of Internet sites and e-mail addresses. Name and subject indexes. The current year is available in pdf format on the Wyoming Secretary of State official Internet page (http://soswy.state.wy.us/director/dir-toc.htm). — *JD*

Collective Biographies

DB107 **Progressive Men of the State of Wyoming.** - Chicago, IL : A.W. Bowen & Co., 1903. - 965 p. ; ports. - (Western Americana 22021).

Class Numbers:
Library of Congress F760
OCLC 6398383   6840370 (microfiche)
LCCN a 15-2727
Notes:
Available in microfiche reproduction: Ann Arbor, MI: Xerox Univ. Microfilm, 1975. 12 microfiches, 11 x 15 cm.

• Brief lives of about 1,100 citizens prominent in a range of professions and occupations. Entries arranged randomly, with an index of names. — *LMcD*

DB108 Woods, Lawrence Milton, 1932- . - **Wyoming Biographies.** - Worland, WY : High Plains Publ. Co., 1991. - 224 p. ; ports.

Class Numbers:
Library of Congress CT269
ISBN 0962333379
OCLC 24708117
LCCN 91-70461
Notes:
Includes bibliographical references (p. 207-210); index

• Biographical sketches, alphabetically arranged, of 380 influential men and women who helped shape Wyoming history, economics, culture, and politics through the territorial period until statehood, 1868-1890. The work contains an introductory essay entitled, "Wyoming in 1890," describing the territory's settlement, cattle industry, Native Americans, and legislative activity. Each entry includes birth and death dates and brief career highlights. — *GK*

Place-Names

DB109 Urbanek, Mae Bobb. - **Wyoming Place Names.** - Missoula, MT : Mountain Pr. Publ. Co., 1988. - 233 p. ; ill.

Class Numbers:
Library of Congress F759
ISBN 0878422048 (pbk.)
OCLC 15366611
LCCN 87-5755

• Urbanek's alphabetical list of place-names draws information from a multitude of sources with the goal of identifying the sources for place-names, so she ignores those named for topographic or biological features (e.g., Cottonwood Creek), and omits names whose origins she cannot identify. What remains is still fairly substantial. Towns and cities are located within counties. For mountains and peaks, Urbanek gives altitude as well as location and source of name. The amount of information for each entry varies. No index. — *MB*

Almanacs   Canada

DB110 Erwin, Marie H. - **Wyoming Historical Blue Book : A Legal and Political History of Wyoming, 1868-1943**. - Denver, CO : Bradford-Robinson Printing Co., 1946. - xxiii, 1471 p. ; ill. (some col.), ports., maps.

> Class Numbers:
> > Library of Congress JK7616
>
> OCLC 10082693
> Notes:
> > In part a Works Progress Administration project

• A snapshot of Wyoming state government during its first 75 years. Blue books, a class of state publications containing almanac-like information about state government, usually contain sections for sketches of legislators (with portraits), the procedure for presenting and debating bills, state offices and officeholders, the state constitution, members of the constitutional convention, important governmental buildings, lists of counties with dates of establishment, state flag, bird, and flower, and the like. This blue book has all that, but covers a much longer period than the usual legislative session, so is valuable for its factual and authoritative view of early Wyoming history. Index. — *RB*

DB111 Roberts, Philip J. - **Wyoming Almanac** / [by] Phil Roberts, David L. Roberts, Steven L. Roberts. - Laramie, WY : Skyline West Pr./Wyoming Almanac, 1994. - 439, [21] p. ; ill.

> Class Numbers:
> > Library of Congress F761
>
> ISBN 0914767216
> OCLC 31160317
> LCCN 94-66659

• A collection of statistics, trivia, lists, firsts, and interesting facts rather than a source for serious researchers, but its sources, editors, and contributing editors are nonetheless authoritative. Organized in broad categories such as the natural world, disasters, people, and arts, it includes burial places of the famous, fictional Wyomingites, river agreements, four worst years for forest fires, famous hats, most common marriage months, bank failures, earthquakes, fatal air crashes, famous hotels, presidential visits, dinosaur finds, and POW camps in Wyoming. With its coverage of difficult-to-research topics, lively language, and visually appealing format, it is fun to read, reflective of the state, and useful at a reference desk. An index would improve access but the broad topic arrangement makes it browsable. — *JD*

DB112 Weir, Thomas R., ed. - **Atlas of the Prairie Provinces** / ed., Thomas R. Weir ; cartographer, Geoffrey Matthews. - Toronto, ON : Oxford Univ Pr., 1971. - 31 leaves of col. maps. ; 39 x 55 cm.

> Class Numbers:
> > Library of Congress G1150
>
> ISBN 0195401786
> OCLC 2656644
> LCCN 72-183649

• Covers physical elements (relief, soil, precipitation, temperature), population (distribution and composition), and resource use (agriculture, natural resources, transportation, manufacturing). Given its age, the atlas is now primarily of historical interest but remains useful for its emphasis on the similarities among Manitoba, Saskatchewan, and Alberta—the Prairie provinces. — *LMcD*

Alberta

Bibliographies

DB113 Boultbee, Paul G., comp. - **A Central Alberta Bibliography**. - [Red Deer, AB] : Red Deer College Pr., 1986. - 58 p.

> Class Numbers:
> > Library of Congress Z1392.A4
>
> ISBN 0889950318
> OCLC 15341227

• Almost 800 items either about the region or written by authors located there, regardless of subject. Edmonton and Calgary are excluded; articles and theses are omitted. Arranged under 20 categories such as religion, literature, education, history, and agriculture. — *LMcD*

DB114 Dew, Ian F. - **Bibliography of Material Relating to Southern Alberta Published to 1970**. - [Lethbridge, AB] : Univ. of Lethbridge, Learning Resources Centre, 1975. - 407 leaves.

> Class Numbers:
> > Library of Congress F1076
>
> National Library of Canada Z1392
> OCLC 9920874

• Extensive bibliography of approximately 3,200 works, many of which deal with the southern portion of the Prairie provinces as a whole. Items about Calgary after 1890 are excluded. Organized by broad topic including native peoples, society, economy, wildlife, vegetation, and climate.

The largest sections are concerned with history and land, including geology, paleontology, and hydrology. Works whose titles do not convey their content are annotated. Although dated, sections remain useful. — *LMcD*

DB115 Krotki, Joanna E. - **Local Histories of Alberta : An Annotated Bibliography**. - 2nd ed. - [Edmonton, AB] : Dept. of Slavic and East European Studies, Univ. of Alberta : Central and East European Studies Society of Alberta, 1983. - 430 p. - (Monographs, papers, and reports [Central and East European Ethno-Cultural Groups in Alberta Study Project], 5).

> Class Numbers:
> Library of Congress Z1392.A4   F1078
> National Library of Canada FC3661
> OCLC 12106138
> LCCN 84-230161
> Notes:
> First ed. published 1980

• A list of almost 1,000 histories of communities, schools, churches, and hospitals, arranged by author or sponsoring group. Annotations indicate the villages or districts each history includes as well as ethnic composition of the area. Separate indexes by place-name, ethnic or cultural group, church or denomination, schools or colleges, hospitals, and titles. – *LMcD*

DB116 Provincial Archives of Alberta. Historical Resources Library. - **Alberta's Local Histories in the Historical Resources Library** - 8th ed. - [Edmonton, AB] : Historical Resources Library, [1989]. - 204 p.

> Class Numbers:
> Library of Congress Z1392.A4
> National Library of Canada COP.AL.1.1104
> OCLC 23049155
> LCCN 91-106439

• More than 2,600 histories of communities, churches, and schools. Arranged by community name, with full publication details and indication of indexing. Useful in combination with the more recent *Local Histories of Alberta* (**DB118**). — LMcD

DB117 Riddell, Judie. - **Local Histories of Alberta : A Bibliography of Holdings Found in Calgary Area Repositories** / [by] Judie Riddell, Marlene Knott. - Calgary, AB : Alberta Family Histories Society, 1999. - 65 p.

> Class Numbers:
> National Library of Canada   Z1392 A4
> ISBN 1895717523
> OCLC 43318336

> Notes:
> Electronic book: http://www.afhs.ab.ca/ aids/localhistory/index.html

• Arranged by community, with entries indicating publication information, presence of index, and libraries with copies. The version on the *Alberta Family Histories Society* Internet site (http://www.afhs.ab.ca) is browsable by locality; in some cases a link lists names in a particular book. Extends the coverage of the work by Krotki (**DB116**). — *LMcD*

DB118 Stephen, Marg. - **Alberta Bibliography, 1980-1987, for Adults and Young Adults** / [by] Marg Stephen, Judy Mah. - Edmonton, AB : Young Alberta Book Festival Society, 1987. - 48 p.

> Class Numbers:
> Library of Congress Z1392.A4
> National Library of Canada Z1392 A4
> ISBN 0969314701
> OCLC 16868479

• Organized by broad subject categories such as biography, history, drama, and religion, the bibliography records a fairly narrow segment of Alberta publications. Very briefly annotated except for works whose titles clearly convey their content. Oddly, there is neither author nor title index. Updated by Stephen's *Alberta Bibliography: Books by Alberta Authors and Publishers* (Edmonton: Young Alberta Book Festival Society, 1989-96). *Alberta, 1954-1979: A Provincial Bibliography* (**DB120**) covers the preceding period of Alberta publishing. — *LMcD*

DB119   Strathern, Gloria M., comp. - **Alberta, 1954-1979 : A Provincial Bibliography**. - Edmonton, AB : Univ. of Alberta, Dept. of Printing Services, 1982. - 745 p.

> OCLC 9228930

• About 3,500 books, pamphlets, and theses dealing with aspects of Alberta or written by Albertans. Serial publications, scientific and technical works, most textbooks, and government documents are excluded. The latter are covered, in part, by *Government Publications Relating to Alberta* (**DB127**). Arrangement is by a subject hierarchy adapted from *Guide to Reference Books*, with the humanities and social sciences strongly emphasized. Some entries are very briefly annotated. Author, title, subject, and series indexes. In some respects, a chronological companion to *Peel's Bibliography of the Canadian Prairies to 1953* (**DA78**). — *LMcD*

DB120   Willis, Gordon K. - **A Bibliography of Southeastern Alberta with a Map and Air Photo Catalogue**. - Edmonton, AB : Univ. of Alberta, 1977. - [55] p.

> Class Numbers:
> Library of Congress Z1392.A34
> OCLC 25432262

• The estimated 500 entries study the region from geological, environmental, social, historical, and agricultural perspectives; a considerable number are government publications or theses. Arranged by author, but lacks a subject index. The maps are listed as found in agency catalogs; the aerial photographs are enumerated by location and National Topographic series number. Some overlap with *Bibliography of Material Relating to Southern Alberta* (DB115). — *LMcD*

Manuscripts ; Archives

DB121 Archival Records of Alberta [Internet Site]. - [Edmonton, AB] : Archives Society of Alberta, 2000?- . - http://www.archivesalberta.org/general/database.htm

> Access Date: Apr. 2006
> Fees: None

• The site provides three related databases that document the people, places, and historical events of Alberta. The ANA (Archives Network of Alberta) Database contains more than 9,000 descriptive records from 40 museums, libraries, historical societies, and archives. Exploration, politics, religion, and natural resources are some of the areas covered. Alberta InSight makes accessible roughly 30,000 photographs from 18 archives. Some of the major categories include buildings, environment and nature, agriculture, farming and personal life, First Nations, railways, and public events. Alberta InWord supplies online versions of a variety of materials: diaries, letters, campaign literature, organizational minutes, radio transcripts, election pamphlets, and unpublished biographies. The largest sections cover agriculture, immigration and homesteading, politics and government, and women, whose approximately 1,500 items are drawn from ten institutions. All three databases are searched with Cinemage software. "Simple Search" indexes nine fields (titles, subjects, topics, creator etc.), while "Boolean Search" has as many as 17. The databases can be browsed by name, topic, repository, provenance, and title. The site delivers a wealth of primary resources about Alberta and points to numerous specialized repositories. — *LMcD*

DB122 A Preliminary Guide to Archival Sources Relating to Southern Alberta / comp. and ed. by members of the Univ. of Lethbridge Regional History Project, Barbara Huston [et al.]. - [Lethbridge, AB : Univ. of Lethbridge Regional History Project], 1979. - 21, [77] leaves.

> Class Numbers:
> Library of Congress F1078   Z1392.A4
> OCLC 7551087
> LCCN 81-457940

• Guide to more than 700 collections; the majority are located at the Glenbow Archives, Provincial Archives of Alberta, or the Galt Museum in Lethbridge, although other institutions are also represented. Entries provide a brief description of contents and size. Some of the collections are included in *Archival Records of Alberta* (DB122). There is a useful description of collections from federal departments such as Agriculture, Labour, and Interior with material dealing with southern Alberta ; these are located at the Public Archives of Canada (now Library and Archives Canada). — *LMcD*

DB123 University of Alberta. Archives. - **From the Past to the Future : A Guide to the Holdings of the University of Alberta Archives** / project coordinator, Bryan Corbett ; contributors : Gertrude Bloor McLaren [et al.]. - Edmonton, AB : Univ. of Alberta Archives, 1992. - xxiii, 284 p. ; ill.

> Class Numbers:
> Library of Congress CD3649.E36
> ISBN 0888647700
> OCLC 25707912
> LCCN 92-213040
> Notes:
> Also accessible as: http://www.ualberta.ca/
>   ARCHIVES/
> Includes bibliographical references; index

• Guide to records of administrative offices and academic divisions (faculties, departments, research centers, and affiliated colleges) of the largest university in the Prairie provinces. Entries provide a brief description of each unit, its history and purpose, directors, and summary holdings. The guide also describes the archives of approximately 75 organizations, such as the Riel Project, and 130 individuals, most with a connection to the University as staff or graduates. The online version updates the records of individuals to the end of 1996. — *LMcD*

DB124 University of Calgary. Libraries. Special Collections Division. - **Mapping the Territory : A Guide to the Archival Holdings, Special Collections, University of Calgary Library** / comp., Jean M. Moore ; ed., Marlys Chevrefils, Apollonia Steele. - Calgary, AB : Univ. of Calgary Pr., 1994. - 150 p. ; ill.

> Class Numbers:
> Library of Congress CD3649.C3
> ISBN 1895176530   0585173311 (electronic bk.)
> OCLC 31290690
> LCCN 91-137795
> Notes:
> Also accessible as: http://www.ucalgary.ca/
>   UofC/departments/UARC/
> Electronic book:
>   http://www.netLibrary.com/ urlapi.asp?action=
>   summary&v=1&bookid= 17644

• Among the collections Moore and her colleagues describe are many in areas of strength at the Univ. of

Calgary : music, architecture, and literature. Notable prairie writers include Robert Kroetsch (**BC72**), W.O. Mitchell (**BC74-BC75**), George Ryga (**BC77**), Guy Vanderhaege, and Rudy Wiebe (**BC78**). Prairie historians include James H. Gray and Grant MacEwan. Entries typically provide a biographical or historical sketch, collection context, physical description, and availability of finding aids. — *LMcD*

Government Publications

DB125 Alberta Queen's Printer [Internet Site]. – Edmonton, AB : Alberta Government, 2002- . - http://www.qp.gov.ab.ca/

> Access Date: July 2006
> Fees: None

• As a record of official publications, the *Queen's Printer* Internet site continues printed checklists issued under various titles such as *Government of Alberta Publications (GAP) Catalogue*. Search options are few: title or browsing by year back to 1996, with the yearly lists arranged by issuing agency. Descriptive information is brief but sometimes leads to full text. The site contains the official *Alberta Gazette* as well as acts and regulations, with searching by title, chapter or regulation number, and responsible ministry. Formatted full text can be downloaded for a fee, but is also available in html at no charge. — *LMcD*

DB126 Forsyth, Joseph. - **Government Publications Relating to Alberta : A Bibliography of Publications of the Government of Alberta from 1905 to 1968, and of Publications of the Government of Canada Relating to the Province of Alberta, from 1867 to 1968.** - High Wycombe, [Eng.] : University Microfilms, [1972?]. - 8 v. (xxxv, 3039 p.).

> Call Numbers
> National Library of Canada Z1373.5 A45
> OCLC 48999671
> Notes:
> Thesis (Fellowship)—Library Association, 1971.

• A century of official documents dealing with the political, economic, and social dimensions of Alberta. The title, though cumbersome, clearly indicates the work's scope. The introduction (p. xvii-xxxv) outlines the structure of the Alberta government and gives a brief history and function of major departments. Vols. 1-3 list 4,000 provincial documents, arranged by issuing agency; v. 4-5 provide a complete listing of Alberta statutes as well as Northwest Territories ordinances relating to Alberta and in force as of 1968; v. 6 lists approximately 800 federal publications. Vol. 7 provides author, title and series indexes, and v. 8 a subject index and keyword index to the statutes. Holdings, mainly of federal libraries, are indicated. — *LMcD*

Encyclopedias

DB127 Our Future Our Past : the Alberta Heritage Digitization Project [Internet Site]. – Calgary, AB : Univ. of Calgary Pr., 1999- . - http://www.ourfutureourpast.ca/

> OCLC 47864677
> Access Date: May 2006
> Fees: None

• AHDP brings together a multitude of resources exploring the multifaceted history of Alberta. Organized largely by format, it consists of several sections, each with its own search options. The art area provides 3,500 works and exhibition catalogs from the Nickle Arts Museum at the Univ. of Calgary; it can be searched by artist, subject, medium, title, object, and keyword. The Calgary Stampede archives has images, corporate records and printed ephemera of one of the city's most distinctive cultural events. Early newspapers of more than 40 communities are online; coverage varies by title and they can be browsed by date or by place. A series of educational modules for K-12 students covers themes such as cowboy culture, prairie agriculture, and First Nations peoples. The Isabel Campbell Collection of 1,200 photographs of the Grande Prairie area is searchable by subject and date. The Alberta Airphoto Collection contains 30,000 images of urban areas in the province, taken between 1924 and 1952. The legal section includes statutes, ordinances, and Legislative Assembly bills, debates, and journals. Perhaps the most substantial area of the Internet site contains an estimated 700 local histories, with Boolean searching by author, title, subject, and full text. Other areas are devoted to medical history, multiculturalism, municipal bylaws, and folklore. The Internet site provides a rich and growing collection of material on the history and culture of Alberta. — *LMcD*

Chronologies

DB128 Levasseur-Ouimet, France. - **D'année en année, de 1659 à 2000 : une présentation synchronique des événements historiques franco-albertains.** - Edmonton, AB : Institut du patrimoine, Faculté Saint-Jean, 2003. - 422 p. : ill., ports.

> Class Numbers:
> National Library of Canada FC3700.5
> ISBN 9782980495816
> OCLC 51274834

• A chronological synopsis of the history of the francophone community of Alberta, divided into 11 time periods. Each section begins with an overview essay providing context for the span of years that follow. Years are presented in terms of noteworthy events—national, provincial, and local—in areas such as religion, politics, history, education, media, and various cultural forms (music, dance, theater). Entries within individual years consist of single paragraphs for each element, carefully documented with bibliographic references. The subject index includes individuals as well as place-names. Convincingly demonstrates the contributions of French Canadians to the development of a region sometimes viewed as an Anglophone monolith. – *LMcD*

Collective Biographies
See also **Who's Who in Southern Alberta, AC17**

DB129 Blue, John, 1874-1945. - **Alberta, Past and Present : Historical and Biographical**. - Chicago, IL : Pioneer Historical Publ. Co., 1924. - 3 v. ; ports.

> Class Numbers:
> > Library of Congress F1076
> > National Library of Canada FC3661
> > OCLC 14018840

• Following a conventional history (v. 1), volumes 2-3 contain biographies of an estimated 800 Albertans of varying degrees of prominence. In lieu of alphabetical arrangement, each volume has a name index. Similar in scale and approach to counterpart works for Saskatchewan **(DB172)** and Manitoba **(DB149)** of roughly the same era. — *LMcD*

DB130 MacRae, Archibald Oswald. - **History of the Province of Alberta**. - [Calgary, AB?] : Western Canada History Co., 1912. - 2 v. (1042 p.) ; ill., ports.

> Class Numbers:
> > Library of Congress F1076
> > National Library of Canada FC3655
> > OCLC 7209297
> > LCCN 15-14551
> > Notes:
> > > Electronic book:
> > > > http://www.ourroots.ca/e/toc.aspx?id=9034
> > > > (v.1)
> > > Electronic book:
> > > > http://www.ourroots.ca/e/toc.aspx?id=9090
> > > > (v.2)
> > > Includes bibliographical references

• The first volume covers the early history of the province in fairly standard fashion. Of greater interest is the second volume, consisting of biographical accounts of 584 men and, tellingly, only two women. Individuals included appear to represent a cross-section of turn-of-the-century Alberta society in background and occupation. About one quarter of the biographies have photographs. The reference value of the work has been enhanced by *Pioneer Albertans, 1912: An Index to Biographies of over 500 Pioneer Albertans, with Cross-References to 950 Spouses and Mothers, Compiled from*

History of Alberta *by Archibald Oswald MacRae, Ph.D.*, by Margaret Mann and Paul Shaw (Nanaimo, BC : Nanaimo Family History Society, 1998). — *LMcD*

DB131 **Who's Who in Alberta : A Biographical Directory**. - Saskatoon, SK : Lyone Publications, 1974. - 224 p. ; ports.

> Class Numbers:
> > Library of Congress F1075.8
> > National Library of Canada FC3655
> > Notes:
> > > Electronic book (1st ed., 1969) :
> > > > http://www.ourfutureourpast.ca/loc_hist/toc.
> > > > aspx?id=2363

• Biographical information on approximately 2,000 individuals from a wide variety of occupations and backgrounds, arranged alphabetically. — *LMcD*

Atlases

DB132 **The Atlas of Alberta : A Special Project of** *Alberta Report*, the Weekly Newsmagazine. - Edmonton, AB : Interwest Publications, 1984. - 160 p. ; ill. col. maps ; 35 cm.

> Class Numbers:
> > Library of Congress G1165
> ISBN 0969185219
> OCLC 12370621
> LCCN 84-245831
> Notes:
> > Scales differ

• The first section illustrates the cartographic history of Alberta, beginning with David Thompson's 1813 map and ending with a coal mine map of Edmonton (1971). An overview includes maps of rural municipalities, regions of the province, and a gazetteer. Much of the work consists of detailed street maps of 39 major cities and towns, indicating schools, churches, hotels, and points of interest. The concluding section covers natural resources. More popular in approach than the scholarly *Atlas of Alberta* **(DB134)**. — *LMcD*

DB133 University of Alberta. Dept. of Geography. - **Atlas of Alberta**. - Edmonton, AB : Univ. of Alberta Pr., in association with the Univ. of Toronto Pr., 1969. - 158 p. (chiefly col. maps) ; 44 cm.

> Class Numbers:
> > Library of Congress G1165
> OCLC 93833
> LCCN 78-653863
> Notes:

Official centennial project of the Government of
Alberta and the Univ. of Alberta.

• An exceedingly thorough atlas, arranged by broad
categories (relief and geology, water, soil, wildlife,
population, agriculture), with maps, sometimes full-page,
that in many cases show features in fine detail. An end-
paper map shows a projection of the world with Alberta,
not unexpectedly, at the center. Some maps are now out of
date (highway traffic, air traffic, retail markets, number of
telephone calls, metropolitan areas), and maps are confined
to Alberta, so that some geographic features that verge into
other provinces (e.g., the Cypress Hills) stop at the border.
Index of place-names. Thorough, as one might expect from
a university's Department of Geography, but needing to be
updated. — *RB*

Gazetteers

**DB134   Gazetteer of Canada : Alberta = Répertoire
géographique du Canada : Alberta.** - 3rd ed. – Ottawa, ON
: Published for the Canadian Permanent Committee on
Geographical Names by the Geographical Services
Division, Canada Centre for Mapping, Dept. of Energy,
Mines and Resources Canada, 1988. - 64 p. ; fold. map.

> Class Numbers:
> > Library of Congress F1075.4
> ISBN 0660539942
> OCLC 21046074
> LCCN 89-202093
> Notes:
> > Available in ASCII format on 3.5-inch floppy
> > > diskettes, CD-ROM, and electronic transfer
> > First ed. pub. in 1958
> > Text in English and French

• Approximately 9,000 names, with latitude, longitude, and
map reference. — *LMcD*

Place-Names

DB135   Place Names of Alberta. - Calgary, AB :
Alberta Culture and Multiculturalism and Friends of
Geographical Names of Alberta Society : Univ. of Calgary
Pr., 1991-1996. - 4 v. ; ill., maps.

> Class Numbers:
> > Library of Congress F1070.4
> National Library of Canada FC3656
> ISBN 0585213925 (electronic bk.)
> > 0919813739 (v.1)   091981395X (v.2)
> > 091895176441 (v.3)   189517659X (v.4)
> > 0919813917 (set)
> OCLC 26131065
> Notes:

Contents: v. 1. Mountains, Mountain Parks,
and Foothills / ed. and introd. by Aphrodite
Karamitsanis; v. 2. Southern Alberta / ed. and
introd. by Aphrodite Karamitsanis; v. 3.
Central Alberta / ed. and introd. by Tracey
Harrison; v. 4. Northern Alberta / ed. and
introd. by Merrily K. Aubrey Electronic book
(v. 1): http://www.ourfutureourpast.ca/
loc_hist/toc.aspx?id=4053
Electronic book (v. 2): http://www.ourfutur
eourpast.ca/loc_hist/toc.aspx?id=4054
Electronic book (v. 3): http://www.ourfutureour
past.ca/loc_hist/ toc.aspx?id=4055
Electronic book (v. 4): http://www.ourfutureour
past.ca/ loc_hist/toc.aspx?id=4056

• Volumes 2-3 cover the prairie regions of the province, with
arrangement by local name. The work includes communities
of various sizes (towns, villages, hamlets), provincial parks,
and geographical features such as lakes, coulees, and fords.
Entries supply information on the derivation and
significance of names. Additional elements include National
Topographic System number, legal description (section,
range, township, and meridian), latitude and longitude, and
direct distance to nearest significant population center.
Combines features of a gazetteer with local history ; has
numerous photographs in color and extensive bibliographies.
The most comprehensive source, among a number of similar
works, on Alberta toponymy. — *LMcD*

DB136   Canadian Board on Geographic Names. -
Place-Names of Alberta. - Ottawa, ON : Publ. for the
Geographic Board by the Dept. of the Interior, 1928. - 138
p. ; fold. map.

> Class Numbers:
> > Library of Congress F1076
> OCLC 2203539
> LCCN 28-18075

DB136a   Holmgren, Eric J. - **Over 2000 Place Names of
Alberta** / by Eric J. Holmgren and Patricia M. Holmgren.
- Expanded 3rd ed. - Saskatoon, SK : Western Producer
Prairie Books, 1976. – 301, [9] p. ; [8] leaves of plates, ill.,
map, ports.

> Class Numbers:
> > Library of Congress F1075.4
> National Library of Canada FC3656
> ISBN 0919306675   0919306756 (pbk.)
> OCLC 3344842
> LCCN 77-361631
> Notes:
> > Bibliography: p. [307]-[309]
> First ed. has title : *2000 Place Names of Alberta*

**DB136b   Mardon, Ernest G., 1928-   . - Community
Names of Alberta** / Ernest G. Mardon and Austin A.

Mardon ; ed. by Larry Erdos. - Expanded 2d ed. - Edmonton, AB : Golden Meteorite Pr., 1998. - xxiv, 426 p. ; [1] folded leaf plate, map.

Class Numbers:
Library of Congress F1075.4
ISBN 1895385679   1895385695 (pbk.)
OCLC 43913326
LCCN 00-302340
Notes:
First ed. published 1973

• The Canadian Board on Geographic Names laid the foundation for later works in *Place-Names of Alberta*, giving brief location and naming information for communities, post offices, many natural features, and all railway stations. Eric Holmgren's *Over 2000 Place-Names of Alberta* builds on the 1928 work, corrects inaccuracies, and places greater emphasis on the historical background of names. Perhaps the most interesting is Ernest Mardon's *Community Names of Alberta*, which covers almost 2,000 places, listing location, foundation date, population figures in 1972 and 1997, and the colorful origins of many names. The detailed index includes personal names, occupations, and country/province/state of the original settlers who influenced the selection of place-names. — *LMcD*

Manitoba

Bibliographies

DB137 A Bibliography of Manitoba Local History : A Guide to Local and Regional Histories Written about Communities in Manitoba / Christopher Hackett, ed. - [Winnipeg, MB?] : Manitoba Historical Society, 1989. - 156 p.

Class Numbers:
Library of Congress F1063   Z1392.M35
ISBN 0921950004
OCLC 26310540
LCCN 90-186389
Notes:
Includes bibliographical references (p. xv) ;
indexes
Rev. ed. of: *Local History in Manitoba*. 1976

• In addition to the expected works covering towns, rural municipalities, churches and schools, the bibliography also includes ethnic and religious groups with a significant presence in Manitoba. The main part consists of almost 1,000 entries, arranged by author or title, followed by extensive geographical and subject indexes. Reflecting Winnipeg's dominant position in the province, a separately numbered section of 330 items covers the city and the Red River Settlement, with its own subject index. Articles in Manitoba Historical Society journals are excluded. For most works, at least one library location is provided. — *LMcD*

DB138   Scott, Michael M., comp. and ed. - **A Bibliography of Western Canadian Studies Relating to Manitoba** / comp. and ed. for the Western Canada Research Council. - Winnipeg, MB : [s.n.] ; [Western Canada Research Council], 1967. - 79 leaves.

Class Numbers:
National Library of Canada   Z1392 M35
OCLC 2030947

• Separate sequences for theses (most from the Univ. of Manitoba), published studies (drawn from the Manitoba Provincial Library and Univ. of Manitoba), articles, and reports, arranged by broad subject categories such as history and literature. Some sections are out of date, but overall the work retains a measure of utility. — *LMcD*

Manuscripts ; Archives

DB139 Haglund, Diane. - **Directory of Archives in Manitoba**. - Winnipeg, MB : Manitoba Council of Archives, 1989. - 50 p.

Class Numbers:
Library of Congress CD3646.M3
ISBN 0969343116
OCLC 23769277
LCCN 91-137795
Notes:
Indexes

• Lists 45 archival repositories, giving contact information, description of facilities and services, historical background, and specialties. French archives are described in French. A thematic index groups archives by type: church, law, medical, military, etc. Under its later name, the Association for Manitoba Archives sponsors *Manitoba Archival Information Network* (http:// scaa.usask.ca/main/), a database of materials at the collection level in 17 institutions. MAIN in turn is linked to *Saskatchewan Archival Information Network* (http://scaa.usask. ca/sain/), organized by the Saskatchewan Council for Archives and Archivists. SAIN contains collection descriptions from 18 Saskatchewan archives. MAIN and SAIN can be searched separately or simultaneously in basic (title, names, keywords), browse or advanced modes. — *LMcD*

DB140 Inventory of Archival Material in Western Manitoba / K.S. Coates, J.C. Everitt, W.R. Morrison, eds. ; Roberta Kempthorne, principal researcher ; Deb Chapman, Jacquie Mackalski, Colleen Snell, associate researchers. - [Brandon, MB] : Brandon Univ. Pr., 1987-1989. - 3 v.

Class Numbers:
Library of Congress CD3646.M3

OCLC 22108370
LCCN 90-172760

• A guide to historical records (for example, minutes, school registers, membership lists, graveyard transcriptions, tax and assessment rolls, unpublished family histories) in repositories or private collections in approximately 125 communities. Arranged by community, then by collection; entries include location, contact information, conditions of access, and description. Lists of collections by category (e.g., agriculture, businesses, cemeteries, churches, community clubs, health care facilities, municipalities, school divisions, service clubs, sports teams). The guide assembles information on the resources in a remarkably diverse, if sometimes obscure, range of organizations. — *LMcD*

DB141 University of Manitoba Libraries. Dept. of Archives and Special Collections. - **A Guide to the Major Holdings of the Department of Archives and Special Collections, the University of Manitoba Libraries** / comp. by Richard E. Bennett [et al.]. - Winnipeg, MB : Dept. of Archives and Special Collections, Univ. of Manitoba, 1993. - 138 p. ; ill.

Class Numbers:
National Library of Canada CD3649 W5
ISBN 0919932002
OCLC 28024675
Notes:
Also accessible as : http://www.umanitoba.
ca/libraries/ units/archives/
Index

• A directory of the University's manuscripts and archives, where prairie literature and western agriculture are major strengths. The literary collections include prairie writers (Frederick Grove, Dorothy Livesay [BC73] and Ralph Connor, among others), publishing houses (Alberta's NeWest Press, Saskatchewan's Thistledown Press, and Manitoba's Turnstone Press), and the Prairie Theatre Exchange. Collections are listed by name of individual or organization. Entries provide a brief history or biographical sketch, contents note, size, any restrictions, and finding aids. The archives contain records of administrative and academic units, arranged by originating office. Entries provide a brief history of each, contents description, and collection size. The electronic version lists additional collections and has links to online finding aids. — *LMcD*

Government Publications

DB142   **Manitoba Government Publications Monthly Checklist = Publications du Gouvernement du Manitoba, Liste Mensuelle.** - Winnipeg, MB : Legislative Library, 1975-   . Monthly.

Class Numbers:
National Library of Canada Z1373.5
OCLC 2249877
LCCN cn 75-82887
Notes:
Text in English only, 1975-1988 ; text in English and French, 1989-

• Arranged by department, agency, committee, etc., under the ministry to which they report. The current ten issues are available on the *Manitoba Legislative Library* Internet site (http://www.gov.mb.ca/chc/leg-lib/checklist.html). — *LMcD*

Encyclopedias

DB143 The Encyclopedia of Manitoba / Ingeborg Boyens, managing ed. - Winnipeg, MB : Great Plains Publ., 2007. - 814 p. : ill. (some col.), maps (chiefly col.).

Class Numbers:
National Library of Canada FC3354
OCLC 150223490
Notes:
"Recommended Reading" : p. 784-797
Index

• The approximately 2,000 entries in this colorful work combine to present a panorama of Manitoba. Comprehensive in scope, it draws on the expertise of several hundred contributors to provide concise but thorough coverage of a wide variety of topics in the history, culture, economy, and physical environment of Manitoba. Short accounts of most communities, brief biographies of persons as disparate as TV game show host Monty Hall and the considerably more cerebral Marshall McLuhan as well as many figures of lesser celebrity, and significant historical events are only some of the encyclopedia's major elements; in fact, almost every facet of life in the province is well represented. Entries are sprinkled with boldface type leading to additional information in related items. A dozen longer essays treat broad subjects such as geography, politics, and agriculture. Manitoba has a smaller prairie zone than its sister provinces but that area contains the majority of the province's population; the distribution of entries accordingly reflects the dominance of the prairie region. Almost 1,000 illustrations enhance the text. A welcome addition to the ranks of jurisdiction-specific encyclopedias. Essential. – *LMcD*

DB144 Hamilton, Gwain E. - **In the Beginning.** - Steinbach, MB : Derksen Printers, 1967. - 362 p. ; ill., port.

Class Numbers:
Library of Congress F1063
OCLC 159693
LCCN 75-499785

Notes:

"Source material" : p. 359-362

Electronic book: http://www.ourroots.ca/e/toc. aspx?id=757

• An alphabetic arrangement of significant places, people, terminology, organizations, and events in the history of Manitoba. Popular rather than overtly academic but a convenient source of information nonetheless. — *LMcD*

Collective Biographies

See also **Representative Men of Manitoba, History in Portraiture, AC20**

DB145 Bryce, George, 1844-1931. - **A History of Manitoba, its Resources and People.** – Toronto, ON : Canada History Co., 1906. - 692 p. ; ports.

Class Numbers:

Library of Congress F1063

National Library of Canada FC3361

OCLC 4620168

Notes:

Electronic book: http://peel.library.ualberta.ca/ cocoon/peel/2915.html

• Following a fairly traditional and uncritical history of the province, the second half of the book consists of biographical accounts of an estimated 400 prominent figures, some with photographs, from various elements of Manitoba society. Not organized alphabetically, but there is an index of names. — *LMcD*

DB146 Harvey, Robert, b. 1884. - **Pioneers of Manitoba.** - Winnipeg, MB : Prairie Publ. Co., 1970. - 82 p. ; map, ports.

Class Numbers:

Library of Congress F1061.8

OCLC 694442

LCCN 73-162877

• Biographical sketches, two or three pages in length, of 24 notable Manitobans who promoted the development of the province in diverse ways; half are not included in the much larger *Dictionary of Manitoba Biography* (**AC18**). Nellie McClung, celebrated suffragist and prairie novelist, is the sole woman included. Not arranged alphabetically. — *LMcD*

DB147 Manitoba Library Association. - **Pioneers and Early Citizens of Manitoba : A Dictionary of Manitoba**

Biography from the Earliest Times to 1920. - Winnipeg, MB : Peguis Publ., 1971. - 268 p. ; map.

Class Numbers:

Library of Congress F1061.8

National Library of Canada FC3355

ISBN 0919566014

OCLC 521310

LCCN 72-191541

Notes:

Bibliography: p. 266-268

Electronic book: http://www.mhs.mb.ca/docs/ people/pioneers.shtml

• Biographical accounts of important figures in the history and development of Manitoba. No photographs or portraits. Many of the individuals also appear in *Dictionary of Manitoba Biography* (**AC18**). — *LMcD*

DB148 Pioneers and Prominent People of Manitoba / [ed., Walter McRaye ; historical introd. by W. J. Healy]. – Winnipeg, MB : Canadian Publicity Co., 1925. - 353 p. ; ill.

Class Numbers:

Library of Congress F1061.8

National Library of Canada FC3355

OCLC 12741951

• Directory of an estimated 500 men and women who contributed to the evolution of Manitoba. The single-paragraph entries provide biographical facts and are not arranged alphabetically. Given the name of the publisher, one wonders about the basis for inclusion, but over time the work has acquired genealogical and historical interest. Some overlap of coverage with *The Story of Manitoba* (**DB150**) but the latter contains more detailed information. — *LMcD*

DB149 Schofield, Frank Howard, 1859-1929. - **The Story of Manitoba.** - Winnipeg, MB : S.J. Clarke, 1913. - 3 v. ; ports., maps.

Class Numbers:

Library of Congress F1063

National Library of Canada FC3231

OCLC 12797578

LCCN 15-5765

Notes:

Electronic book: http://www.ourroots.ca/e/toc. aspx?id= 6049 (v.3)

Electronic book: http://www.ourroots.ca/e/toc. aspx?id= 6055 (v.1)

Electronic book: http://www.ourroots.ca/e/toc. aspx?id= 8218 (v.2)

• The initial volume is a general history of the area that eventually became Manitoba. The other volumes consist of brief biographies of an estimated 1,100 Manitobans prominent in a variety of fields. Not arranged alphabetically, the sketches appear to be uniformly laudatory; *Dictionary of Canadian Biography* (**AC15**) provides a more objective assessment of some of the better-known figures. — *LMcD*

Atlases

DB150 Manitoba. Surveys and Mapping Branch. - **Atlas of Manitoba** / Thomas R. Weir, ed. – Winnipeg, MB : Surveys and Mapping Branch, Dept. of Natural Resources, 1983. - 1 atlas (157 p.) ; col. maps ; 40 cm.

> Class Numbers:
> Library of Congress G1155
> ISBN 0771100019
> OCLC 10824965
> LCCN 84-675011
> Notes:
> Cover title : *Manitoba Atlas*
> Includes index
> Scales differ

• The 317 maps are organized in four thematic sections covering the physical and biological environment (climate, vegetation, geology, hydrology, wildlife), people (distribution, rural/urban, ethnicity, language, religion), primary economy (agriculture, mining, forestry), and secondary economy (manufacturing, labor, transportation). The concluding section consists of reference maps (statistical and administrative divisions) and a gazetteer. Many of the social and economic maps are dated, but the atlas provides an overview of the province. — *LMcD*

DB151 Warkentin, John, 1928- , ed. - **Manitoba Historical Atlas : A Selection of Facsimile Maps, Plans, and Sketches from 1612 to 1969** / ed. with introd. and annotations by John Warkentin and Richard I. Ruggles. - Winnipeg, MB : Historical and Scientific Society of Manitoba, 1970. - 585 p. ; ill., maps ; 30 cm.

> Class Numbers:
> Library of Congress G1156.S1
> OCLC 204948
> LCCN 71-654514
> Notes:
> Bibliography: p. 575-585

• A collection of 312 maps and plans illustrating the evolution of Manitoba. Divided into historically significant time periods: 1612-1800, 1801-1869, and 1870-1969, each with essays providing context. The 17th- and 18th-century items are arranged chronologically to show the spread of exploration. The 19th- and 20th-century maps are arranged thematically (boundaries, settlement surveys, land surveys, communication, early settlement patterns, among others), then by date. Each map has a brief analysis and bibliographic description on the facing page. A

scholarly compilation illustrating the development of both Manitoba and historical cartography. — *LMcD*

Gazetteers

DB152 Gazetteer of Canada : Manitoba = **Répertoire toponymique du Canada : Manitoba.** – Ottawa, ON : Published for the Canadian Permanent Committee on Geographical Names by the Centre for Topographic Information, Geomatics Canada, Natural Resources Canada, and the Land Information Branch, Manitoba Natural Resources, 1999. - xxvii, 127 p. ; col. maps.

> Class Numbers:
> Library of Congress F1061.4
> National Library of Canada FC3356
> ISBN 0660607867
> OCLC 41431910
> Notes:
> Available in ASCII format on 3.5-inch floppy
> diskettes, CD-ROM, and electronic transfer
> First ed. published in 1955
> Text in English and French

• Approximately 17,200 names, with latitude, longitude, and map references. — *LMcD*

Place-Names

DB153 Geographical Names of Manitoba. - [Winnipeg, MB] : Manitoba Conservation, 2000. - 323 p. : ill., col. map.

> Class Numbers:
> Library of Congress F1061.4
> National Library of Canada FC3356
> ISBN 0771115172
> OCLC 46618791
> LCCN 2003-386198
> Notes:
> Includes bibliographical references (p. 308-
> 319)
> Prepared by Manitoba Geographical Names
> Program

• A guide to the location, history and origin of 12,000 names of communities and natural features. Many small settlements, school districts, and railway points are excluded. Names are followed by a map reference in the National Topographic System 1:50,000 series, brief location note and derivation. Glossary of native root words used in names (p. iv). Related works include J.B. Rudnyckyj's *Manitoba : Mosaic of Place Names* (Winnipeg, MB : Canadian Institute of Onomastic Sciences, 1970), covering 1,400 names, and Penny Ham's *Place Names of Manitoba* (Saskatoon,SK: Western Producer Prairie Books, 1980), 1,800 names. Both provide more information about fewer places but in a more interesting way. All three titles build on the original work in the Geographic Board of Canada's *Place-Names of Manitoba* (Ottawa: King's Printer, 1933). – *LMcD*

Almanacs

DB154   **Almanach français du Manitoba** / Bureau de direction du Centre d'études franco-canadiennes de l'Ouest, Collège de Saint-Boniface ; Edmond Cormier et al.]. - Saint-Boniface, MB : Centre d'études franco-canadiennes de l'Ouest, Collège de Saint-Boniface, 1984. - 176 p. ; ill., ports.

> Class Numbers:
> National Library of Canada FC3361
> ISBN 0919841058
> OCLC 15965487

• Curious amalgam of almanac and local history ; some of the almanac information, especially political, is out of date. Provides a snapshot, literally, of 55 communities with a substantial franco-phone population. Each is allotted two pages for a brief history and a description of the area as of the early 1980s. Maps locate the municipalities, not all of which are in the prairie region of the province. Although not scholarly, the work conveniently identifies French communities in Manitoba and summarizes their development. — *LMcD*

Saskatchewan

Bibliographies

DB155 Arora, Ved Parkash. - **The Saskatchewan Bibliography.** - Regina, SK : Saskatchewan Provincial Library, 1980. - 787 p.

> Class Numbers:
> Library of Congress Z1392.S2
> ISBN 0919059007   0919059015 (pbk.)
> LCCN 81-142259
> Notes:
> Electronic book: http://www.ourroots.ca/e/
> toc.aspx?id=1370 (supplement)

• Major topical areas include agriculture, economy, education, ethnic groups, history, Indians, literature, politics, and religion. Dates of coverage are 1905-1979; the editor excludes articles and treats government publications selectively. Includes author, title, and subject indexes and indicates holding institutions. Useful as a starting point for research on Saskatchewan. A first supplement (694 p.) covering 1979-1993, by the same author and publisher, appeared in 1993. — *LMcD*

DB156 Lyle, Guy Redvers. - **British Emigration into the Saskatchewan Valley : The Barr Colony, 1903, its Bibliographical Foundation.** - [Atlanta, GA?] : [s.n.], 1975. - 57 leaves.

> Class Numbers:
> National Library of Canada FC3217.4
> OCLC 3221333
> Notes:On spine : *The Barr Colony, 1903 : its
> Bibliographical Foundation*
> Photocopy of typescript

• Bibliography of writings related to a British settlement established in Saskatchewan under particularly inauspicious circumstances—inadequate preparation compounded by climatic and agricultural ignorance as well as claims of profiteering. Sections treat the founders of the colony, official material (correspondence, government publications, plans, contemporary records), contemporary newspaper articles, first-hand accounts, and secondary sources. Partially annotated. — *LMcD*

DB157 Saskatchewan Local Histories at the Legislative Library / comp. by Kim Heidebrecht and Liza Leutenegger ; ed. by Leslie Polsom. – Regina, SK : Saskatchewan Legislative Library, 2006. - 238, 38 p.

> Class Numbers:
> National Library of Canada FC3511
> ISBN 0973952601
> OCLC 68815121
> Notes:
> Includes index

• Bibliography of approximately 900 histories of Saskatchewan settlements of various sizes (cities, towns, villages) as well as individual churches, school districts, rural municipalities, First Nations reserves, and Hutterite colonies. Histories of the province and associations such as service clubs are not included. Arranged by title. Some of the community histories are available electronically at *Our Roots* Internet site (**AD13**). Although the indexing is not as detailed as that of *Saskatchewan Local History Directory* (**DB159**), the bibliography includes newer works not included in the latter. — *LMcD*

Manuscripts ; Archives

DB158 Maier, Sharon, comp. - **Saskatchewan Local History Directory : A Locality Guide to Community and Church Histories in the Prairie History Room, Regina Public Library.** - Corrected and reprinted ed. - Regina, SK : Prairie History Room, Regina Public Library, 2002. – 2 v.

> Class Numbers:
> National Library of Canada FC 3544.9

Notes:

Originally produced 1990

• Arranged by locality (communities, rural municipalities, school districts, Indian reserves, post offices, and named settlements), with author, title, date and call number of the books listed. The full text of some of the local histories is available on the *Our Roots* Internet site (**AD13**). — *LMcD*

DB159 Saskatchewan Archives Board. - **Guide des sources historiques des francophones aux Archives de la Saskatchewan**. - [Régina, SK] : Société historique de la Saskatchewan, 1992. - 102 p. ; ports. - (Saskatchewan Archives reference series, 1).

Class Numbers:
Library of Congress F1074.7.F83
National Library of Canada Z1392 S27
ISBN 0920895050
OCLC 27217003
Notes:
First ed., 1983
Foreword in English; introd. in English and French

• A guide to collections documenting the history and experiences of French-speaking communities and individuals in Saskatchewan, held by the Saskatchewan Archives Board. Arrangement is in part by format: federal and provincial publications; documents from organizations concerned with preserving French culture and language; histories of French communities, parishes and dioceses, listed by place; personal papers and newspaper clippings of individuals and families, arranged by surname. Other sections contain audiovisual material and oral histories, listed by interviewee with place and date; Saskatchewan newspapers listed by place, with publication dates and frequency; photos, selectively listed. Entries provide brief descriptions, extent and format; finding aids (*répertoire donné*) are indicated. Some of the material is also listed in *Guide des sources bibliographiques des communautés francophones de la Saskatchewan* (**CC30**). — *LMcD*

DB160 University of Saskatchewan. Archives. - **The University of Saskatchewan Archives : Guide to Holdings** / contributors : Cheryl Avery [et al.]. - [Saskatoon, SK] : Univ. of Saskatchewan Archives, 1994. - 276 leaves ; [20] leaves of plates ; ill., ports.

Class Numbers:
National Library of Canada CD3649 S37
OCLC 32543745
Notes:
Also accessible as : http://www.usask.ca/
archives/index.php
Includes bibliographical references ; index

• The first part consists of the *fonds* (records) of administrative offices, academic colleges and their subject departments, and service units. The second contains fonds of individuals and related organizations. Entries indicate inclusive dates, formats, size, short history or biographical sketch, brief description, and finding aids. University chronology on p. iv-viii. The online version can be searched or browsed by ten elements such as title, name, subject, and provenance. — *LMcD*

Government Publications

DB161 Checklist of Saskatchewan Government Publications [Internet Site]. – Regina, SK : Legislative Library of Saskatchewan, 1997– . - http://www.legassembly.sk.ca/leglibrary/

Access Date: Apr. 2006
Notes:
Also issued in paper: annual, 1976-1981; monthly,
July 1982-
Fees: None

• A monthly list of provincial documents, arranged by issuing agency, beginning with January 1997. The usefulness is reduced by the lack of a search mechanism (apart from Adobe Acrobat's in the individual issues) and cumulations. The Legislative Library also compiled a historical listing of Saskatchewan government publications (**DB163**). — *LMcD*

DB162 MacDonald, Christine. - **Publications of the Governments of the North-West Territories, 1876-1905 and of the Province of Saskatchewan, 1905-1952**. - Regina, SK : Legislative Library, 1952. - 109 p.

Class Numbers:
Library of Congress Z1373.5
OCLC 3078887
LCCN 53-38784

• Arranged in separate sequences by departments, bureaus, commissions, crown corporations, and miscellaneous committees ; serials and special publications listed under each. Lacks title index. — *LMcD*

Encyclopedias

DB163 The Encyclopedia of Saskatchewan. - Regina, SK : Univ. of Regina, Canadian Plains Research Center, 2005. - xx, 1071 p. ; ill. (some col.), col. maps.

Class Numbers:
Library of Congress F1071
National Library of Canada FC3504
ISBN 0889771758
OCLC 57639332

Notes:

Includes bibliographical references ; indexes

• More than 2,300 entries, by 750 contributors, examine all facets of the historic, economic, cultural, and social life of Saskatchewan. Entries are signed and many include brief bibliographies; highlighted terms lead to related information. Twenty-one detailed thematic essays provide overviews of major areas such as aboriginals, agriculture, health, history, politics, social policy, and women. Appendixes list contributors and entries arranged by broad subject. Index of names referred to in the text. Visually appealing, in part because of striking photos by the renowned prairie photographer Courtney Milne. Lavishly illustrated with more than 1,000 maps, graphs, and photos. *E-Sask*, the online version with video and audio clips, updated statistical information, and additional photographs, is available without charge at http://esask. uregina.ca. The thematic essays and selected entries also have French translations. A project celebrating the province's centennial in 2005, the encyclopedia is the definitive reference work on Saskatchewan. — *LMcD*

Atlases

DB164 Atlas of Saskatchewan / director and ed., Ka-iu Fung ; assistant eds., Bill Barry, Michael Wilson ; technical (GIS) consultant, Lawrence Martz ; computer cartographers, Gerald Romme, Keith Bigelow, Elise Pietroniro. - 2nd ed. - Saskatoon, SK : Univ. of Saskatchewan, 1999. - 336 p. : col. ill., col. maps. ; 35 cm.

Class Numbers:

Library of Congress G1160

ISBN 0888803877

OCLC 42138149

LCCN 2004-396457

Notes:

Also available on CD-ROM

First ed. publ. 1969

Includes bibliographical references (p. 288-293) ;

indexes

• The broadly based atlas is organized thematically, with sections examining major physical and human dimensions of Saskatchewan—archaeology, history, physical environment, wildlife, natural resources, population, economy, and urban environment. A great deal of very specific information is presented through eye-catching maps, explanatory text, photos, and graphs, combining to provide a multidimensional portrait of the province. Includes gazetteers of physical features and settlements. A fundamental reference for the physical, economic, and social environment of Saskatchewan. — *LMcD*

Gazetteers

DB165 Gazetteer of Canada : Saskatchewan = Répertoire toponymique du Canada : Saskatchewan. – Ottawa, ON : Published for the Canadian Permanent Committee on Geographical Names by the Centre for Topographic Information, Geomatics Canada, Natural Resources Canada, and the SaskGeomatics Division, Saskatchewan Property Management Corporation, 1998. - xx, 93 p. ; 1 folded col. map.

Class Numbers:

Library of Congress F1070.4

National Library of Canada FC3506

ISBN 0660605406

OCLC 48441654

Notes:

Available in ASCII format on 3.5-inch flop-

py diskettes, CD-ROM, and electronic transfer

First ed. published in 1957

Text in English and French

• Offers 12,500 names of populated places, geographical features, federal and provincial parks, and First Nations reserves, with latitude, longitude and reference to the map (scale 1:50 000) inserted in the pocket. — *LMcD*

Place-Names

DB166 Barry, Bill, 1942-   . - Geographic Names of Saskatchewan. - Regina, SK : People Places Publ., 2005. - 480 p. ; maps.

Class Numbers:

Library of Congress F1070.4

National Library of Canada FC3506

ISBN 1897010192

OCLC 61526351

LCCN 2006-365511

Notes:

Includes bibliographical references (p. 475)

• Dictionary of name origins both for communities of various sizes and for physical features. Entries include grid references to maps on front and back inside covers and official provincial road maps, legal land description, location, dates of operation (rural post offices), and derivation of name. Places not in boldface are essentially defunct. Features honoring military personnel and marked with a poppy symbol are described in the author's *Age Shall Not Weary Them: Saskatchewan Remembers its War Dead* (Regina, SK: People Places Publ., 2005; 512 p.). Builds on Barry's earlier works from the same publisher: *People Places: Contemporary Saskatchewan Place Names* (2003; 288 p.) and *People Places: The Dictionary of Saskatchewan Place Names* (1998 ; 416 p.). There is inevitably a certain amount of overlap among the three. In *People Places: Saskatchewan and its Names* (Regina, SK: Canadian Plains Research Center, Univ. of Regina, 1997; 202 p.), on the other hand, Barry takes a somewhat unusual approach to provincial toponymy. Instead of a straightforward alphabetical listing of places and name origins, the book has a thematic arrangement. Place names are organized by categories such as First Nations, railways, ethnic or religious origins, occupations (fur traders, politicians, North West Mounted Police, etc.) and an intriguing group called simply "The Bizarre." The most interesting work among several similar titles. — *LMcD*

DB167   Russell, E. T. - What's in a Name? : The Story behind Saskatchewan Place Names. –3rd ed. with new

foreword - Calgary, AB : Fifth House Publ., 1997. - 350 p. ;
map, ports.

Class Numbers:
    Library of Congress F1070.4
    National Library of Canada FC3506
    ISBN 1895618983
    OCLC 37368858
    Notes:
        1st ed. publ. 1968

• Vignettes, in alphabetical order, of more than 1,800 place-names.
Entries provide a description of the place and source of the name.
Interesting, if not always entirely reliable; Barry (**DB167**), who has
made a career of studying Saskatchewan toponymy, holds the view that
Russell is more frequently wrong than right. — *LMcD*

Chronologies

DB168   Bitner, Ruth, 1951- . - **Saskatchewan History
: Centennial Timeline, 1905-2005** / by Ruth Bitner and
Leslee Newman ; assisted by Brenda Mundell and Christa
Nicholat ; introd. by J. William Brennan. - Saskatoon, SK :
Saskatchewan Archives Board, 2005. - 30 p. ; ill.

Class Numbers:
    Library of Congress F1071
    National Library of Canada COP.SA.2.2005-103
    ISBN 0969144504 (pbk.)   9780969144502 (pbk.)
    OCLC 62227536
    LCCN 2005-434689
    Notes:
        Electronic book: http://olc.spsd.sk.ca/DE/
            saskatchewan100/timelinecover.htm
• A chronological approach to Saskatchewan history, with each
year typically allotted three or four significant events. Entries are
necessarily brief and decidedly eclectic, ranging from the popular,
such as major sports victories, to more lasting political, social, and
cultural developments. The introduction summarizes Saskatchewan history previous to 1905; the work concludes with lists
of premiers, population figures from decennial censuses, and
incorporation dates of cities. An interesting compilation of facts to
pique the browser's curiosity. — *LMcD*

Collective Biographies

DB169   Black, Norman Fergus, 1876-1964. - **History
of Saskatchewan and the North West Territories.** - Regina,
SK : Saskatchewan Historical Co., 1913. - 2 v. (xxx, 1010
p., [53] leaves of plates) ; ill., ports.

Class Numbers:
    Library of Congress F1071

National Library of Canada FC3511
OCLC 25440748
Notes:
    2nd ed. (Regina, SK : North West Historical Co.,
    [1913] ; xxiv, 605p.) published as *History of
    Saskatchewan and the Old North West*, without
    the biographies

• Another example of a format, popular in the early decades of the
previous century, combining history and laudatory collective
biography; the Alberta and Manitoba counterparts are **DB130**
and **DB149**. The reference value is chiefly in the biographical
accounts of an estimated 450 men of the time, significant in a
variety of professions and trades. Not arranged alphabetically but
has an index of names. — *LMcD*

DB170   Hawkes, John, 1851-1931. - **The Story of
Saskatchewan and its People.** - Chicago, IL : S.J. Clarke,
1924. - 3 v. (2084 p.) ; ill., ports.

Class Numbers:
    Library of Congress F1071
    National Library of Canada FC3511
    OCLC 11579779
    LCCN 58-52724
    Notes:
        Electronic book: http://www.ourroots.ca/e/toc.
            aspx?id=718 (v.1)
        Electronic book: http://www.ourroots.ca/e/toc.
            aspx?id=719 (v.2)
        Electronic book: http://www.ourroots.ca/e/toc.
            aspx?id=720 (v.3)

• The first half of the set consists of a general history of the
province; the remainder contains biographical sketches of an
estimated 900 prominent figures in politics, law, medicine, and
other fields. Not in alphabetical order but each volume has an
index. More detailed and interesting than *Pioneers and Prominent
People of Saskatchewan* (**DB172**), also published in 1924. — *LMcD*

DB171 Pioneers and Prominent People of Saskatchewan.
– Winnipeg, MB : Canadian Publicity Co., 1924. - 343 p.

Class Numbers:
    Library of Congress F1073
    National Library of Canada FC3505
    OCLC 21958413

• Biographical listing of approximately 475 individuals, arranged
in random order. Less useful than the much larger *The Story of
Saskatchewan and its People* (**DB171**), issued the same year.
Counterpart to the Manitoba work (**DB149**) from the same
publisher; some of the introductory material is identical with only
provincial names changed. — *LMcD*

DC : HISTORY, LOCAL

Scope   Lists titles covering regions that bridge political boundaries (Northern Plains) or that are contained within a political jurisdiction (Flint Hills); and titles that treat local political jurisdictions contained within states or provinces (counties, cities or towns).

General Works

DC1   Kammen, Carol. - **Encyclopedia of Local History** / [by] Carol Kammen and Norma Prendergast. - Walnut Creek, CA : AltaMira Pr., 2000. - 539 p. ; ill. - (American Association for State and Local History book series).

> Class Numbers:
> Library of Congress E180
> ISBN 0742503992
> LCCN 00-60560

• Kammen (history, Cornell Univ.) and Prendergast (art historian) provide a guide to aid individuals in locating sources to conduct research and explore trends for public, local, and regional history. They make readers aware of the emergence of various fields in history and of changing methodologies in order to explore pertinent local history resources. The entries point researchers to source materials, historical fields, bibliographical materials, libraries, and Internet sites. Contributors provide commentary on a number of subjects, among them agricultural history, American Indian history, and geographical entries for the Midwest and Western United States. There is no entry for rural history despite the vast scholarship reported in this field over the last 20 years. Appendixes list ethnic groups, religious groups, state historical organizations, and National Archives and Records Administration facilities. — *GK*

REGIONS

Deserts

DC2   Mares, Michael A. - **Encyclopedia of Deserts**. - Norman, OK : Univ. of Oklahoma Pr., 1999. - xxxvii, 654 p. ; ill., maps.

> Class Numbers:

> Library of Congress GB611
> ISBN 0806131446Z0585194785 (electronic bk.)
> OCLC 39905751
> LCCN 98-44437
> Notes:
> Electronic book:
> http://www.netLibrary.com/urlapi.asp?
> action=summary&v=1&bookid=15791
> Includes bibliographical references ; index
> Publ. in collaboration with the Oklahoma Museum
> of Natural History, Univ. of Oklahoma

• A survey of deserts around the world, Mares's encyclopedia has just enough of Plains interest to deserve consideration. Its entries (listed at the front by categories—"Geographic Areas and Desert Regions," "Mountains, Rivers, Plains, and Places," "Conservation, National Parks, Monuments, and Reserves," "General Desert Types, Geology, Landforms, Soils," "Life Forms in Deserts," "Bacteria," "Plants," "Animals," "Invertebrates," "Vertebrates," "Native Peoples," and "Climate") blanket the subject and include topics that will interest Prairies-Plains readers: "Great American Desert," "Texas Desert," "Llano Estacado," "Dirt Bikes," "Off-Road Vehicles," "Overgrazing," "Artesian Basin," "Groundwater," "Grassland," "Cottonwood," "Grasshoppers," "Agriculture in Deserts," "Aridity." Entries, alphabetically arranged, are written for educated adults and have bibliographies. The editor surveys deserts in a six-page introductory essay. Roster of contributors; index of subjects and places that prints article titles in boldface capitals. — *RB*

Flint Hills

DC3   Hoy, James F., ed. - **The Essential Flint Hills : A Bibliography** / assistant eds., James Hewitt and Karen Rupp. - Emporia, KS : Center for Great Plains Studies, Emporia State Univ., 1989. - 48 p.

> Class Numbers:
> Library of Congress F687.F56
> OCLC 21797306

• Hoy (director, Center for Great Plains Studies, Emporia State Univ.) has compiled an author list of about 125 books (including fiction), articles, master's theses, and occasional newspaper articles having to do with the Flint Hills, that granitic outcropping of gently undulating hills in central Kansas. He annotates all the citations and ranges widely as to subject matter--cattle, petroleum, the Pike exploration, towns and counties, grasses, the proposed Prairie National Park. Citations are as full as is necessary to locate the sources in libraries. There are no indexes. Unhappily, Hoy published too early to catch *PrairyErth*, William Least Heat-Moon's exhaustive celebration of Chase County, a title still missing from the revision (below). — *RB*

DC3a   Hoy, James F. - **Life and Lore of the Tallgrass Prairie : An Annotated Bibliography of the Flint Hills of Kansas**. - Emporia, KS : College of Liberal Arts and Sciences, Emporia State University, 1991. - 2 v. ; ill., map.

> Notes:
>   Issued as v. 24, nos. 1&2 (winter-spring 1991) and
>   nos. 3&4 (summer-fall 1991) of *Heritage of the
>   Great Plains*

• The bibliography focuses on a geologically and culturally distinctive region of Kansas; a few items on the adjoining Osage Hills of Oklahoma are also included. The approximately 625 works are organized by subject. Volume 1 deals with social history, with sections on ranching, memoirs, various cultural forms, ethnicity, and history, both local and family. The second volume is devoted to natural history and early settlement. Among the geological and biological topics are flora and fauna of the area, range management, water, soils, and minerals. The settlement portion covers archaeology, Native Americans, explorers, travel and transportation. Each topical section is prefaced by a brief but useful overview. Lacks author and title indexes. The bibliography appears to have met its goal of comprehensive coverage of the Flint Hills. —*LMcD*

Northern Plains

DC4   Native American and Northern Plains Historical Resources Guide [Internet Site]. - [Vermillion, SD : I.D. Weeks Library], Univ. of South Dakota, 2001. - http://www.usd.edu/jstor/

> Access Date: May 2006
> Notes:
>   Made possible by a Project JSTOR Campus Development
>   Mini-Grant
>   Provides access to articles selected from JSTOR's journal
>   database and to selected materials from the University
>   of South Dakota's Archives and Special Collections: the
>   Richardson Manuscript Collection and the Chilson
>   Collection of Western Americana
> Fees: None

• Compiled at the I.D. Weeks Library, this site consists of citations to articles in the JSTOR journal archive and in the Richardson Manuscript Collection and the Chilson Collection of Western Americana at the Weeks Library that have to do with the Northern Plains (chiefly the Dakotas) and with Indians of that region. The site has three parts, all accessible from the home page: an explanation of the project, a search window, and a browse button. "Browse" presents an alphabetic grid; each letter opens to headings

(topics, personal names, places, events) that in turn present single-line entries; clicking on those opens an entry with full bibliographic details. No full text is available. "Browse" has the great advantage of presenting headings in context and giving a sense of the site's scope and content. It will be principally useful to students at the University of South Dakota, where the special collections it indexes may be found, but is potentially useful to all Plains students. — *RB*

Southern Plains

DC5   Rader, Jesse Lee, 1883-   . - **South of Forty : From the Mississippi to the Rio Grande, a Bibliography**. - Norman, OK : Univ. of Oklahoma Pr., 1947. - 336 p.

> Class Numbers:
>   Library of Congress Z1251.S83
>   OCLC 1038801
>   LCCN 47-5360

• Exhaustive rather than selective, the bibliography covers an area bounded by the 40th parallel (the border between Kansas and Nebraska), the Mississippi River, the Gulf of Mexico, and the Rio Grande. It was a busy landscape for the nearly 400 years covered by the bibliography as French, English, and Spanish explorers pushed in from three sides, traders and immigrant settlers arrived, and Native peoples were pushed first out of and then onto the Plains. Entries range from Acosta's 1590 treatise on Indians to the 1827 constitution of the Cherokee Nation and a 1936 report on the architecture of Texas missions. Arranged by author, the 3,793 entries give complete bibliographic citations and physical descriptions for official documents, monographs, theses, and serials. Printing histories and brief annotations are sometimes added. Indexed by names and topics. — *JD*

Southwest, New

DC6   Borderlands Sourcebook : A Guide to the Literature on Northern Mexico and the American Southwest / ed. by Ellwyn R. Stoddard, Richard L. Nostrand, and Jonathan P. West. - Norman, OK : Univ. of Oklahoma Pr. ; publ. under the sponsorship of the Association of Borderlands Scholars, 1983. - 445 p. ; maps.

> Class Numbers:
>   Library of Congress F786   Z1251.S8
>   ISBN 0806117184
>   OCLC 8763887
>   LCCN 82-40331
> Notes:
>   Includes bibliographical references (p. [305]-437); index

• The editors cover states of Mexico that border the U.S. (Coahuila, Chihuahua, Sonora) and states of the U.S. that touch Mexico (California, Arizona, New Mexico, and Texas, as well as Utah), of which only Texas and New Mexico will be of interest to Prairies-Plains study. The book's first part contains four essays that address borderlands issues in broad terms. The second part, "Major Topical Concerns," contains 53 essays divided into five categories: history and archaeology, geography and the environment, the economy, politics, the law, demography, and society and culture. Among the historical essays, "Texas History" and "Border Cities" are likely to be of interest. The essays in Parts 2 to 5 each begin with a handy map of the area discussed. The index can also help locate essays of interest. Part 3, in addition to two short essays, consists of bibliographies of books, articles, dissertations, unpublished materials, and miscellaneous resources. The arrangement is alphabetical by author, but the date of publication is offset to the left of each entry for easy reference to recent publications. — *MB*

DC7   Dobie, James Frank, 1888-1964. - **Guide to Life and Literature of the Southwest : Rev. and Enl. in Both Knowledge and Wisdom**. - Dallas, TX : Southern Methodist Univ. Pr., 1952. - 222 p. ; ill.

> Class Numbers:
> Library of Congress Z1251.S8
> OCLC 577272
> Notes:
> 1st ed., 1943
> First publ. in J.W. Rogers's *Finding Literature on the Texas Plains*, 1931
> Guide to the course taught by the author at the Univ. of Texas

• For his classic bibliography, the Texas folklorist and social critic chose works that "interpret the region" though they naturally lean towards Texas and Western lore. The entries in the emphatically idiosyncratic guide are organized by chapters such as "Indian Culture," "Spanish-Mexican Strains," "Fighting Texians," "Pioneer Doctors," "The Bad Man Tradition," and "Bears and Bear Hunters." Dobie's scholarship, folklorist's perspective, and distinctive humor are evident in the chapter introductions and critical annotations. He is a fine teacher of research methods, recommending search strategies, advocating the value of pamphlets, and lamenting the state of state histories. Indexed by author and title. Available online through Project Gutenberg and netLibrary. — *JD*

DC8   **Society of Southwest Archivists Guide to Archival and Manuscript Repositories** / Kathryn E. Stallard, general ed. ; Jesús F. de la Teja, technical ed. - [Austin, TX] : Society of Southwest Archivists, 1993. - 256 p.

> Class Numbers:
> Library of Congress CD3057
> ISBN 0964016907 (pbk.)

OCLC 30577092
Notes:
> Contents: Arizona / Jean Nudd; Arkansas / Wendy Richter; Louisiana / Alfred E. Lemmon ; New Mexico / Kathleen Ferris; Oklahoma / John Caldwel ; Texas (A-G) / Casey Greene ; Texas (H-Z, El Paso) / Ann Massmann

• A directory and guide to the manuscript and archival collections held by 451 libraries, archives, museums, and other institutions in Arizona, Arkansas, Louisiana, New Mexico, Oklahoma, and Texas. Data were gathered by means of questionnaires mailed to 1,500 institutions, whose responses were regularized and edited by editors for each of the states (two were needed for Texas). Entries are alphabetical by state, city, and institution. Each entry supplies name of institution, address, phone and fax, contact person, type of institution, hours, access, and information about the collections (focus, format, access). Collections vary widely, as do the institutions themselves; for Enid, OK, for example, collections are reported for Phillips Univ. and for the Museum of the Cherokee Strip. Indexes cover special institutional services (humidity controls, exhibits, staff), collection formats (oral histories, postcards), and subjects. Useful, especially for the three Prairies-Plains states included. — *RB*

Counties

DC9   **Counties USA : A Directory of United States Counties** / Darren Smith, managing ed. - 2nd ed. - Detroit, MI : Omnigraphics, c2003. - 672 p. ; ill., maps.

> Class Numbers:
> Library of Congress E154.5
> ISBN 0780805461

• Statistical, descriptive, and contact information for 3,140 counties in the U.S., arranged alphabetically by state. Each state entry begins with a full-page outline map showing counties. Entries include county name, address, telephone/fax numbers, brief description of county location, percentage of foreign-born population, area in square miles, name origin, total population, median age, state rank, population change 1990-1999, per capita income, population below poverty level, unemployment rate, median home value, and average travel time to work. The back endpapers contain statistical tables of the top 25 counties throughout America ranked by population, population growth, per capita income, area in square miles. — *GK*

DC10 Dykstra, DeVee L. - **South Dakota County Population Projections, 2000-2025**. - Vermillion, SD :

State Data Center, Business Research Bureau, Univ. of South Dakota, 2002. - 230 p. ; ill., map.

Class Numbers:
Library of Congress HA635
Government Document South Dakota ED 380:P
943/2000-2025
OCLC 53980140
Notes:
Chiefly tables

• Dykstra (Business Research Bureau, Univ. of South Dakota) provides estimates of the population of South Dakota counties through 2025, based on the 2000 decennial Census. The compilation will be useful for businesses, organizations, and government agencies. It updates and revises data from *South Dakota County Population Projections: 1995-2020* (1997), concerning migration, mortality, and fertility rates. The baby boomer population is the largest age group in the state; counties with the highest population will continue to be located in two areas, the Black Hills and along the I-29 corridor in the southeast. Includes bar graphs, pie charts, and county map. — *GK*

DC11   Filby, P. William, 1911- , comp. - **A Bibliography of American County Histories**. - Baltimore, MD : Genealogical Publ. Co., 1985. - 449 p.

Class Numbers:
Library of Congress E180 ; Z1250
ISBN 0806311266
LCCN 85-80029

• Filby (formerly director, Maryland Historical Society) presents a list of 5,000 county histories published 1880-1920. He provides in a state-by-state arrangement such information for each entry as title, author, place, and date of publication. The sources were compiled from the county history holdings found in the Library of Congress and the New York Public Library. — *GK*

DC12   Kane, Joseph Nathan, 1899- . - **The American Counties : Origins of County Names, Dates of Creation and Organization, Area, Population Including 1980 Census Figures, Historical Data, and Published Sources** / comp. by Joseph Nathan Kane, Charles Curry Aiken. - 5th ed. - Lanham, MD : Scarecrow Pr., 2005. - xxiii, 529 p.

Class Numbers:
Library of Congress E180
ISBN 0810850362
LCCN 82-5982
Notes:
1st ed., 1960
Includes bibliographical references (p. 527-528)

• Kane (compiler of fact-based reference works) supplies for U.S. counties the origins of their names, historical information, geographic area, and population according to data drawn from the 1980 Census. The work is arranged in nine parts: counties listed by county name, date or year organized, name changes, seats, individuals that counties were named after, independent cities, and Alaska boroughs. To locate counties in Western and Great Plains states easily, readers should consult Part 3, "Counties Listed by State," which supplies year and date the state was admitted, names of counties, county seats, legislative statute numbers or chapters, and month, day, and year the county was created. — *GK*

DC13   Munnerlyn, Tom, comp. - **Texas Local History : A Source Book for Available Town and County Histories, Local Memoirs, and Genealogical Records**. - Austin, TX : Eakin Pr., 1983. - 112 p.

Class Numbers:
Library of Congress F386 ; Z1339
ISBN 0890153787
OCLC 9545326
LCCN 89-155167

• Lists histories specific to Texas counties and towns, arranged by county name. Entries under each county are alphabetical by title, and supply prices and publisher or book dealer. A supplemental bibliography (p. 83-90) lists state and regional publications, and a roster called "Sources" lists dealers from whom titles can be purchased. For each county, gives a brief history. No indexes. — *RB*

CITIES AND TOWNS

General Works

See also **Maier, Saskatchewan Local History Directory, DB158**

DC14   Artibise, Alan F.J. - **Canada's Urban Past : A Bibliography to 1980 and Guide to Canadian Urban Studies** / Alan F.J. Artibise and Gilbert A. Stelter. - Vancouver, BC : Univ. of British Columbia Pr., 1981. - xxxix, 396 p.

Class Numbers:
Library of Congress Z7165.C2
ISBN 0774801344
OCLC 7699159
LCCN 81-170677

• Reflecting the multidisciplinary nature of urban studies, Artibise and Stelter's bibliography draws on the literature of several of the social sciences including geography, sociology, economics, political science, demography, and history. Almost 1,000 of the 7,054 entries deal with the prairies. Organized by region or province: chapter 9 covers Western Canada in general, chapters 10 through 12 Manitoba, Saskatchewan, and Alberta respectively. Each has a uniform structure of general works followed by sections on individual major cities, with a composite group on other communities. The portions on Winnipeg, Calgary, and Edmonton are divided into general, pre-1921 and post-1921 works. "A Guide to Canadian Urban Studies" (p. 273-322) describes sources such as journals, archives, and specialized libraries. Author, place, and subject indexes. Artibise (**DA75**) and Stelter conveniently bring together citations on specific Prairie cities from a variety of perspectives. — *LMcD*

DC15   Beaulieu, C.R. - **Adaptability of Prairie Cities to Climate : A Bibliography** / by C.R. Beaulieu, E.E. Wheaton. – Saskatoon, SK : Saskatchewan Research Council, 1998. - 37 p. - (SRC publication; no. 10442-2E98).

> Class Numbers:
> Library of Congress QC 985.5.P7
> OCLC 171110524
> Notes:
> Funded by Alberta Environmental Protection and the
> Prairie Adaptation Network, a partnership of
> Saskatchewan Energy and Mines and the Saskatchewan
> Research Council

• An author listing, without annotations, of 430 items dealing with the use of climatic information in urban planning and development in the Plains environment. Climate encompasses a number of distinct elements and many of the works examine its influence on major concerns such as urban water quality, health, air quality, transportation, and sustainable infrastructure. A companion piece to the authors' *Adaptability of Urban Planning and Development to Climate: A Preliminary Literature Review and Annotations with Emphasis on the Canadian Prairies* (Saskatoon, SK : Saskatchewan Research Council, 1998; 17 p.). In view of the vulnerability of the Plains region to the effects of global warming, the two publications provide a useful overview and list of resources on a subject of increasing importance. — *LMcD*

DC16   McLennan, David, 1961-   . - **Our Towns : Saskatchewan Communities from Abbey to Zenon Park.** - Regina, SK : Canadian Plains Research Center, University of Regina, 2008. - 468 p. : ill. (some col.). - (Trade books based in scholarship, 23).

> Class Numbers:
> National Library of Canada FC3661
> ISBN 9780889772090

OCLC 181078253
> Notes:
> Includes bibliographical references

• McLennan provides snapshots, both textual and literal, of 725 communities located the length and breadth of Saskatchewan. The profiles provide a remarkable amount of information considering the number of places covered, typically including a concise history, name origin, ethnic background of the original settlers, and population statistics. Major historical events, circumstances of economic rise and—all too often—fall, local landmarks and attractions, and local offspring of noteworthy achievement help convey the distinctive nature of individual communities. Sumptuously illustrated with more than 1,000 captivating photographs, both historical and contemporary. Appendixes list source material and municipal status of each place. Clearly a labor of love by the author (who spent five years and covered 55,000 kilometers in assembling his material), his affection for the province apparent on every page.— *LMcD*

DC17   Moffat, Riley Moore, 1947-   . - **Population History of Western U.S. Cities and Towns, 1850-1990.** - Lanham, MD : Scarecrow Pr., 1996. - 344 p. ; chiefly tables.

> Class Numbers:
> Library of Congress HA218
> ISBN 0810830337
> OCLC 32274538
> LCCN 95-14583
> Notes:
> Includes bibliographical references (p. xi)

• Provides population data for an estimated 14,000 communities that have at any time had at least 200 residents; all the Plains states are included. Figures were compiled from the Bureau of the Census decennial censuses as well as state and territorial censuses, augmented by numbers from the *Rand McNally Commercial Atlas* and various Polk state directories over many years. Organized alphabetically by state and by location within each state. Riley has done a real service in bringing together a mass of historical figures at the individual community level in one convenient place. —*LMcD*

DC18   Reps, John William. - **Views and Viewmakers of Urban America : Lithographs of Towns and Cities in the United States and Canada, Notes on the Artists and Publishers, and a Union Catalog of Their Work, 1825-1925.** - Columbia, MO : Univ. of Missouri Pr., 1984. - 570 p. ; ill. (some col.).

> Class Numbers:
> Library of Congress NE2454 Z5961.U5
> ISBN 0826204163
> LCCN 83-6495

Notes:
    Includes bibliographical references (p. 87-94); index

• Among the most popular of printed images from the early 1830s to the early 20th century, were eye level, mid-level, and bird's eye views of U.S. and Canadian cities and towns, many detailed enough to label every building and street. Views were not limited to the larger cities. Itinerant artists traveling the Plains produced views of Billings, Montana in 1904; Bismarck, North Dakota in 1883; Sumner, Kansas in 1857; Omaha, Nebraska in 1868; Tulsa, Oklahoma in 1918 and many more, especially of towns in Kansas and Nebraska. Part 1 describes ways views were drawn, printed and sold and discusses their reliability and application. Part 2 has biographies of 51 artists, artist-publishers, lithographers and printers. Part 3 is a catalog of nearly 4,500 lithographs of 2,400 cities. Entries include place, date, title, size, artist, lithographer, printer, publisher and special features such as keys and vignettes, as well as institutions holding copies and catalogs or checklists citing the views. Thirteen color and 90 black-and-white views are reproduced in the text and an index by people and cities is included. For historical research and urban studies.— *JD*

Cities

DC19   Lack, Paul D. - **The History of Abilene : Facts and Sources** / by Paul D. Lack [et al.]. - [Abilene, TX] : McMurry College, 1981. - 101 p. ; maps.

    Class Numbers:
        Library of Congress HA730.A63
        LCCN 81-186360
    Notes:
        Bibliography: p. 74-94

• Lack combines a historical abstract of statistics and a bibliography of resources about Abilene, TX. The statistical portion supplies charts, tables, and maps of population, geography, climate, economics, political trends, transportation, communication, and education. The bibliographic portion cites newspaper articles, books, periodical articles, and maps, and unpublished histories and manuscript collections. — *JB*

DC20   Winnipeg, a Centennial Bibliography : A Centennial Project of the Manitoba Library Association / ed. by D. Louise Sloane, Janette M. Roseneder, Marilyn J. Hernandez. – Winnipeg, MB : Armstrong Printers, 1974. - 140 p.

    Class Numbers:
        Library of Congress Z1392 W55
        OCLC 1256379
        LCCN 74-188748

• The almost 1,440 items related to Manitoba's capital and surrounding area are organized by subjects such as politics, city planning, transportation, and education. Topics of national importance--the Red River Settlement, the 1869-1870 rebellions, and the Winnipeg general strike of 1919, for example--are covered in the history section. A useful source of information on the city long considered the gateway to the Canadian West. — *LMcD*

Towns

DC21   Burns, Nancy, 1944–   . - **The Collapse of Small Towns on the Great Plains : A Bibliography**. - Emporia, KS : School of Graduate and Professional Studies of the Emporia State University, 1982. - 36 p. - (Emporia State research studies, v. 31 no. 1).

    Class Numbers:
        Library of Congress HC107.A17   Z7165.U5 G73
        OCLC 10950364

• Much of Burns's slim publication is an essay summarizing works on the factors that led to the decline of small towns and the almost inevitable phenomenon of ghost towns. Technological advances such as diesel trains replacing steam engines, introduction of the telegraph and rural mail delivery, and the automobile, in particular, played significant roles. Changes in farming practices, environmental conditions such as prolonged drought, the exhaustion of resource-based economies, and rural-urban migration hastened the demise of many small communities. The bibliography, arranged by author, contains approximately 210 citations to books, articles, and theses. Although not comprehensive, it lists a significant part of the writings on the social and economic situation of small plains towns.— *LMcD*

GHOST TOWNS

UNITED STATES

DC22   Baker, T. Lindsay. - **Ghost Towns of Texas**. - Norman, OK : Univ. of Oklahoma Pr., 1986. - 196 p. ; ill., maps

    Class Numbers:
        Library of Congress F387
        ISBN 0806119977 0585214018 (electronic bk.)
        OCLC 13426490
        LCCN 86-40067
    Notes:
        Bibliography: p. 177-185
        Electronic book: http://www.netLibrary.com/
            urlapi.asp?action=summary&v=1&bookid=15331

DC22a Baker, T. Lindsay. - **More Ghost Towns of Texas**. - Norman, OK : Univ. of Oklahoma Pr., 2003. - 210 p. ; ill., maps.

> Class Numbers:
> Library of Congress F387
> ISBN 806135182
> LCCN 2002-40921
> Notes:
> Includes bibliographical references (p. 185-202);
> index
> Review by David Wharton: *Great Plains Quarterly*
> 24.4 (fall 2004): 296-297

• Both of Baker's books about Texas ghost towns are mixes of deserted towns and towns whose population is so low they are no longer viable communities. Selection is based on tangible remains visitors can see, public access, and distribution across the state. Since entries are arranged alphabetically, an outline state map shows town locations by number. For each town, Baker provides description, location on a road map, basic history of the town, photographs, and current status. Bibliography; index. — *JB*

DC23 Fitzgerald, Daniel C. - **Ghost Towns of Kansas : A Traveler's Guide**. - Lawrence, KS : Univ. Pr. of Kansas, c1988. - 348 p. ; ill., maps

> Class Numbers:
> Library of Congress F679.3 .F58 1988
> ISBN 0700603670 0700603689 (pbk.)
> LCCN 88-26
> Notes:
> Bibliography: p. 327

• Organized by sections of the state, Fitzgerald's book defines nine areas of the state: northeast, east central, southeast, etc. Each chapter describes four to 18 ghost towns, providing a highway map of that section with ghost towns marked in small capitals. Entries include fairly detailed historical information about each place; many include black-and-white illustrations or photos. End matter includes a brief bibliography and a detailed index of personal and place-names. Although designed as a traveler's guide, the book stands up well as a historical resource. — *MB*

DC23a Fitzgerald, Daniel C. - **Faded Dreams : More Ghost Towns of Kansas**. - Lawrence, KS : Univ. Pr. of Kansas, 1994. - 318 p. ; ill., maps.

> Class Numbers:
> Library of Congress F679.3
> ISBN 070060667X 0700606688 (pbk.)
> LCCN 93-42117
> Notes:
> Includes bibliographical references (p. [299]) ; index

• The sequel to *Ghost Towns of Kansas* (above) is a travel guide to more than 100 towns. The author defines a ghost town not just as an abandoned or nonexistent town but one that is a "shadowy remnant of what it once was." Major indicators are loss of two-thirds of a town's population or business district and a bleak economic future. Some towns featured have few remnants while others have a post office, stores, and community life. Narratives, organized by nine geographical regions, describe each town's founding, settlement, history, and demise and include facts, colorful anecdotes, and excerpts from reminiscences, interviews, archival records, letters, and newspaper articles. Route maps and photographs. Indexed by place and personal name. — *JD*

DC24 Florin, Lambert. - **Ghost Towns of the West**. - [New York] : Promontory Pr., 1971. - 872 p. ; ill.

> Class Numbers:
> Library of Congress F591
> ISBN 0883940132
> OCLC 1177004
> LCCN 73-90741

• A guide to communities either abandoned entirely or in apparently irreversible decline in 13 Western states, British Columbia, and the Yukon. Coverage of the Plains area is limited to Colorado, Montana, New Mexico, Texas, and Wyoming, and ranges from a low of four settlements in Texas to 32 in New Mexico. Arrangement is alphabetical under each state. The historical and descriptive accounts are chatty and full of interesting detail; the effect is fascinating at the individual level but somewhat sobering collectively. Profiles vary from a single paragraph to six or seven pages, almost all with at least one photograph. More complete guides for several jurisdictions in the region will be found in this section. — *LMcD*

DC25 Harris, Linda G. - **Ghost Towns Alive : Trips to New Mexico's Past** / photographs by Pamela Porter. - Albuquerque, NM : Univ. of New Mexico Pr., 2003. - 242 p. ; ill.

> Class Numbers:
> Library of Congress F797
> ISBN 826329071
> LCCN 2003-9194
> Notes:
> Includes bibliographical references (p. 235-236) ;
> index
> Review by David Pike: *Great Plains Quarterly* 25.2
> (spring 2005): 130-131
> Table of contents: http://www.loc.gov/catdir/toc/
> ecip043/2003009194.html

• A roster of about 70 abandoned towns in varying states of disintegration in New Mexico, arranged by 11 regions (e.g., the eastern plains, the Black Range, the Mogollon, the Bootheel). For each site, Harris provides location and a highly personal description, sometimes reaching several pages, that gives location of the town, history, and current state or condition. Most towns are abandoned, but a few still have inhabitants. Numerous illustrations, chiefly photographs. Index of persons, places, topics. For Prairies-Plains research, sections of greatest interest are east and southeast of Santa Fe. — *JB, RB*

DC26   Miller, Donald C., 1933-   . - **Ghosts on a Sea of Grass : Ghost Towns of the Plains : Colorado, Kansas, Montana, Nebraska, New Mexico, North Dakota, Oklahoma, South Dakota, Texas, Wyoming.** - Missoula, MT : Pictorial Histories Publ. Co., 1990. - 238 p. ; ill.

Class Numbers:
Library of Congress F591
ISBN 0929521331
OCLC 21954983
LCCN 90-60032
Notes:
Index

• Miller arranges his directory alphabetically by state, then by the name of the extinct city or town. Information about each town includes its location, when it was established, and what happened to cause its abandonment. Lavishly illustrated with contemporary black-and-white photos of people, buildings, and ruins. Very useful for historians or fanciers of ghost towns. — *MB*

DC27   Parker, Watson. - **Black Hills Ghost Towns** / [by] Watson Parker and Hugh K. Lambert. - Chicago, IL : Sage Books, 1974. - 215 p. ; ill., maps

Class Numbers:
Library of Congress F657.B6
ISBN 0804006377
LCCN 73-1501
Notes:
Bibliography: p. 214-215

• Parker and Lambert (writers, Oshkosh, WI, and Northbrook, IL) list 600 ghost towns located in the Black Hills of South Dakota in this guide for tourists, students, and historians. These towns thrived during the mining boom in the area, 1890-1940. The localities are described by county, section, and township, drawing on information from newspapers, maps, and books. The 1970 Census provides information about both places still populated and those that are not. Maps, illustrations, and selected bibliography. — *GK*

DC28   Fryer, Harold. - **Ghost Towns of Southern Alberta.** - Surrey, BC : Heritage House, 1982. - 2 v. : ill., maps. - (Frontier series, no. 39-40).

Class Numbers:
Library of Congress F1076
National Library of Canada FC3667.3
ISBN 0919214967 (v. 1)0919214983 (v. 2)
OCLC 9569986

• Brief but colorful accounts of approximately 50 communities, traditional ghost towns as well as trading posts, way stations, mining camps, and police forts no longer inhabited. Numerous black-and-white photos enliven the text. The Internet site *Ghost Towns of Alberta* (http://www.ghosttownpix.com/alberta/index.html),   by Johnnie Bachusky and Susan Foster, covers some of the same communities and includes contemporary photos.— *LMcD*

DC29   Moore, Frank. - **Saskatchewan Ghost Towns.** - [Regina, SK? : F. Moore], 1982. - 44 p. : ill.

Class Numbers:
National Library of Canada FC3517.3
OCLC 15983533
Notes:
Accompanied by map entitled: *Ghost Towns in Saskatchewan*
Electronic book: http://www.ourfutureourpast.ca/loc_hist/toc.aspx?id=8523

• Informal accounts of 108 communities that have become essentially defunct or disappeared outright. Location, brief history and reasons for decline are given. The accompanying large folded map identifies 293 ghost towns and indicates the degree of abandonment (e.g., 3/4 ghosted), with symbols. — *LMcD*

DC30   Mulligan, Helen. - **Ghost Towns of Manitoba** / by Helen Mulligan and Wanda Ryder. - Surrey, BC : Heritage House, 1985. - 160 p. ; ill., map.

Class Numbers:
Library of Congress F1063
ISBN 0919214703
OCLC 13396686
LCCN 85-188604

• Brief histories of approximately 40 abandoned communities in southern Manitoba. The numerous illustrations add a melancholy note to the recurring theme of optimistic beginnings gone awry. The arrangement is roughly geographical rather than alphabetically by town name. — *LMcD*

E   Science and Technology

EA : EARTH SCIENCES

Scope Lists sources in geology, meteorology, and paleontology. Other earth sciences (e.g., oceanography and volcanology) have little application to the Prairies-Plains region.

GEOLOGY ; MINERALOGY

General Works

EA1   Bibliography and Index of Geology / American Geological Institute; Geological Society of America. - v. 33 (1969)- . [Alexandria, VA, etc.] : American Geological Institute [etc.], 1969- . - Monthly.

> Class Numbers:
> > Library of Congress Z6031
> ISSN 0098-2784
> OCLC 2240713
> LCCN 75-642313
> Notes:
> > Annual cumulation includes a list of serial citations which is augmented by: *GeoRef Serials List*
> > Monthly with annual cumulations
> > Preceding titles: *Bibliography and Index of Geology Exclusive of North America*, ISSN 0376-1673; *Bibliography of North American Geology*, ISSN 0740-6347 (**EA1A**)

EA1a   Bibliography of North American Geology / Geological Survey (U.S.). - [1st] (1906/1907)- [64th] (1970). Washington, DC : U.S. Govt. Print. Off., 1907-1970. Annual.

> Class Numbers:
> > Library of Congress QE75
> OCLC 2177447
> LCCN gs 09-427
> Notes:
> > Library files frequently begin with a cumulative volume, John M. Nickles, *Geologic Literature in North America, 1785-1918*. Washington, DC : U.S. Govt. Print. Off., 1922. (USGS 746). In 2 v., Bibliography and Index. The introduction lists Bulletins cumulated in this volume
> > Preceding title: Fred Boughton Weeks, 1864- : *Bibliography and Index of North American Geology, Paleontology, Petrology, and Mineralogy*
> > Published in series: Geological Survey *Bulletin*
> > Succeeding title: *Bibliography and Index of Geology*, ISSN 0098-2784 (**EA1**)

• Until the advent of *GeoRef* (**EA2**), this set with its preceding and succeeding titles was the standard retrieval source for geologic research about North America. Covers all aspects of geology and all regions of the North American continent. All the issues are published as U.S. Geological Survey *Bulletins*, so may be available in that format in depository libraries, although many libraries bind and shelve the set separately. The bibliographies are arranged by author but each is accompanied by an elaborate index that uses broad topics as entry points ("Ground water," "Mineral exploration," "Rivers") subdividing them by place and topic. All the Plains states and Prairie provinces are included, but there are regional entries neither for "Plains" nor "Great Plains." An exhaustive record of geologic publication (books, government publications, journal articles) that provides access to Plains topics. — *RB*

EA2   GeoRef [Internet Site] / American Geological Institute. - Alexandria, VA : American Geological Institute, 1997- . - http://www.agis.org/georef/

> Access Date : Apr. 2006
> Fees: Subscription

• *GeoRef* picks up the indexing formerly published in the printed *Bibliography of North American Geology* (1906-1970, **EA1a**) and its successor, *Bibliography and Index of Geology* (1969- , **EA1**). *GeoRef* presently covers the geoscience literature of the world: for North America, 1693 to the present, and for the remainder of the world, 1933 to the present. It contains about 2.6 million records, with 80,000 added per year, representing articles, books, maps, conference papers, reports, theses, and all publications of the U.S. Geological Survey. "Search" allows searching in author, title, and subject fields (or all of them), and "Advanced" provides three search windows linked by Boolean operators and offering searches in 24 fields, plus four more specific to GeoRef. Display is by tagged format. A third search format, "Find Citation," provides six search windows for requesting journal articles when only a specific citation is wanted. Indexing is extremely thorough and elaborate, often providing dozens of subject identifiers. The site will be fruitful for Plains studies: "Great Plains" produced 5,108 entries, "Aquifer" 13,354 (although "Ogallala Aquifer" produced none), "Sand Hills" 141, "Permian Basin" 1,308, and "Llano Estacado" 114. — *RB*

UNITED STATES

Colorado

EA3   Eckel, Edwin B. - Minerals of Colorado / by Edwin B. Eckel, Robert R. Cobban, Shirley K. Mosburg. - Golden, CO : Fulcrum Publ., 1997. - 665 p. ; ill. (some col.), col. maps.

> Class Numbers:

Library of Congress TN24.C6
ISBN 1555913652
OCLC 36900724
LCCN 97-14815
Notes:
    Includes bibliographical references (p. [557]-665)
    Sponsored by the Friends of Mineralogy, Colorado
        Chapter, and the Denver Museum of Natural History

• The authors do not intend their book to be a field guide

describing where and how to find minerals, but a summary of known facts about minerals found in Colorado, including those new to mineralogy (called "type minerals"), of which they supply a two-page list, followed by a brief list of those discredited. Then comes a list of mineral localities, arranged by county, and more detailed descriptions of the localities. A map of Colorado shows numbered locations of mineral localities, and there are a half dozen maps of regions of Colorado. The largest part of the book consists of an alphabetic list of

Site List 15
Geological Surveys

U.S. Geological Survey http://www.usgs.gov

USGS provides information about geology, climatography, landscape, physiography, natural resources, and natural hazards in all states. "Science in Your Backyard" at the USGS Internet site links to state-by-state real time flood, drought, stream flow, and groundwater data; real time and historic earthquake data; maps and remote sensing data; and information on water, recreational, mineral, and biological resources. The site also links to affiliated state Water Science Centers and Fish and Wildlife Research Units, and to directory information for all state USGS offices. A "Maps, Products, and Publications" tab provides access to USGS publications. "USGS Library" is an online catalog of 300,000 book, map, and serial records, and "Publications Warehouse" provides citations and some full-text access to 67,000 serial titles and maps. Links lead to geological data, water data, and maps for all states. The site provides access and order information for software, data sets, digital satellite data, aerial photographs, and real time monitoring data.

State and Provincial Geological Surveys

Every state has a Geological Survey office, administered by the State Geologist and often affiliated with a university or other state agency. Their Internet sites offer a variety of resources, including bibliographies, online databases, statistics, digital maps, and field guides.

United States

Colorado Geological Survey
    http://geosurvey.state.co.us

Kansas Geological Survey
    http://www.kgs.ku.edu

Montana Bureau of Mines and Geology
    http://www.mbmg.mtech.edu

Nebraska Geological Survey
    http://csd.unl.edu/surveyareas/geology.asp

New Mexico Bureau of Geology and Mineral Resources
    http://geoinfo.nmt.edu

North Dakota Geological Survey
    http://www.state.nd.us/ndgs

Oklahoma Geological Survey
    http://www.ogs.ou.edu

South Dakota Geological Survey
    http://www.sdgs.usd.edu

Texas Bureau of Economic Geology
    http://www.beg.utexas.edu

Wyoming State Geological Survey
    http://www.wsgs.uwyo.edu

Canada

Alberta Geological Survey
    http://www.ags.gov.ab.ca

Manitoba Geological Survey
    http://www.gov.mb.ca/iedm/mrd/index.html?/
        index.html

Saskatchewan Industry and Resources
    http://www.ir.gov.sk.ca

Water Science Centers

Colorado Water Science Center
    http://co.water.usgs.gov

Kansas Water Science Center
    http://ks.water.usgs.gov

Water Resources of Montana
    http://mt.water.usgs.gov

Water Resources of Nebraska
    http://ne.water.usgs.gov

Water Resources of New Mexico
    http://nm.water.usgs.gov

continued on following page

minerals, giving for each the mineral name, its chemical formula, crystalline structure, and locations where samples have been found; all the sections of each entry refer to the bibliography at the end. An appendix gives previously unpublished chemical analyses of minerals. The bibliography (109 double-column pages) is an author list. A section at the center provides photographs of minerals, 32 p. in color, eight in black-and-white. Intended for professional geologists, but of probable use to amateur rock hounds. — *RB*

---

continued from previous page

North Dakota Water Science Center
http://nd.water.usgs.gov

Water Resources of Oklahoma
http://ok.water.usgs.gov

South Dakota Water Science Center
http://sd.water.usgs.gov

USGS Activities in Texas: Water Resources

Water Resources of Wyoming
http://wy.water.usgs.gov

Fish and Wildlife Research Units

Colorado Cooperative Fish and Wildlife Research Unit
http://www.colostate.edu/Dept/coopunit

Kansas Cooperative Fish and Wildlife Research Unit
http://www.k-state.edu/kscfwru

Montana Cooperative Fishery Research Unit
http://www.montana.edu/mtcfru

Nebraska Cooperative Fish and Wildlife Research Unit
http://snr.unl.edu/necoopunit

New Mexico Cooperative Fish and
Wildlife Research Unit
http://leopold.nmsu.edu/fwscoop/

Oklahoma Cooperative Fish and Wildlife Unit
http://www.vpr.okstate.edu/ocfwr.htm

South Dakota Cooperative Fish and Wildlife Research Unit [South Dakota State University]
http://wfs.sdstate.edu/wfsci.htm

Texas Cooperative Fish and Wildlife Research Unit
http://www.tcfwru.ttu.edu

Wyoming Cooperative Fish and Wildlife Research Unit
http://uwadmnweb.uwyo.edu/fish_wild/

Kansas

EA4   KGS Online Bibliography of Geology [Internet Site] / Janice H. Sorensen . - [Lawrence, KS] : Kansas Geological Survey, 1990s-   . - http://www.kgs.ku.edu/Magellan/Bib/index.html

> OCLC 83466298
> Access Date : May 2007
> Notes:
>> Includes data from the print publications: *Bibliography of Kansas Geology, 1985-1989* / Janice H. Sorensen (**EA5**); *Bibliography of Kansas Geology, 1823-1984* / Janice H. Sorensen, Scott J. Johnsgard, and Christopher Wozencraft (**EA5a**)
>> Updated periodically by KGS staff
>> Fees: None

• A site of uncertain size, searchable by county (a pulldown list is in alphabetic order), by author (chosen from an alphabetic grid), and by "index terms" (i.e., keywords, with principal terms and subordinate terms chosen from a grid). Materials are drawn chiefly from earth science journals and publications of geological surveys (especially the Kansas Geological Survey). Responses, displayed in a standardized format, show title, author, publication, and year. Since the site picks up the content of the two printed bibliographies of Kansas geology that preceded it (**EA5, EA5a**) and has added other sources, it is the standard site for the bibliography of Kansas geology. Searching is tightly controlled, hence it is not case sensitive and requires none of the common limiting characters; users are advised to avoid quotation marks, commas, or Booleans, but simply enter author names, rock units, or keywords of interest. It is gratifying that KGS has converted two publications to machine-readable form and added additional citations, but designers need to supply as well the number of records available at the site, the dates of coverage, and the date the site was first made available. — *RB*

EA5   Sorensen, Janice H. - Bibliography of Kansas Geology, 1823-1984 / by Janice H. Sorensen, Scott J. Johnsgard, and Christopher Wozencraft. - Lawrence, KS : Kansas Geological Survey, 1989. - xxiv, 418 p. ; maps. - (Kansas Geological Survey. Bulletin, 221).

> Class Numbers:
>> Library of Congress Z6034.U5 K33
> LCCN 90-623189
> Notes:
>> Included in *KGS Online Bibliography of Geology* (**EA4**)

EA5a   Sorensen, Janice H. - Bibliography of Kansas Geology, 1985-1989. - Lawrence, KS : Kansas Geological Survey, 1994. - 158 p. ; ill. - (Kansas Geological Survey. Bulletin, 234).

> Class Numbers:
>> Library of Congress QE113

OCLC 31313377

Notes:

    Included in *KGS Online Bibliography of Geology* (**EA4**)

    Index

• The standard bibliography of Kansas geology until conversion of records to machine-readable form (**EA4**). The base file cites about 9,500 records, the supplement about 2,400. Entries are listed by senior author, with other authors cross-referenced to the principal entry. There are indexes by subject (with numerous cross-references, e.g., "Equus beds aquifer see under Ground water--Aquifers"), by county subarranged by topic, and by rock-unit (i.e., rock-stratigraphic names used in the papers cited). Useful and carefully prepared. —*RB*

Montana

EA6   Alt, David D. - **Roadside Geology of Montana** / [by] David Alt and Donald W. Hyndman. - Missoula, MT : Mountain Pr. Publ. Co., 1986. - 427 p. ; ill.

    Class Numbers:

        Library of Congress QE133

    ISBN 0878422021

    OCLC 13903972

    LCCN 86-17954

    Notes:

        Bibliography: p. 421; index

• Consisting of five chapters, this guide offers first an illustrated general introduction to Montana's geological features, followed by four chapters, each of which deals with a specific section of the state: northwest, southwest, central, and east. Each begins with an illustrated narrative and includes a number of driving tours along highways (e.g., US 12, Garrison to Helena; Interstate 90, Missoula to Butte). The tours are accompanied by detailed maps which point out significant geologic features. Photos and cross-section geologic drawings enhance the narrative information. Glossary; index. —*MB*

EA7   James, Harold Lloyd, 1912- . - **Bibliography and Index of Montana Geology** / comp. by H.L. James and Kay Yost. - Butte, MT : Montana Bureau of Mines and Geology, 1990-. - 7 v. - (Montana Bureau of Mines and Geology. Special publication, 98, 101, 104, 105, 107, 108, 109).

    Class Numbers:

        Library of Congress QE133   Z6034.U5

    OCLC 25328121

    LCCN 92-621104

    Notes:

        Contents: v. 1, 1856-1929; v. 2, 1930-1959; v. 3, 1960-1969; v. 4, 1970-1974; v. 5, 1975- 1979; v. 6, 1980-

1982; v. 7, 1983-1985

Prepared in cooperation with the American Geological Institute

• All seven volumes are author lists with subject indexes, providing an uninterrupted record of publishing about geology and related subjects, from the first white settlements in Montana through 1985. The subject indexes give access to Prairies-Plains topics under such headings as "Great Plains," "Eastern Montana," and "Lignite." Kept up to date after 1985 by *GeoRef* (**EA2**). Primarily for professional geologists. —*RB*

Nebraska

EA8   Maher, Harmon D., 1955- . - **Roadside Geology of Nebraska** / [by] Harmon D. Maher Jr., George F. Engelmann, and Robert D. Shuster. - Missoula, MT : Mountain Pr. Publ. Co., 2003. - 264 p. ; ill. (some col.), col. maps.

    Class Numbers:

        Library of Congress QE135

    ISBN 0878424571 (pbk.)

    LCCN 2002-10930

    Notes:

        Includes bibliographical references (p. 251-254); index

• Much of Nebraska geology is invisible, and that which is visible is often subtle. Its most remarkable features are the Sand Hills, the largest stretch of sand in the Western Hemisphere, and the Ogallala Aquifer, a massive underground source of water. The remainder of the state, apart from land devoted to agriculture, varies from salt deposits in the east to badlands in the west, and the entire state teems with fossil deposits. In this guide, one of a series of state guides intended for nonspecialists, a detailed "Geologic Summary of Nebraska" is followed by route-by-route descriptions of the landscape, underlying strata, and fossil records. It highlights areas of particular interest (called "Geolocalities"), many of which are state or national parks or monuments. Simplified geologic maps, tables, photographs, a glossary, suggested readings, and recommended Internet sites all help in understanding the geology of the state and region. Geologic history underlies both the history of human settlement in Nebraska and current issues like water regulations and the effect of humans on the Plains ecosystem. A useful resource for travelers and nonspecialists looking for information about geology, paleontology, anthropology, history, ecology, and natural resources. —*JD*

EA9   Sandy, John H. - **Bibliography of Nebraska Geology, 1843-1976** / [by] John H. Sandy, Jay Fussell. - [Lincoln, NE] : Conservation and Survey Div., Institute of Agriculture and Natural Resources, Univ. of Nebraska–Lincoln, 1983. - 198 p. ; map.

Class Numbers:
  Library of Congress QE135 Z6034.U5
  OCLC 9713973
  LCCN 83-622156
Notes:
  Indexes

• Between 1843, when the economic interests of the frontier drove geological surveys in the Plains states, through 1976, when computers had become the tools for storing and retrieving geological information rather than simply modeling or mapping it, geology developed as a discipline, and the Conservation and Survey Division was charged as Nebraska's modern organization to investigate and record state geology. This bibliography records research conducted during that era. Arranged alphabetically by senior author, entries include master's theses, dissertations, books, articles, government publications, and reports. Entries lack annotations but titles tend to be fully descriptive, and indexes cover joint authors and keywords. The bibliography has been digitized as one of the texts in *Western Waters Digital Library : The Platte River Basin in Nebraska* (http://libtextcenter.unl.edu/westernwaters/index. html). Some of the sources cited in the bibliography have also been selected for *Western Waters*. —*JD*

New Mexico

EA10 Wright, Anne Finley. - **Bibliography of Geology and Hydrology, Eastern New Mexico**. - Albuquerque, NM : U.S. Geological Survey, 1979. - 170 p. ; map. - (Water resources investigations, 79-76).

  Class Numbers:
    Library of Congress GB701 QE143 Z6034.U5N53
    OCLC 5626080
    LCCN 79-603769

• An author list, chiefly of journal articles and government publications, having to do with the geology, hydrology, chemistry, and geography of the High Plains of eastern New Mexico. There are no indexes, and while none is needed for authors, finding materials about oil and gas production, Carlsbad Caverns, the Roswell area, or the Ogallala formation requires scanning the entire file. Only for durable researchers. —*RB*

North Dakota

EA11 **Collective Bibliography of North Dakota Geology [Internet Site]** / a collaborative effort of the North Dakota State University Libraries and the North Dakota Geological Survey ; Lura Joseph, [project leader]. - Fargo, ND : North Dakota State Univ. Libraries, 1998-   . - http://dp3.lib.ndsu.nodak. edu/ndgs/

Class Numbers:
  Library of Congress Z6034.U5
  OCLC 39026023
  Access Date : May 2006
  Fees: None

• Consisting of approximately 5,100 citations published 1806-2002, the database merges and updates *Annotated Bibliography of the Geology of North Dakota, 1806-1959* (1972) and *Annotated Bibliography of the Geology of North Dakota, 1960-1979* (1981), both by M.W. Scott, and *Bibliography of the Geology of North Dakota, 1980-1993* (1996), by L. Greenwood et al. (all three published in the "North Dakota Geological Survey Miscellaneous Series"). "Simple Search" provides keyword, Boolean, customized displays, sorting, and browsing by author. "Advanced Search" includes keyword, author, date, title, source, annotation, print resource, and record number. An attractive alternative for readers who lack access to the commercial *GeoRef* database (**EA2**). —*LMcD*

South Dakota

EA12 DeWitt, Ed. - **BHBIB : Bibliography of Black Hills Geology, 1852-1988** [microform] / by Ed DeWitt, Margaret Clemensen, and Rachel Barari. - Denver, CO : U.S. Dept. of the Interior, Geological Survey ; [distr. by Books and Open-File Reports Section], 1989. - 1 microfiche ; negative. - (Open-file report, 89-443A).

  Class Numbers:
    Government Document I 19.76:89-443 A

• DeWitt, Clemensen (both U.S. Geological Survey, Denver), and Barari (database administrator, Univ. of South Dakota) provide a bibliography of 3,676 references on the geology of the Black Hills and Wyoming. The entries do not cover the areas of the Bad Lands (SD) or the Powder River Basin (WY). The records are listed in alphabetical order. The subject fields addressed are maps, economic geology, geochronology, structural, petrology, geophysics, mineralogy, metallurgy, geochemistry, paleontology, petroleum, stratigraphy, engineering, hydrology, paleontology, and expeditions. Publications included in the bibliography are federal and state government documents, journals, periodicals, magazines, books, theses, and dissertations. The work is available in two other formats, print and floppy disk (the latter in open file and ASCII). —*GK*

EA13 O'Harra, Cleophas Cisney, 1866-1935. - **A Bibliography of the Geology and Mining Interests of the Black Hills Region**. - Rapid City, SD : [South Dakota School of Mines and Technology], 1917. - 216 p. ; front. (folded map). - (South Dakota School of Mines and

Technology. Bulletin, 11).

Class Numbers:
    Library of Congress TN24.S8
    LCCN gs 17-344

• O'Harra (president, South Dakota State School of Mines) cites and provides annotations to 1,200 sources related to the Black Hills, encompassing the region east of the Pine Ridge Reservation, north to the North Dakota line, and south to the bend of the Niobrara River. Publications cited include reports, journals, articles, and books. O'Harra lists entries chronologically, citing each entry by author, 1814-1917. The main topics addressed are geology and mining, plus related subjects such as mineralogy, petrography, geography, paleontology, mineralogy, and metallurgy. A foldout map of the area precedes the title page. — *GK*

Texas

EA14 Bibliography and Index of Texas Geology. - Austin, TX : Bureau of Economic Geology, Univ. of Texas, 1959-1990. - 5 v.

Class Numbers:
    Library of Congress QE167; Z6034.U5
    OCLC 985246 (v. [1])   651520 (v. [2])
        2719012 (v. [3]) 8229132 (v. [4]) 23101756 (v. [5])
    LCCN 59-63220 (v. [1])   73-620786 (v.[2] 77-622653
        (v. [3]) 82-621025 (v. [4]) 91-621908 (v. [5])
    Notes:
        Contents: v. [1], 1933-1950, by Roselle M. Girard; v. [2], 1951-1960, by Elizabeth T. Moore and Margaret D. Brown; v. [3], 1961-1974, by E. T. Moore; v. [4], 1975-1980, by Amanda R. Masterson; v. [5], 1981-1985, by Amanda R. Masterson and Lana Dieterich
        Indexes

• Five volumes that cover publications relating to the geology of Texas, 1933-1985. The first volume is typeset, the others are reproduced either from typescript or computer printout. All are author lists, but all have subject indexes that enable identification of materials relating to the Plains portion of Texas: "Amarillo Uplift," "High Plains," "Panhandle," "Palo Duro Basin." The last two volumes also have author indexes that identify secondary authors. The five volumes allow access to about 13,500 publications. Although the set is a logical candidate for loading to an Internet site, none appears to have been created; compilation ceased with 1985. *GeoRef* (**EA2**) covers material published after 1985. — *RB*

Wyoming

EA15 Bovee, Gladys G. - Bibliography and Index of Wyoming Geology, 1823-1916. - Cheyenne, WY : S.A. Bristol Co., 1918. - 2 p. l., p. [319]-446. 23 cm. -

(Wyoming. State Geologist. Bulletin 17).

Class Numbers:
    Library of Congress Z6034 U5
    OCLC 4636939
    Notes:
        Reprinted in 1969 by Frontier Print and Mailing Co.

• Encompassing the years of the establishment and explosive growth of the state geological surveys, Bovee's bibliography of over 700 books, articles, pamphlets, and reports is comprehensive for state and U.S. Geological Survey publications and nearly comprehensive for other publications. Topics include paleontology, petrology, and mineralogy. Arranged by year of publication, entries include brief annotations. Author index and an extensive index by topic and location. — *JD*

EA15a Troyer, Max Loraine, 1916- . - Bibliography of Wyoming Geology, 1917-1945. - Laramie, WY : Univ. of Wyoming, 1969. - 73 p. - (Geological Survey of Wyoming. Bulletin, 53).

Class Numbers:
    Library of Congress Z6034.U5 W8

• Compiled from U.S. Geological Survey publications and holdings at the University of Wyoming, Troyer's bibliography includes scholarly, technical, and professional works published as books, pamphlets, proceedings, reports, theses, and articles. General textbooks and reference books are excluded. Though the unannotated entries are organized by author, a classified subject index groups them under broad headings: general, economic geology, historical geology, mineralogy, paleontology, petrology, physical geology, physiographic geology, underground water, and Yellowstone National Park. — *JD*

CANADA

EA16 Geological Atlas of the Western Canada Sedimentary Basin / comp. by Grant Mossop and Irina Shetsen . - Calgary, AB : Canadian Society of Petroleum Geologists, 1994. - 1 atlas (510 p.); ill. (chiefly col.), maps (chiefly col.) ; 45 x 59 cm.

Class Numbers:
    Library of Congress G1151
    ISBN 0920230539
    OCLC 31161111
    Notes:
        "Published jointly by the Canadian Society of Petroleum Geologists and the Alberta Research Council, in sponsorship association with the Alberta Department of Energy and the Geological Survey of Canada"
        Electronic book: http://www.ags.gov.ab.ca/publications/
        Scales differ

• The WCSB, principal source of oil and natural gas in Canada, includes regions of Alberta and Saskatchewan. The atlas consists of chapters, each by a different team of geologists, basically arranged by geological period. Division chapters are heavily illustrated and include index map, correlation charts, reference logs, and various types of technical maps; the text provides context for the illustrated material and includes references to important writings. Thematic chapters examine geological, geophysical, geochemical, and geotechnical elements of strata; they summarize information, much like a review article, and provide citations. Three-quarters of the atlas consists of maps, cross-sections and additional illustrations; it is intended to provide a foundation for environmentally sustainable resource development. — *LMcD*

Alberta

EA17   Alberta Society of Petroleum Geologists. - **Annotated Bibliography of Geology of the Sedimentary Basin of Alberta and of Adjacent Parts of British Columbia and Northwest Territories, 1845-1955** / comp. and ed. by R.G. McCrossan [et al.]. - Calgary, AB : [Alberta Society of Petroleum Geologists], 1958. - 499 p. ; folded maps.

> Notes:
>
> Title on spine: *Bibliography of Alberta Geology 1845-1955*

• An author listing of approximately 1,500 references, mostly scientific articles or survey reports, on a range of geological subjects. Graduate theses without annotations appear in a separate alphabetical list. Given the geographic expanse covered, however, many of the items do not deal with the Prairies. The exceptionally thorough subject index (p. 209-406) consists of major areas such as economic geology, historical geology, paleontology, petrology, and mineralogy, each subdivided as necessary. Entries are arranged by alphabetical location or National Topographic Reference System number, followed by author and year. The location index is in two parts: large or irregular geographic areas listed alphabetically, and NTS numbers, both divided by subject. Index of place names in Alberta and British Columbia with NTS equivalents. The *GeoRef* database (**EA2**) covers post-1955 publications. Intended mainly for the use of the oil industry, but of wider interest. — *LMcD*

EA18   Powter, C. B. - **A Bibliography of Baseline Studies in Alberta : Soils, Geology, Hydrogeology, Ground Water** / by C.B. Powter, H.P. Sims. - Edmonton, AB : Alberta Dept. of Environment, Research Management Division, 1982. - 97 p. - (Report (Alberta. Reclamation Research Technical Advisory Committee) ; RRTAC 82-2).

> Class Numbers:
>
> Library of Congress Z6034.C19   QE186
>
> OCLC 10825965
>
> LCCN 82-200205

• Cites chiefly documents from government agencies such as the Alberta Research Council, Geological Survey of Canada, and the Alberta Dept. of the Environment, with additional consultants' reports. Arranged by the broad subject categories indicated in the title; within each group, entries are listed alphabetically by geographic location. Intended to identify sources for reclamation research and environmental assessments. Databases such as *Water Resources Abstracts* (**EB31**), *GeoRef* (**EA2**) and *Environmental Sciences and Pollution Management* list more current publications. — *LMcD*

Manitoba

EA19   **Bibliography of Manitoba Geology (BMG) [Internet Site]** / updated and maintained by the Mineral Resources Library. - Winnipeg, MB : Mineral Resources Library, Manitoba Industry, Economic Development and Mines, 1982. - http://www.gov.mb.ca/iedm/mrd/info/library/bmgintro.htm

> Access Date : July 2005
>
> Notes:
>
> Supersedes *Bibliography of Manitoba Geology 1795 to 1988*, by L. E. Chackowsky (Winnipeg: Manitoba Energy and Mines, Mines Branch, 1989)
>
> Fees: None

• Almost 12,000 citations to reports, maps, articles, conference papers, and theses, reaching as far back as 1795. The Inmagic interface provides Basic (keyword, title, author, National Topographic System number, year) and Advanced searches (an additional ten elements, many of which can be browsed). A comprehensive source on Manitoba geology and the counterpart to Alberta (**EA17**) and Saskatchewan (**EA21**). — *LMcD*

Saskatchewan

EA20   **Geological Atlas of Saskatchewan [Internet Site]** / Saskatchewan Industry and Resources. - Regina, SK : Saskatchewan Industry and Resources, 1982. - http://www.ir.gov.sk.ca/

> Access Date : Apr. 2006
>
> Notes:
>
> Also issued as CD-ROM
>
> Fees: None

• The site provides interactive bedrock and surface geological maps. Mine locations, mineral deposits, oil and gas data, regional geological maps, and topographical base maps are among the elements that can be manipulated. Geological datasets are in ArcView/ArcExplorer format. — *LMcD*

EA21   Kupsch, Walter Oscar, 1919-   . - **Annotated Bibliography of Saskatchewan Geology**. - Regina, SK : Dept. of Mineral Resources, 1973-1979. - 2 v. (xxiii, 421 p. ; xxx, 140 p.); fold. col. maps. - (Saskatchewan Dept. of Mineral Resources. Report, 9 and 9 suppl.).

> Class Numbers:
>   Library of Congress QE194   Z6034.C19
> OCLC 2615639
> LCCN 76-376375
> Notes:
>   Contents: v.1, 1823-1970; v. 2, 1970-1976

• Cites an estimated 3,300 geological and geophysical reports, papers and maps, arranged by author. Entries include National Topographic System numbers used on the accompanying maps, and subject keywords. Subject and geographic location (NTS number) indexes. Later material is covered by the American Geological Institute's *Bibliography and Index of Geology* (**EA1**) and its online version *GeoRef* (**EA2**). — *LMcD*

METEOROLOGY ; CLIMATOLOGY

UNITED STATES

EA22   **High Plains Regional Climate Center [Internet Site]** / United States. National Oceanic and Atmospheric Administration. High Plains Regional Climate Center. University of Nebraska-Lincoln. - Lincoln, NE : High Plains Regional Climate Center, 2001-   . - http://www.hprcc.unl.edu/

> OCLC 466240836
> Access Date : Jan. 2006
> Notes:
>   Updated daily
> Fees: Access is free; fees charged for some data

• One of six regional climate centers at public universities, HPRCC serves Colorado, Iowa, Kansas, Nebraska, the Dakotas, and Wyoming. Most data are free, but HPRCC charges for some data sets. Free data include Historical Data Summaries (tables and charts of averages and extremes of temperature, precipitation, snowfall, and snow depth), averages of cooling and heating degree days by weather station, maps of current climate summaries and 30-year normals, and a regional climate atlas. Fee-based services, offered online or through the HPRCC office,

include the near real time Automated Weather Data Network (offering, e.g., hourly and daily updates by city for air temperature, precipitation, relative humidity, soil temperature, solar radiation, wind speed, wind direction), drought indexes 1895-present, average temperature and precipitation records 1895-present, and crop yield data 1972-1996. The site links to weather services maintained by Lincoln and by the state of Nebraska and to other sources of climatic information. Useful to researchers and practitioners in agriculture, conservation, business, insurance, natural resources. — *JD*

EA23   Visher, Stephen Sargent, 1887-1967. - **Climatic Atlas of the United States**. - Cambridge, MA : Harvard Univ. Pr., 1954. - 403 p. ; 1031 maps, diagrs.

> Class Numbers:
>   Library of Congress G1201.C8
> LCCN map 53-383
> Notes:
>   "Sources of the maps": p. 395-400
>   Bibliography: p. 393-395

• All maps show the entire U.S., depicting general patterns of temperature; winds, atmospheric pressure and storms; sunshine; atmospheric humidity and evaporation; precipitation; and consequences on agriculture, topography, health, land and water, soil erosion, lakes and rivers. They illustrate the climatic effect of the rain shadow of the Rockies, a determining factor in the economy and culture of the Great Plains. Though the maps are not detailed and the data not as precise as those gathered today, the atlas can be used as a baseline for Plains climate change or in conjunction with regional atlases or data. The list of references and map sources is a font of information for research in greater depth about historical climate and weather. Indexed by author, title, and map topic. — *JD*

Kansas

EA24   Goodin, Douglas G. - **Climate and Weather Atlas of Kansas : An Introduction** / [by] Douglas G. Goodin [et al.]. - Lawrence, KS : Kansas Geological Survey, 1995. - 24 p. ; ill. (some col.). - (Kansas Geological Survey. Educational series, 12 ; ISSN 0731-616X).

> Class Numbers:
>   Library of Congress G4200.C8   QE113
>   Government Documents Kansas E 54.109:12
> OCLC 34620105
> Notes:
>   Includes bibliographical references

• This large format pamphlet consists entirely of charts and maps. Maps include a guide to locations of weather stations in Kansas; physiography (e.g., High Plains, lowlands); mean, maximum, and minimum temperatures in various locations in the state for each season of the year; and maps showing average annual dates of first and last freezes by two-week increments. Charts include selected record-breaking precipitation events, 1960-1990, and precipitation patterns, including snowfall. Glossary; reading list. – MB

Nebraska

EA25   Climatic Atlas of Nebraska / project director, Merlin P. Lawson ; contributing authors, Merlin P. Lawson, Kenneth F. Dewey, Ralph E. Neild ; cartographer, John D. Magill. - Lincoln, NE : Univ. of Nebraska Pr., 1977. - 88 p. ; ill., maps (2 in pocket) ; 24 x 31 cm.

Class Numbers:
 Library of Congress G1451.C8
ISBN 080320924X
OCLC 2965910
LCCN 77-6643
Notes:
 Appendix: State and federal climatological publications:
  p. 87-88

• One of three atlases produced by the Nebraska Atlas Project (the others cover agriculture and economic conditions, **G8** and **CF4**), this climatic atlas' charts and maps present historical data about temperature, humidity, precipitation, and wind. The atlas has two distinct functions: in keeping with the principle announced in the foreword ("Prediction is the goal of the climatologist"), the compilers have accumulated data that may be used today in predicting state climate patterns and extremes; and they describe the climate that has propelled Nebraska's settlement and economic development. The beginning dates for data vary depending on when accurate records began to be kept, but begin as early as 1850. Precipitation in the Dust Bowl years and other periods of drought is well-chronicled. The final chapter discusses perceived fluctuations in climate. The appendix is a selective but useful list of weekly, monthly, and annual sources of Nebraska climatological information. — *JD*

Oklahoma

EA26 Johnson, Howard L. - **Atlas of Oklahoma Climate** / Howard L. Johnson and Claude E. Duchon. - Norman, OK ; London : Univ. of Oklahoma Pr., 1995. - 1 atlas (xii, 32, [104] p.) ; ill., maps.

Class Numbers:
 Library of Congress G1366.C8J6
ISBN 0806126892
OCLC 31374247
LCCN 94-38763
Notes:
 Includes bibliographical references
 Scale not given

• Maps and charts, accompanied by some textual information. The table of contents simply lists six sections: introduction, geography and weather, annual climate, seasonal climate, wind and humidity, and climate and agriculture. The list of illustrations is much more detailed. The majority of the charts, tables, and maps appear in the section for seasonal climate. Climatological maps of the state show county boundaries. There is no index, compensated for by the detailed list of illustrations. — *MB*

Droughts

EA27   Wilhite, Donald A. - **Drought in the Great Plains : A Bibliography** / [comp. and ed. by Donald A. Wilhite, Richard O. Hoffman]. - [Lincoln, NE] : Agricultural Experiment Station, Univ. of Nebraska-Lincoln, Institute of Agriculture and Natural Resources, [1980]. - 75 p. - (Agricultural Experiment Station, University of Nebraska-Lincoln. Miscellaneous publication, MP 39).

Class Numbers:
 Library of Congress QC929.D8   Z6683.D7
OCLC 6898750
LCCN 80-624036
Notes:
 Indexes
 Supplements: Supplement 1, [1983]. 48 p.; Supplement 2,
  [1987]. 60 p.

• Based on a bibliography for participants in a 1979 National Science Foundation workshop, Research in Great Plains Drought Management Strategies, this work lists scholarly literature on the occurrence, impact, and mitigation of drought on the Plains. The "recurring phenomenon" (Introd.) of drought on the Great Plains creates lasting interest in the nature of past droughts and makes this resource still valuable. Confirming the preface's assertion that the literature specific to this topic is "rich and abundant," the base volume includes over 4,000 unannotated entries for published works dating back to the 19th century and for current research projects. Two supplements (1983 and 1987) add 1,349 new entries and expand coverage to popular magazines and newspapers. Author and subject indexes. For scientists and historians. — *JD*

CANADA

EA28   Longley, Richmond Wilberforce. - **Bibliography of Climatology for the Prairie Provinces 1957-1969** / bibliography eds., Richmond W. Longley, John M. Powell. - Edmonton, AB : Univ. of Alberta Pr., 1971. - 64 p. - (Studies in geography. Bibliographies, 1).

> Class Numbers:
>   Library of Congress Z6683.C5
> ISBN 0888640021
> OCLC 589544
> LCCN 72-171549

• An author listing of 665 scientific articles and reports dealing with Prairie weather. The subject index identifies many elements including the extremes, both destructive (floods, blizzards, tornadoes etc.) and benign (chinooks), characteristic of the area. A regional update to M.K. Thomas's *A Bibliography of Canadian Climate, 1763-1957* (Ottawa: Information Canada, 1961) and a companion to Longley's own *The Climate of the Prairie Provinces* (Ottawa: Information Canada, 1972). Historical statistics (maximum/minimum/mean temperature, total rain/snow/precipitation, wind speed and direction) at the micro level are available for individual communities and weather stations, in some cases going back many decades, in Environment Canada's *National Climate Archive* (http://www.climate. weatheroffice.ec.gc.ca/). — *LMcD*

EA29   Wheaton, Elaine E. - **Impacts of a Variable and Changing Climate on the Prairie Provinces : A Preliminary Integration and Annotated Bibliography** / prepared for the Canadian Climate Centre [and] Environment Canada. - Saskatoon, SK : Saskatchewan Research Council, 1994. - 140 p. ; ill. - (SRC publication, E-2900-7-E-93).

> Class Numbers:
>   Library of Congress QC981.8.C5
> OCLC 31527974

• Literature review of the environmental, social, and economic effects of climate change and global warming on the prairies. Factors considered include air and water quality, energy, agriculture, forest and wetland ecosystems, tourism, and health. The bibliography proper (p. 34-100) of 770 items is listed by author and forms half the volume. A useful synthesis and reference list for areas such as resource management and environmental protection. — *LMcD*

PALEONTOLOGY

EA30   Kues, Barry S. - **Bibliography of New Mexico Paleontology** / [by] Barry S. Kues and Stuart A. Northrop. - Albuquerque, NM : Univ. of New Mexico Pr., 1981. - 150 p.

> Class Numbers:
>   Library of Congress QE747.N6Z6033.P2
> ISBN 0826306004   9780826306005
> OCLC 7812758
> LCCN 81-14765
> Notes:
>   Index
>   Reproduced from typescript

• An author list of just over 2,000 items, chiefly journal articles and publications of government agencies (principally geological surveys) and geological societies. The only index is organized by geologic period, subarranged by major taxon. Finding materials that bear on the New Mexico plains region (the Pecos River basin and east) is therefore highly inconvenient. Little else exists on New Mexico paleontology. — *RB*

EARTHQUAKES

EA31   Frohlich, Cliff, 1947-   . - **Texas Earthquakes** / [by] Cliff Frohlich and Scott D. Davis. - Austin, TX : Univ. of Texas Pr., 2002. - 275 p. ; ill. - (Peter T. Flawn series in natural resource management and conservation, 2).

> Class Numbers:
>   Library of Congress QE535.2.U6
> ISBN 0292725507 0292725515 (pbk.)
> LCCN 2002-4972
> Notes:
>   Includes bibliographical references (p. 257-268); index
>   Table of contents: http://www.loc.gov/catdir/toc/
>   fy036/2002004972.html

• Nine chapters provide information about Texas along with information about earthquakes in general; two chapters specifically cover Texas earthquakes. The 68 illustrations consist of maps, line drawings, and cartoons, and 14 tables accompany the text. Regional information is provided by maps showing the areas where a specific earthquake was felt, and in the tables "Texas Earthquakes of Magnitude of 3.0 or More" and "Regional Earthquakes Felt in Texas." The title page contains a map showing the locations of all earthquakes felt in Texas, 1847-2001. List of references and subject index. — *MS*

EB : ENVIRONMENT ;
NATURAL RESOURCES

Scope This section includes titles that are concerned with the environment, ecology, and endangered species, and with several topics having to do with natural resources: forests (despite their supposed scarcity in the Prairies-Plains region), grasslands, land resources and use, and water.

General Works

EB1   Meisel, Max, 1892–   . - **A Bibliography of American Natural History**. - Brooklyn, NY : Premier Publ. Co., 1924-1929. - 3 v.

> Class Numbers:
> Library of Congress Z7408.U5
> OCLC 3399110
> LCCN 24-30970
> Notes:
> Subtitle: The Pioneer Century, 1769-1865; The Rôle Played by the Scientific Societies; Scientific Journals; Natural History Museums and Botanic Gardens; State Geological and Natural History Surveys; Federal Exploring Expeditions in the Rise and Progress of American Botany, Geology, Mineralogy, Paleontology and Zoology

• Cited works about the "pioneer century" in the Plains include geological surveys, travel and exploration accounts, and species descriptions. Part A (v. 1) lists 700 titles arranged by author with a classified subject index and a geographical index by city, county, state, and region. Brief notes on scope, plan, arrangement, and content are added as needed. Listed separately are 1,500 biographies and bibliographies of 600 principal American naturalists. Part B (v. 2 and 3) lists publications of 230 institutions, which are arranged chronologically by their date of founding. Their publications are categorized as history, bibliography, reports, and papers on natural history. A separate section covers self-published books and papers, obscure articles and papers, and foreign serials. Appendixes to Part B include chronological tables of publications, an index of authors and naturalists, an index of institutions, and a supplement to volume 1. Some titles appear in both Parts A and B. — *JD*

EB2   Merchant, Carolyn. - **The Columbia Guide to American Environmental History**. - New York : Columbia Univ. Pr., 2002. - 448 p. - (Columbia Guides to American History and Cultures).

> ISBN 0231112335   9780231112321

> 9780231112338
> LCCN 2001-56192
> Notes:
> Book review (H-Net): http//www.h-net.org/review/ hrev-a0d5r0.aa

• An extremely useful review of the environmental history of the United States, beginning with the land as it was regarded and managed by Indians before the Europeans came, through the conservation movements of the late 20th century. Ten chapters review briefly the interaction between people and the environment, attending to the Plains region among others (chapters on "Plains Indians and the Westward Movement," "The European Transformation of the Plains," "European Settlement of the Great Plains," "The Rancher's Frontier," "The Farmer's Frontier," "Land Law in the Arid West," and an entire section on Indian land policy). An alphabetical section has brief entries for agencies, concepts, laws, and people, and a chronology covers prehistory through 2000 CE. A section of resources lists films, videos, and Internet sites. The book ends with a bibliographic essay that usefully summarizes the most important publications covered in each of the book's chapters, and with a hundred-page bibliography arranged by broad topics. Important for students or scholars taking up study of the Plains environment and people's interaction with it. — *RB*

EB3   The Natural Environment : An Annotated Bibliography on Attitudes and Values / comp. by Mary Anglemyer and Eleanor R. Seagraves . - Washington, DC : Smithsonian Institution Pr., 1984. - 268 p.

> Class Numbers:
> Library of Congress QH75   Z7405.N38
> Government Documents SI 1.17/2:En8
> ISBN 087474220X
> OCLC 9732177
> LCCN 83-600323
> Notes:
> Index
> Sponsored by Global Tomorrow Coalition

• Residents of the fragile and diverse Great Plains have recently become acutely aware of its declining water resources and decreasing biodiversity. This multidisciplinary bibliography, while three decades old and international in approach, applies to these current local issues. Its entries catalog a variety of attitudes toward the natural environment and their effects. The writings, drawn from education, philosophy, religion, sciences, business, and the humanities, display attitudes ranging from mystical to determined exploitation. Entries include a report on values in the electric power industry, a scholarly article on Spinoza and ecology, classics like Aldo Leopold's *A Sand County Almanac*, and wide-ranging forecasts like the Club of Rome's *Beyond the Age of Waste*. The bibliography's stance is that all attitudes must be considered and adjusted in the interest of preserving the environment. Organized by broad categories, the 857 entries include monographs, chapters, and articles. Annotations supply such details as quotations, author information, and summaries of theme, relevance, and audience. Great Plains attitudes, issues, and ethical positions that shape them are shared across regions and cultures. — *JD*

EB4   Rockwell, David B. - **The Nature of North America : A Handbook to the Continent : Rocks, Plants, and Animals** / ill. by Janet McGahan. - New York : Berkley Books, 1998. - 379 p. ; ill., maps.

> Class Numbers:
>   Library of Congress QH102
>   ISBN 0425165876   0425165485 (pbk.)
>   LCCN 98-27182
>   Notes:
>   Index

• Rockwell (natural resources conservation specialist) provides a comprehensive reference work on the broad patterns affecting natural history in North America. Subject sections include geology, water, soil, climate, plants, invertebrates, fish, amphibians, reptiles, birds, and mammals. Of interest for those researching the American West are essays on the Rocky Mountains, Black Hills, Colorado Desert/ Plateau/River, Yellowstone, and the Great Plains. Animals discussed are the prairie vole, white-tailed deer, Wyoming toad, grizzly bears, coyotes, cougars, and mountain lions. Also supplies information concerning prairie plant adaptations to drought conditions, grassland prairies, and sagebrush. Numerous illustrations, tables, charts, line drawings, and maps. — *GK*

EB5   Shirley, Shirley. - **Restoring the Tallgrass Prairie : An Illustrated Manual for Iowa and the Upper Midwest.** - Iowa City, IA : Univ. of Iowa Pr., 1994. - 330 p. ; ill. - (A Bur Oak original).

> Class Numbers:
>   Library of Congress SB434.3.S48
>   ISBN 087745468X   0877454698 (pbk.)
>   OCLC 29954202
>   LCCN 94-7374
>   Notes:
>   Includes bibliographical references (p. 315-322); index

• The first part of Shirley's volume consists of a guide to prairie restoration, including chapters on site planning, seed selection, site preparation, and planting. But the greater part of the volume supplies an extensive list of about 110 species of wildflowers and grasses. Each entry includes a line drawing, name and classification, location, description, propagation, germination, harvest, attractants, and

comments. A glossary, an interesting pictorial glossary, a chronological blooming list, butterfly habitats, family characteristics, sources for seeds and plants, a brief list of organizations that sponsor restoration, a bibliography, and an index complete the volume. — *MB*

Collective Biographies

EB6   Axelrod, Alan, 1952- . - **The Environmentalists : A Biographical Dictionary from the 17th Century to the Present** / [by] Alan Axelrod and Charles Phillips. - New York : Facts on File, 1993. - 258 p. ; ill.

> Class Numbers:
>   Library of Congress S926.A2
>   ISBN 0816027153
>   LCCN 92-38773
>   Notes:
>   Includes bibliographical references; index

• Profiles cover contemporary organizations, authors, activists, administrators, and scientists who have shaped U.S. environmental policy, study, or philosophy, along with historical personalities who made landmark contributions to the field. Many, such as the Grassland Heritage Foundation and John Wesley Powell (who pioneered the study of water use in arid lands), have had a significant impact on the Great Plains. Individual entries give birth and death dates, professional biographies, achievements, highly selected lists of publications, and sometimes one or two sources for further reading. Organizational entries (interfiled with individuals) give directory information, mission, and history. Illustrated with portraits and scenic photographs. Biographies are indexed by names and topics. — *JD*

UNITED STATES

EB7   Huber, Thomas Patrick. - **Colorado : The Place of Nature, the Nature of Place.** - Niwot, CO : Univ. Pr. of Colorado, 1993. - 296 p. ; ill., maps.

> Class Numbers:
>   Library of Congress F776
>   Government Document Colorado
>   UCB20/10.2/N21/1993
>   ISBN 0870812890   0870812904 (pbk.)
>   0585004447 (electronic bk.)
>   LCCN 93-21472
>   Notes:
>   Electronic book: http://www.netLibrary.com/urlapi.asp?
>   action=summary&v=1&bookid=310
>   Includes bibliographical references; index

• Overviews of the landforms, geology, ecology, climate, vegetation, fauna, ecosystems, and special features of the state and of 12 natural places: Mount Evans, Crested Butte, Steamboat Lake, Florissant Fossil Beds, Garden of the Gods, Comanche National Grassland, Tamarack Ranch, Silverton, Piceance Creek Basin, Great Sand Dunes, Slumgullion Slide, and Colorado National Monument. Each place is unique but intended to represent the general pattern of Colorado landscapes. Intended to inform, tantalize, and sensitize students and travelers, the book can be read as a narrative or used as a reference source. Additional readings for each place include books, popular magazines, and technical reports that can jump-start further research. Diagrams of geologic formations; black-and-white photographs of landscapes; and a list of maps published by the U.S. Geological Survey, Bureau of Land Management, and Forest Service are included. Indexed by personal names, common names of plants and animals, features, and locations. — *JD*

EB8   Johnsgard, Paul A. - **A Guide to the Tallgrass Prairies of Eastern Nebraska**. - [Lincoln, NE] : School of Biological Sciences, Univ. of Nebraska-Lincoln, 2006. - 90 p. ; ill., maps.

Class Numbers:
    Library of Congress QH541.5.P7
    OCLC 67226357
    Notes:
        Includes bibliographical references (p. 87-90)

• Johnsgard enumerates the plants and animals of the tallgrass prairies, which he asserts are now 95 percent gone. His slim volume compiles some results of studies of the areas that remain. Part 1 describes the ecology of the tallgrass prairie and its subtypes. Part 2 covers plants with a checklist of plants; relative frequencies; the 20 most abundant fall forbs; typical shrubs, forbs, grasses and sedges; English-Latin and Latin-English equivalents; and identification keys to common forbs. Part 3 covers animals, supplying a detailed description of prairie chickens, checklists of birds, and sections on mammals, typical reptiles and amphibians, typical butterflies, and grasshoppers, mantids, and walking sticks. Part 4 gives locations and visitor information for tallgrass prairies by county, along with location maps for some, citing popular and scholarly works. Though the guide is not comprehensive and much of the information is drawn from previous publications by Johnsgard and others, he provides a convenient guide for tallgrass prairie aficionados. — *JD*

EB9   Johnsgard, Paul A. - **The Nature of Nebraska : Ecology and Biodiversity**. - Lincoln, NE : Univ. of Nebraska Pr., 2001. - xxiii, 402 p. ; ill.

Class Numbers:
    Library of Congress QH105.N2
    ISBN 0803225962

OCLC 458795507
LCCN 2001-27065
Notes:
    Includes bibliographical references (p. 259-393); index
    Table of contents: http://www.loc.gov/catdir/toc/fy031/
        2001027065.html

• Johnsgard devotes the first 200 pages to vivid descriptions of the diverse geology, landforms, biomes, natural communities, and ecoregions that sustain Nebraska's diverse natural life-forms. He defines ecological regions and biological communities in greater detail by supplying information about terrestrial community types, profiles of keystone and typical species, and vignettes of endangered and declining species. Illustrations include maps, charts, and Johnsgard's line drawings of inhabitants. The 200 pages of appendixes contain the only current comprehensive checklist of Nebraska flora and fauna. It provides common names and brief descriptions of species' primary habits and status. Although Johnsgard omits information about current range, population, and distribution, references in the appendixes cite important updates to earlier species accounts. The revised taxonomy updates earlier works. The appendixes include a guide to Nebraska's 400 public access natural areas and preserves, an index to selected Museum Notes from the Univ. of Nebraska State Museum, an index to *NEBRASKAland* notes about Nebraska flora and fauna, a glossary, extensive references to technical and popular literature, and general and county indexes. An important compilation. — *JD*

EB10   Texas Center for Policy Studies. - **Texas Environmental Almanac** / comp. by Mary Sanger and Cyrus Reed. - 2nd ed. - Austin, TX : Univ. of Texas Pr., 2000. - 387 p. ; ill., maps.

Class Numbers:
    Library of Congress GE155.T4
    ISBN 0292777493 (pbk.)
    OCLC 44517874
    LCCN 99-6872

• Intending to provide timely information about the environment of Texas, this almanac covers water quality, land, wildlife and biodiversity, air quality, energy, municipal waste, and industrial waste. Each topic has an essay that focuses on a special aspect of the topic or a strong influence on the topic. There are many maps, graphs, and tables, and a detailed index. — *JB*

CANADA

EB11   Robinson, Jill M., comp. - **Seas of Earth : An Annotated Bibliography of Saskatchewan Literature as it**

Relates to the Environment. - Regina, SK : Canadian Plains Research Center, Univ. of Regina, 1977. - 139 p. ; ill. - (Canadian plains reports, 2).

Class Numbers:
    Library of Congress F1071   Z1392.S2
  ISBN 0889770107
  OCLC 4465989
  LCCN 78-316923

• A combination of commentary and bibliography of approximately 140 works, both imaginative and nonfiction, that consider natural forces of the Prairies. Chapters examine fiction, pioneer accounts, histories, travel accounts, and biographies for the role played by the prairie environment. Within each, several titles receive two- or three-page analyses, followed by supplementary bibliographies of additional titles. Aimed at a high school audience, but worthwhile for anyone interested in one of the enduring themes of Saskatchewan writing. — *LMcD*

EB12   Saskatchewan Environmental Directory. - [1st] (1992)-   . Regina, SK : Saskatchewan Environment and Public Safety, 1992-   . - Annual.

Class Numbers:
  Library of Congress GE20
  National Library of Canada HC117
  OCLC 30842943
  LCCN 95-640746; cn 94-801220
  Notes:
    Electronic book: http://www.se.gov.sk.ca/corporate/ whoswho/
    Issued 1993- by Saskatchewan Environment and Resource Management

• Lists government departments (federal, provincial, and municipal), major resource companies, environmental consultants, environmental law firms, media, and nongovernmental agencies. Entries provide contact information and brief description of areas of focus. — *LMcD*

Natural Resurces

General Works; Ecology

EB13   Annotated Bibliography of Natural Resource Information, Southwestern North Dakota / comp. by North Dakota Game and Fish Dept. and Ecology Consultants Inc. ; performed for Western Energy and Land Use Team, Office of Biological Services, Fish and Wildlife Service, U.S. Dept. of the Interior. - [Washington, DC] :

Biological Services Program, Fish and Wildlife Service, U.S. Dept. of the Interior, 1977. - 215 p. ; map. - (FWS/OBS, 77/32).

Class Numbers:
  Library of Congress Z5322.E2
  OCLC 4868569
  Notes:
    Indexes

• Intended to assist researchers working on the Regional Environmental Test Area project, of which southwestern North Dakota was a part, this bibliography, completed in summer 1977, reports results of a literature search covering geology, hydrology, topography, land use, mineral use, vegetation, and wildlife. Entries list published and unpublished works–books, articles, government agency publications, theses and dissertations, etc. Entries provide abstracts and cross-references; indexes by subject, geographic location, taxonomic classification, and author. — *JB*

EB14   Geological Survey (U.S.). - **Status and Trends of the Nation's Biological Resources**. - Fort Collins, CO : U.S. Dept. of the Interior, U.S. Geological Survey ; Washington, DC : U.S. Govt. Print. Off, 1998. - 2 v. (964 p.) ; ill. (some col., col. maps)

Class Numbers:
  Library of Congress QH104
  Government Document I 19.202:ST 1.V1-2
  ISBN 016053285X
  LCCN 97-35780
  Notes:
    Also accessible as: http://biology.usgs.gov/s+t/SNT/ index.htm
    Includes bibliographical references; indexes

• Described in the foreword as "the first large-scale assessment of the health of the nation's plants, animals, and ecosystems," the document is peer-reviewed by scientists but geared to a wider audience of managers, policymakers, and the general public. Part 1 describes general factors (such as fire, water use, nonindigenous species) that affect biological resources. Part 2 considers regional trends in 14 geographical areas (the Plains are covered by two sections, "The Grasslands" and "The Southwest"). In subsections like "Tall Grass Prairie Butterflies and Birds," texts, statistical tables, maps, illustrations, and charts synthesize the status and trends in the ecosystems and document changes in habitats, numbers, and ranges of specific species. References are cited in each subsection. List of common and scientific names, glossary, index. Widely available on the Internet, the report is officially posted on the USGS site (http://biology.usgs.gov/s+t/SNT/index.htm). The "Grass-lands" section can be downloaded in pdf format from the *Northern Prairie Wildlife Research Center* Internet site; (**EC1**). — *JD*

EB15   H. John Heinz III Center for Science, Economics, and the Environment. - **The State of the Nation's Ecosystems : Measuring the Lands, Waters, and Living Resources of the United States** / [ed. by] the H. John Heinz III Center for Science, Economics, and the Environment. - Cambridge, UK ; New York : Cambridge Univ. Pr., 2002. - 270 p. ; col. ill., col. maps.

> Class Numbers:
> > Library of Congress QH104
> > ISBN 0521525721 (pbk.)
> > LCCN 2002-73890
> > Notes:
> > > Includes bibliographical references
> > > Table of contents: http://www.loc.gov/catdir/toc/
> > > cam031/2002073890.html

• Chemical, physical, biological, and production indicators of the health of six ecosystems are identified in this report for policymakers and the public. All six ecosystems, coasts and oceans, farmlands, forests, fresh waters, grasslands and shrublands, and urban and suburban areas, cover parts of the Great Plains. Current conditions and historic trends in indicators in each ecosystem are described with tables, maps, charts, and accompanying text. Many indicators relate to major Plains environmental, economic, and policy issues such as pesticides in farmland streams, established nonnative species, production of food and fiber and water withdrawals, and croplands prone to wind erosion. National reporting varies; some statistics cover single states, others broad geographic regions. Data sources are clearly cited and graphics indicate gaps in important data. Extensive technical notes define ecosystems, indicators, and methodologies. A good companion to the USGS *Status and Trends of the Nation's Biological Resources* (**EB14**). — *JD*

EB16   LaRoe, Edward Terhune. - **Our Living Resources : A Report to the Nation on the Distribution, Abundance, and Health of U.S. Plants, Animals, and Ecosystems** / [ed. by] Edward T. LaRoe [et al.]. - Washington, DC : U.S. Dept. of the Interior. National Biological Service, 1995. - 530 p. ; ill. (some col.), maps, charts.

> Class Numbers:
> > Library of Congress QH104
> > LCCN 95-198061
> > Notes:
> > > Accessible as: http://purl.access.gpo.gov/GPO/LPS13985
> > > Includes bibliographical references ; index

• Presenting text, tables, maps, and charts on species and ecosystems, this report addresses itself to scientists, managers, and general readers. Following an introduction to biodiversity and the role of federal agencies, part 2 covers the distribution, abundance, and health of plants, animals, ecosystems, and ecoregions. Overviews are supplemented with trends in specific species and habitats, such as eagles in Colorado and migratory birds in North Dakota. It covers the ecoregion of the Great Plains, discussing trends in indicator species of environmental change: birds, fish, and coyotes. Part 3 covers the special issues of global climate change, human influences, nonnative species, and habitat assessment. Many of the examples, such as purple loosestrife, wild horses on public lands, wildlife mortality ascribed to pesticides, and agricultural ecosystems are important Plains issues. Glossary and thorough subject index that includes both common and scientific species names. Complements *State of the Nation's Ecosystems* (**EB15**) and its follow-up report, *Status and Trends of the Nation's Biological Resources* (**EB14**). — *JD*

EB17   **Natural Resources Data Bank [Internet Site]** / Nebraska Dept. of Natural Resources. - [Lincoln, NE] : Department of Natural Resources, 2000?-   . - http://www.dnr.state.ne.us/databank/dbindex.html

> Access Date : Jan. 2006
> Notes:
> > Fees: access is free; fees charged for requests requiring data processing.

• *Data Bank* supplies data and mapped data about Nebraska land and water resources. The spatial/Geographic Information System and relational/tabular databases are suitable only for specialized, technologically astute users. Topics include demographics, soils, groundwater, surface water, wells, dams, and reservoirs. More suitable for general readers are "Nebraska Interactive Maps," displaying wells, groundwater, water level, climate station, Census results, and other information. Some specialized data are available at the site, some must be downloaded or requested from the Department of Natural Resources (fees charged). Projects that have used *Data Bank* data and maps include base maps, soil surveys, farm and ranch planning, background images, and floodplain delineations. — *JD*

EB18   **Statewide Digital Data Bases [Internet Site]**. - Lincoln, NE : University of Nebraska-Lincoln, Center for Advanced Land Management Information Technologies (CALMIT) ; University of Nebraska-Lincoln. School of Natural Resources. Conservation and Survey Division (CSD), 2000?-   . - http://csd.unl.edu/general/gis-datasets.asp

> OCLC 44207355
> Access Date: Jan. 2006
> Fees: None

• CALMIT and CSD have assembled a set of spatial databases for Geographic Information Systems (GIS) mapping. Primarily focused on state conservation and natural resources, the Internet site does not include data with less than statewide coverage. Available databases are both listed by title in a table of contents and described in brief records. The brief records display a small image of the mapped data and a description of the data, along with links to the metadata, data in ARC/INFO export format, and larger map images in JPEG format. The data descriptions cover source, methodology, scale, date, related data, and planned updates. Topics include active mineral operations; bedrock geology; center pivot irrigation systems; railroads; depth-to-water; slope; land use and land cover; streams; ranges and townships; and native vegetation. The data are useful for both researchers and practitioners. The database choices are clearly presented and defined. — *JD*

ENDANGERED SPECIES

EB19   Campbell, Linda. - **Endangered and Threatened Animals of Texas : Their Life History and Management**. - Austin, TX : Texas Parks & Wildlife, Resource Protection Div., Endangered Resources Branch ; distr. by Univ. of Texas Pr., 1995. - 130 p. ; ill. (some col.), maps.

> Class Numbers:
> Library of Congress QL84.22.T4
> LCCN 96-154960
> Notes:
> > Table of contents: htp://www.loc.gov/catdir/toc/
> > texas051/96154960.html

• In six categories (mammals, birds, reptiles, amphibians, fish, and invertebrates) Campbell provides two-page essays for each species. Species accounts give common and scientific names and cover habitat, life history, current threats and reasons for decline, and recovery efforts. Each essay notes the species status on both federal and state lists, contains a map showing historic and current range, a color photograph, and references. Some essays are followed by material on habitat rehabilitation. A description of the endangered species process, and a list of state endangered and threatened species comprise the appendixes. — *MS*

EB20   Crawford, Mark, 1954-   . - **Habitats and Ecosystems : An Encyclopedia of Endangered America**. - Santa Barbara, CA : ABC-CLIO, 1999. - 398 p.

> Class Numbers:
> Library of Congress QH76
> ISBN 0874369975   1576074536 (electronic bk.)
> OCLC 43164895
> LCCN 00-698072
> Notes:
> > Companion to: Mark Crawford, *Toxic Waste Sites: An*
> > *Encyclopedia of Endangered America*. Santa Barbara, CA:
> > ABC-CLIO, 1997
> > Electronic book: http://www.netLibrary.com/urlapi.asp?

action=summary&v=1&bookid=71363
Includes bibliographical references (p. 361-375); index

• Crawford has compiled a register of habitats and ecosystems that are home to endangered and threatened plant and animal species in the United States. Arranged alphabetically by state, the register uses local names (e.g., Cheyenne Bottoms) to locate habitat sites, supplying only the county name and keeping exact locations carefully vague (e.g., "north of Medora"); there are no maps. Many properties are owned by the Nature Conservancy. Besides county name, Crawford gives for habitats a brief description and lists some endangered and threatened species. End matter includes a glossary, lists of national and state organizations concerned with wildlife preservation, endangered and threatened flora and fauna (arranged by state), an excellent bibliography that cites general references then references by state, and an index, principally of site names. All Prairies-Plains states are included. Useful in identifying endangered or threatened species and their habitats. — *RB*

EB21   **An Illustrated Guide to Endangered or Threatened Species in Kansas** / [by] Joseph T. Collins [et al.] ; foreword by John E. Hayes Jr. - Lawrence, KS : Univ. Pr. of Kansas, 1995. - 140 p. ; col. ill., maps. - (Kansas nature guides).

> Class Numbers:
> Library of Congress   QH76.5.K2
> ISBN 0700607269
> LCCN 95-19590
> Notes:
> > Publ. in cooperation with the Kansas Dept. of Wildlife and
> > Parks with advice and assistance of Kansas Natural History
> > Museum, Kansas Biological Survey, U.S. Fish and Wildlife
> > Service

• For use by both amateurs and professionals, this guide covers 60 animal species classified by Kansas or federal agencies as endangered or threatened in 1995. Accounts include a color photo, official status, description, size, habitat reproduction, food, critical habitat in Kansas, and a range map. Can be used as a field guide or as a comparison to the current status of wildlife in the Plains. List of suggested books and index by popular and scientific names. — *JD*

GRASSLANDS

EB22   **Annotated Bibliography of Fire Literature Relative to Northern Grasslands in South-Central Canada and North-Central United States** / Kenneth F. Higgins [et al.]. - [Brookings, SD?] : U.S. Fish and Wildlife Service, South Dakota Cooperative Fish and Wildlife Research Unit, South Dakota State University, 1989. - 20 p.

Class Numbers:
  Library of Congress SD421.5
  OCLC 21290895
  LCCN 89-621920
Notes:
  Electronic book: http://agbiopubs.sdstate.edu/articles/
    EC762.pdf

• An author list, with subject index, of approximately 200 items related to both natural and planned fires on the Prairies. The effects on specific species of animals, birds and vegetation; fire prevention and suppression in various locations and seasons; and controlled burning are among the aspects of fire ecology covered. — *LMcD*

EB23   Moul, Francis. - **The National Grasslands : A Guide to America's Undiscovered Treasures** / photography by Georg Joutras. - Lincoln, NE : Univ. of Nebraska Pr., 2006. - 204 p. ; color ill., maps.

Class Numbers:
  Library of Congress QH104.5 W4
  ISBN 0803283202
  OCLC 64065811

• Combining natural history, political history, environmental status reports, and grasslands advocacy, Moul's well-documented introductory overview will interest students and scholars of the Plains. It reports on grassland droughts, land use, economic importance, relief programs, and the history of the establishment and management of national grasslands. A reference and travel guide to each grassland in the U.S. and the National Grasslands of Canada follows. Entries, which quote grassland officials, biologists, ranchers, and others with extensive knowledge of the grasslands, vividly portray the varied terrain, climate, wildlife, flora, public facilities, and special features of each. Maps are included. The fine color photographs will appeal to all fans of Western landscapes. —*JD*

EB24   Pemble, Richard H. - **Native Grassland Ecosystems East of the Rocky Mountains in North America : A Preliminary Bibliography** / [by] Richard H. Pemble, Ronald L. Stuckey, Lynn Edward Elfner. - [Grand Forks, ND : Univ. of North Dakota Pr., 1975?]. - 466 p.

Class Numbers:
  Library of Congress QH104
Notes:
  Publ. as a supplement to: Midwest Prairie Conference
    (4th: 1974), which had special title: *Prairie: A Multiple
    View*

• Author list, without annotations, of approximately 7,000 items on the grassland biome of North America. Most

studies focus on the Great Plains but coverage extends eastward as far as Ohio and Ontario. Early travel accounts, agricultural development, habitat destruction, prairie restoration, and plant and animal distribution are among the themes. Lack of a subject arrangement or topical index limits the bibliography's usefulness and only the most determined would plod through the entire work. Fortunately keyword searching is possible through the online version available in the "Ecology and Natural Collections" section of the University of Wisconsin Digital Collections Internet site (http://digicoll.library.wisc.edu/ cgi-bin/EcoNatRes/EcoNatRes-idx?id=EcoNatRes. NAPC04s), opening up for exploration the large amount of frequently obscure material assembled here. — *LMcD*

LAND

EB25   **Agricultural Land Resource Atlas of Alberta**. - Rev. ed. - Edmonton, AB : Alberta Agriculture, Food and Rural Development, Resource Management and Irrigation Division, Conservation and Development Branch, 2005. - 1 atlas (50 p.) ; col. maps ; 44 cm.

Class Numbers:
  Library of Congress G1166.J3
  OCLC 67672301
  LCCN 2006-627732
Notes:
  "Agriculture and Agri-Food Canada–Agriculture et
    agroalimentaire Canada."
  Available as: http://www1.agric.gov.ab.ca
  Originally publ. 1997
  Scale ca. 1:3,150,000

• An atlas that focuses on environmental impacts of agriculture in Alberta. The 25 maps cover risks (surface and groundwater quality, erosion, air quality, and biodiversity) as well as elements such as precipitation, soils, frost-free periods, and wetlands. Each map contains a description, data sources, potential uses, limitations, and sources for additional information. Useful to the agricultural sector and environmentalists. — *LMcD*

EB26   U.S. Dept. of Agriculture. Soil Conservation Service. - **Land Resource Regions and Major Land Resource Areas of the United States**. - Rev. ed. - Washington, DC : U.S. Dept. of Agriculture. Soil Conservation Service, 1981. - 156 p. ; maps (some col.). - (U.S. Dept. of Agriculture. Agricultural handbook, 296).

Class Numbers:
  Library of Congress HD110.5.U5

• Identifies and describes major land resource areas (MLRAs) of the U.S., including Alaska, Hawai'i, Puerto

Rico, and the U.S. Virgin Islands. The handbook provides for each MLRA its current land use, elevation and topography, climate, water, soils, and potential natural vegetation. The 182 MLRAs are numbered and discussed in numerical order, but are arranged by 25 land resource regions that group MLRAs with similar characteristics (e.g., "Northern Great Plains Spring Wheat Region," "Southwestern Prairies Cotton and Forage Region"). A foldout map shows in color the land resource regions and MLRAs. A brief bibliography is followed by appendixes that include the areas of land resource units and MLRAs and provide a classification of soils. The Prairies-Plains region is divided among six land resource regions. — *RB*

WATER

General Works

EB27   Encyclopedia of Water Science / ed. by B.A. Stewart, Terry A. Howell. - New York : Marcel Dekker, 2003. - 1076 p. ; ill., maps.

Class Numbers:
    Library of Congress S494.W3
    ISBN 0824709489
    LCCN 2003-55700
Notes:
    Includes bibliographical references; index

• Howell (agricultural engineer, U.S. Dept. of Agriculture) and Stewart (professor of soil science, West Texas A&M Univ.) have assembled 250 articles on the management, treatment, and protection of water resources. An international team of professionals wrote on such topics as current laws and regulations, irrigation, agricultural economics, agro-forestry, erosion control, and groundwater sanitation. Four articles pertain to the Great Plains region: Platte River, rural water supply, Dust Bowl era, and groundwater law in the Western U.S. Includes illustrations, maps, and graphs. — *GK*

EB28   National Water Summary / Geological Survey (U.S.). - [1st] (1984)-   . [Reston, VA] : U.S. Dept. of the Interior, Geological Survey ; Washington, DC : U.S. Govt. Print. Off., 1984-   . - Biennial.

Class Numbers:
    Library of Congress GB701
    Government Document I 19.13/3: ; I 19.13:
    OCLC 12379142
    LCCN 85-644161
Notes:
    Frequency varies: annual, 1983-1987
    Includes bibliographical references

Series: United States Geological Survey. Water-supply paper 0886-9308
    Some vols. distributed to depository libraries in microfiche

• Designed for the general public, the series focuses on trends in water, a primary concern in the Plains states. Each volume focuses on selected topics such as hydrologic events, water quality, water supply and use, floods and droughts, stream water quality, surface water resources, and wetland resources. Maps and graphs illustrate trends in the nature, distribution and magnitude of water supplies; state-by-state summaries of trends; and articles on water-related themes. Supplemented with glossaries. Useful for comparisons with current data, which is available through the "Water Resources of the U.S." page of the U.S. Geological Survey Internet site (http://water.usgs.gov) and on state geological survey sites. The USGS page offers national and state-by-state analyses, tables, maps, datasets, and real-time data on water. — *JD*

EB29   Nebraska Water Resources Center. - Water Resources Publications Related to the State of Nebraska / Nebraska Water Resources Center, Institute of Agriculture and Natural Resources, Univ. of Nebraska-Lincoln. - [Lincoln, NE] : Nebraska Water Resources Center, 1982. - 165 p. - (NWRC publication, 7).

Class Numbers:
    Library of Congress Z7935
    OCLC 8789962
Notes:
    Indexes

• An unannotated list of difficult-to-identify books, articles, maps, and reports published by federal agencies, state agencies, University of Nebraska units, Nebraska Natural Resources Districts, and other organizations, useful for those seeking historical data and research reports on surface and ground water supplies, quality, use, economics, laws, and effects on the rest of the environment. Topics include magnitude and frequency of floods; deep well statistics; geology of the Republican River; drought patterns; and irrigation practices. Organized by publishing agency and subdivided by broad topics and dates. Author index but, unfortunately, no subject index. The Internet site of the publisher's successor, the Water Center of the School of Natural Resources at University of Nebraska-Lincoln, http://watercenter.unl.edu, is the best source for current information and research reports. — *JD*

EB30 Surf Your Watershed [Internet Site]. - Washington, DC : Environmental Protection Agency, 2000s-. - http://cfpub1.epa.gov/surf/locate/index.cfm

Access Date: May 2008
Fees: None

• Since both surface and ground water are subjects of contention in the Plains, this site will interest a wide range of users. Watersheds can be searched ten ways, some clearly intended for researchers and water professionals while others might be used by interested citizens and students. The search modes are zip code, city name, watershed name, state stream, eight-digit USGS hydrologic cataloging code, county name, national estuary program, community water system identification number, and large ecosystem. Watersheds may also be chosen by clicking on a map of the continental U.S. Information specific to each watershed includes maps, citizen groups at work, environmental Internet sites, impairments, and links to watersheds upstream and downstream. The site also links to state water assessments of biological health and water quality, related EPA databases on topics such as such as hazardous waste and community water sources, and USGS water data for the state and the U.S. This gem is hidden in the complex and seminavigable EPA Internet site. — *JD*

EB31   Water Resources Abstracts [Internet Site]. - Bethesda, MD : Cambridge Scientific Abstracts, 1994- . - http://www.csa.com

> Class Numbers:
>> Library of Congress TC1
>
> OCLC 36888825
> Access Date: July 2006
> Notes:
>> Continues the print and online title *Selected Water Resources Abstracts* produced by the U.S. Geological Survey.
>
> Fees: Subscription

• Concentrating on water supply and treatment, this site covers issues whose solutions are essential to the future of the Plains. They include groundwater, water supply and conservation, water quantity management and control, watershed protection, water resources planning, and water law. Providing abstracts of journals, books, proceedings, technical reports, and government documents in physical science, life science, engineering, and law published from 1967 to the present, the site is updated monthly with approximately 1,000 new records and includes foreign language and international material. The premier source on water literature, it can be used in conjunction with the USGS page, *Water Resources in the U.S.* (http://www.water.usgs.gov) and with state geological survey sites for nearly complete coverage of Plains water and water issues. — *JD*

Aquifers

EB32   Kansas Geological Survey. - **An Atlas of the Kansas High Plains Aquifer** / prepared by the Kansas Geological Survey and the Kansas Water Office. -

Lawrence, KS : Kansas Geological Survey, 2000. - 1 v. (various foliations) ; col. maps, charts. - (Kansas Geological Survey. Educational series, 14).

> Class Numbers:
>> Government Publication Kansas E 54.2:H 638/draft
>
> OCLC 58527371
> Notes:
>> Draft
>>
>> The sections in this draft (except Section P) can be found at the Internet site: http://www.kgc.ku.edu/HighPlains/atlas

• Charts, graphs, and maps at this site provide data of interest to policymakers, farmers, ranchers, conservationists, and researchers in the High Plains. Topics include surface water and its interaction with groundwater, High Plains aquifers, estimated life expectancy of aquifers, irrigated acreage and cropping trends. Technical appendixes cover, e.g., atlas terminology, data sources, concepts, and measurements. A historical overview of the decline in saturated thickness graphically summarizes the data and points to the need for water sustainability. The simple explanations, clear graphics, and well-presented data give the site appeal to general audiences. The Internet version is silent about updating, but it offers useful links in the atlas pages. — *JD*

Groundwater

EB33   Borton, Robert L. - Bibliography of Ground-Water Studies in New Mexico. - Santa Fe, NM : New Mexico State Engineer, 1972. - 28 p. - (New Mexico State Engineer. Special publication).

> Class Numbers:
>> Library of Congress TD224.N6 Z7935
>
> OCLC 699493
> Notes:
>> Supplemented by: *Bibliography of Ground-Water Studies in New Mexico, 1873-1977* (Santa Fe, NM: New Mexico State Engineer, 1978, OCLC 4144692) 121 p.; and by: *Bibliography of Ground-Water Studies in New Mexico, 1848-1979* (Santa FE, NM: New Mexico State Engineer, 1980. OCLC 7282072) 46 p. Both comp. by Borton

• These three bibliographies cite studies of ground-water in all parts of New Mexico, where finding water is a matter of the first importance. All three are author lists. The first has 284 entries and lacks any indexes, so finding entries having to do with the Plains region of the state requires scanning all the entries. The 1978 supplement, with 446 entries, has indexes by areas (including Great Plains, High Plains, New Mexico by region, New Mexico counties [a map at the front identifies all the counties], Northern High Plains, Southern

High Plains, and "Specific Areas" [among them the Llano Estacado]). The 1980 supplement has 116 entries and is arranged like the 1972 supplement. — *RB*

EB34 Colorado Geological Survey. - **Ground Water Atlas of Colorado** / [by] Ralf Topper [et al.] ; Jason C. Wilson, GIS and cartography. - Denver, CO : Colorado Geological Survey, 2003. - 1 atlas (210 p.) ; col. ill., col. maps 28 x 44 cm. - (Colorado Geological Survey. Special publication, 53).

> Class Numbers:
> Library of Congress G1501.C34
> ISBN 1884216587
> LCCN 2003-683863
> Notes:
> Includes bibliographical references
> Scales differ

• Topper and Wilson (Colorado Geological Survey and GIS, cartography) provide an atlas for use as a comprehensive reference guide to Colorado's complex ground water resources. They include location, geography, geology, water quality, and hydrologic characteristics of its aquifers. The purpose of the atlas is to give information to policy makers, developers, district water managers, technical staff, and the public to enable decisions concerning ground water. Chapters 1-3 address ground water in a geological, hydrological, and legal context, while chapters 4-7 focus on the major aspects of the state's major aquifer systems. The only appendix is a water terminology glossary. — *GK*

EB35 University of Nebraska-Lincoln. Conservation and Survey Division. - **The Groundwater Atlas of Nebraska**. - Lincoln, NE : Conservation and Survey Div., Univ. of Nebraska-Lincoln, 1998. - 1 atlas (32 p.) ; ill. (some col.), maps (some col.) ; 28 cm. - (Resource atlas, 4a).

> Class Numbers:
> Library of Congress G1451.C34
> Notes:
> Scale: 1:3,000,000
> Supported by the Groundwater Foundation (Lincoln, NE)

• Nebraska has a lot of water, but most of it is underground—facts central to an understanding of the state's history, farming and ranching, natural resources, and economic development. Decline in the amount of underground water and its relation to surface water underlie recent struggles over water law and public policy. The Conservation and Survey Division is the agency charged to "investigate and interpret the geologically related natural resources of the state" (Foreword). The atlas' maps, diagrams, and analysis describe regional conditions (e.g., average annual discharge

of streams and reservoirs, topographic regions, groundwater regions, geology, locations of test wells, depth to the water table, surface water irrigation projects, irrigation wells, average annual precipitation, rises and declines in groundwater levels). Includes selected references and glossary. More detailed annual information may be found at the Division's *Groundwater Levels Map Archives* site (http://csd.unl.edu/ surveyareas/gwmaparchives.asp). — *JD*

Irrigation

EB36 **Great Plains Irrigation, 1975-80 : A Literature Review** / Curtis A. Everson; Rodney L. Sharp. - Washington, DC : U.S. Dept. of Agriculture, Economic Research Service, 1981. - 69 p.

> Class Numbers:
> Library of Congress S616.U6   Z5074.I7
> Government Document A 1.60/3:22
> LCCN 81-603133

• Cites 467 studies published 1975-1980 treating various aspects of irrigation in Great Plains states. Intended for individual farmers and agribusiness firms. Has sections for, e.g., "Economics of Irrigation with Limited Water," "Energy Use and Conservation," "Irrigation Efficiency," "Water Quality." Cites many studies from agricultural extension services of individual states, which may make some publications ticklish to locate. — *RB*

Limnology

EB37 **Atlas of Alberta Lakes** / ed. by Patricia Mitchell, Ellie Prepas ; writers, J.M. Crosby [et al.] ; contributors, W.M. Tonn, P.A. Chambers. - Edmonton, AB : Univ. of Alberta Pr., 1990 [1997]. - 675 p. ; ill. (some col.), col. maps ; 37 cm.

> Class Numbers:
> Library of Congress G1166.C3
> ISBN 0888642148   0888642156 (pbk.)
> OCLC 21447458
> LCCN 93-676504
> Notes:
> Electronic book: http://sunsite.ualberta.ca/Projects/
> Alberta-Lakes/
> Includes bibliographical references (p. 661-665), glossary, and index

• Covers 100 lakes, selected for availability of scientific data as well as their recreational or economic value; lakes in national parks are excluded. The first part explains scientific terms and discusses features of Alberta drainage basins and lake basins, water quality, and biology. Each chapter examines a single lake, arranged by river basin. Description (location, facilities, access) and history are followed by detailed information including soils, water levels, area, volume, depth, fish, surrounding plants and animals, and bibliography. Numerous tables and graphs; species list (animals in taxonomic order; plants in alphabetical order by common name). User's guide on endpapers. Informative for both recreational users and scientists. — *LMcD*

EB38 Atton, F. M. - **Bibliography of Limnology and Aquatic Fauna and Flora of Saskatchewan** / by F.M. Atton, R.P. Johnson, and N.W. Smith. - [Regina, SK?] : Saskatchewan Dept. of Tourism and Renewable Resources, 1974. - 34 p. - (Fisheries report ; no. 10).

Class Numbers:
Library of Congress QH106.2.S27   Z5322.F7
OCLC 3541348
LCCN 77-372600

• An author list of works examining Saskatchewan's lakes and streams. Representative areas include water chemistry and physics, water levels, evaporation rates, ice formation and other aspects of limnobiology; groundwater is not included. Geological reports are included only if treating a particular body of water. Citations range in date from 1836 to 1972. The subject index groups major categories subdivided by specific topic. Later works are covered by Cambridge Scientific Abstracts' *Water Resources Abstracts* (**EB31**). — *LMcD*

Rivers

EB39 Bartlett, Richard A., ed. - **Rolling Rivers : An Encyclopedia of America's Rivers**. - New York : McGraw-Hill, 1984. - 398 p. ; ill.

Class Numbers:
Library of Congress GB1215
ISBN 0070039100
OCLC 10807295
LCCN 83-18745
Notes:
Includes bibliographies; index

• Bartlett's encyclopedia covers the 117 rivers he believes have been most important in the history of the U.S. The rivers are arranged by region (East Coast, Northeast Mississippi Valley, Northwest Mississippi Valley, Southeast and Texas, Great Basin and Arizona, Pacific Coast and Alaska), then alphabetically by river. For each, Bartlett provides some basic facts in a text box at the beginning (source, length, tributaries, mouth, agricultural products, industries), then an essay that summarizes the river's significance and reviews its place in American history.

Essays end with a brief reading list and are signed. Although the editor pointedly thanks the contributors with whom he worked, there is no roster; they are named only at the ends of their essays. The rivers of the Prairies-Plains region that the work covers are the Bighorn/Wind, Kansas, Missouri, Platte, Red (of the North), Arkansas, Neosho-Grand, Pecos, and Red (of the South), as well as tributaries discussed in passing. Useful as a starting point. — *RB*

EB40 Burke, Vincent J. - **Missouri River Natural Resources Bibliography** / by Vincent J. Burke, Lynn Rebbeor Shay, and Sharon B. Whitmore. - Springfield, VA : distr. by National Technical Information Service ; [Reston, VA?] : U.S. Dept. of the Interior, U.S. Geological Survey, [1997]. - 157 p.

Class Numbers:
Library of Congress Z7165.U6   HC107.A172
Government Document I 19.210:1997-0002
    I 73.11:1997-0002
Notes:
Indexes
U.S. Dept. of the Interior, U.S. Geological Survey, Environmental and Contaminants Research Center

• Funded by the U.S. Geological Survey's Lower Missouri River Ecosystem Initiative, Burke (Univ. of Missouri), Shay (Univ. of North Carolina-Wilmington), and Whitmore (U.S. Fish & Wildlife Service) provide 2,232 descriptive references regarding the Missouri River. This river is the longest (2,250 mi.) in America, flowing through Montana, the Dakotas, Nebraska, Iowa, Kansas, and Missouri. The study intends to assist researchers and administrators in managing the Missouri River floodplain. It cites documents, reports, and papers on the subjects of ecology, biology, geology, geography, hydrology, sociology, policy, and law. The annotations are listed alphabetically by author; author and keyword indexes. — *GK*

EB41 Cochran, Anita. - **A Selected, Annotated Bibliography on Fish and Wildlife Implications of Missouri Basin Water Allocations**. - [Boulder, CO] : Institute of Behavioral Science, Univ. of Colorado, 1975 [1997]. – 71 p.

Class Numbers:
Library of Congress Z7935
Notes:
Index

• Completed as part of a research assessment by the Office of Biological Services, U.S. Fish & Wildlife Service, this annotated bibliography cites 1,500 sources. The study was charged to provide a selective list of sources that would aid decisions about water allocation for the Upper Missouri River Basin. Subject matter ranges through geology, biology, engineering, law, and social issues. The bibliography's five sections list general reference works, resource data, development, water quality, and biotic impacts. Citations are alphabetically arranged by author. Subject index. — *GK*

EB42   Graves, John, 1920-   . - **Texas Rivers** / photographs by Wyman Meinzer. - Austin, TX : Texas Parks & Wildlife Pr., 2002. - 144 p. ; col. ill., maps.

> Class Numbers:
> Library of Congress F392.A17
> LCCN 2002-4965
> Notes:
> Table of contents: http://www.loc.gov/catdir/toc/FY0621/
> 2002004965.html

• Consists of six essays accompanied by lavish photographs, describing the Canadian, Lower Neches, Pecos, Llano, Brazos Clear Fork, and Upper Sabine Rivers. Except for the Lower Neches, all originate west of the 98th meridian. Essays and photographs were originally published in *Texas Parks & Wildlife* magazine. Bibliography. — *MS*

EB43   Kuzmiak, John M. - **Bibliography of Selected Water-Resources Information for the Arkansas River Basin in Colorado through 1985** : [Microform] / by John M. Kuzmiak and Hyla H. Strickland ; prepared in cooperation with the Southeastern Colorado Water Conservancy District. - Denver, CO : U.S. Dept. of the Interior, U.S. Geological Survey ; [distr. by] Earth Science Information Center, Open-File Reports Section, 1994. - 266 p. ; map. - (U.S. Geological Survey open-file report, 94-331).

> Class Numbers:
> Government Document I 19.76:94-331
> OCLC 33158941
> Notes:
> Distributed to depository libraries in microfiche
> Includes bibliographical references (p. 13); indexes
> Reproduction: Microfiche. [Denver, CO : U.S. Geological
> Survey, 1995?] 3 microfiches; negative

• A bibliography that cites publications of all types (books, reports, journal articles) having to do with the supply of water, surface and subsurface, in the Arkansas River Basin of southeastern Colorado. The principal list is by senior author (other authors are cross-referred), where full bibliographic information is provided; other indexes (subjects, counties, and hydrologic units) provide enough information to locate the full description in the author index. The bibliography attempts to be complete through 1985. Uses scientific format for description (author, date, title). The entire bibliography has potential for Plains studies, and the subject index helps isolate topics of particular interest

(e.g., "Great Plains," "Precipitation," "Ground-water levels," "Water law"). The fiche version is difficult to read (and on machines still maintained by libraries, to focus) and requires backing-and-forthing among the fiches. For specialists. — *RB*

EB44   Penn, James R. - **Rivers of the World : A Social, Geographical, and Environmental Sourcebook**. - Santa Barbara, CA : ABC-CLIO, 2001. - xxv, 357 p. ; ill., maps.

> Class Numbers:
> Library of Congress GB1201.4
> ISBN 1576070425   1576075796 (electronic bk.)
>   781576070420   9781576075791 (electronic bk.)
> OCLC 47696430   50296830 (electronic bk.)
> LCCN 2001-4556
> Notes:
> Electronic book: http://www.netLibrary.com/urlapi.asp?
> action=summary&v=1&bookid=70980
> Includes bibliographical references (p. 331-338)

• Of the Prairies-Plains rivers that might have been mentioned in a work that sets out to describe the world's rivers, Penn mentions eight: the Big Sioux (a smaller tributary of the Missouri), Gila, Missouri, Platte, Red (North and South), Rio Grande, and Saskatchewan. Missing are the Arkansas, Canadian, Kansas, Pecos, Niobrara, Cheyenne, Republican, Yellowstone, and Qu'Appelle. The articles themselves are brief (even the Missouri rates only a little more than two pages), and while they are factual and well-written, leave one thirsting for more. At the end are a glossary, bibliography, and index. Outline maps at the beginning show the approximate position of rivers in the continents of the world, with country maps for Britain, the U.S., and Canada. For beginning students. — *RB*

EB45   **The Platte River : An Atlas of the Big Bend Region** / general ed., Allan Jenkins [et al.]. - [Kearney, NE] : Univ. of Nebraska-Kearney, 1993. - 194 p. ; ill. (some col.), maps (some col.) 28 cm.

> Class Numbers:
> Library of Congress F672.P6
> Government Document Nebraska C2800 X001 -1993
> LCCN 95-620406
> Notes:
> Includes bibliographical references

• An atlas arranged in four broad sections: "Geography/Climate/Biology," "History/Literature/Art," "Economics/Agriculture/Demography," and "Water/Law/ People." The first section discusses plant and animal life, the second covers a handful of writers and artists, the third deals with specific social issues, and the fourth discusses water policy and highlights the effect of the region on selected persons. Well illustrated in both color and black-

and-white. The atlas supplies more than 20 maps and graphs of the Big Bend region and several appendixes of its flora and fauna. No index. — *MB*

EB46   Rivers of North America / ed. by Arthur C. Benke & Colbert E. Cushing. - Amsterdam ; Boston, MA : Elsevier/Academic Pr., 2005. - xxiii, 1144 p. ; col. ill., col. maps.

> Class Numbers:
> Library of Congress QH102.R58
> ISBN 0120882531
> OCLC 5903378
> LCCN 2005-8909
> Notes:
> Includes bibliographical references
> Review by M.J. Zwolinsky: *Choice* 43.9 (June 2006): review 43-5639
> Table of contents: http://www.loc.gov/catdir/toc/ecip0510/2005008909.html

• Organized by river basin, each chapter begins with an overview of the region, covering its physiography, climate, landscape, land use, and rivers. As many as five rivers are given detailed descriptions, including geomorphology, hydrology, ecology, and human impact. For comparative purposes, up to 12 additional rivers are summarized under a variety of physical and biological elements (area, discharge, major fish and plant species, water quality, land use, population density, etc.), with a topographic map and graph of monthly air temperature, precipitation, and runoff. Among the rivers given major coverage are the Arkansas, Canadian, and Red (Southern Plains basin), Brazos (Gulf Coast), and the Missouri, Yellowstone, and Platte (Missouri River basin); the Milk, Cheyenne, Big Sioux, Niobrara, Kansas, Cimarron, and Washita are among the Plains rivers given briefer treatment. Numerous full-color photographs, extensive bibliographies, appendix of common and scientific names, glossary, and index of rivers. An attractive and useful source intended for scientists, environmentalists, and anyone interested in the state of the continent's rivers. — *LMcD*

EC : BIOLOGY

Scope. Works having to do with plants and animals of the Prairies-Plains region, native or introduced.

ANIMALS

General Works

EC1 Northern Prairie Wildlife Research Center [Internet Site] / Jamestown, ND : Northern Prairie Wildlife Research Center, U.S. Dept. of the Interior, U.S. Geological Survey, 1998-   . - http://www.npwrc.usgs.gov/

> Class Numbers:
> Library of Congress   QL84.22.N9
> OCLC 38563585
> Access Date: May 2006
> Fees: None

• The NPWRC conducts environmental and biological research on the northern Great Plains in support of natural resource management. As part of its educational mandate, the "Biological Resources" section of the Internet site provides several hundred full-text documents, arranged by type (identification tools, checklists, distributions, species accounts, etc.), by taxon (waterfowl, mammals, endangered/threatened species, etc.) and by geographical area (Great Plains, state/province, etc.) The publications database contains citations for more than 1,300 papers written by staff; many are available online. The database is searchable by keyword, title, author, source, year, and reprint number. Entries include citation, abstracts, keywords, taxonomy, and geographical area. A useful clearinghouse for environmental studies of the northern Plains. — *LMcD*

EC2   Ogaard, Louis A. - The Fauna of the Prairie Wetlands : Research Methods and Annotated Bibliography / in collaboration with Jay A. Leitch, Donald F. Scott, and William C. Nelson. - Fargo, ND : Agricultural Experiment Station, North Dakota State Univ., 1981. - 23 p.; map. - (North Dakota Research Report; no. 86).

> Class Numbers:
> Library of Congress QL114.5   S99
> OCLC 8660921
> LCCN 82-623106
> Notes:

Electronic book:
   http://pc6.psc.state.nd.us/jurisdiction/
   Includes bibliographies; index

• Review of zoological studies of waterfowl, nongame birds, mammals, and cold-blooded animals, with an emphasis on species characteristic of the Prairie Pothole Region, an area of the northern Plains marked with grass-covered wetlands. No subject index but the bibliography is brief enough (approximately 90 items) to be quickly searched. Useful for naturalists with an interest in pothole ecosystems. — *LMcD*

UNITED STATES

Colorado

EC3   Beidleman, Richard G. - Annotated Bibliography of Colorado Vertebrate Zoology, 1776-1995 / [by] Richard G. Beidleman, Reba R. Beidleman, and Linda H. Beidleman. - Colorado Springs, CO : Univ. Pr. of Colorado, 2000. - 447 p.

> Class Numbers:
> Library of Congress   QL606.52.U6
>   Z7996.V4
> ISBN 0870815571 9780870815577
> OCLC 43694313
> LCCN 00-28989
> Notes:
>   Index

• An immense bibliography, about 11,000 items with brief annotations, drawn chiefly from journals (of which a list is provided, p. 437-438) and government agency publications. An opening section lists general works on natural history, followed by sections for fishes, amphibians, reptiles, birds, and mammals. Reflecting the fascination birds hold for observers, their section is far the longest. Subsections under each major subdivision include a general section further subdivided by general topics, national and state parks and grasslands, population studies, and materials of professional interest (e.g., entries about mammalogists), followed by studies of specific species, arranged by taxon. In each subsection, entries are alphabetical by author. An index lists common and taxonomic names. Journal articles were checked page by page to identify species discussed, hence some articles appear more than once. — *RB*

Kansas

EC4   Gress, Bob. - Watching Kansas Wildlife: A Guide to 101 Sites / [by] Bob Gress and George Potts. - Lawrence, KS: publ. for the Kansas Dept. of Wildlife and Parks by Univ.

Pr. of Kansas, 1993. - 104 p.; ill. (some col.), col. maps.

 Class Numbers: Library of Congress QL177
   Government Document Kansas F 1.2:W 324
 ISBN 0700605940
 OCLC 27171612
 LCCN 92-41094
 Notes:
   Includes bibliographical references
     (p. 102-104); index

• Kansas offers abundant wildlife, bison to tiny screech owls, on its limited federal and state public lands. Organized into six geographic regions, entries for parks, reservoirs, lakes, wildlife areas, and other sites describe the landscape and wildlife, driving directions, ownership, size, and contact information. Icons indicate the most commonly sited animals, recreational facilities, and amenities. The introduction has viewing tips, viewing etiquette, the 12 most exceptional sites, an index to the best sites for viewing the 12 most popular animals, and descriptions of four general types of habitats. Maps of each region and color photographs of animals and landscapes add interest. List of recommended field guides and other references. — *JD*

Montana

EC5 Thompson, Larry S. - **An Index to Montana Wildlife Literature, 1950-1976**. - Helena, MT : Montana Dept. of Natural Resources and Conservation, 1976. - [52] p.; maps. - (Montana. Energy Division. Research report, 1).

 Class Numbers: Library of Congress QL188
   Z7998.M65
 OCLC 3604719
 LCCN 77-621991

• An author bibliography of approximately 500 scientific and technical references, including theses, on "non-domestic terrestrial vertebrates." Instead of a traditional subject index, Thompson takes a novel approach, using a series of state maps devoted to individual species or groups of species such as upland game birds, elk, mountain goats, and bighorn sheep. On each map the location of particular studies is indicated at the county level with the author's name, giving a quick sense of geographical distribution. *A List of Literature Pertaining to Wildlife Research and Management in Montana* by R. Mackie and H. Yeager (Helena, MT: Research Section, Game Management Division, Montana Fish and Game Dept., 1966; 75 p.) covers earlier studies. — *LMcD*

Texas

EC6 Hodge, Larry D. - **Official Guide to Texas Wildlife Management Areas** / foreword by Andrew

Sansom. - Austin, TX : Texas Parks & Wildlife Pr., 2000. - 258 p.; ill., maps.

 Class Numbers:
   Library of Congress SK451
 ISBN 1885696353
 LCCN 00-11017
 Notes:
   Includes bibliographical references (p. 251-253)
   Table of contents:
     http://www.loc.gov/catdir/toc/texas
       041/00011017.html

• Organized by geographic regions, including "Prairies and Lakes," "Panhandle Plains," "Hill Country," and "South Texas Plains." Each section begins with a quote from Aldo Leopold and a map of the region showing subdivisions. The detailed profiles note location, driving times from the major Texas cities, information about lodging, local points of historical interest, and the history and geography of the area. Available recreational activities (hunting, fishing, cycling, hiking, camping, sightseeing, wildlife viewing, and bird watching) are described in detail. Color photographs throughout the text. Sidebars called "Insiders Corner" cover a variety of topics, including wildlife restoration, local history, and behavioral guidelines for visitors. Subject index. — *MS*

CANADA

Saskatchewan

EC7 Schurr, Carol D. - **Saskatchewan Fish and Wildlife Bibliography**. - Saskatoon, SK : Saskatchewan Environment and Resource Management, Fish and Wildlife Branch, 2000. - 74 p. - (Fish and Wildlife Technical Report, 00-03).

 Class Numbers:
   Library of Congress QH106.2.S2
   National Library of Canada COP.SA.2.2001-20
 OCLC 46671106
 Notes:
   Electronic book: http://www.siast.sk.ca/~wood
     land/dos/lrc/Frames/printedbibliojan15.pdf

• Includes an estimated 900 reports issued by Saskatchewan Environment and its predecessors, 1949-1999. The fishery studies include surveys of individual species, aquaculture, sport, and recreational fishing. Many of the wildlife reports examine habitat management in specific geographic areas, habitat mapping, and inventories, and include some environmental studies on, e.g., acid rain and waterfowl damage. Arranged by author and date; no title or subject indexes but each citation includes keywords derived from the title. Intended for aquatic and wildlife biologists as well as environmentalists. — *LMcD*

AMPHIBIANS AND REPTILES

EC8   Carpenter, Charles Congden, 1921-   . - **Oklahoma Herpetology : An Annotated Bibliography** / [by] Charles C. Carpenter and James J. Krupa. - Norman, OK : Univ. of Oklahoma Pr., 1989. - 258 p.; ill.

> Class Numbers:
>   Library of Congress QL653.O5Z7996.R4
> ISBN 0806122102
> LCCN 88-38318
> Notes:
>   An Oklahoma Museum of Natural History
>   publication
>   Indexes

• Carpenter and Krupa cite 1,536 publications (principally journal articles) that treat Oklahoma amphibians and reptiles. The main list is arranged by author in scientific format, with journal titles abbreviated (but no key is given), and telegraphically brief annotations that consist of a brief statement of content if the title is not self-explanatory (e.g., "Range map and literature review"), one or more terms from a list of 23 specified in the introduction, and the genera described. Indexes by genus and key words, and by common name. Except for the cover and frontispiece (neither of which identifies the amphibian shown), no illustrations. — *RB*

EC9   Conant, Roger, 1909-   . - **A Field Guide to Reptiles and Amphibians of Eastern and Central North America** / ill. by Isabelle Hunt Conant. - Boston, MA : Houghton Mifflin, 1975, 1958. - 616 p.; ill., 48 plates (part col.). - (Peterson field guide series, 12).

> Class Numbers:
>   Library of Congress QL651
> ISBN 0395199794
>   0395904528 (pbk.)
> LCCN 74-13425
> Notes:
>   Bibliography: p. 585-594
>   First publ. 1958 under title: *A Field Guide to
>   Reptiles and Amphibians of the United States
>   and Canada East of the 100th Meridian*

• The area covered by this volume includes Manitoba and provinces to the east, the vertical stack of states, North Dakota to Texas, and all states to the Atlantic Coast, thereby including most of the Plains region. Introductory material includes advice about catching specimens and caring for them in

captivity. Following this is a substantial section of color plates that depict several species on each page, cross-referenced to the species accounts that comprise the greater part of the book. The species accounts are divided into categories for crocodilians, turtles, lizards, amphibians, snakes, salamanders, and toads and frogs. The species descriptions are cross-referenced to the plates and where applicable, to figures. Information for each entry includes a physical description, habitat, a range map, and information about similar species. Short glossary; bibliography; index. — *MB*

EC10   Dixon, James Ray. - **Texas Snakes : A Field Guide** / [by] James R. Dixon and John E. Werler; line drawings by Regina Levoy. - Austin, TX : Univ. of Texas Pr., 2005. - 364 p.; ill. (chiefly col.), col. maps. - (Texas natural history guides).

> LCCN 2004-26120
> Notes:
>   Includes bibliographical references
>   (p. 345-353); index
>   Table of contents: http://www.loc.gov/catdir/
>   toc/fy0601/2004026120.html

• A useful field guide, with copious introductory matter: a list of threatened Texas snakes; more than 20 pages about poisonous snakes; classification and identification; taxonomic issues; organization of families, species, and subspecies; checklist of Texas snakes; and keys for identification. Species accounts are divided into four groups (blind snakes, Colubrids, coral snakes, and vipers) arranged alphabetically by scientific name. Accounts provide a distribution map, description, comparable snakes, size, habitat, and a photograph in color. Includes glossary, bibliography, and indexes of common and scientific names. — *RB*

EC11   Fischer, Tate D. - **A Field Guide to South Dakota Amphibians** / by Tate D. Fischer [et al.]. - [Brookings, SD]: Dept. of Wildlife and Fisheries Sciences, South Dakota State Univ., 1999. - 52 p.; ill (some col.), col. maps. - (South Dakota Agricultural Experiment Station. Bulletin, 733).

> Class Numbers:
>   Library of Congress QL653.S8
>   Government Document South Dakota
>   ED 175:B 874/733
> ISBN 0965893677
> OCLC 42630880
> Notes:
>   Includes bibliographical references (p. 51-52)
>   Issued by: U.S. Fish and Wildlife Service;
>   U.S. Geological Survey, Biological Resources Div.;
>   South Dakota Cooperative Fish and Wildlife
>   Research Unit; South Dakota Dept. of Game, Fish
>   & Parks; South Dakota State Univ.

• Fischer (Dept. of Wildlife, South Dakota State Univ.) and his colleagues make the case for the vital role amphibians play in a region's ecosystem—they are sensitive to changes in their aquatic environment and have importance in the food chain as prey for mammals and birds. The book has sections for frogs and toads (order Anura), consisting of true toads (Bufonidae), treefrogs (Hylidae), and spadefoots (Pelobatidae), and for salamanders (order Caudata), consisting of mudpuppies (Proteidae) and tiger salamanders (Ambystomatidae). The entry for each amphibian includes color photographs. — *GK*

EC12 Hammerson, Geoffrey A. - **Amphibians and Reptiles in Colorado**. - 2nd ed. - [Boulder?, CO] : Colorado Div. of Wildlife; Niwot, CO: Univ. Pr. of Colorado, 1999. - xxii, 484 p.; ill. (some col.), maps.

> ISBN 0870815210
> LCCN 99-10312

• A carefully prepared, clearly written field guide. The introductory matter includes a history of herpetology in Colorado, a description of the environment influencing the occurrence of amphibians and reptiles (with descriptions of the Great Plains region of the state and its various habitats, among them plains, grassland, and sandhills), human impact on herpetological habitat, advice as to observing and photographing amphibians and reptiles, and a key to the sections found in the species accounts. The accounts themselves are divided into amphibians (salamanders and frogs and toads) and reptiles (turtles, lizards, and snakes). Each species account has sections for recognition (physical characteristics), distribution with a map showing occurrences, conservation status, habitat, activity, reproduction and growth, food, and taxonomy. The book ends with a key giving successive characteristics to observe in identifying the species of an individual specimen. Since more species and greater occurrences of amphibians and reptiles are found in Colorado's Plains regions east of the mountains than in any other part of the state, Hammerson's book will be useful to Plains naturalists. — *RB*

EC13 Hudson, George Elford, 1907-   . - **The Amphibians and Reptiles of Nebraska**. - Lincoln, NE : Univ. of Nebraska, Conservation and Survey Division, 1972, 1942. - 146 p.; plates, maps. - (Nebraska conservation bulletin, 24 [Mar. 1972]).

> Class Numbers:
> Library of Congress QL653.N2
> OCLC 8027292
> LCCN a 43-2242
> Notes:
> Includes bibliographical references (p. 111-114)
> Reprint of 1942 ed.

• Based on specimens collected for the project and several hundred borrowed from U.S. museums, this work begins by discussing the economic value and beneficial activities of cold-blooded mammals and reviewing earlier records and publications. A table reflecting the profound and diverse effects of Nebraska's physiographic conditions shows the presence of 57 species in five biotic regions, from the deciduous forests of the Missouri River bluffs where snakes feel welcome to the hostile buttes and badlands of the panhandle. A descriptive key to species aids in identification. Species entries, organized by class, order, and family supply general identification, coloration, size, structure, habits, general range, and distribution by Nebraska counties, including distribution maps. Appendixes provide a glossary, bibliography, and diagrams and photographs of each species. Common names appear in the entries but are not indexed. Although nomenclature and distribution data are out of date, this source provides excellent data for comparison with more recent regional surveys. — *JD*

EC14 Russell, Anthony Patrick, 1947-   . - **The Amphibians and Reptiles of Alberta : A Field Guide and Primer of Boreal Herpetology** / [by] Anthony P. Russell, Aaron M. Bauer; colour photographs by Wayne Lynch; ill. by Irene McKinnon. - 2nd ed. - Calgary, AB : Univ. of Calgary Pr., 2000. - 292 p.; 28 p. of plates, ill., charts, tables.

> Class Numbers:
> Library of Congress QL654
> National Library of Canada QL654
> ISBN 1552380386
> LCCN 00-344558
> Notes:
> Includes bibliographical references (p. 211-262);
> index

• Since the number of species of amphibians and reptiles in Alberta is small (salamanders, frogs, turtles, lizards, and snakes, 18 species in all), the species accounts in this catalog take up comparatively little space. This allows the authors to characterize amphibians and reptiles in general, to advise how to observe them, and to provide a checklist and keys for Alberta specimens. They also offer a section on zoogeography of Alberta herpetofauna, natural history (life cycles, food, and predators), reactions to cold and aridity (amphibians and reptiles are most numerous in the arid southeastern section of Alberta), defense mechanisms, and relations to human beings. Glossary, 40-page bibliography, and index. — *RB*

EC15 Shaw, Charles E. - **Snakes of the American West** / [by] Charles E. Shaw and Sheldon Campbell. - New York : Knopf [distr. by Random House], 1974. - 328 p.; ill. (part col.).

Class Numbers:
  Library of Congress QL665
ISBN 0394488822
LCCN 73-7304
Notes:
  Bibliography: p. 271-280

• Guide to 70 species found in 11 states including Colorado, Montana, New Mexico, and Wyoming. Sections describe general characteristics (anatomy and physiology, feeding, mating, hibernation) and give tips on keeping snakes as pets. The principal division is between harmless and venomous snakes; within each, species are arranged in increasing order of evolutionary complexity. Accounts provide description and identification guide, habitat, diet, and distribution map; the frequent anecdotes add a popular dimension to the scientific narrative. Appendixes cover life spans and distinguish subspecies. Vivid colored photographs attract the reader's attention; a useful introduction to western herpetology. — *LMcD*

EC16   Tennant, Alan, 1943- . - **Texas Snakes**. - 3rd ed. - Lanham [TX] : Taylor Trade Publ., 2006. - xx, 263 p.; col. ill. - (Lone Star field guide).

Class Numbers:
  Library of Congress QL666.O6
ISBN 1589792092
LCCN 2005-19889
Notes:
  Rev ed. of Tennant's *A Field Guide to Texas Snakes*
  Table of contents: http://www.loc.gov/catdir/toc/
    ecip0515/2005019889.html

• Consists of six general essays covering snakes and the law, the evolution of snakes, Texas snake habitats, snake venom poisoning and antidotes, scalation, and an identification key, and 110 entries describing species and subspecies of snakes. Species accounts include color photographs and treat venom, abundance, size, habitat, prey, reproduction, coloring, scale, similar snakes, and behavior. The essay on habitat provides a county map of Texas divided into regions, including Prairies and High Plains. Prairies are further subdivided into tallgrass and coastal, and the High Plains into short- and tallgrass. The essay contains a useful chart cross-referencing snakes by region. Entries run approximately one page. — *MS*

EC17   Werler, John E. - **Texas Snakes : Identification, Distribution, and Natural History** / [by] John E. Werler and James R. Dixon; line drawings by Regina Levoy. - Austin, TX : Univ. of Texas Pr., 2000. - 437 p.; ill. (some col.), maps.

ISBN 0292791305

LCCN 99-6329
Notes:
  Table of contents:
    http://www.loc.gov/catdir/
      enhancements/fy0609/99006329-t.html

• An elaborately produced catalog of snakes native to Texas. The introduction treats such matters as the aversion people feel toward snakes and myths about them, snakebite and its hazards, the biotic provinces of Texas (two of which, Kansan and Balconian, cover the Plains region of the state), and classification and identification. A checklist of Texas snakes and a key to species precede the entries for specific species, arranged by family. Each species account, accompanied by a distribution map, gives description, comparable snakes, size, habitat, behavior, feeding, and reproduction. A section of 200 splendid photographs in color follows p. 206. At the end of the book are a glossary, 14-page bibliography, and indexes of scientific and common names. — *RB*

BIRDS

General Works

EC18   **The Birds of North America**. - No. 1 (1992) - no. 716 (2002). Washington, DC : American Ornithologists' Union, 1992-2002. Irregular.

Class Numbers:
  Library of Congress QL681
LCCN 93-641491
Notes:
  Cumulative indexes: no. 1-680 (1 v.), no. 1-716 (1 v.)
  Each year's issues accompanied by a cumulative
    corrigenda
  Issued as fascicles, 40 per release, 716 altogether
  Issued jointly by: American Ornithologists' Union
    and Academy of Natural Sciences of
    Philadelphia (1992-1999); by: American Orni-
    thologists' Union, Cornell Laboratory of
    Ornithology, and Academy of Natural
    Sciences (2000-2002)

EC18a   **Birds of North America Online [Internet Site]**. - Ithaca, NY : Cornell Laboratory of Ornithology and the American Ornithologists' Union, 2004-   . - http://bna.birds.cornell.edu/BNA/

Class Numbers:
  Library of Congress QL681
OCLC 57240924
Access Date: Aug. 2006
Fees: Subscription

• Accounts for 716 species, providing detailed information on a range of elements: distinguishing characteristics, distribution, systematics, migration, habitat, food habits, behavior, breeding, demography, conservation, appearance, and measurements; extensive bibliographies of 100 to 300 references for each species. Searchable by species name and keywords; browsable by family and alphabetically. Guides to birds in individual Plains states and provinces are relatively commonplace, but the keyword capability of BNA provides more flexibility and precision in searching; birds of southwestern Oklahoma or ducks common to both Kansas and Nebraska, for example, are easily identified. The Internet site includes all 18,000 pages of the 18-volume printed set published 1992-2002; the additional features of frequent updates, sound and video clips, and image galleries are major enhancements. An excellent resource, both comprehensive in coverage and beautiful in execution, for anyone with even a passing interest in birds. — *LMcD*

EC19   Johnsgard, Paul A. - **Birds of the Great Plains : Breeding Species and Their Distribution**. - Lincoln, NE : Univ. of Nebraska Pr., 1979. - xlv, 539 p.; [8] leaves of plates, ill.

> Class Numbers:
> Library of Congress QL683.G68
> ISBN 803225504
> LCCN 79-1419
> Notes:
> Bibliography: p. 513-533; index

• Although Johnsgard's book is intended for a broad, nontechnical audience interested in the breeding behaviors of birds rather than for professional ornithologists, it is not a field guide. The organization of entries follows the American Ornithologists' Union's *Check-List of North American Birds*. The area covered by Johnsgard is about 500,000 square miles, extending from the Canadian border south to the Oklahoma-Texas border and from the eastern border of Kansas to the western border of Nebraska. The introductory section includes descriptions and maps of the topography, precipitation, and plant communities of the region. Entries for species, which are arranged by scientific name, discuss breeding habits and habitat, nest location, clutch size and incubation, breeding time, breeding biology, and suggested readings. A marginal map shows the range for each species. Black-and-white line drawings accompany the title page for each family. Thirty color plates occupy a center spread. Appendix A provides a map and information about wildlife refuges that offer bird-watching opportunities. Appendix B charts the abundance and breeding status at selected parks and refuges. Bibliography arranged by state; index by common name. — *MB*

EC20   Johnsgard, Paul A. - **Hawks, Eagles & Falcons of North America : Biology and Natural History**. - Washington, DC: Smithsonian Institution Pr., 1990. - 403 p.; [31] p. of plates, ill (some col.), maps.

> Class Numbers:
> Library of Congress QL696.F3
> ISBN 0874746825
> LCCN 89-48558
> Notes:
> Includes bibliographical references (p. 367-397); index

• Preceding part 1 are 32 pages of attractive color plates. Part 1 discusses, in general terms, comparative biology, evolution, classification, foraging ecology, comparative behavior, reproductive biology, and conservation. These chapters are enhanced with tables, charts, maps, and line drawings. Part 2 contains the natural histories of individual species, each treated in great detail, including a full-page range map which allows the reader to identify species native to the Great Plains region. Entries include other vernacular names, distribution, subspecies, physical description (both adult and juvenile), measurements, weights, identification, habitat and ecology, foods and foraging, social behavior, breeding biology, and evolutionary relationships. Appendixes include the origins of both common and scientific names of Falconiformes, a glossary, field identification views, and anatomical drawings of Falconiformes. The bibliography is extensive. Index of common and scientific names. — *MB*

EC21   Johnsgard, Paul A. - **North American Owls : Biology and Natural History**. - 2nd ed. - Washington, DC : Smithsonian Institution Pr. - 298 p.; [32] p. of plates, ill. (some col.).

> Class Numbers:
> Library of Congress QL696.S8
> National Library of Canada QL696
> ISBN 1560989394
> LCCN 2002-21015
> Notes:
> 1st ed.: 1988
> Includes bibliographical references (p. 271-289); index
> Table of contents: http://www.loc.gov/catdir/toc/fy037/2002021015.html

• Part 1 discusses the comparative biology of owls–e.g., comparative ecology, comparative behavior. Part 2 covers the natural histories of North American owls, by families. For each species (e.g., barn owl, Tyto alba), information is provided about other common names, range, subspecies, weights and measurements, keys to identification, vocalization, habitat, movement, foraging behavior, social behavior, and breeding characteristics. Full-page range maps are given for most species. Illustrations include line drawings, watercolors, and color photos. While not all the species are found in the Plains region, many are, which can easily be determined by examining the range maps. Supplementary material includes several appendixes, a glossary, an extensive bibliography, and a good index. —*MB*

EC22 Wassink, Jan L. - **Watchable Birds of the Black Hills, Badlands, and Northern Great Plains**. - Missoula, MT: Mountain Pr. Publ., 2006. - 231 p.; ill. (chiefly col.), map.

> Class Numbers:
> Library of Congress QL683.G68
> ISBN 0878425268 9780878425266
> OCLC 70291993
> LCCN 2006-22086
> Notes:
> Includes bibliographical references (p. 216-219); index

• A field guide for beginning or occasional bird watchers, limited to the area's 82 most commonly sited birds. It covers the Plains east of the Rocky Mountains to the eastern border of the Dakotas and Nebraska, a region that includes a significant part of the Missouri River Basin. Introductory information explains how to use the guide, provides hints for observing birds, and specifies ethical behavior in bird watching. Species accounts, arranged by family, include a color photograph, common and scientific names, notable markings, status (native or migratory), location of hot spots for viewing, and a description of the bird. Includes a brief glossary, suggested readings, birding destinations arranged by state, and a species index. — *JB*

UNITED STATES

Colorado

EC23 **Colorado Breeding Bird Atlas** / Hugh E. Kingery, ed.; ill. by Radeaux. - [Denver, CO] : Colorado Bird Atlas Partnership; Colorado Div. of Wildlife, 1998. - 636 p.; ill. (some col.), maps (some col.); 28 cm.

> Class Numbers:
> Library of Congress QL684.C6
> ISBN 0966850602
> LCCN 98-74577
> Notes:
> Includes bibliographical references (p. 600-630); index

• Prepared with great care by ornithologists associated with the Colorado Bird Atlas Partnership assisted by 1,300 field observers, this atlas of birds that breed in Colorado

accounts for 253 species. Front matter describes the methods used in making observations and the selection of atlas blocks, lists all the observers, and establishes codes used to classify breeding and habitat. Sixteen pages of color plates contain photographs of habitats, typical nest locations, and adult and fledgling birds. Species accounts take up the greater part of the book, arranged by families and species. Each species is presented in a double-page spread that has sections describing habitat, breeding, and distribution, accompanied by a map showing breeding evidence and by line drawings of the species. A list of "Supplemental Species Accounts" lists 11 additional species whose breeding status did not meet the criteria for inclusion in the principal list. At the end are a 30-page bibliography and an index of common and scientific names. A splendid catalog, handsomely presented. —*RB*

Kansas

EC24 Busby, William H., 1955-   . - **Kansas Breeding Bird Atlas** / by William H. Busby and John L. Zimmerman; illustrated by Dan Kilby, Robert Mengel, and Orville Rice. - Lawrence, KS : Univ. Pr. of Kansas, 2001. - 466 p.; ill., maps.

> Class Numbers:
> Library of Congress QL684.K2
> ISBN 0700610553
> LCCN 00-62032
> Notes:
> Includes bibliographical references (p. 457-459); index
> Review by H.N. Cunningham Jr.: *Choice* 39 (Nov. 2001): review 39-1573

• A catalog of 203 birds that breed in Kansas, based on sightings by ornithologists and nearly 200 field volunteers over the six years 1992-1997. The introduction describes methods of establishing priority sighting blocks and recording sightings, and also supplies an extremely clear and thorough explanation of Kansas geography and physiography. The catalog proper assigns a double facing-page spread to each species, giving common and scientific names, a description of the species and its habitat, a line drawing showing salient characteristics, an outline map of the state showing possible, probable, and confirmed sightings, and a smaller outline map of abundance by stratum. Appendixes include statistics about priority blocks (latitude, longitude, region, county, total species, hours in the field), statistics of special blocks (e.g., Cheyenne Bottoms), a bibliography, and an index of common and scientific names. Useful for ornithologists and birders. — *RB*

EC25 Cable, Ted T. - **Birds of Cimarron National Grassland** / [by] Ted T. Cable, Scott Seltman, Kevin J. Cook. - Fort Collins, CO : U.S. Dept. of Agriculture, Forest Service, Rocky Mountain Forest and Range Experiment Station, 1996. - 108 p.; ill. - (USDA Forest Service general technical report, RM 281).

Class Numbers:
Library of Congress   QL684.K2

• The report addresses academic, recreational and managerial interests. Parts 1 and 2 describe the Grassland and its administration. Parts 3-4 offer the main attractions: an ornithological history of southwest Kansas with historical bird counts and surveys; 355 species accounts based on historical records and publications; and a site guide for birders. Focusing on statistics rather than descriptions, species accounts give status and seasonal range, high counts, nesting records, and remarks on distribution and frequency. A small fraction of accounts are illustrated with black-and-white photographs. Part 5 discusses management of birds and grasslands. Since birds fail to respect political boundaries, the bibliography includes sources on other Plains states. —*JD*

EC26 Goodrich, Arthur Leonard, 1905-   . - **Birds in Kansas**. - Topeka, KS : printed by F. Voiland Jr., State Printer, 1946. - 340 p.; ill., maps. - (Kansas. State Board of Agriculture. Report, 24.267 [June 1945]).

Class Numbers:
Library of Congress S63
Government Document Kansas A 1.3:64/267
OCLC 2650688
LCCN 46-22614
Notes:
Includes bibliographies; index

• Emphasizing birds' economic and aesthetic value, Goodrich's work is an educational tool rather than a list of species accounts or a field guide. Introductory chapters cover topics such as beneficial services, nesting, songs, and bird morphology. Selected lists of common water and land birds include simple line drawings, a few color plates, and eloquent descriptions of appearance, behavior, and benefits. A systematic list of additional birds by order and family provides similar, but generally briefer, descriptions. No range or distribution data are provided. A list of common colloquial names, state birds, seasonal finding lists, and an index by common and scientific names are included. —*JD*

EC27 Thompson, Max C. - **Birds in Kansas** / [by] Max C. Thompson and Charles Ely; foreword by John E. Hayes Jr. - Lawrence, KS : Univ. of Kansas Museum of Natural History; distr. by Univ. Pr. of Kansas, 1989-1992. - 2 v. (404, 424 p.); ill., maps. - (University of Kansas. Museum of Natural History. Public education series, 11-12).

Class Numbers:
Library of Congress QL684.K2
ISBN 0893380261 (v. 1)
089338027X (v. 1 pbk.)
0893380393 (v. 2)
0893380407 (v. 2 pbk.)
OCLC 19741630
LCCN 89-5017
Notes:
Includes bibliographical references
(v. 2, p. [409]-413); index

• Volume 1 identifies and describes 222 species of non-songbirds in 41 broad categories, and v. 2, 207 species of songbirds in 24 broad categories. Both volumes are intended for both general readers and professional ornithologists, giving common and scientific names and following the sequence of species in the American Ornithologists' Union's *Check-List of North American Birds*. Most entries are accompanied by a black-and-white photo and a map showing which Kansas counties have reported sightings, a status report, and information about breeding, habits and habitat, field marks, food, and time of year when the species has been sighted. Volumes end by listing literature cited and with an index to common, generic, and scientific names. — *MB*

EC28 Zimmerman, John L., 1933-   . - **Birds of Konza :The Avian Ecology of the Tallgrass Prairie**. - Lawrence, KS : Univ. Pr. of Kansas, 1993. - 186 p.

Class Numbers:
Library of Congress QL684.K2
ISBN 0700605975
OCLC 27187276
LCCN 92-42414
Notes:
Includes bibliographical references (p. 171-179);
index

• The Konza prairie is located south of Manhattan, KS. Zimmerman deals with the avian communities found in grasslands, woodlands, and rock outcroppings. He includes numerous charts and graphs, an annotated list of resident species, and a checklist of times of year species may be sighted. A unique visual guide to the relative abundance of various birds through the year. Glossary, bibliography, and index. — *MB*

EC29 Zimmerman, John L., 1933-   . - **A Guide to Bird Finding in Kansas and Western Missouri** / [by] John L. Zimmerman and Sebastian T. Patti; ill. by Robert M. Mengel. - Lawrence, KS : Univ. Pr. of Kansas, 1988. - 244 p.; ill., maps.

Class Numbers:
Library of Congress QL684.K2

ISBN 0700603654 0700603662 (pbk.)
LCCN 87-34655
Notes:
     Bibliography: p. 227-228; index

• Not a catalog of bird species, but of places in Kansas and western Missouri where they are likely to be seen. The authors describe sites in detail and sometimes with humor, and list bird species likely to be seen at each site. They class sites according to environment, among them forest-prairie mosaic, tallgrass prairie, sand prairie, cedar hills prairie, mixed-grass prairie, sandsage prairie and shortgrass prairie, and the I-70 transect. They include a checklist of birds of the region, a list of specialty species, and indexes to common names and place-names. To be used in planning birding expeditions, or kept in the glove compartment while visiting the Plains. — *RB*

Nebraska

EC30   Birds of Nebraska : An Interactive Guide [Internet Site] / Nebraska Game and Parks Commission. - Lincoln, NE : Nebraska Game and Parks Commission, 2000?. -http://www.ngpc.state.ne.us/wildlife/guides/birds/findbirds.asp

     Access Date: Aug. 2005
     Notes:
          Updated frequently
     Fees: None

• Four hundred thirty-nine bird species found currently or historically in Nebraska can be browsed alphabetically by order name or searched by common or scientific name. The site resembles a field guide: entries include taxonomy, appearance, habitat, status and range, and call. General information includes interesting behaviors and best viewing times and locations. The site supplies photographs for about half the birds, sound files for most, and links to entries for similar birds. Information is drawn from Nebraska Ornithologists' Union records. Contributions of photographs and sound files are solicited to expand the database. The photos, sound files, and clearly written text make this source attractive for birders and students. — *JD*

EC31   Ducey, James E. - Nebraska Birds: Breeding Status and Distribution / maps by Remote Sensing Applications Laboratory, Univ. of Nebraska at Omaha; ill. by Paul A. Johnsgard. - Omaha, NE: Simmons-Boardman Books, 1988. - 148 p.; ill., maps.

     Class Numbers:
          Library of Congress QL684.N2
     ISBN 0911382070
     OCLC 18486580

LCCN 88-60758
Notes:
     Includes bibliographical references (p. 135-142);
     index

• Ducey's summary of breeding birds of Nebraska begins with useful histories of birders and of birds. It draws on publications of the Nebraska Ornithologists' Union and the unpublished records its amateur observers began to keep in the mid-1880s. Species accounts, organized by family, describe nesting status and general range and cite records from three periods: early through 1920, 1921-1960, and post-1960. Accompanying maps show ranges shaded by county for each period. Includes an extensive bibliography and an index by location and common name. Documentation of changes in bird status over time, implying changes in habitat, is particularly useful. — *JD*

EC32   Johnsgard, Paul A. - The Birds of Nebraska. - Rev. ed. - Lincoln, NE: P.A. Johnsgard, 2006. - 153 p.; maps.

     Class Numbers:
          Library of Congress QL682.N2
     OCLC 63203190
     Notes:
          Includes bibliographical references (p. 142-143);
          index
          Previous ed. publ. by: Lincoln, NE: School of
          Biological Sciences, Univ. of Nebraska-Lincoln,
     2000

• Part 1, valuable for amateur birdwatchers and professional ornithologists, begins with a month-by-month timeline of bird appearances and migrations in Nebraska, followed by sections on fundamentals of birdwatching; optical equipment and acoustic aids; a guide to print and Internet field guides; vernacular and technical names; monitoring of bird populations; and sources of information on finding birds in Nebraska. Part 2 accounts for 445 bird species reported at least once in Nebraska from prehistoric times to the present, based on an actual specimen or proven occurrence. Organized by 23 families, entries include common and Latin names, range maps, migration, habitats, and comments on behavior, population or appearance. Johnsgard is the foremost authority on Nebraska birds. Despite his fame as a bird illustrator, this book has no depictions of birds other than his well-known etching of a prairie chicken on the cover. References, checklist of Nebraska birds by family, and species index. — *JD*

EC33   Johnsgard, Paul A. - The Birds of Nebraska and Adjacent Plains States. - Lincoln, NE : Nebraska Ornithologists' Union, 1996. - 144 p.; maps. - (Nebraska

Ornithologists' Union. Occasional papers, 6).

Class Numbers:
    Library of Congress QL684.N2
OCLC 37271019
Notes:
    5th printing with corrections
    Index

• Johnsgard's revision of *Revised Checklist of Nebraska Birds* (Nebraska Ornithologists' Union, 1958) lists birds "convincingly reported" at least once. It includes "420 species, including 53 'accidental' vagrants, in addition to 19 hypothetical species and 12 unsuccessfully introduced, extirpated, extinct or probably extinct species" (Introd.). Entries, by family, describe temporal occurrence, relative abundance, geographic or ecological distribution, migration patterns, and habitats. Descriptions focus on Nebraska but include other Plains states. Sightings are listed or summarized. Range maps in an appendix show density of bird population in Nebraska. Reference sources for Nebraska and the region are cited, and there is an index of common names. An HTML version is available at NOU's Internet site. Johnsgard is an authority on birds and has written widely on Nebraska birds and bird life. — *JD*

EC34 Lingle, Gary R. - **Birding Crane River : Nebraska's Platte** / ill. by William S. Whitney and Ernest V. Ochsner. - Grand Island, NE : Harrier Publ., 1994. - 121 p.; ill, maps; 22 cm.

Class Numbers:
    Library of Congress QL684.N2
LCCN 94-76921
Notes:
    Includes bibliographical references (p. 107-109); index

• A spiral-bound guide to bird populations in the area of south central Nebraska that lies on the twice-annual migratory flyway of the sandhill cranes. It has the following sections: introductory information about the physical characteristics of the region, birding in the seven-county area (with detailed foldout maps), comments on the 30 bird species most common to the area, and an extended chart showing the months during the year when much larger numbers of species may be seen. Includes information about local organizations and contact persons, a bibliography, an index, and black-and-white line drawings. — *MB*

EC35 Mollhoff, Wayne J. - **The Nebraska Breeding Bird Atlas 1984-1989.** - Lincoln, NE : Nebraska Game and Parks Commission, 2001. - 233 p.; ill. - (Nebraska technical series, 20; Nebraska Ornithologists' Union occasional papers, 7).

Class Numbers:
    Library of Congress QL684.N4
    Government Document Nebraska G1000
    H055 -2001
OCLC 48800857
Notes:
    Includes bibliographical references; index

• Because of its environmental diversity, Nebraska provides an excellent laboratory for analyzing bird distribution. Mollhoff intends "to provide ... maps depicting breeding distribution, based on systematic statewide data collection within discrete survey blocks ... collected within a specific time period" (Pref.). The atlas documents the relation of birds to vegetation and provides data allowing documentation of changes over time. Data were gathered and plotted for seven regions rather than counties because county data vary. Species accounts supply range, status, habitat, and phenology (timing of the breeding cycle). Field workers regularly surveyed 443 three-square-mile blocks of the state; activity in those blocks is noted on maps accompanying species accounts. Appendixes include a list of 38 species not reported by field workers and descriptions of blocks with tables of sightings. Bibliography of literature cited; index by common name. — *JD*

EC36 Sharpe, Roger S., 1941-   . - **Birds of Nebraska : Their Distribution & Temporal Occurrence** / [by] Roger S. Sharpe, W. Ross Silcock, and Joel B. Jorgensen. - Lincoln, NE : Univ. of Nebraska Pr., 2001. - 520 p.; [15] p. of plates, col. ill., maps.

Class Numbers:
    Library of Congress QL684.N2
ISBN 0803242891
OCLC 45008663
LCCN 00-64925
Notes:
    Includes bibliographical references (p. [485]-507); index

• In a volume as large as this, illustrations might be expected, but the only plates show habitat areas rather than the birds themselves, for whom there are neither line drawings nor photographs. A rival work, Stan Tekiela's *Birds of Nebraska: Field Guide* (**EC37**), has beautiful color photos of 117 species. Sharpe et al. include about 400 species because they track birds that use Nebraska flyways as well as species commonly found throughout the year. Nebraska species are diverse, the result of the state's diverse geomorphology, water resources, and climate. Introductory text that explains use of "species accounts" is followed by vegetation and land use maps. The editors arrange birds by type (e.g., loons, grebes, pelicans) and for each species supply status (common or rare, seasonal presence, population), documentation, distribution and ecology by season, taxonomy, likely habitat, first evidence, finding tips. The data are drawn from records of the Nebraska Ornithological Union, much of it recorded by bird enthusiasts over the years. Includes a history of Nebraska ornithology, a substantial bibliography, and an index by common and scientific names. — *MB, JD*

EC37 Tekiela, Stan. - **Birds of Nebraska : Field Guide**. - Cambridge, MN : Adventure Publications, Inc., 2003. - 287 p.; ill. (chiefly col.).

> Class Numbers:
> Library of Congress QL684.N2
> ISBN 1591930170

• As befits a field guide, this book is pocket-sized, but it is packed with information for Nebraska birders, including a page of text and a full color page of photos for each of 117 species of Nebraska birds. The entries are organized by the dominant color of the bird for easy identification. Each entry includes the common and Latin name, a state map for habitat, size, and descriptions of male, female, juvenile, nest, and eggs, with additional notes regarding behaviors. — *MB*

New Mexico

EC38 Baley, Florence Merriam, b. 1863. - **Birds of New Mexico** / with contributions by the late Wells Woodbridge Cooke ... ill. with colored plates by Allan Brooks, plates and text figures by the late Louis Agassiz Fuertes and ... drawings, photographs, and maps; based mainly on field work of the Bureau of Biological Survey, U. S. Dept. of Agriculture. - [Santa Fe, NM]: New Mexico Dept. of Game and Fish in cooperation with the State Game Protective Association and the Bureau of Biological Survey, 1928. - xxiv, 807 p.; front., ill., plates (part col.), maps.

> Class Numbers:
> Library of Congress QL684.N6
> LCCN 29-27060
> Notes:
> "Literature cited": p. 763-793

• Although more recent field guides to New Mexico birds exist, Baley's classic is based on careful and extensive scientific observation. The lengthy introduction, besides a general overview, discusses zonal distributions, the value of birds in given environments, a list of refuges and conservation areas, field reports from researchers, locations visited by project observers, and a glossary of technical terms. Birds are grouped by type–e.g., shore birds, owls, perching birds. Entries give common and scientific names, description, habitat range, general habits, food, state records of sightings, and additional literature. Some entries include black-and-white illustrations or refer to the section of

plates in color. Includes maps, list of sources, extensive table of contents, index. Much more than an amateur bird watcher's field guide. — *JB*

North Dakota

EC39 Stewart, Robert E. - **Breeding Birds of North Dakota**. - Fargo, ND : Tri-College Center for Environmental Studies, 1975. - 295 p.; [9] col. leaves of plates, ill.

> Class Numbers:
> Library of Congress QL684.N9
> OCLC 2070539
> LCCN 75-36527
> Notes:
> Bibliography: p. 273-280
> Electronic book: http://www.npwrc.usgs.gov/
> resource/birds/bbofnd/bbofnd.htm

• An atlas of 185 species, based on field work, 1961-1970, supplemented by historical records. An introductory chapter examines the different ecological areas of North Dakota and the types of birds located in each. Organized by family; species accounts include breeding range, habitat, nesting information, distribution map, and some photographs. Species index and appendix of common and scientific names of plants. Illustrated with black-and-white photos and colored drawings of birds, nests, and habitats. The photos, mostly half or full-page, are often unclear. For each species there is a county line map of species distribution and density. — *LMcD*

Oklahoma

EC40 Grzybowski, Joseph Anthony, 1946-   . - **Oklahoma Ornithology : An Annotated Bibliography** / [by] Joseph A. Grzybowski and Gary D. Schnell. - Norman, OK : publ. by the Univ. of Oklahoma Pr. for the Stovall Museum of Science and History, 1984. - 175 p.

> Class Numbers:
> Library of Congress QL684.O5
> ISBN 0806118121
> LCCN 83-40327
> Notes:
> A Stovall Museum publication
> Indexes

• This briefly annotated bibliography supplies just over 1,550 citations that constitute "the primary basis of our knowledge of Oklahoma birds" (Pref.). Entries cite journal articles, dissertations, and theses, assembled from "citations in pertinent publications, personal correspondence, curriculum vitae of authors known to have worked in Oklahoma, our general knowledge of ornithology, and chance"–a fair and accurate description of the way most bibliographies are put together. The Preface has tables of families and subfamilies of birds found in Oklahoma, and families for which there are more than 60 references. The principal list, arranged alphabetically by author, uses scientific format. Annotations consist of family and subfamily names, a descriptive term drawn from a list of 21 keywords, and, occasionally, a brief supplementary statement (e.g., "Sight record"). Appendixes list Christmas bird counts, Oklahoma birds in seasonal reports, and Oklahoma surveys of breeding and winter birds, with citations to the appearance of these counts in journals, especially those published by the National Audubon Society. Indexes of keywords (the same 21 used in annotations), bird families, and English names and subfamilies, all refer to numbered entries in the bibliography. No illustrations. — *RB*

EC41   Oklahoma Breeding Bird Atlas / Dan L. Reinking, ed. - Norman, OK : Univ. of Oklahoma Pr., 2004. - 519 p.; port.

> Class Numbers:
> Library of Congress QL684.O5
> ISBN 0806136146 0806136146 (pbk.)
> OCLC 53099091
> Notes:
> Book review (E-STREAMS): http://www.e-streams.com/es0802/es0802%5F3955.html
> Includes bibliographical references
> Project administered by George M. Sutton, Avian Research Center and the Oklahoma Biological Survey

• Following a brief introduction and a general discussion of Oklahoma vegetation are the species accounts, with a two-page spread devoted to each species. Each entry includes an attractive color photo, a distribution map, and a narrative that offers a general description, breeding habits, nesting ecology, distribution and abundance (both historical and current), population trends, and bibliographic references. The appendixes include the project data forms and observation form. The bibliography (p. 475-511) is quite extensive. The species index refers to both common and scientific name. — *MB*

EC42   Sutton, George Miksch, 1898-   . - **Fifty Common Birds of Oklahoma and the Southern Great Plains**. - Norman, OK : Univ. of Oklahoma Pr., 1977. - 113 p.; col. ill.

> Class Numbers:
> Library of Congress QL684.O5
> ISBN 0806114398

> 0585169233 (electronic bk.)
> OCLC 3167366
> LCCN 77-24336
> Notes:
> Electronic book:
> http://www.netLibrary.com/urlapi.asp?action=summary&v=1&bookid=15103

• Covering 50 species common to large areas of the state, the page-long entries are well-written narratives augmented by colored drawings on the facing page. Based on the author's extensive personal observations, they do not offer the detailed species accounts or identification keys common to field guides, nor do they have the data on distribution and range useful for comparison over time. Nevertheless, the anecdotal, expert and thoroughly delightful descriptions of birds and bird behavior will be of interest to new and experienced enthusiasts. A list of the approximately 400 species known in Oklahoma is included. — *JD*

EC43   Sutton, George Miksch, 1898-   . - **Oklahoma Birds : Their Ecology and Distribution : with Comments on the Avifauna of the Southern Great Plains**. - Norman, OK : Univ. of Oklahoma Pr., 1967. - 674 p.; ill., maps.

> Class Numbers:
> Library of Congress QL684.O5
> OCLC 1975738
> LCCN 67-10209
> Notes:
> Bibliography: p. 643-646

• A catalog, arranged by taxon, of birds observed in all counties of Oklahoma. Sutton summarizes in standardized format but literate prose each family's general appearance, diet, habits, distribution, and like matters, and for each species, recorded sightings in Oklahoma. Maps show counties of Oklahoma and divisions of the state during its territorial period. Illustrations are confined to about 30 line drawings. Index of common and taxonomic names. Since observations are keyed by author name to items in the four-page bibliography, no author index is needed. — *RB*

South Dakota

EC44   The Birds of South Dakota / by Dan A. Tallman, David L. Swanson, and Jeffrey S. Palmer. - 3rd ed. - Aberdeen, SD : South Dakota Ornithologists' Union, 2002. - xxvi, 441 p.; col. ill., col. maps.

> Class Numbers:
> Library of Congress QL684.S8
> ISBN 0929918061

OCLC 50504454

LCCN 91-60391

Notes:

   1st ed., 1978

   Includes bibliographical references

      (p. 421-437); index

   Major underwriters: U.S. Fish & Wildlife

      Service and South Dakota Dept. of Game,

      Fish and Parks

• Earlier editions (1978, 1991) were issued cooperatively by the South Dakota Ornithologists' Union. Tallman (biology, Northern State Univ.), Swanson (biology, Univ. of South Dakota), and Palmer (natural science, Dakota State Univ.) add information about occurrence of species in South Dakota, arranged by families. They supply seasonal numbers, geographic distribution, habitat, and nesting and migration habits. Includes color photographs, illustrations of physiographic divisions and vegetation, and observation maps. A comprehensive work. — *GK*

EC45   Peterson, Richard Allan, 1942- . - **The South Dakota Breeding Bird Atlas**. - Aberdeen, SD : South Dakota Ornithologists' Union, 1995. - 1 atlas (ix, 276 p.); maps.

   Class Numbers:

      Library of Congress G1446.D4

      ISBN 1883120047

      LCCN 95-69083

   Notes:

      Also available in electronic version:

         http://www.npsc.nbs.gov/resouce/distr/birds/

         sdatlas/sdatlas.htm

      Includes bibliographical references; index

      Scale not given

      South Dakota state map insert inside back cover

• Peterson's atlas was the result of a project to document the status and distribution of breeding bird species in South Dakota, 1988-1993. Seventy-one volunteers gathered information about nesting birds in the state in order to address ecological concerns and conservation management. Includes distribution maps of birds on a county basis and 14 tables that provide breeding behavior, habitat categories, and density of population. The species account section includes the common and scientific names, legend (confirmed, possible, probable, and observed sightings), number of reports, habitat elements, frequency of occurrence, and abundance estimates. — *GK*

Texas

EC46   Lockwood, Mark. - **Basic Texas Birds : A Field Guide** / photographs by Greg W. Lasley, Tim Cooper, and

Mark W. Lockwood. - Austin, TX : Univ. of Texas Pr., 2007. - 403 p.; col. ill., maps (chiefly col.). - (Texas natural history guides).

   Class Numbers:

      Library of Congress QL684.T4

      ISBN 0292713495 (pbk.) 9780292713499 (pbk.)

      OCLC 74569351

      LCCN 2006-35914

   Notes:

      Includes bibliographical references

         (p. 391-393); index

      Table of contents: http://www.loc.gov/catdir/toc/

         ecip073/2006035914.html

• Describes 180 species of birds, including common and some rarer species that have been observed in Texas. Entries include common and scientific names, background, similar species, a county map of Texas showing status and distribution, and a color photograph. The introductory material supplies a description and a map showing the physical and geographic regions of Texas, which can be used in conjunction with maps in the entries to identify birds of the Prairies-Plains region. Appendixes list birds by common name and the 629 bird species observed in Texas and documented by the Texas Ornithological Society as of 2006. Concludes with a glossary and a brief list of references. — *MS*

EC47   Lockwood, Mark W. - **Birds of the Texas Hill Country** / drawings by Clemente Guzman III. - Austin, TX : Univ. of Texas Pr., 2001. - 228 p.; ill. (some col.), maps. - (Corrie Herring Hooks series, 50).

   Class Numbers:

      Library of Congress QL684.T4

      ISBN 029274725X 0292747268 (pbk.)

      LCCN 2001-939

   Notes:

      Book review (E-STREAMS):

         http://www.estreams.com/es0509/

         es0509_2113.html

      Includes bibliographical references

         (p. 211-215)

      Table of contents: http://www.loc.gov/catdir/

         toc/ecip0421/2001000939.html

• The 26 counties that make up what is called the Texas Hill Country are located on the Edwards Plateau, the southernmost extension of the Great Plains. Some 420 resident and migratory species that have been observed in the Hill Country are described in this annotated list. It supplies information about status and distribution, gives common and scientific names, and lists parks and exceptional birding locations. It includes line drawings and 32 plates in color. Two tables list the most common species on the Edwards Plateau, and show the seasonal distribution of birds in the region. Bibliography; index. — *MS*

EC48   Seyffert, Kenneth D. - **Birds of the Texas Panhandle** / ill. by Carolyn Stallwitz. - College Station, TX : Texas A&M Univ. Pr., 2001. - 501 p.; ill., map. - (W.L. Moody, Jr., natural history series, 29).

Class Numbers:
Library of Congress QL684.T4
ISBN 1585440914 1585440965 (pbk.)
LCCN 00-44316
Notes:
Bibliography: p. 473-491; index

• Seyffert brings up to date three earlier works, Warren M. Pulich's *The Birds of North Central Texas* (College Station, TX: Texas A&M Univ. Pr., 1988), H.C. Oberholser's *The Bird Life of Texas* (Austin, TX: Univ. of Texas Pr., 1974), and Paul Johnsgard's *Birds of the Great Plains* (1979; **EC19**). His species accounts list 442 species, 406 based on confirmed observations, and 36 "Species of Uncertain Occurrence," observed in the 26 counties of the Panhandle. For each species, he briefly cites its status (common, vagrant, frequent visitor, whether the species breeds in the Panhandle), occurrence (sightings he has recorded or those found in the literature), nesting behavior if the species breeds in the Panhandle, and where in museums specimens may be found. Line drawings are infrequent but show good detail. Front matter summarizes the topographic and climatic environment of the Panhandle and lists (not in alphabetic order) the terminology used in the species accounts. An appendix lists species by county, and an index refers to common and scientific names. — *RB*

CANADA

General Works

EC49   Lynch, Wayne. - **Wild Birds Across the Prairies** / text and photography by Wayne Lynch; assisted by Aubrey Lang. – Calgary, AB : Fifth House Publ., 1999. – 138 p.; col. ill., col. map

Class Numbers:
Library of Congress QL685.5 P7
ISBN 1894004213
OCLC 40396020

• Heavily illustrated field guide to 85 species of the Northern Plains by one of Canada's premier nature photographers. Organized by family, with a physical description of the family, number of species and number of prairie species in particular. The species accounts provide detailed information on field identification, location, wintering grounds, diet and feeding habits, breeding biology, and a section of unusual facts. Includes a checklist of species. — *LMcD*

Alberta

EC50   **The Atlas of Breeding Birds of Alberta** / ed. by Glen P. Semenchuk. - Edmonton, AB : Federation of Alberta Naturalists, 1992. - 391 p. : col. ill., col. maps.

Class Numbers:
Library of Congress QL685.5.A3
ISBN 0969613407
OCLC 26804377
Notes:
Bibliography: p. 349-383

• A record of the breeding status and distribution of Alberta birds between 1987 and 1991. Each species has a color photograph for visual identification as well as a description of habitat, breeding season, migratory pattern, and conservation situation. Distribution maps locate data on the six natural areas of the province, one of which is the grassland region. Separate nomenclature indexes in English, French, and Latin; trilingual index of migratory species. Extensive bibliography of historical references, general references and references by family. Updates *The Birds of Alberta* (Edmonton: Alberta Dept. of Industry and Development, 1966) by W.R. Salt and A.L. Wilk. — *LMcD*

EC51   Ealey, David M. - **A Bibliography of Alberta Ornithology** / [by] David M. Ealey, Martin K. McNicholl. - 2nd ed. - Edmonton, AB : Natural History Section, Provincial Museum of Alberta, 1991. - 751 p.; ill. - (Natural history occasional paper; no. 16).

Class Numbers:
Library of Congress QL685.5.A4
National Library of Canada
COP.AL.2.1991-307
OCLC 24537492
LCCN 92-120093
Notes:
First ed., 1981

• Almost 7,500 studies, published and unpublished, on Alberta birds. Ealey employs the same 20 broad categories used in his companion bibliography on Alberta mammals (**EC83**). Species accounts, paleontology, ecology, behavior, disease, management and conservation, and habitat studies are among the major divisions. Domesticated bird species and poultry are not included. Citations include subject keywords, species, and location information. Author, subject, species, and location indexes make the bibliography easy to use. — *LMcD*

EC52   Salt, Walter Raymond, 1905-   . - **The Birds of Alberta : With Their Ranges in Saskatchewan & Manitoba** / [by] W. Ray Salt & Jim R. Salt. - Edmonton,

AB : Hurtig, 1976. - 498 p.; ill. (some col.), maps.

Class Numbers:
    Library of Congress QL695.5.A4
ISBN 0888301081 9780888301086
OCLC 3016117
LCCN 77-356675
Notes:
    Indexes

• Although expressly not intended as a field guide, this work has many of the hallmarks of one. Arranged according to the American Ornithologists' *Union Checklist of North American Birds*, the book provides for each of the approximately 300 species with a presence in Alberta a description, identifying elements, nesting behavior, range, notes, and small outline maps showing distribution for the Prairie provinces. Most also have a color photo or painting. Additional features include a checklist, hypothetical list (reported in Alberta but undocumented), and indexes of scientific and common names. — *LMcD*

Manitoba

EC53   McNicholl, Martin K. - **Manitoba Bird Studies, 1744-1983 : A Bibliography**. - Winnipeg, MB : Manitoba Natural Resources; Manitoba Museum of Man & Nature, 1985. - 290 p.

Class Numbers:
    Library of Congress QL685.5; Z5334 C3
OCLC 14356477
LCCN 86-166144

• An author list of about 1,500 entries, the majority journal articles. Appendixes list biographical works on ornithologists, arranged by author; secondary authors and biographical works, arranged by biographee; and sources. The absence of topical, species, and geographical indexes substantially increases the tedium of searching. — *LMcD*

Saskatchewan

EC54   Smith, Alan R. - **Atlas of Saskatchewan Birds**. - Regina, SK : Saskatchewan Natural History Society, 1996. - 456 p.; ill., maps. - (Manley Callin series, 4; Saskatchewan Natural History Society. Special publication, 18).

Class Numbers:
    Library of Congress QL685.5.S2
ISBN 092110412X
OCLC 43661601
Notes:
    Includes bibliographical references (p. 436-448) and
      index

• Treats approximately 400 species, not all of which are found in the Prairie region. Listed by English name of subspecies, followed by scientific and French vernacular names. Individual species information consists of a map (1:50,000 grid, with breeding data and seasonal status represented symbolically), species summary, and species accounts (indicating variations in status or abundance). Describes provincial biotic regions. Several appendixes: annotated list of species recorded 25 or fewer times (listed by English name, with map location, date, age, sex, breeding status, record type, and references); Christmas bird counts; breeding bird survey; common and scientific names of plants, insects, reptiles, and mammals in the text; gazetteer, bibliography, and index of English and scientific names. More informative for birdwatchers is the author's *Saskatchewan Birds* (EC55). — *LMcD*

EC55   Smith, Alan R. - **Saskatchewan Birds** / [by] Alan Smith, with contributions from Eloise Pulos, Andy Bezener, and Chris Fisher. - Edmonton, AB : Lone Pine Publ., 2001. - 176 p. : col. ill., col. maps.

Class Numbers:
    Library of Congress QL685.5
National Library of Canada QL685.5 S2
ISBN 1551053047
OCLC 46624967
Notes:
    Includes bibliographical references and indexes

• Field guide to 145 species. Identifying elements for each include description, size, status, habitat, nesting and feeding habits, sound, similar species, best sites for viewing, and range maps. Glossary, species checklist, indexes of scientific and common names. Handy guide, in nontechnical language, for bird enthusiasts. — *LMcD*

BUTTERFLIES

EC56   **Atlas of North Dakota Butterflies [Internet Site]** / information provided by Ronald A. Royer. - Jamestown, ND : Northern Prairie Wildlife Research Center Online, 2004. – http://www.npwrc.usgs.gov/resource/insects/bflynd/index.htm

Class Numbers:
    Library of Congress QL551.N63
OCLC 38911678
Access Date: May 2006
Notes:
    Based on the author's *Butterflies of North Dakota:*
      An Atlas and Guide (Minot, ND: Minot State

Univ., 2003)
Fees: None

• Organized by family and subfamily, the atlas covers approximately 150 species. Each indicates naming conventions, habitat, larval food, adult flight, references, and distribution map at the county level. Color photographs show male and female specimens, as well as upper and lower wing surfaces. Updated at the end of each season, the atlas provides the most current species information for the state. — *LMcD*

EC57   The Butterflies of Manitoba / [by] P. Klassen [et al.]. - Winnipeg, MB : Manitoba Museum of Man and Nature, 1989. - 290 p.; ill. (some col.), maps.

    Class Numbers:
        Library of Congress QL552.B88
        ISBN 0920704166
        LCCN 89-191570
    Notes:
        Includes bibliographical references (p. 259-263);
            index

• Identification guide to 144 species of butterflies occurring in Manitoba. Preliminary material discusses taxonomy, life history, distribution, and conservation. Species accounts consist of description, similar species, life cycle, habitat, range, Manitoba records, subspecies, remarks, and distribution maps. Twenty-seven colored plates show life-size views (dorsal and ventral) of each species. Glossary. Appendixes cover collecting, food plants, locations of collection sites, and flight periods. Intended for both amateur and professional entomologists. — *LMcD*

EC58   Hooper, Ronald R. - **The Butterflies of Saskatchewan** / with photographs by Ron Long; drawings by F.W. Lahrman and J. Pickering. - [Regina, SK] : Saskatchewan Dept. of Natural Resources, [1973]. - 216 p.; ill. (part col.).

    Class Numbers:
        Library of Congress QL552
        LCCN 74-150706
    Notes:
        Bibliography: p. 202-204

• For 135 species, briefly discusses habits, life histories, where to look for butterflies, collecting and mounting of specimens. Area locations of distribution records are keyed to a zonal map of the province. Each chapter covers a single family with its subfamilies and includes an identification chart. The species accounts provide common and scientific names, description of appearance, range, habits and photographs, usually black-and-white. Checklist and separate indexes of plants, scientific, and common names. — *LMcD*

EC59   Marrone, Gary M. - **Field Guide to Butterflies of South Dakota**. - Pierre, SD : South Dakota Dept. of Game, Fish, and Parks, 2002. - 478 p.; ill. (chiefly col.), maps.

    Class Numbers:
        Library of Congress QL551.S8
        Government Document South Dakota GA
            200: W 645:B 982
        ISBN 0971246319
        OCLC 51530340
        LCCN 2002-141290
    Notes:
        Includes bibliographical references (p. 472-474);
            index

• Marrone (fisheries biologist, South Dakota Dept. of Game, Fish, and Parks) provides a comprehensive guide to 177 species of South Dakota butterflies, with county maps that illustrate distribution and habitat. Describes in detail life stages (pupa, caterpillar, butterfly), supplies 700 color photographs to help identify specimens, and provides a butterfly checklist, seasonal calendar, list of species, and glossary. — *GK*

FISHES

EC60   Atton, F. M. - **Atlas of Saskatchewan Fish** / presented to Fisheries Branch, Dept. of Parks and Renewable Resources, by F.M. Atton and J.J. Merkowsky. - Regina, SK : Fisheries Branch, 1983. - 281 p.; ill., maps. - (Fisheries technical report; 83-2).

    Class Numbers:
        Library of Congress QL 626.5 S2
        OCLC 28023321
    Notes:
        Includes bibliographical references: p. 263-278

• Occurrence data and distribution maps for 58 native and 10 introduced species. Species records are arranged by English name, followed by Latin name and map number, drainage basin and drainage system, and source of information keyed to the bibliography. Species maps show distribution on a base map of the province's eight drainage basins. — *LMcD*

EC61   Bailey, Reeve Maclaren. - **Fishes of South Dakota** / by Reeve M. Bailey and Marvin O. Allum. - Ann Arbor, MI : Museum of Zoology, Univ. of Michigan, 1962. - 131 p.; ill., maps, tables. - (University of Michigan. Museum of Zoology. Miscellaneous publications, 119).

    Class Numbers:
        Library of Congress QK628.S7
        OCLC 1892833
        LCCN 62-63614

Notes:
> Bibliography: p. 126-131

• Bailey and Allum (South Dakota State College) seek to identify fishes based on information from 137 collecting stations in South Dakota. The state has 93 species, 2 subspecies, and 6 introduced species. Includes sections for the history of South Dakota, ichthyology, hypothetical occurrence, hybridization, hydrographic interchanges, and origins of South Dakota fish fauna. Annotations include the physical characteristics found in each species. One plate, five distribution maps, map of collecting agencies, nine tables. — *GK*

EC62   **A Bibliography of Fisheries Biology in North and South Dakota [Internet Site]** / [by] John B. Owen and Alice K. Owen. - [Jamestown, ND] : Northern Prairie Wildlife Research Center, 1995-. - http://www.npwrc.usgs.gov/resource/literatr/fishbibl/index.htm

> Class Numbers:
>> Library of Congress SH222.N9
>> Z5974.U6
> OCLC 35633155
> Access Date: May 2007
> Version: Sep. 30, 2002
> Fees: None

• Approximately 1,200 citations, the earliest dating back to 1858, to scientific studies and theses. Although the focus is on the Dakotas, items related to adjacent states and Manitoba with a common river basin are also included. Searchable by keyword, author, year, title, source, and abstract. Intended for aquatic biologists. — *LMcD*

EC63   Brown, Claudeous Jethro Daniels, 1904–   . - **Fishes of Montana**. - Bozeman, MT : Montana State Univ., 1971. - 207 p.; ill., maps.

> Class Numbers:
>> Library of Congress QL628.M9
> OCLC 195355
> LCCN 77-155934
> Notes:
>> Bibliography: p. 191-197

• Distribution data on 80 species, of which 52 were considered native, is based on specimens at Montana State University, surveys by Montana Fish and Game, and other publications. A glossary, keys to species in each family, and an introduction to fish collecting and will aid nonspecialists. Entries have a clear drawing, a distribution map showing rivers and tributaries, description, range, life history, habitat, size, food, and recreational and commercial value. Appendixes include references, an index by common and scientific name, a map of stream drainages, and a list of fish by drainage area. A well-formatted guide that is also useful to researchers identifying changes in species and distribution. — *JD*

EC64   Fedoruk, Alex N. - **Checklist of and Key to the Freshwater Fishes of Manitoba : Preliminary**. - Winnipeg, MB : Dept. of Mines, Resources and Natural Resources, Canada Land Inventory Project, 1969. - 98p. : ill.

> Class Numbers:
>> Library of Congress QL626 M35
> OCLC 184742735
> Notes:
>> 1971 ed. has title: *Freshwater Fishes of Manitoba: Checklist and Keys* (Winnipeg: Dept. of Mines, Resources & Environmental Management; 120 p.)
>> Includes bibliographical references and index

• An inventory of 82 species, native or introduced, of freshwater fish found in Manitoba. The key consists of pairs of descriptive statements designed to lead progressively to identification and small line drawings. Glossary of terms and index. Informative but drab in appearance. — *LMcD*

EC65   Joseph, Timothy W. - **An Annotated Bibliography of the Rare Fishes of the Upper Missouri River System** / Ecology Consultants Inc. - Fort Collins, CO : Dept. of the Interior, Fish and Wldlife Service, Office of Biological Services, Western Energy and Land Use Team; Washington, DC : U.S. Govt. Print. Off., 1977. - [287] p.

> Class Numbers:
>> Government Document I 49.18:Up 6 m

• Joseph (Ecology Consultants Inc.) cites 590 sources, with annotations, concerning endangered or threatened fish species in the Upper Missouri River system. The bibliography has two parts: the status, history, environment, and habitats of rare fishes, and distribution maps. For convenience, 70 subject headings are printed in the right-hand margins; citations are listed alphabetically by author and are cross-indexed. The study was sponsored by the Environmental Protection Agency. — *GK*

EC66   Thomas, Chad, 1970-   . - **Freshwater Fishes of Texas : A Field Guide** / [by] Chad Thomas, Timothy H. Bonner, and Bobby G. Whiteside. - College Station, TX : Texas A&M Univ. Pr., 2007. - 220 p.; ill. (chiefly col.), maps (chiefly col.). - (River books; TxAM nature guides).

> Class Numbers:
>> Library of Congress QL628.T4
> ISBN 1585445703   9781585445707
> LCCN 2006-29777
> Notes:
>> Table of contents: http://www.loc.gov/catdir/toc/ecip0620/2006029777.html

• Describes 161 species of fish, native and nonnative. Each species account consists of a double spread: a color photograph labeled with the scientific and common names on the left, and text describing range, habitat, characteristics, dimensions, coloration, and comments on the right. Maps that show the range of habitat accompany the text and allow identification of fish found in the Plains region of Texas. Introductory essays cover drainage regions, common fish counts and measurements, phylogeny of fishes, and a key to fish families. The appendix consists of colored plates that illustrate the counting of pharyngeal teeth. The glossary is accompanied by colored illustrations showing fish anatomy. Brief list of references. — *MS*

INSECTS

EC67 Acorn, John, 1958-   . - **Ladybugs of Alberta : Finding the Spots and Connecting the Dots**. - Edmonton, AB : Univ. of Alberta Pr., 2007. - xxix, 169 p.; ill. (chiefly col.), ports. (some col.). - (Alberta insects series).

> Class Numbers:
> Library of Congress QL596.C65
> LCCN 2007-277237
> Notes:
> Includes bibliographical references: p. 165-169
> Table of contents: http://www.loc.gov/catdir/toc/
> fy0713/2007277237.html

• In the first regional guide to North American ladybugs, Acorn (conservation biology, Univ. of Alberta) manages to make an unlikely subject not only informative but also entertaining. He discusses life cycle, ladybug study in Alberta, introduced species, and conservation in an informal and sometimes humorous style. The 75 species covered are arranged by subfamily, followed by English name, and eye-catching names they are: Episcopalian ladybug, Flying saucer ladybug, and Twice-stabbed ladybug, among many others. Species accounts, each introduced by a rhyming couplet, provide scientific name and pronunciation, English name (some coined by the author) and origin, identification, notes, colored photographs, and distribution map. Checklist, glossary, and list of helpful resources. Since many of the species described are widely distributed across the continent, the guide is useful well beyond Alberta. – *LMcD*

EC68 Capinera, John L. - **Field Guide to Grasshoppers, Crickets, and Katydids of the United States** / [by] John L. Capinera, Ralph D. Scott, and Thomas J. Walker. - Ithaca, NY : Cornell Univ. Pr., 2004. - 249 p.; 48 p. of plates, ill. (some col.).

> Class Numbers:
> Library of Congress QL508.A2
> ISBN 0801442605 0801489482 (pbk.)

LCCN 2004-10727
Notes:
> Includes bibliographical references (p. [229]-231);
> index

• Designed for amateurs, students, and professionals. Uses pictorial keys, color illustrations, and nontechnical language to simplify identification of species of the order Orthoptera, which have significant presence and ecological impact in the Great Plains. A primer on Orthoptera appearance and body parts, life history, biogeography, collection and preservation, sound production, and harmful effects precedes the species accounts. Accounts cover common species, about a third of the total in the U.S. and Canada, giving distribution, range maps, identification, ecology, and similar species. Includes pronunciation of scientific names, a glossary, selected readings, and an index by scientific name, common name, and topic. — *JD*

EC69 Fairweather, Mary Lou. - **Field Guide to Insects and Diseases of Arizona and New Mexico Forests**. - Albuquerque, NM : USDA Forest Service, Southwestern Region, 2006. - 269 p.; chiefly col. ill.

> Class Numbers:
> Library of Congress SB763.A6
> Government Document A 13.36/2:D 63/2
> OCLC 80550527
> LCCN 2007-361110
> Notes:
> Includes bibliographical references (p. 233-
> 246); indexes
> Table of contents: http://0-www.loc.gov.library.
> unl.edu:80/catdir/toc/fy-0705/2007361110.html

• Sturdy and spiral-bound for use in the field, Fairweather's field guide covers insects and diseases with significant ecological or economic impact on recreation, wildlife, wood production and watershed quality. Insects and diseases are organized by type: forest insect defoliators; sap sucking insects, gall formers, and mites; bark beetles; wood borers; cone and seed insects; bud and shoot insects; insects of wood products; foliar diseases; stem decays and stains; cankers; stem and cone rusts of pine; mistletoes; root disease; noninfectious disorders and animal damage. Entries give hosts, symptoms/signs, biology, effects, similar insects and diseases, and references to the bibliography. Color photographs of adults, larvae, eggs, and damage aid identification. Includes glossary, selected bibliography, host index and a general index with common and scientific names. Pages are color tabbed for easy reference. — *JD*

EC70 **Nebraska Insects** / ed. by Stephen V. Johnson, Lynne K. Reiske. - Lincoln, NE : Nebraska Dept of Agriculture, Bureau of Plant Industry, 1988. - 1 v. (loose-leaf); ill. (chiefly col.).

Class Numbers:
    Library of Congress SB934.5.N2
    OCLC 20754342
Notes:
    Includes bibliographical references

• A useful general reader's introduction to insects' beneficial and detrimental effects, structure, life cycle, and taxonomy in practical loose-leaf format. It covers only a few hundred of the estimated 10,000 species found in Nebraska, focusing on insects with strong economic and agricultural impact. Organized by food source (e.g., livestock, forage legumes, corn), species entries give descriptions of egg, larva, pupa, and adult; life history; and damage caused. Clear color photos of insects at various stages of the life cycle, silhouettes showing actual size, and photos of characteristic damage all aid in identification. Includes brief lists of beneficial insects and insects that affect humans, a glossary, and list of references. —*JD*

EC71   Pfadt, Robert E. - **Field Guide to Common Western Grasshoppers**. - 3rd edition - [Laramie, WY[: Wyoming Agricultural Experiment Station, 2002. - 1 v. (various pagings); ill., (some col.), col. maps 29 cm. - (Bulletin 912; U.S. Dept. of Agriculture. Technical bulletin, 1809).

Class Numbers:
    Library of Congress S131
    Government Document A 1.36:1809/PACK.1
    OCLC 50602147
Notes:
    Available online: http://www.sidney.ars.usda.gov/
        grasshopper/ID%5FTools/F%5FGuide/index.htm
    Includes bibliographical references

• Spiral bound fact sheets based on observation, field notes, and published information, describe 60 of about 400 species common in the 17 western states. Nearly all inhabit the Great Plains. General information includes external anatomy, nymphal characters, scientific and common names, species, populations, life history, life cycle, behavior, collection and survey, grasslands and food plants, along with a glossary and selected references. Four-page Fact Sheets, more complete than the usual species accounts, are arranged alphabetically by scientific name. They cover distribution and habitat, economic importance, food habits, migratory habits, identification, hatching, nymphal development, adults and reproduction, population, ecology, daily activity, and references to published literature. Maps show geographic range; charts show years of outbreaks and other data; and up to ten color photographs show nymphs, male and female adults, color patterns, body parts and egg pods. Captions include measurements. Indexed by common name and topic. —*JD*

EC72   Wheeler, George Carlos, 1897- . - **The Ants of North Dakota** / [by] George C. Wheeler and Jeanette Wheeler. - Grand Forks, ND : Univ. of North Dakota, 1963. - 326 p.; ill., maps.

Class Numbers:
    Library of Congress QL568.F7
    OCLC 1029134
    LCCN 63-63430
Notes:
    Bibliography: p. 316-320

• The first third of the Wheelers' work introduces the family Formicidae in general; methods of studying ants; and North Dakota physiography, climate, soils, and biota. Species accounts are organized by the four subfamilies. Based on existing collections and field notes, information includes description, habitat, nests, habits, mimicry, range, state records, and other literature, along with range maps, photographs, and drawings. A chapter on biogeography of ants in North Dakota uses maps, tables, and text to discuss paleontology, relations to other species, geographical and ecological distributions, subspecies, and endemic species. Appendixes include a glossary, pronunciation, derivation of names, and literature cited. Indexed by ant genus, species, and subspecies, as well as by names of related plants and animals. The work seems too technical for its intended audience of amateurs. Though the taxonomy may be out of date, it is useful for comparisons with current ecological and distribution data. —*JD*

MAMMALS

UNITED STATES

General Works

EC73   Choate, Larry L. - **The Mammals of the Llano Estacado**. - Lubbock, TX : Museum of Texas Tech, 1997. - 240 p.; ill., maps. - (Museum of Texas Tech University. Special publications, 40).

Class Numbers:
    Library of Congress QL719.T4
    ISBN 0964018861
    OCLC 38303220
Notes:
    Includes bibliographical references (p. 209-221)

• The Llano or Southern High Plains, a mesa in western Texas and eastern New Mexico, is or has been home to at least 74 species of mammals. Based on specimens and prior literature, the species accounts, organized by order and family, include identification keys to the orders, species distributions, distribution maps, tables of distributions by county, summaries of the literature, species descriptions, specimens examined, and additional literature. Discussions of the unique environment and zoogeography of the region with tables, maps, and photographs give context. A bibliography of the literature cited is included along with a county-by-county list of the exact localities of the specimens examined. For specialists. — *JD*

distribution, description, natural history and selected references. Names include derivation of the scientific name and list common names. Ranges are roughly mapped to illustrate distribution. Natural history of the species includes ecology, behavior, reproduction, development, molt, food habits, and parasites. Separate chapters cover the general Plains environment and introduced species. Glossary, literature cited, and additional readings. — *JD*

EC74 Jones, J. Knox. - **Guide to Mammals of the Plains States** / [by] J. Knox Jones Jr., David M. Armstrong, Jerry R. Choate. - Lincoln, NE : Univ. of Nebraska Pr., 1985. - xvii, 371 p.; ill.

> Class Numbers:
> Library of Congress QL719.G73
> ISBN 0803225628 0803275579 (pbk.)
> OCLC 11234314
> LCCN 84-21012
> Notes:
> Bibliography: p. [347]-361; index

• Jones (biology, Texas Tech Univ.), Armstrong (natural sciences, Univ. of Colorado), and Choate (zoology, Fort Hays State Univ.) provide a handbook of 138 native and eight introduced species of mammals that live in the Plains states of North and South Dakota, Nebraska, Kansas, and Oklahoma. The book is arranged by mammalian order and family; keys and glossaries allow quick identification by species. For each mammal, the authors arrange information in five categories: distribution, description, habitat, reproduction, and further readings, and supply 140 black-and-white photographs and 94 maps that show distribution of mammals in the five states. — *GK*

EC76 Turner, Ronald W. - **Mammals of the Black Hills of South Dakota and Wyoming**. - Lawrence, KS : Univ. of Kansas, 1974. - 178 p.; ill. - (University of Kansas. Museum of Natural History. Miscellaneous publication, 60).

> Class Numbers:
> Library of Congress QL719.B55
> OCLC 879484
> LCCN 74-622589
> Notes:
> Bibliography: p. 166-178

• Turner (World Health Organization) describes the mammalian fauna of 62 species in 44 genera found in the Black Hills of South Dakota and Wyoming. He divides the work into environment (geography, geology, climate, soils, hydrography, vegetation, Pleistocene history, influence of man on the environment), accounts of species (orders Insectivora, Chiroptera, Lagmorpha, Rodentia, Carnivora, Artiodactyla), species of unverified occurrence, and factors influencing distribution. Bibliography of sources; geographic coordinates of the region, p. 6. — *GK*

Colorado

EC77 Fitzgerald, James P., 1940-   . - **Mammals of Colorado** / [by] James P. Fitzgerald, Carron A. Meaney, David M. Armstrong. - [Denver, CO] : Denver Museum of Natural History, 1994. - 467 p.; ill., maps.

> Class Numbers:
> Library of Congress QL719.C6
> ISBN 0870813331
> LCCN 94-1626
> Notes:
> Bibliography: p. 413-457
> Revision of: Robert R. Leichleitner, *Wild Mammals of Colorado*. Boulder, CO: Pruit Publ. Co., 1969

• A catalog of nine orders of mammals native to and presently found in Colorado, intended for undergraduate and secondary students of zoology and mammals. Species accounts are classed by order, Marsupialia through Artiodactyla, giving for each species a detailed description, natural history (habitat, feeding patterns, migration), and distribution in Colorado. Black-and-white photographs

EC75 Jones, J. Knox. - **Mammals of the Northern Great Plains** / [by] J. Knox Jones [et al.]. - Lincoln, NE : Univ. of Nebraska Pr., 1983. - 379 p.; ill.

> Class Numbers:
> Library of Congress QL719.G73
> ISBN 0803225571 9780803225572
> OCLC 8282163
> LCCN 82-2693
> Notes:
> Bibliography: p. [361]-375; index

• Jones covers wild mammals of Nebraska, North Dakota, and South Dakota, "the northern part of the great interior grasslands of North America," in a "comprehensive yet semitechnical" approach intended for specialists and nonspecialists (Pref.). Arranged in conventional phylogenetic order with the class Mammalia, orders, families, and genera briefly described. Species accounts, arranged alphabetically under genus, use data mostly derived from field studies in the region, and include name, accompany each account, as do distribution maps for North America and for Colorado. Front matter includes 26 pages on the landscape of Colorado, a general discussion of mammals, and "People and Wild Mammals in Colorado," a history of accommodation and conflict between people and the mammalian population. There is no index, but appendixes supply conversion factors for metric measures and a glossary, and a thorough bibliography occupies 45 pages. — *RB*

Nebraska

EC78   Jones, J. Knox. - **Distribution and Taxonomy of Mammals in Nebraska**. - Lawrence, KS : Univ. of Kansas, Museum of Natural History, 1964. - 356 p.; ill., maps. - (University of Kansas. Museum of Natural History. Publications, v. 16 no.1).

> Class Numbers:
> Library of Congress QH1
> OCLC 997577
> LCCN 64-65199
> Notes:
> Bibliography: p. 341-356

• Eighty-one species of native mammals live in Nebraska; many also inhabit other parts of the U.S. Front matter describes the history of the published record with regard to Nebraska animals, the state's diverse environment, and factors affecting distribution and speciation. Jones examined 10,339 specimens of 86 species held by museums, universities, and private collectors to develop the species accounts, which devote general discussion to each species' characteristics and distribution, and supply scientific name, common name, literature citations, geographic distribution in Nebraska, external and cranial measurements, variations, records of occurrence, and additional localities. Nebraska distribution maps are set into U.S. distribution maps. Reports unverified occurrences and includes an extensive list of references. Changes in nomenclature and mammalian distribution since 1964 make this work a historical or baseline source. — *JD*

New Mexico

EC79   Bailey, Vernon, 1864-1942. - **Mammals of the Southwestern United States (with Special Reference to New Mexico)**. - New York : Dover Publ., 1971, 1931. - 412 p.; ill., maps, 22 plates.

> Class Numbers:
> Library of Congress QL719.N6
> ISBN 0486227391
> LCCN 70-156908
> Notes:
> Bibliography: p. 395-399

Originally publ. 1931 under title:
Mammals of New Mexico

• Most of the text (as the subtitle indicates) is concerned with New Mexico mammals. Field studies were carried out by the Bureau of Biological Survey, U.S. Dept. of Agriculture. The introduction covers history, geographic variations, useful and injurious species, game protection, and control of noxious species. The greater part of the guide is devoted to individual mammalian species; its entries list scientific and common names, where and when data were collected, general characteristics, and measurements, also listing as applicable distribution, habitat, general habits, food habits, breeding, economic influence, and hibernation habits. Maps show habitat range. Illustrated with black-and-white photographs; detailed index. Although the survey was conducted between 1890 and 1930, this is considered a classic study of mammals of the southern Plains. — JB

Oklahoma

EC80   Owen, Robert D. - **Oklahoma Mammalogy : An Annotated Bibliography and Checklist** / [by] Robert D. Owen and Gary D. Schnell. - Norman, OK : Univ. of Oklahoma Pr., 1989. - 230 p.

> Class Numbers:
> Library of Congress QL 719 Z7996.M3
> ISBN 0806121858
> OCLC 18589146
> LCCN 88-27959
> Notes:
> Index

• Contains more than 1,200 citations to books, journal articles, dissertations, and reports issued prior to 1987 on the mammals of Oklahoma. Entries, arranged alphabetically by author, list author, title, date of publication, and publisher. The family and keyword index must be used to locate entries for any given species. The family and keyword index is arranged alphabetically by scientific name, then alphabetically by topic (e.g., behavior, bibliographies, ecology). Brief index to common names. — MB

South Dakota

EC81   Higgins, Kenneth F. - **Wild Mammals of South Dakota**. - Pierre, SD : South Dakota Dept. of Game, Fish, and Parks, 2000. - 278 p.; ill. (some col.), maps.

> Class Numbers:
> Library of Congress QL719.S6
> Government Document South Dakota
> GA 200:W 645/M 311
> ISBN 0965893669   9780965893664

OCLC 43841439

Notes:

    Funded in part by Federal Aid in Wildlife
      Restoration Program

    Includes bibliographical references (p. 250-252)

• Higgins's book, the result of a project conducted by the South Dakota Game, Fish, and Parks Department and the Wildlife Research Unit (South Dakota State Univ.), serves as a field guide intended for naturalists, amateurs to experienced professionals, describing 95 species of wild mammals found in the state. Each species is accompanied by a color photograph, scientific name, brief description, basic history, and a map in color that depicts current distribution and population statistics. — *GK*

Texas

EC82 Schmidly, David J., 1943-　. - **The Mammals of Texas**. - Austin, TX : Univ. of Texas Pr., 2004. - 501 p.; ill. (some col.), maps. - (Corrie Herring Hooks series, 59).

    Class Numbers:

      Library of Congress QL719.T4

    ISBN 0292702418 (pbk.)

    Notes:

      1st ed. by William B. Davis: Austin, TX: *Texas Parks
        and Wildlife, Nongame and Urban Program*; distr. by
        Univ. of Texas Pr., 1974.

      Book review (E-STREAMS): http://www.e-streams.
        com/es0802/es0802_3958.html

      Includes bibliographical references (p. [477]-479)

      Table of contents: http://www.loc.gov/catdir/toc/
        ecip0419/2003026430.html

• A guide to the 11 orders of mammals found in Texas, including Cetacea (found in waters off the coast). For each order, the authors provide a key to the order, then list families by scientific name. Within each family, species are listed by common name, e.g., mule deer. For each species, entries include description, distribution, habits, and often, a distribution map and black-and-white photo. Appendixes include a list of selected references, a guide to measurement methods, and a glossary. No subject index. — *MB*

CANADA

Alberta

EC83 Ealey, D. M. - **A Bibliography of Alberta Mammalogy** / prepared for Provincial Museum of Alberta. - Edmonton, AB : Alberta Culture, Historical Resources Division, 1987. - 400 p. - (Natural history occasional paper; no. 8).

    Class Numbers:

      Library of Congress QL721.5.A3

      Z7996.M3

    OCLC 20530793

    LCCN 89-120878

    Notes:

      Includes bibliographical references (p. 12-19);
        indexes

• Ealey groups 3,800 items under 20 major subject categories such as species counts, ecology, paleontology, and behavior. The largest sections deal with status and distribution, along with management and conservation. Studies of domesticated mammals and livestock are excluded. A considerable number of unpublished wildlife management reports and environmental impact assessments are included. Citations indicate subject, species, and location information; separate author, subject, species, and geographical indexes. — *LMcD*

EC84 Stelfox, J. Brad. - **A Selected Bibliography of Research, Management, and Biology of Alberta's Native Ungulates** / by J.B. Stelfox, L. Peleshok, and M.T. Nietfeld. - 2nd ed. - [Vegreville, AB] : Alberta Environmental Centre, 1991. - 110 p.

    Class Numbers:

      Library of Congress QL737.U4

      National Library of Canada COP.AL.2.1992-213

    ISBN 0773205470 9780773205475

    OCLC 26261542

    LCCN 93-206754

• Approximately 2,400 items in a variety of formats, published from the 1940s to 1991, examining nine species of hoofed mammals in Alberta: deer, caribou, elk, moose, pronghorn, mountain goat, bighorn sheep, and bison. Entries are alphabetically arranged under topics such as game ranching, habitat classification, hunting, and provincial surveys; geographic and species indexes would have facilitated more precise searching. Intended for environmental management agencies and academic researchers. — *LMcD*

BADGERS

EC85 Long, Charles Alan, 1936-　. - **The Badgers of the World** / by Charles A. Long and Carl Arthur Killingley. - Springfield, IL : C.C. Thomas, 1983. - xxiv, 404 p.; ill. (some col.).

    Class Numbers:

      Library of Congress QL737.C25

    ISBN 0398047413

    LCCN 82-10393

    Notes:

      Bibliography: p. 369-384; index

• Although Long surveys badgers over the entire world, the section on North American badgers is extensive, where their range is principally the Prairies-Plains and the mountain West. Besides photos, maps, line drawings, and tabular data, Long provides descriptive characteristics of badgers, their geographic variation and distribution, natural history (e.g., senses, locomotion, habitats, and reproduction), behavior, and status. — *MB*

BISON

EC86   Arthur, George W. - **A Buffalo Round-Up : A Selected Bibliography**. - [Regina, SK] : Canadian Plains Research Center, Univ. of Regina, c1985. - 153 p. - (Canadian plains bibliographies, 2).

> Class Numbers:
> > Library of Congress Z7997.B57

• Arthur's guide to the literature on both the Plains bison and the wood bison updates earlier works such as G. Miller's *The American Bison (Bison Bison): An Initial Bibliography* (1977). It attempts to be inclusive, except it excludes fiction and juvenile works. The 2,521 numbered entries, arranged alphabetically by author, enforce reliance on the extensive subject index, which runs 25 pages. The index entries are arranged by topic and region, e.g., "Frontier and Pioneer Life - Prairie Provinces." — *MB*

EC87   McDonald, Jerry N. - **North American Bison : Their Classification and Evolution**. - Berkeley, CA : Univ. of California Pr., 1981. - 316 p.; [8] leaves of plates, ill.

> Class Numbers:
> > Library of Congress QL737.U53 M27
> ISBN 0520040023
> OCLC 6487736
> LCCN 80-36831
> Notes:
> > Bibliography: p. [286]-309

• Besides an extensive section on classification, McDonald's volume also addresses morphological variation and models of bison adaptation to different environments. The work also offers a wealth of statistical data regarding the historical range and habitat of the various species of bison and pays particular attention to skeletal morphology. Illustrations are plentiful. An extensive bibliography (p. 286-309) should be especially useful to students and scholars. The subject index is too brief. — *MB*

EC88   Plumb, Glenn E. - **A Bibliography on Bison (Bison Bison)** / [by] Glenn E. Plumb, Jerrold L. Dodd, and J. Brad Stelfox. - Laramie, WY : Agricultural Experiment Station, 1992. - 23 p. - (Wyoming Agricultural Experiment Station. Miscellaneous publication, 71).

> Class Numbers:
> > Library of Congress Z7997.B57
> Notes:
> > Electronic book: http://www.npwrc.usgs.gov/
> > resource/literatr/bisonbib/index.htm

• Almost 600 scientific reports, articles, and theses on perhaps the most iconic of Plains animals. Popular articles as well as most historical and archaeological materials are excluded. Multiple search points (keyword, author, date, title, source, category); browsable by broad categories such as social organization, diseases, and growth. Narrower in focus than *A Buffalo Round-Up: A Selected Bibliography* (**EC86**) and intended for biologists conducting research on the bison. — *LMcD*

EC89   Steelquist, Robert. - **Field Guide to North American Bison : A Natural History and Viewing Guide to the Great Plains Buffalo**. - Seattle, WA : Sasquatch Books, 1998. - 46 p.; ill. - (Sasquatch field guide series).

> Class Numbers:
> > Library of Congress QL737.U53
> ISBN 1570610533 1570611343 (pbk.)
> LCCN 97-51773
> Notes:
> > Includes bibliographical references (p. 45-46)
> > Title page: Greater Yellowstone Coalition

• An extensive species account of wild bison, Steelquist's field guide summarizes their evolution, taxonomy, distribution, description, social order, seasonal cycle, habitat, uses by Plains Indians, the "great killing" that decimated them by the end of the 19th century, and recent rebirth. The physical description covers size, physique, horns, fur, speed, senses, sounds, body language, life span, feeding, and predators. The habitat description discusses their effects on the environment through grazing, rubbing posts, buffalo chips, wallows, trails, buffalo birds, and prairie dogs. Describes viewing areas for public, tribal, and private herds, maps, resources and organizations. Bison as domesticated animals are not covered. — *JD*

COYOTES

EC90   Bekoff, Marc. - **A General Bibliography on the Coyote (Canis Latrans)**. - Boulder, CO : Coymar Pr., 1974. - 26 leaves.

> Class Numbers:
> > Library of Congress Z7997.C65

• Drawing from books, journal articles, government publications, and popular periodicals in all aspects of coyote natural history, Bekoff groups resources by topic. Entries are not annotated, and appear only once under the category of highest relevance. Topical divisions include general references, taxonomy, anatomy, morphology, genetics, pathology, disease, physiology, serology, reproduction, behavior, hybrids, ecology, distribution, methods of study, population control, movements and activity, predator-prey relations, and relations with non-prey animals. Includes an addendum dated Oct. 1974. — *JB*

DEER

EC91   Rue, Leonard Lee. - **The Deer of North America**. - Guilford, CT : Lyons Pr., 2004. - 544 p.; [16] p. of plates, ill. (some col.), map.

> Class Numbers:
> Library of Congress QL737.U55
> ISBN 1592284655
> OCLC 57724165
> LCCN 97-8276
> Notes:
> Includes bibliographical references
> (p. 509-525); index

• A complete guide to all species of deer in North America–white tail, black tail, mule, and Sitka–all but the latter native to Prairies-Plains. Sections cover the animal and its behavior, life cycle by season, and deer management, made vivid by numerous black-and-white photographs. Appendixes list foods by season and daily activity cycles. Generous bibliography; detailed index. — *JB*

FERRETS

EC92   Reading, Richard P. - **Black-Footed Ferret Annotated Bibliography, 1986-1990** / by Richard P. Reading, Tim W. Clark. - Billings, MT: U.S. Dept. of the Interior, Bureau of Land Management, Montana State Office, 1990. - 22 p.; ill. - (Montana Bureau of Land Management. Wildlife technical bulletin, 3).

> Class Numbers:
> Library of Congress Z7997.B59
> Government Document I 53.34:M 76/no.3
> LCCN 91-601180
> Notes:
> Index

• Reading and Clark base their 118 citations on journal articles, books, dissertations, and some popular articles and government reports (but no newspaper articles), building on D.E. Casey et al.'s "Annotated Bibliography of the Black-Footed Ferret," *Great Basin Naturalist Memoirs* 8 (1986): 185-208. They include some references on prairie

dogs because prairie dogs are ferret prey. Their bibliography surveys the black-footed ferret population during the period the species was nearly eliminated by canine distemper (in 1990, the wild population was extinct; only 18 ferrets were being bred in captivity in the hope they could be returned to the wild). Entries are bibliographically complete, although nonbiologists may not be familiar with some journal abbreviations; all entries have annotations. The bibliography proper is preceded by a subject index that employs only seven subject terms and by a list of sources. — *RB*

FOXES

EC93   **Bibliography for Swift Foxes (Vulpes Velox) [Internet Site]** / by Marsha A. Sovada. - Jamestown, ND : Northern Prairie Wildlife Research Center Online, 1998. - http://www.npwrc.usgs.gov/resource/literatr/swiftlit/swiftlit.htm

> OCLC 46611421
> Access Date: Aug, 2005
> Fees: None

• Author listing of approximately 450 studies of a small fox native to the Plains; arranged in separate sections by format–peer-reviewed articles, theses, other publications, and unpublished reports. Most citations are species-specific but there are also guides to fauna and other general sources. The database can be searched by keyword, title, author, year, source, and section. Results can be sorted by author, title, and year. — *LMcD*

PRAIRIE DOGS

EC94   Clark, Tim W. - **Annotated Prairie Dog Bibliography, 1973 to 1985**. - Billings, MT : U.S. Bureau of Land Management; Helena, MT : U.S. Fish and Wildlife Service, 1986. - 32 p.; ill.

> Class Numbers:
> Library of Congress QL737.R46
> Government Document I 53.17:P 88
> Notes:
> Publ. in cooperation with Montana Dept. of Fish,
> Wildlife, and Parks

• Cites 201 numbered entries concerning prairie dogs published during the 13-year period indicated by the title. Entries are arranged alphabetically by author; there is neither index nor table of contents. Illustrations consist of a single page with four black-and-white photographs of prairie dog species. Entries supply standard bibliographical information and annotations 50 to several hundred words in length. Extends the coverage of two earlier works published in 1971 and 1973. — *MB*

EC95   Hassien, Fred. - **Prairie Dog Bibliography**. - [Washington, DC] : U.S. Dept. of the Interior, Bureau of Land Management, 1976. - 28 p. - (United States. Bureau of Land Management. Technical note T/N 279).

Class Numbers:
> Library of Congress Z7996.R6
> Government Document I 53.20:279

• Consists of 437 entries that cite journal articles, books, theses, bulletins, and proceedings dealing with prairie dogs. Literature outside the U.S. is omitted, as are early entries from T.W. Clark's "Towards a Literature Review of Prairie Dogs" *Journal of Wyoming Range Management*, no. 286 (1971): 29-44, although Clark's later entries are included. Entries cover behavior, description, distribution, ecology, management, morphology, physiology, parasites, diseases, pest control, and predators. Entries are not annotated. One of the few bibliographies devoted to a common prairie animal. — *JB*

EC96   Knowles, Craig J. - **Review of Black-Tailed Prairie Dog : Literature in Relation to Rangelands Administered by the Custer National Forest** / prepared by Craig J. and Pamela R. Knowles. - [Billings, MT: Custer National Forest], 1994. - [80] p.; ill.

Class Numbers:
> Library of Congress QL737.R68
> OCLC 39283194
> Notes:
>> Includes bibliographical references (p. 48-61)

• Brief but informative, this volume concerned with prairie dog management on the Northern Plains covers habitat, social behavior, reproduction, ecology, population dynamics, disease, and range relationships. The section on prairie dog control includes a historical overview and examines management in north central Montana. Ample tables and graphs illustrate the text and a section on associated species (ferret, fox, badger, bobcat, bison, pronghorn, and various birds). Bibliography; appendixes. — *JB*

PLANTS

General Works

EC97   Boon, William. - **Nature's Heartland : Native Plant Communities of the Great Plains Illustrated in Seasonal Color : A Photo-Essay of Woodland Plants and Prairie** / William Boon and Harlen Groe. - Ames, IA : Iowa State Univ. Pr., 1990. - 361 p.

Class Numbers:
> Library of Congress QK135

ISBN 0813811635
LCCN 89-26952
Notes:
> Includes bibliographical references (p. 347-351) and index

• Organized by vegetation zones, this volume covers quite a bit of the U.S., hence only some of the sections are relevant to study of the Prairies-Plains region. The sections that pertain include dry prairie, marsh prairie, wet prairie, mixed floodplain, and farmstead-windbreak. In each section, plants are listed alphabetically by scientific name. Each page contains a short description, several color photos, a map of the range, and brief information on habitat, form, foliage, flower, and fruit. The volume emphasizes trees, many of which cannot be found in the Plains region. The book ends with an extensive illustrated glossary, a good bibliography, and an index by common and scientific name. — *MB*

EC98   **Control of Invasive Exotic Plants in the Great Plains : Annotated Bibliography [Internet Site]** / Diane Larson and Kristin Freitag. - Jamestown, ND : USGS, Northern Prairie Wildlife Research Center, [1996]. - http://www.npwrc.usgs.gov/resource/literatr/exotic/

Class Numbers:
> Library of Congress SB612.A17
> OCLC 43876474
> Access Date: May 2007
> Notes:
>> Version: 30 Sept 2002
> Fees: None

• A small bibliography, a mere 18 items at present, on a large problem: rapidly-spreading alien species that cause significant economic loss and environmental damage. Searchable by keyword, scientific name, common name, family, location, control measure, and habitat. Lists of species and control measures. — *LMcD*

EC99   **Flora of North America : North of Mexico** / ed. by Flora of North America Editorial Committee. - New York : Oxford Univ. Pr., 1993-. - v. 1 - (In progress).

Class Numbers:
> Library of Congress QK110
> ISBN 0195137299 (set) 9780195137293 (set)
> OCLC 26803793
> LCCN 92-30459
> Notes:
>> Includes bibliographical references; indexes
>> To be complete in about 30 v.

• Intended for, and written by, professional botanists, and being edited by the Flora of North America Editorial Committee, *Flora* is a heroic effort to catalog all the species of plants identified by botanists and reported in the literature, occurring in the continental United States (including Alaska and the Aleutian Islands), the Florida Keys, Canada, Greenland, and St. Pierre and Miquelon. Arranged by family, species accounts include distribution maps and occasional line drawings, often showing several species from a family. Descriptions of species are telegraphic, omitting most verbs and keeping tightly to a formula (roots, plants, common stock, trophophore, etc.), emphasizing consistency in style and content and holding to a strict technical vocabulary. Each volume ends with a bibliography and index for that volume, and a general bibliography and index are planned for the last volume. Plants of the Prairies-Plains are assuredly covered comprehensively, but *Flora*'s taxonomic arrangement means it will necessarily be reserved for use after species of interest have been identified elsewhere. — *RB*

EC100   Great Plains Flora Association. - **Atlas of the Flora of the Great Plains** / Great Plains Flora Association, William T. Baker [et al.]; R.L. McGregor, coordinator; T.M. Barkley, ed. - Ames, IA : Iowa State Univ. Pr., 1977. - 600 p.; maps. - (Div. of Biology, Kansas Agricultural Experiment Station, Kansas State Univ. Contribution, 1283-B; Dept. of Botany, North Dakota Agricultural Experiment Station, North Dakota State Univ. Contribution, 658).

> Class Numbers:
> Library of Congress G1421.J9
> ISBN 081380154
> LCCN 76-54301
> Notes:
> Includes bibliographical references (p. x); index
> Precursor to *Flora of the Great Plains* (**EC101**)

• The editors provide a unique approach to information about plants on the Great Plains. Most of the book consists of maps (four to a page) showing the distribution of 2,217 species in the region between the Canadian border and the Texas Panhandle and including the eastern half of the corridor from Montana through New Mexico and the four states from Minnesota to Arkansas. The limits of the Great Plains (as the editors define the region) are shown on each map. The maps show county outlines; locations of plant species in the region are shown by black dots within counties. The table of contents lists the 150 families of plants, divided into vascular cryptogams, conifers, dicots, and monocots. A detailed index lists common and scientific names, preceded by a list of 850 taxa that occur rarely in the region, with references to states and counties where the taxa can be found. — *MB*

EC101   Great Plains Flora Association (U.S.). - **Flora of the Great Plains** / Ronald L. McGregor, coordinator; T.M. Barkley, ed., Ralph E. Brooks and Eileen K. Schofield,

associate eds. - Lawrence, KS : Univ. Pr. of Kansas, 1986. - 1392 p.; maps. - (Division of Biology, Kansas Agricultural Experiment Station, Kansas State Univ. Contribution, 84-135-B; Department of Botany, North Dakota Agricultural Experiment Station, North Dakota State Univ. Contribution, 1254).

> Class Numbers:
> Library of Congress QK135
> ISBN 070060295X
> OCLC 13093762
> LCCN 86-23
> Notes:
> Bibliography: p. 5-6; index

• An exhaustive technical volume that treats all the vascular plants occurring naturally in the Great Plains. The region is defined as the area from the base of the Rocky Mountains east to the beginnings of continuous forest, and from the Canadian border to the Texas panhandle. This includes all or part of 13 states. The systematic descriptions do not include any illustrations and occupy more than 1,200 pages. For specialists. Glossary; index. — *MB*

EC102   **Historical Common Names of Great Plains Plants [Internet Site]** / [Elaine A. Nowick]. - [Lincoln, NE : Agriculture Network Information Center, 2006]. - http://www.unl.edu/agnicpls/gpcn/index.html

> Access Date: May 2007
> Fees: None

• Lists over 8,000 common native and naturalized plant names drawn from nearly 200 sources, including personal journals, first-person accounts of explorations, ethnobotanical literature, medical botany texts, cooperative extension publications, species accounts, popular wildflower guides, field notes, and dictionaries. Indian plant names are included as are names common outside the Plains. Most sources date from prior to 1940 but the compiler plans to add more recent common names. Common names are listed alphabetically with spelling that conforms to "Common Names for Vascular Plants" (John T. Kartesz and John W. Thieret, *Sida* 14.3 [1991]: 421-434). Non-English common names are spelled as in the original work. Entries include dates of usage in a published source, alternate spellings, a number referencing a separate list of sources, and the scientific name. Scientific names in the entry link to a record giving family, origin (native or introduced), scientific synonyms, and all common names. Includes a separate species index by scientific name. Compiled by a librarian and AgNIC (Agriculture Network Information Center) subject specialist for plant science at the AgNIC partner institution, University of Nebraska-Lincoln. Intended for prairie restorationists, the site will also interest gardeners and historians. Simple, sleek, and functional. — *JD*

EC103 Larson, Gary E. - **Aquatic and Wetland Vascular Plants of the Northern Great Plains**. - Fort Collins, CO : United States Dept. of Agriculture, Forest Service, Rocky Mountain Forest and Range Experiment Station, [1993]. - 681 p.; ill. (some col.), maps - (General technical report RM, 238).

> Class Numbers:
> > Library of Congress QK135
> Notes:
> > Electronic version: http://www.npwrc.usgs.gov/
> > > resource/1999/vascplnt/vascplnt.htm
> > Includes bibliographical references (p. 5); index

• Meticulous species descriptions and a diagnostic key to the taxa aid in identifying 500 species growing in water or saturated soils of the Plains, where they have ecological importance and grow in unique combinations. Arranged by family, species entries give common name, flowering and fruiting periods, habitat, distribution, and nomenclatural synonyms. Some entries are illustrated with photographs or simple line drawings. Range maps showing the county-by-county occurrence of specimens are exact but rudimentary and difficult to read. A glossary and index by common and scientific names are included. Not a pretty field guide, but a working document for professionals and students. — *JD*

EC104 Ogaard, Louis A. - **Wetland Vegetation of the Prairie Pothole Region : Research Methods and Annotated Bibliography** / in collaboration with Jay A. Leitch [et al.]. - Fargo, ND : Agricultural Experiment Station, North Dakota State Univ., 1981. - 50 p. - (North Dakota Research Report, 85).

> Class Numbers:
> > Library of Congress QK135 S99
> OCLC 8659989
> LCCN 82-623105
> Notes:
> > Electronic book: http://pc6.psc.state.nd.us/
> > > jurisdtion/aml/articles/no-85-nd-research-rpt.pdf
> > Index

• Following literature reviews of primary production (energy accumulated by plants), nutrient cycling, and plant distribution, Ogaard provides about 240 citations to scientific literature analyzing freshwater vegetation in the Prairie wetlands, a swath consisting of much of the southern Prairie provinces, a narrow strip of northern Montana, and portions of North and South Dakota. — *LMcD*

EC105 Stephens, Homer A. - **Woody Plants of the North Central Plains**. - Lawrence, KS : Univ. Pr. of Kansas, 1973. - xxx, 530 p.; ill.

> Class Numbers:
> > Library of Congress QK484.G7
> ISBN 0700601074 9780700601073
> OCLC 834763
> LCCN 72-97834
> Notes:
> > Bibliography: p. 517

• An extremely thorough catalog of woody and suffrutescent plants in the Plains states of the Dakotas, Nebraska, and Kansas. In the catalog proper, entries are arranged by scientific name. Each species is treated to two full pages that supply family name (families are grouped), species name with variants, common name, and descriptions of leaves, flowers, fruit, twigs, trunk, habitat, and range. Occurrences are shown on an outline map of the four states, and the text has a facing page with line drawings of twigs, leaves, flowers, fruit, and other features. At the end come a list of species not included, a page of references, a glossary, and an index of common and scientific names. Compilation required eight years and was conducted in all seasons, the author and an assistant traveling in a camper—a notable example of scientific persistence and thoroughness. — *RB*

EC106 Stubbendieck, James L. - **North American Wildland Plants : A Field Guide** / [by] James Stubbendieck, Stephan L. Hatch, L.M. Landholt; ill. by Kelly L. Rhodes Hays, Bellamy Jansen, and Debra Meier; maps by Kathleen Lonergan-Orr. - 6th ed. - Lincoln, NE : Univ. of Nebraska Pr., 2003. - 501 p.; ill.

> Class Numbers:
> > Library of Congress SB193.3.N67
> ISBN 0803243065   0803293062 (pbk.)
> LCCN 2003-42698
> Notes:
> > Includes bibliographical references (p. 469-480);
> > > index
> > Rev. ed. of: James Stubbendieck. *North American
> > > Range Plants*. 5th ed., c1997

• The 6th ed. of Stubbendieck's well-known source describes 200 of the most important species of grasses, grass-like plants, forbs, and woody plants, selected for their abundance, desirability, or noxious properties. This edition increases the number of riparian and wetlands plants to 10 percent and emphasizes plants across and within ecosystems. The guide is well-designed for identification of plants by professionals, students, identification teams, and amateur botanists. One-page species descriptions give common names, life span, origin, and season of growth, followed by fruit, floral, vegetative, and growth characteristics; forage value; food and medicinal uses; livestock losses; and habitat. On the page facing the description are a clear drawing labeled to highlight specific parts, a list of synonyms, and a range map. Includes an introduction to wildland plants, a plant morphology, a glossary, an authorities list, selected references, and an index by common and scientific names. — JD

UNITED STATES

Colorado

EC107   Interneter, William Alfred, 1918- . - **Colorado Flora : Eastern Slope** / [by] William A Interneter, Ronald C. Wittmann. - 3rd ed. - Boulder, CO : Univ. Pr. of Colorado, 1990. - xl, 521 p.; ill.

> Class Numbers:
>   Library of Congress QK150
> ISBN 0870815220
> OCLC 21600935

• Includes an introductory section listing botanists honored by Colorado plant names. Has sections for "Key to the Families," "Ferns and Fern Allies," "Gymnosperms," and "Angiosperms," of which the latter is by far the largest. Supplementary material includes line drawings, a glossary, and a single index for both common and scientific names. Entries within sections are arranged alphabetically by scientific name. Provides for each family a brief description and list of distinctive features. — MB

Kansas

EC108   **Kansas Wildflowers and Grasses [Internet Site]** / maintained by Mike Haddock; ill. by Dean Haddock. - Manhattan, KS : Kansas State Univ., 1997- . - http://www.lib.ksu.edu/wildflower/

> Class Numbers:
>   Library of Congress QK161
> OCLC 43693622
> Access Date: Apr. 2006
> Fees: None

• Haddock uses six files to present some 450 species of native and introduced plants: wildflowers by color; wildflowers and grasses by time of flowering and flower color; grasses; sedges, rushes and other grass-like plants; common name; and scientific name. The entries give scientific and common names, cite the person who first identified and named the plant, and supply specimen location, life cycle, height, and flowering time, followed by concise descriptions of stem, leaves, inflorescence, flower, and fruit. Notes add information about habitat, range, characteristics, history and uses. Nearly 2,000 color

photographs, comparative drawings of morphological characteristics, and a glossary aid in identifying plants. A bibliography and a nomenclature authority list complete a site that is beautifully designed and easy to use. The author has published a field guide based on the site, *Wildflowers and Grasses of Kansas* (**EC153**). — JD

EC109   Stephens, Homer A. - **Trees, Shrubs, and Woody Vines in Kansas**. - Lawrence, KS : Univ. Pr. of Kansas, 1969. - 250 p.; ill.

> Class Numbers:
>   Library of Congress QK484.K2
> OCLC 11597
> LCCN 69-10357

• Designed for students, teachers, general readers, and others unfamiliar with the conventional plant identification keys, Stephens's guide describes 114 species of native and naturalized plants that have woody stems and winter buds that are more than six inches above the ground. Accounts are organized by family and use popular names. Each has a distribution map, clear description, and several black-and-white photographs. Appendixes list excluded species, measurements of selected woody plants, measurements of the growth of nine trees over 30 years, and an index by scientific and popular names. Based on the 1950 edition of *Gray's Manual of Botany*, hence scientific names will be out of date. — JD

Nebraska

EC110   Kaul, Robert B. - **The Flora of Nebraska: Keys, Descriptions, and Distributional Maps of All Native and Introduced Species that Grow Outside Cultivation : with Observations about Their Past, Present, and Future Status** / [by] Robert B. Kaul, David M. Sutherland, Steven B. Rolfsmeier. - Lincoln, NE : Conservation and Survey Div., School of Natural Resources, Institute of Agriculture and Natural Resources, Univ. of Nebraska-Lincoln, 2006. - 966 p.; [16] p. of plates, ill. maps, col. plates.

> Class Numbers:
>   Library of Congress QK172
> ISBN 1561610089 9781561610082
> OCLC 124042424
> LCCN 2006-937185
> Notes:
>   Bibliography: p. 19-20; indexes

• A new standard work that reevaluates and remaps all native and naturalized species of vascular plants (ferns, fern allies, conifers, and flowering plants) in Nebraska, adding to and deleting from previous lists. All plants included were collected at least once in Nebraska, are represented in at least one Nebraska herbarium, and grow (or can grow) outside cultivation. A few grow near the borders of Nebraska and are considered likely to move into state. The introduction covers the physical and biological characteristics of Nebraska; the state's botanical history; and the current status of flora and vegetation, illustrated by a color statewide distribution map. Plants are organized by family with brief descriptions of the species as they exist in Nebraska. Accepted and common names are included along with synonyms and misapplied and invalid names. Maps indicate counties in which at least one specimen has been found, from 1804 (Meriwether Lewis's descriptions) through 2005. Additional matter includes a guide to Nebraska counties; an index to families; diagnostic keys to the four phyla; glossary and gazetteer; bibliography; an ordinal placement of angiosperm families in the APG [Angiosperm Phylogeny Group] system; a complete index; and an index to genera. Though they designed the book for botanists, the authors tested the material with nonbotanists to ensure clarity for all adult readers. — *JD*

EC111   Nebraska Florasearch [Internet Site]. - Lincoln, NE : Nebraska Statewide Arboretum, 2000?– . - http://arboretum.unl.edu/florasearch.html

> Access Date: Jan. 2006
> Fees: None

• A field guide, *FloraSearch* has components for identifying Nebraska plants, determining which are native to Nebraska, and finding Nebraska plants by common and scientific names. The site's centerpiece, "Which Wildflower Is It?," a comprehensive database of Nebraska wildflowers accompanied by clear photographs in color, can be searched by common name, botanic name, plant family, flower color, biotic regions, height, foliage texture, and month of blooming. Search keys can be combined. "What Tree or Shrub Is It?" offers similar search options, along with mature height, mature spread, soil moisture and sun/shade requirements for native tree and shrubs. More limited searches cover grasses, plants by region, and plants by family. The site also lists wildflower viewing areas with links to their Internet sites, offers advice about landscaping "Nebraska style," and provides links to regional and conservation sites. An extremely useful and thorough site. — *JD*

EC112   Pound, Roscoe. - The Phytogeography of Nebraska : General Survey / [by] Roscoe Pound and Frederic E. Clements. - New York : Arno Pr., 1977. - 442 p.; [3] leaves of plates (1 folded), maps. - (History of ecology; Nebraska. University. Botanical Seminar. Contributions from the Botanical Survey of Nebraska).

> Class Numbers:
> Library of Congress QK172
> ISBN 0405104170

OCLC 3071583
LCCN 77-74248
Notes:
> Bibliography: p. 22-30; index
> Reprint of the ed. publ. by Botanical Seminar,
>   Lincoln, NE, in series: "University of Nebraska
> Botanical Survey of Nebraska" (1900)

• Now dated, this volume includes information about the physical characteristics of Nebraska (river systems, geology, climate, vegetation, and ecology) just over 100 years ago. It focuses on plant life, but there are no illustrations. Extensive index. Historical in value. — *MB*

North Dakota

EC113   North Dakota Vegetation : A Bibliography [Internet Site] / B.L. Heidel and D.S. Rogers. - [Jamestown, ND] : Northern Prairie Wildlife Research Center Online, 2002. - http://www.npwrc.usgs.gov/resource/literatr/ndveg/ndveg.htm

> Class Numbers:
> Library of Congress QK179
> OCLC 35624924
> Access Date: June 2006
> Notes:
> Based on the authors' *North Dakota Vegetation*
>   (Grand Forks, ND: Institute for Ecological
>   Studies, University of North Dakota, 1984.
> Contribution Series no. 4)
> Fees: None

• An author listing of almost 1,200 citations on vegetation research and management in North Dakota. Works on similar plant types in adjacent states and provinces are also included. Contains articles, reports, and unpublished theses, all unannotated. Searchable by keyword. Useful for biologists and environmentalists concerned with vegetation of the northern plains. — *LMcD*

EC114   Stevens, Orin Alva, b. 1885. - Handbook of North Dakota Plants. - Fargo, ND : North Dakota Agricultural College, 1950. - 324 p.; ill., maps.

> Class Numbers:
> Library of Congress QK179
> OCLC 2760237
> LCCN 51-62007
> Notes:
> Sponsored by the North Dakota Institute for
>   Regional Studies

• Stevens (botany, North Dakota Agricultural College) describes native and introduced wild plants found in North Dakota. The introductory chapter contains general information on the names of plants, physiography, topography, soils, vegetation types, distribution of species, and plant characters (roots, stems, leaves). Common names are used to identify types and families, but scientific terms of genera and species are printed in italics. The work is arranged by 100 families (listed at p. 300 ff.); each family has a brief description followed by a key to species with each plant listed in numerical order. Distribution maps and illustrations. — *GK*

Oklahoma

EC115   Johnson, Forrest L. - **Oklahoma Botanical Literature** / [by] Forrest L. Johnson and T.H. Milby. - Norman, OK : Univ. of Oklahoma Pr., 1989. - 150 p.

> Class Numbers:
> > Library of Congress QK181 Z5358.U5
> > ISBN 080612198X
> > LCCN 88-31247
> > Notes:
> > > Indexes
> > > Publ. for the Oklahoma Biological Survey, Univ. of Oklahoma, Norman

• Lists 850 resources consisting primarily of articles, theses, and dissertations published through 1987. Citations are arranged by author and annotated with one or two keywords. Extensively indexed by author, county, geographical region, a Duck and Fletcher index (based on a 1930s effort to map Oklahoma vegetation), general vegetation, and subject based on the keywords accompanying the citations. — *MS*

South Dakota

EC116   Ball, John Jeffrey. - **Shrubs for South Dakota** / [by] John Ball, David F. Graper, [and] Carol M.F. Wake . - Brookings, SD : South Dakota State Univ., Cooperative Extension Service, 2000. - 110 p.; col. ill., col. map. - (South Dakota State University. Cooperative Extension Service. Extension circular, 904).

> Class Numbers:
> > Library of Congress QK186
> > Government Document South Dakota
> > > ED 550:Ec 1/904
> > ISBN 0913062146
> > OCLC 45440355
> > Notes:
> > > Indexes

• Ball (arboriculture), Graper (horticulture), and Wake (biology, all South Dakota State Univ.) offer a general guide

to introduced and native shrubs that can be grown in South Dakota. Entries in five sections ("Deciduous and Broadleaf Evergreen Shrubs," "Vines," "Conifer Shrubs," "Plants with Ornamental Characteristics," "Summer Key") are arranged in sections by botanical name, followed for native species by the Lakota name. Color photographs accompany each entry, along with icons that indicate leaf color, flower, fruit, wildlife value, soil tolerance, and shade requirements. Appendixes include a glossary and black-and-white illustrations of flower types, leaf shapes, and bud arrangement. — *GK*

EC117   Ode, David J. - **Dakota Flora : A Seasonal Sampler**. - Pierre, SD : South Dakota State Historical Society Pr., 2006. - 260 p.; col. ill.

> Class Numbers:
> > Library of Congress QK179
> > ISBN 0974919543   9780974919546
> > OCLC 63472897
> > LCCN 2006-3755
> > Notes:
> > > Includes bibliographical references; index
> > > Previous versions of entries published in *South Dakota Conservation Digest*, 1987-2005.
> > > Table of contents: http://0-www.loc.gov.livrary. unl.edu:80/catdir/toc/ecip067/2006003755.html

• Eighty-two wild plants are categorized by the season in which they flower or fruit. Personal and anecdotal descriptions of about 500 words cover the plants' biology and cultural significance, including hardiness, habitat, wildlife use, medicinal uses, economic importance, and appearance in literature. Some, like the stonyhills muhly, are noted as rare; others, like the three-nerved fleabane, flourish along the roadsides each summer. Exceptional color photographs of plants and surroundings. Not a traditional field guide or species account, but a detailed and expertly written source for plant identification and lore. Appendixes cover scientific names, an annotated list of plant field guides, a bibliography, and an index by popular names, scientific names, earlier observers, and locations. — *JD*

EC118   Van Bruggen, Theodore. - **Vascular Plants of South Dakota**. - Ames, IA : Iowa State Univ. Pr., 1976. - 538 p.

> LCCN 76-3747

• The introductory section contains geologic maps of South Dakota and a brief explanation of the geography and climate of the area. A two-page list summarizes families found in the region, and there are also a statistical summary and a brief description of the groups: "Ferns and Fern Allies," "Gymnosperms," "Monocotyledons," "Dicotyledons." The principal list is arranged first by characteristics, then alphabetically by scientific name. Extensive bibliography of sources, including both a general section and a list of sources arranged by family. Glossary; index of common and scientific names. — *MB*

Texas

EC119 Everitt, James H. - **Trees, Shrubs & Cacti of South Texas** / [by] James H. Everitt, D. Lynne Drawe, Robert I. Lonard. - Rev. ed. - Lubbock, TX : Texas Tech Univ. Pr., 2002. - 249 p.; col. ill., col. maps.

> Class Numbers:
> Library of Congress QK188
> ISBN 0896724735 (pbk.)
> LCCN 2001-5009
> Notes:
> Includes bibliographical references (p. 239-248);
> index

• Describes 201 species (22 cacti, 170 trees and shrubs) divided into 60 families. Includes native and nonnative species found in the 14 southernmost counties of Texas, nine of which are completely located in the South Texas Plains, as are the westernmost regions of the remaining four. Species accounts consist of color photographs, scientific and common names, and brief descriptions of each plant and its location. An essay covers plant identification keys. Concluding material consists of a glossary and a set of line drawings of leaf forms. — *MS*

CANADA

General Works

EC120 Budd, Archibald C. - **Budd's Flora of the Canadian Prairie Provinces** / [by] Archibald C. Budd [et al.]. - Rev. and enlarged ed. / by J. Looman and K.F. Best - Hull, Quebec : available from Canadian Government Publ. Centre; [Ottawa, Ont.] : Research Branch, Agriculture Canada, 1987. - 863 p.; ill. - (Research Branch, Agriculture Canada. Publication, 1662).

> Class Numbers:
> Library of Congress QK203.P7
> National Library of Canada
> COP.CA.2.1987-3673
> Government Document Canada A53-1662/1979
> ISBN 0660102331 0660125242
> OCLC 22339480
> Notes:
> 1987 revision undertaken by J. Waddington
> Indexes

• Intended for botanists, farmers, ranchers, and agricultural

specialists, Budd's attempts to describe all species naturally occurring in the Prairie provinces. Introductory material includes line drawings of types of flowers, fruits, and leaves to help readers understand the descriptive information, since entries offer only a few line drawings of species. Then come keys to the main groups and to families. Entries are arranged in taxonomic order. Back matter includes a good glossary and indexes to common and scientific names. There is neither bibliography nor illustrations in color; hence, a volume like *Wildflowers of the Northern Great Plains* (**EC164**) makes an ideal complement. — *MB*

EC121 Lahring, Heinjo, 1957- . - **Water and Wetland Plants of the Prairie Provinces**. - Regina, SK : Canadian Plains Research Center, 2003. - 326 p.; ill. (some col.). - (Canadian Plains Studies, 44; ISSN 0397-6290).

> Class Numbers:
> National Library of Canada QH106.2.P6
> ISBN 0889771626
> OCLC 52837103
> Notes:
> Includes bibliographical references; index

• A field guide to approximately 400 species of aquatic and marshland plants occurring in the Prairies and Northern Plains states. An introductory essay discusses the biogeography of the region, hardiness zones, wetland classification, plant categories and wetland ecology. Entries include botanical name and family, synonyms, common names, description, distribution and habitat, special features, and related species. More than 600 colored photos and black-and-white line drawings accompany the text. Species are organized by ferns, monocots (grasses, sedges, rushes) and woody dicots (shrubs). Arrangement of families generally corresponds to that of *Flora of Alberta* (**EC122**) and Budd's *Flora of the Canadian Prairie Provinces* (**EC120**), which this work supplements. Glossary and indexes to family names, scientific names, and common names. Useful for gardeners, as well as amateur and professional botanists. — *LMcD*

Alberta

EC122 Moss, Ezra Henry, 1892-1963. - **Flora of Alberta : A Manual of Flowering Plants, Conifers, Ferns, and Fern Allies Found Growing without Cultivation in the Province of Alberta, Canada**. - 2nd ed. / rev. by John G. Packer - Toronto, ON; Buffalo, NY : Univ. of Toronto Pr., 1983. - 687 p.; ill.

> Class Numbers:
> Library of Congress QK203.A4
> ISBN 0802025080 9780802025081
> OCLC 12217114
> LCCN 84-179310
> Notes:
> Bibliography: p. [613]; index

• Guide to 1,775 plant species, arranged by the Englerian system of classification with genera and species alphabetically within family. Botanical keys aid in identification. Species accounts include descriptions and a brief listing of general North American distribution. For native species, more than 1,100 small dotmaps indicate distribution within Alberta. Comprehensive in coverage but the lack of any illustrations may limit its appeal for amateur botanists. — *LMcD*

CACTI

EC123   Powell, A. Michael. – **Cacti of Texas : A Field Guide : with Emphasis on the Trans-Pecos Species** / [by] A. Michael Powell, James F. Weedin, and Shirley A. Powell. – Lubbock, TX : Texas Tech Univ. Pr., 2008. – 400 p.; col. ill., maps. – (Grover E. Murray studies in the American Southwest).

   ISBN 9780896726116 (pbk.)
   LCCN 2007-30415

• A field guide to cacti found in Texas and neighboring states that opens by describing what constitutes a cactus and follows with a key to the distinguishing characteristics of the 12 cactus genera. Accounts of individual species give scientific and common names and describe stems, areoles, spines, flowers, fruits, and range in Texas and other states and in Mexico. Glossary; indexes of scientific and common names. — *RB*

DISEASES AND PESTS

See also **Common Insect Pests of Trees in the Great Plains, EC141**

EC124   Whitney, E.D., ed. - **Compendium of Beet Diseases and Insects** / ed. by E.D. Whitney and James E. Duffus. - [Saint Paul, MN]: APS Pr., 1986. - 76 p.; [31] p. of plates, ill. (some col.). - (The disease compendium series of the American Phytopathological Society).

   Class Numbers:
      Library of Congress SB608.S88
   ISBN 0890540705
   LCCN 86-71222
   Notes:
      Includes bibliographies; index

• For field workers, extension specialists, plant pathologists, entomologists and specialty growers, the compendium describes diseases and pests of sugar beets, a major crop in parts of the Great Plains. Part 1 covers biotic diseases and disorders including fungi, bacteria, viruses, and parasites,

Part 2 major insects and arthropods, and Part 3 abiotic disorders including nutritional deficiencies, herbicide damage, environmental conditions, and genetic disorders. Entries give symptoms, causes, control, and selected references. Includes a key for disease diagnosis, a glossary, and an index by common and scientific names. Two appendixes show the scientific classifications and life histories of beet insects and pests. Illustrated with drawings, diagrams, photographs, statistical tables, and 243 color plates. — *JD*

ETHNOBOTANY

EC125   Kindscher, Kelly. - **Edible Wild Plants of the Prairie : An Ethnobotanical Guide** / drawings by Carol Kuhn. - Lawrence, KS : Univ. Pr. of Kansas, 1987. - 276 p.; ill

   Class Numbers:
      Library of Congress   QK98.5.U6
   ISBN 0700603247   0700603255 (pbk.)
   LCCN 87-6162
   Notes:
      Bibliography: p. 255-266; index

• Most of this interesting book consists of 49 short chapters about Prairie plant species that have significant food use. Arrangement is by scientific name following the scheme in *Flora of the Great Plains* (**EC101**). Each chapter is headed by the common and scientific name and a full-page line drawing of the plant. Sections in each chapter identify other common names, Indian names, background information on the scientific name, physical description, habitat, parts used, food use, and cultivation. A range map is also provided. Following the 49 chapters, two parts provide briefer descriptions of 11 grasses and 22 other plants with minor food uses. Glossary, bibliography, and an index of scientific and common names. — *MB*

EC126   Kindscher, Kelly. - **Medicinal Wild Plants of the Prairie : An Ethnobotanical Guide** / drawings by William S. Whitney . - Lawrence, KS : Univ. Pr. of Kansas, 1992. - xi, 340 p.; ill., maps.

   Class Numbers:
      Library of Congress   E78.G73
   ISBN 0700605266 0700605274 (pbk.)
   LCCN 91-38471
   Notes:
      Includes bibliographical references
      (p. 299-313); index

• A handbook of native plants used by Indians, emphasizing traditional beliefs about their medicinal value. Arranged alphabetically by botanical name, the profiles of 43 major plants contain a wealth of information: numerous common names, Indian names and their English equivalents, scientific name, description, habitat, distribution map, parts used, Indian use, Anglo folk use, medical history, scientific research, harvesting and cultivation, and a full-page line drawing. An additional 60 plants of lesser significance have briefer accounts. Despite the title, the work is not a herbal guide for self-treatment; the introduction repeatedly makes the point that it provides "descriptions not prescriptions." The intention is to increase knowledge of the uses of Prairie plants to further their conservation. Valuable for those with an interest in Prairie plants in general, as well as in their past uses and potential therapeutic benefits. — *LMcD*

EC127   Moerman, Daniel E. - **Native American Ethnobotany**. - Portland, OR : Timber Pr., 1998. - 927 p.

> Class Numbers:
> > Library of Congress E98.B7
> ISBN 0881924539
> LCCN 97-32877
> Notes:
> > Includes bibliographical references
> > > (p. [619]-623); indexes
> > Incorporates: *Moerman's Medicinal Plants of Native*
> > > *America* (Ann Arbor, MI: Museum of
> > > Anthropology, Univ. of Michigan, 1986)
> > Previous ed.: New York: Garland, 1977

• Using information from 206 published sources on ethnobotany, Moerman lists 4,029 different plants used in 44,691 ways by 291 different societies. Use falls into five categories: food, medicine, fiber, dye, and other. Information was added only if some use of the plant was made by tribes north of the Rio Grande; if it was based on original work with tribes rather than secondary sources; and if the source used reasonably clear scientific plant names, preferably from botanists. Within the five categories, Moerman identifies 186 specific plant uses, such as cold remedy, red dye, cordage, baby food, candy, paint, and cleaning agent. Entries, in alphabetical order by scientific name of plant, with common names and synonyms noted, are organized by main category of use, tribe, and specific use. Uses are described in some detail; e.g., among the Lakota, Monarda fistulosa was an eye medicine applied by an "infusion of leaves used on a cloth placed on sore eyes overnight." Reference numbers for each use are keyed to the bibliography. Two tables list uses by tribes and tribes by uses. Separate indexes by synonyms and common names. Moerman's revealing look about cultural adaptation to and exploitation of the environment can also be used to study tribes, folklore, medicine, textiles, food, anthropology, and botany. — *JD*

FERNS

EC128   Petrik-Ott, Aleta Jo. - **The Pteridophytes of Kansas, Nebraska, South Dakota, and North Dakota, U.S.A.** - Vaduz [Liechtenstein] : J. Cramer; [distr. Forest

Grove, OR : ISBS], 1979. - 332 p.; ill., maps. - (Beihefte zur Nova Hedwiga, Heft 61).

> Class Numbers:
> > Library of Congress QK504   QK525.5.G73
> ISBN 3768254615
> OCLC 5232122
> LCCN 79-670364
> Notes:
> > Bibliography: p. 299-309; indexes

• Botanist Petrik-Ott seeks to classify pteridophytes found in four central Plains states (Kansas, Nebraska, and the Dakotas). Three sections deal with the keys to species of ferns and fern allies, genera of lycopodiophyta, and polypodiophyta. Ferns are treated separately from fern allies, with divisions by subclass, order, and families. Includes 66 distribution maps, 122 plates, glossary, and index to Latin and English common names. — *GK*

EC129   Yarborough, Sharon C. - **Ferns and Fern Allies of the Trans-Pecos and Adjacent Areas** / [by] Sharon C. Yarborough & A. Michael Powell. - Lubbock, TX : Texas Tech Univ. Pr., 2002. - 116 p.; ill., maps.

> Class Numbers:
> > Library of Congress QK525.5.T6
> ISBN 089672476X (pbk.)
> OCLC 48263684
> LCCN 2001-6536
> Notes:
> > Includes bibliographical references (p. 108-109);
> > > index

• Describes 64 species of true ferns and 14 related species of spikemosses and scoring rushes. Entries provide scientific names, common names, synonyms, and locations. Line drawings and distribution maps accompany the entries. Also included are a quick identification code, a checklist of ferns and related species, a glossary and a list of references. — *MS*

FUNGI

EC130   Bisby, Guy Richard. - **The Fungi of Manitoba and Saskatchewan** / ... with the collaboration of A.H.R. Buller ... John Dearness [et al.]; preface by H.T. Güssow. - Ottawa, ON : National Research Council of Canada, 1938. - 189 p.; 13 plates, folded map. - (Memoirs on Canadian Fungi).

> Class Numbers:
> > Library of Congress QH606.C2
> OCLC 4924279
> LCCN 40-165

Notes:

Bibliography: p. 174-183

• Arranged by species and subspecies, with references to the bibliography. The brevity of the descriptions (typically one or two lines) and the dearth of illustrations preclude use as a field guide. — *LMcD*

EC131   Stubbs, Ansel Hartley. - **Wild Mushrooms of the Central Midwest**. - Lawrence, KS : Univ. Pr. of Kansas, 1971. - 135 p.

ISBN 1700600671
LCCN 76-107330
Notes:

Illus. with color photographs and drawings by Chester E. Moore

• Limited to the central portion of the Midwest: Kansas, Missouri, Colorado, Nebraska, Iowa, Oklahoma, and Arkansas. The book intends to provide descriptions of common species and should be seen as a guide to further study. A growing season calendar is provided for the principal varieties. For each variety, provides a line drawing and a text description of the caps, stems, and habitat. Reference is made to the location of a color photo in the center photo section. Additional material includes a chart of characteristics used for identifying varieties. A brief selective bibliography and an index round out the volume. — *MB*

GRASSES

EC132   Johnson, James Russell, 1941-   . - **Grassland Plants of South Dakota and the Northern Great Plains** / [by] James R. Johnson and Gary E. Larson; ed. by Mary Brashier. - Brookings, SD : South Dakota State Univ., College of Agricultural & Biological Sciences, South Dakota Agricultural Experiment Station, 1999. - 288 p.; ill. (some col.). - (South Dakota Agricultural Experiment Station. Bulletin, 566).

Class Numbers:

Library of Congress QK186
ISBN 0913062065
OCLC 42890856
Notes:

Includes bibliographical references (p. 268-269); index

Revision of Johnson's *Plants of South Dakota Grasslands* (1982)

• In a book intended to be a general guide for researchers, botanists, farmers, tourists, and environmentalists, Johnson and Larson (agricultural extension and biology, South

Dakota State Univ.) provide color photographs and descriptions of 289 plant species found in the grass hills of central and western South Dakota, extending into the southern part of the Nebraska Sandhills. The editors hope to direct attention to the diminishing range of grasslands caused by industrialization and population growth. Entries are arranged alphabetically by family, genus, and species and give scientific names. The authors add a glossary and a comments section that addresses the importance of grasslands to food supply and to medicinal use by American Indians. — *GK*

EC133   Loflin, Brian. - **Grasses of the Texas Hill Country** / by Brian Loflin and Shirley Loflin; Stephan L. Hatch, scientific advisor. - College Station, TX : Texas A&M Univ. Pr., 2006. - 195 p.; col. ill., col. maps. - (Louise Lindsey Merrick Natural Environment Series, 40; TAM Nature Series).

Class Numbers:

Library of Congress QK495.G74
ISBN 1585444677
    1585445002 (pbk.)
    9781585444670
    9781585445004 (pbk.)
OCLC 59147750
LCCN 2005-10823
Notes:

Includes bibliographical references (p. [187]-188); index

Table of contents: http://www.loc.gov/catdir/toc/ ecip0511/2005010823.html

• This "photographic identification handbook" of 70 grasses important to agriculture, business, land stabilization, and wildlife, or known for their beauty, is designed for naturalists, ranchers, land stewards, and educators. It begins with descriptions of the Hill Country's 19 counties and ten vegetational areas. For easy identification, species accounts are categorized by the structure of the grass seedhead rather than by taxonomic category. Full-page color photographs of grasses against a black background are placed opposite one-page accounts that include key features, uses, habitat, growing season, and additional photographs. Icons indicate origin (native or introduced), longevity (annual or perennial), season of growth (warm or cool), grazing response (decreaser, increaser, invader) and toxicity. Bibliography, glossary, and index by common and scientific name. — *JD*

EC134   **PrairieMap : A GIS Database for Prairie Grassland Management in Western North America [Internet Site]**. - Bozeman, MT : Montana State University, Big Sky Institute, 2003-   . - http://bsi.montana.edu/ prairiemap/

OCLC 52817068

Access Date: May 2007

Notes:

Originally developed by the Snake River Field
Station of the USGS Forest and Rangeland
Ecosystem Science Center, Boise, ID

Fees: None

• *PrairieMap* serves as a repository of geospatial information on ecological aspects of the Prairie grasslands, with an emphasis on their conservation and management. Downloadable datasets detail conditions such as the distribution of Prairie falcons in New Mexico, agricultural land use in Wyoming, and black-tailed Prairie dog towns in Saskatchewan. Although the database is arranged in no discernible order, it provides sufficient descriptive elements (layer name, theme, state, data format, and projection scale) to identify relevant items. The site also includes a number of Prairie and grassland documents in pdf. Useful for environmentalists, land managers, and geographic information specialists. — *LMcD*

EC135   Shaw, Robert Blaine, 1949-   . - **Grasses of Colorado**. - Boulder, CO : Univ. Pr. of Colorado, 2008. - 768 p.; ill., maps, tables.

Class Numbers:

Library of Congress QK495.G74

ISBN 9780870818837

OCLC 154701409

LCCN 2007-37115

Notes:

Includes bibliographical references; index

• Covering grasses that have been collected in the state outside of cultivation, the guide is "meant to assist students, botanists, ecologists, agronomists, range scientists, naturalists" and others working with wild and domesticated animals, soil conservation, land use, cultivated grasses, and grass usage. It is compiled from sources dating from 1935 to the present. Introductory matter covers the physiography and ecoregions of Colorado, grass structures, and identification keys. Accounts of Colorado's 335 species in 14 families include range maps, synonyms, vernacular names, life span, origin, season, floral characteristics, vegetative characteristics, habitat, and comments. To aid in the difficult task of initial identification in the field, line diagrams supplement the detailed descriptions. A glossary, list of cited references, an index by scientific and popular names, and an index by subfamilies, tribes and genera complete the work. — *JD*

LEGUMES

EC136   Stubbendieck, James L. - **Common Legumes of the Great Plains : An Illustrated Guide** / by James Stubbendieck and Elverne C. Conard; ill. by Bellamy Parks

Jansen. - Lincoln, NE : Univ. of Nebraska Pr., 1989. - xxi, 330 p.; ill. 26 cm.

Class Numbers:

Library of Congress QK495.L52

ISBN 0803242042

LCCN 88-27690

Notes:

Includes bibliographical references (p. 307-311); index

• Stubbendieck and Conard (agronomy, Univ. of Nebraska-Lincoln) identify 180 species of native legumes vital for food supply, fertilizer, and prevention of soil erosion on the Great Plains. The introduction defines the Great Plains, a region of 500 million acres in 13 states and three Canadian provinces. Legumes included are those consumed by livestock and wildlife rather than humans. The work supplies life span, origin, and height for plants, listing them by common name and abbreviating scientific names (family, genus, species). Includes distribution maps and detailed black-and-white illustrations for 107 species. — *GK*

PASTURE AND RANGE PLANTS

EC137   Frisina, Michael Redvers, 1948-   . - **Montana Sagebrush Bibliography** / [by] Michael R. Frisina, John J. McCarthy, Carl L. Wambolt. - [Helena, MT] : Montana Fish, Wildlife & Parks, 2001. - 60 p.; ill. (some col.).

Class Numbers:

Library of Congress QK495.C74

OCLC 55011839

Notes:

Electronic book: http://www.fwp.state.mt.us/
insidefwp/fwplibrary/sage.pdf

• Sagebrush is a prominent feature of the western reaches of the Plains landscape, particularly in a state such as Montana. The first part of the work contains background information on big sagebrush (Artemisia tridentata), an identification key, and color photos of subspecies. The bibliography consists of 450 citations arranged by author. Scientific papers and theses are included but environmental assessments and impact statements are not. The scope is broader than the title suggests as the bibliography includes material on vegetation, wildlife, and soils in Montana. Author and subject indexes. Intended for Montana land managers but of interest to those in similar environmental areas. — *LMcD*

EC138   Looman, J. - **111 Range and Forage Plants of the Canadian Prairies**. - [Ottawa, ON] : Agriculture Canada, 1983. - 255 p.

Class Numbers:
  Library of Congress SB193.3.C3
  ISBN 0660113872
  LCCN C83-097205-6

• The 111 range plants are organized into groups: grasses, herbs, legumes, poisonous plants, rushes and sedges, and trees and shrubs, the largest section being grasses. Each section is arranged alphabetically by common name, e.g., bent grasses, blue grasses, brome grasses. Each plant is described on two facing pages, text on the verso and a full-page line drawing on the recto. Text pages are generally about half filled; entries provide scientific names and descriptive information about range and characteristics. At the back, a key to preferred common names serves as an index. This book needs color illustrations and a better index. — *MB*

EC139   Phillips Petroleum Company. - **Pasture and Range Plants**. - Bartlesville, OK : Phillips Petroleum Co., 1963. - 176 p.

Class Numbers:
  Library of Congress QK938 .P7
  LCCN 63-11000
  Notes:
    Bibliography: p. 171-172
    Originally publ. as a series of six booklets

• Guide to grassland plants commonly found in the Great Plains, with arrangement by common name under the categories of grasses, legumes, forbs, woody plants, and poisonous plants. Colored illustrations clearly show distinguishing features; the accompanying text describes each plant and its growing habits, preferred soils, distribution, and agricultural value, if any. Index of scientific and common names. The second edition, revised by Robert A. Nicholson, was published Hays, KS: Fort Hays State University, 2006. — *LMcD*

Trees

EC140   Ball, John Jeffrey. - **Trees for South Dakota** / by John J. Ball and David F. Graper. - [Brookings, SD] : Cooperative Extension Service, South Dakota State Univ., 1995. - 65 p.; ill. (some col.), col. maps. - (South Dakota State University. Cooperative Extension Service. Extension circular, 903).

Class Numbers:
  Library of Congress QK186
  OCLC 36956882
  Notes:
    Index

• Ball (arboriculture) and Graper (horticulture, both South Dakota State Univ.) provide a guide to South Dakota native or introduced trees. Their guide has five sections: deciduous trees,

coniferous trees, glossary, "More Trees for South Dakota," and keys to identify species. Each tree is characterized by growth rate, mature size, landscape features, and pest/disease issues. Icons indicate adaptability to soil, moisture requirements, power line compatibility, and planting aids. The sections describing trees are arranged alphabetically by botanical name and include the Lakota name if the tree is indigenous. Color photographs; distribution maps, which indicate climate zones for planting. — *GK*

EC141   Common Insect Pests of Trees in the Great Plains [Internet Site]. - [Lincoln, NE] : U.S. Dept of Agriculture, Forest Service; Nebraska Cooperative Extension Service, [1986?]. - http://www.unl.edu/nac/insectpest.html

OCLC 56393095
Access Date: June 2007
Notes:
  Great Plains Agricultural Council publication, 119
  Includes bibliographical references
  Nebraska Cooperative Extension Service. EC,
    v. 86-1548
  This publication is a cooperative effort of the Rocky
    Mountain Forest and Range Experiment Station,
    USDA Forest Service, and the Univ. of Nebraska
    Cooperative Extension Service
  Fees: None

• A guide to rapid identification and management of Plains tree pests, designed for people with no formal training in entomology. Produced originally as a printed field guide, it is now available on the Internet in pdf format with the introduction, table of contents, appendixes, and the 80 pest descriptions linked as separate files. Entries are organized under the general categories hardwood and conifers, with subcategories by damage type: defoliators, borers, and sapsucking insects. All gall insects are listed separately. Entries are by common name followed by the scientific name, a color photo, and information on hosts, identification, life cycle, damage, and control. A glossary has the title, "Common and Scientific Names of Insect Pests and Host Plants with Scientific Equivalents." Includes selected references and a "Pesticide Precautionary Statement." The separate pdf files make navigation of the Internet version cumbersome but the information is clear and concise and the photos of high enough quality to aid in identification. — *JD*

EC142   Herman, Dale E. - **Trees and Shrubs for Northern Great Plains Landscapes** / [by] Dale E. Herman, Vernon C. Quam. - Fargo, ND : NDSU Extension Service, 2006. - 272 p.; col. ill. - (North Dakota State University. Extension Service. Circular, F-1309).

Class Numbers:
  Library of Congress SB435.5
  OCLC 82943530

Notes:
  Glossary

• Intended to be a starting point for home gardeners selecting woody plants for landscaping. Introductory material covers tree growth above and below ground; general care and pest management; tree nomenclature; species by common and scientific name; quick guide to tree and shrub characteristics; and glossary. Species accounts include pictures in color, general description, environmental requirements, and related information. Allows a quick review of native and planted trees on the northern Great Plains. —*JB*

EC143   Kuhns, Michael Richard. - **Trees of Nebraska** / by Michael Kuhns and David Mooter. - [Lincoln, NE : Univ. of Nebraska, Institute of Agriculture and Natural Resources], 1992. - 75 p.; ill. (some col.). - (Nebraska Cooperative Extension Service, EC 92-1774-x).

  Class Numbers:
    Library of Congress QK484.N2
  OCLC 27097148

• A field identification guide that covers 97 species of trees, most native to Nebraska, others commonly planted or naturalized to the wild. Introductory sections about parts of trees and scientific nomenclature and a tree identification key help general readers understand species descriptions. Entries are organized by family under broad headings of gymnosperms and angiosperms, and species entries describe leaves, twigs, fruit, bark, and wood in vivid detail. Line drawings are numerous and clear. General comments cover usefulness, native range, and growth and flower characteristics. Glossary; landscaping guide; index by scientific name. —*JD*

EC144   Petrides, George A. - **A Field Guide to Western Trees : Western United States and Canada** / ill. by Olivia Petrides. - Boston, MA : Houghton Mifflin, 1992. - 308 p.; 50 p. of plates, ill. (some col.). - (Peterson field guide series, 44I).

  Class Numbers:
    Library of Congress QK133
    National Library of Canada QK133
  ISBN 0395467306   0395467292 (pbk.)
  OCLC 23940266
  LCCN 91-21904
  Notes:
    Includes bibliographical references (p. 293-296); index
    Sponsored by the National Audubon Society, the National Wildlife Federation, and the Roger Tory Peterson Institute

• All native and introduced trees from the Great Plains west and from the Arctic tree line to the Mexican border are described with clear identification characteristics, color

photographs of 387 species, and 295 approximate range maps. For ease of use, phylogenetic order and technical terms were rejected in favor of six groupings of similar-looking trees and commonly understood words. Comparison charts and color drawings help general readers distinguish among the six groups and their associated species. A key to trees in leafless condition; taxonomic list; glossary; references; and index by common and scientific names are included. —*JD*

EC145   Read, Ralph A. - **Bibliography of Great Plains Forestry**. - Fort Collins, CO : Rocky Mountain Forest and Range Experiment Station, 1961. - 176 p.

  Class Numbers:
    Library of Congress SD391
  OCLC 70497971
  Notes:
    Index

• Tree planting began to flourish on the Plains in the 1870s when homesteaders planted trees to "prove up" their claims, land sales agents claimed that tree planting would improve the climate, and the Arbor Foundation was founded in Nebraska. The protection of trees is a necessity for farms and ranches on the Plains and windbreaks are a topic of continuing interest. This bibliography was published 100 years after the initial flurry of planting, during a period of renewed interest in tree planting and land use, "to bring together the world's literature on the subject of windbreaks for over the past 80 years." Unannotated citations for books, reports, scholarly articles and popular articles published in the U.S and Canada are listed alphabetically by author under the headings "Great Plains Region," "Natural Forests of the Plains," "Afforestation in Sandhills and Nebraska National Forest," "Prairie States Forestry Project (1935-42)," "Planting Stock Production," "Growing Windbreaks," "Protecting Windbreaks," "Influences and Values of Windbreaks," "Other Tree Plantations," and "Farm Orchards and Gardens." A separate author list covers publications from other countries. Subject index. For foresters, scientists, environmentalists, historians, farmers and ranchers. —*JD*

WEEDS

EC146   Barkley, Theodore Mitchell, 1934-   . - **Field Guide to the Common Weeds of Kansas** / prepared for Kansas Agricultural Experiment Station and Division of Biology, Kansas State Univ. - Lawrence, KS : publ. for Kansas State Univ. by the Univ. Pr. of Kansas, 1983. - 164 p.; ill.

  Class Numbers:
    Library of Congress SB612.K2

ISBN 070060233X
LCCN 82-21914
Notes:
    Includes bibliographical references; index

• Designed for easy identification of annual and perennial plants commonly considered "weeds" in Kansas yards, roadsides, barnyards, cultivated fields, and other areas that have been disturbed by human use, Barkley's guide does not cover native vegetation of natural areas or uncommon weeds. A finding list to the weed groups is followed by species accounts with line drawings and range maps. Distribution maps and other data are based on specimens in regional herbaria. Glossary, selected references, and index by popular and scientific names. Scientific names may have changed since publication. — *JD*

EC147   Davis, Linda W. - **Weed Seeds of the Great Plains : A Handbook for Identification**. - Lawrence, KS : publ. for the Cooperative Extension Service of Kansas State Univ. by Univ. Pr. of Kansas, 1993. - 145 p.

    Class Numbers:
        Library of Congress SB612.G73
        Government Document Kansas E 46.2:W 394
        ISBN 0700606513
        OCLC 27976628
        LCCN 98-15615

• Covers the panhandle of Texas, most of Oklahoma, all of Kansas, Nebraska, North and South Dakota, the eastern parts of Colorado, Wyoming, and Montana, the western edges of Minnesota, Iowa, and Missouri, and the prairie portions of Manitoba, Saskatchewan, and Alberta. Introductory material describes methodology, cites sources, and provides a finding list for identification (organized by color, size, and other distinctive characteristics). Descriptions of 280 seed varieties are organized systematically by families, then alphabetically by genera. Each entry includes scientific name, common name, shape and structure, surface characteristics, size, and notes. A section of color plates at the center of the book illustrates all 280 varieties. At the end are a text glossary, an illustrated glossary, and an index of common and scientific names. — *MB*

EC148   Stubbendieck, James L. - **Weeds of the Great Plains**. - Lincoln, NE : Nebraska Dept. of Agriculture, Bureau of Plant Industry in cooperation with the University of Nebraska-Lincoln, 2003. - xiv, 605 p.

    Class Numbers:
        Library of Congress SB612 G73
        Government Document Nebraska A5560
            H001-2003
        ISBN 0939870005
        OCLC 52367437

Notes:
    Previous editions published as *Weeds of Nebraska and the Great Plains*

• Developed to help scientists, farmers, ranchers, and homeowners identify common and particularly damaging weeds, the species accounts are necessarily detailed but clear. The introduction is an excellent primer for nonscientists on the characteristics used to identify plants and the terminology used to describe them. Entries are organized by family and indexed by common and scientific names. They give succinct descriptions of growth form, life span, origin, flowering dates, reproduction, plant characteristics (height, inflorescence, flower, fruit, seed, leaves, stems, underground parts), where found, uses and values, poisoning and losses, historical uses, similar species, and other characteristics. Color photographs show the color, form, important characteristics and differences from similar plants. Botanical drawings show additional identifying characteristics and details. Glossary and selected references. — *JD*

WILDFLOWERS

EC149   Barr, Claude A. - **Jewels of the Plains : Wild Flowers of the Great Plains Grasslands and Hills**. - Minneapolis, MN : Univ. of Minnesota Pr., 1983. - 236 p.

    Class Numbers:
        Library of Congress QK135
        ISBN 0816611270
        OCLC 8667005
        LCCN 82-13691
    Notes:
        Bibliography: p. 215-223; index

• The greater part of this book consists of a 175-page list of native plants, organized alphabetically by scientific name. Entries also include common names and corresponding color plates, where applicable (the 119 color plates are gathered at the center of the book). The descriptive information, sometimes anecdotal, is drawn from Barr's personal observations gathered over 65 years living in western South Dakota. Supplementary information includes a glossary, a substantial bibliography, and a good subject index. Barr, author of 100 of these articles, is well known for his work with prairie wildflowers. — *MB*

EC150   Brown, Paul Martin. - **Wild Orchids of the Prairies and Great Plains Region of North America** / with original artwork by Stan Folsom. - Gainesville, FL : Univ. Pr. of Florida, 2006. - 342 p.; ill (some col.), col. maps.

    Class Numbers:
        Library of Congress QK495.O64
        ISBN 0813029759 9780813029759
        OCLC 70660314

LCCN 2006-46143

Notes:

    Includes bibliographical references (p. 321-326); index

• Like tropical orchids, those of the Great Plains rely on fungi and thus live in very specific habitats. The field guide shows likely locations and identifying characteristics of 64 species, nine varieties, eight hybrids, and 71 forms in North Dakota, South Dakota, Nebraska, Kansas, Texas, New Mexico, Colorado, Wyoming, Alberta, Manitoba, Saskatchewan, and other Prairie areas of the U.S. Orchids are organized by genus with a brief diagnostic key to the genus followed by entries in alphabetical order by scientific name. Accounts have alternate names, color photographs, line drawings, distribution maps, and descriptions of habitat, range, and flowering times. A references and resources section has a checklist of names with common and alternate Latin names; names by state and province; regional orchid statistics; rare, threatened, and endangered species; synonyms and misapplied names; changes to Carlyle Luer's nomenclature for orchids; cryptic species, species pairs, and varietal pairs; recommendation for orchid hunting in specific Prairie regions; hunting tips and tricks; new discoveries; an orchid distribution matrix; flowering time chart; glossary and bibliography. The soft, sturdy cover has built-in rulers for field measurements. One of a series on wild orchids of North America; a unique compilation that is highly informative and beautifully presented. — *JD*

EC151   Farrar, Jon, 1947-   . - **Field Guide to Wildflowers of Nebraska and the Great Plains**. - Lincoln, NE : Nebraskaland Magazine; Nebraska Game and Parks Commission, 1990. - 215 p.; [1] leaf of plates, ill. (some col.), col. map.

    Class Numbers:

        Library of Congress QK172

    ISBN 096259590X

    LCCN 90-6524

    Notes:

        Includes bibliographical references (p. 209); index

• Opens by describing Nebraska's wildflower regions (e.g., tallgrass prairie, Sandhills prairie), with a color map of the regions. The guide proper is arranged by color of the flowers, then by common physical characteristics. Each entry supplies a color photo and common name, scientific name, family, flowering season, distribution, habitat, description, and other general information. A glossary, references, and an index round out the volume. The illustrated glossary is particularly helpful, since it offers line drawings depicting varieties of leaf shape, leaf margin, leaf types and arrangements, as well as stem, root, and flower types. — *MB*

EC152   Gates, Frank C. - **Wild Flowers in Kansas : Report of the Kansas State Board of Agriculture for the Quarter**

Ending December, 1932 / ill. by Mrs. Albert Dickens. - Topeka, KS : Kansas State Printing Plant; W.C. Austin, State Printer, 1934. - 295 p.; ill. - (Kansas. State Board of Agriculture. Report. v. 51 no. 204-B).

    Class Numbers:

        Library of Congress QK161

    OCLC 3622948

    Notes:

        "References and very incomplete list of useful books": p. 8-9

• Prefatory material includes an introduction with identification keys and description of finding lists, references, a list of orders and families, and keys to the families. The flowers are organized according to the key, e.g., submerged, aquatic with floating leaves. Line drawings, four to a page, follow the textual matter. End matter includes a glossary and an index with popular and scientific names interspersed. Of particular interest is a finding list organized by color of plant and time of year. — *MB*

EC153   Haddock, Michael John. - **Wildflowers and Grasses of Kansas : A Field Guide**. - Lawrence, KS : Univ. Pr. of Kansas, 2005. - 374 p.; ill. (chiefly col.).

    Class Numbers:

        Library of Congress QK161

    LCCN 2004-15157

    Notes:

        Includes bibliographical references (p. 359-361); index

        Table of contents: http://www.loc.gov/catdir/toc/ ecip0419/2004015157.html

• Of the 2,100 species of vascular plants in Kansas, this field guide describes 323, both native and introduced. A few trees and shrubs with unique or showy blooms are included but most species are wildflowers, grasses, and sedges. Many occur in other parts of the central Great Plains. Species are grouped into four broad categories based on flower color and organized alphabetically by family and scientific name. Illustrated with color photographs, entries give common name, flowering period, height, distribution and habitat, life span, basic morphological characteristics, and comments. An introduction to basic plant morphology, a finding aid, and a glossary will aid nonspecialists. A bibliography of 45 sources and an index by family, genus, species and common name are included. Additional species are described on the author's Internet site (http://www.lib.ksu. edu/wildflower) but its entries are less full. Though designed as a field guide, its coated paper may deter use in the field. — *JD*

EC154   Holloway, Joel Ellis. - **A Dictionary of Common Wildflowers of Texas & the Southern Great**

Plains / written and comp. by Joel E. Holloway; ed. by Amanda Neill. - Fort Worth, TX : TCU Pr., 2005. - 178 p.; ill.

Class Numbers:
Library of Congress QK188
ISBN 087565309X
142372402X (electronic bk.)
9780875653099
OCLC 60550549
61451157 (electronic bk.)
LCCN 2005-15304
Notes:
Electronic book: http://www.netLibrary.com/
urlapi.asp?action=summary&v=1&bookid=139639
Includes bibliographical references; index

• Intended as a companion to field guides, this dictionary's entries provide scientific and common names and etymology for wildflowers of the region. Index of common names. —JB

EC155 Kirkpatrick, Zoe Merriman, 1935- . - **Wildflowers of the Western Plains : A Field Guide** / David K. Northington, scientific advisor; forewords by Benny J. Simpson and David K. Northington; drawings by Phillis Unbehagen . - Austin, TX : Univ. of Texas Pr., 1992. - xx, 240 p.; ill. (some col.), col. map. - (The Corrie Herring Hooks series, 20).

Class Numbers:
Library of Congress QK135
ISBN 0282790619 0292790627 (pbk.)
LCCN 91-3232
Notes:
Includes bibliographical references (p. 229-230);
index

• The wildflowers described thrive in the high elevations and semiarid conditions of the Plains in a range bounded on the east by the 99th meridian (the 26-inch rainfall line) and on the west by the Rockies, stretching north into Manitoba and south across the Rio Grande. Most are common herbaceous plants with a few shrubs, small trees and rare species. Entries are organized by family and species. Families are introduced with a summary of characteristics and color photographs. Species entries give common and scientific names and describe the plant, fruit, flower, and range of distribution; a few have line drawings. Remarks are more plentiful than in most field guides, giving personal observations, folklore, recipes, and medicinal uses. A guide to plant names and plant families, outline of plant diagnostic features, an illustrated glossary of plant parts, a bibliography, and an index by scientific and common names are all helpful. —JD

EC156 Ladd, Douglas M. - **Tallgrass Prairie Wildflowers : A Falcon Field Guide** / photos by Frank

Oberle and others. - Helena, MT : Falcon Pr., 1995. - 262 p.; ill. (some col.) , col. map.

Class Numbers:
Library of Congress QK128
ISBN 0585349010 (electronic bk.)
LCCN 95-6990
Notes:
"A Nature Conservancy book"–Cover
Electronic book: http://www.netLibrary.com/
urla[i.asp?action=summary&v=1&bookid=34719
Includes bibliographical references (p. [253]-254);
index

• Ladd arranges his colorful guide by the predominant color of the blossom–blue and purple, pink, red and orange, yellow, white, and green. He adds a section for grasses, sedges, and rushes. Additional material includes an essay on tallgrass prairies, a glossary, a directory of habitats, a bibliography, and an index. Each entry supplies a color photo, common name, scientific name, plant family, description, and information on habitat/range, often adding miscellaneous comments. — MB

EC157 Loughmiller, Campbell. - **Texas Wildflowers : A Field Guide** / [by] Campbell and Lynn Loughmiller; foreword to the first ed. by Lady Bird Johnson. - Austin, TX : Univ. of Texas Pr., 2006. - xxiv, 278 p.; ill. (chiefly col.), col. map. - (Texas Natural History Guides).

Class Numbers:
Library of Congress QK188
ISBN 0292712863
OCLC 61262398
LCCN 2005-23299
Notes:
Includes bibliographical references
(p. 251-254); index
Table of contents: http://www.loc.gov/catdir/
toc/fy0661/2005023299-t.html

• In a state known for wildflowers, a wide array of guidebooks is available, of which the Loughmillers' is one of the standards. Providing plant taxonomy and nomenclature, detailed description, and full-color photographs for the most common species and for rarer and more unusual plants, it will be useful both for beginners and experienced wildflower enthusiasts. Other titles of interest include James Kavanagh's *Texas Trees & Wildflowers* ([S.l.]: Waterford Press, 2001), designed as a quick reference to common species of trees and wild plants. Although Marshall Enquist's *Wildflowers of the Texas Hill Country* (Austin, TX: Lone Star Botanical, 1987) would seem to be a regional guide, it includes flowers found in all parts of Texas. It has numerous color photographs and descriptions, and advice concerning best soil for growth and months for optimal blooms. For outstanding photography of Texas wildflowers, Laurence E. Parent and Patricia Caperson's *Wildflowers Across Texas* (Portland, OR: Graphic Arts

Center, 2002) has 112 pages of color photographs and an introduction by Laura Bush. — *JB*

EC158   Native Wildflowers of the North Dakota Grasslands [Internet Site] / [Harold A. Kantrud]; photographs by Kurt A. Adolfson and Jack Lefor. - Jamestown, N.D. : Northern Prairie Wildlife Research Center, 1997-   . - http://npwrc.usgs.gov

    Class Numbers:
        Library of Congress QK179
    OCLC 39455031
    Access Date: May 2008
    Fees: None

• Orisginating as a series of newspaper articles, Kantrud's handbook provides short descriptions of 225 species. Arranged by botanical family name, the accounts include life history, identifying characteristics, locale within the state, nomenclatural history, and colored photographs. No maps or index. A popular guide to wildflowers of the Northern Plains. — *LMcD*

EC159   Owensby, Clenton E., 1940-   . - Kansas Prairie Wildflowers. - Ames, IA : Iowa State Univ. Pr., 1980. - 124 p.; ill. 23 cm.

    Class Numbers:
        Library of Congress QK161
    ISBN 0813808502
    LCCN 80-17791
    Notes:
        Includes bibliographical references (p. 120); indexes

• Introductory material covers Prairie wildflower ecology, nomenclature, morphology, and use of the keys. Of particular interest are schematics of plant structure, defining petal types and leaf shapes, parts, and arrangements. The wildflower entries are arranged by the color of the bloom and within that by the key given for each section, wherein the organization is by specific structural characteristics. Each item supplies a color photo and text that gives popular and scientific names, blooming season, descriptive information and a small outline map of Kansas showing the habitat area. There is a good glossary, a very brief list of references, a scientific name index, and a separate common name index. — *MB*

EC160   Runkel, Sylvan T. - Wildflowers of the Tallgrass Prairie : The Upper Midwest / Sylvan T. Runkel and Dean M. Roosa; foreword by John Madson. - Ames, IA : Iowa State Univ. Pr., 1989. - 279 p.

    LCCN 87-34482

• Organized by wildflower common names into 131 short chapters, each of which contains a color photo of a specimen and descriptive information including the scientific name, other common names, habitat, and textual description. Supplementary material includes a glossary, bibliography, and index. — *MB*

EC161   Van Bruggen, Theodore. - Wildflowers of the Northern Plains and Black Hills. - 2nd ed. - Interior, SD : Badlands Natural History Association, 1976. - 84 p. - (Badlands Natural History Association. Bulletin, 3).

    Class Numbers:
        Library of Congress QK135 b.V35
    ISBN 0912410035
    LCCN 79126933
    Notes:
        Includes bibliography
        1st ed., 1971

• This second edition extends the first by 20 pages. There is no table of contents. The flower identification pages are organized by the color of the bloom, beginning with yellow and continuing with white, red, and blue. All other hues are incorporated into these four choices. Each entry (three to a page) contains a 2-inch x 2-inch color photo and descriptive information, including common name, scientific name, family, blooming season and additional information including size and habitat. An index, by both common and scientific name, is included. There is also a bibliography listing 13 selected items. — *MB*

EC162   Vance, Fenton R., 1907-   . - Wildflowers across the Prairies / [by] F.R. Vance [et al.]. - 3rd ed. - Vancouver : Greystone Books, 1999. - 382 p.; ill. (some col.).

    Class Numbers:
        Library of Congress QK203.P7
    ISBN 1550547038
    OCLC 43719203
    Notes:
        Includes bibliographical references (p. 374); indexes

• "A book for field use and for reading enjoyment by both casual and serious observers of plants" (Pref.), this wildflower guide describes 400 species in Alberta, Saskatchewan, Manitoba, and parts of the Plains states of Montana, Wyoming, North Dakota, and South Dakota. Arranged taxonomically with one plant per page, except where comparisons of similar plants are presented, entries include color photographs, sketches, and brief descriptions of the flowers, fruit, leaves, growth habit, and habitat. Changes in range and abundance are inevitable and the guide notes that several of the plants were rare at the time of the first edition or perhaps had already vanished. New to this edition is a section on grasses, sedges, and rushes (p. 315-370). The guide may now prove useful, not simply in identification, but in tracking changes in flora and the surrounding environment. Glossary, bibliography, index of common and scientific names, index of plant families, and color index to plants. Some botanical names may have changed. — *JD*

EC163   Wildflowers and Weeds of Kansas / Janet E. Bare. - Lawrence, KS : Regents Pr. of Kansas, 1979. - 509 p.; [8] leaves of plates, ill.

> Class Numbers:
>> Library of Congress QK161
>
> ISBN 0700601767
> OCLC 4004252
> LCCN 78-16862

• Introductory material provides information on the physical geography of Kansas with maps, the structure of flowering plants, and illustrations of plant characteristics, e.g., leaf margins. Following that is a key to families. Entries, organized according to the key, include many color and black-and-white photos besides textual descriptions, and supply common name, scientific name, color, blooming season, habitat, description, and cross-references to appropriate color plates, as applicable. Appendixes include a substantial glossary and citations to sources. Exhaustive index. — *MB*

EC164   Wildflowers of the Northern Great Plains / [by] F. R. Vance [et al.]. - 3rd ed. - Minneapolis, MN : Univ. of Minnesota Pr., 1999. - 382 p.; ill. (some col.); map.

> Class Numbers:
>> Library of Congress QK203.7
>
> ISBN 081663484X
> Notes:
>> Includes bibliographical references
>>> (p. 374); index
>>
>> Includes new section on grasses, sedges,
>>> and rushes

• Describes nearly 400 species of flowering plants found in the northern part of the Great Plains, from Kansas north and west into the Prairie provinces, including Nebraska, the Dakotas, Manitoba, Saskatchewan, and Alberta. Entries are arranged in taxonomic order; the index permits locating plants by common name or genus. Entries include a color photo and a description that covers the plant's size, fruit, leaves, habitat, and season; many entries also have line drawings. Glossary; bibliography. — *MB*

F : Health and Medicine

Scope   Lists titles having to do with medicine and the health of citizens in the Prairies-Plains region.

See also the section "Health and Medicine," in section **CD, Indians, CD99-CD100.**

F1   Colorado Health Information Dataset : CoHID [Internet Site] / Colorado Dept. of Public Health and Environment. - [Denver, CO] : Colorado Dept. of Public Health and Environment, 2000s-. - http://www.cdphe.state.co.us/cohid/index.html

> OCLC 48528868
> Access Date: May 2008
> Fees: None

• Health, birth, morbidity, and mortality statistics are available for neighborhoods, communities, counties, and regions of the state. Vital statistics and health statistics on behavioral risk factors, birth defects, cancer incidents, injury hospitalization, pregnancy risks, and tobacco attitudes and behaviors are available in searchable datasets.

Cancer incidence data, for example, can be searched and sorted by geographic location, age, race/ethnicity, gender, diagnosis year (1990 to the present), and cancer site. With its interdisciplinary focus on public health and the environment, the agency has produced datasets for a variety of researchers. Details of the data collection and restrictions on use are clearly stated. Many of the same statistics are also available in text and table format on the sponsoring agency's Internet site at http://www.cdphe.state.co.us/stats.html. — *JD*

F2   Dartmouth Medical School. Center for the Evaluative Clinical Sciences. - **The Dartmouth Atlas of Health Care : The Great Plains States**. - Chicago, IL : American Hospital Publishing, Inc., 1996. - 1 v. atlases ; col. ill., col. maps.

> Class Numbers:
>   Library of Congress G1201.E5
> ISBN 1556481764
> OCLC 38865129
> LCCN 96-11510
> Notes:
>   Available online in pdf: http://www.dartmouthatlas.org/;
>   *The Great Plains States* is segment 6 of the online
>   version

Site List 16
Public Health

Nearly all states and provinces in the Plains region have agencies responsible for the health of citizens, and nearly all maintain Internet sites whose purpose is to make available statistics of health and disease (often including vital statistics), broadcast developments in health care, and in some cases supply directories of health professionals and state or provincial health agencies.

UNITED STATES

Colorado Department of Public Health and
    Environment.
    http://www.cdphe.state.co.us/

Kansas Department of Health and Environment.
    http://www.kdheks.gov/
[Maintains Center for Health and Environmental
    Statistics].
    http://www.kdheks.gov/ches/

Montana Department of Public Health & Human
    Services.
    http://www.dphhs.mt.gov/

Nebraska Health and Human Services System.
    http://www.hhs.state.ne.us/

New Mexico Department of Health.
    http://www.health.state.nm.us/

North Dakota Department of Health.
    http://www.health.state.nd.us/

Oklahoma State Department of Health.
    http://www.health.state.ok.us/

South Dakota Department of Health.
    http://www.state.sd.us/DOH/

Texas Department of State Health Services.
    http://www.tdh.state.tx.us

Wyoming Department of Health.
    http://wdh.state.wy.us/

CANADA

Alberta Health & Wellness.
    http://www.health.gov.ab.ca/

Manitoba Health.
    http://www.gov.mb.ca/health/

Saskatchewan Health – Healthy People, a Healthy
    Province.
    http://www.health.gov.sk.ca/

• Attempts to assess the level of medical care available to residents of the Great Plains, with an eye to making accessibility to hospitals and health care more equal in all sections of the United States. The Great Plains is defined as Kansas, Nebraska, the Dakotas, Minnesota, Iowa, and Missouri, and the work is an atlas only in the sense that it displays analyses of health care on standard maps of the region. The Plains section opens with an introductory discussion of methods, comparisons, and benchmarks that is repeated in every section of the Atlas. The first section, "The Geography of Health Care in the Great Plains States," shows on regional maps hospital service areas in regions identified by the largest population center (Fargo, Rapid City, Lincoln, Wichita, etc.), identifying the availability of hospital services. Subsequent sections show by means of statistical tables and maps: acute care hospital resources and expenditures, the Medicare program, the physician workforce, the use of hospitals for medical and surgical conditions, and hospital beds and Medicare reimbursements. Presents a clear picture of heath care availability in the region, but is now ten years old, so can be presumed to be out of date in some respects. The Internet version simply duplicates in pdf the printed version, with no search enhancements. — *RB*

F3 A Guide to Sources of Medical History in the University of Alberta Archives. - [Edmonton, AB] : [University of Alberta], 1984. - 25 leaves.

    Class Numbers:
        Library of Congress R 463 A3
        OCLC 65806839
    Notes:
        Electronic book: http://www.ourfutureourpast.ca/loc_
            hist/toc.aspx?id=5369

• Guide to papers and records of Edmonton medical organizations and physicians connected with the Univ. of Alberta. Entries begin with a brief historical or biographical note, followed by an indication of collection size, finding aids, restrictions, and conclude with a collection description. — *LMcD*

F4 Manitoba's Research on Aging : An Annotated Bibliography, 1950-1982. - [Winnipeg, MB] : Manitoba Association on Gerontology, 1982. - 269 p.

    Class Numbers:
        Library of Congress Z7164 O4
        OCLC 15940609

• Arranged by subject categories such as education, health care, needs assessment, senior centers, and social policy. Annotations are given twice, in formats for professionals in the field and interested general readers. Author index. Partially updated by sources such as *AgeLine* (http:

//www.aarp.org) and *Abstracts in Social Gerontology* (Newbury Park, CA: Sage, 1990-). A Manitoba counterpart to *Saskatchewan Aging*, **F6**. — *LMcD*

F5 The Nebraska Health Information Project Databook [Internet Site] / Nebraska Center for Rural Health Research. - [Omaha, NE] : Univ. of Nebraska Medical Center, 1995-   . - http://www.unmc.edu/nebraska/databooks/2003-databook/default.htm

    Class Numbers:
        Library of Congress RA407.4.N2
        OCLC 37388092 (print)   54671511 (online)
        Access Date: Jan. 2006
    Notes:
        Available in print, online, or CD-ROM
    Fees: None

• *Databook*, accessible from the Nebraska Health Information Project home page, provides statistics of availability, cost, and quality of medical care in Nebraska. Tables cite the sources of statistics–government and commercial publications, authoritative Internet sites, and local unpublished data. Six chapters, each beginning with a summary, cover demographics and geography, health professionals, health care facilities, insurance and health expenditures, health status, and hospital discharges. Specific tables, maps, and charts treat, for example, medically underserved areas by county, health facilities by type and county, insurance status, HIV incidence cross-tabulated by age, race, and risk, and rate of preventable hospitalizations. Some tables supply comparisons over time, and some statistics are compiled by county or region. Databook is posted on the Internet in pdf format beginning with the issue for 2003. — *JD*

F6 Saskatchewan Aging : An Annotated Bibliography on Research in Saskatchewan, 1945 to the Present. - Regina, SK : Senior Citizens' Provincial Council, 1983. - 166 p.

    Class Numbers:
        Library of Congress Z6663.A3
        National Library of Canada COP.SA.2.1985
        OCLC 16064024
    Notes:
        A joint project of the Senior Citizens' Provincial
            Council and the Saskatchewan Gerontology
            Association; Louise Boynton et al., compilers
        Electronic book: http://www.ourfutureourpast.ca/
            loc_hist/toc.aspx?id=8515

• Cites gerontological studies, both in journals and grey literature such as reports from service agencies, dealing with Saskatchewan. Arranged by broad subjects including demography, needs, housing, health care, income, retirement, and leisure. The organization is somewhat unusual: the scholarly abstracts of the first half are followed by "lay translations" of the same items, although frequently the two are identical. Author and subject indexes. *Manitoba's Research on Aging* (**F4**) is an equivalent source. *AgeLine* (http://www.aarp.org) and *Abstracts in Social Gerontology* (Newbury Park, CA: Sage, 1990-) cover some later material. — *LMcD*

F7   Senior Citizen Services : Midwestern States. -1st ed. - Detroit, MI : Gale Research Inc., 1993-   . Annual.

>   Class Numbers:
>   Library of Congress HV1468.A14
>   LCCN 93-640584 sn 93-33175
>   Notes:
>   Covers Illinois, Indiana, Iowa, Kansas, Michigan,
>   Minnesota, Missouri, Nebraska, North Dakota,
>   Ohio, South Dakota, Wisconsin

• An index to 15,000 providers of senior citizen services in 12 Midwestern states, Ohio in the east to Nebraska in the west, arranged alphabetically by state, then by agency. Information for each entry includes name of agency, address, phone, contact person or director, area served, and type of services offered. Prior to each state's list of service providers is a "geographic/service" index. At the back of the volume is an extensive index by agency name, which, since agency names tend to resemble one another, is not likely to be often used. — *MB*

F8   University of Texas Southwestern Medical School at Dallas. Library. - **Texas Medical History in the Library of the University of Texas Southwestern Medical School** / comp. and ed. by Violet M. Baird. - Dallas, TX : Friends of the Medical Library of the Univ. of Texas Southwestern Medical School, 1972. - 91 p.

>   Class Numbers:
>   Library of Congress Z6661.U5
>   LCCN 76-187337

• A catalog of 246 items—histories, monographs, pamphlets, documents, and manuscripts—relating to Texas medical history purchased with funds donated by Friends of the Medical Library of the University of Texas Southwestern Medical School and deposited in the library. The catalog has sections for monographs, pamphlets, and documents prior to 1900; monographs and pamphlets after 1900; biography and autobiography; Texas medical history; and general Texas history. Many items, especially in the first three sections, have annotations; entries in each section are arranged alphabetically by author or other entry (sometimes by catch phrases). The catalog was compiled by the collection's librarian, so is carefully complete. Of historical interest. — *RB*

G : Agriculture

Scope Covers farming and cattle and sheep raising, the trades that have been close to the hearts and interests of many Prairies-Plains people since the first white settlements.

General Works

G1 **AGRICOLA [Internet Site]** / National Agricultural Library (U.S.). - [Washington, DC] : National Agricultural Library, 1970- . - http://agricola.nal.usda.gov/

Class Numbers:
Library of Congress S494.5.A8
OCLC 40441401
Access Date: Nov. 2005
Notes:
Accesses NAL's Online Public Access Catalog and Journal Article Citation Index
Available on subscription from various online vendors
Compiled by: Bethesda, MD: National Agricultural Library, 1970–
Index to materials acquired by NAL and cooperating insti tutions. Includes journal articles, monographs, series, materials in nonprint formats. International in scope, 1970-1985; 1985+ focuses on U.S.-related publications
Updated daily
Fees: Subscription

• *AGRICOLA* is the catalog of the world's largest agriculture library, the National Agricultural Library, which holds 3.5 million items and administers a national network of state land-grant and USDA field libraries. It includes articles, monographs, theses, livestock registries, agricultural statistics, inventions and patents, bibliographies, plant databases, image galleries, manuscript guides, research reports, and technical reports published from 1970 to the present. It provides full text of many publications and links to Internet sites. The vast range of topics includes many of interest to Great Plains producers, researchers, and businesses, including animal science, grain science, water resources, farming techniques, rural development, marketing and trade, and laws and regulations. — *JD*

G2 Arntzen, Charles J., ed. - **Encyclopedia of Agricultural Science** / ed. by Charles J. Arntzen [and] Ellen M. Ritter. - San Diego, CA : Academic Pr., 1994. - 4 v.

Class Numbers:
Library of Congress S411

ISBN 0122266706 0122266714 (v. 1)
0122266722 (v. 2) 0122266730 (v. 3)
0122266749 (v. 4)
LCCN 94-3143
Notes:
Includes bibliographical references; index
Table of contents: http://www.loc.gov/catdir/toc/els032/94003143.html

• The editors (both at Texas A&M Univ.) provide about 180 articles written by specialists that cover large topics in agriculture, each a small treatise on its subject. Among the articles of particular interest to Prairies-Plains researchers will be "Desertification of Drylands," "Dryland Farming," "Grain, Feed, Crop Storage," "Ground Water," ten articles on rangeland, and 13 on soil. All the articles are listed at the beginning of each volume, and all end with bibliographies. Volume 4 lists U.S. colleges and universities offering academic programs in agriculture, U.N. agricultural and related organizations, a roster of contributors, a subject index, and an index of articles related to the separate articles (essentially, a cross-reference list). The style is faceless and impersonal, and provides a fresh home for passive voice. — *RB*

G3 **Encyclopedia of Rural America : The Land and the People** / ed. by Gary Goreham. - Santa Barbara, CA : ABC-CLIO, 1997. - 2 v. (861 p.); ill., maps.

Class Numbers:
Library of Congress E169.12
ISBN 0874368421
LCCN 97-23320
Notes:
Includes bibliographical references (p. 789-807); index

• The focus of this set rests on rural life in the United States. Goreham and his advisory board concentrate on topics that apply across the rural U.S. and treat them with scientific impartiality. Two pages in the front matter list the topics covered in both volumes, making it possible to locate topics relevant to Plains interest: "American Indians," "Barns," "Drought," "Dryland farming," "Feedlots," "Grain elevators," "Groundwater," "Ranching," "Rural women," "Soil," "Theology of the land," "Wheat industry." The text includes illustrations, charts, and graphs. Entries are signed and end by citing further readings. Volume 2 concludes with a substantial selected bibliography, illustration credits, and a roster of contributors. The subject index allows location of topics that do not have their own entries, e.g., "Great Plains," states, "Rural attitudes," and expands topics for which there are separate articles, e.g., "Land." — *MB, RB*

G4 **The Land Institute [Internet Site]**. - Salina, KS : The Land Institute, 2002- . - http://www.landinstitute.org

OCLC 51783666
Access Date: Jan. 2006
Fees: None

• The Institute works to develop natural agriculture as an alternative to annual crops. Its site is emphatically organizational, presenting news about the Institute, its members and supporters, and activities, written in polemical language, but it provides bibliographies at a main page "Publications" link. The bibliographies fall under three main headings, "Science," "General," and "Prairie Writers," and include books and both technical and general interest articles as well as links to Internet pages on sustainable agriculture and organic agriculture. Topics include agrarianism, biotechnology, ecosystems, soils, and world view. "Prairie Writers" includes articles by members of Prairie Writers Circle, a group of newspaper commentators writing about ecology and sustainability. An array of indexes by date, author, and subject are confusing to use but can provide helpful information. The Institute's archives can be searched by keyword. Citations link to the full text of many articles as reprints or pdf files. — *JD*

G5   **Nebraska Rural Poll [Internet Site]** / Univ. of Nebraska-Lincoln. Center for Applied Rural Innovation. - Lincoln, NE : Univ. of Nebraska-Lincoln, 2001 −   . - http://cari.unl.du/ruralpoll/topics.htm

Class Numbers:
    Library of Congress HD1775.N2
OCLC 47835714 (CARI)
Access Date: Jan. 2006
Notes:
    Updated annually
Fees: None

• In 2005, 68 percent of rural Nebraskans were satisfied with their marriages, but only 23 percent with their jobs and 9 percent with their retirement security. Trends in these and other measures of well-being have remained stable for the past ten years. The figures are drawn from the Nebraska Rural Poll conducted by the Center (CARI), which coordinates public access to University of Nebraska information and program support regarding rural economic and social well-being. CARI has conducted the poll every year since 1996, using responses to questions about core issues and key topics to inform state and federal legislators and others of the "aggregated voice of rural Nebraska." Topics vary from year to year, but have included perceptions of safety and crime, taxes for education and public assistance, water priorities, use of technology, and alternative energy sources. CARI analyzes responses by age, gender, education, income and marital status, community size, and region, and observes trends in ongoing questions concerning quality of life and community satisfaction. The site lacks a search engine but groups reports of

questionnaire responses under broad categories (e.g., "Agricultural Policy," "Community Satisfaction," "County Government") and holds reports from earlier years until the issue is resubmitted to the 7,000 respondents. — *JD*

G6   Rogers, Earl M., comp. - **A List of References for the History of Agriculture in the Great Plains.** - Davis, CA : Agricultural History Center, University of California, 1976. - 90 p.

Class Numbers:
    Library of Congress S441
OCLC 2772713
Notes:
    A cooperative project by the Agricultural History Branch, Economic Research Service, U.S. Dept. of Agriculture, and the Agricultural History Center.

• Defining the Great Plains as Kansas, Nebraska, North Dakota, Oklahoma, and South Dakota, Rogers's bibliography includes books, articles, theses, and reports that cover the region as a whole, a state or group of states, or a local region. Scholarly and popular works are included; works without a historical approach are excluded. Briefly annotated citations are organized by author under headings such as land policy and use, crops, livestock, technology, institutions, and states and territories. The topics remain fresh and the information applicable to current concerns such as irrigation and drought; public land use; and agrarian politics. A good source for farm and ranch journals and reminiscences. Indexed by author. — *JD*

G7   Rogers, Earl M. - **A List of References for the History of Agriculture in the Mountain States.** - Davis, CA : Agricultural History Center, Univ. of California, 1972. - 91 p.

Class Numbers:
    Library of Congress Z5071
OCLC 1147146
Notes:
    "A cooperative project by the Agricultural History Branch, Economic Research Service, U.S. Dept. of Agriculture, and the Agricultural History Center."

• Covering the eastern parts of Colorado, Montana, New Mexico, and Wyoming, as well as other montane states, Rogers's bibliography cites articles, monographs, chapters, theses, and bulletins. A few cover the West or the entire mountain state region though most cover individual states or local areas. Primary works, cowboy reminiscences, and contemporary accounts are excluded. Very briefly annotated entries are classified by major topics, including Indian agriculture, land and land use, crops, livestock, agricultural movements, institutions, and states. The section on Indian agriculture, which encompasses crops, livestock, land, and land use, is especially useful. Indexed by author. — *JD*

Atlases

See also **Agricultural Land Resource Atlas of Alberta, EB25**

G8   **Agricultural Atlas of Nebraska** / project director, Merlin P. Lawson; ed. by James H. Williams, Doug Murfield ; foreword by James H. Zumberge ; cartographer, John D. Magill. - Lincoln, NE : Univ. of Nebraska Pr., 1977. - 110 p. ; ill., col. maps ; 24 x 32 cm.

Class Numbers:
    Library of Congress G1451.J1
    ISBN 0803208944
    OCLC 2213283
    LCCN 76-16169

• One of three atlases produced by the Nebraska Atlas Project (the others cover climate and economic conditions, **EA25** and **CF4**), established "to provide a geographical inventory of the state of Nebraska" (Foreword). The atlas provides a graphical and statistical view of the state's agricultural base, and acts as both a historical document and a baseline against which the tremendous changes since the atlas' publication in 1977 may be studied. The data, compiled primarily by the State-Federal Division of Agricultural Statistics, begin as early as 1900 and cover climate, soil, water, farms, production, economics, and marketing. Charts and maps include such topics as irrigation wells drilled 1900-75, value of crops 1930-73, cattle on farms 1900-73, average farm size 1900-69, percentage of land irrigated, farm production expenses, petroleum expense, acres harvested, crop production, cash receipts, egg production, bee colonies, and hired labor expense. The accompanying text supplies context, additional statistics, and detailed analyses. A work of great clarity and scholarship. — *JD*

G9   **Agroclimatic Atlas of Alberta, 1971-2000** / Shane Chetner, editor-in-chief and the Agroclimatic Atlas Working Group. - Edmonton, AB : Alberta Agriculture, Food and Rural Development, 2003. - 97 p. : col. maps ; 28 cm.

Class Numbers:
    Library of Congress S600.64.C2
    National Library of Canada COP.AL.2.2004-275
    OCLC 55977068
    LCCN 2005-362325
    Notes:
        Electronic book: http://www1.agric.gov.ab.ca
        Includes bibliographical references (p. 89-92)

Previous ed. by Peter Dzikowski and Richard T. Heywood published in 1989

• Provides climatic information significant to agriculture in Alberta. Numerous maps illustrate factors such as precipitation, soils, and temperature. The Internet site includes additional maps for 30-year periods back to 1901. — *LMcD*

G10   Fung, Ka-iu, 1948-   . - **Atlas of Saskatchewan Agriculture** / [by] Kai-iu Fung, Stuart H. Gage. - Saskatoon, SK : Extension Division, University of Saskatchewan, 1978. - 141 p. ; maps ; 28 cm.

Class Numbers:
    Library of Congress G1161.J1
    OCLC 4875265
    LCCN 83-245254
    Notes:
        Contents: Climate and Land Use; Crop and Livestock
            Characteristics; Farm Population and Land
            Tenure Characteristics

• A graphical representation of Saskatchewan agriculture in the form of choropleth (drawn on a quantitative areal basis) and isoline (contour) maps. The monochrome display is sometimes difficult to decipher and advances in cartography have not been kind to the atlas. The age of the statistics makes the work primarily of historical interest. — *LMcD*

G11   United States. Dept. of Agriculture. - **Atlas of American Agriculture : Physical Basis Including Land Relief, Climate, Soils, and Natural Vegetation of the United States** / prepared under supervision of O.E. Baker (Bureau of Agricultural Economics) ; contributions from the Weather Bureau [et al.]. - Washington, DC : U.S. Govt. Print. Off., 1936. - 1 v. (various pagings) ; ill., col. maps

Class Numbers:
    Library of Congress G1201.J1
    LCCN agr 36-297
    Notes:
        Contents: Land Relief / F.J. Marschner, 1936; Climate:
            Temperature, Sunshine, and Wind / Joseph B. Kincer, 1
            928; Climate: Frost and the Growing Season / William
            Gardner Reed; Climate: Precipitation and Humidity /
            Joseph B. Kincer, 1922; Soils of the United States / C.F.
            Marbut, 1935; The Physical Basis of Agriculture:
            Natural Vegetation, Grassland and Desert Shrub / H.L.
            Shantz; Forests / Raphael Zon, 1924
        Includes bibliographical references

• Originally issued as six fascicles beginning in 1922, this atlas was a milestone in cartography and in the science of agriculture. Today, it is a good source of Great Plains historical data on climate and plant distributions. Because soils in large areas of the western Great Plains were not yet extensively mapped, the level of information on soil composition, depth, and distribution varies. Each section includes impressively detailed color maps, explanatory texts, photographs, numerous tables, and selected readings. No index. Appendixes provide a list of common plant names and their scientific equivalents and a selected bibliography. Changes in climate and land use will renew interest in this record of the condition of agriculture early in the 20th century. — *JD*

Statistical Compendiums

G12   Nebraska. Dept. of Agriculture and Economic Development. - **Nebraska Agricultural Statistics : Historical Record, 1866-1954** / [by] Nebraska Dept. of Agriculture and Inspection cooperating with the U.S. Dept. of Agriculture, Agricultural Marketing Service, Agricultural Estimates ; assembled by Thelma M. Mahr. - [Lincoln, NE] : State-Federal Division of Agricultural Statistics, 1957. - 176 p. ; map.

> Class Numbers:
> Library of Congress S451.N2
> OCLC 5372918
> LCCN 57-63899

• Assembles nearly 90 years' crop and livestock statistics drawn from a variety of statistical series prepared by numerous U.S. and Nebraska agencies (the federal *Census of Agriculture*, *Nebraska Annual Farm Census*, annual statewide surveys, field agent reports, and other sources). Extensive tables cover, e.g., number and size of farms; farm tenancy; farm income; land use; individual crop yield, production, price, and value; individual livestock numbers, production, disposition, and income; prices, indexes, and ratios; wages. Most data are annual and statewide, although some tables are arranged by month, season, or county. Beginning dates for tables vary widely. Data were reconciled with the U.S. Census on a regular basis. — *JD*

G13   South Dakota Agricultural Statistics Service. - **100 Years of South Dakota Agriculture, 1900-1999**. - Sioux Falls, SD : South Dakota Agricultural Statistics Service, 2000. - 54 p. ; ill.

> Class Numbers:
> Library of Congress S113
> OCLC 43611213
> LCCN 00-325416

• The South Dakota Agricultural Statistics Service here reports data about major crops and livestock in South Dakota throughout the 20th century. This publication includes statistics for crops (corn, sorghum, soybeans, sunflowers, wheat, oats, barley, rye, flaxseed, alfalfa, hay) and livestock (cattle, hogs, sheep, poultry). Some tabulated

data are incomplete because data were not recorded during certain periods. In many instances, state agencies did not keep statistics until World War II. — *GK*

FARMING

General Works

G14   Dyson, Lowell K., 1929–   . - **Farmers' Organizations**. - Westport, CT : Gre4wood Pr., 1986. - 383 p. - (Greenwood encyclopedia of American institutions, 10).

> Class Numbers:
> Library of Congress HD1484
> ISBN 0313221499
> OCLC 12420996
> LCCN 85-17529
> Notes:
> Index

• Dyson describes 133 national and local farm organizations intended for owners, tenants, or workers. Some (e.g., National Farmers Union) still exist; others have merged or died. Includes unions (Sheepshearers' Union), commodity and breed groups (Dairy Farmers of America), and interest groups (International Flying Farmers). Some were national organizations with local membership, like the Farm Holiday Association, which recruited heavily in the Great Plains in the early 1930s, and some, like the Oklahoma Renters Union and Knights of Reciprocity (Kansas), were local. Others (e.g., National Colored Progressive Farmers' Union, which operated in Texas and Oklahoma, and the ubiquitous Four-H Club), attracted specific populations. Unhappily, the many organizations devoted to the needs of farm women are excluded. Entries, based on primary and secondary sources, range from a paragraph to ten pages. Each ends with information about sources and strategies for research. Three appendixes list headquarters by state, chief executive officers of selected farm organizations, and estimated membership of selected farm organizations. Useful to researchers in labor issues, history, farming, sociology, and politics. — *JD*

G15   Loucks, William L. - **Windbreak Bibliography**. - [Lincoln, NE?] : Forestry Committee, Great Plains Agricultural Council, [1983]. - 111 p. - (Great Plains Agricultural Council publication, 113).

> Class Numbers:
> Library of Congress Z5991
> LCCN 89-111131
> Notes:
> Index of topics, p. 108-111
> Reproduced from typescript

• Loucks's bibliography, arranged by author, lists about 1,700 items drawn primarily from periodicals and government publications. The index is arranged by broad subjects, many heavily posted ("Management" has about 275 entries), that refer to item numbers. Although a good share of entries have some bearing on the use of windbreaks on the Plains, where they were heavily planted in the 1930s, those entries cannot be identified except by scanning them all. — *RB*

BARBED WIRE

G16   Campbell, Robert O. - **Barriers : An Encyclopedia of United States Barbed Fence Patents** / [by] Robert O. Campbell [and] Vernon L. Allison. - Denver, CO : Western Profiles Publ. Co., 1986. - 460 p. ; ill.

> Class Numbers:
>   Library of Congress TS271
>   ISBN 0937231002
>   LCCN 86-50126
>   Notes:
>   Bibliography: p. 457-460

• Campbell and Allison's practical guide to the identification of barbed wire, also a comprehensive source on barbed wire patents, draws from over 500 U.S. Patent Office records beginning in 1867 for barbed wire, barbed picket fencing, barbed cattle guards, fencing hand tools, and tool and die machinery. Foreign patents and those without clear illustrations and descriptions are excluded. Organized chronologically, entries give date, name of patent holder, patent number, drawings, and salient excerpts from the files. The complexity and sheer number of the designs depict the development of an industry and its importance to the cattle business. Seven chapters divide the entries into time periods and summarize innovations and popular styles. An index by patent holder and a bibliography are included. Provides access to primary materials and functions as a collector's handbook. — *JD*

G17   Glover, Jack. - **"Bobbed" Wire : An Illustrated Guide to the Identification and Classification of Barbed Wire** / ill. by Gary Odle - Wichita Falls, TX : Terry Bros., 1966. - 49 leaves ; ill.

> Class Numbers:
>   Library of Congress TS271
>   OCLC 2569737
>   LCCN 66-4208

• A marketing tool for commercial trading posts, Glover's guide is also an identification guide for collectors and dealers. Of the thousands of variations of barbed wire, 160 of the "major" wires are illustrated by clear drawings captioned with names or types. Patent dates are usually given but patent numbers, unfortunately, are omitted.

Glover apparently hoped his own entry numbers would become standard classifications. Twenty fencing tools and staples are also included. Criteria for inclusion and the arrangement are unclear though similar wires appear to be grouped. — *JD*

FARM BUILDINGS

G18   Noble, Allen George, 1930-   . - **The Old Barn Book : A Field Guide to North American Barns and Other Farm Structures** / [by] Allen G. Noble and Richard K. Cleek ; ill. by M. Margaret Geib. - New Brunswick, NJ : Rutgers Univ. Pr., c1995. - 222 p. ; ill., map.

> Class Numbers:
>   Library of Congress NA8230
>   ISBN 0813521726   0813521734 (pbk.)
>   OCLC 31434972
>   LCCN 94-41300
>   Notes:
>   Based on v. 2, *Barns and Farm Structures*, of Noble's
>   *Wood, Brick, and Stone*. Amherst, MA: Univ. of
>   Massachusetts Pr., 1984
>   Includes bibliographical references (p. [201]-210); index

• The authors' field guide to the rural landscape describes barns and other farm structures. Their design varies with local materials, climate, economics, ethnic group, use, and technology. On the Plains, windmills, storm cellars, and German barns are common, but other forms and combinations also occur. The book supplies an overview of barn types and specific barn features (wall materials, foundations, roof design, hay hoods, ventilators, dormers, bridges and entries, porches, windows, wall openings and doors, sheds, decorations). Types of barns include crib, crib-derived, ethnic, newer, and special purpose. Other farm buildings (in a separate section) include chicken houses, windmills, granaries, hay barracks, fences, summer kitchens, cisterns, storm cellars, and privies. Entries include location and distribution, range maps, sketches, and photographs. The book ends with a list of structures common or important in specific locales (limestone barns and fence posts in Kansas, hay stackers in Wyoming, Czech barns in South Dakota). Sources of information are arranged by barn type, and the index refers to places, features, barn types, and use. For architectural, agricultural, and cultural historians and enthusiasts. The work on which the guide is based offers additional information. — *JD*

GRAIN

G19   Aldis, David F. - **Review of Literature Related to Engineering Aspects of Grain Dust Explosions** / by David F. Aldis and Fang S. Lai. - [Washington, DC] : [U.S.] Dept. of Agriculture, Science and Education Administration, 1979. - 42 p. ; ill. - (United States. Dept. of Agriculture. Miscellaneous publication, 1375).

Class Numbers:
  Government Document A 1.38:1375
Notes:
  Bibliography: p. 32-37
  Prepared in cooperation with Kansas State University

• A critical review of published literature on grain dust explosions, principally devoted to a topical survey arranged by general categories: definitions, causes and effects of explosions, theoretical analysis, and prevention methodologies, each subdivided as appropriate. The remaining fourth of this pamphlet contains an alphabetical list of works cited and a glossary of terms. The survey section is enhanced with charts and illustrations. Usefulness diminished by its age. — *MB*

Site List 17
Agriculture Information Networks

AgNIC Agricultural Network Information Center
http://www.agnic.org

Supported by the National Agricultural Library, AgNIC is a cooperative of universities, research institutions, government agencies, and nonprofit organizations that supplies expert current and historical information about agriculture and related areas. Topics of interest to Prairies-Plains researchers include viticulture, medicinal plants, farmland preservation, animal waste management, water quality, sustainable agriculture, beef cattle production, western rangelands, and specific crops. AgNIC's database includes images, full-text documents, and lists of publications, and services such as discussion groups, calendar of events, news, and reference and expert services.

National Agricultural Library http://agricola.nal.usda.gov

The world's largest agricultural library, NAL holds 3.5 million items and administers a national network of state land-grant and USDA field libraries, NAL's catalog, *AGRICOLA* (**G1**), provides full text of many publications, links to Internet sites, and includes a vast range of topics and formats of interest to Prairies-Plains producers, researchers, and businesses, many focusing specifically on the region or its states. Topics include livestock registries, agricultural statistics, inventions and patents, bibliographies, plant databases, image galleries, manuscript guides, research reports, and technical articles. NAL offers reference service ("Ask a Question") and spotlights intriguing material in "Browse by Subject."

Cooperative Extension System
The nationwide CES system maintains state offices at land-grant universities that serve a network of local offices. Local offices are staffed by specialists who provide "useful, practical, and research-based information to agricultural producers, small business owners, youth, consumers, and others in rural

G20   Grain & Milling Annual. - (1990?)-   . Kansas City, MO : Sosland Publ. Co., 1990s-   . Annual.

Class Numbers:
  Library of Congress TS2120
  LCCN 98-660582   sn 97-33510
Notes:
  "A joint publication of Milling & Baking News and World Grain"
  Preceding title: *North American Grain and Milling Annual*; ISSN 1082-1740

• A directory of the grain industry, this annual includes North American grain companies and elevators, milling companies and mills, industry statistics, and a buyer's guide

areas and communities of all sizes" on topics such as pets, food, nutrition, agriculture, and natural resources. The federal partner, the Dept. of Agriculture's Cooperative State Research, Education, and Extension Service (http://www.csrees.usda.gov), offers links to all state extension office Internet sites and experiment stations, directory information, and e-mail links to local offices.

State Offices:

Colorado State Univ. Cooperative Extension
  http://www.ext.colostate.edu

Kansas State Univ. Research and Extension
  http://www.oznet.ksu.edu

Montana State Univ. Extension Service
  http://extn.msu.montana.edu

Univ. of Nebraska. Cooperative Extension
  http://www.extension.unl.edu

New Mexico State Univ. Cooperative Extension Service
  http://www.cahe.nmsu.edu/ces

North Dakota State Univ. NDSU Extension Service
  http://www.ext.nodak.edu

Oklahoma State Univ. Cooperative Extension Service
  http://www2.dasnr.okstate.edu

South Dakota State Univ. Cooperative Extension
  http://www3.sdstate.edu/CooperativeExtension

Texas A&M University. Texas Cooperative Extension http://texasextension.tamu.edu

Univ. of Wyoming. Cooperative Extension Service
  http://uwadmnweb.uwyo.edu/UWces

for equipment, products, services, and manufacturers. Directory entries give location, phone, fax, e-mail, URL, selected personnel, facility type, license, loadout and receiving capabilities, railroad, switching carrier, capacities, and products. A trade publication used by purchasers, the annual offers classifieds, highlighted listings, and other advertisements. Portions of the annual available on the publisher's Internet site (http://www.world-grain.com) include selected current and historical industry statistics and a search engine for companies, mills, and elevators by company name, personnel, type of location, and type of grain. —*JD*

G21   Grain Elevators of North America. - [1st ed.] (1900?) - 5th ed. (1942). - Chicago, IL : Grain & Feed Journals, 1900s-1942. - Irregular.

> OCLC 29804216
> Notes:
>> 5th ed. (1942); no more published
>> Each edition contains only new material
>> Earlier eds. publ. under title: *Plans of Grain Elevators*; publ. by Grain Dealers Journal

• Devoted to the design, construction, and equipping of grain elevators; written for grain dealers. Each edition describes new elevator designs. The classification scheme for elevators is based on type of grain and type of construction. An index lists elevators by class and location. Entries include blueprints, plans, photographs, and detailed description of operation. The industry had to apply new technology to cope with power limitations, grain dust explosions, and fire hazards. Includes advertisements. For architectural, farm, and grain industry historians. —*JD*

G22   Wrigley, Colin W., ed.-in-chief. - Encyclopedia of Grain Science / ed.-in-chief, Colin Wrigley ; ed. by Harold Corke and Charles Walker. - Oxford, UK : Academic, 2004. - 3 v. ; ill.

> Class Numbers:
>> Library of Congress SB188.4
> ISBN 0127654909 (set) 0127654917 (v. 1)
>> 0127654925 (v. 2)   0127654933 (v. 3)
> LCCN 2004-104693
> Notes:
>> Includes bibliographical references; index
>> Review by H.F. Smith: *Choice* 42.7 (Mar. 2005): review 42-3777

• Although this encyclopedia assuredly considers grains, agricultural methods, diseases, crop genetics, and a host of other topics of concern to researchers, farmers, and residents of the Prairies-Plains region, it is pitched at such a distant level of discourse and is so lacking in any regional

component that Prairies-Plains readers will be able to use it only to fix the context of a line of inquiry. The editors (Wrigley is with Food Science Australia, Corke with Univ. of Hong Kong, and Walker with Kansas State Univ.) and a host of contributors take up cereals, barley, wheat, maize, soybeans, stored grain, all of Plains interest, but even when they talk of "Grain Production and Consumption" (v. 2, p. 61-134), and include North America, their analysis does not descend below the country level of Canada, the U.S., and Mexico. An able work, compiled by specialists for specialists, but only tangentially useful in Prairies-Plains research. — *RB*

SOILS AND SOIL MANAGEMENT

See also Powter, **A Bibliography of Baseline Studies in Alberta, EA18**

G23   Aandahl, Andrew Russell, 1912-   . - Soils of the Great Plains : Land Use, Crops, and Grasses. - Lincoln, NE : Univ. of Nebraska Pr., 1982. - 282 p. ; col. ill.

> Class Numbers:
>> Library of Congress S599.A1
> ISBN 0803210116   9780803210110
> OCLC 7554389
> LCCN 81-7435
> Notes:
>> Bibliography: p. 275-276; index
>> One folded col. map laid in

• Written for students, farmers, ranchers, conservationists and others interested in developing the Plains in ways adapted to its environment. The centerpiece is a soil map (in pocket) published in 1972, which used a new classification system recently developed by the USDA, based on soil temperature and moisture, factors of great interest to a dry region with cycles of drought. The book itself is organized by 18 principal soil types—about 800 soil series. Entries for each soil type describe the soil as it exists in each of 195 Great Plains regions or "mapping units" distinguished on the soil map. Descriptions have a paragraph for each of three factors: (1) general characteristics such as topography and particle size; (2) soil composition; and (3) land use, crops, and grasses. Land use and crop information is from Census data and soil survey reports; the information on grasses was drawn from reports of the Soil Conservation Service. An appendix, which may be the section of greatest interest, has color photographs of landscapes and soil profiles for 70 of the 800 soil series, alphabetically arranged. Includes an essay on range use and management, a plant names list, suggested readings, and an index by soil series. While a more up-to-date soil taxonomy exists for the U.S. (**G26**), this is a classic, still cited for its soil descriptions and photographic profiles. — *JD*

G24 Cann, M.C. - **The Impacts of Soil Degradation on Crop Yields in the Canadian Prairies : An Annotated Bibliography** / [by] M. Cann, J. Dumanski and M. Brklacich ; ed. by V. Kirkwood. - Ottawa, ON : Research Branch, Agriculture Canada, 1992. - 227 p. - (CLBRR contribution ; no. 92-73).

> ISBN 0662202198
> OCLC 31527974
> Notes:
>> Includes bibliographical references (p. 207-227)

• The work begins with a literature review of soil degradation in relation to fertility. The annotations are extensive and include summary methods, degradation type, crop type, land management, location, impact results, productivity abstract, and key words. When no Canadian studies could be located, reports from Midwestern U.S. states are included. Organized by degradation type (wind and water erosion, compaction, salinization, and acidification), grouped by crop. Separate lists of annotated and unannotated references, both listed by author. The *AGRICOLA* database (http://agricola.nal.usda.gov/; **G1**), freely available at the National Agricultural Library Internet site, indexes more recent material. — *LMcD*

G25 National Agricultural Library (U.S.). - **A Selected Bibliography on Weather-Crop Relations in the Great Plains** / comp. in the Library of the U.S. Dept. of Agriculture by Elizabeth Gould Davis. - Washington, DC : National Agricultural Library, 1956. - 16 p.

> Class Numbers:
>> Library of Congress Z8883.A4
> OCLC 63982857
> LCCN 57-60683

Site List 18
Agricultural Statistics Services

The most important state agricultural statistics sources are periodicals published by the state Agricultural Statistics Services, which are field offices of the Dept. of Agriculture National Agricultural Statistics Service (NASS). Prairies-Plains state services publish annual agricultural statistical summaries and weekly crop condition and weather reports. Other publications vary by state. Many of these periodicals have long histories, though beginning dates are difficult to determine and changes in title and agency are frequent. Current issues and some backfiles can be found at "Statistics by State" at NASS' Internet site (http://www.nass.usda.gov). That site also offers state data from Census of Agriculture and other sources, agricultural overviews, and interactive state statistical maps.

Colorado
> *Ag Update*. Biweekly, 1981- .
> *Colorado Agricultural Statistics Bulletin*. Annual, 1883?- .

Kansas
> *Crop Weather*. Weekly.
> *Kansas Farm Facts*. Annual.

Montana
> *Crop Weather Report*. Weekly.
> *Montana Crop and Livestock Reporter*. Biweekly, 1979- .
> *Montana Agricultural Statistics*. Annual.

Nebraska
> *Nebraska Weather and Crops*. Bimonthly.
> *Agri-Facts*. Semimonthly.
> *Nebraska Agricultural Statistics*. Annual, 1923- .

New Mexico
> *Weekly Ag Update*. 1977- .
> *New Mexico Agricultural Statistics*. Annual, 1962- .

North Dakota
> *North Dakota Crop, Livestock & Weather Report*. Weekly, 1956- .
> *North Dakota Farm Reporter*. Biweekly, 1975- .
> *North Dakota Annual Statistics Bulletin*.

Oklahoma
> *Oklahoma Crop Weather*. Weekly.
> *Oklahoma Farm Statistics*. Biweekly, 1981- .
> *Oklahoma Agricultural Statistics*. Annual, 1976- .

South Dakota
> *South Dakota Crop and Livestock Reporter*. Biweekly.
> *South Dakota Agriculture*. Annual.
> *County Level Land Rents and Values*. Annual.

Texas
> *Texas Crop Weather*. Weekly.
> *Agricultural Facts*. Monthly.
> *Texas Agricultural Statistics*. Annual, 1994- .

Wyoming
> *Crop-Weather Report*. Weekly.
> *Range Review*. Monthly
> *Wyoming Agricultural Statistics*. Annual.

• Davis's 188-item bibliography is useful for anyone researching the history of land use, drought, agricultural methods, and crop development in the Great Plains. Unannotated citations are arranged under five headings: "General," "Economic Aspects," "Crops," "Range, Forage and Livestock," and "Research Methodology." "Crops" has subheadings for general, barley, beets, corn, oats, sorghum, and wheat. The books, articles, theses, and government reports date from 1916 to 1955 and relate events and data as far back as 1866. Representative titles are "Frequency, Extent, and Severity of Drought Since 1881" (1935), "Is the West Drying Up?" (1936), "Institutional Methods of Meeting Weather Uncertainty in the Great Plains" (1950), and "Farmers' Adaptation to Income Uncertainty" (1950). Notes give the experiment station, government agency, university, association, or company responsible for the research. *— JD*

G26   United States. Natural Resources Conservation Service. - **Soil Taxonomy : A Basic System of Soil Classification for Making and Interpreting Soil Surveys**. - 2nd ed. - Washington, DC : U.S. Dept of Agriculture, Natural Resources Conservation Service, 1999. - 869 p. : ill. (some col.), maps ; 29 cm. - (Agriculture Handbook, 436).

    Class Numbers:
        Library of Congress S21   S592.16
        Government document A 1.76:436
    OCLC 42281600
    Notes:
        Two folded colored maps in pocket.

• This standard source on soil classification provides scientists with descriptions and data on soils worldwide. It forms the basis for soil surveys used to study crops, forage, conservation, wildlife habitat, recreational development and other topics of interest to the Plains. Following chapters on taxonomy, nomenclature, diagnostic characteristics, and application to soil surveys, twelve soil types and their distribution are described in highly technical detail. With no index by location, two color maps in the pocket are essential for understanding the distribution of soils in the Great Plains. Text and maps are available in pdf format from the USDA Internet site at http://purl.access.gpo.gov/GPO/ LPS37493. *— JD*

WINDMILLS

G27   Baker, T. Lindsay. - **A Field Guide to American Windmills** / foreword by Donald E. Green. - Norman, OK : Univ. of Oklahoma Pr., 1985. - 516 p. ; ill.

    Class Numbers:
        Library of Congress TJ825

    ISBN 0806119012
    OCLC 10948414
    LCCN 84-40272
    Notes:
        Bibliography: p. 459-503; index

• In Part 1, Baker provides a footnoted, heavily illustrated history of American windmills, which were a mark of white settlement in the Plains and are still used to draw water for cattle. Part 2 is a windmill identification guide to some 100 common windmills, organized by manufacturer and model, with silhouettes, photographs, and detailed descriptions of the models' operations. Two appendixes list windmill manufacturers and over 1,000 known windmill models (e.g., Everlasting, Sanspareil, Vaneless Governor, Hewitt's Sancho Panza). The bibliography of sources includes catalogs, manufacturers' trade literature, farm implement periodicals, business directories, sales brochures, government publications, books, articles, and interviews. Locations are noted for all archival records. A scholarly work that will also interest hobbyists. *— JD*

CATTLE TRADE

General Works

G28   Adams, Ramon Frederick, 1889-1976. - **The Rampaging Herd : A Bibliography of Books and Pamphlets on Men and Events in the Cattle Industry**. - Norman, OK : Univ. of Oklahoma Pr., 1959. - 46 p. ; facsims.

    Class Numbers:
        Library of Congress Z5074.L7
    LCCN 59-7957

• Adams sees cattle and cattlemen as civilizing influences preparing the way for European settlers. The bibliography is celebratory, avoiding issues such as habitat destruction, appropriate land use, and displacement of tribes, but it covers a wide range of materials of interest to both scholars and amateur historians and is especially useful for finding accounts of life on the Plains. Most entries are primary sources from the 19th and early 20th centuries, including government pamphlets, railroad advertisements, brand books, memoirs, reminiscences, and travelers' accounts. Secondary sources include county histories, travel guides, and biographies. Cowboy songs and poetry, animal science, and cattle industry titles are excluded. Although the title implies women will be ignored, they are covered in a section of works by and about women. Entries offer detailed physical descriptions and notes about rarity, and a few have brief annotations, but the lengthy titles of early works make explanations unnecessary. Indexed by author, title, and subject. *— JD*

G29   Reese, William S. - **Six Score : The 120 Best Books on the Range Cattle Industry**. - Austin, TX : Jenkins Publ. Co., 1976. - 85 p. ; facsims. - (Contributions to bibliography series).

Class Numbers:
Library of Congress SF196.U5   Z5074.C33
OCLC 2468470
LCCN 76-8956
Notes:
Index

• The author's choice of the "best and most representative" books about the cattle industry from 1835 to 1972 include ranch, county, and industry histories; works on Western art, music, folklore, and culture; and fiction. Primary documents include autobiographies, promotional literature, brand books, and government reports. The geographic focus is balanced: works on the West, the Great Plains, and each of the Plains states are included, though books on Texas ranching are distinctly in the majority. Geared to collectors, the entries provide detailed physical descriptions of first editions and dust jackets, along with annotations on contents, references to previous bibliographies, and reproductions of nine title pages. Some titles are rare. Indexed by author and title. — *JD*

G30   Rouse, John E. - **Cattle of North America**. - Norman, OK : Univ. of Oklahoma Pr., 1973. - 650 p. ; ill. - (World cattle, 3).

Class Numbers:
Library of Congress SF196.A43
ISBN 0806110236
LCCN 72-861
Notes:
Bibliography: p. 637-641

• Rouse (rancher, Wyoming) in the third volume of this series provides a comprehensive guide to the history of cattle, breeds, management practices, marketing, auction procedures, government regulations, diseases, and slaughterhouse facilities in North America. Part 4 contains information on breeds commonly found in the U.S., particularly those raised in the Prairies-Plains and Southwest: Holstein, Herefords, Longhorns, and Black Angus (Aberdeen-Angus). Includes illustrations, four appendixes, 13 figures and maps, and a bibliography. — *GK*

G31   Vallentine, John F. - **Range Science : A Guide to Information Sources** / [by] John F. Vallentine [and] Phillip L. Sims. - Detroit, MI : Gale Research Co., 1980. - 231 p. - (Natural world information guide series, v. 2 ; Gale information guide library).

Class Numbers:
Library of Congress Z5074.R27
ISBN 0810314207
LCCN 80-14361
Notes:
Indexes

• Although the sections on online literature searching are obsolete and the lists of relevant journals and organizations need updating, the primary chapter, "Selected Literature of Range Science," is a useful bibliography of titles relating to livestock, ranches, wildlife, watersheds, grazing, plants, natural resources, economics, and range research and education published during a period of growth in range science. Many are difficult to identify and locate (e.g., agricultural experiment station bulletins, state and federal technical reports, state agency bulletins, and conference papers). Organized by broad subject with author, organization, title, and subject indexes. Of interest to historical and applied research. — *JD*

BRANDS

G32   Ford, Gus Lee. - **Texas Cattle Brands : A Catalog of the Texas Centennial Exposition Exhibit, 1936**. - Dallas, TX : Clyde C. Cockrell Co., [1936?]. - 240 p.

Class Numbers:
Library of Congress SF103.T4
OCLC 2521456

• Consists of three main sections covering brands, branding irons, and portraits of prominent ranchers. Entries listing 789 brands used from the Spanish period until the 1930s are organized chronologically, provide information about the brand holder(s) and their property, and are accompanied by line drawings. Entries covering branding irons are organized numerically and are accompanied by line drawings. Introductory essays cover the Texas Cattleman's Association, brands as sign of possession, and Texas cattle. Two indexes of popular names, the first of brands, the second of branding irons. Four historical maps and one map showing cattle trails complete the catalog. A revised index, *Index, Texas Cattle Brands*, ed. by Vera Meek Wimberley was published: Conroe, TX: Montgomery County Genealogical and Historical Society, 1990. — *MS*

G33   **Nebraska Brand Book [Internet Site]** / Nebraska Brand Committee. - Alliance, NE : Nebraska Brand Committee, 2000?-   . - http://nbc.nol.org/brandbook/book.cgi

OCLC 21540719 (print)
Access Date: Jan. 2006
Notes:
Producer varies: 1941– , Nebraska Brand Committee;

1908-1941, various state agencies

Title varies: *Nebraska Livestock Brand Book*; *State of Nebraska Official Brand Book*; *Official Brand Book of the State of Nebraska*

Updated weekly

Fees: None

• The Nebraska Brand Committee, created by the legislature in 1941 to inspect cattle and investigate cases of missing or stolen cattle, produces *Brand Book* to assist in identifying ownership of cattle. Brands are still the primary visual means for the identification of cattle ownership, and the *Brand Book* Internet site provides the most current information about brands. Its nearly 35,000 entries of expired or active brands may be browsed in its entirety or searched by brand number, brand images (numbers, letters, shapes), brand owner, county, brand position, or renewal date. Editions in print of *Brand Book* are produced every four years, and the Nebraska Library Commission distributes copies on microfiche to Nebraska depository libraries. Although designed for the cattle industry, Brand Book offers unique information for researchers in the history of ranching, ranches and ranch families, and brands. — *JD*

COWHANDS

G34   Porter, Willard H., 1920-   . - **Who's Who in Rodeo**. - Oklahoma City, OK : Powder River Book Co. ; distr. by National Cowboy Hall of Fame, 1982. - 224 p. ; [4] leaves of plates, ill.

Class Numbers:
    Library of Congress GV1833.5
    ISBN 093215412
    OCLC 9174738
    LCCN 82-62362
Notes:
    Includes bibliographies; index

• Since rodeos are important in Great Plains culture, Plains states are well represented in lists of rodeos and rodeo cowboys. Cowboys honored in Rodeo Hall at the National Cowboy Hall of Fame (NCHF) include men and women, old-time cowboys, and modern athletes. Porter covers them in two sections: elected honorees and automatic inductees who are Professional Rodeo Cowboys Association (PRCA) All-Around Champion cowboys of the year. Two-page biographies focus on their rodeo careers but include some personal information. Entries include photographs—portraits, memorabilia, and action shots. A bibliography with each entry cites articles from local publications (e.g., *Wyoming Eagle, Laramie Daily Boomerang* [WY], *Duncan Daily Banner* [OK]) and specialized periodicals (e.g., *Persimmon Hill* [NCHF], *Western Horseman*). The citations omit page numbers. Appendixes consist of a

cumulative list of nominations to the NCHF; descriptions of rodeo contests and events; rodeo groups and associations; a glossary of range, ranch, and rodeo terms; and an index by name. The front matter includes a joint index by name of honoree or inductee. A good source for Western culture, rodeo culture, and individuals like Lucille Mulhall, the Oklahoma rancher who was the first woman billed as a cowgirl, and Bill Pickett, the black cowboy who originated the no longer acceptable "bite-em-down" style of bulldogging. — *JD*

G35   Rickey, Don. - **$10 Horse, $40 Saddle : Cowboy Clothing, Arms, Tools, and Horse Gear of the 1880's** / by Don Rickey Jr. ; illustrated by Dale Crawford. - Ft. Collins, CO : Old Army Pr., 1976. - 135 p. ; ill.

Class Numbers:
    Library of Congress F594
    LCCN 76-9411
Notes:
    Bibliography: p. 134-135

• Open range Plains cowboys, whose numbers peaked in the mid-1880s, were a brief phenomenon with lasting appeal. Their accoutrements, generally cheap, functional, and influenced by their Texas origins, did not resemble those of movie cowboys. To show the look of the real cowboy of that period, the authors depict items in four categories—clothing, gear, weapons, and tools—with drawings and text. Specific entries include hats, chaps, revolvers, knives, quirts, and branding irons. An entertaining and instructive work on real life cowboys and a send-up of the myth. Much of the information came from interviews with nine men who had been cowboys in the 1880s. Includes biographical sketches of the informants and sources for further reading on the open range cattle era. — *JD*

G36   Slatta, Richard W., 1947-   . - **The Cowboy Encyclopedia**. - Santa Barbara, CA : ABC-CLIO, 1994. - 474 p. ; ill.

Class Numbers:
    Library of Congress E20
    ISBN 0874367387
    LCCN 94-19824
Notes:
    Includes bibliographical references (p. 427-451); index

• Arranged in traditional alphabetic format with an index, entries in Slatta's encyclopedia include persons, fictional characters, places, organizations, expressions, and concepts. Some entries are merely cross-references, others a single line of a few words. In that sense the book often doubles as a dictionary of cowboy terms, but most entries have more detail. The handful of illustrations are more decorative than functional. Appendix A is a guide to film and video sources, Appendix B lists a selection of pertinent museums, Appendix C cites two dozen periodicals, with addresses, phone numbers, and descriptions, and Appendix D covers a sampling of annual events, with contact information. Many of the contact numbers are likely to be out of date. Bibliography of about 500 items. — *MB*

RANGE MANAGEMENT

G37   Abouguendia, Zoheir M. - **Management and Improvement of Saskatchewan Rangeland : A Selected Bibliography** / prepared by Z. Abouguendia, J. Haraldson, J. Valby. - [Saskatoon, SK] : Saskatchewan Research Council, 1981. - 80 p. - (SRC technical report , 112 ; SRC publication C-805-22-B-81).

> Class Numbers:
>   Library of Congress SF85.4.C2
>   OCLC 15979341

• Lists 534 items on range ecology published 1923-1981. The scope is larger than the title would suggest, since many of the publications deal with the Northern Plains generally, not solely Saskatchewan. Fertilization, grazing effects, range evaluation, and soils are some of the areas covered. Major topics such as forage plants, grasslands, range plants, and parklands are subdivided by aspect. Author, subject, and chronological indexes. — *LMcD*

SHEEP

G38   **Montana Sheep Directory** / [Montana Dept. of Agriculture in cooperation with the Montana Wool Growers Association]. - Helena, MT : Montana Dept. of Agriculture, 2007. - 56 p. : ill.

> Class Numbers:
>   Library of Congress HD9436.M6
> OCLC 124082663
> Notes:
> Electronic book: http://agr.mt.gov/business/SheepDir/
>   Sheepindex.asp
> Index

• Descriptions of sheep breeds with producers of each, and lists of industry services, supplies, and contacts mainly, but not exclusively, located in Montana. — *LMcD*

WOMEN

G39   **Texas Women on the Cattle Trails** / ed. by Sara R. Massey. - College Station, TX : Texas A&M Univ., 2006. - 326 p. ; ill., map. - (Sam Rayburn series on rural life, 13).

> Class Numbers:
>   Library of Congress F391
> ISBN 9781585445431
> LCCN 2006-1539
> Notes:
> Review by Judy Alter: *Great Plains Quarterly* 28.1 (winter 2008): 77-78

• An introductory overview of women and cattle drives sets the stage for the biographies that follow and contrasts stereotypical images of Western women with the realities that research reveals. The period of coverage (1868-1889) is divided into three periods. Most of the biographies treat women who were well-known ranchers' wives or ran their own ranches; a few were trail hands or traveled with drives as an adventure. Entries range from five to 15 pages and have ample photographs and maps. Excellent bibliography and index. — *JB*

H : Military Science ; War

Scope   Includes works on military history in general, in so far as they are concerned with Western wars and engagements, the enlisted men who did the fighting (even some officers), the Indians who were their opponents, and descriptions of forts and outposts. See also the heading "Wars" in Section **CD, INDIANS, CD125-133.**

General Works

H1   Fredriksen, John C. - **America's Military Adversaries : From Colonial Times to the Present**. - Santa Barbara, CA : ABC-CLIO, 2001. - 621 p. ; ill.

Class Numbers:
    Library of Congress E181
    ISBN 1576076032 1576076040 (electronic bk.)
    OCLC 52467882 (electronic bk.)
    LCCN 2001-5293
        Bibliography: p. 546-595; index
        Electronic book: http://www.netLibrary.com/urlapi.asp?
            action-summary&v=1&bookid=76042

• Fredriksen (an independent scholar specializing in military history) arranges this encyclopedia by the names of 223 leaders who opposed the U.S. in any of its wars from earliest colonization through the 1991 Gulf War. Entries are headed by the opponent's name and birth-death dates and a brief statement of his (or in the case of Tokyo Rose, her) role in opposition (Crazy Horse is a "Sioux War Chief"). Entries vary considerably in length, and all are followed by useful bibliographies. For the Prairies-Plains region, all the opponents are Indians, who can be easily identified by two appendixes that list subjects by occupation ("Cheyenne War Chief") and by conflict (all Indian opponents are listed under "Frontier Wars"). Confederate generals constitute the largest number of entries. Fredriksen wrote all the entries, which are factual and straightforward but written in a supple style. Fifty-page general bibliography; index.— *RB*

H2   **A Guide to the Sources of United States Military History** / ed. by Robin Higham. - Hamden, CT ; North Haven, CT : Archon Books, 1975-1998. – 559 p.

Class Numbers:
    Library of Congress E181   Z1249.M5
    ISBN 0208014993
    LCCN 75-14455
    Notes:

Supplement I, ed. by Higham and Donald J. Mrozek.
    Hamden, CT: Archon Books. 300 p.; covers works publ.
    1973-1978
Supplement II, ed. by Higham and Mrozek. Hamden, CT:
    Archon Books, 1986. 332 p.; covers works publ. 1978-
    1983
Supplement III, ed. by Higham and Mrozek. Hamden,
    CT: Archon Books, 1993. 531 p.
Supplement IV, ed. by Higham and Mrozek. North
    Haven, CT: Archon Books, 1998. 580 p.

• The base volume's 19 chapters deal with topics ranging from "Colonial Forces" to "The Navy 1941-1973." The Indian Wars of the Great Plains do not earn a separate category; they are covered in the chapter titled "Civil-Military Relations, Operations, and the Army, 1865-1917." This chapter includes a bibliographic essay and a list of nearly 300 items of interest. Each of the four supplemental volumes follows the same organization, but with some modern additions that are not applicable to Plains studies.— *MB*

H3   Hacker, Barton C., 1935-   . - **World Military History Bibliography : Premodern and Nonwestern Military Institutions and Hardware**. - Leiden ; Boston, MA: Brill, 2003. - 834 p. - (History of warfare, v. 16).

Class Numbers:
    Library of Congress D25   Z6724
    ISBN 9004129979
    LCCN 2003-51938
    Notes:
        Index

H3a   Hacker, Barton C., 1935-   . - **World Military History Annotated Bibliography : Premodern and Nonwestern Military Institutions (Works Published before 1967)**. - Leiden ; Boston, MA : Brill, 2005. – 305 p. - (History of warfare, v. 27 ; ISSN 1385-7827).

Class Numbers:
    Library of Congress Z6724   D25
    ISBN 9004140719
    LCCN 2005-295185

• Hacker (Smithsonian Institution) focuses on "studies of preclassical and indigenous nonwestern military institutions" published 1967-1997, including studies of specific engagements or wars only so far as they illuminate the book's principal concern, the place of military institutions in society. Entries (they are unnumbered, but there are about 7,000) are arranged according to the categories cited in the contents note above, each having several subcategories. Entries are carefully complete, and many include brief annotations. Prairies-Plains students will find several categories fruitful: in part 1, "Disease and Conquest"; in part 5, "Precontact North America"; in part

6, "Western North America" and "National Indian Wars." Anyone interested in the roles of war and the military in building and destroying societies will find useful citations in part 8. Name index. An unusual and serious approach to the study of war and the military. The 2005 addition covers works published before 1967, and considers "medieval and early modern West European military institutions only in the context of European colonialism and imperialism" (Preface). The arrangement differs slightly; Prairies-Plains researchers will find relevant titles in two sections, in Part 6 under the subheading "Precontact North America," and in Part 7 under "Plains."— *RB*

H4   Kinnell, Susan K., ed. - **Military History of the United States : An Annotated Bibliography** / foreword by Timothy K. Nenninger. - Santa Barbara, CA : ABC-CLIO, 1986. - 333 p.

     Class Numbers:
        Library of Congress E181   Z1249 M5
     ISBN 0874364744
     OCLC 14214876

• More useful at the time of publication than in today's online research world, Kinnell's bibliography draws its entries from *America: History and Life*. Organized by time periods, 16th century to 1985, entries include scholarly articles and book reviews published between 1974 and 1985, and dissertations. An extremely thorough subject index uses the style of the print AHL in which each index entry is assigned a set of subject terms that rotate so that citations appear under each term. As a guide to military history, it naturally focuses on military people, institutions, and tactics. Events in the Great Plains can be searched by locations, military personnel, battles, and topics. Author index.— *JD*

H5   Marley, David F. - **Wars of the Americas : A Chronology of Armed Conflict in the New World, 1492 to the Present**. - Santa Barbara, CA : ABC-CLIO, 1998. - 722 p. ; ill,. maps.

     Class Numbers:
        Library of Congress E18.75
     ISBN 0874368375 1576075044 (electronic bk.)
     LCCN 98-21209
     Notes:
        Electronic book: http://www.netLibrary.com/urlapi.asp? action=summary&v=1&bookid=56905
        Includes bibliographical references (p. 677-689); index

• Includes only conflicts confined to the Western Hemisphere. Some entries treat specific wars, others cover clusters of wars or confrontations. Illustrated with maps, photographs, and drawings, entries have brief introductions followed by briefer descriptions of wars, battles, skirmishes, and significant events. A list of further readings is included

but sources for the entries are not cited. Though not a scholarly work, it provides an overview of the political evolution of the continent and an introduction to conflicts on the Plains, particularly in the 19th century. Indexed by names of battles and participants.— *JD*

Soldiers

H6   **Soldiers West : Biographies from the Military Frontier** / ed. by Paul Andrew Hutton ; introd. by Robert M. Utley. - Lincoln, NE : Univ. of Nebraska Pr., 1987. - 276 p. ; ill., ports.

     Class Numbers:
        Library of Congress F591
     ISBN 080322334X   0803272251 (pbk.)
     OCLC 14130937
     LCCN 86-19283
     Notes:
        Includes bibliographies; index

• This work investigates the military role in the trans-Mississippi West by exploring major figures and their contributions on the frontier. Each military leader is featured in an article written by a noted scholar. The introduction is written by Robert M. Utley, an eminent frontier military historian. A photograph of each individual accompanies each essay. Contributor list, four maps.— *GK*

H7   O'Neal, Bill, 1942- . - **Fighting Men of the Indian Wars : A Biographical Encyclopedia of the Mountain Men, Soldiers, Cowboys, and Pioneers Who Took up Arms during America's Westward Expansion**. - Stillwater, OK : Barbed Wire Pr., 1991. - 255 p. ; ill.

     Class Numbers:
        Library of Congress E81
     ISBN 093526907X
     OCLC 24544129
     LCCN 91-36114
     Notes:
        Includes bibliographical references (p. 235-244); index

• A biographical dictionary of 100 individuals who fought against Indian peoples, including such well-known figures as Jim Bridger, George Custer, George Crook, and Jedediah Smith. Entries, alphabetically arranged, provide birth and death dates and places, professions, and chronological accounts of each subject's combat activities, concluding with references for further reading. Some entries have portraits. Introductory material includes statistics, e.g., Indian wars by year and location, and Medals of Honor awarded by date. The extensive bibliography includes both books and articles, and the detailed index cites both persons and place-names, including references to 91 forts.— *MB*

H8　　Schubert, Frank N. - **On the Trail of the Buffalo Soldier : Biographies of African Americans in the U.S. Army, 1866-1917**. - Wilmington, DE : Scholarly Resources Inc., 1995. - 519 p. ; port.

　　Class Numbers:
　　　Library of Congress U52
　　ISBN 0842024824
　　LCCN 93-46408
　　Notes:
　　　Includes bibliographical references

• Organized alphabetically in the familiar who's-who arrangement, Schubert's volume contains thousands of entries for black Americans who fought in the Indian Wars throughout the Prairies-Plains region. Most are quite brief, containing little information of substance. The bibliography that follows the entries includes books, articles, newspapers, U.S. government publications, archival collections, and military records. Several appendixes include lists of those killed in action and those who received the Medal of Honor. No index, but the 2004 supplement (below) has an index to both volumes.— *MB*

H8a　　Schubert, Irene, 1939-　, comp. and ed. - **On the Trail of the Buffalo Soldier II : New and Revised Biographies of African Americans in the U.S. Army, 1866-1917** / comp. and ed. by Irene Schubert, Frank N. Schubert. - Lanham, MD : Scarecrow Pr., 2004. - 502 p.

　　Class Numbers:
　　　Library of Congress U52
　　ISBN 0842050795
　　LCCN 2003-23427
　　Notes:
　　　Includes bibliographical references (p. 349-352); index
　　　Table of contents: http://www.loc.gov/catdir/toc/
　　　　ecip0410/2003023427.html

• This edition incorporates new data (1,000 revised and 2,000 new entries) that appeared on databases or was supplied by the descendants of soldiers responding to publication of the first edition. Appendixes include lists of battles involving buffalo soldiers and of soldiers who received Certificates of Merit. The indexing is something of a maze, with many opportunities to get lost among extended listings under main headings. Individuals are listed under place-names within states, not itself a problem except for the confusion caused by many type fonts and indentions. Indexing also leads to entries in the 1995 edition that were not included in this one.— *MB*

Forts ; Outposts

H9　　Cragg, Dan. - **Guide to Military Installations**. - Mechanicsburg, PA : Stackpole Books, 2000. - xx, 411 p. ; ill., maps.

　　Class Numbers:
　　　Library of Congress UA26.A2
　　ISBN 0811727815 (pbk.)
　　OCLC 46640663
　　LCCN 2001-20961
　　Notes:
　　　1st ed., 1983
　　　Index

• Chatty discussions, short on factual information, of U.S. military bases in the United States and in other countries. U.S. installations are arranged alphabetically by state, then by Air Force, Army, Marine Corps, and Navy. All the Plains states are represented (some by only a single installation). No index.— *RB*

H10　　Frazer, Robert Walter, 1911-　. - **Forts of the West : Military Forts and Presidios, and Posts Commonly Called Forts, West of the Mississippi River to 1898**. - Norman, OK : Univ. of Oklahoma Pr., 1965. - xxxvii, 246 p. ; ill., maps.

　　Class Numbers:
　　　Library of Congress UA26.A6
　　ISBN 0585194092 (electronic bk.)
　　OCLC 569354 ; 44959015 (electronic bk.)
　　LCCN 65-24196
　　Notes:
　　　Bibliography: p. 190-226
　　　Electronic book: http://www.netLibrary.com/urlapi.asp?
　　　　action=summary&v=1&bookid=15007

• Because the nomenclature of military posts is inconsistent and the characteristics of a fort ill-defined, Frazer covers military posts either officially or commonly called forts, ignoring establishments officially and commonly known as agencies, redoubts, cantonments, camps, depots, or barracks. French, Mexican, and Spanish forts are included. The introduction discusses the history and types of Western military posts. Arranged by state, entries give date established; location; purpose; name, rank, and unit of the person establishing the post; origin of the name; name changes; date of abandonment; and present status and disposition. Maps for each state show locations of forts relative to rivers and lakes, which frequently determined their sites. An appendix lists forts established specifically as Civil War posts. Bibliography of published sources and an index by people, organizations, locations, and tribes. — *JD*

H11　　Hannings, Bud. - **Forts of the United States : An Historical Dictionary, 16th through 19th Centuries**. - Jefferson, NC : McFarland, 2006. - 738 p. ; ill.

　　Class Numbers:
　　　Library of Congress UG410
　　ISBN 078641796X 9780786417964
　　OCLC 614684130

LCCN 2005-26328

Notes:

    Includes bibliographical references; index

    Table of contents: http://www.loc.gov/catdir/toc/
        ecip0519/2005026328.html

• Forts, Pony Express depots, stage stations, trading posts, blockhouses, garrison houses and fortified villages are listed in alphabetical order by state. The 6,000 entries, which range in length from one sentence to one page, describe the establishment, uses, significant events, and current status of the forts. In the Plains, many were outposts during the Plains Indian Wars and protectors of the Indian agencies. Many have disappeared or exist as ruins, but some remain in service and some are cared for as part of the National Park Service. Contact and visitor information are included for outposts that currently have an official status as a military establishment or park. Appendixes relevant to the Plains include a checklist of Pony Express depots by state; Spanish missions and presidios; a timeline of conflicts; and a checklist by state of 20th-century forts, posts, bases and stations. Bibliography of primary and secondary sources and thorough index by name, fort, and location. A starting place for new researchers that is also enormously useful for historians and travelers. — *JD*

H12   Hart, Herbert M. - **Old Forts of the Far West** / drawings by Paul J. Hartle. - Seattle, WA : Superior Publ. Co., 1965. - 192 p. ; ill., maps, ports.

    Class Numbers:

        Library of Congress UA26.W4

    OCLC 711591

    LCCN 65-23448

    Notes:

        Bibliography: p. 186-189

• The states included are California, Nevada, Utah, Arizona, Colorado, New Mexico, and Texas, the latter three falling in the Prairies-Plains region. The 60 forts the volume describes are arranged thematically, (e.g., "Campaigning with Crook") so not all forts of interest will be found in the same section of the book. Descriptions of seven forts in Texas comprise the first chapter; other chapters treat forts in the Plains region, including Fort Collins, CO and Fort Bascom, NM. Entries are well-illustrated with black-and-white photos and line drawings. A directory of 545 old forts, arranged by state, is particularly helpful, since most of them are not discussed in the text. A bibliography and index complete the volume.— *MB*

H13   Prucha, Francis Paul. - **A Guide to the Military Posts of the United States, 1789-1895.** - Madison, WI :

State Historical Society of Wisconsin, 1964. - 178 p. ; ill., maps (part col.).

    Class Numbers:

        Library of Congress UA26.A6 P7

    LCCN 64-63571

    Notes:

        Bibliography: p. 159-178

• Military forts served to protect against infiltration by the British, Spanish, and Indians as the white migrant population moved westward, 1789-1895. The work is arranged in five parts: general history of the military on the frontier; list of regular army posts or installations in alphabetical order, providing the name, location, and dates of operation; seven sectional maps; supplementary information that includes temporary forts of the Seminole Wars and a statistical table of Army strength; selected bibliography. — *GK*

H14   Roberts, Robert B. - **Encyclopedia of Historic Forts : The Military, Pioneer, and Trading Posts of the United States.** - London : Collier Macmillan ; New York : Macmillan, 1964. - 894 p. ; ill.

    Class Numbers:

        Library of Congress UA26 .A45

    ISBN 002926880X

    LCCN 86-28494

    Notes:

        Includes bibliographical references (p. 865-867)

• Roberts's compilation lists for researchers and students fortifications located in the U.S., including Alaska and Hawaii. Entries, all written by the compiler, are arranged alphabetically by state, list forts alphabetically by keyword (Fort Carson, CO, under C) and give alternate names, brief historical description, and years of operation. Both active installations and those no longer in use are listed. Western trading posts, usually named for the men who established them, were then often used by the Army as local population grew. All Prairies-Plains states are represented. Occasionally presents odd insights: a monument at Fort Riley, KS, erected to commemorate "the tragedy of Wounded Knee" (p. 299) seems actually to honor the 7th Cavalry. Entries lack bibliographies, but there is a general bibliography, a list of state archives and libraries, an index to forts, and a glossary .— *GK*

Western Wars ; Engagements

H15   Hatch, Thom, 1946- . - **Custer and the Battle of the Little Bighorn : An Encyclopedia of the People, Places, Events, Indian Culture and Customs, Information**

Sources, Art and Films. - Jefferson, NC : McFarland, 1997. - 229 p. ; ill., maps.

    Class Numbers:

      Library of Congress E83.876

    ISBN 0786401540 9780786401543

    OCLC 35207940

    LCCN 96-34688

    Notes:

      Index

• As the title testifies, Hatch's encyclopedia focuses more on Custer and the U.S. military than on the Plains Indians. It attempts to guide readers overwhelmed by the extensive literature with a reference-style digest of the battle's people, places, technology, and equipment, and places the battle in context by covering both other events of the time and Plains Indian culture. Most entries range from 200 to 400 words, though some, like the biographies of Custer and Crazy Horse, are significantly longer. The enormous literature of the battle is characterized by interpretation, theory, contradiction, uncertainty, and nuance that are not--and possibly cannot be--conveyed by the entries; for example, Hatch's description of the killing of Crazy Horse is controverted by much of the literature. The source lists accompanying most entries along with entries on significant authors, books, articles, artists, artwork, and movies will be valuable to researchers looking for primary and secondary sources.— *JD*

H16   Purcell, L. Edward. - **Encyclopedia of Battles in North America, 1517 to 1916** / [by] L. Edward Purcell and Sarah J. Purcell. - New York : Facts on File, 2000. - 383 p. ; maps. - (Facts on File library of American history).

    Class Numbers:

      Library of Congress E46.5

    ISBN 0816033501

    LCCN 99-38634

    Notes:

      Includes bibliographical references (p. 345-362); index

• The Purcells, who wrote all the entries but do not identify themselves, describe battles from 1517 to 1916, most not relevant to the Prairies-Plains region. Those that are consist chiefly of engagements between whites (usually Army detachments) and Indians, among them Batoche, Rosebud Creek, Washita, Adobe Walls, Sand Creek, Wounded Knee, and, of course, the Little Bighorn. Engagements are listed alphabetically by the common name of the battle (e.g., Alamo, Beecher's Island), giving the location, date, and war. The battle is described, including key personnel, casualties, and outcome. Entries end with suggested readings. Maps accompany some entries. Supplementary material includes a glossary, alphabetical list of battles, list of battles by year and date, bibliography, and index. The index is the most useful way to identify Plains engagements, since it lists battles by state. —*MB, RB*

Contributors

Robert Balay (*RB*) has been Head of Reference at Yale and Reference Editor at *Choice*. He was General Editor of the 11th edition of *Guide to Reference Books* (1996) and compiler of *Early Periodical Indexes* (2000).

Mel Bohn (*MB*) is Reference Librarian Emeritus at the University of Nebraska-Omaha and past Editor of *Nebraska Library Association Quarterly*.

Jean Piper Burton (*JB*) is Associate Professor in Library Services for Cataloging and Technical Services at West Chester University of Pennsylvania, where she also has charge of collection development for women's studies.

Jeanetta Drueke (*JD*) oversees e-mail reference service and Love Library reference desk service at the University of Nebraska-Lincoln, where she also is subject specialist for art and art history, grants and foundations, and Great Plains studies. She has published articles on active learning in library instruction, scriptoriums and e-text centers, local organization research, and British Parliamentary Papers.

Gayla Koerting (*GK*) was most recently Special Collections Librarian at the I.D. Weeks Library, University of South Dakota (Vermillion) and is presently Curator of Government Records, Nebraska State Historical Society in Lincoln.

Larry McDonald (*LMcD*) is a Reference Librarian at the University of Regina (Saskatchewan) and liaison to the University's Canadian Plains Research Center.

Lisa Mitten (*LM*) is Social Sciences Editor at *Choice*. Previously, she was for 14 years anthropology bibliographer at the University of Pittsburgh. She is past president of the American Indian Library Association, was Assistant Editor of *Native America in the Twentieth Century* (1994), edited the Native American periodicals section of *Magazines for Libraries* (10th ed., 2000), has been a consultant for the National Museum of the American Indian, and created and maintains a Web site, *Native American Sites* (**CD6**). She is a mixed-blood Mohawk.

Marcella Stark (*MS*) is a reference librarian retired from the Central University Libraries, Southern Methodist University (Dallas). She was a contributor to the 11th edition of *Guide to Reference Books* and a reviewer for *Choice*. She teaches a research methods course for the Master of Liberal Studies program at SMU.

NAMES

Names of authors, editors, compilers, and in some cases, sponsors appearing in bibliographic entries and in annotations are indexed. Names of illustrators, cartographers, and advisors are ignored. Names in contents notes are not indexed. Names of organizations or, in a few instances, of personal authors listed in organization rosters in Site Lists are unnumbered, so show page numbers instead of entry numbers. Alphabetization is word by word, hence organization names ending in a full stop (University of Alberta.) follow the same name that lacks a full stop. Names beginning "Mc" and "Mac" are not interfiled but are filed as spelled.

TITLES

Titles indexed include those in bibliographic entries, in notes, and in annotations. Section or chapter titles in Contents notes are not indexed. Initial articles are omitted in all languages. Titles listed in organization rosters in Site Lists are unnumbered, so show page numbers instead of entry numbers. Titles beginning with numbers sort to the head of the file; they also appear at the appropriate places in the alphabetic list ("$10 Horse" as "Ten Dollar Horse"). Filing is word by word ("Kansas Wildflowers" precedes "Kansas.gov"). Abbreviations and acronyms ("BHBIB") file as spelled. With regard to Internet sites in the main text or in Site Lists, it is often difficult to distinguish titles from organization names, hence any organization name appearing with an Internet site will be listed here.

N

O

Y

Z

SUBJECTS

Subject entries are drawn for the most part from subject added entries in records derived from the Library of Congress or the Online Catalog Library Center. Where needed, some entries have been added to supplement those records. Entries are alphabetized word by word. Titles and Internet sites listed in Site Lists have no subject entries, so do not appear in this index.

Civil rights—Handbooks, manuals, etc. CD7
Clothing CD93
Clothing—Catalogs BD3
Directories CD31, CD51
Encyclopedias CD28, CD29, CD30, CD32, CD33,
CD34, CD35, CD119, EC127
Ethnobotany EC125, EC127
Ethnobotany—Great Plains EC126
Ethnobotany—Prairie provinces EC126
First contact with Europeans CD96
Folklore CD97, CD119
Folklore—Bibliographies CB7
Food EC125
Government relations CD43, CD120, CD125
Government relations—Bibliographies CD101
Government relations—Biographies CD50
Government relations—Sources—Bibliographies—Catalogs
CD20
Great Plains—Archival resources CD22
Great Plains—Audiotape catalogs CD53
Great Plains—Bibliographies CD4, CD17, CD64, DC4
Great Plains—Biographies—Bibliographies CD47
Great Plains—Internet sites DC4
Great Plains—Encyclopedias CD23
Great Plains—Guidebooks CD128
Great Plains—History CD25
Great Plains—History—19th century—Bibliographies
CD98
Great Plains—Indexes CD85
Great Plains—Pictorial works CD85
Great Plains—Portraits CD85
Great Plains—Religion —Bibliographies BA27, CD98
Great Plains—Rites and ceremonies—Bibliographies
BA27
Health and Hygiene—Bibliographies CD99
History CD1, CD2, CD39, CD41a, CD44, CD45, CD125
History—Chronology CD38, CD132
History—Guidebooks CD133
History—Handbooks, manuals, etc. CD56
History—Maps CD36, CD37
History—Sources—Bibliographies—Catalogs CD20
History—Statistics CE9
Housing—Prairie provinces—Bibliographies CD124
Implements—Texas CB23
Indexes CD8
Intellectual life CD106, CD107, CD111, CD114
Intellectual life—Bibliographies
CD108, CD108a, CD109, CD109a, CD113
Internet sites CD6
Jewelry CD91
Juvenile literature—Bibliographies CD14
Languages BB18
Languages—Bibliographies BB22
Languages—Study and teaching—Bilingual method—
Bibliographies BB19
Legal status, laws, etc. CD102, CD103, CD105, CD123
Legal status, laws, etc.—Cases—Digests CD104
Legal status, laws. etc.—Handbooks, manuals, etc. CD7
Library resources CD5
Maps CD36, CD37
Material culture CD55
Medical Care—Bibliographies CD99
Medicine—Encyclopedias BA26, CD100
Montana—Bibliographies CD59
Museums—Guidebooks CD133
Music—Bibliographies CB7, CD116
Music—Discography CD117
Music—History and criticism CD117

Music—History and criticism—Bibliographies CB7, CD116
New Mexico—Bibliographies DB44, DB45
Oklahoma—Antiquities—Bibliographies CB19
Oklahoma—Antiquities—Catalogs CB20
Oklahoma—History—Pictorial works—Catalogs DA40
Oklahoma—Religion and mythology BB42
Pictorial works BD6
Pictorial works—Catalogs BD4
Politics and government CD120
Politics and government—Handbooks, manuals, etc. CD7
Population CE8
Population—Maps CD36
Portraits CD44
Prairie provinces—Economic conditions—Statistics CD69
Prairie provinces—Social conditions—Bibliographies CD124
Prairie provinces—Social conditions—Statistics CD69
Reference books—Bibliographies CD18
Religion—Encyclopedias BA24, BA25, BA26, CD100
Rites and ceremonies—Encyclopedias
BA25, BA26, CD100
Saskatchewan—Abstracts CD70
Saskatchewan—Antiquities—Bibliographies CB18
Saskatchewan—Biographies CD48
Saskatchewan—Directories CD72
Social conditions CD120
Social life and customs CD39
Social life and customs—Handbooks, manuals, etc. CD56
South Dakota—Antiquities—Bibliographies CB24
South Dakota—Archival resources CD21
South Dakota—Bibliographies CD21, DB73
South Dakota—Directories CD52
Statistics CE8
Study and teaching—Southwest, New—Exhibitions CB3
Texas—Antiquities CB23
Texas—Bibliographies CD15
Texas—History—Sources CD24
Texas—Texas Panhandle—Bibliographies CB22
Treaties CD102, CD105, CD122, CD123
Urban residence—Prairie provinces—Bibliographies
CD124
Urban residence—Prairie provinces—Maps CD69
Urban residence—Prairie provinces—Statistics CD69
Warfare CD132
Warfare—Encylopedias CD129
Wars CD125, CD126, CD132
Wars—1861-1865—Encyclopedias CD131
Wars—1866-1895—Encyclopedias CD131
Wars—1866-1895—Guidebooks CD128
Wars—Encylopedias CD129
Wars—Guidebooks CD133
West (U.S.)—Biographies H7
West (U.S.)— Encyclopedias CD57, DA43
Wars—West (U.S.)—Guidebooks CD130
West (U.S.)—History—Manuscripts—Catalogs DA39
West (U.S.)—History—Pictorial works—Catalogs DA40
West (U.S.)—History—Sources—Bibliographies—Catalogs
DA39
West (U.S.)—Pictorial works BD2
Indians of South America—Encyclopedias CD119
Folklore CD119
Indians of the Arctic CD26
Indians of the Subarctic CD26
Indigenous peoples—Canada—Internet sites CD68
Industries—Colorado—Directories CF3
Kansas—Directories CF3
Nebraska— Directories CF3
Oklahoma—Directories CF3
Wyoming—Directories CF3

O

V

W